THE SACRED KURRAL OF TIRUVALLUVA NAYANAR

THE SACRED KURRAL

OF

TIRUVALLUVA NAYANAR

WITH

INTRODUCTION, GRAMMAR, TRANSLATION, NOTES, LEXICON AND CONCORDANCE
(IN WHICH ARE REPRINTED FR. BESCHI'S AND F. W. ELLIS VERSIONS)

REV. G. U. POPE

GYAN

Published by

Gyan Publishing House
5, Ansari Road
Daryaganj, New Delhi-110002
Phone: 011-47034999, 9811692060
E-mail: books@gyanbooks.com

Distribution Network
gyanbooks.com
India, USA, Canada, UK, Australia, France

ISBN : 978-81-212-3977-6 (PB)
First Published, 1886

2nd Impression 2020

Printed at: Gyan Press, Delhi.

The Sacred Kurral of Tiruvalluva Nayanar
Author: Rev. G. U. Pope

PREFACE.

I AM thankful, after so many years, to see, at length, the completion of this work, projected at the very outset of my Oriental studies—a work which has cost much time and labour, and completes the series of Tamiḻ books by which I have tried to help forward the study of this admirable language among both Europeans and Natives.*

It is primarily intended to make classical Tamiḻ easier to English students, while to Native students it may afford means for a more comprehensive and fruitful study of their greatest classic author, who has sung of so many topics, *Musaeo contingens cuncta lepore,* 'touching all things with poetic grace.' The Grammatical Introduction (pp. xv.–xxiv.), together with the Handbook, and a careful use of the Lexicon and Concordance, aided by the English and Latin versions, will make it easy to master the great work of this very influential teacher of men.†

---

* These are—

1. 'A First Catechism of Tamil Grammar.' [In Tamil.] This was published in 1842. The C. V. E. S. alone has sold 350,000 copies. The C. R. S. and various Missionary Societies, and the Madras Government also, have reprinted it in very many editions.
2. 'The Second Catechism.' [In Tamil.] Published in 1844. The C. V. E. S. has sold 75,000, and it is very largely used.
3. 'The Third Catechism,' with Native Authorities, being a larger Grammar of Tamil, in both its dialects. [In Tamil.] 2nd Edition. 8vo. 411 pp.
4. 'A Tamil Handbook for English Students,' in three parts. 4th Edition.
5. 'A Tamil Prose Reader,' with references to the Handbook.
6. 'A Tamil Poetical Anthology,' with references to the third Grammar.

These works can be obtained from the publishers of this book, and the Author will be glad to assist any student who will communicate with him, at the Indian Institute, Oxford.

† Since this work was sent to the press, I have seen a charming little volume entitled, 'Tales and Poems of South India,' from the Tamil, by Rev. E. J. Robinson. (T. Woolmer, 1885.) Had I known of this earlier, I should have felt it less necessary to publish a translation. I cordially recommend this interesting and scholarly little volume. I have not seen the edition edited by M. Murugêça Mutali and translated by J. Lazarus. (Madras, 1885.) In an elegant little volume of translations from Tamil authors, and other miscellanies, entitled *Indische Sinnpflanzen und Blumen*, by the late lamented Dr. Graul (Erlangen, 1865), the accomplished author has given translations in metre

Anyone living in India, and having the assistance of a Munshi, or Native teacher, should use also one of the editions published by சருவணை பெருமாள் ஐயர். The verbal commentary and paraphrase will be very useful; yet it is only by much loving thought and reiteration of the couplets themselves that their full force and beauty can be apprehended. The Commentary constitutes, in such cases, rather a pair of crutches than a pair of wings.

It would have been possible to illustrate each chapter with parallel passages from Sanskrit authors, from poets of many languages and times, and from Holy Scripture. This I have done here and there, especially where it might seem that the author was translating, as from Manu, for example; but, after careful study, and especially after comparison with Böhtlingk's *Indische Sprüche* (which resembles the Kurraḷ, though much of that collection is of more recent date than our poet), it would seem that, except the few I have indicated, it is not probable that Tiruvaḷḷuvar translated a *çloka* from Sanskrit.

I may say here that it is hard to discern the least reason to imagine (with M. Jules Vinson,* *Mélanges orientaux*, Sept. 1883. Paris: Leroux) that we have not before us the original work of the poet as he planned it. It is certainly not an anthology, but the perfect and most elaborate work of one master. The third part might be deemed separable, but the manner even there is quite peculiar to our bard. As one link in a chain of evidence, the following is remarkable. The poet uses தொடி nine times as equivalent to 'lady,' but never uses the same epithet twice. So with இறை. There is a studied variety in epithets throughout.

A brief notice of Father Beschi, the greatest of Tamiḷ scholars, may be of interest. Father Constantius Josephus Beschius (Constantio Josepho Beschi) was an Italian Jesuit, and was appointed to the South Indian Missions in 1700, and died at Manaparai in 1742. He lived at Âvûr, near Trichinopoly, assuming the dress, and conforming to the habits of a Hindû *guru*. He studied Tamiḷ, Telugu, Sanskrit, Hindustânî, and Persian; and from 1736 to 1740 we find him Dîwân, or chief minister (Ch. LXIV.) to Chandâ Sahêb. [See my *Text-Book of Indian History*, 3rd ed. p. 270.]

---

of the choicest couplets of 'der tamulische Gnomen-Dichter Tiruvalluvar.' In the *Maximes traduites des Courals de Tirou Valluvar*, by P. G. de Dumast (Nancy, 1854), the poetry of the Tamil bard is somewhat diluted; but the pamphlet is interesting.

* Speaking of the Çintâmaṇi, he says:—'On ne pourrait guère regarder comme antérieurs que le recueils de sentences morales intitulés Kuraḷ de Tiruvalluva et Nâlaḍiyâr; mais, à mon avis, ces recueils, sous leur forme actuelle sont des compilations relativement récentes.'

In regard to the *Nâlaḍi* this is the case (Introd. p. xiii.); but not as to the *Kurral*.

His works a e numerous.

The தேம்பாவணி, *Têmbâvaṇi*, 'The Unfading Garland,' is an epic in 3,615 quatrains. It was intended to serve as a summary of the Gospel history, and is full of legends. In style it is thoroughly Tamiḷ. The student will find some fine passages; but, as a whole, it is monotonous.

Of his pro e writings the very admirable *Vêdiyar Oṛukkam*, வேதியர் ஒழுக்கம், 'The Duties of Catechists,' is the best. It is in part adapted from the writings of S. Gregory the Great; and is the best model I know for the student of Tamiḷ prose.

His grammars of high Tamiḷ (செந்தமிழ்) and of low Tamiḷ (கொடுந் தமிழ்) were written in Latin, but have been translated into English, the former by Mr. Babington, M.C.S., and the latter by Mr. Horst and Mr. Mahon He also wrote or edited a grammar in Tamiḷ, தொன்னூல் விளக்கம்; and dictionaries in Tamiḷ-French, Tamiḷ-Portuguese, and Tamiḷ-Latin; and one of the poetical dialect, called the சதுரகராதி, 'The four-fold Dictionary.'

The Adventures of Guru Noodle (பரமார்த்தகுரு) is a very amusing story in eight chapters, intended to ridicule the native Rabbis, whom, however, he did not disdain to imitate pretty closely in many things. This is translated into many native languages; and an edition, with English translation, vocabulary and praxis, was published in London, in 1832, by Mr. B. G. Babington, of the Madras Civil Service.

The MS. from which I have edited the Latin translation of the *Kurraḷ* (generally attributed to Beschi) belongs to the India Office Library, and is supposed to be the only one in existence. It seems to have been written at least a century ago. This copy (not quite perfect) belonged to Francis Whyte Ellis. Some missing chapters have been supplied by Thomas Brotherton of the S. P. G., I know not from what copy. One shee of the India Office MS. is in the handwriting of William Henry Drew. Dr. Graul used this MS. for his work. Sir Walter Elliot presented it to the Library in 1877. It was evidently transcribed by a native, and mistakes occur. The Latin, it will be seen, is tinged with Tamiḷ, but will help the student more than a more strictly classical version. The Editor has had to amend the text occasionally, but has generally allowed even doubtful things to appear as in the MS.

Beschi was known by three names or titles. These are தைரிய நாத சுவாமி (S. *Dairya-nâtha-svâmi*), வீரமா முனிவர் (S. *Vîra-mahâ-muni*), and عصمتی سنیاسی (*'Iṣmatî Sannyâsî*).

Of these the first was his official designation as a Christian priest, and is a translation of 'Constantius,' with *Nâtha* (=Lord) and *Svâmi* (the usual title of a Hindû *guru*). The second title was given him by the Hindû *literati*, and is also equivalent to 'Constantius,' with the addition of the words 'great devotee.' The third was given him by

Chandâ Sahêb, and signifies 'the Chaste or Noble Ascetic,' and is also intended, more or less, to reproduce his Christian name.

[See 'A Brief Sketch of the Life and Writings of Father Beschi,' by A. Muttusâmi Piḷḷai. *Madras Lit. Journal*, April 1840.]

I have in transliteration used *rr* for ற, and have, therefore, written *Kurraḷ*. In this I follow the example of Beschi. But my chief reason for this course is that in pronunciation it is nothing but a strong double *r*. In common Tamiḷ ற is constantly used for ர, and in the cognate languages the rough or double *r* is hardly used at all. The very signs ற and ఱ (the Telugu equivalent, now well-nigh obsolete) seem to be from a doubling of the ர and ర.

The kind patronage of the Secretary of State for India in Council, and of the Madras Government, has enabled me to publish this work.

To Dr. R. Rost, Librarian of the India House, I am indebted for much kindly assistance, without which this volume would not have been published.

Mr. F. Pincott, M.R.A.S., has rendered me invaluable assistance throughout. This gentleman has minimised for me the confessedly great labour of publishing such a book in England.

Works of reference I could command at the British Museum, the India House Library, and the Oxford Indian Institute; but I have often felt the lack of the advice and assistance of Native scholars which I enjoyed for many happy years in India. I have examined and used most of the books, Native and European, relating to the Kurraḷ; but have often departed from traditional renderings; and, as no Native eye has seen my MS., I must bear the entire responsibility in such cases.

That this publication may be useful in promoting the real study of Tamiḷ, and so help those who go to South India as officers of Government, or as missionaries, better to understand the mind of the people among whom they live and work, is my one desire in sending it forth.

Quod faxit D. O. M.

G. U. POPE.

INDIAN INSTITUTE, OXFORD.
Sept. 1, 1886.

CONTENTS.

ERRATA.

[Please to correct before using the book.]

Couplet	14,	*for*	குண்றி	*read*	குன்றி
	70,	,,	லென்றுஞ்	,,	லென்னுஞ்
	91,	,,	வீர	,,	லீர
	96,	,,	ன	,,	ன்
	131,	,,	ம	,,	ம்
	190,	,,	மண்ணு	,,	மன்னு
	207,	,,	லீ	,,	வீ
	209,	,,	ற	,,	ற்
	223,	,,	யீதல	,,	யீதல்
	265,	,,	கெய	,,	கெய்
	311,	,,	றா	,,	றர்
	322,	,,	லந்	,,	லாந்
	346,	,,	ருக	,,	ருக்
	354,	,,	வெய	,,	வெய்
	433,	,,	துனை	,,	துணை
	461,	,,	ழிப்	,,	ழிப
	491,	,,	னல	,,	னல்
	608,	,,	ர்க	,,	ர்க்
Chap. c., title,		,,	ஹ	,,	ை

ERRATA.

A புள்ளி (·) may be supplied in 109 (ம்), 323 (ன்), 346 (க்). 352 (ம்), 354 (ய்), 501 (ன்). In 12 (ப்பா).

[Correct these in text. *They are all correct in the Concordance.*]

Intro. p. iii., l. 37, *for* வளு *read* வள்.

xx., l. 33, *read* Telugu

Verse 13,	*for*	நி	*read*	நீ.
26,	,,	யார்	,,	யர்.
74,	,,	2nd பீ	,,	வீ.
135,	,,	முடைய	,,	மில.
273,	,,	ர	,,	யா.
279,	,,	கொடு	,,	கோடு.
287,	,,	ந்	,,	ங்.
313,	,,	ரூா	,,	ரூ.
338,	,,	{ குடு	,,	குட.
		{ யுடு	,,	யுட.
443,	,,	ரை	,,	ரைப்.
472,	,,	ஓ	,,	ஒ.
517,	,,	இநீகை	,,	இதீகை.
586,	,,	சொ	,,	சோ.
601, line 2,	*for*	ச்	,,	மாய்ந்து.
605 (notes, p. 272),	*for*	[illegible]	,,	நீர்.
614, line 2,	*for*	லெ	,,	வா.
627,	*for*	முடு	,,	முட.
629,	,,	டு	,,	ட்டு.
650,	,,	ரை	,,	ரைபா.
674 (p. 279), *read* reliquiae.				
700,	*for*	ற	*read*	பு.
714,	,,	தெருளி	,,	ஞெள்ளி.
823	,,	ஞா	,,	ஞ.
1103,	,,	ணி	,,	ணிணி.
1194,	,,	ழிய	,,	இயி.

Page 275 (notes), l. 3, *for* etibus *read* etatibus

The following should have been inserted in page [56].

ப

பகடு 'a bullock,' 624, Nâl. 2.

பகவன் [S. *Bhagavân*], 'the revered one,' 1.

பகு. **1.** (§ 68; பகுந்து and பக்கு, 56 III.) 'be divided.' பக (§ 168) 'so that disunion ensues,' 187. பக்குவிடும் (§ 254) 'will be split, wrecked,' 1068. **2.** (§ 64; S. *bhaj*; comp. வகு), 'divide, share.' பகுத்து 'having shared,' 322. (See பாத்து.) பகவு (§ 190) 'a slice, bit,' 889.

பகல். **1.** (§ 148) 'Disunion,' 851, 852. **2.** 'Day-time,' 481, 999. [Comp. பால்; S. *bhaga*; H.B. Pt. II. p. 37.] முற்பகல், பிற்பகல் (§ 225) 'forenoon, afternoon,' 319.

பகை. **1.** 'Enmity,' 146, 207, 434, 450, 861, 867, 871–80, 995. **2.** 'Hostile act, provoking enmity,' 1225. **3.** 'A foe,' 304, 674, 723, 727, 734, 744, 830, 863, 875, 882. உட்பகை 'Civil dissension,' 735, 881–890. பகைமாட்சி, Ch. LXXXVII. பகைத்திறந்தெரிதல், Ch. LXXXVIII. மட்பகை [மண் + பகை], 'a potter's knife, the divider (foe) of the earthen vessel,' 883. பகை-மை 'hostility, 709. பகை-வர் (§ 184) 'foes,' 465, 817, 869, 877, 878.

பச (§ 66; comp. பசு), 'grow sallow, wear a green and sickly aspect.' பசந்து, 1232, 1278. பசந்த, 1181. பசந்தது, 1238. பசந்தாள், 1188. பசக்க 'let . . . grow sallow,' 1189. [Intro. p. xx.; Opt., § 140.] பசப்பு 'sallowness,' 1182–90, 1239–40. பசப்புறுபருவரல், Ch. CXIX. பசலை 'sallowness from love-sickness: *green and yellow melancholy*,' 1183.

INTRODUCTION.

I.—GENERAL INTRODUCTION.

The weaver of Mayilâpûr, known now only as Tiruvaḷḷuvar, was undoubtedly one of the great geniuses of the world; but his fame belongs to South India alone, and to only one great race there. He is the venerated sage and lawgiver of the Tamiḷ people, of whom there are about ten millions inhabiting the Central and Southern Karnatic.

M. Ariel, in a letter to Burnouf published in the *Journal Asiatique* (Nov.–Dec. 1848) speaks of Tiruvaḷḷuvar's great work as 'the masterpiece of Tamiḷ literature—one of the highest and purest expressions of human thought.' Again, he says: 'That which above all is wonderful in the Kurraḷ is the fact that its author addresses himself, without regard to castes, peoples or beliefs, to the whole community of mankind; the fact that he formulates sovereign morality and absolute reason; that he proclaims in their very essence, in their eternal abstractedness, virtue and truth; that he presents, as it were, in one group the highest laws of domestic and social life; that he is equally perfect in thought, in language and in poetry, in the austere metaphysical contemplation of the great mysteries of the Divine Nature, as in the easy and graceful analysis of the tenderest emotions of the heart.'

It is strange that the poet and his one great work are both without a name.* The author himself is commonly known as Tiru-vaḷḷuva-nâyanâr (*lit.* 'the sacred devotee, priest, or soothsayer of the Parraya caste'). Tradition says he was a weaver, and of those who are regarded as the refuse of all the castes—the *pariah* tribe. Their priests, soothsayers, teachers, or 'prophets' are styled *Vaḷḷuvar.* But he does not

* 'Ce livre sans nom, par un autre sans nom.'—Ariel. Dr. Barth, *Religions of India*, translated by Rev. J. Wood, p. 157 (Trübner's Oriental Series, 1882), speaks of this work as 'that admirable collection of stanzas in the Tamil (*sic*) language, which is instinct with the purest and most elevated religious emotion.'

write as a priest, and it would be impossible to gain from his writings any idea of the kind of temple in which he lit the sacred lamp and presented the offerings of his people. It is strange that the title by which alone the greatest poet of South India is known should be one indicating an origin most degrading and contemptible in the eyes of the vast multitudes of whom he has been for ten centuries the Oracle. The last has indeed become first. A wild and utterly incredible tradition assigns him a Brâhman father and a no-caste mother; and represents the poetess *Avvai* (='old woman': her name, too, is unknown) as his sister, while several other poets, of whom some fragments remain, were his brothers. All that we certainly know is that he was a *pariah*, and a weaver; lived at S. Thomé, or Mayilâpûr, now a suburb of Madras; and had an intimate friend, probably a patron, called Êlêla-çiṅkan (='Lion of the surf'), who was the captain of a small vessel.

The poet's home was a place around which there still lingers a strange oriental beauty, and which has probably not changed much since the time when the passer-by might have heard the click of the shuttle mingling with the low chaunt of his melodious verse. I may be pardoned for dwelling on my recollections of this interesting spot, since in 1840 my missionary life began there, and while visiting the villages around, that enthusiasm for the great Tamil poet was first kindled which has been an important factor in my life. Mayilâpûr, or Mayilai, is 'the town of peacocks,' and the name seems to indicate a place of groves and gardens around old temples. There is a sacred tank still, with a belt of cocoa-nut palms, and a square of old leaf-covered native houses in any one of which the poet might have lived. The sea-shore is close by, and Êlêla-çiṅkan's successors (I fear much degenerated) dwell there yet. The poet could hear the boom of the surf-waves, and pondered often, doubtless, on the shore of what he calls the *nâma-nîr*, 'the gruesome wave.' (149.)

A higher interest is imparted to the spot and its neighbourhood, at least to Christians, by the tradition (so long and lightly discredited, but now generally acknowledged to be authentic) that here S. Thomas preached, and here met his death by a spear (*vêl*) such as the poet often speaks of, and was here buried.* Mayilâpûr to us is better known as S. Thomé: In this neighbourhood a Christian community has existed from the earliest times. Here are fine old Armenian and Portuguese churches; and a Christian inscription of the 5th century. Here Pantaenus of Alexandria taught; and we are quite warranted in imagining Tiruvaḷḷuvar, the thoughtful poet, the eclectic, to whom the teaching of the Jains was as familiar as that of every Hindû sect, who was not hin-

* The reader may find a full discussion of this subject in Dr. German's learned and instructive work, *Die Kirche der Thomas Christen.*

dered by any caste prejudices from familiar intercourse with foreigners, whose one thought was to gather knowledge from every source, whose friend the sea-captain would bring him tidings of every stranger's arrival (coming from Ceylon, perhaps, in his own dhoney): we may fairly, I say, picture him pacing along the sea-shore with the Christian teachers, and imbibing Christian ideas, tinged with the peculiarities of the Alexandrian school, and day by day working them into his own wonderful *Kurraḷ*.

The East and the West have influenced one another in a very real and not yet thoroughly understood way from the earliest times. It is undoubtedly a noteworthy fact that from this Mayilâpûr, on which the eyes of Christendom have ever rested as the one sacred spot in India of Apostolic labour, comes the one Oriental book, much of whose teaching is an echo of the 'Sermon on the Mount.'

The name குறள் *Kurraḷ* is given *par excellence* to this the poet's great and only work; which consists of 133 chapters, each containing 10 couplets; and thus numbers 2,660 lines.

Kurraḷ means 'anything short' (√*kurr*, Sans. √*kṛit*, Lat. *curt-us* Gr. κειρ, A.S. *sceor-t*), and is properly the name of the couplet, as being the shortest species of stanza in the Tamiḷ language (p. xxvi.).

Tiruvaḷḷuvar's poem is thus by no means a long one; though in value it far outweighs the whole of the remaining Tamiḷ literature, and is one of the select number of great works which have entered into the very soul of a whole people, and which can never die. According to a custom not unknown in Europe, a series of verses (most of them very modern) bearing the names of all the great Tamiḷ poets is prefixed to the *Kurraḷ*, under the name of 'The Garland of Tiruvaḷḷuvar,' and exhausts the subject of his excellence with every variety of hyperbole.

Several of these are neat. One, by பரணர் (Paraṇar), says that as மால் (Vishṇu), when he appeared as Vâmana (குறள் *kurraḷ* means 'dwarf' also), or the dwarf, measured with two steps heaven and earth, so with the two lines of his diminutive Veṇpa-footed kurraḷ-verse has Tiruvaḷḷuvar measured the universe.

[மாலுங் குறளாய் வளர்ந்திரண்டு மாணடியான்
ஞால' முழுது' நயந்த' ளந்தான்;
வாலறிவன்
வளுளுவருந் தங்குறள்வெண் பாவடியால் வையத்தார்
உள்ளுவ வெல்லாம் அளந்தார் ஓர்ந்து.]

Complete in itself, the sole work of its author, it has come down the stream of ages absolutely uninjured,—hardly a single various reading of any importance being found,—and every rival sect in the Tamiḷ country claims the *Kurraḷ* as its own, and has furnished it with commentary and critical apparatus accordingly.

Tradition declares that Tiruvaḷḷuvar composed his *Kurraḷ* at the request of his neighbours, in order that the Tamiḷ people might have a *Vêdam* of their own; and it was doubtless intended to become the abiding authority on all ethical subjects for the Tamiḷ country. The author must have already possessed a great reputation, or this request would not have been made; yet there are no traces of any other writings of his.

The *Kurraḷ*, when finished, is said to have been taken by its author to Madura, where there was a college of learned Tamiḷ scholars, supposed to have been founded in the days of *Vamça Çêkhara*, an ancient king of the Pâṇḍya kingdom. In this college Çiva himself had condescended to appear as the forty-ninth professor, especially devoting himself to the exposition of the Tamiḷ language. The god also bestowed on the college a sacred bench of sòlid diamond, on which no one could sit who was not a faultless scholar. [See Wilson's *Hist. Sketch of the Kingdom of Pâṇḍya.*] Lists are given of the forty-eight members of this academy, but there are no genuine remains of their writings. The result of the appearance of Tiruvaḷḷuvar is variously stated. The general idea is that the high-caste assembly would not permit him to take his seat on the bench with the learned paṇḍits, on account of his want of caste; but that, meekly acquiescing in his own exclusion, he simply requested permission to lay his book on the end of the seat. On this being granted, the book was placed where the poet should have been seated, and the whole bench at once disappeared, leaving the learned professors afloat in the Lotus-tank. This story is obviously inconsistent with the idea which is equally prevalent, that the president was Kapilar, himself a Pariah, and a brother of Tiruvaḷḷuvar.

The truth seems to be that the Madura school of Tamiḷ literature, now too full of Sanskrit influences, was supreme till the advent of the S. Thomé poet, whose fame at once eclipsed that of the southern sages.

There are no data whatever which may enable us to fix with precision the period at which our poet flourished. I think between A.D. 800 and 1000 is its probable date. The style is not archaic—far less so than that of the *Çîvaga Çintâmaṇi*. Remembering that its author was not fettered by caste prejudices, that his greatest friend was a sea-captain, that he lived at S. Thomé, that he was evidently an 'eclectic,' that Christian influences were at the time at work in the neighbourhood, and that many passages are strikingly Christian in their spirit, I cannot feel any hesitation in saying that the Christian Scriptures were among the sources from which the poet derived his inspiration.

Dr. Graul, a devoted student of Tamiḷ literature, published an edition in Leipzig and in London, in 1856, with German and Latin translations. It is very valuable, though incomplete—owing to his lamented death—and has serious misprints.

Mr. F. W. Ellis, an Oriental scholar of extraordinary ability, printed a small portion of the *Kurraḷ*, with copious notes and illustrations. The sheets of this unfinished work (304 pages) can still be had.

The Rev. W. H. Drew, a missionary of the London Society in Madras, published an edition of 63 chapters, with English Translation, and additional notes by the fine old scholar, Râmânuja Kavirâyar,* with the Tamiḷ commentary of Parimêlaṛagar. This is, as far as it goes, the best edition.

The purely native editions, issued under the editorship of the late learned paṇdit Çarvaṇaperumâlaiyar of Madras, are very correct and valuable.

Twelve native commentators have illustrated by verbal commentaries the whole text; but the student will do well to disregard the meanings read into the verses by persons, native or European, who are anxious to prove that the Tamiḷ sage taught their own favourite dogmas. Tiruvaḷḷuvar is generally very simple, and his commentators very profound.

In regard to the philosophico-theological system taught in the *Kurraḷ* various opinions have naturally been held. Every Hindû sect claims the great poet, and strives to interpret his verses so as to favour its own dogmas. Something on these subjects will be found in the notes to each chapter. The Jains especially consider him their own, and he has certainly used several of their technical terms, and seems to have been cognizant of the latest developments of that system.

There is one couplet, however, that is destructive of the idea that Tiruvaḷḷuvar was a Jain. In Ch. III., fourth couplet, a story regarding Indra is referred to as proving that ascetics have power over the gods. The sage was Gautama, who cursed Indra for deceiving the sage's wife, Ahalyâ. Now, according to Jain ideas, a sage could have no wife, nor could he feel the emotion of anger, nor had he the power to inflict punishment. A Jain would not believe the story, and could scarcely use it as the author of the *Kurraḷ* has done. But, in as far as it is Oriental, Tiruvaḷḷuvar's teaching is just such as the study of Hindûism,

* With reference to my old Pandit, I venture to quote words used elsewhere:—'In many ways we fail to understand the people of India. Hindûs are often spoken of as apathetic. I should term them fervid. My first teacher of Tamiḷ was a most learned scholar, long dead (peace to his ashes!), who possessed more than any man I have known the *ingenium perfervidum*. He was a profound and zealous Vaishṇavite. I remarked one day a long white line or scar on his neck, where his rosary of huge Eleocarpus beads hung, and ventured to ask him (I had to wait on such occasions for the *mollia tempora fandi!*) its history. "Well," said he, "when I was a boy, I could learn nothing. Nothing was clear to me, and I could remember nothing. But I felt my whole soul full of an intense love of learning. So, in despair, I went to a temple of *Sarasvatî* (the goddess of learning), and, with a passionate prayer, I cut my throat and fell bleeding at her feet. In a vision she appeared to me, and promised I should become the greatest of Tamiḷ scholars. I recovered, and from that day, by her grace, I found all things easy, and *I am what she said I should be.*" I believe he was so; and from that noble enthusiastic teacher I learnt to love Tamiḷ and to reverence its ancient professors.'

in the light of Çankara's reforms, combined with that of the Jain system in its later developments, and of the *Bhagavadgîtâ*, might have produced.

There is no trace in the *Kurraḷ* of many things, systems, doctrines, and practices, current in South India at different periods, because, I suppose, they had been eliminated from the sage's own eclectic system of faith and practice, and because his work is didactic, and not controversial.

What philosophy he teaches seems to be of the eclectic school as represented by the *Bhagavadgîtâ*.*

Of *Bhakti*—that compound of πίστις and ἀγάπη, the introduction of which into India I still think (with Weber) is mainly due to the influence of Christianity—the first chapter of the *Kurraḷ* is a beautiful exposition.

The *Kurraḷ* owes much of its popularity to its exquisite poetic form. A *kurraḷ* is a couplet (Third Gram., 187) containing a complete and striking idea expressed in a refined and intricate metre. No translation can convey an idea of its charming effect. It is truly an 'apple of gold in a network of silver.' Something of the same kind is found in Greek epigrams, in Martial, and the Latin elegiac verse. There is a beauty in the periodic character of the Tamiḻ construction in many of these verses that reminds the reader of the happiest efforts of Propertius. Probably the Tamiḻ sage adopted it as being the best representative in Tamiḻ of the Sanskrit *çloka*.

The brevity rendered necessary by the form gives an oracular effect to the utterances of the great Tamiḻ 'Master of the sentences.' They are the choicest of moral epigrams.

The selection of the most difficult metre in the language—one permitting no deviations from strict rule, and requiring such wonderful condensation—for a long work, showed that the author intended to expend upon it his utmost of power, and to make it a 'possession for ever,' a 'delight of many generations.'

The laws of the Veṇpâ metre, in which the *Kurraḷ* is composed, are very curious, and, in fact, unique in prosody. They will be explained farther on; but the student of Tamil is referred to my *Third Tamiḻ Grammar* for a more complete exposition. In the *Clavis humaniorum litterarum sublimioris Tamulici idiomatis*, by the great Beschi, the whole subject of Tamil poetry is discussed. The late lamented Dr. A. C. Burnell, M.C.S. (among his very many benefactions to Oriental learning), issued a reprint of this valuable work, which is most faithful to its native sources, the best of which are printed in my Third Grammar.

The following is an analysis of the whole *Kurraḷ*, as given in the Commentary of *Parimêlaragar*.

* Barth, *Religions of India*, p. 192 (Trübner, 1882).

It is divided into three BOOKS treating of Virtue, Wealth, and Pleasure. The *Nannûl*, a standard Tamil Grammar of much later date, has the rule :—

'The benefit derived from a treatise must be the attaining to Virtue, Wealth, Enjoyment, Heaven (Deliverance).' In the 26th *çloka* of the *Hitopadêça* the same enumeration is given :

धर्म्मार्थकाममोक्षाणां *Dharmmârtha-kâma-mokshâṇâm.*

Our author treated of only three of these. Did he leave his work incomplete ? or did he refrain from any exposition of *Vîḍu* or *Moksha* because he resolved to take only the practical view of things ? I suppose he was not satisfied with the glimpses he had obtained of man's future, and waited for light ; or, perhaps, he thought his people not prepared for higher teaching. Ch. xxxv.—xxxvii. give us his nearest approach to the subject.

BOOK I.—VIRTUE. Ch. I.—XXXVIII.

The Tamil word is ARRAM [Comp. S. *ṛi*=*ar*, from whence *rita* and *riti*]=S. D'HARMA.

§ I. INTRODUCTION. Ch. I.—IV.

1. The praise of *God.**
2. The excellence of *rain.*
3. The greatness of *those who have renounced: Ascetics.*
4. The commendation of the *strength of virtue:* 'ad virtutem sectandum hortatio.'

[Beschi makes Ch. I.—III. the Preface, 'Prologus,' and Ch. IV. the Introduction.]

§ II. VIRTUE IN DOMESTIC LIFE. Ch. V.—XXIV.

5. Domestic life : *married life.*
6. The goodness of the help to domestic life : *the wife.*
7. The gain of sons : *children.*
8. The possession of affection : *love of family.*
9. The cherishing *of guests : hospitality.*
10. The utterance of pleasant things : *kindly speech.*
11. The recognition of benefits conferred : *gratitude.*
12. Impartial *justice.*
13. The possession of *restraint : self-control.*
14. The possession of *decorous conduct.* [S. ÂCHÂRA.]
15. Not coveting another's wife.
16. The possession of *forbearance.*
17. Absence of *envy.*
18. Absence of *covetousness.*
19. Not *speaking evil* of the absent.
20. Not uttering *profitless words.*
21. Dread of *evil deeds.*
22. The recognition of *duty.*
23. Giving.
24. Renown.

---

* Though his first chapter is 'The Praise of God,' theology is no part of his general subject and he scarcely alludes to a Divine Being in the remaining chapters.

§ III. VIRTUE IN A LIFE OF RENUNCIATION: ASCETIC VIRTUE. Ch. XXV.—XXXVII.

§ IV. DESTINY.

BOOK II.—WEALTH. Ch. XXXIX.—CVIII. [PROPERTY.]

[Beschi: 'rerum proprietates.' Graul: 'de bonis': 'vom Gute.' Ariel: 'la fortune.']

§ I. ROYALTY. Ch. XXXIX.—LXIII.

§ II. MINISTERS OF STATE. Ch. LXIV.—LXXIII.

§ III. Essentials of a State. Ch. lxxiv.—xcv.

74. The land.
75. The fort.
76. The method of collecting revenue.
77. The excellence of the army.
78. Military spirit.
79. Friendship: allies.
80. Scrutiny of friendship.
81. Familiarity.
82. Evil friendship.
83. Faithless friendship.
84. Folly.
85. Unwisdom.
86. Hostility.
87. The excellence of hate: how to make enmity profitable.
88. Skill in the conduct of quarrels.
89. Secret enmity: treachery.
90. Giving no offence to the great.
91. Uxoriousness: 'not going in the wife's way.'
92. Wanton women.
93. Abstinence from 'toddy.'
94. Gaming.
95. Medical art.

§ IV. Appendix. Ch. xcvi.—cviii.

96. Nobility.
97. Honour.
98. Greatness.
99. Perfect excellence.
100. Courtesy.
101. Wealth without benefit.
102. The possession of shame.
103. The way to sustain the family.
104. Agriculture.
105. Poverty.
106. Mendicancy.
107. The dread of mendicancy.
108. Vileness.

BOOK III.—LOVE. [Sexual Love.] Ch. cix.—cxxxiii.

§ I. Concealed Love. Ch. cix.—cxv. 'The gand'harva Marriage.'

109. Mental disturbance caused by the Princess' beauty.
110. Recognition of the signs (of mutual love).
111. Rejoicing in the embrace.
112. The praise of her beauty.
113. Declaration of love's special grace.
114. Abandonment of reserve.
115. The rumour.

§ II. Wedded Life. Ch. cxvi.—cxxxiii. 'The açura Marriage.'

116. Not enduring separation.
117. Complainings of absence.
118. Eyes consumed with grief.
119. Grief's pallor.
120. Solitary anguish.
121. Sad memories.
122. Visions of the night.
123. Lament at eventide.
124. Wasting away.
125. Soliloquies.
126. Reserve overcome.
127. Longing for return.
128. Full declaration.
129. Longing for re-union.
130. Dissatisfaction with herself.
131. Pouting.
132. Petty jealousies.
133. The pleasures of temporary variance.

In the Notes I have striven to remove difficulties from the path of the beginner. The poem will not at first reveal all its beauties to the student. The whole scope and connection of Chapters v.–xxiv. should be studied to show the beauty of the life of the Tamiḷ householder as the South-Indian *vates sacer* contemplates it. The ideal householder leads on earth a consecrated life (50), not unmindful of any duty to the living, or to the departed (42). His wife, the glory of his house, is modest and frugal; adores her husband; guards herself, and is the guardian of his house's fame (VI.). His children are his choicest treasures; their babbling voices are his music; he feasts with the gods when he eats the rice their tiny fingers have played with; and his one aim is to make them worthier than himself (VII.). Affection is the very life of his soul: of all his virtues the first and greatest. The sum and source of them all is love (VIII.). His house is open to every guest, whom he welcomes with smiling face and pleasant word, and with whom he shares his meal (IX.). Courteous in speech (X.), grateful for every kindness (XI.), just in all his dealings (XII.), master of himself in perfect self-control (XIII.), strict in the performance of every assigned duty (XIV.), pure (XV.), patient and forbearing (XVI.), with a heart free from envy (XVII.), moderate in desires (XVIII.), speaking no evil of others (XIX.), refraining from unprofitable words (XX.), dreading the touch of evil (XXI.), diligent in the discharge of all the duties of his position (XXII.), and liberal in his benefactions (XXIII.), he is one whom all unite to praise (XXIV.).

It is not irreverent to put side by side with this the words which I feel sure he had heard, or at least the summary of them (Phil. iv. 6–8):

> 'Whatsoever things are pure,
> whatsoever things are honourable,
> whatsoever things are just,
> whatsoever things are of good report,
> if there be any virtue, and if there be any praise,
>   think on these things.'

Tradition* (reflecting, doubtless, in many things the spirit of a much later age) says that the life of the poet in *Mayilâpûr*, with his wife *Vâçuki*, was in perfect accordance with these chapters. She was the embodiment of all the *Kurraḷ* requires in the 'help to household life.'

In his youth, her father, *Mârka-çakâyan*, struck with his virtues, offered the poet his daughter in marriage. Tiruvaḷḷuvar was inclined to marry, because domestic virtue is the highest, yet resolved first to try the maiden's temper and gifts; and accordingly replied: 'If she will take this sand and make it into rice for me, I will take her as my wife.' *Vâçuki* meekly took the basket of sand, and, feeling sure that what the holy man ordained was possible and right, proceeded to boil

* The *Tiruvaḷḷuvar Çarittiram* (திருவள்ளுவர் சரித்திரம்) and the *Mahâ-nîti-çûḷâmaṇi* (மகாநீதிசூளாமணி) will satisfy the most enthusiastic lover of traditions.

it; and, as (v. 55) the virtuous woman is said to have power with the gods, so it came to pass with her; a miracle was wrought on her behalf, and she brought him the rice for which he asked. So she became his wife, faithful and obedient.

In after years, when the poet's fame had spread through all the Tamil country, one day a noble stranger came to the weaver's cottage, and asked the question (so much discussed in those times), 'Which is greater—domestic life, or a life of asceticism?' The sage, while courteously entertaining the stranger, gave no reply in words to the question. The enquirer was left to see domestic life in its perfect grace, and judge for himself. What he saw was this. One day when *Vâçuki* was drawing water from the well the sage suddenly called her, and the obedient wife instantly came, *leaving the bucket hanging mid-way in the well.*

Another day, when the good housewife brought her husband his morning meal of cold rice, he complained that it *burnt his mouth!* when she, unquestioning, and unhesitating in her attention to his comfort, instantly began to fan it. Another day, at noon, when the glaring light was everywhere, the sage, who was at work at his loom, let fall his shuttle, and *called for a light to seek it!* The wife, with unquestioning obedience, lit a lamp and brought it him!

The enquirer had learnt his lesson: 'Where such a wife is found, domestic life is the best. Where such a wife is not, the life of the ascetic is to be preferred.'

So the poet and his *Vâçuki*, this Griselda of the Tamil olden days, lived, till the time that she must leave him, and gain 'release.' The dying wife looked wistfully at her husband. 'What is it?' said he. 'When you married me, and on that day I stood and spread the rice for you (literally, *for you, my god*), you gave me a commandment to place always, with your meals, a cup of water and a needle. I know not why it was.' 'It was,' he replied, 'that if a grain of rice were spilt, I might pick it up and purify it.' Satisfied, the meek *Vâçuki* closed her eyes for ever.

She had never during her whole married life questioned her lord's command! And also, it is clear, no grain of rice had ever been spilt!

As he lay that night, after her death and cremation, and pondered, he was heard to exclaim (there are many various readings of the verse):—

அடிசிற் கினியாளே! அன்புடையாளே!
படிசொற் றவறாத பாவாய்!
அடிவருடிப்
பின்றூங்கி முன்னெழுந்த பேதையே! போதியோ?
என்றூங்கும் என்கண் இரா?

'Sweet as my daily food! O full of love! O wife,
Obedient ever to my word! Chafing my feet,
The last to sleep, the first to rise, O gentle one!
By night, henceforth, what slumber to mine eyes?'

Whatever may be thought of these characteristic traditions, it is the singular glory of the poet to have drawn this picture of the perfect householder; and it speaks loudly in favour of the Tamiḷ race that these couplets are enshrined in the hearts of the whole people. Dynastic changes, Muhammadan raids, and irruptions of alien races, through a dozen centuries, have changed many things in the South:

'Old times are changed, old manners gone,
And strangers fill the *Pâṇḍyan's* throne,'

but the Tamiḷ race preserves many of its old virtues, and has the promise of a noble future. Their English friends, in teaching them all that the West has to impart, will find little to unteach in the moral lessons of the *Kurraḷ* rightly understood. Sir A. Grant says: "Humility, charity, and forgiveness of injuries, being Christian qualities, are not described by Aristotle." Now these three are everywhere forcibly inculcated by the Tamiḷ moralist. These are the themes of his finest verses. So far, then, we may call this Tamiḷ poet Christian; and to understand him, to free him from mistaken glosses, to teach his works, to correct their teaching where it is misleading, and to supplement it where it is defective, would seem to be the duty of all who are friends of the race that glories in the possession of this poetical masterpiece. Sir A. Grant (*Aris. Ethics*, I. 81), treating of Greek morality 'before the birth of Moral Philosophy,' says truly: 'It is obvious that such a code as this could only arise among an essentially moral and noble race.' This is precisely what I claim for the Tamiḷ-speaking peoples, and on the same ground. We shall not do all the good we might do among them till we more unreservedly recognize this.

No doubt many couplets in this remarkable work say more to us than they did to those for whom they were written. Many of these epigrammatic masterpieces have a profound significance, of which their author himself was hardly conscious. Their resemblance to the gnomic poetry of Greece is remarkable as to their subjects, their sentiments, and the state of society when they were uttered.

Something must be said regarding the Third Book on 'Love.'

Of this Mr. Drew said, that 'it could not be translated into any European language without exposing the translator to infamy.' But this is only true in regard to certain of the commentaries upon it, which are simply detestable. I am persuaded that it is perfectly pure in its tendency, and in the intention of its wise and high-souled composer. Its title is *Kâmattu-pâl*, 'the division which treats of *kâma*,' and this means *Lust* or *Love*.

Kâman is the Hindû Cupid. Hindû ideas differ from our own. This prejudice kept me from reading the third part of the *Kurraḷ* for some years; but the idea occurred to me very forcibly that he who wrote:

'Spotless be thou in mind! This only merits virtue's name;
All else, mere pomp and idle sound, no real worth can claim,' [34.]

could not have covered himself with the spotted infamy of singing a song of lust. Thus I ventured at length to read and study it, rejecting commentators, when I was able fairly to appreciate its spirit; and, as the result, I translate it, believing that I shall be regarded as having done good service in doing so. Dr. Graul has published it in German and in Latin, M. Ariel in French.

The late Dr. Graul wrote: 'Ich selbst halte mich, für vollkommen entschuldigt nicht bloss, sondern selbst verbunden, auch das dritte Buch dem abendländischen Publicum anheimzugeben. Ist doch der *Kurraḷ* in allem seinen drei Theilen ein Spiegel des indischen, speciell de tamulischen Volksgeistes, und es würde in der That etwas fehlen, wenn man den dritten Theil, der ein so helles Licht auf das häusliche Leben wirft, weglassen Wolte, bloss weil ein paar Andrücke darin vorkommen, die an die freire Art des Morgenlandes erinnern.'

'To the pure all things are pure.'

I may add that many give to the whole a mystical interpretation, an idea with which commentators on the book of Canticles have made us familiar. Its interpretation as an allegory exhibiting the play [S. *lîlâ*] of the Divine Spirit with the embodied soul, would be in harmony with much that is found in Muhammadan literature as well as in Sanskrit, especially in Buddhist writers. Yet I can hardly think that Tiruvaḷḷuvar's tone of mind would lead him to this method of teaching spiritual truths.

In the Notes I have introduced many stanzas from the நாலடி (*Nâladi*), the work which stands next in estimation to the *Kurraḷ* among the Tamiḻ people. The tradition regarding the *Nâladi-nânnûrru*, or '400 Quatrains,' is that 8,000 sages brought their verses to the King of Madura, who, to test their worth, caused the palmyra leaves on which they were written to be thrown into the River Vaikai. Those that floated against the current were to be preserved. Three collections of leaves stood the test; one was found to contain these 400, and the two others consisted of similar collections of verses, which are extant under the names of *Paṛa-moṛi* (பழமொழி='Old words') and *Arra-nerri-*

çâram (அறநெறிச்சாரம்='Essence of the way of Virtue'). The two latter works are inferior.

I suppose that the meaning of the tradition is, that these are verses of various ancient Tamiḷ poets, which the stream of time has not been able to sweep away into oblivion. Since they were not allowed to perish, they may be presumed to have been the most popular, perhaps the most worthy, c mpositions of those olden times. The authors seem to have been Jains. Perhaps we may refer them to the time of Kûna Pâṇḍya, some time in the eleventh century A.D.

They are of very unequal value, often obscure, sometimes trivial. The prevailing tone is cynical, and we miss in them the healthy humanity of Tiruvaḷḷuvar. They have been forced by a later native editor into an arrangement harmonizing with that of the *Kurraḷ*; the result of which is, that the title of a chapter often affords no clue to its contents. They are mostly of much later date, I think, than the *Kurraḷ*, and often seem to indicate an acquaintance with it. I must mention that, though by different unknown hands, I feel sure I can see the work of one principal writer in about half of them. He was a Tamiḷian Antisthenes.

Though often very beautiful, these verses especially lack the condensation and vigour of our poet; and I have often felt tempted to exclaim, when noting how much less they are able to say in a quatrain than Tiruvaḷḷuvar in a couplet:

νήπιοι, οὐδὲ ἴσασιν, ὅσῳ πλέον ἥμισυ παντὸς!

The student of the *Kurraḷ* should, however, thoroughly master the *Nâladi*.

In regard to the translation, I may venture to say that it is faithful, and that I have not read into the rendering a single idea or thought which there were not good grounds for supposing that the poet intended to convey. I thought it best to try to give a metrical translation. The Tamiḷ scholar will see that I have tried to reproduce even the rhythm in many cases, but I could not retain the inimitable grace, condensation, and point of the original.

Nothing, not even a corrupt Greek chorus, so defies the efforts of the student as does very much of the high Tamiḷ poetry. The poetical dialect of Tamiḷ allows every kind and any amount of ellipsis, so that a line is often little else than a string of crude forms artfully fitted together. The best compositions are quatrains or couplets, each containing a complete idea: a moral epigram. Their construction resembles that of a design in mosaic. The materials fitted together are sometimes mere bits of coloured glass, but sometimes also very precious stones and pure gold. And the design? Why you walk round it, and try to catch it in all lights, and feel at first, and often for a long time, as if it meant nothing at all, till you catch some hint, and at once it lies revealed, something to be thought of again and again, some bit of symbolism it may be, not unfrequently grotesque, often quaint, but sometimes also of rare beauty.

Especially of Tiruvaḷḷuvar it may be said, as Archbishop Trench says of S. Augustine (*S. Augustine as an Interpreter of Scripture*, p. 154): 'He abounds in short and memorable, and, if I might so call them, epigrammatic sayings, concentrating with a forceful brevity the whole truth which he desires to impart into some single phrase, forging it int a polished shaft, at once pointed to pierce, and barbed that it shall n. lightly drop from, the mind and memory.'

II.—THE GRAMMAR OF THE KURRAL.

§ 1. To the student of the *Handbook*, it will at first seem as though the *Kurraḷ* were written in an entirely different language from that to which he has been introduced. The object of these sections is to explain whatever in the language of this poem differs from the ordinary spoken Tamiḷ; and reference will be made to the sections of the *Handbook* (Fourth Edition) throughout.

The Tamiḷ word for grammar is இலக்கணம் [S. लक्षणं ='characteristic']; and the aim of a Grammar should be to state lucidly and in convenient order the characteristic FACTS of a language, and then to analyse, classify, and explain them. Here the facts can be verified by reference to the Concordance.

§ 2. The *Kurraḷ* is composed in pure Tamiḷ, that is, with scarcely any admixture of Sanskrit. This will appear from the Vocabulary and Concordance, which will enable the student to form an independent judgment on many points of grammar. Whatever may be the original connection between what Tamiḷians call the *Vaḍa-moṛi* (வட-மொழி= 'northern speech') and the *Ten-moṛi* (தென்-மொழி='southern speech'), it is obvious that Tamiḷ is not a dialect of Sanskrit, but an independent language with a copious and original vocabulary, having a very clear and philosophical grammatical system, very highly cultivated, and in every respect equal to Sanskrit itself.

This is the mother of the South Indian languages. To these languages the term *Drâviḍian* has been given, but the epithet is unsuitable, as Drâviḍam includes Guzerat and the Mahratta country also, and is, in fact, a name for all the country south of the Nerbuda. The

பஞ்சதிராவிடம் (*Pañça-Tirâviḍam*), or 'five-fold Drâviḍam,' includes Tamiḻ, Telegu, Kanarese, Mahrattî, and Guzaratî. This inappropriate name has been given to this family of languages because the word Tamiḻ itself is supposed to be a corruption of the Sanskrit *drâviḍa*. This idea is opposed by Native scholars.* The derivation of the word தமிழ் is uncertain. The following suggestions have been made: (1) Since ழ் is a formative of very common use (இகழ், புகழ், &c.), it is suggested that தமிழ் is from the root தமி 'alone,' and that it means 'the incomparable.' (2) It is said to be=தீமொழி or தேன்மொழி 'the sweet or honey speech.' Neither of these seems probable. Since the one native designation for the original language of the South was *Ten-moṛi* (தென்மொழி)='southern speech,' may not the word Tamiṛ be simply a corruption of this? [தென்மொழி, தெம்மொழி, தமிழ்.]

Believing this to be the true origin of the word, I prefer to call the family of South Indian languages the Tamiḻian, as it is certain that for the study of each dialect of them Tamiḻ must be the language of reference.

Of this pure and primitive Tamiḻ this work of Tiruvaḻḻuvar is the most finished specimen, and may fitly be termed 'a well of (Tamiḻ) undefiled.' The very few words introduced from the Sanskrit are made to assume a Tamiḻ garb, under which it is hard to recognize them. Thus, உலகு represents S. लोक, அரசு the S. राजन्, அமைச்சு the S. अमात्यः, மாந்தன் the S. मानुषस्. Many Sanskrit words in universal use now, such as வேதம், கோபம், சாட்சி, are not found in the *Kurraḷ*, which uses only மறை, வெகுளி and கரி. In the *Nâlaḍi* many more Sanskrit derivatives are found, and there is in general a much less exquisite use of words.

§ 3. The form of the text presents a difficulty to the student. I have printed it as its author wrote it, with two differences only. In the poet's time the mute mark, or புள்ளி, was not used: எழுத்து was written எழுதது. Nor was there any distinction between எ and ஏ, or between ஒ and ஓ, except in some cases a புள்ளி over the short letter lengthened it; thus எ, எ் ; ஒ, ஒ். I have not introduced stops, and a small space is left between the metrical feet; but as in Tamiḻ there is a cæsura, in general, between every word, this does not make it more difficult to construe. The laws of combination are mainly those given in Appendix VIII. to the *Handbook* (Part ii. pp. 41–44).

In regard to orthography we find அவ் for ஔ. See கௌவை and அவ்வித்து. We have தொறும் and தோறும், ஓடு and ஒடு.

ம் is used for ன் in terminations; thus, அறன் for அறம்.

---

* The student, when he is able, may study with advantage the grammar of *Puttamittiranâr* (புத்தமித்திரனார்), called the *Viruçôriyam* (வீரசோழியம்). The preface by Tâmôtaram Piḻḻai of Jaffna discusses this subject ably.

ல் and ன் are interchangeable, with a preference for ன். We have எனின் or எனில், and the term. of the third case is in ஆல் or ஆன். Thus அல் for அன் is occasionally used in 1st pers. sing. of verbs.

Poetry mostly prefers ன்.

Clipt forms are used, as என் for என்னை. This is required by the need for condensation.

But this can all be best studied in the Concordance.

§ 4. The greatest difficulty to the learner arises from Ellipsis, which in all its forms rules over Tamiḷ poetry. The metre, requiring much to be compressed into two lines, having but seven feet between them, renders constant ellipsis indispensable. This is its difficulty, and this also is one of its great beauties.

(1) The finite verb is omitted whenever this is possible. Couplets 1 and 2 have no verb; and, in general, words are omitted whenever (the author thinks that) no ambiguity arises from their omission.

(2) There are six kinds of ellipsis (தொகை) enumerated by Tamiḷ authors (Third Gram. 151–157), and numerous examples of all of these occur in the *Kurraḷ*. These are:

(*a*) Ellipsis of casal signs in nouns, &c. [வேற்றுமைத்தொகை]. In the *Kurraḷ* the noun itself, or its inflexional base, is normally used for every case. It may, indeed, be said that case-endings are never used, except when hopeless ambiguity would result from their suppression. The fourth case (dative) alone is generally found in full. Thus in 2: வாலறிவனற்றாடொழாஅர் = பரிசுத்த அறிவையுடைய இறைவனது நல்லபாதங்களை வணங்கார். ஆனால். In 14: ஏரின் = ஏரினால்.

The inflexional base of nouns in ம் ends in அத்து: hence பெருக்கத்து, சுருக்கத்து (963) are case vii. [comp. 21, 213, 161].

Under this head may be included the ellipsis of the pluralising particle in அஃறிணை nouns (H. B. 29). கள் only occurs a few times: மக்கள் (60, 65), பூதங்களை (271), மற்றையவர்கள் (263), and one or two others.

(*b*) Ellipsis of verbal inflections [வினைத்தொகை]. Here the root of the verb is used as an adjective.

The theory is, that the relative participle (செய் கிற, செய் த, செய் யும், H. B. § 74), drops its termination, and becomes an aoristic shortened enlargement of the noun to which it is prefixed. This is not unknown in prose; thus அறி-முகம் is 'an acquaintance.' Thus are used in 5 (சேர்), 6 (தீர்), 13 (விரி), 218 (அறி); and compare roots கழி, அறி, அல், இல் in Vocabulary. ஆ, போ, 371.

(*c*) Ellipsis of connecting particle, when one noun is used as an attribute of another [பண்புத்தொகை or குணத்தொகை]. This resembles the Sanskrit *karma-dhâraya* compounds. Thus in 8 (அறவாழி), 216 (பயன்மரம்), 198 (அரும்பயன்). Comp. H. B. §§ 130–133. செந்தண்மை 30. See 346–47 புல்லறிவு, அருமறை.

(*d*) Ellipsis of particle denoting comparison (உவமைத்தொகை). This is, in fact, equal to what we call metaphor. Comp. 6.

(*e*) Ellipsis of உம். [உம்மைத்தொகை.] Comp. 4, 43.

(*f*) Ellipsis of other words. [அன்மொழித்தொகை.] Under this head fall most Tamiḻ compounds. Thus in 13 (விரிநீர்வியனுலகம்), besides வினைத் in விரி(ந்த)நீர் ; and பண்புத் in விய(னுள்ள உலகம்); there is அன் .. தொ in நீராற் சூழப்பட்ட='the vast world surrounded by the spreading ocean.'

In regard to the whole subject, the *Vîrasoṛiyam* has a chapter called the தொகைப்படலம், in which an elaborate attempt is made to show that தொகை is the Sanskrit *samâsa*. It will appear, I think, that the Tamiḻ method of arrangement is better. The rule is simply this: When a noun has one or more enlargements of any kind, these may be prefixed to it without any inflexional increment, in their crude form (root, stem, or inflexional base), with or without euphonic insertions, so as to form one compound word. The expansion of these is not easy in many cases.

A group of elegant words of constant use in Tamiḻ poetry, which are chiefly appellations of females, comes under this head. They are examples of metonomy. Compare in Concordance ஒளியிழை (1329)='*she with* bright jewels'; கனங்குழை (1081)='*she with* ponderous ear-rings.'

We may sum this up as far as relates to the enlargement of subjects or objects:

The meaning of a noun is extended or defined—

I. By composition. Noun + noun: மனக்கவலை 'mental anxiety'; and there may be an ellipsis of case-sign, of adjective sign, or of several words. See Third Gram. 152–7. This is வேற்றுமைத்தொகை or பண்புத்தொகை.

II. By a relative participle, with or without connected words: i.e. *a relative clause.* நல்லாற்றி னின்றதுணை: 'an assistance that has stood in a good path.'

III. By a verbal root prefixed, with or without connected words. This is called வினைத்தொகை. It is the preceding with an ellipsis of the participial or temporal affixes.

Thus some of the most beautiful expressions in the poem are built up. I append a few examples:

(1) இருள்சேரிருவினையும். Here வினை is plural, is enlarged by இரு with உம்='the two kinds of action.' This is enlarged by சேர், for சேரும், with its subject இருள்='to which darkness clings.'

(2) விரிநீர்வியனுலகம். Here உலகம் is enlarged by வியன் and by விரிநீர் (itself a compound)='the broad world, surrounded by the wide waters.'

§ 5. The Declension of the Noun in the *Kurraḷ* is not very different from H. B. Part ii. App. ix.

(1) The second case. With அன், 32.

(2) The third case. ஆல் with அன், 2. இன் for ஆல், 14. இனல், 102, 129. ஆன்=ஆல், 24, 39, 93. ஒடு, 195, 236. ஓடு, 37, 73.

(3) The fourth case. [illegible]க்கு, 67. அன்பிற்கு, 71. நலக்கு (=நலத்துக்கு, 149. நிலக்கு, 570.

(4) The fifth case. இல்=போல், 9. இல்='from,' 16, 97. இன்= 'than,' 31, 32, 48. With உம், 64.

(5) The sixth case. இன, 80. அன், 257.

(6) The seventh case (or abl. of place where) is formed with the aid of the particles கண், 34, 52, 117, 135, 223. மாட்டு (inf. base of மாடு), 5, 94. உள், 13, 47. உழை, 168. உழி, 545. இடை, 7. மிசை, 3. முன், 59. பின், 225. கட்டு (see கண்). இல், 46. இன், 123

(7) The eighth case. பரத்த, 1311. தெவ்விர், 771. நெஞ்சே, 1291.

ஏ is often inserted when there is ellipsis of case. கணமேயும் (29)= 'even for a moment.'

Neuter nouns, when primitives, are used either as sing. or plural. Thus எழுத்து in 1. [Comp. 5, 4, 9.]

Nouns masc. and fem. (உயர்திணை) form their pl. in (1) அர், 14. (2) ஆர், 911. (3) இர், 920, Ch. xcii. (4) ஓர், 18, 30, 923.

Derivative neuters in து make pl. in அ, or அவை, 157, 8.

§ 6. Predicates, and the finite verb in general.

(1) The ordinary forms of the present tense of the finite verb do not occur in the *Kurraḷ*. Tiruvaḷḷuvar does not use any form corresponding to H. B. § 34.

(2) The past tense, as in H. B. § 70*, is found, and sometimes is the predicate, as அமர்த்தன, 1084. கொண்டார், 1183.

(3) But the future is most often found. This is used as a true aorist, expressing what belongs to any time or all times. And of this (if, indeed, it can properly be called *future*) the general form in உம் is the commonest; செய்யும், answering to Telugu కొట్టును. Comp. 166.

(4) Besides these the negative verb, and the imperative, optative, and prohibitive moods, are extensively employed. Comp. 33, 140, 882.

(5) Whenever the verb 'to be' is used with its complement as the predicate, the verb of incomplete predication, or copulative verb, is omitted. See 2[illegible]

(6) In considering predicative relation as expressed in the *Kurraḷ*, it is necessary to examine certain roots which are in constant use; such as இல், which *denies existence*; அல், which *excludes a quality*; அர் 'rare, hard'; நல் 'good'; உள் 'existence, inner being.' From these nouns are formed in மை.

In the Concordance the uses of these roots are shown. They occur as the (or in the) predicate of a very great number of these verses.

To these roots (and to many others) personal terminations are added, and the result is what Tamiḷ grammarians call the வினைக்குறிப்பு= 'verb-sign.' These seem to be really nouns, e.g. அரிது='that which is hard,' and by the omission of the substantive verb='it is hard,' 7.

§ 7. General view of the VERB in the *Kurraḷ*.

1. The ROOT of a pure Tamiḷ verb is generally the most ancient form, the philological root, as far as Tamiḷ is concerned. It is used

(1) as an *imperative* [thus, பெய், 55. இடு, 552];

(2) with an ellipsis of inflexional particles, as a kind of adjective, as shown above [வினைத்தொகை; thus, 301, செல்லிடம்];

(3) for the infinitive, as in Telugu, where the usage is more general, [thus, 805, நோதக்க=நோகத்தக்க, 'things calculated *to cause pain*'].

2. The root receives certain formatives which are convenient for euphonic or other purposes. These are

(*a*) உ (with doubling of final consonant often): செல், செல்லு.

(*b*) கு, with or without a nasal, for intransitives and க்கு for transitives; போகு, ஆகு, 371. ஆக்கு, அடங்கு. To these are added particles by which new stems are formed, causals and others. H. B. 160, &c.

3. An infinitive in அ is in constant use. என, 37. வைக்க, 50. There is nothing remarkable in its use.

Sometimes ப் is inserted, and then the infin. seems to be future,= 'to be about to be.' இருப்ப, 67. மோப்ப, 90. An anomaly is காட்டிய, 1313, for காட்ட. H. B. § 168–71.

4. The next is an aoristic form in உம். உடற்றும், 13. ஈனும், 31. ஒல்லும், 33. எய்தும், 145. போகும (போம) படுக்கும், 372. This is used as the third person singular or plural of all genders, and also as an aoristic relative participle. H. B. § 74. This is reckoned as the future tense third person singular and plural. But it is one of the oldest and simplest verbal forms, having no temporal particle, being *root*+உம் with or without கு or க்கு. Thus in Telegu we have పంపును='he, she, they send, will send' [Tel. ను =Tam. ம்].

5. An optative mood, or courteous imperative, with a corresponding prohibitive, is the next in importance. Of this we have the following forms:

(i.) Positive. செயல், 33. செய்க, 36. நினைக்க, 250. கொள்கு (for கொள்க), 875. வாழி (S.), 1242. காண்கம் (pl.), 1301. அயர்கம் (pl.), 1268.

(ii.) Neg. or Prohib. எனல், 196. மறவற்க, 106, 439. படாதி, 1210. Since அல் added to a root makes an optative, either positive or negative [see 196, where எனல்='call,' or 'do not call'], it seems as if it were a verbal noun in அல். with ellipsis of வேண்டும் and வேண்டாம் respectively. The plural adds மின: இரவன்மின், 1067; நில்லன்மின், 771.

6. The next thing to be considered is *tense*. In the *Kurraḷ* there are but two tenses, a past and a future or aorist. There is also a negative aoristic form. As regards these nothing need be added to what is given in the H. B., except some forms with அளபெடை, or lengthening of vowels. [§ 12.]

The pronominal endings by which person, number, and gender are distinguished are:

Sing. 1 pers. ஏன், அன், அல். [Comp. யான்.] என்றேன், 1315, தும்மினேன், 1317. அறிந்தேன், 1083. புலப்பேன், 1267. புலப்பல், 1259. நோவல், 1236. பருகுவன், 1266.

Very irregular is உரைக்கு, 1181="I shall tell."

Sing. 2 pers. ஆய், இ, ஐ. [Comp. நீ.] சேறி, 1292. காய்தி, 1246. பெறுதிபுலத்தை, 1301. செருஅஅய, 1200.

Sing. 3 pers. *mas.* அன். (ஆர் honorific.) [Comp. அவன்.] நீங்கியான். *Fem.* ஆள், அனள். [Comp. அவள்.] ஊடிஞள், 1314. கொண்டனள், 1315. எழுவாள், 55. *Neut.* து, changed into று. [Comp. அது.] பிறங்கிற்று, 23. எய்தின்று, 1240.

Plur. 1 pers. ஏம், ஆம், உம், அம், நம். [Comp. யாம்.] அற்றேம், 88. இழந்தேம், 593. அறிவாம், 36. கள்வேம், 282. எண்ணுவம், 467. பெறுகுவம், 1328. வாழுநம், 1193. இழத்தும், 1250. வாற்தும், 971.

Plur. 2 pers. ஈர், இர். [Comp. நீர்.] சூடினீர், 1313. மறைத்திர், 1318. ஆகுதிர், 1319.

Plur. 3 pers. *m. f.* ஆர், அர், ப. [Comp. அவர்.] தும்மிஞர், 1312. வாழ்வார், 6. நீந்துவர், 10. என்ப, 60. கருதுப, 337.

Plur. 3 pers. *neut.* அ. [Comp. அவை.] தேய்ந்த, 1261. நாணின, 1231.

The temporal middle particles are as in common prose; but no example of the present tense is found in the *Kurraḷ*. [We find இறவாநின்ற, 1157, which is in form a rel. part. of the present, for ஆநின்று is, in higher language, a mid. temp. particle of the present. H. B. § 33. It may be that இறவா is p. verb. part. and நின்ற to be taken in its ordinary sense.]

7. The defective forms, both பெயர் எச்சம் and வினைஎச்சம், are as in H. B. § 74–78.

I. வினைஎச்சம் (H. B. 97). நின்று, 11. வழங்கி, 11. தெரிந்து, 23. விஞய் (விஞவி), 594. ஓரா, 548. எனின், 2. அற்ருல், 943. பொய்ப்பின், 13. ஆஞல், 53. உண்டேல், 368 [see ஏல்]; and with உம் [H. B.

§ 100]. கற்றும், 728. உணர்ந்தும், 417. கற்பினும், 373. ஆயினும், 52. [See ஆனும்.] படுபாக்கு, 164.

The infin. mood (so called) is a வினையெச்சம்.

(1) In addition to what is said in H. B. regarding the (so called) infinitive mood, or adverbial part. in அ, I may direct the reader to the use of என, ஆக, போல, குன்ற, ஆற்ற, நோக்க [see Concordance].

(2) A future infin. is found. See இருப்ப, மோப்ப.

(3) A form in பாக்கு is used in 136, 164, 1312.

(4) The root is used for the infinitive. See கோள், நோ.

(5) காட்டிய for காட்ட is an infin. of purpose, 1313.

II. பெயர் எச்சம். The aorist in உம் has been already explained. நின்ற, 41. தக்க, 51. அளாவிய, 64, 419.

8. The neg. aorist, and other forms (H. B. § 110–22), are much as in prose; but இல் and அல் are often used. [See these roots in Lex.]

Sing. 1 pers. நண்ணேன், 1311. அறியேன், 1083.

Sing. 2 pers. சொல்லாய், 1241. படாதி, 1210.

Sing. 3 pers. *m.* நாணன், 1018. உண்ணன், 1001. *f.* தொழாள், 55. *n.* செல்லாது, 18. வேண்டா, 37.

Plur. 1 pers. அறியலம், 1257.

Plur. 2 pers. அறியீர்.

Plur. 3 pers. *m. f.* தொழாஅர், 2. செய்கலாதார், 26. பேணலர், 1016. *n.* சேரா, 5

Adv. part. நல்காது, 17. இழக்கா, 35. படாமை, 38. கரவா, 527. சிதையாமல், 578.

Rel. part. கல்லாத, 397. வணங்கா, 9.

9. Participial nouns in great variety occur. H. B. 87–89. It may be said in general that *any form of a tense may be used as a noun also*; thus, ஏகினன்='he passed over,' or 'he that passed over.' Comp. தக்கார், 51. அடங்கியான், 124. சேர்ந்தார், 3. ஈன்றாள், 923. சான்றோன், 69. கற்றது, 2. மிக்கவை, 158. These are all past.

The following are future or aorist: கெடுப்பது, 15. வருவது, 39. காப்பான், 24. என்போர், 30 தெரிவான், 27. ஆள்பவர், 383. களையுநர், 879. வீழுநர், 1193. தோற்கிற்பவர் [கு+இன்], 159, 515. படுவ, 17. அற்குப, 333, 1232, 1233. அஞ்சுமவன் is unique, 727.

The following are negative: சேராதார், 10. கேளாதவர், 66. காவாதான், 435. கல்லார், 408.

These forms resemble Greek participles with the article.

10. From these the transition is easy to the குறிப்புவினை. Any crude form, inflexional base, or root, may be treated as a verb. In general we find that the terminations which mark person and number may be added to nouns, thus making derivatives which resemble verbs, and are called so by Tamiḷ grammarians.

These quasi-verbal forms are of constant use in poetry, and give to it much of its terseness and beauty.

Take, for example, உடை 'possession.' We get 1 pers. sing. உடையேன் 'I (am) a possessor.' This may be used as a noun, or as a finite verb, active or passive. [See Concordance, *sub voce.*]

முதல் 'that which stands first,' is used in the first couplet in this way. It takes the term. of the 3 pers. sing. and plur. neuter (H. B. § 31), with euphonic change making முதற்று='it has for its first'; முதல= 'they have for their first.' These are passive: 'All letters are A-firsted.'

The free use of these appellatives gives an indescribable life and energy to many verses. Nouns are not dead, but invested with powers of action, and thus a vigour, terseness and clearness are given to many verses which nothing else could give. A beautiful example of the terseness of this construction is found in the following invocation: அன்பர்க்கடியனேனுடையவப்பனே! 'O Father of me who am the humble servant of all that love.' [அன்பு+ஆர். அடி, அடியன், அடியனேன் 'I who am a slave,' in 6th case.]

The following Table exhibits the types which occur in the *Kurraḷ*:—

	Term.	
SING. 1 pers.	ஏன் அன	உடையேன், 1133.
2 pers.	ஐ	வல்லை. வேலை, 1221. கண்ணை, 1222. நீரை, 11[illegible].
3 p. *m.*	அன்	அறிவன். உள்ளன். எளியன், 386.
f.	அள்	பசையினள், 1098. நல்லாள், 924, 1111.
n.	து	முதற்று, 1. அரிது, 8. கண்ணது, 1222. இனிது. அனைத்து, பா[illegible]ற்று. வற்று, 1079. மாட்டு. நணியது, 3[illegible].
PLUR. 1 pers.	ஏம் அம்	உளேம், 1204. வள்ளி[illegible]பம், 598. காதலம், 1314.
2 pers.	ஈர்	உடையீர்.
3 p. *m. f.*	(ஆர் அர், ஓ. அவர்	நீரர், 1319. காதலவர். இலர், 1242. தமர், 443. உளர், 1204. பெரியார், 444. தொழிலோர், 560. அறிவினவர், 914.
n.	அ	முதல, 1. அரிய. தீய. இனிய. அனைய, பால.

Comp. H. B. § 184.

§ 8. The derivatives from verbal roots are very numerous and varied. Comp. H. B. § 143-9, 154, 190. The following types are found in this work: வேண்டுகல், 4. ஒரால், 153. மாற்றல், 7. செயல், 26. அகறல் (அகலல்), 1325. சேறல் (செல்லல்), 1256. கோறல் (கொல்லல்), 254. காண்டல், 1213. கோள், 9, 220. ஊண், 44. பேறு, 60. நோய், 320. வீடு, ஒத்து, 134. எழுத்து, 1. தகுதி, 111. பிறவி, 10. உண்டி, 945. ஆட்சி, 252. உணர்ச்சி, 453. கொல்லி, 306. வேண்டாமை, 4. பார்வல், 1152. பொருள், 307. புகழ்மை, 533. நோன்மை, 48. வாழ்க்கை, 46. நடை, 59. பொறை, 153. வைப்பு, 24. சோர்வு, 56. அடக்கம், 121. எச்சம், கிடந்தமை, 959. [These are all explained in the appended Lexicon.]

§ 9. Some anomalous forms are found with அளபெடை. This is really the lengthening a long syllable by writing after it its corresponding short letter; thus, தொழார் is written தொழாஅர், 2. [Comp. ἠέλιος for ἥλιος.]

A short syllable is first lengthened, and then tripled by அளபெடை; thus, எடுப்பதும் becomes எடுப்பதூஉம், 15.

The following cases require elucidation:

(1) அளைஇ, 91 (=அளைந்து). ஐ takes as its short, இ. நசைஇ, 1263.

(2) அழீஇ, 182 (=அழித்து).

(3) மரீஇ, 227 (=மருவி). ஓரீஇ, 42 (=ஒருவி). கொளீஇ, 938.

(4) தாஅயது, 610 (=தாவியது).

Here it seems especially to appear in the past verb. part.

§ 10. Another form of which our author makes constant use, and which is a mark of his style, is apparently a verbal part., where a relative might be expected, followed by a குறிப்புவினை, or an adverbial particle thus,

(1) கொன்றன்ன, 109. தளிர்த்தற்று, 78. கண்டனையர், 277. கொன்றுங்கு, 532. தக்காங்கு, 561.

(2) நினைத்தக்கால், 1296. கற்றகடைத்தும், 823. Comp. செயதவக்கண்ணும், 312, and காவாக்கால், 301.

(3) In தோய்வன்ன, 308, and கொள்வற்று, 1187, we seem to have verbal nouns தோய்வு 'as when they cling,' கொள்வு 'like the seizing.'

III.—METRE OF THE KURRAḶ.

In studying the metre of these couplets we must regard—

§ I. அசை='syllables,' or elements of the metrical foot. These are-

(1) நிரையசை, consisting of two syllables, of which the former is short by nature and position, and the latter long or short; thus, இல, மிசை, பயன், are நிரையசைகள். In classical metres it equals a *pyrrhic* (⏑ ⏑) or *iambus* (⏑ —).

(2) நேர். This is long by nature, or by position (any vowel followed by two consonants); or it is the remaining syllable of a word, long or short; thus, வா, வார்த்.

But வான is நேர்நேர், for வா is a நேர் and ன is the remaining syllable, and is long, as the last syllable in a hexameter line, or a syllable *in pausâ*. அகர is நிரைநேர் (⏑ ⏑ —) or *anapæst*.

§ II. சீர் foot,' or elements of the metrical line.

Each word must form a foot. This is the general rule; but words closely connected, as in apposition, may be taken together as one foot. Thus, the first couplet consists of seven feet, each a single word, except எழுத்தெல்லாம், which is two words in apposition. In the குறள் these சீர் are of three kinds:

(1) அசைச்சீர், consisting of a single அசை: —[1], ⏑ ⏑[2].

(2) இயற்சீர், consisting of two அசைகள்: — —[3], ⏑ ⏑ —[4], — ⏑ ⏑[5], ⏑ ⏑ ⏑ ⏑[6].

(3) வெஃண்சீர, consisting of the four இயற்சீர் with an additional நேர்: — — —[7], ⏑ ⏑ — —[8], — ⏑ ⏑ —[9], ⏑ ⏑ ⏑ ⏑ —[10].

These ten metrical feet have technical names:

1. நாள் (—). 2. மலர் (⏑ ⏑).

[Each of these may take a short உ at the end: காசு (— ⏑) பிறப்பு (⏑ ⏑ ⏑). They only occur in the seventh foot of a *kurraḷ*.]

3. தேமா (— —). 4. புளிமா (⏑ ⏑ —).
5. கூவிளம் (— ⏑ ⏑). 6. கருவிளம் (⏑ ⏑ ⏑ ⏑).
7. தேமாங்காய் (— — —). 8. புளிமாங்காய் (⏑ ⏑ — —).
9. கூவிளங்காய் (— ⏑ ⏑ —). 10. கருவிளங்காய் (⏑ ⏑ ⏑ ⏑ —).

Observe (*a*) the long syllable is marked by a stress of the voice, and a short pause; and its length is independent, in many cases, of the actual metrical quantity; (*b*) the last foot in every குறள் being நாள், கா(சு), மலர் or பிறப்(பு), the effect of a catalectic syllable is produced. The deficiency is compensated for by the pause, and a slight prolongation of the closing syllable of the couplet.

The first couplet is scanned:

{ புளிமா புளிமா புளிமாங்காய் தேமா
(அகர முதல வெழுத்தெல்லா மாதி
{ புளிமா புளிமா பிறப்(பு)
(பகவன் முதற்றே யுலகு.

§ III. அடி 'line.' The குறள் is a couplet of seven feet, divided into lines of 4 and 3 feet, or 3 and 4 feet. The division is marked by the rhyme. Of the 1330 couplets, 909 have 4 and 3, while 421 have 3 and 4. There may be a doubt as to one or two of these.

§ IV. எதுகை 'rhyme.' Rhyme in Tamil is in the beginning of the line, and is strictly *the identity of the second letter*, the first being of the same metrical quantity. Six kinds are enumerated. Sometimes there is no rhyme, but a repetition of the entire foot, 201.

(i.) இடையாசெதுகை: identity of 2nd letter. As in 1, அகர rhymes with பகவன். Here க is repeated, the preceding syllable in both lines being short. So in 2, கற் with நற்; in 6, பொறி with நெறி.

(ii.) தலையாசெதுகை: where *the whole foot is identical, with the exception of the first letter* (or syllable, as we should say). This is elegant, and is extended sometimes to the second and even third foot. In 8, அறவாழி rhymes with பிறவாழி.

(iii.) கடையாசெதுகை: when the last syllable of the foot is repeated.

(iv.) ஆசெதுகை: when ய, ர, ல, ழ are disregarded. Thus, in 3, மலர் மிசை rhymes with நிலமிசை, 206.

(v.) இனவெதுகை: when a letter of the same class is substituted. (H.B. Intro. p. 9.) So 112, செப்ப is made to rhyme with எச்ச, 211.

(vi.) மூன்றாமெழுத் தொன்றெதுகை: consonance of third letter, 881.

§ V. மோனை 'alliteration' (Third Gram. 183.) The letter which begins each line should begin at least one other foot in the line. But it is considered sufficient if one of its class is found to commence one of the other feet. For this purpose the classes are:

1. அ, ஆ, ஐ, ஔ.
2. இ, ஈ, எ, ஏ.
3. உ, ஊ, ஒ, ஓ.

Also ச may be represented by த; ஞ by ந் and ம் by வ. Thus, அகர corresponds to ஆதி, 1. The யாப்பருங்கலம் (Third Gram. ii.) distinguishes—

(1) இணைமோனை, consonance in	1 and 2		வேண்டுதல் வேண்டாமை, 4.
(2) பொழிப்புமோனை	,,	1 ,, 3	வானின் றுலகம் வழங்கி, 11.
(3) ஒரூஉத்தொடை	,,	1 ,, 4	அகர முதல எழுத்தெல்லா மாதி, 1.
(4) கூழை	,,	1 2 3	see 19.
(5) மேற்கதுவாய்	,,	1 3 4	see 13.
(6) கீழ்க்கதுவாய்	,,	1 2 4	see 200.

Many lines in the குறள் have no மோனை; but there is generally some alliteration. Comp. 186.

§ VI. தளை: 'connection, or rhythmic sequence of feet.' In the குறள் (and in the நாலடி) the connection peculiar to the metre, which is the வெண்பா, is strictly observed. Its rule is thus expressed:

மாமுன்னிரையும்
விளமுன்னேருங்
காய்முன்னேரும்.

'after மா comes a நிரை,
after விளம் come a நேர்,
after காய் comes a நேர்.'

(முன் here means 'after.') This provides

(1) That a foot ending in மா should always be followed by one beginning with a நிரை:

தேமா or புளிமா	+	(மலர்) புளிமா கருவிளம் or கருவிளங்காய்.

(2) A foot ending in விளம் must be followed by one beginning with a நேர்:

கூவிளம் or கருவிளம்	+	(நாள்) தேமா தேமாங்காய் or கூவிளங்காய்.

(3) A foot ending in காய் must be followed by one beginning with a நேர்:

தேமாங்காய் புளிமாங்காய் or கூவிளங்காய் கருவிளங்காய்	+	(நாள்) தேமா தேமாங்காய் கூவிளங்காய்.

It will be seen on examination that, according to this rule,

(*a*) No குறள் can consist wholly of *spondees*;

(*b*) A குறள் might be framed entirely of *molossi* or *choriambi*;

(*b*) A குறள் may consist wholly of *anapæsts*, or of *dactyls* (excepting in all cases the *catalectic* last foot).

Thus the variety of rhythms in the குறள் is astonishingly great. The first couplet is anapæstic with a single *Ionic a minore* and one spondee:

⏑ ⏑ — ⏑ ⏑ — ⏑ ⏑ — — — —
⏑ ⏑ — ⏑ ⏑ — ⏑ ⏑ (⏑)

§ VII. ஓசை 'tone' or 'rhythm.' In the குறள (and in the வெண்பா in general) the tone, or rhythm is called செப்பலோசை, which seems to mean 'the recitative or didactic tone,' from செப்பு 'declare.' Three kinds are distinguished:—

(1) When only the feet called இசைச்சீர் are used, it is called தூங்கிசைச்செப்பல், or "the *balanced* recitative." The following are all of this kind :—3, 23, 28, 39, 63, 80, 92, 98, 124, 131, 133, 152, 153, 188, 193, 195, 202, 215, 224, 239, 265, 270, 280, 283, 304, 310, 341, 342, 347, 385, 391, 418, 419, 425, 429, 431, 444, 449, 451, 457, 465, 467, 477, 483, 488, 505, 508, 522, 531, 535, 594, 623, 625, 633, 637, 651, 652, 664, 666, 690, 693, 703, 706, 760, 774, 783, 785, 796, 811, 847, 856, 863, 873, 961 975, 978, 979, 980, 1010, 1031, 1042, 1048, 1052, 1055, 1085, 1093, 1105, 1108, 1116, 1118, 1121, 1159, 1193, 1199, 1200, 1201, 1211, 1213, 1224, 1235, 1238, 1242, 1266, 1273, 1277, 1289, 1301, 1309, 1322, 1324. Here the rhythm is lively, and the number of short syllables is generally double the number of the long; but the effect is somewhat monotonous.

(2) When only the வெண்சீர் (except in the seventh foot, are used, it is called ஏந்திசைச் செப்பல்="*grave* recitative." Only one couplet (397) is of this kind :

— — — — — — — — — — ⌣ ⌣ —

— ⌣ ⌣ — — — — — (⌣)

Here the effect is very heavy.

(3) When இயற்சீர் and வெண்சீர் are intermingled we have the ஒழுகிசைச்செப்பல்=" the *mixed* recitative." All not mentioned above are of this kind. In this class, comprising the great majority of couplets, the rhythm has an inexhaustible variety. According to the number of வெண்சீர் introduced is the gravity of the tone ; thus, 12, 110, 758, 735 have but one இயற்சீர், while the first couplet has only one வெண்சீர்.

Much more might be said in regard to the Tamiḷ metres, which are entirely different from the Sanskrit or Telugu metrical systems ; but the student who feels an interest in the subject will find what is here given a sufficient introduction to the subject, at least, as far as the குறள் is concerned.

BOOK I.—VIRTUE.

திருவள்ளுவநாயனார் அருளிச்செய்த
திருக்குறள்.

THE SACRED KURRAL OF TIRUVALLUVA-NÂYANÂR.

BOOK I. — VIRTUE. அறத்துப்பால.

§ I.—INTRODUCTION. பாயிரம்.

CHAPTER I. அதிகாரம் க.

கடவுள் வாழ்த்து.—THE PRAISE OF GOD.

1. அகர முதல வெழுத்தெல்லா மாதி
பகவன் முதற்றே யுலகு (க)

A, as its first of letters, every speech maintains;
The 'Primal Deity' is First through all the world's domains.

2. கற்றதனா லாய பயனென்கொல் வாலறிவ
னற்றா டொழாஅ ரெனின் (உ)

No fruit have men of all their studied lore,
Save they the 'Purely Wise One's' feet adore.

3. மலர்மிசை யேகினான் மாணடி சேர்ந்தார்
நிலமிசை நீடுவாழ் வார் (ங)

His feet, 'Who o'er the full-blown flower hath past,' who gain
In bliss long time shall dwell above this earthly plain.

4. வேண்டுதல் வேண்டாமை யில்லா னடிசேர்ந்தார்க்
கியாண்டு மிடும்பை யில (ச)

His foot, 'Whom want affects not, irks not grief,' who gain
Shall not, through every time, of any woes complain.

5. இருள்சே ரிருவினையுஞ் சேரா விறைவன்
பொருள்சேர் புகழ்புரிந்தார் மாட்டு (ரு)

The men, who on the 'King's' true praise delight to dwell,
Affects not them the fruit of deeds done ill or well.

6. பொறிவாயி லைந்தவித்தான் பொய்தீ ரொழுக்க
நெறிநின்றார் நீடுவாழ் வார் (௬)

Long live they blest, who 've stood in path from falsehood freed;
His, 'Who quenched lusts that from the sense-gates five proceed.'

7. தனக்குவமை யில்லாதான் றாள்சேர்ந்தார்க் கல்லான்
மனக்கவலை மாற்ற லரிது (௭)

Unless His foot, 'to Whom none can compare,' men gain,
'Tis hard for mind to find relief from anxious pain.

8. அறவாழி யந்தணன் றாள்சேர்ந்தார்க் கல்லாற்
பிறவாழி நீந்த லரிது (௮)

Unless His feet, 'the Sea of Good, the Fair and Bountiful,' men gain,
'Tis hard the further bank of being's changeful sea to attain.

9. கோளில் பொறியிற் குணமிலவே யெண்குணத்தான்
றாளை வணங்காத் தலை (௯)

Before His foot, 'the Eight-fold Excellence,' with unbent head
Who stands, like palsied sense, is to all living functions dead.

10. பிறவிப் பெருங்கட னீந்துவர் நீந்தா
ரிறைவ னடிசேரா தார் (௰)

They swim the sea of births, the 'Monarch's' foot who gain;
None others reach the shore of being's mighty main.

CHAPTER II. அதி. ௨.

வான்சிறப்பு.—The Excellence of Rain.

11. வானின் றுலகம் வழங்கி வருதலாற்
றானமிழ்த மென்றுணரற் பாற்று (௧)

The world its course maintains through life that rain unfailing gives;
Thus rain is known the true ambrosial food of all that lives.

12. துப்பார்க்குத் துப்பாய துப்பாக்கித் துப்பார்க்குத்
துப்பாய தூஉ மழை (௨)

The rain makes pleasant food for eaters rise;
As food itself, thirst-quenching draught supplies.

13. விண்ணின்று பொய்ப்பின் விரிநீர் வியனுலகத்
துண்ணின் றுடற்றும் பசி (௩)

If clouds, that promised rain, deceive, and in the sky remain,
Famine, sore torment, stalks o'er earth's vast ocean-girdled plain.

14. ஏரி னுழாஅ ருழவர் புயலென்னும்
வாரி வளங்குன்றிக் கால் (௪)

If clouds their wealth of waters fail on earth to pour,
The ploughers plough with oxen's sturdy team no more.

15. கெடுப்பதூஉங் கெட்டார்க்குச் சார்வாய்மற் றாங்கே
யெடுப்பதூஉ மெல்லா மழை (௫)

'Tis rain works all: it ruin spreads, then timely aid supplies;
As, in the happy days before, it bids the ruined rise.

16. விசும்பிற் றுளிவீழி னல்லான்மற் றாங்கே
பசும்புற் றலைகாண் பரிது (௬)

If from the clouds no drops of rain are shed,
'Tis rare to see green herb lift up its head.

17. நெடுங்கடலுந் தன்னீர்மை குன்றுந்
தடிந்தெழிலி தானல்கா தாகி விடின் (௭)

If clouds restrain their gifts and grant no rain,
The treasures fail in ocean's wide domain.

18. சிறப்பொடு பூசனை செல்லாது வானம்
வறக்குமேல் வானோர்க்கு மீண்டு (௮)

If heaven grow dry, with feast and offering never more
Will men on earth the heavenly ones adore.

19. தானந் தவமிரண்டுந் தங்கா வியனுலகம்
வானம் வழங்கா தெனின் (௯)

If heaven its watery treasures ceases to dispense,
Through the wide world cease gifts, and deeds of 'penitence.'

20. நீரின் றமையா துலகெனின் யார்யார்க்கும்
வானின் றமையா தொழுக்கு (௰)

When water fails, functions of nature cease, you say;
Thus when rain fails, no men can walk in 'duty's ordered way.'

CHAPTER III. அதி. ௩.

நீத்தார்பெருமை.—THE GREATNESS OF ASCETICS.

21. ஒழுக்கத்து நீத்தார் பெருமை
விழுப்பத்து வேண்டும் பனுவற் றுணிவு (௧)

The settled rule of every code requires, as highest good,
Their greatness who, renouncing all, true to their rule have stood.

22. துறந்தார் பெருமை துணைக்கூறின் வையத்
திறந்தாரை யெண்ணிக்கொண் டற்று (௨)

As counting those that from the earth have passed away,
'Tis vain attempt the might of holy men to say.

23. இருமை வகைதெரிந் தீண்டறம் பூண்டார்
பெருமை பிறங்கிற் றுலகு (௩)

Their greatness earth transcends, who, way of both worlds weighed,
In this world take their stand, in virtue's robe arrayed.

24. உரனென்னுந் தோட்டியா னோரைந்துங் காப்பான்
வரனென்னும் வைப்புக்கோர் வித்து (௪)

He, who with firmness' curb the five restrains,
Is seed for soil of yonder happy plains.

25. ஐந்தவித்தா னாற்ற லகல்விசும்பு ளார்கோமா
னிந்திரனே சாலுங் கரி (௫)

Their might who have destroyed 'the five,' shall soothly tell
Indra, the lord of those in heaven's wide realms that dwell.

26. செயற்கரிய செய்வார் பெரியார் சிறியர்
செயற்கரிய செய்கலா தார் (௬)

Things hard in the doing will great men do;
Things hard in the doing the mean eschew.

27. சுவையொளி யூறோசை நாற்றமென் றைந்தின்
வகைதெரிவான் கட்டே யுலகு (௭)

Taste, light, touch, sound, and smell: who knows the way
Of all the five,—the world submissive owns his sway.

28. நிறைமொழி மாந்தர் பெருமை நிலத்து
மறைமொழி காட்டி விடும் (௮)

The might of men whose word is never vain,
The 'secret word' shall to the earth proclaim.

29. குணமென்னுங் குன்றேறி நின்றார் வெகுளி
கணமேயுங் காத்த லரிது (௯)

The wrath 'tis hard e'en for an instant to endure
Of those who virtue's hill have scaled, and stand secure.

30. அந்தண ரென்போ ரறவோர்மற் றெவ்வுயிர்க்குஞ்
செந்தண்மை பூண்டொழுக லான் (௰)

Towards all that breathe, with seemly graciousness adorned they live;
And thus to virtue's sons the name of 'Anthanar' men give.

CHAPTER IV. அதி. ௪.

அறன்வலியுறுத்தல்.—ASSERTION OF THE STRENGTH OF VIRTUE.

31. சிறப்பீனுஞ் செல்வமு மீனு
மறத்தினூஉங் காக்க மெவனோ யுயிர்க்கு (௧)

It yields distinction, yields prosperity ; what gain
Greater than virtue can a living man obtain ?

32. அறத்தினூஉங் காக்கமு மில்லை யதனை
மறத்தலி னூங்கில்லை கேடு (௨)

No greater gain than virtue aught can cause ;
No greater loss than life oblivious of her laws.

33. ஒல்லும் வகையா லறவினை யோவாதே
செல்லும் வாயெல்லாஞ் செயல் (௩)

To finish virtue's work with ceaseless effort strive,
What way thou may'st, where'er thou see'st the work may thrive.

34. மனத்துக்கண் மாசில னாத
லனைத்தற னாகுல நீர பிற (௪)

Spotless be thou in mind ! This only merits virtue's name ;
All else, mere pomp of idle sound, no real worth can claim.

35. அழுக்கா றவாவெகுளி யின்னாச்சொன் னான்கு
மிழுக்கா வியன்ற தறம் (௫)

'Tis virtue when, his footsteps sliding not through envy, wrath,
Lust, evil speech—these four, man onwards moves in ordered path.

36. அன்றறிவா மென்னா தறஞ்செய்க மற்றது
பொன்றுங்காற் பொன்றாத் துணை (௬)

Do deeds of virtue now. Say not, 'To-morrow we 'll be wise';
Thus, when thou diest, shalt thou find a help that never dies.

37. அறத்தா றிதுவென வேண்டா சிவிகை
பொறுத்தானோ டூர்ந்தா னிடை (௭)

Needs not in words to dwell on virtue's fruits: compare
The man in litter borne with them that toiling bear !

38. வீழ்நாள் படாஅமை நன்றாற்றி னஃதொருவன்
வாழ்நாள் வழியடைக்குங் கல் (௮)

If no day passing idly, good to do each day you toil,
A stone 't will be to block the way of future days of moil.

39. அறத்தான் வருவதே யின்பமற் றெல்லாம்
புறத்த புகழு மில (௯)

What from virtue floweth, yieldeth dear delight;
All else extern, is void of glory's light.

40. செயற்பால தோரு மறனே யொருவற்
குயற்பால தோரும் பழி (௰)

'Virtue' sums the things that should be done;
'Vice' sums the things that man should shun.

பாயிரமுற்றும்.

END OF INTRODUCTION.

§ 2. DOMESTIC VIRTUE. இல்லறம்

CHAPTER V. அதி. ரு.

இல்வாழ்க்கை.—Domestic Life.

41. இல்வாழ்வா னென்பா னியல்புடைய மூவர்க்கு
நல்லாற்றி னின்ற துணை (௧)

The men of household virtue, firm in way of good, sustain
The other orders three that rule professed maintain.

42. துறந்தார்க்குந் துவ்வா தவர்க்கு
மிறந்தார்க்கு மில்வாழ்வா னென்பான் றுணை (௨)

To anchorites, to indigent, to those who 've passed away,
The man for household virtue famed is needful help and stay.

43. தென்புலத்தார் தெய்வம் விருந்தொக்க
லானென்றாங் கைம்புலத்தா றோம்ப றலை (௩)

The manes, God, guests, kindred, self, in due degree,
These five to cherish well is chiefest charity.

44. பழியஞ்சிப் பாத்தூ ணுடைத்தாயின் வாழ்க்கை
வழியெஞ்ச லெஞ்ஞான்று மில் (௪)

Who shares his meal with others, while all guilt he shuns,
His virtuous line unbroken though the ages runs.

45. அன்பு மறனு முடைத்தாயி னில்வாழ்க்கை
பண்பும் பயனு மது (௫)

If love and virtue in the household reign,
This is of life the perfect grace and gain.

46. அறத்தாற்றி னில்வாழ்க்கை யாற்றிற்
புறத்தாற்றிற் போஒய்ப் பெறுவ தெவன் (௬)

If man in active household life a virtuous soul retain,
What fruit from other modes of virtue can he gain?

47. இயல்பினா னில்வாழ்க்கை வாழ்பவ னென்பான்
முயல்வாரு ளெல்லாந் தலை (௭)

In nature's way who spends his calm domestic days,
'Mid all that strive for virtue's crown hath foremost place.

48. ஆற்றி னொழுக்கி யறனிழுக்கா வில்வாழ்க்கை
நோற்பாரி னோன்மை யுடைத்து (௮)

Others it sets upon their way, itself from virtue ne'er declines;
Than stern ascetics' pains such life domestic brighter shines.

49. அறனெனப் பட்டதே யில்வாழ்க்கை யஃதும்
பிறன்பழிப்ப தில்லாயி னன்று (கூ)

The life domestic rightly bears true virtue's name ;
That other too, if blameless found, due praise may claim.

50. வையத்துள் வாழ்வாங்கு வாழ்பவன் வானுறையுந்
தெய்வத்துள் வைக்கப் படும் (௰)

Who shares domestic life, by household virtues graced,
Shall, mid the gods, in heaven who dwell, be placed.

CHAPTER VI. அதி. சா.

வாழ்க்கைத் துணைநலம்.—THE GOODNESS OF THE HELP TO DOMESTIC LIFE.

51. மனைத்தக்க மாண்புடைய ளாகித்தற் கொண்டான்
வளத்தக்காள் வாழ்க்கைத் துணை (க)

As doth the house beseem, she shows her wifely dignity ;
As doth her husband's wealth befit, she spends : helpmeet is she.

52. மனைமாட்சி யில்லாள்க ணில்லாயின் வாழ்க்கை
யெனைமாட்சித் தாயினு மில் (உ)

If household excellence be wanting in the wife,
Howe'er with splendour lived, all worthless is the life.

53. இல்லதெ னில்லவண் மாண்பானா
லுள்ளதெ னில்லவண் மாணாக் கடை (ங)

There is no lack within the house, where wife in worth excels,
There is no luck within the house, where wife dishonoured dwells.

54. பெண்ணிற் பெருந்தக்க யாவுள கற்பென்னுந்
திண்மையுண் டாகப் பெறின் (ச)

If woman might of chastity retain,
What choicer treasure doth the world contain ?

55. தெய்வந் தொழாஅள் கொழுநற் றொழுதெழுவாள்
பெய்யெனப் பெய்யு மழை (ரு)

No god adoring, low she bends before her lord ;
Then rising, serves : the rain falls instant at her word !

56. தற்காத்துத் தற்கொண்டாற் பேணித் தகைசான்ற
சொற்காத்துச் சோர்விலாள் பெண் (சா)

Who guards herself, for husband's comfort cares, her household's fame
In perfect wise with sleepless soul preserves,—give her a woman's name !

57. சிறைகாக்குங் காப்பெவன் செய்யு மகளிர்
நிறைகாக்குங் காப்பே தலை (௭)

Of what avail is watch and ward?
Honour 's a woman's safest guard.

58. பெற்றாற் பெறிற்பெறுவர் பெண்டிர் பெருஞ்சிறப்புப்
புத்தேளிர் வாழு முலகு (௮)

If wife be wholly true to him who gained her as his bride,
Great glory gains she in the world where gods in bliss abide.

59. புகழ்புரிந் தில்லிலோர்க் கில்லை
யிகழ்வார்முன் னேறுபோற் பீடு நடை (௯)

Who have not spouses that in virtue's praise delight,
They lion-like can never walk in scorners' sight.

60. மங்கல மென்ப மனைமாட்சி மற்றத
னன்கல நன்மக்கட் பேறு (௰)

The house's 'blessing,' men pronounce the house-wife excellent;
The gain of blessèd children is its goodly ornament.

CHAPTER VII. அதி. ௭.

புதல்வரைப்பெறுதல்.—The Obtaining of Sons.

61. பெறுமவற்றுள் யாமறிவ தில்லை
யறிவறிந்த மக்கட்பே றல்ல பிற (௧)

Of all that men acquire, we know not any greater gain,
Than that which by the birth of learned children men obtain.

62. எழுபிறப்புந் தீயவை தீண்டா
பழிபிறங்காப் பண்புடை மக்கட் பெறின் (௨)

Who children gain, that none reproach, of virtuous worth,
No evils touch them, through the sev'n-fold maze of birth.

63. தம்பொரு ளென்பதம் மக்க ளவர்பொரு
டந்தம் வினையான் வரும் (௩)

'Man's children are his fortune,' say the wise;
From each one's deeds his varied fortunes rise.

64. அமிழ்தினு மாற்ற வினிதே
தம்மக்கள் சிறுகை யளாவிய கூழ் (௪)

Than gods' ambrosia sweeter far the food before men laid,
In which the little hands of children of their own have play'd.

65. மக்கண்மெய் தீண்ட லுடற்கின்ப மற்றவர்
சொற்கேட்ட லின்பஞ் செவிக்கு (௫)

To parent sweet the touch of children dear;
Their voice is sweetest music to his ear.

66. குழலினி தியாழினி தென்ப தம்மக்கண்
மழலைச்சொற் கேளா தவர் (௬)

'The pipe is sweet,' 'the lute is sweet,' by them 't will be averred,
Who music of their infants' lisping lips have never heard.

67. தந்தை மகற்காற்று நன்றி யவையத்து
முந்தி யிருப்பச் செயல் (௭)

Sire greatest boon on son confers, who makes him meet
In councils of the wise to fill the highest seat.

68. தம்மிற்றம் மக்க ளறிவுடைமை மாநிலத்து
மன்னுயிர்க் கெல்லா மினிது (௮(

Their children's wisdom greater than their own confessed,
Through the wide world is sweet to every human breast.

69. ஈன்ற பொழுதிற் பெரிதுவக்குந்
தன்மகனைச் சான்றோனெனக் கேட்ட தாய் (௯)

When mother hears him named 'fulfill'd of wisdom's lore,'
Far greater joy she feels, than when her son she bore.

70. மகன்றந்தைக் காற்று முதவி
யிவன்றந்தை யென்னோற்றான் கொல்லென்னுஞ் சொல்
(௰)

To sire, what best requital can by grateful child be done?
To make men say, 'What merit gained the father such a son?'

CHAPTER VIII. அதி. ௮.

அன்புடைமை.—The Possession of Love.

71. அன்பிற்கு முண்டோ வடைக்குந்தா ழார்வலர்
புன்கணீர் பூச றரும் (௧)

And is there bar that can even love restrain?
The tiny tear shall make the lover's secret plain.

72. அன்பிலா ரெல்லாந் தமக்குரிய ரன்புடையா
ரென்பு முரியர் பிறர்க்கு (௨)

The loveless to themselves belong alone;
The loving men are others' to the very bone.

73. அன்போ டியைந்த வழக்கென்ப வாருயிர்க்
கென்போ டியைந்த தொடர்பு (௩)

Of precious soul with body's flesh and bone,
The union yields one fruit, the life of love alone.

74. அன்பீனு மார்வ முடைமை யதுவீனு
நண்பென்னு நாடாச் சிறப்பு (௪)

From love fond yearning springs for union sweet of minds;
And that the bond of rare excelling friendship binds.

75. அன்புற் றமர்ந்த வழக்கென்ப வையகத்
தின்புற்றா ரெய்துஞ் சிறப்பு (௫)

Sweetness on earth and rarest bliss above,
These are the fruits of tranquil life of love.

76. அறத்திற்கே யன்புசார் பென்ப வறியார்
மறத்திற்கு மஃதே துணை (௬)

The unwise deem love virtue only can sustain,
It also helps the man who evil would restrain.

77. என்பி லதனை வெயில்போலக் காயுமே
யன்பி லதனை யறம் (௭)

As sun's fierce ray dries up the boneless things,
So loveless beings virtue's power to nothing brings.

78. அன்பகத் தில்லா வுயிர்வாழ்க்கை
வன்பாற்கண் வற்றன் மரந்தளிர்த் தற்று (௮)

The loveless soul, the very joys of life may know
When flowers, in barren soil, on sapless trees, shall blow.

79. புறத்துறுப் பெல்லா மெவன்செய்யும் யாக்கை
யகத்துறுப் பன்பி லவர்க்கு (௯)

Though every outward part complete, the body's fitly framed;
What good, when soul within, of love devoid, lies halt and maimed?

80. அன்பின் வழிய துயிர்நிலை யஃதிலார்க்
கென்புதோல் போர்த்த வுடம்பு (௰)

Bodies of loveless men are bony framework clad with skin;
Then is the body seat of life, when love resides within.

CHAPTER IX. அதி. ௯.

விருந்தோம்பல்.—Cherishing Guests.

81. இருந்தோம்பி யில்வாழ்வ தெல்லாம்
விருந்தோம்பி வேளாண்மை செய்தற் பொருட்டு (௧)

All household cares and course of daily life have this in view,
Guests to receive with courtesy, and kindly acts to do.

82. விருந்து புறத்ததாத் தானுண்டல் சாவா
மருந்தெனினும் வேண்டற்பாற் றன்று (௨)

Though food of immortality should crown the board,
Feasting alone, the guests without unfed, is thing abhorred.

83 வருவிருந்து வைகலு மோம்புவான் வாழ்க்கை
பருவந்து பாழ்படுத லின்று (௩)

Each day he tends the coming guest with kindly care;
Painless, unfailing plenty shall his household share.

84. அகனமர்ந்து செய்யா ளுறையு
முகனமர்ந்து நல்விருந் தோம்புவா னில் (௪)

With smiling face he entertains each virtuous guest;
'Fortune' with gladsome mind shall in his dwelling rest.

85. வித்து மிடல்வேண்டுங் கொல்லோ விருந்தோம்பி
மிச்சின் மிசைவான் புலம் (௫)

Who first regales his guest, and then himself supplies,
O'er all his fields, unsown, shall plenteous harvests rise.

86. செல்விருந் தோம்பி வருவிருந்து பார்த்திருப்பா
னல்விருந்து வானத் தவர்க்கு (௬)

The guest arrived he tends, the coming guest expects to see;
To those in heavenly homes that dwell a welcome guest is he.

87 இனைத்துணைத் தென்பதொன் றில்லை விருந்தின்
றுணைத்துணை வேள்விப் பயன் (௭)

To reckon up the fruit of kindly deeds were all in vain;
Their worth is as the worth of guests you entertain.

88. பரிந்தோம்பிப் பற்றற்றே மென்பர்
விருந்தோம்பி வேள்வி தலைப்படா தார் (௮)

With pain they guard their stores, yet 'All forlorn are we,' they 'll cry,
Who cherish not their guests, nor kindly help supply.

89. உடைமையு ளின்மை விருந்தோம்ப லோம்பா
மடமை மடவார்க ணுண்டு (௯)

To turn from guests is penury, though worldly goods abound;
'Tis senseless folly, only with the senseless found.

90. மோப்பக் குழையு மனிச்ச முகந்திரிந்து
நோக்கக் குழையும் விருந்து (ம)

The flower of the 'Anicha' withers away,
If you do but its fragrance inhale;
If the face of the host cold welcome convey,
The guest's heart within him will fail.

CHAPTER X. அதி. ௧0.

இனியவைகூறல்.—The Utterance of Pleasant Words.

91. இன்சொலா லீர மளைஇப் படிறிலவாஞ்
செம்பொருள் கண்டார்வாய்ச் சொல் (௧)

Pleasant words are words with all pervading love that burn;
Words from his guileless mouth who can the very truth discern.

92. அகனமர்ந் தீதலி னன்றே
முகனமர்ந் தின்சொல னாகப் பெறின் (௨)

A pleasant word with beaming smile 's preferred,
Even to gifts with liberal heart conferred.

93. முகத்தா னமர்ந்தினிது நோக்கி
யகத்தா னினிசொ லினதே யறம் (௩)

With brightly beaming smile, and kindly light of loving eye,
And heart sincere, to utter pleasant words is charity.

94. துன்புறூஉந் துவ்வாமை யில்லாகும் யார்மாட்டு
மின்புறூஉ மின்சொ லவர்க்கு (௪)

The men of pleasant speech that gladness-breathe around,
Through indigence shall never sorrow's prey be found.

95. பணிவுடைய னின்சொல னாத லொருவற்
கணியல்ல மற்றுப் பிற (௫)

Humility with pleasant speech to man on earth,
Is choice adornment; all besides is nothing worth.

96. அல்லவை தேய வறம்பெருகு
நல்லவை நாடி யினிய சொலின் (௬)

Who seeks out good, words from his lips of sweetness flow;
In him the power of vice declines, and virtues grow.

97. நயனீன்று நன்றி பயக்கும்
பயனீன்று பண்பிற் றலைப்பிரியாச் சொல் (௭)

The words of sterling sense, to rule of right that strict adhere,
To virtuous action prompting, blessings yield in every sphere.

௯௮. சிறுமையு ணீங்கிய வின்சொன்
மறுமையு மிம்மையு மின்பந் தரும் (௮)

Sweet kindly words, from meanness free, delight of heart
In world to come and in this world impart.

99. இன்சொ லினிதீன்றல் காண்பா னெவன்கொலோ
வன்சொல் வழங்கு வது (௯)

Who sees the pleasure kindly speech affords,
Why makes he use of harsh, repellant words?

100. இனிய வுளவாக வின்னாத கூறல்
கனியிருப்பக் காய்கவர்ந் தற்று (௰)

When pleasant words are easy, bitter words to use,
Is, leaving sweet ripe fruit, the sour unripe to choose.

CHAPTER XI. அதி. ௧௧.

செய்ந்நன்றியறிதல்.—THE KNOWLEDGE OF BENEFITS CONFERRED: GRATITUDE.

101. செய்யாமற் செய்த வுதவிக்கு
வையகமும் வானகமு மாற்ற லரிது (௧)

Assistance given by those who ne'er received our aid,
In debt by gift of heaven and earth but poorly paid.

102. காலத்தி னாற்செய்த நன்றி சிறிதெனினு
ஞாலத்தின் மாணப் பெரிது (௨)

A timely benefit,—though thing of little worth
The gift itself,—in excellence transcends the earth.

103. பயன்றூக்கார் செய்த வுதவி
நயன்றூக்கி னன்மை கடலிற் பெரிது (௩)

Kindness shown by those who weigh not
What the return may be;
When you ponder right its merit,
'Tis vaster than the sea.

104. தினைத்துணை நன்றி செயினும்
பனைத்துணையாக் கொள்வர் பயன்றெரி வார் (௪)

Each benefit to those of actions' fruit who rightly deem,
Though small as millet-seed, as palm-tree vast will seem.

105. உதவி வரைத்தன் றுதவி
யுதவி செயப்பட்டார் சால்பின் வரைத்து (௫)

The kindly aid's extent is of its worth no measure true;
Its worth is as the worth of him to whom the act you do.

106. மறவற்க மாசற்றார் கேண்மை
துறவற்க துன்பத்துட் டுப்பாயார் நட்பு (௬)

Kindness of men of stainless soul remember evermore!
Forsake thou never friends who were thy stay in sorrow sore!

107. எழுமை யெழுபிறப்பு முள்ளுவர் தங்கண்
விழுமந் துடைத்தவர் நட்பு (௭)

Through all seven worlds, in seven-fold birth,
Remains in mem'ry of the wise,
Friendship of those who wiped on earth,
The tears of sorrow from their eyes.

108. நன்றி மறப்பது நன்றன்று நன்றல்ல
தன்றே மறப்பது நன்று (௮)

'Tis never good to let the thought of good things done thee pass away;
Of things not good, 'tis good to rid thy memory that very day.

109. கொன்றன்ன வின்னா செயினு மவர்செய்த
வொன்றுநன் றுள்ளக் கெடும் (௯)

Effaced straightway is deadliest injury,
By thought of one kind act in days gone by.

110. எந்நன்றி கொன்றார்க்கு முய்வுண்டா முய்வில்லை
செய்ந்நன்றி கொன்ற மகற்கு (௰)

Who every good have killed, may yet destruction flee;
Who 'benefit' has killed, that man shall ne'er 'scape free!

CHAPTER XII. அதி. ௧௨.

நடுவுநிலைமை.—IMPARTIALITY.

111. தகுதி யெனவொன்று நன்றே
பகுதியாற் பாற்பட் டொழுகப் பெறின் (௧)

If justice, failing not, its quality maintain,
Giving to each his due,—'tis man's one highest gain.

112. செப்ப முடையவ னாக்கஞ் சிதைவின்றி
யெச்சத்திற் கேமாப் புடைத்து (௨)

**The just man's wealth unwasting shall endure,
And to his race a lasting joy ensure.**

113. நன்றே தரினு நடுவிகந்தா மாக்கத்தை
யன்றே யொழிய விடல் (௩)

**Though only good it seem to give, yet gain
By wrong acquired not e'en one day retain!**

114. தக்கார் தகவில ரென்ப தவரவர்
எச்சத்தாற் காணப் படும் (௪)

**Who just or unjust lived shall soon appear:
By each one's offspring shall the truth be clear.**

115. கேடும் பெருக்கமு மில்லல்ல நெஞ்சத்துக்
கோடாமை சான்றோர்க் கணி (௫)

**The gain and loss in life are not mere accident;
Just mind inflexible is sages' ornament.**

116. கெடுவல்யா னென்ப தறிகதன் னெஞ்ச
நடுவொரீஇ யல்ல செயின் (௬)

**If, right deserting, heart to evil turn,
Let man impending ruin's sign discern!**

117. கெடுவாக வையா துலக
நடுவாக நன்றிக்கட் டங்கியான் றாழ்வு (௭)

**The man who justly lives, tenacious of the right,
In low estate is never low to wise man's sight.**

118. சமன்செய்து சீர்தூக்குங் கோல்போ
லமைந்தொருபாற் கோடாமை சான்றோர்க் கணி (௮)

**To stand, like balance rod that level hangs and rightly weighs,
With calm unbiassed equity of soul, is sages' praise.**

119. சொற்கோட்ட மில்லது செப்ப மொருதலையா
வுட்கோட்ட மின்மை பெறின் (௯)

**Inflexibility in word is righteousness,
If men inflexibility of soul possess.**

120. வாணிகஞ் செய்வார்க்கு வாணிகம்
பேணிப் பிறவுந் தமபோற் செயின் (௰)

**As thriving trader is the trader known,
Who guards another's interests as his own.**

CHAPTER XIII. அதி. ௧௩.

அடக்கமுடைமை.—The Possession of Self-restraint.

121. அடக்க மமரரு ளுய்க்கு
மடங்காமை யாரிரு ளுய்த்து விடும் (௧)

Controul of self does man conduct to bliss th' immortals share;
Indulgence leads to deepest night, and leaves him there.

122. காக்க பொருளா வடக்கத்தை
யாக்க மதனினூஉங் கில்லை யுயிர்க்கு (௨)

Guard thou as wealth the power of self-controul;
Than this no greater gain to living soul!

123. செறிவறிந்து சீர்மை பயக்கு
மறிவறிந் தாற்றி னடங்கப் பெறின் (௩)

If versed in wisdom's lore by virtue's law you self restrain,
Your self-repression known will yield you glory's gain.

124. நிலையிற் றிரியா தடங்கியான் றோற்ற
மலையினு மாணப் பெரிது (௪)

In his station, all unswerving, if man self subdue,
Greater he than mountain proudly rising to the view.

125. எல்லார்க்கு நன்றாம் பணித லவருள்ளுஞ்
செல்வர்க்கே செல்வந் தகைத்து (௫)

To all humility is goodly grace; but chief to them
With fortune blessed,—'tis fortune's diadem.

126. ஒருமையு ளாமைபோ லைந்தடக்க லாற்றி
னெழுமையு மேமாப் புடைத்து (௬)

Like tortoise, who the five restrains
In one, through seven worlds bliss obtains.

127. யாகாவா ராயினு நாகாக்க காவாக்காற்
சோகாப்பர் சொல்லிழுக்குப் பட்டு (௭)

Whate'er they fail to guard, o'er lips men guard should keep;
If not, through fault of tongue, they bitter tears shall weep.

128. ஒன்றானுந் தீச்சொற் பொருட்பய னுண்டாயி
னன்றாகா தாகி விடும்

Though some small gain of good it seem to bring,
The evil word is parent still of evil thing.

129. தீயினாற் சுட்டபு ணுள்ளாறு மாறாதே
நாவினாற் சுட்ட வடு (௯)

In flesh by fire inflamed, nature may throughly heal the sore;
In soul by tongue inflamed, the ulcer healeth nevermore.

130. கதங்காத்துக் கற்றடங்க லாற்றுவான் செவ்வி
யறம்பார்க்கு மாற்றி னுழைந்து (௰)

Who learns restraint, and guards his soul from wrath,
Virtue, a timely aid, attends his path.

CHAPTER XIV. அதி. ௧௪.

ஒழுக்கமுடைமை.—The Possession of Decorum

131. ஒழுக்கம் விழுப்பந் தரலா
னொழுக்க முயிரினு மோம்பப் படும் (௧)

'Decorum' gives especial excellence; with greater care
'Decorum' should men guard than life, which all men share.

132. பரிந்தோம்பிக் காக்க வொழுக்கந்
தெரிந்தோம்பித் தேரினு மஃதே துணை (௨)

Searching, duly watching, learning,—'decorum' still we find
Man's only aid: toiling, guard thou this with watchful mind.

133. ஒழுக்க முடைமை குடிமை
யிழுக்க மிழிந்த பிறப்பாய் விடும் (௩)

'Decorum' 's true nobility on earth;
'Indecorum's' issue is ignoble birth.

134. மறப்பினு மோத்துக் கொளலாகும் பார்ப்பான்
பிறப்பொழுக்கங் குன்றக் கெடும் (௪)

Though he forget, the Brâhman may regain his Vêdic lore;
Failing in 'decorum due,' birthright 's gone for evermore.

135. அழுக்கா றுடையான்க ணாக்கம்போன் றில்லை
யொழுக்க முடையான்க ணுயர்வு (௫)

The envious soul in life no rich increase of blessing gains,
So man of 'due decorum' void no dignity obtains.

136. ஒழுக்கத்தி னொல்கா ருரவோ
ரிழுக்கத்தி னேதம் படுபாக்க றிந்து (௬)

The strong of soul no jot abate of 'strict decorum's' laws,
Knowing that 'due decorum's' breach foulest disgrace will cause.

137. ஒழுக்கத்தி னெய்துவர் மேன்மை
இழுக்கத்தி னெய்துவ ரெய்தாப் பழி (எ)

'Tis source of dignity when 'true decorum' is preserved;
Who break 'decorum's' rules endure e'en censures undeserved.

138. நன்றிக்கு வித்தாகு நல்லொழுக்கந் தீயொழுக்க
மென்று மிடும்பை தரும் (அ)

'Decorum true' observed a seed of good will be;
'Decorum's breach' will sorrow yield eternally.

139. ஒழுக்க முடையவர்க் கொல்லாவே தீய
வழுக்கியும் வாயாற் சொலல் (கூ)

It cannot be that they who 'strict decorum's' law fulfil,
E'en in forgetful mood, should utter words of ill.

140. உலகத்தோ டொட்ட வொழுகல்
பலகற்றுங் கல்லா ரறிவிலா தார் (ω)

Who know not with the world in harmony to dwell,
May many things have learned, but nothing well.

CHAPTER XV. அதி. கரு.

பிறனில் விழையாமை.—Not Coveting another's Wife.

141. பிறன்பொருளாட் பெட்டொழுகும் பேதைமை ஞாலத்
தறம்பொருள் கண்டார்க ணில் (க)

Who laws of virtue and possession's rights have known,
Indulge no foolish love of her by right another's own.

142. அறன்கடை நின்றாரு ளெல்லாம்
பிறன்கடை நின்றாரிற் பேதையா ரில் (உ)

No fools, of all that stand from virtue's pale shut out,
Like those who longing lurk their neighbour's gate without.

143. விளிந்தாரின் வேறல்லார் மன்ற
தெளிந்தாரிற் றீமை புரிந்தொழுகு வார் (ங)

They're numbered with the dead, e'en while they live,—how otherwise?
With wife of sure confiding friend who evil things devise.

144. எனைத்துணைய ராயினு மென்னாந்
தினைத்துணையுந் தேரான் பிறனில் புகல் (ச)

How great soe'er they be, what gain have they of life,
Who, not a whit reflecting, seek a neighbour's wife?

145. எளிதென வில்லிறப்பா னெய்துமெஞ் ஞான்றும்
விளியாது நிற்கும் பழி (௫)

'Mere trifle!' saying thus, invades the home; so he ensures
A gain of guilt that deathless aye endures.

146. பகைபாவ மச்சம் பழியென நான்கு
மிகவாவா மில்லிறப்பான் கண் (௬)

Who home invades, from him pass nevermore,
Hatred and sin, fear, foul disgrace: these four.

147. அறனியலா னில்வாழ்வா னென்பான்
பிறனியலாள் பெண்மை நயவா தவன் (௭)

Who sees the wife, another's own, with no desiring eye,
In sure domestic bliss he dwelleth ever virtuously.

148. பிறன்மனை நோக்காத பேராண்மை சான்றோர்க்
கறனொன்றோ வான்ற வொழுக்கு (௮)

Manly excellence, that looks not on another's wife,
Is not virtue merely, 'tis full 'propriety' of life.

149. நலக்குரியார் யாரெனி னாமநீர் வைப்பிற்
பிறற்குரியா டோடோயா தார் (௯)

Who 're good indeed, on earth begirt by ocean's gruesome tide?
The men who touch not her that is another's bride.

150. அறன்வரையா னல்ல செயினும்
பிறன்வரையாள் பெண்மை நயவாமை நன்று (௰)

Though virtue's bounds he pass, and evil deeds hath wrought;
At least, 'tis good if neighbour's wife he covet not.

CHAPTER XVI. அதி. ௧௬.

பொறையுடைமை.—THE POSSESSION OF PATIENCE: FORBEARANCE.

151. அகழ்வாரைத் தாங்கு நிலம்போலத் தம்மை
யிகழ்வார்ப் பொறுத்த றலை (௧)

As earth bears up the men who delve into her breast,
To bear with scornful men of virtues is the best.

152. பொறுத்த லிறப்பினை யென்று மதனை
மறத்த லதனினு நன்று (௨)

Forgiving trespasses is good always;
Forgetting them hath even higher praise.

153. இன்மையு ளின்மை விருந்தொரால்
வன்மையுள் வன்மை மடவார் பொறை (௩)

The sorest poverty is bidding guest unfed depart;
The mightiest might to bear with men of foolish heart.

154. நிறையுடைமை நீங்காமை வேண்டிற்
பொறையுடைமை போற்றி யொழுகப் படும் (௪)

Seek'st thou honour never tarnished to retain;
So must thou patience, guarding evermore, maintain.

155. ஒறுத்தாரை யொன்றாக வையாரே வைப்பர்
பொறுத்தாரைப் பொன்போற் பொதிந்து (௫)

Who wreak their wrath as worthless are despised;
Who patiently forbear as gold are prized.

156. ஒறுத்தார்க் கொருநாளை யின்பம்
பொறுத்தார்க்குப் பொன்றுந் துணையும் புகழ் (௬)

Who wreak their wrath have pleasure for a day;
Who bear have praise till earth shall pass away.

157. திறனல்ல தற்பிறர் செய்யினு நோனொந்
தறனல்ல செய்யாமை நன்று (௭)

Though others work thee ill, thus shalt thou blessing reap:
Grieve for their sin, thyself from vicious action keep!

158. மிகுதியான் மிக்கவை செய்தாரைத் தாந்தந்
தகுதியான் வென்று விடல் (௮)

With overweening pride when men with injuries assail,
By thine own righteous dealing shalt thou mightily prevail.

159. துறந்தாரிற் றூய்மை யுடைய
ரிறந்தார்வா யின்னாச்சொ னோற்கிற் பவர் (௯)

They who transgressors' evil words endure
With patience, are as stern ascetics pure.

160. உண்ணாது நோற்பார் பெரியர் பிறர்சொல்லு
மின்னாச்சொ னோற்பாரிற் பின் (௰)

Though 'great' we deem the men that fast and suffer pain,
Who others' bitter words endure, the foremost place obtain.

CHAPTER XVII.

அழுக்காறாமை.—NOT ENVYING. அதி. ௧௭.

161. ஒழுக்காறுக் கொள்க வொருவன்றன் னெஞ்சத்
தழுக்கா றிலாத வியல்பு (௧)

As 'strict decorum's' laws, that all men bind,
Let each regard unenvying grace of mind.

162. விழுப்பேற்றி னஃதொப்ப தில்லையார் மாட்டு
மழுக்காற்றி னன்மை பெறின் (௨)

If man can learn to envy none on earth,
'Tis richest gift,—beyond compare its worth.

163. அறனாக்கம் வேண்டாதா னென்பான்
பிறனாக்கம் பேணா தழுக்கறுப் பான் (௩)

Nor wealth nor virtue does that man desire, 'tis plain,
Whom others' wealth delights not, feeling envious pain.

164. அழுக்காற்றி னல்லவை செய்யா
ரிழுக்காற்றி னேதம் படுபாக் கறிந்து (௪)

The wise through envy break not virtue's laws,
Knowing ill-deeds of foul disgrace the cause.

165. அழுக்கா றுடையார்க் கதுசாலு மொன்னார்
வழுக்கியுங் கேடீன் பது (௫)

Envy they have within! Enough to seal their fate!
Though foemen fail, envy can ruin consummate.

166. கொடுப்ப தழுக்கறுப்பான் சுற்ற
முடுப்பதூஉ முண்பதூஉ மின்றிக் கெடும் (௬)

Who scans good gifts to others given with envious eye,
His kin, with none to clothe or feed them, surely die.

167. அவ்வித் தழுக்கா றுடையானைச் செய்யவ
டவ்வையைக் காட்டி விடும் (௭)

From envious man good fortune's goddess turns away,
Grudging him good, and points him out misfortune's prey.

168. அழுக்கா றெனவொரு பாவி
திருச்செற்றுத் தீயுழி யுய்த்து விடும் (௮)

Envy, embodied ill, incomparable bane,
Good fortune slays, and soul consigns to fiery pain.

169. அவ்விய நெஞ்சத்தா னாக்கமுஞ்
செவ்வியான் கேடு நினைக்கப் படும் (௯)

To men of envious heart, when comes increase of joy,
Or loss to blameless men, the 'why' will thoughtful hearts employ.

170. அழுக்கற் றகன்றாரு மில்லை யஃதிலார்
பெருக்கத்திற் றீர்ந்தாரு மில் (௰)

No envious men to large and full felicity attain;
No men from envy free have failed a sure increase to gain.

CHAPTER XVIII. அதி. ௧௮.

வெஃகாமை.—NOT COVETING.

171. நடுவின்றி நன்பொருள் வெஃகிற்
குடிபொன்றிக் குற்றமு மாங்கே தரும் (௧)

With soul unjust to covet others' well-earned store,
Brings ruin to the home, to evil opes the door.

172. படுபயன் வெஃகிப் பழிப்படுவ செய்யார்
நடுவன்மை நாணு பவர் (௨)

Through lust of gain, no deeds that retribution bring
Do they, who shrink with shame from every unjust thing.

173. சிற்றின்பம் வெஃகி யறனல்ல செய்யாரே
மற்றின்பம் வேண்டு பவர் (௩)

No deeds of ill, misled by base desire,
Do they, whose souls to other joys aspire.

174. இலமென்று வெஃகுதல் செய்யார்
புலம்வென்ற புன்மையிற் காட்சி யவர் (௪)

Men who have conquered sense, with sight from sordid vision freed,
Desire not others' goods, e'en in the hour of sorest need.

175. அஃகி யகன்ற வறிவென்னாம் யார்மாட்டும்
வெஃகி வெறிய செயின் (௫)

What gain, though lore refined of amplest reach he learn,
His acts towards all mankind if covetous desire to folly turn?

176. அருள்வெஃகி யாற்றின் கணின்றான்
பொருள்வெஃகிப் பொல்லாத சூழக் கெடும் (௬)

Though, grace desiring, he in virtue's way stand strong,
He's lost who wealth desires, and ponders deeds of wrong.

177. வேண்டற்க வெஃகியா மாக்கம் விளைவயின்
மாண்டற் கரிதாம் பயன் (எ)

Seek not increase by greed of gain acquired;
That fruit matured yields never good desired.

178. அஃகாமை செல்வத்திற் கியாதெனின்
வெஃகாமை வேண்டும் பிறன்கைப் பொருள் (அ)

What saves prosperity from swift decline?
Absence of lust to make another's cherished riches thine!

179. அறனறிந்து வெஃகா வறிவுடையார்ச் சேருந்
திறனறிந் தாங்கே திரு (கூ)

Good fortune draws anigh in helpful time of need,
To him who, schooled in virtue, guards his soul from greed.

180. இறலீனு மெண்ணாது வெஃகின்
விறலீனும் வேண்டாமை யென்னுஞ் செருக்கு (ம)

From thoughtless lust of others' goods springs fatal ill;
Greatness of soul that covets not shall triumph still.

CHAPTER XIX. அதி. கக.

புறங்கூறாமை.—NOT BACKBITING.

181. அறங்கூறா னல்ல செயினு மொருவன்
புறங்கூறா னென்ற லினிது (க)

Though virtuous words his lips speak not, and all his deeds are ill,
If neighbour he defame not, there 's good within him still.

182. அறனழீஇ யல்லவை செய்தலிற் றீதே
புறனழீஇப் பொய்த்து நகை (உ)

Than he who virtue scorns, and evil deeds performs, more vile
Is he that slanders friend, then meets him with false smile.

183. புறங்கூறிப் பொய்த்துயிர் வாழ்தலிற் சாத
லறங்கூறு மாக்கந் தரும் (ரு)

'Tis greater gain of virtuous good for man to die
Than live to slander absent friend, and falsely praise when nigh.

184. கண்ணின்று கண்ணறச் சொல்லினுஞ் சொல்லற்க
முன்னின்று பின்னோக்காச் சொல் (ச)

In presence though unkindly words you speak, say not
In absence words whose ill result exceeds your thought.

185. அறஞ்சொல்லு நெஞ்சத்தா னன்மை
புறஞ்சொல்லும் புன்மையாற் காணப் படும் (௫)

The slanderous meanness that an absent friend defames,
'This man in words owns virtue, not in heart,' proclaims.

186. பிறன்பழி கூறுவான் றன்பழி யுள்ளுந்
திறன்றெரிந்து கூறப் படும் (௬)

Who on his neighbours' sins delights to dwell,
The story of his sins, culled out with care, the world will tell.

187. பகச்சொல்லிக் கேளிர்ப் பிரிப்பர்
நகச்சொல்லி நட்பாட றேற்றா தார் (௭)

With friendly art who know not pleasant words to say,
Speak words that sever hearts, and drive choice friends away.

188. துன்னியார் குற்றமுந் தூற்று மரபினா
ரென்னைகொ லேதிலார் மாட்டு (௮)

Whose nature bids them faults of closest friends proclaim,
What mercy will they show to other men's good name?

189. அறனோக்கி யாற்றுங்கொல் வையம்
புறனோக்கிப் புன்சொ லுரைப்பான் பொறை (௯)

'Tis charity, I ween, that makes the earth sustain their load
Who, neighbours' absence watching, tales of slander tell abroad.

190. ஏதிலார் குற்றம்போற் றங்குற்றங் காண்கிற்பிற்
றீதுண்டோ மன்னு முயிர்க்கு (௰)

If each his own, as neighbours' faults would scan,
Could any evil hap to living man?

CHAPTER XX. அதி. ௨௰.

பயனிலசொல்லாமை.—The not Speaking Profitless Words.

191. பல்லார் முனியப் பயனில சொல்லுவா
னெல்லாரு மெள்ளப் படும் (௧)

Words without sense, while chafe the wise,
Who babbles, him will all despise.

192. பயனில பல்லார்முற் சொல்லல
னயனில நட்டார்கட் செய்தலிற் றீது (௨)

Words without sense, where many wise men hear, to pour
Than deeds to friends ungracious done offendeth more.

193. நயனில னென்பது சொல்லும்
பயனில பாரித் துரைக்கு முரை (௩)

Diffusive speech of useless words proclaims
A man who never righteous wisdom gains.

194. நயன்சாரா நன்மையி னீக்கும்
பயன்சாராப் பண்பில்சொற் பல்லா ரகத்து (௪)

Unmeaning, worthless words, said to the multitude,
To none delight afford, and sever men from good.

195. சீர்மை சிறப்பொடு நீங்கும் பயனில
நீர்மை யுடையார் சொலின் (௫)

Gone are both fame and boasted excellence,
When men of worth speak words devoid of sense.

196. பயனில்சொற் பாராட்டு வானை மகனெனல்
மக்கட் பதடி யெனல் (௬)

Who makes display of idle words' inanity,
Call him not man,—chaff of humanity!

197. நயனில சொல்லினுஞ் சொல்லுக சான்றோர்
பயனில சொல்லாமை நன்று (௭)

Let those who list speak things that no delight afford,
'Tis good for men of worth to speak no idle word.

198. அரும்பய னாயு மறிவினார் சொல்லார்
பெரும்பய னில்லாத சொல் (௮)

The wise, who weigh the worth of every utterance,
Speak none but words of deep significance.

199. பொருடீர்ந்த பொச்சாந்துஞ் சொல்லார்
மருடீர்ந்த மாசறு காட்சி யவர் (௯)

The men of vision pure, from wildering folly free,
Not e'en in thoughtless hour, speak words of vanity.

200. சொல்லுக சொல்லிற் பயனுடைய
சொல்லற்க சொல்லிற் பயனிலாச் சொல் (௰)

If speak you will, speak words that fruit afford,
If speak you will, speak never fruitless word.

CHAPTER XXI. அதி. ௨௧.

தீவினையச்சம்.—DREAD OF EVIL DEEDS.

201. தீவினையா ரஞ்சார் விழுமியா ரஞ்சுவர்
தீவினை யென்னுஞ் செருக்கு (௧)

With sinful act men cease to feel the dread of ill within;
The excellent will dread the wanton pride of cherished sin.

202. தீயவை தீய பயத்தலாற்
தீயவை தீயினு மஞ்சப் படும் (௨)

Since evils new from evils ever grow,
Evil than fire works out more dreaded woe.

203. அறிவினு ளெல்லாந் தலையென்ப தீய
செறுவார்க்குஞ் செய்யா விடல் (௩)

Even to those that hate make no return of ill;
So shalt thou wisdom's highest law, 'tis said, fulfil.

204. மறந்தும் பிறன்கேடு சூழற்க சூழி
னறஞ்சூழுஞ் சூழ்ந்தவன் கேடு (௪)

Though good thy soul forget, plot not thy neighbour's fall,
Thy plans shall 'virtue's Power' by ruin to thyself forestall.

205. இலனென்று தீயவை செய்யற்க செய்யி
னிலனாகு மற்றும் பெயர்த்து (௫)

Make not thy poverty a plea for ill;
Thy evil deeds will make thee poorer still.

206. தீப்பால தான்பிறர்கட் செய்யற்க
நோய்ப்பால தன்னை யடல்வேண்டா தான் (௬)

What ranks as evil spare to do, if thou would'st shun
Affliction sore through ill to thee by others done.

207. எனைப்பகை யுற்றாரு முய்வர்
வினைப்பகை வீயாது பின்சென் றடும் (௭)

From every enmity incurred there is to 'scape a way;
The wrath of evil deeds will dog men's steps, and slay.

208. தீயவை செய்தார் கெடுத னிழறன்னை
வீயா தடியுறைந் தற்று (௮)

Man's shadow dogs his steps where'er he wends;
Destruction thus on sinful deeds attends.

209. தன்னைத்தான் காதல னாயி னெனைத்தொன்றுந்
துன்னற்க தீவினைப் பால் (௯)

Beware, if to thyself thyself is dear,
Lest thou to aught that ranks as ill draw near!

210. அருங்கேட னென்ப தறிக
மருங்கோடித் தீவினை செய்யா னெனின் (௰)

The man, to devious way of sin that never turned aside,
From ruin rests secure, whatever ills betide.

CHAPTER XXII. அதி. ௨௨.

ஒப்புரவறிதல்.—The Knowledge of what is Befitting a Man's Position.

211. கைம்மாறு வேண்டா கடப்பாடு மாரிமாட்
டென்னாற்றுங் கொல்லோ வுலகு (௧)

Duty demands no recompense; to clouds of heaven,
By men on earth, what answering gift is given?

212. தாளாற்றித் தந்த பொருளெல்லாந் தக்கார்க்கு
வேளாண்மை செய்தற் பொருட்டு (௨)

The worthy say, when wealth rewards their toil-spent hours,
For uses of beneficence alone 'tis ours.

213. புத்தே ளுலகத்து மீண்டும் பெறலரிதே
யொப்புரவி னல்ல பிற (௩)

To 'due beneficence' no equal good we know,
Amid the happy gods, or in this world below.

214. ஒத்த தறிவா னுயிர்வாழ்வான் மற்றையான்
செத்தாருள் வைக்கப் படும் (௪)

Who knows what 's human life's befitting grace,
He lives; the rest 'mongst dead men have their place.

215. ஊருணி நீர்நிறைந் தற்றே யுலகவாம்
பேரறி வாளன் றிரு (௫)

The wealth of men who love the 'fitting way,' the truly wise,
Is as when water fills the lake that village needs supplies.

216. பயன்மர முள்ளூர்ப் பழுத்தற்றாற் செல்வ
நயனுடை யான்கட் படின் (௬)

A tree that fruits in th' hamlet's central mart,
Is wealth that falls to men of liberal heart.

217. மருந்தாகித் தப்பா மரத்தற்றாற் செல்வம்
பெருந்தகை யான்கட் படின் (௭)

Unfailing tree that healing balm distils from every part,
Is ample wealth that falls to him of large and noble heart.

218. இடனில் பருவத்து மொப்புரவிற் கொல்கார்
கடனறி காட்சி யவர் (௮)

E'en when resources fail, they weary not of 'kindness due,'—
They to whom Duty's self appears in vision true.

219. நயனுடையா னல்கூர்ந்தா னாதல்
செயுநீர்மை செய்யா தமைகலா வாறு (௯)

The kindly-hearted man is poor in this alone,
When power of doing deeds of goodness he finds none.

220. ஒப்புரவி னல்வருங் கேடெனி னஃதொருவன்
விற்றுக்கோட் டக்க துடைத்து (௰)

Though by 'beneficence' the loss of all should come,
'Twere meet man sold himself, and bought it with the sum.

CHAPTER XXIII. அதி. உ௩.

ஈகை.—Giving.

221. வறியார்க்கொன் றீவதே யீகைமற் றெல்லாங்
குறியெதிர்ப்பை நீர துடைத்து (க)

Call that a gift to needy men thou dost dispense,
All else is void of good, seeking for recompense.

222. நல்லா றெனினுங் கொளறீது மேலுலக
மில்லெனினு மீதலே நன்று (உ)

Though men declare it heavenward path, yet to receive is ill;
Though upper heaven were not, to give is virtue still.

223. இலனென்னு மெவ்வ முரையாமை யீதல
குலனுடையான் கண்ணே யுள (௩)

'I 've nought' is ne'er the high-born man's reply;
He gives to those who raise themselves that cry.

224. இன்னா திரக்கப் படுத லிரந்தவ
ரின்முகங் காணு மளவு (௪)

The suppliants' cry for aid yields scant delight,
Until you see his face with grateful gladness bright.

225. ஆற்றுவா ராற்றல் பசியாற்ற லப்பசியை
மாற்றுவா ராற்றலிற் பின் (ரு)

'Mid devotees they 're great who hunger's pangs sustain,
Who hunger's pangs relieve a higher merit gain.

226. ஆற்றா ரழிபசி தீர்த்த லஃதொருவன்
பெற்றான் பொருள்வைப் புழி (சா)

Let man relieve the wasting hunger men endure;
For treasure gained thus finds he treasure-house secure.

227. பாத்தூண் மரீஇ யவனைப் பசியென்னுந்
தீப்பிணி தீண்ட லரிது (எ)

Whose soul delights with hungry men to share his meal.
The hand of hunger's sickness sore shall never feel.

228. ஈத்துவக்கு மின்ப மறியார்கொ றாமுடைமை
வைத்திழக்கும் வன்க ணவர் (அ)

Delight of glad'ning human hearts with gifts do they not know,
Men of unpitying eye, who hoard their wealth, and lose it so?

229. இரத்தலி னின்னாது மன்ற
நிரப்பிய தாமே தமிய ருணல் (கூ)

They keep their garners full, for self alone the board they spread;—
'Tis greater pain, be sure, than begging daily bread!

230. சாதலி னின்னாத தில்லை யினிததூஉ
மீத லியையாக் கடை (ய)

'Tis bitter pain to die! 'Tis worse to live
For him who nothing finds to give!

CHAPTER XXIV. அதி. உச.

புகழ்.—Renown.

231. ஈத லிசைபட வாழ்த லதுவல்ல
தூதிய மில்லை யுயிர்க்கு (க)

See that thy life the praise of generous gifts obtain;
Save this for living man exists no real gain.

232. உரைப்பா ருரைப்பவை யெல்லா
மிரப்பார்க்கொன் றீவார் மேனிற்கும் புகழ் (உ)

The speech of all that speak agrees to crown
The men that give to those that ask, with fair renown.

233. ஒன்றா வுலகத் துயர்ந்த புகழல்லாற்
பொன்றாது நிற்பதொன் றில் (௩)

Save praise alone that soars on high,
Nought lives on earth that shall not die.

234. நிலவரை நீள்புக ழாற்றிற்
புலவரைப் போற்றாது புத்தே ளுலகு (௪)

If men do virtuous deeds by world-wide ample glory crowned,
The heavens will cease to laud the sage for other gifts renowned.

235. நத்தம்போற் கேடு முளதாகுஞ் சாக்காடும்
வித்தகர்க் கல்லா லரிது (௫)

Loss that is gain, and death of life's true bliss fulfilled,
Are fruits which only wisdom rare can yield.

236. தோன்றிற் புகழொடு தோன்றுக வஃதிலார்
தோன்றலிற் றோன்றாமை நன்று (௬)

If, man you walk the stage, appear adorned with glory's grace;
Save glorious you can shine, 'twere better hide your face.

237. புகழ்பட வாழாதார் தந்நோவார் தம்மை
யிகழ்வாரை நோவ தெவன் (௭)

If you your days will spend devoid of goodly fame,
When men despise, why blame them? You 've yourself to blame.

238. வசையென்ப வையத்தார்க் கெல்லா
மிசையென்னு மெச்சம் பெறாஅ விடின் (௮)

Fame is virtue's child, they say; if, then,
You childless live, you live the scorn of men.

239. வசையிலா வண்பயன் குன்று
மிசையிலா யாக்கை பொறுத்த நிலம் (௯)

The blameless fruits of fields' increase will dwindle down,
If earth the burthen bear of men without renown.

240. வசையொழிய வாழ்வாரே வாழ்வா
ரிசையொழிய வாழ்வாரே வாழா தவர் (௰)

Who live without reproach, them living men we deem;
Who live without renown, live not, though living men they seem.

இல்லறவியன் முற்றும்.

END OF THE SECTION ON 'DOMESTIC VIRTUE.'

§ 3. ASCETIC VIRTUE. துறவறவியல்.

i. Religious Observances. விரதம்.

CHAPTER XXV. அதி. உரு.

அருளுடைமை.—The Possession of Benevolence.

241. அருட்செல்வஞ் செல்வத்துட் செல்வம்
பொருட்செல்வம் பூரியார் கண்ணு முள (க)

Wealth 'mid wealth is wealth of 'kindliness';
Wealth of goods the vilest too possess.

242. நல்லாற்ற னாடி யருளாள்க
பல்லாற்றாற் றேரினு மஃதே துணை (உ)

The law of 'grace' fulfil, by methods good due trial made,
Though many systems you explore, this is your only aid.

243. அருள்சேர்ந்த நெஞ்சினார்க் கில்லை
யிருள்சேர்ந்த வின்னா வுலகம் புகல் (௩)

They in whose breast a 'gracious kindliness' resides,
See not the gruesome world, where darkness drear abides.

244. மன்னுயி ரோம்பி யருளாள்வாற் கில்லென்ப
தன்னுயி ரஞ்சும் வினை (ச)

Who for undying souls of men provides with gracious zeal,
In his own soul the dreaded guilt of sin shall never feel.

245. அல்ல லருளாள்வார்க் கில்லை வளிவழங்கு
மல்லன்மா ஞாலங் கரி (ரு)

The teeming earth's vast realm, round which the wild winds blow,
Is witness, men of 'grace' no woeful want shall know.

246. பொருணீங்கிப் பொச்சாந்தா ரென்ப
ரருணீங்கி யல்லவை செய்தொழுகு வார் (சா)

Gain of true wealth oblivious they eschew,
Who 'grace' forsake, and graceless actions do.

247. அருளில்லார்க் கவ்வுலக மில்லை
பொருளில்லார்க் கிவ்வுலக மில்லா தியாங்கு (எ)

As to impoverished men this present world is not;
The 'graceless' in yon world have neither part nor lot.

248. பொருளற்றார் பூப்ப ரொருகா
லருளற்றா ரற்றார்மற் றாத லரிது (௮)

Who lose the flower of wealth, when seasons change, again may bloom;
Who lose 'benevolence,' lose all; nothing can change their doom.

249. தெருளாதான் மெய்ப்பொருள் கண்டற்றாற் றேரி
னருளாதான் செய்யு மறம் (௯)

When souls unwise true wisdom's mystic vision see,
The 'graceless' man may work true works of charity.

250. வலியார்முற் றன்னை நினைக்கதான் றன்னின்
மெலியார்மேற் செல்லு மிடத்து (௰)

When weaker men you front with threat'ning brow,
Think how you felt in presence of some stronger foe.

CHAPTER XXVI. அதி. ௨௬.

புலான்மறுத்தல்.—The Renunciation of Flesh.

251. தன்னூன் பெருக்கற்குத் தான்பிறி தூனுண்பா
னெங்ஙன மாளு மருள் (௧)

How can the wont of 'kindly grace' to him be known,
Who other creatures' flesh consumes to feed his own?

252. பொருளாட்சி போற்றாதார்க் கில்லை
யருளாட்சி யாங்கில்லை யூன்றின் பவர்க்கு (௨)

No use of wealth have they who guard not their estate;
No use of grace have they with flesh who hunger sate.

253. படைகொண்டார் நெஞ்சம்போ னன்றூக்கா தொன்ற
னுடல்சுவை யுண்டார் மனம் (௩)

Like heart of them that murderous weapons bear, his mind
Who eats of savoury meat, no joy in good can find.

254. அருளல்ல தியாதெனிற் கொல்லாமை கோறல்
பொருளல்ல தவ்வூன் றினல் (௪)

'What's grace, or lack of grace'? 'To kill' is this, that 'not to kill';
To eat dead flesh can never worthy end fulfil.

255. உண்ணாமை யுள்ள துயிர்நிலை யூனுண்ண
வண்ணாத்தல் செய்யா தளறு (௫)

If flesh you eat not, life's abodes unharmed remain;
Who eats, hell swallows him, and renders not again.

256. தினற்பொருட்டாற் கொள்ளா துலகெனின் யாரும்
விலைப்பொருட்டா லூன்றருவா ரில் (௬)

'We eat the slain,' you say, 'by us no living creatures die';
Who'd kill and sell, I pray, if none came there the flesh to buy?

257. உண்ணாமை வேண்டும் புலாஅல் பிறிதொன்றன்
புண்ண துணர்வார்ப் பெறின் (௭)

With other beings' ulcerous wounds their hunger they appease;
If this they felt, desire to eat must surely cease.

258. செயிரிற் றலைப்பிரிந்த காட்சியா ருண்ணா
ருயிரிற் றலைப்பிரிந்த வூன் (௮)

Whose souls the vision pure and passionless perceive,
Eat not the bodies men of life bereave.

259. அவிசொரிந் தாயிரம் வேட்டலி னொன்ற
னுயிர்செகுத் துண்ணாமை நன்று (௯)

Than thousand rich oblations, with libations rare,
Better the flesh of slaughtered beings not to share.

260. கொல்லான் புலாலை மறுத்தானைக் கைகூப்பி
யெல்லா வுயிருந் தொழும் (௰)

Who slays nought,—flesh rejects,—his feet before
All living things with claspèd hands adore.

CHAPTER XXVII. அதி. ௨௭.

தவம்.—PENANCE.

261. உற்றநோய் நோன்ற லுயிர்க்குறுகண் செய்யாமை
யற்றே தவத்திற் குரு (௧)

To bear due penitential pains, while no offence
He causes others, is the type of 'penitence.'

262. தவமுந் தவமுடையார்க் காகு
மவமதனை யஃதிலார் மேற்கொள் வது (௨)

To 'penitents' sincere avails their 'penitence';
Where that is not, 'tis but a vain pretence.

263. துறந்தார்க்குத் துப்புரவு வேண்டி
மறந்தார்கொன் மற்றை யவர்க டவம் (௩)

Have other men forgotten 'penitence,' who strive
To earn for penitents the things by which they live?

264. ஒன்னார்த் தெறலு முவந்தாரை யாக்கலு
மெண்ணிற் றவத்தான் வரும் (௪)

Destruction to his foes, to friends increase of joy,
The 'penitent' can cause, if this his thoughts employ.

265. வேண்டிய வேண்டியாங் கெய்தலாற் செய்தவ
மீண்டு முயலப் படும் (௫)

That what they wish may, as they wish, be won,
By men on earth are works of painful 'penance' done.

266. தவஞ்செய்வார் தங்கருமஞ் செய்வார் மற்றல்லா
ரவஞ்செய்வ ராசையுட் பட்டு (௬)

Who works of 'penance' do, their end attain,
Others, in passion's net ensnared, toil but in vain.

267. சுடச்சுடரும் பொன்போ லொளிவிடுந் துன்பஞ்
சுடச்சுட நோற்கிற் பவர்க்கு (௭)

The hotter glows the fining fire, the gold the brighter shines;
The pain of penitence, like fire, the soul of man refines.

268. தன்னுயிர் தானறப் பெற்றானை யேனைய
மன்னுயி ரெல்லாந் தொழும் (௮)

Who gains himself in utter self-control,
Him worships every other living soul.

269. கூற்றங் குதித்தலுங் கைகூடு
நோற்றலி னாற்ற றலைப்பட் டவர்க்கு (௯)

E'en over death the victory he may gain,
If power by penance won his soul obtain.

270. இலர்பல ராகிய காரண நோற்பார்
சிலர்பலர் நோலா தவர் (௰)

The many all things lack! The cause is plain;
The 'penitents' are few. The many shun such pain.

CHAPTER XXVIII. அதி. ௨௮.

கூடாவொழுக்கம்.—Inconsistent Conduct.

271. வஞ்ச மனத்தான் படிற்றொழுக்கம் பூதங்க
ளைந்து மகத்தே நகும் (௧)

Who with deceitful mind in false way walks of covert sin,
The five-fold elements his frame compose, deride within.

272. வானுயர் தோற்ற மெவன்செய்யுந் தன்னெஞ்சந்
தானறி குற்றப் படின் (௨)

What gain, though virtue's semblance high as heaven his fame exalt,
If heart dies down through sense of self-detected fault?

273. வலியி னிலைமையான் வல்லுருவம் பெற்றம
புலியின்றோல் போர்த்துமேய்ந் தற்று (௩)

As if a steer should graze wrapped round with tiger's skin,
Is show of virtuous might when weakness lurks within.

274. தவமறைந் தல்லவை செய்தல்
புதன்மறைந்து வேட்டுவன் புட்சிமிழ்த் தற்று (௪)

'Tis as a fowler, silly birds to snare, in thicket lurks,
When, clad in stern ascetic garb, one secret evil works.

275. பற்றற்றே மென்பார் படிற்றொழுக்க
மெற்றெற்றென் றேதம் பலவுந் தரும் (௫)

'Our souls are free,' who say, yet practise evil secretly,
'What folly have we wrought!' by many shames o'erwhelmed, shall cry.

276. நெஞ்சத்திற் றுறவார் துறந்தார்போல்
வஞ்சித்து வாழ்வாரின் வன்கணா ரில் (௬)

In mind renouncing nought, in speech renouncing every tie,
Who guileful live,—no men are found than these of 'harder eye.'

277. புறங்குன்றி கண்டனைய ரேனு
மகங்குன்றி மூக்கிற் கரியா ருடைத்து (௭)

Outward, they shine as 'kunri' berry's scarlet bright;
Inward, like tip of 'kunri' bead, as black as night.

278. மனத்தது மாசாக மாண்டார் நீராடி
மறைந்தொழுகு மாந்தர் பலர் (௮)

Many wash in hallowed waters, living lives of hidden shame;
Foul in heart, yet high upraised of men in virtuous fame.

279. கணைகொடிது யாழ்கோடு செவ்விதாங் கன்ன
வினைபடு பாலாற் கொளல் (௯)

Cruel is the arrow straight, the crookèd lute is sweet,
Judge by their deeds the many forms of men you meet.

280. மழித்தலு நீட்டலும் வேண்டா வுலகம்
பழித்த தொழித்து விடின் (௰)

What 's the worth of shaven head or tresses long,
If you shun what all the world condemns as wrong?

CHAPTER XXIX. அதி. உகூ.

கள்ளாமை.—THE ABSENCE OF FRAUD.

281. எள்ளாமை வேண்டுவா னென்பா னெனைத்தொன்றுங்
கள்ளாமை காக்கதன் னெஞ்சு (க)

Who seeks heaven's joys, from impious levity secure,
Let him from every fraud preserve his spirit pure.

282. உள்ளத்தா லுள்ளலுந் தீதே பிறன்பொருளைக்
கள்ளத்தாற் கள்வே மெனல் (உ)

'Tis sin if in the mind man but the thought conceive:
'By fraud I will my neighbour of his wealth bereave.'

283. களவினா லாகிய வாக்க
மளவிறந் தாவது போலக் கெடும் (௩)

The gain that comes by fraud, although it seem to grow
With limitless increase, to ruin swift shall go.

284. களவின்கட் கன்றிய காதல்
விளைவின்கண் வீயா விழுமந் தரும் (ச)

The lust inveterate of fraudful gain,
Yields as its fruit undying pain.

285. அருள்கருதி யன்புடைய ராதல்
பொருள்கருதிப் பொச்சாப்புப் பார்ப்பார்க ணில் (ரு)

'Grace' is not in their thoughts, nor know they kind affection's power,
Who neighbour's goods desire, and watch for his unguarded hour.

286. அளவின்க ணின்றொழுக லாற்றார்
களவின்கட் கன்றிய காத லவர் (சா)

They cannot walk restrained in wisdom's measured bound,
In whom inveterate lust of fraudful gain is found.

287. களவென்னுங் காரறி வாண்மை
யளவென்னு மாற்றல் புரிந்தார்க ணில் (எ)

Practice of fraud's dark cunning arts they shun,
Who long for power by 'measured wisdom' won.

288. அளவறிந்தார் நெஞ்சத் தறம்போல நிற்குங்
களவறிந்தார் நெஞ்சிற் கரவு (அ)

As virtue dwells in heart that 'measured wisdom' gains;
Deceit in hearts of fraudful men established reigns.

289. அளவல்ல செய்தாங்கே வீவர்
களவல்ல மற்றைய தேற்றா தவர் (௯)

Who have no lore save that which fraudful arts supply,
Acts of unmeasured vice committing straightway die.

290. கள்வார்க்குத் தள்ளு முயிர்நிலை கள்ளார்க்குத்
தள்ளாது புத்தே ளுலகு (௰)

The fraudful forfeit life and being here below;
Who fraud eschew the bliss of heavenly beings know.

CHAPTER XXX. அதி. ௩௰.

வாய்மை.—VERACITY.

291. வாய்மை யெனப்படுவ தியாதெனின் யாதொன்றுந்
தீமை யிலாத சொலல் (௧)

You ask, in lips of men what 'truth' may be:
'Tis speech from every taint of evil free.

292. பொய்ம்மையும் வாய்மை யிடத்த புரைதீர்ந்த
நன்மை பயக்கு மெனின் (௨)

Falsehood may take the place of truthful word,
If blessing, free from fault, it can afford.

293. தன்னெஞ் சறிவது பொய்யற்க பொய்த்தபின்
றன்னெஞ்சே தன்னைச் சுடும் (௩)

Speak not a word which false thy own heart knows,
Self-kindled fire within the false one's spirit glows.

294. உள்ளத்தாற் பொய்யா தொழுகி னுலகத்தா
ருள்ளத்து ளெல்லா முளன் (௪)

True to his inmost soul who lives,—enshrined
He lives in souls of all mankind.

295. மனத்தொடு வாய்மை மொழியிற்
றவத்தொடு தானஞ் செய்வாரிற் றலை (௫)

Greater is he who speaks the truth with full consenting mind,
Than men whose lives have penitence and charity combined.

296. பொய்யாமை யன்ன புகழில்லை
யெய்யாமை யெல்லா வறமுந் தரும் (௬)

No praise like that of words from falsehood free;
This every virtue yields spontaneously.

297. பொய்யாமை பொய்யாமை யாற்றி னறம்பிற
செய்யாமை செய்யாமை நன்று (எ)

If all your life be utter truth, the truth alone,
'Tis well, though other virtuous acts be left undone.

298. புறந்தூய்மை நீரா னமையு
மகந்தூய்மை வாய்மையாற் காணப் படும் (அ)

Outward purity the water will bestow;
Inward purity from truth alone will flow.

299. எல்லா விளக்கும் விளக்கல்ல சான்றோர்க்குப்
பொய்யா விளக்கே விளக்கு (கூ)

Every lamp is not a lamp in wise men's sight;
That 's the lamp with truth's pure radiance bright.

300. யாமெய்யாக் கண்டவற்று ளில்லை யெனைத்தொன்றும்
வாய்மையி னல்ல பிற (ய)

Of all good things we 've scanned with studious care,
There 's nought that can with truthfulness compare.

CHAPTER XXXI. அதி. ௩௧.

வெகுளாமை.—The not being Angry.

301. செல்லிடத்துக் காப்பான் சினங்காப்பா
னல்லிடத்துக் காக்கினென் காவாக்கா லென் (க)

Where thou hast power thy angry will to work, thy wrath restrain;
Where power is none, what matter if thou check or give it rein?

302. செல்லா விடத்துச் சினந்தீது செல்லிடத்து
மில்லதனிற் றீய பிற (உ)

Where power is none to wreak thy wrath, wrath impotent is ill;
Where thou hast power thy will to work, 'tis greater evil still.

303. மறத்தல் வெகுளியை யார்மாட்டுந் தீய
பிறத்த லதனான் வரும் (௩)

If any rouse thy wrath, the trespass straight forget;
For wrath an endless train of evils will beget.

304. நகையு முவகையுங் கொல்லுஞ் சினத்திற்
பகையு முளவோ பிற (ச)

Wrath robs the face of smiles, the heart of joy,
What other foe to man works such annoy?

305. தன்னைத்தான் காக்கிற் சினங்காக்க காவாக்காற்
றன்னையே கொல்லுஞ் சினம் (௫)

If thou would'st guard thyself, guard against wrath alway;
'Gainst wrath who guards not, him his wrath shall slay.

306. சினமென்னுஞ் சேர்ந்தாரைக் கொல்லி
யினமென்னு மேமப் புணையைச் சுடும் (௬)

Wrath, the fire that slayeth whoso draweth near,
Will burn the helpful 'raft' of kindred dear.

307. சினத்தைப் பொருளென்று கொண்டவன் கேடு
நிலத்தறைந்தான் கைபிழையா தற்று (௭)

The hand that smites the earth unfailing feels the sting;
So perish they who nurse their wrath as noble thing.

308. இணரெரி தோய்வன்ன வின்னா செயினும்
புணரின் வெகுளாமை நன்று (௮)

Though men should work thee woe, like touch of tongues of fire,
'Tis well if thou canst save thy soul from burning ire.

309. உள்ளிய வெல்லா முடனெய்து முள்ளத்தா
லுள்ளான் வெகுளி யெனின் (௯)

If man his soul preserve from wrathful fires,
He gains with that whate'er his soul desires.

310. இறந்தா ரிறந்தா ரனையர் சினத்தைத்
துறந்தார் துறந்தார் துணை (௰)

Men of surpassing wrath are like the men who've passed away;
Who wrath renounce, equals of all-renouncing sages they!

CHAPTER XXXII. அதி. ௩௨.

இன்னாசெய்யாமை.—NOT DOING EVIL.

311. சிறப்பீனுஞ் செல்வம் பெறினும்
பிறர்க்கின்னா செய்யாமை மாசற்றார் கோள் (௧)

Though ill to neighbour wrought should glorious pride of wealth secure,
No ill to do is fixed decree of men in spirit pure.

312. கறுத்தின்னா செய்தவக் கண்ணு
மறுத்தின்னா செய்யாமை மாசற்றார் கோள் (௨)

Though malice work its worst, planning no ill return, to endure,
And work no ill, is fixed decree of men in spirit pure.

313. செய்யாமை செற்றார்க்கு மின்னாத செய்தபி
னுய்யா விழுமந் தரும் (௩)

Though unprovoked thy soul malicious foes should sting,
Retaliation wrought inevitable woes will bring.

314. இன்னாசெய் தாரை யொறுத்த லவர்நாண
நன்னயஞ் செய்து விடல் (௪)

To punish wrong, with kindly benefits the doers ply;
Thus shame their souls; but pass the ill unheeded by.

315. அறிவினா னாகுவ துண்டோ
பிறிதினோய் தந்நோய்போற் போற்றாக் கடை (௫)

From wisdom's vaunted lore what doth the learner gain,
If as his own he guard not others' souls from pain?

316. இன்னா வெனத்தா னுணர்ந்தவை
துன்னாமை வேண்டும் பிறன்கட் செயல் (௬)

What his own soul has felt as bitter pain,
From making others feel should man abstain.

317. எனைத்தானு மெஞ்ஞான்றும் யார்க்கு
மனத்தானா மாணாசெய் யாமை தலை (௭)

To work no wilful woe, in any wise, through all the days,
To any living soul, is virtue's highest praise.

318. தன்னுயிர்க் கின்னாமை தானறிவா னென்கொலோ
மன்னுயிர்க் கின்னா செயல் (௮)

Whose soul has felt the bitter smart of wrong, how can
He wrongs inflict on ever-living soul of man?

319. பிறர்க்கின்னா முற்பகற் செய்யிற் றமக்கின்னா
பிற்பகற் றாமே வரும் (௯)

If, ere the noontide, you to others evil do,
Before the eventide will evil visit you.

320. நோயெல்லா நோய்செய்தார் மேலவா
நோய்செய்யார் நோயின்மை வேண்டு பவர் (௰)

O'er every evil-doer evil broodeth still;
He evil shuns who freedom seeks from ill.

CHAPTER XXXIII. அதி. ௩௩.

கொல்லாமை.—Not Killing.

321. அறவினை யாதெனிற் கொல்லாமை கோறல்
பிறவினை யெல்லாந் தரும் (௧)

What is the work of virtue? 'Not to kill';
For 'killing' leads to every work of ill.

322. பகுத்துண்டு பல்லுயி ரோம்புத னூலோர்
தொகுத்தவற்று ளெல்லந் தலை (௨)

Let those that need partake your meal; guard everything that lives:
This the chief and sum of lore that hoarded wisdom gives.

323. ஒன்றாக நல்லது கொல்லாமை மற்றதன
பின்சாரப் பொய்யாமை நன்று (௩)

Alone, first of good things, is 'not to slay';
The second is, no untrue word to say.

324. நல்லா றெனப்படுவ தியாதெனின் யாதொன்றுங்
கொல்லாமை சூழு நெறி (௪)

You ask, What is the good and perfect way?
'Tis path of him who studies nought to slay.

325. நிலையஞ்சி நீத்தாரு ளெல்லாங்
கொலையஞ்சிக் கொல்லாமை சூழ்வான் றலை (௫)

Of those who 'being' dread, and all renounce, the chief are they,
Who, dreading crime of slaughter, study nought to slay.

326. கொல்லாமை மேற்கொண் டொழுகுவான் வாழ்நாண்மேற்
செல்லா துயிருண்ணுங் கூற்று (௬)

Ev'n death, that life devours, their happy days shall spare,
Who law, 'Thou shall not kill,' uphold with reverent care.

327. தன்னுயிர் நீப்பினுஞ் செய்யற்க தான்பிறி
தின்னுயிர் நீக்கும் வினை (௭)

Though thine own life for that spared life the price must pay,
Take not from aught that lives gift of sweet life away.

328. நன்றாகு மாக்கம் பெரிதெனினுஞ் சான்றோர்க்குக்
கொன்றாகு மாக்கங் கடை (௮)

Though great the gain of good should seem, the wise
Will any gain by slaughter won despise.

329. கொலைவினைய ராகிய மாக்கள்
புலைவினையர் புன்மை தெரிவா ரகத்து (௯)

Whose trade is 'killing,' always vile they show,
To minds of them who what is vileness know.

330. உயிருடம்பி னீக்கியா ரென்பர்
செயிருடம்பிற் செல்லாத்தீ வாழ்க்கை யவர் (௰)

Who lead a loathèd life in bodies sorely pained,
Are men, the wise declare, by guilt of slaughter stained.

விரதமுற்றும்.

END OF 'RELIGIOUS OBSERVANCES.'

§ 3. ASCETIC VIRTUE—*continued.*

ii. Wisdom. ஞானம்.

CHAPTER XXXIV. அதி. ௩௪.

நிலையாமை.—Instability.

331. நில்லா தவற்றை நிலையின வென்றுணரும்
புல்லறி வாண்மை கடை (௧)

Lowest and meanest lore, that bids men trust secure,
In things that pass away, as things that shall endure!

332. கூத்தாட் டவைக்குழாத் தற்றே பெருஞ்செல்வம்
போக்கு மதுவிளிந் தற்று (௨)

As crowds round dancers fill the hall, is wealth's increase;
Its loss, as throngs dispersing, when the dances cease.

333. அற்கா வியல்பிற்றுச் செல்வ மதுபெற்றா
லற்குப வாங்கே செயல் (௩)

Unenduring is all wealth; if you wealth enjoy,
Enduring works in working wealth straightway employ.

334. நாளென வொன்றுபோற் காட்டி யுயிரீரும்
வாள துணர்வார்ப் பெறின் (௪)

As 'day' it vaunts itself; well understood, 'tis 'knife,'
That daily cuts away a portion from thy life.

335. நாச்செற்று விக்குள்மேல் வாராமு னல்வினை
மேற்சென்று செய்யப் படும் (௫)

Before the tongue lie powerless, 'mid the gasp of gurgling breath,
Arouse thyself, and do good deeds beyond the power of death.

336. நெருந லுளனொருவ னின்றில்லை யென்னும்
பெருமை யுடைத்திவ் வுலகு (௬)

Existing yesterday, to-day to nothing hurled!—
Such greatness owns this transitory world.

337. ஒருபொழுதும் வாழ்வ தறியார்
கருதுப கோடியு மல்ல பல (௭)

Who know not if their happy lives shall last the day,
In fancies infinite beguile the hours away!

338. குடம்பை தனித்தொழியப் புட்பறந் தற்றே
யுடம்போ டுயிரிடை நட்பு (அ)

Birds fly away, and leave the nest deserted bare ;
Such is the short-lived friendship soul and body share.

339. உறங்கு வதுபோலுஞ் சாக்கா
டுறங்கி விழிப்பது போலும் பிறப்பு (௯)

Death is sinking into slumbers deep ;
Birth again is waking out of sleep.

340. புக்கி லமைந்தின்று கொல்லோ வுடம்பினுட்
டுச்சி லிருந்த வுயிர்க்கு (௰)

The soul in fragile shed as lodger courts repose :—
Is it because no home's conclusive rest it knows ?

CHAPTER XXXV. அதி. ௩௫.

துறவு.—Renunciation.

[Beschi introduces this Chapter with the following note :—

"This should form the fourth book of this work, since it was the design of the Author to include in his poem the four most esteemed things, அறம் பொருள் இன்பம் வீடு. But he has not assigned to வீடு a separate Book, because (1) it is very brief, being only three Chapters ; and (2) it really belongs to the first Book, since only by virtues can 'emancipation' (வீடு) be sought. Of these துறவு is the first."

The Tam. Com. arranges Ch. XXXIV.–XXXVII. under the head of ஞானம் or *wisdom*, 'which is gained by obedience to the laws laid down in the section on விரதம் [Ch. XXV.–XXXIII.], and which secures *emancipation* (மோட்சம், வீடு).']

341. யாதனின் யாதனி னீங்கியா
னோத லதனி னதனி னிலன் (க)

From whatever, aye, whatever, man gets free,
From that, aye, from that, no more of pain hath he !

342. வேண்டி னுண் டாகத் துறக்க துறந்தபி
னீண்டியற் பால பல (உ)

'Renunciation' made—ev'n here true pleasures men acquire ;
'Renounce' while time is yet, if to those pleasures you aspire.

343. அடல்வேண்டு மைந்தின் புலத்தை
விடல்வேண்டும் வேண்டிய வெல்லா மொருங்கு (௩)

'Perceptions of the five' must all expire ;—
Relinquished in its order each desire.

344. இயல்பாகு நோன்பிற்கொன் றின்மை யுடைமை
மயலாகு மற்றும் பெயர்த்து (௪)

'Privation absolute' is penance true;
'Possession' brings bewilderment anew.

345. மற்றுந் தொடர்ப்பா டெவன்கொல் பிறப்பறுக்க
லுற்றார்க் குடம்பு மிகை (௫)

To those who sev'rance seek from being's varied strife,
Flesh is burthen sore; what then other bonds of life?

346. யானென தென்னுஞ் செருக்கறுப்பான்
வானோர்க் குயர்ந்த வுலகம் புகும் (௬)

Who kills conceit that utters 'I' and 'mine,'
Shall enter realms above the powers divine.

347. பற்றி விடாஅ விடும்பைகள் பற்றினைப்
பற்றி விடாஅ தவர்க்கு (௭)

Who cling to things that cling and eager clasp,
Griefs cling to them with unrelaxing grasp.

348. தலைப்பட்டார் தீரத் துறந்தார் மயங்கி
வலைப்பட்டார் மற்றை யவர் (௮)

Who thoroughly 'renounce' on highest height are set:
The rest, bewildered, lie entangled in the net.

349. பற்றற்ற கண்ணே பிறப்பறுக்கு
மற்று நிலையாமை காணப் படும் (௯)

When that which clings falls off, severed is being's tie;
All else will then be seen as instability.

350. பற்றுக பற்றற்றான் பற்றினை யப்பற்றைப்
பற்றுக பற்று விடற்கு (௰)

Cling thou to that which He, to Whom nought clings, hath bid thee cling,
Cling to that bond, to get thee free from every clinging thing.

CHAPTER XXXVI. அதி. ௩௬.

மெய்யுணர்தல்.—KNOWLEDGE OF THE TRUE.

351. பொருளல் லவற்றைப் பொருளென் றுணரு
மருளானா மாணாப் பிறப்பு (௧)

Of things devoid of truth as real things men deem;—
Cause of degraded birth the fond delusive dream!

352. இருணீங்கி யின்பம பயக்கு
மருணீங்கி மாசறு காட்சி யவர்க்கு (௨)

Darkness departs, and rapture springs to men who see
The mystic vision pure, from all delusion free.

353. ஐயத்தி னீங்கித் தெளிந்தார்க்கு
வையத்தின் வான நணிய துடைத்து (௩)

When doubts disperse, and mists of error roll
Away, nearer is heav'n than earth to sage's soul.

354. ஐயுணர் வெய்தியக் கண்ணும் பயனின்றே
மெய்யுணர் வில்லா தவர்க்கு (௪)

Five-fold perception gained, what benefits accrue
To them whose spirits lack perception of the true?

355. எப்பொரு ளெத்தன்மைத் தாயினு
மப்பொருண் மெய்ப்பொருள் காண்ப தறிவு (௫)

Whatever thing, of whatsoever kind it be,
'Tis wisdom's part in each the very thing to see.

356. கற்றீண்டு மெய்ப்பொருள் கண்டார் தலைப்படுவர்
மற்றீண்டு வாரா நெறி (௬)

Who learn, and here the knowledge of the true obtain,
Shall find the path that hither cometh not again.

357. ஓர்த்துள்ள முள்ள துணரி னொருதலையாப்
பேர்த்துள்ள வேண்டா பிறப்பு (௭)

The mind that knows with certitude what is, and ponders well,
Its thoughts on birth again to other life need not to dwell.

358. பிறப்பென்னும் பேதைமை நீங்கச்
சிறப்பென்னுஞ் செம்பொருள் காண்ப தறிவு (௮)

When folly, cause of births, departs; and soul can view
The truth of things, man's dignity—'tis wisdom true.

359. சார்புணர்ந்து சார்பு கெடவொழுகின் மற்றழித்து
சார்தரா சார்தரு நோய் (௯)

The true 'support' who knows—rejects 'supports' he sought before—
Sorrow that clings and all destroys, shall cling to him no more.

360. காமம் வெகுளி மயக்க மிவைமூன்றி
னாமங் கெடக்கெடு நோய் (௰)

When lust and wrath and error's triple tyranny is o'er,
Their very names for aye extinct, then pain shall be no more.

CHAPTER XXXVII. அதி. ௩௭.

அவாவறுத்தல்.—The Extirpation of Desire.

361. அவாவென்ப வெல்லா வுயிர்க்கு மெஞ்ஞான்றுந்
தவாஅப் பிறப்பீனும் வித்து (௧)

The wise declare, through all the days, to every living thing
That ceaseless round of birth from seed of strong desire doth spring.

362. வேண்டுங்கால் வேண்டும் பிறவாமை மற்றது
வேண்டாமை வேண்ட வரும் (௨)

If desire you feel, freedom from changing birth require!
'Twill come, if you desire to 'scape, set free from all desire.

363. வேண்டாமை யன்ன விழுச்செல்வ மீண்டில்லை
யாண்டு மஃதொப்ப தில் (௩)

No glorious wealth is *here* like freedom from desire;
To bliss like this not even *there* can soul aspire.

364. தூஉய்மை யென்ப தவாவின்மை மற்றது
வாஅய்மை வேண்ட வரும் (௪)

Desire's decease as purity men know;
That, too, from yearning search for truth will grow.

365. அற்றவ ரென்பா ரவாவற்றார் மற்றையா
ரற்றாக வற்ற திலர் (௫)

Men freed from bonds of strong desire are free;
None other share such perfect liberty.

366. அஞ்சுவ தோரு மறனே யொருவனை
வஞ்சிப்ப தோரு மவா (௬)

Desire each soul beguiles;
True virtue dreads its wiles.

367. அவாவினை யாற்ற வறுப்பிற்
றவாவினை தான்வேண்டு மாற்றான் வரும் (௭)

Who throughly rids his life of passion-prompted deed,
Deeds of unfailing worth shall do, which, as he plans, succeed.

368. அவாவில்லார்க் கில்லாகுந் துன்ப மஃதுண்டேற்
றவாஅது மேன்மேல் வரும் (௮)

Affliction is not known where no desires abide;
Where these are, endless rises sorrow's tide.

Cause oı

369. இன்ப மிடையறா தீண்டு மவாவென்னுந்
துன்பத்துட் டுன்பங் கெடின் (௯)

When dies away desire, that woe of woes,
Ev'n here the soul unceasing rapture knows.

370. ஆரா வியற்கை யவாநீப்பி னந்நிலையே
பேரா வியற்கை தரும் (௰)

Drive from thy soul desire insatiate;
Straightway is gained the moveless blissful state.

ஞானம் முற்றும்.

THE END OF 'WISDOM.'

துறவறவியன் முற்றும்.

THE END OF THE SECTION ON 'ASCETIC VIRTUE.'

---

§ 4. FATE. ஊழ்.

CHAPTER XXXVIII. அதி. ௩௮.

371. ஆகூழாற் றோன்று மசைவின்மை கைப்பொருள்
போகூழாற் றோன்று மடி (௧)

Wealth-giving fate power of unflinching effort brings;
From fate that takes away idle remissness springs.

372. பேதைப் படுக்கு மிழவூ ழறிவகற்று
மாகலூ ழுற்றக் கடை (௨)

The fate that loss ordains makes wise men's wisdom foolishness;
The fate that gain bestows with ampler powers will wisdom bless.

373. நுண்ணிய நூல்பல கற்பினு மற்றுந்த
னுண்மை யறிவே மிகும் (௩)

In subtle learning manifold though versed man be,
The wisdom, truly his, will gain supremacy.

374. இருவே றுலகத் தியற்கை
திருவேறு தெள்ளிய ராதலும் வேறு (௪)

Two-fold the fashion of the world: some live in fortune's light;
While other some have souls in wisdom's radiance bright.

375. நல்லவை யெல்லாஅந் தீயவாந் தீயவு
நல்லவாஞ் செல்வஞ் செயற்கு (௫)

All things that good appear will oft have ill success;
All evil things prove good for gain of happiness.

376. பரியினு மாகாவாம் பாலல்ல வுய்த்துச்
சொரியினும் போகா தம (௬)

Things not your own will yield no good, howe'er you guard with pain;
Your own, howe'er you scatter them abroad, will yours remain.

377. வகுத்தான் வகுத்த வகையல்லாற் கோடி
தொகுத்தார்க்குந் துய்த்த லரிது (௭)

Save as the 'sharer' shares to each in due degree,
To those who millions store enjoyment scarce can be.

378. துறப்பார்மற் றுப்புர வில்லா
ருறற்பால வூட்டா கழியு மெனின் (௮)

The destitute might with ascetics merit share,
If fate to visit with predestined ills would spare.

379. நன்றாங்கா லல்லவாக் காண்பவ
ரன்றாங்கா லல்லற் படுவ தெவன் (௯)

When good things come, men view them all as gain;
When evils come, why then should they complain?

380. ஊழிற் பெருவலி யாவுள மற்றொன்று
சூழினுந் தான்முந் துறும் (௰)

What powers so great as those of Destiny? Man's skill
Some other thing contrives; but fate 's beforehand still.

அறத்துப்பான் முற்றிற்று.

THE END OF BOOK I. ON VIRTUE.

BOOK II.—WEALTH.

BOOK II. — WEALTH. பொருட்பால்.

§ 1.—ROYALTY. அரசியல்.

CHAPTER XXXIX. அதி. ௩௯.

இறைமாட்சி.—The Greatness of a King.

381. படைகுடி கூழமைச்சு நட்பரணாறு
உடையா னரசரு ளேறு (௧)
An army, people, wealth, a minister, friends, fort: six things—
Who owns them all, a lion lives amid the kings.

382. அஞ்சாமை யீகை யறிவூக்க மிந்நான்கு
மெஞ்சாமை வேந்தற் கியல்பு (௨)
Courage, a liberal hand, wisdom, and energy: these four
Are qualities a king adorn for evermore.

383. தூங்காமை கல்வி துணிவுடைமை யிம்மூன்று
நீங்கா நிலனாள் பவர்க்கு (௩)
A sleepless promptitude, knowledge, decision strong:
These three for aye to rulers of the land belong.

384. அறனிழுக்கா தல்லவை நீக்கி
மறனிழுக்கா மான முடைய தரசு (௪)
Kingship, in virtue failing not, all vice restrains,
In courage failing not, it honour's grace maintains.

385. இயற்றலு மீட்டலுங் காத்தலுங் காத்த
வகுத்தலும் வல்ல தரசு (௫)
A king is he who treasure gains, stores up, defends,
And duly for his kingdom's weal expends.

386. காட்சிக் கெளியன் கடுஞ்சொல்ல னல்லனேன்
மீக்கூறு மன்ன னிலம் (௬)
Where king is easy of access, where no harsh word repels,
That land's high praises every subject swells.

387. இன்சொலா லீத்தளிக்க வல்லாற்குத்
தன்சொலாற் றான்கண் டனைத்திவ் வுலகு (௭)

With pleasant speech, who gives and guards with powerful liberal hand,
He sees the world obedient all to his command.

388. முறைசெய்து காப்பாற்று மன்னவன் மக்கட்
கிறையென்று வைக்கப் படும் (௮)

Who guards the realm and justice strict maintains,
That king as god o'er subject peoples reigns.

389. செவிகைப்பச் சொற்பொறுக்கும் பண்புடை வேந்தன்
கவிகைக்கீழ்த் தங்கு முலகு (௯)

The king of worth, who can words bitter to his ear endure,
Beneath the shadow of his power the world abides secure.

390. கொடையளி செங்கோல் குடியோம்ப னான்கு
முடையானாம் வேந்தர்க் கொளி (௰)

Gifts, grace, right sceptre, care of people's weal:
These four a light of dreaded kings reveal.

CHAPTER XL. அதி. ௪௰.

கல்வி.—LEARNING.

391. கற்க கசடறக் கற்பவை கற்றபி
னிற்க வதற்குத் தக (௧)

So learn that you may full and faultless learning gain,
Then in obedience meet to lessons learnt remain.

392. எண்ணென்ப வேனை யெழுத்தென்ப விவ்விரண்டுங்
கண்ணென்ப வாழு முயிர்க்கு (௨)

The twain that lore of numbers and of letters give
Are eyes, the wise declare, to all on earth that live.

393. கண்ணுடைய ரென்பவர் கற்றோர் முகத்திரண்டு
புண்ணுடையர் கல்லா தவர் (௩)

Men who learning gain have eyes, men say;
Blockheads' faces pairs of sores display.

394. உவப்பத் தலைக்கூடி யுள்ளப் பிரித
லனைத்தே புலவர் தொழில் (௪)

You meet with joy, with pleasant thought you part;
Such is the learned scholar's wondrous art!

395. உடையார்மு னில்லார்போ லேக்கற்றுங் கற்றார்
கடையரே கல்லா தவர் (௫)

With soul submiss they stand, as paupers front a rich man's face;
Yet learned men are first; th' unlearned stand in lowest place.

396. தொட்டனைத் தூறு மணற்கேணி மாந்தர்க்குக்
கற்றனைத் தூறு மறிவு (௬)

In sandy soil, when deep you delve, you reach the springs below;
The more you learn, the freer streams of wisdom flow.

397. யாதானு நாடாமா லூராமா லென்னொருவன்
சாந்துணையுங் கல்லாத வாறு (௭)

The learned make each land their own, in every city find a home;
Who, till they die, learn nought, along what weary ways they roam!

398. ஒருமைக்கட் டான்கற்ற கல்வி யொருவற்
கெழுமையு மேமாப் புடைத்து (௮)

The man who store of learning gains,
In one, through seven worlds, bliss attains. [Comp. 126.]

399. தாமின் புறுவ துலகின் புறக்கண்டு
காமுறுவர் கற்றறிந் தார் (௯)

Their joy is joy of all the world, they see; thus more
The learners learn to love their cherished lore.

400. கேடில் விழுச்செல்வங் கல்வி யொருவற்கு
மாடல்ல மற்றை யவை (௰)

Learning is excellence of wealth that none destroy;
To man nought else affords reality of joy.

CHAPTER XLI. அதி. ௪௧.

கல்லாமை.—Ignorance.

401. அரங்கின்றி வட்டாடி யற்றே
நிரம்பிய நூலின்றிக் கோட்டிக் கொளல் (௧)

Like those at draughts would play without the chequered square,
Men void of ample lore would counsels of the learned share.

402. கல்லாதான் சொற்கா முறுதன் முலையிரண்டு
மில்லாதாள் பெண்காமுற் றற்று (௨)

Like those who doat on hoyden's undeveloped charms are they,
Of learning void, who eagerly their power of words display.

403. கல்லா தவரு நனிநல்லர் கற்றார்முற்
சொல்லா திருக்கப் பெறின் (௩)

The blockheads, too, may men of worth appear,
If they can keep from speaking where the learned hear!

404. கல்லாதா னொட்பங் கழியநன் றாயினுங்
கொள்ளா ரறிவுடை யார் (௪)

From blockheads' lips, when words of wisdom glibly flow,
The wise receive them not, though good they seem to show.

405. கல்லா வொருவன் றகைமை தலைப்பெய்து
சொல்லாடச் சோர்வு படும் (௫)

As worthless shows the worth of man unlearned,
When council meets, by words he speaks discerned.

406. உளரென்னு மாத்திரைய ரல்லாற் பயவாக்
களரனையர் கல்லா தவர் (௬)

'They are': so much is true of men untaught;
But, like a barren field, they yield us nought!

407. நுண்மா ணுழைபுல மில்லா னெழினல
மண்மாண் புனைபாவை யற்று (௭)

Who lack the power of subtle, large, and penetrating sense,
Like puppet, decked with ornaments of clay, their beauty's vain pretence.

408. நல்லார்கட் பட்ட வறுமையி னின்னாதே
கல்லார்கட் பட்ட திரு (௮)

To men unlearned, from fortune's favour greater evil springs
Than poverty to men of goodly wisdom brings.

409. மேற்பிறந்தா ராயினுங் கல்லாதார்
கீழ்ப்பிறந்துங் கற்றா ரனைத்திலர் பாடு (௯)

Lower are men unlearned, though noble be their race,
Than low-born men adorned with learning's grace.

410. விலங்கொடு மக்க ளனைய
ரிலங்குநூல் கற்றாரோ டேனை யவர் (௰)

Learning's irradiating grace who gain,
Others excel, as men the bestial train.

CHAPTER XLII. அதி. ௪௨.

கேள்வி.—HEARING.

411. செல்வத்துட் செல்வஞ் செவிச்செல்வ மச்செல்வஞ்
செல்வத்து ளெல்லாந் தலை (௧)

Wealth of wealth is wealth acquired by ear attent;
Wealth mid all wealth supremely excellent.

412. செவிக்குண வில்லாத போழ்து சிறிது
வயிற்றுக்கு மீயப் படும் (௨)

When 'tis no longer time the listening ear to feed,
With trifling dole of food supply the body's need.

413. செவியுணவிற் கேள்வி யுடையா
ரவியுணவி னான்றாரோ டொப்பர் நிலத்து (௩)

Who feed their ear with learned teachings rare,
Are like the happy gods oblations rich who share.

414. கற்றில னாயினுங் கேட்க வஃதொருவற்
கொற்கத்தி னூற்றாந் துணை (௪)

Though learning none hath he, yet let him hear alway;
In weakness this shall prove a staff and stay.

415. இழுக்க லுடையுழி யூற்றுக்கோ லற்றே
யொழுக்க முடையார்வாய்ச் சொல் (௫)

Like staff in hand of him in slippery ground who strays,
Are words from mouth of those who walk in righteous ways.

416. எனைத்தானு நல்லவை கேட்க
வனைத்தானு மான்ற பெருமை தரும் (௬)

Let each man good things learn, for e'en as he
Shall learn, he gains increase of perfect dignity.

417. பிழைத்துணர்ந்தும் பேதைமை சொல்லா
ரிழைத்துணர்ந் தீண்டிய கேள்வி யவர் (௭)

Not e'en through inadvertence speak they foolish word,
With clear discerning mind who've learning's ample lessons heard.

418. கேட்பினுங் கேளாத் தகையவே கேள்வியாற்
றோட்கப் படாத செவி (௮)

Where teaching hath not oped the learner's ear,
The man may listen, but he scarce can hear.

419. நுணங்கிய கேள்விய ரல்லார்
வணங்கிய வாயின ராத லரிது (௯)

'Tis hard for mouth to utter gentle, modest word,
When ears discourse of lore refined have never heard.

420. செவியிற் சுவையுணரா வாயுணர்வின் மாக்க
ளவியினும் வாழினு மென் (௰)

His mouth can taste, but ear no taste of joy can give!
What matter if he die, or prosperous live?

CHAPTER XLIII. அதி. ௪௩.

அறிவுடைமை.—The Possession of Knowledge.

421. அறிவற்றங் காக்குங் கருவி
செறுவார்க்கு முள்ளழிக்க லாகா வரண் (௧)

True wisdom wards off woes,
  A circling fortress high;
Its inner strength man's eager foes
  Unshaken will defy.

422. சென்ற விடத்தாற் செலவிடா தீதொரீஇ
நன்றின்பா லுய்ப்ப தறிவு (௨)

Wisdom restrains, nor suffers mind to wander where it would;
From every evil calls it back, and guides in way of good.

423. எப்பொருள் யார்யார்வாய்க் கேட்பினு மப்பொருண்
மெய்ப்பொருள் காண்ப தறிவு (௩)

Though things diverse from divers sages' lips we learn,
'Tis wisdom's part in each the true thing to discern.

424. எண்பொருள வாகச் செலச்சொல்லித் தான்பிறர்வாய்
நுண்பொருள் காண்ப தறிவு (௪)

Wisdom hath use of lucid speech, words that acceptance win,
And subtle sense of other men's discourse takes in.

425. உலகந் தழீஇய தொட்ப
மலர்தலுங் கூம்பலு மில்ல தறிவு (௫)

Wisdom embraces frank the world, to no caprice exposed;
Unlike the lotus flower, now opened wide, now petals strictly closed.

426. எவ்வ துறைவ துலக முலகத்தோ
டவ்வ துறைவ தறிவு (௬)

As dwells the world, so with the world to dwell
In harmony—this is to wisely live and well.

427. அறிவுடையா ராவ தறிவா
ரறிவிலா ரஃதறி கல்லா தவர் (௭)

The wise discern, the foolish fail to see,
And minds prepare for things about to be.

428. அஞ்சுவ தஞ்சாமை பேதைமை
யஞ்சுவ தஞ்ச லறிவார் தொழில் (௮)

Folly meets fearful ills with fearless heart;
To fear where cause of fear exists is wisdom's part.

429. எதிரதாக் காக்கு மறிவினார்க் கில்லை
யதிர வருவதோர் நோய் (௯)

The wise with watchful soul who coming ills foresee;
From coming evil's dreaded shock are free.

430. அறிவுடையா ரெல்லா முடையா
ரறிவிலா ரென்னுடைய ரேனு மிலர் (௰)

The wise is rich, with ev'ry blessing blest;
The fool is poor, of everything possessed.

CHAPTER XLIV. அதி. ௪௪.

குற்றங்கடிதல்.—The Correction of Faults.

431. செருக்குஞ் சினமுஞ் சிறுமையு மில்லார்
பெருக்கம் பெருமித நீர்த்து (௧)

Who arrogance, and wrath, and littleness of low desire restrain,
To sure increase of lofty dignity attain.

432. இவறலு மாண்பிறந்த மானமு மாணா
வுவகையு மேத மிறைக்கு (௨)

A niggard hand, o'erweening self-regard, and mirth
Unseemly, bring disgrace to men of kingly birth.

433. தினைத்துணையாங் குற்றம் வரினும்
பனைத்துணையாக் கொள்வர் பழிநாணு வார் (௩)

Though small as millet-seed the fault men deem;
As palm-tree vast to those who fear disgrace 'twill seem.

434. குற்றமே காக்க பொருளாகக் குற்றமே
யற்றந் தரூஉம் பகை (௪)

Freedom from faults is wealth; watch heedfully
'Gainst these, for fault is fatal enmity.

435. வருமுன்னர்க் காவாதான் வாழ்க்கை
யெரிமுன்னர் வைத்தூறு போலக் கெடும். (௫)

His joy who guards not 'gainst the coming evil day,
Like straw before the fire shall swift consume away.

436. தன்குற்றம் நீக்கிப் பிறர்குற்றங் காண்கிற்பி
னென்குற்ற மாகு மிறைக்கு (௬)

Faultless the king who first his own faults cures, and then
Permits himself to scan the faults of other men.

437. செயற்பால செய்யா திவறியான் செல்வ
முயற்பால தன்றிக் கெடும் (௭)

Who leaves undone what should be done, with niggard mind,
His wealth shall perish, leaving not a wrack behind.

438. பற்றுள்ள மென்னு மிவறன்மை
யெற்றுள்ளு மெண்ணப் படுவதொன் றன்று (௮)

The greed of soul that avarice men call,
When faults are summed, is worst of all.

439. வியவற்க வெஞ்ஞான்றுந் தன்னை
நயவற்க நன்றி பயவா வினை (௯)

Never indulge in self-complaisant mood,
Nor deed desire that yields no gain of good.

440. காதல காத லறியாமை யுய்க்கிற்பி
னேதில வேதிலார் நூல் (௰)

If, to your foes unknown, you cherish what you love,
Counsels of men who wish you harm will harmless prove.

CHAPTER XLV. அதி. ௪௫.

பெரியாரைத் துணைக்கோடல்.—Seeking the Aid of Great Men.

441. அறனறிந்து மூத்த வறிவுடையார் கேண்மை
திறனறிந்து தேர்ந்து கொளல் (௧)

As friends the men who virtue know, and riper wisdom share,
Their worth weighed well, the king should choose with care.

442. உற்றநோய் நீக்கி யுறாஅமை முற்காக்கும்
பெற்றியார்ப் பேணிக் கொளல் (௨)

Cherish the all-accomplished men as friends,
Whose skill the present ill removes, from coming ill defends.

443. அரியவற்று ளெல்லா மரிதே
பெரியாரை பேணித் தமராக் கொளல் (௩)

To cherish men of mighty soul, and make them all their own,
Of kingly treasures rare, as rarest gift is known.

444. தம்மிற் பெரியார் தமரா வொழுகுதல்
வன்மையு ளெல்லாந் தலை (௪)

To live with men of greatness that their own excels,
As cherished friends, is greatest power that with a monarch dwells.

445. சூழ்வார்கண் ணாக வொழுகலான் மன்னவன்
சூழ்வாரைச் சூழ்ந்து கொளல் (௫)

The king, since counsellors are monarch's eyes,
Should counsellors select with counsel wise.

446. தக்கா ரினத்தனாய்த் தானொழுக வல்லானைச்
செற்றார் செயக்கிடந்த தில் (௬)

The king, who knows to live with worthy men allied,
Has nought to fear from any foeman's pride.

447. இடிக்குந் துணையாரை யாள்வாரை யாரே
கெடுக்குந் தகைமை யவர் (௭)

What power can work his fall, who faithful ministers
Employs, that thunder out reproaches when he errs.

448. இடிப்பாரை யில்லாத வேமரா மன்னன்
கெடுப்பா ரிலானுங் கெடும் (௮)

The king with none to censure him, bereft of safeguards all,
Though none his ruin work, shall surely ruined fall.

449. முதலிலார்க் கூதிய மில்லை
மதலையாஞ் சார்பிலார்க் கில்லை நிலை (௯)

Who owns no principal, can have no gain of usury;
Who lacks support of friends, knows no stability.

450. பல்லார் பகைகொளலிற் பத்தடுத்த தீமைத்தே
நல்லார் தொடர்கை விடல் (௰)

Than hate of many foes incurred, works greater woe
Ten-fold, of worthy men the friendship to forego.

CHAPTER XLVI. அதி. சசு.

சிற்றினஞ்சேராமை.—Avoiding mean Associations.

451. சிற்றின மஞ்சும் பெருமை சிறுமைதான்
சுற்றமாய்ச் சூழ்ந்து விடும் (க)

The great of soul will mean association fear;
The mean of soul regard mean men as kinsmen dear.

452. நிலத்தியல்பா னீர்திரிந் தற்றாகு மாந்தர்க்
கினத்தியல்ப தாகு மறிவு (உ)

The waters' virtues change with soil through which they flow;
As man's companionship so will his wisdom show.

453. மனத்தானா மாந்தர்க் குணர்ச்சி
யினத்தானா மின்னா னெனப்படுஞ் சொல் (ங)

Perceptions manifold in men are of the mind alone;
The value of the man by his companionship is known.

454. மனத்து ளதுபோலக் காட்டி யொருவற்
கினத்து ளதாகு மறிவு (ச)

Man's wisdom seems the offspring of his mind;
'Tis outcome of companionship we find.

455. மனந்தூய்மை செய்வினை தூய்மை யிரண்டு
மினந்தூய்மை தூவா வரும் (ரு)

Both purity of mind, and purity of action clear,
Leaning on staff of pure companionship, to man draw near.

456. மனந்தூயார்க் கெச்ச நன்றாகு
மினந்தூயார்க் கில்லை நன்றாகா வினை (சு)

From true pure-minded men a virtuous race proceeds;
To men of pure companionship belong no evil deeds.

457. மனநல மன்னுயிர்க் காக்க
மினநல மெல்லாப் புகழுந் தரும் (எ)

Goodness of mind to lives of men increaseth gain;
And good companionship doth all of praise obtain.

458. மனநல நன்குடைய ராயினுஞ் சான்றோர்க்
கினநல மேமாப் புடைத்து (அ)

To perfect men, though minds right good belong,
Yet good companionship is confirmation strong.

459. மனநலத்தி னாகு மறுமைமற் றஃது
மினநலத்தி னேமாப் புடைத்து (கூ)

Although to mental goodness joys of other life belong,
Yet good companionship is confirmation strong.

460. நல்லினத்தி னூங்குந் துணையில்லைத் தீயினத்தி
னல்லற் படுப்பதூஉ மில் (ய)

Than good companionship no surer help we know;
Than bad companionship nought causes direr woe.

CHAPTER XLVII. அதி. சஎ.

தெரிந்துசெயல்வகை.—Acting after due Consideration.

461. அழிவதூஉ மாவதூஉ மாகி
வழிபயக்கு மூதியமுஞ் சூழ்ந்து செயல் (க)

Expenditure, return, and profit of the deed
In time to come: weigh these—then to the act proceed.

462. தெரிந்த வினத்தொடு தேர்ந்தெண்ணிச் செய்வார்க்
கரும்பொருள் யாதொன்று மில் (உ)

With chosen friends deliberate; next use thy private thought;
Then act. By those who thus proceed all works with ease are wrought.

463. ஆக்கங் கருதி முதலிழக்குஞ் செய்வினை
யூக்கா ரறிவுடை யார் (ங)

To risk one's all and lose, aiming at added gain,
Is rash affair, from which the wise abstain.

464. தெளிவி லதனைத் தொடங்கா
ரிளிவென்னு மேதப்பா டஞ்சு பவர் (ச)

A work of which the issue is not clear,
Begin not they reproachful scorn who fear.

465. வகையறச் சூழா தெழுதல்
பகைவரைப் பாத்திப் படுப்பதோ ராறு (ரு)

With plans not well matured to rise against your foe,
Is way to plant him out where he is sure to grow!

466. செய்தக்க வல்ல செயக்கெடுஞ்
செய்தக்க செய்யாமை யானுங் கெடும் (சா)

'Tis ruin if man do an unbefitting thing;
Fit things to leave undone will equal ruin bring.

467. எண்ணித் துணிக கருமந் துணிந்தபி
னெண்ணுவ மென்ப திழுக்கு (௭)

Think, and then dare the deed! Who cry,
'Deed dared, we 'll think,' disgraced shall be.

468. ஆற்றின் வருந்தா வருத்தம் பலர்நின்று
போற்றினும் பொத்துப் படும் (௮)

On no right system if man toil and strive,
Though many men assist, no work can thrive.

469. நன்றாற்ற லுள்ளுந் தவறுண் டவரவர்
பண்பறிந் தாற்றாக் கடை (௯)

Though well the work be done, yet one mistake is made,
To habitudes of various men when no regard is paid.

470. எள்ளாத வெண்ணிச் செயல்வேண்டுந் தம்மொடு
கொள்ளாத கொள்ளா துலகு (௰)

Plan and perform no work that others may despise;
What misbeseems a king the world will not approve as wise.

CHAPTER XLVIII. அதி. ௪௮.

வலியறிதல்.—The Knowledge of Power.

471. வினைவலியுந் தன்வலியு மாற்றான் வலியுந்
துணைவலியுந் தூக்கிச் செயல் (௧)

The force the strife demands, the force he owns, the force of foes,
The force of friends: these should he weigh ere to the war he goes.

472. ஒல்வ தறிவ தறிந்ததன்கட் டங்கிச்
செல்வார்க்குச் செல்லாத தில் (௨)

Who know what can be wrought, with knowledge of the means, on this
Their mind firm set, go forth, nought goes with them amiss.

473. உடைத்தம் வலியறியா ருக்கத்தி னூக்கி
யிடைக்கண் முரிந்தார் பலர் (௩)

Ill-deeming of their proper powers, have many monarchs striven,
And midmost of unequal conflict fallen asunder riven.

474. அமைந்தாங் கொழுகா னளவறியான் றன்னை
வியந்தான் விரைந்து கெடும் (௪)

Who not agrees with those around, no moderation knows,
In self-applause indulging, swift to ruin goes.

475. பீலிபெய் சாகாடு மச்சிறுமப் பண்டஞ்
சால மிகுத்துப் பெயின் (௫)

With peacock feathers light you load the wain;
Yet, heaped too high, the axle snaps in twain.

476. நுனிக்கொம்ப ரேறினா ரஃதிறந் தூக்கி
னுயிர்க்கிறுதி யாகி விடும் (௬)

Who daring climbs, and would himself upraise
Beyond the branch's tip, with life the forfeit pays.

477. ஆற்றி னளவறிந் தீக வதுபொருள்
போற்றி வழங்கு நெறி (௭)

With knowledge of the measure due, as virtue bids you, give!
That is the way to guard your wealth, and seemly live.

478. ஆகா றளவிட்டி தாயினுங் கேடில்லைப்
போகா றகலாக் கடை (௮)

Incomings may be scant; but yet, no failure there,
If in expenditure you rightly learn to spare.

479. அளவறிந்து வாழாதான் வாழ்க்கை
யுளபோல வில்லாகித் தோன்றாக் கெடும் (௯)

Who prosperous lives and of enjoyment knows no bound,
His seeming wealth, departing, nowhere shall be found.

480. உளவரைத் தூக்காத வொப்புர வாண்மை
வளவரை வல்லைக் கெடும்

Beneficence that measures not its bound of means,
Will swiftly bring to nought the wealth on which it leans.

CHAPTER XLIX. அதி. ௪௯.

காலமறிதல்.—Knowing the fitting Time.

481. பகல்வெல்லுங் கூகையைக் காக்கை
யிகல்வெல்லும் வேந்தர்க்கு வேண்டும் பொழுது (௧)

A crow will conquer owl in broad daylight;
The king that foes would crush, needs fitting time to fight.

482. பருவத்தோ டொட்ட வொழுக
றிருவினைத் தீராமை யார்க்குங் கயிறு (௨)

The bond binds fortune fast is ordered effort made,
Strictly observant still of favouring season's aid.

483. அருவினை யென்ப வுளவோ
கருவியாற் கால மறிந்து செயின் (௩)

Can any work be hard in very fact,
If men use fitting means in timely act?

484. ஞாலங் கருதினுங் கைகூடுங்
காலங் கருதி யிடத்தாற் செயின் (௪)

The pendant world's dominion may be won,
In fitting time and place by action done.

485. காலங் கருதி யிருப்பர் கலங்காது
ஞாலங் கருது பவர் (௫)

Who think the pendant world itself to subjugate,
With mind unruffled for the fitting time must wait.

486. ஊக்க முடையா னொடுக்கம் பொருதகர்
தாக்கற்குப் பேருந் தகைத்து (௬)

The men of mighty power their hidden energies repress,
As fighting ram recoils to rush on foe with heavier stress.

487. பொள்ளென வாங்கே புறம்வேரார் காலம்பார்த்
துள்வேர்ப்ப ரொள்ளி யவர் (௭)

The glorious ones of wrath enkindled make no outward show,
At once; they bide their time, while hidden fires within them glow.

488. செறுநரைக் காணிற் சுமக்க
விறுவரை காணிற் கிழக்காந் தலை (௮)

If foes' detested form they see, with patience let them bear;
When fateful hour at last they spy,—the head lies there.

489. எய்தற் கரிய தியைந்தக்கா லந்நிலையே
செய்தற் கரிய செயல் (௯)

When hardest gain of opportunity at last is won,
With promptitude let hardest deed be done.

490. கொக்கொக்க கூம்பும் பருவத்து மற்றதன்
குத்தொக்க சீர்த்த விடத்து (௰)

As heron stands with folded wing, so wait in waiting hour;
As heron snaps its prey, when fortune smiles, put forth your power.

CHAPTER L. அதி. ருo.

இடனறிதல்.—Knowing the Place.

491. தொடங்கற்க வெவ்வினையு மெள்ளற்க முற்று
மிடங்கண்ட பின்னல் லது (க)

Begin no work of war, despise no foe,
Till place where you can wholly circumvent you know.

492. முரண்சேர்ந்த மொய்ம்பி னவர்க்கு
மரண்சேர்ந்தா மாக்கம் பலவுந் தரும் (உ)

Though skill in war combine with courage tried on battle-field,
The added gain of fort doth great advantage yield.

493. ஆற்றாரு மாற்றி யடிப விடனறிந்து
போற்றார்கட் போற்றிச் செயின் (ங)

E'en weak ones mightily prevail, if place of strong defence
They find, protect themselves, and work their foes offence.

494. எண்ணியா ரெண்ண மிழப்ப ரிடனறிந்து
துன்னியார் துன்னிச் செயின் (ச)

The foes who thought to triumph, find their thoughts were vain,
If hosts advance, seize vantage ground, and thence the fight maintain.

495. நெடும்புனலுள் வெல்லு முதலை
யடும்புனலி னீங்கி னதனைப் பிற (ரு)

The crocodile prevails in its own flow of water wide,
If this it leaves, 'tis slain by any thing beside.

496. கடலோடா கால்வ னெடுந்தேர்
கடலோடு நாவாயு மோடா நிலத்து (சு)

The lofty car, with mighty wheel, sails not o'er watery main,
The boat that skims the sea, runs not on earth's hard plain.

497. அஞ்சாமை யல்லாற் றுணைவேண்டா
வெஞ்சாமை யெண்ணி யிடத்தாற் செயின் (எ)

Save their own fearless might they need no other aid,
If in right place they fight, all due provision made.

498. சிறுபடையான் செல்லிடஞ் சேரி
னுறுபடையா னூக்க மழிந்து விடும் (அ)

If lord of army vast the safe retreat assail
Of him whose host is small, his mightiest efforts fail.

499. சிறைநலனுஞ் சீரு மிலரெனினு மாந்த
ருறைநிலத்தோ டொட்ட லரிது (௯)

Though fort be none, and store of wealth they lack,
'Tis hard a people's homesteads to attack!

500. காலாழ் களரி னரியடுங் கண்ணஞ்சா
வேலாண் முகத்த களிறு (௰)

The jackall slays, in miry paths of foot-betraying fen,
The elephant of fearless eye and tusks transfixing armèd men.

CHAPTER LI. அதி. ௫௧.

தெரிந்து தெளிதல்.—Selection and Confidence.

501. அறம்பொரு ளின்ப முயிரச்ச நான்கின்
றிறந்தெரிந்து தேறப் படும் (௧)

How treats he virtue, wealth and pleasure? How, when life 's at stake,
Comports himself? This four-fold test of man will full assurance make.

502. குடிப்பிறந்து குற்றத்தி னீங்கி
வடுப்பரியு நாணுடையான் கட்டே தெளிவு (௨)

Of noble race, of faultless worth, of generous pride
That shrinks from shame or stain; in him may king confide.

503. அரியகற் றாசற்றார் கண்ணுந்
தெரியுங்கா லின்மை யரிதே வெளிறு (௩)

Though deeply learned, unflecked by fault, 'tis rare to see,
When closely scanned, a man from all unwisdom free.

504. குணநாடிக் குற்றமு நாடி யவற்றுண்
மிகைநாடி மிக்க கொளல் (௪)

Weigh well the good of each, his failings closely scan,
As these or those prevail, so estimate the man.

505. பெருமைக்கு மேனைச் சிறுமைக்குந் தத்தங்
கருமமே கட்டளைக் கல் (௫)

Of greatness and of meanness too,
The deeds of each are touchstone true.

506. அற்றாரைத் தேறுத லோம்புக மற்றவர்
பற்றிலர் நாணார் பழி (௬)

Beware of trusting men who have no kith or kin;
No bonds restrain such men, no shame deters from sin.

507. காதன்மை கந்தா வறிவறியார்த் தேறுதல்
பேதைமை யெல்லாந் தரும் (எ)

By fond affection led who trusts in men of unwise soul,
Yields all his being up to folly's blind control.

508. தேரான் பிறனைத் தெளிந்தான் வழிமுறை
தீரா விடும்பை தரும் (அ)

Who trusts an untried stranger, brings disgrace,
Remediless, on all his race.

509. தேறற்க யாரையுந் தேராது தேர்ந்தபிற்
றேறுக தேறும் பொருள் (கூ)

Trust no man whom you have not fully tried,
When tested, in his prudence proved confide.

510. தேரான் றெளிவுந் தெளிந்தான்க ணையுறவுந்
தீரா விடும்பை தரும் (ய)

Trust where you have not tried, *doubt* of a friend to feel,
Once trusted, wounds inflict that nought can heal.

CHAPTER LII. அதி. ருஉ.

தெரிந்துவினையாடல்.—Selection and Employment.

511. நன்மையுந் தீமையு நாடி நலம்புரிந்த
தன்மையா னாளப் படும் (க)

Who good and evil scanning, ever makes the good his joy;
Such man of virtuous mood should king employ.

512. வாரி பெருக்கி வளம்படுத் துற்றவை
யாராய்வான் செய்க வினை (உ)

Who swells the revenues, spreads plenty o'er the land,
Seeks out what hinders progress, his the workman's hand.

513. அன்பறிவு தேற்ற மவாவின்மை யிந்நான்கு
நன்குடையான் கட்டே தெளிவு (ந)

A loyal love with wisdom, clearness, mind from avarice free;
Who hath these four good gifts should ever trusted be.

514. எனைவகையாற் றேறியக் கண்ணும்
வினைவகையான் வேறாகு மாந்தர் பலர் (ச)

Even when tests of every kind are multiplied,
Full many a man proves otherwise, by action tried!

515. அறிந்தாற்றிச் செய்கிற்பாற் கல்லால் வினைதான்
சிறந்தானென் றேவற்பாற் றன்று (௫)

No specious fav'rite should the king's commission bear,
But he that knows, and work performs with patient care.

516. செய்வானை நாடி வினைநாடிக் காலத்தோ
டெய்த வுணர்ந்து செயல் (௬)

Let king first ask, 'Who shall the deed perform?' and 'What the deed?'
Of hour befitting both assured, let every work proceed.

517. இதனை யிதனா லிவன்முடிக்கு மென்றாய்ந்
ததனை யவன்கண் விடல் (௭)

'This man, this work shall thus work out,' let thoughtful king command;
Then leave the matter wholly in his servant's hand.

518. வினைக்குரிமை நாடிய பின்றை யவனை
யதற்குரிய னாகச் செயல் (௮)

As each man's special aptitude is known,
Bid each man make that special work his own.

519. வினைக்கண் வினையுடையான் கேண்மை வேறாக
நினைப்பானை நீங்குந் திரு (௯)

Fortune deserts the king who ill can bear
Informal friendly ways of men his toils who share.

520. நாடோறு நாடுக மன்னன் வினைசெய்வான்
கோடாமை கோடா துலகு (௰)

Let king search out his servants' deeds each day;
When these do right, the world goes rightly on its way.

CHAPTER LIII. அதி. ௫௩.

சுற்றந்தழால்.—CHERISHING ONE'S KINDRED.

521. பற்றற்ற கண்ணும் பழைமைபா ராட்டுதல்
சுற்றத்தார் கண்ணே யுள (௧)

When wealth is fled, old kindness still to show,
Is kindly grace that only kinsmen know.

522. விருப்பறாச் சுற்ற மியையி
னருப்பறா வாக்கம் பலவுந் தரும் (௨)

The gift of kin's unfailing love bestows
Much gain of good, like flower that fadeless blows.

523. அளவளா வில்லாதான் வாழ்க்கை
குளவளாக் கோடின்றி நீர்நிறைந் தற்று (௩)

His joy of life who mingles not with kinsmen gathered round,
Is lake where streams pour in, with no encircling bound.

524. சுற்றத்தாற் சுற்றப் படவொழுகல் செல்வந்தான்
பெற்றத்தாற் பெற்ற பயன் (௪)

The profit gained by wealth's increase,
Is living compassed round by relatives in peace.

525. கொடுத்தலு மின்சொல்லு மாற்றி
னடுக்கிய சுற்றத்தாற் சுற்றப் படும் (௫)

Who knows the use of pleasant words, and liberal gifts can give,
Connections, heaps of them, surrounding him shall live.

526. பெருங்கொடையான் பேணான் வெகுளி யவனின்
மருங்குடையார் மாநிலத் தில் (௬)

Than one who gifts bestows and wrath restrains,
Through the wide world none larger following gains.

527. காக்கை கரவா கரைந்துண்ணு
மாக்கமு மன்னநீ ரார்க்கே யுள (௭)

The crows conceal not, call their friends to come, then eat;
Increase of good such worthy ones shall meet.

528. பொதுநோக்கான் வேந்தன் வரிசையா நோக்கி
னதுநோக்கி வாழ்வார் பலர் (௮)

Where king regards not all alike, but each in his degree,
'Neath such discerning rule many dwell happily.

529. தமராகித் தற்றுறந்தார் சுற்ற
மமராமைக் காரண மின்றி வரும் (௯)

Who once were his, and then forsook him, as before
Will come around, when cause of disagreement is no more.

530. உழைப்பிரிந்து காரணத்தின் வந்தானை வேந்த
னிழைத்திருந் தெண்ணிக் கொளல் (௰)

Who causeless went away, then to return, for any cause, ask leave;
The king should sift their motives well, consider, and receive!

CHAPTER LIV. அதி. ௫௪.

பொச்சாவாமை.—UNFORGETFULNESS.

531. இறந்த வெகுளியிற் றீதே
சிறந்த வுவகை மகிழ்ச்சியிற் சோர்வு (௧)

'Tis greater ill, if rapture of o'erweening gladness to the soul
Bring self-forgetfulness, than if transcendent wrath control.

532. பொச்சாப்புக் கொல்லும் புகழை யறிவினை
நிச்ச நிரப்புக்கொன் றாங்கு (௨)

Perpetual poverty is death to wisdom of the wise;
When man forgets himself his glory dies!

533. பொச்சாப்பார்க் கில்லைப் புகழ்மை யதுவுலகத்
தெப்பானூ லோர்க்குந் துணிவு (௩)

'To self-oblivious men no praise'; this rule
Decisive wisdom sums of every school.

534. அச்ச முடையார்க் கரணில்லை யாங்கில்லைப்
பொச்சாப் புடையார்க்கு நன்கு (௪)

'To cowards is no fort's defence': e'en so
The self-oblivious men no blessing know.

535. முன்னுறக் காவா திழுக்கியான் றன்பிழை
பின்னூ றிரங்கி விடும் (௫)

To him who nought foresees, recks not of anything,
The after woe shall sure repentance bring.

536. இழுக்காமை யார்மாட்டு மென்றும்
வழுக்காமை வாயி னதுவொப்ப தில் (௬)

Towards all unswerving, ever watchfulness of soul retain,
Where this is found there is no greater gain.

537. அரியவென் றாகாத வில்லைப்பொச் சாவாக்
கருவியாற் போற்றிச் செயின் (௭)

Though things are arduous deemed, there 's nought may not be won,
When work with mind's unslumbering energy and thought is done.

538. புகழ்ந்தவை போற்றிச் செயல்வேண்டுஞ் செய்யா
திகழ்ந்தார்க் கெழுமையு மில் (௮)

Let things that merit praise thy watchful soul employ;
Who these despise attain through sevenfold births no joy.

539. இகழ்ச்சியிற் கெட்டாரை யுள்ளுக தாந்த
மகிழ்ச்சியின் மைந்துறும் போழ்து (௯)

Think on the men whom scornful mind hath brought to nought,
When exultation overwhelms thy wildered thought.

540. உள்ளிய தெய்த லெளிதுமன் மற்றுந்தா
னுள்ளிய துள்ளப் பெறின் (௰)

'Tis easy what thou hast in mind to gain,
If what thou hast in mind thy mind retain.

CHAPTER LV. அதி. ருரு.

செங்கோன்மை.—The Right Sceptre.

541. ஓர்ந்துகண் ணோடா திறைபுரிந் தியார்மாட்டுந்
தேர்ந்துசெய் வஃதே முறை (௧)

Search out, to no one favour show, with heart that justice loves
Consult, then act; this is the rule that right approves.

542. வானோக்கி வாழு முலகெல்லா மன்னவன்
கோனோக்கி வாழுங் குடி (௨)

All earth looks up to heav'n whence raindrops fall;
All subjects look to king that ruleth all.

543. அந்தணர் நூற்கு மறத்திற்கு மாதியாய்
நின்றது மன்னவன் கோல் (௩)

Learning and virtue of the sages spring,
From all-controlling sceptre of the king.

544. குடிதழீஇக் கோலோச்சு மாநில மன்ன
னடிதழீஇ நிற்கு முலகு (௪)

Whose heart embraces subjects all, lord over mighty land
Who rules, the world his feet embracing stands.

545. இயல்புளிக் கோலோச்சு மன்னவ னாட்ட
பெயலும் விளையுளுந் தொக்கு (௫)

Where king, who righteous laws regards, the sceptre wields,
There fall the showers, there rich abundance crowns the fields.

546. வேலன்று வென்றி தருவது மன்னவன்
கோலதூஉங் கோடா தெனின் (௬)

Not lance gives kings the victory,
But sceptre swayed with equity.

547. இறைகாக்கும் வையக மெல்லா மவனை
முறைகாக்கு முட்டாச் செயின் (௭)

The king all the whole realm of earth protects;
And justice guards the king who right respects.

548. எண்பதத்தா னோரா முறைசெய்யா மன்னவன்
றண்பதத்தாற் றானே கெடும் (௮)

Hard of access, nought searching out, with partial hand
The king who rules, shall sink and perish from the land.

549. குடிபுறங் காத்தோம்பிக் குற்றங் கடிதல்
வடுவன்று வேந்தன் றொழில் (௯)

Abroad to guard, at home to punish, brings
No just reproach; 'tis work assigned to kings.

550. கொலையிற் கொடியாரை வேந்தொறுத்தல் பைங்கூழ்
களைகட் டதனொடு நேர் (௰)

By punishment of death the cruel to restrain,
Is as when farmer frees from weeds the tender grain.

CHAPTER LVI. அதி. ௫௬.

கொடுங்கோன்மை.—The Cruel Sceptre.

551. கொலைமேற்கொண் டாரிற் கொடிதே
யலைமேற்கொண் டல்லவை செய்தொழுகும் வேந்து (௧)

Than one who plies the murderer's trade, more cruel is the king
Who all injustice works, his subjects harassing.

552. வேலொடு நின்றா னிடுவென் றதுபோலுங்
கோலொடு நின்றா னிரவு (௨)

As 'Give' the robber cries with lance uplift,
So kings with sceptred hand implore a gift.

553. நாடொறு நாடி முறைசெய்யா மன்னவ
னாடொறு நாடு கெடும் (௩)

Who makes no daily search for wrongs, nor justly rules, that king
Doth day by day his realm to ruin bring.

554. கூழுங் குடியு மொருங்கிழக்குங் கோல்கோடிச்
சூழாது செய்யு மரசு (௪)

Whose rod from right deflects, who counsel doth refuse,
At once his wealth and people utterly shall lose.

555. அல்லற்பட் டாற்று தழுதகண் ணீரன்றே
செல்வத்தைத் தேய்க்கும் படை (ரு)

His people's tears of sorrow past endurance, are not they
Sharp instruments to wear the monarch's wealth away?

556. மன்னர்க்கு மன்னுதல் செங்கோன்மை யஃதின்றேன்
மன்னுவா மன்னர்க் கொளி (சு)

To rulers' rule stability is sceptre right;
When this is not, quenched is the rulers' light.

557. துளியின்மை ஞாலத்திற் கெற்றற்றே வேந்த
னளியின்மை வாழு முயிர்க்கு (எ)

As lack of rain to thirsty lands beneath,
Is lack of grace in kings to all that breathe.

558. இன்மையி னின்னா துடைமை முறைசெய்யா
மன்னவன் கோற்கீழ்ப் படின் (அ)

To poverty it adds a sharper sting,
To live beneath the sway of unjust king.

559. முறைகோடி மன்னவன் செய்யி
னுறைகோடி யொல்லாது வானம் பெயல் (கூ)

Where king from right deflecting, makes unrighteous gain,
The seasons change, the clouds pour down no rain.

560. ஆபயன் குன்று மறுதொழிலோர் நூன்மறப்பர்
காவலன் காவா னெனின் (ம)

Where guardian guardeth not, udder of kine grows dry,
And Brâhmans' sacred lore will all forgotten lie.

CHAPTER LVII. அதி. ருஎ.

வெருவந்தசெய்யாமை.—Absence of 'Terrorism.'

561. தக்காங்கு நாடித் தலைச்செல்லா வண்ணத்தா
லொத்தாங் கொறுப்பது வேந்து (க)

Who punishes, investigation made in due degree,
So as to stay advance of crime, a king is he.

562. கடிதோச்சி மெல்ல வெறிக
நெடிதாக்க நீங்காமை வேண்டு பவர் (உ)

For length of days with still increasing joys on Heav'n who call,
Should raise the rod with brow severe, but let it gently fall.

563. வெருவந்த செய்தொழுகும் வெங்கோல னாயி
னொருவந்த மொல்லைக் கெடும் (௩)

Where subjects dread of cruel wrongs endure,
Ruin to unjust king is swift and sure.

564. இறைகடிய னென்றுரைக்கு மின்னாச்சொல் வேந்த
னுறைகடுகி யொல்லைக் கெடும் (௪)

'Ah! cruel is our king,' where subjects sadly say,
His age shall dwindle, swift his joy of life decay.

565. அருஞ்செவ்வி யின்னா முகத்தான்
பெருஞ்செல்வம் பேஎய்கண் டன்ன துடைத்து (௫)

Whom subjects scarce may see, of harsh forbidding countenance;
His ample wealth shall waste, blasted by demon's glance.

566. கடுஞ்சொல்லன் கண்ணில னாயி
னெடுஞ்செல்வ நீடின்றி யாங்கே கெடும் (௬)

The tyrant, harsh in speech and hard of eye,
His ample joy, swift fading, soon shall die.

567. கடுமொழியுங் கையிகந்த தண்டமும் வேந்த
னடுமுரண் டேய்க்கு மரம் (௭)

Harsh words and punishments severe beyond the right,
Are file that wears away the monarch's conquering might.

568. இனத்தாற்றி யெண்ணாத வேந்தன்
சினத்தாற்றிச் சீறிற் சிறுகுந் திரு (௮)

Who leaves the work to those around, and thinks of it no more;
If he in wrathful mood reprove, his prosperous days are o'er!

569. செருவந்த போழ்திற் சிறைசெய்யா வேந்தன்
வெருவந்து வெய்து கெடும் (௯)

Who builds no fort whence he may foe defy,
In time of war shall fear and swiftly die.

570. கல்லார்ப் பிணிக்குங் கடுங்கோ லதுவல்ல
தில்லை நிலக்குப் பொறை (௰)

Tyrants with fools their counsels share:
Earth can no heavier burthen bear!

CHAPTER LVIII. அதி. ருஅ.

கண்ணோட்டம்.—BENIGNITY.

571\. கண்ணோட்ட மென்னுங் கழிபெருங் காரிகை
யுண்மையா னுண்டிவ் வுலகு (க)

Since true benignity, that grace exceeding great, resides
In kingly souls, the world in happy state abides.

572\. கண்ணோட்டத் துள்ள துலகிய லஃதிலா
ருண்மை நிலக்குப் பொறை (உ)

The world goes on its wonted way, since grace benign is there;
All other men are burthen for the earth to bear.

573\. பண்ணென்னும் பாடற் கியைபின்றேற்
கண்ணென்னுங் கண்ணோட்ட மில்லாத கண் (ங)

Where not accordant with the song, what use of sounding chords?
What gain of eye that no benignant light affords?

574\. உளபோன் முகத்தெவன் செய்யு
மளவினாற் கண்ணோட்ட மில்லாத கண் (ச)

The seeming eye to face gives no expressive light,
When not with duly meted kindness bright.

575\. கண்ணிற் கணிகலங் கண்ணோட்ட மஃதின்றேற்
புண்ணென் றுணரப் படும் (ரு)

Benignity is eyes' adorning grace;
Without it eyes are wounds disfiguring face.

576\. மண்ணோ டியைந்த மரத்தனையர்
கண்ணோ டியைந்துகண் ணோடா தவர் (சா)

Whose eyes 'neath brow infixed diffuse no ray
Of grace; like tree in earth infixed are they.

577\. கண்ணோட்ட மில்லவர் கண்ணிலர் கண்ணுடையார்
கண்ணோட்ட மின்மையு மில் (எ)

Eyeless are they whose eyes with no benignant lustre shine;
Who 've eyes can never lack the light of grace benign.

578\. கருமஞ் சிதையாமற் கண்ணோட வல்லார்க்
குரிமை யுடைத்திவ் வுலகு (அ)

Who can benignant smile, yet leave no work undone;
By them as very own may all the earth be won.

579. ஒறுத்தாற்றும் பண்பினார் கண்ணுங்கண் ணோடிப்
பொறுத்தாற்றும் பண்பே தலை (௯)

To smile on those that vex, with kindly face,
Enduring long, is most excelling grace.

580. பெயக்கண்டு நஞ்சுண் டமைவர்
நயத்தக்க நாகரிகம் வேண்டு பவர் (௰)

They drink with smiling grace, though poison interfused they see,
Who seek the praise of all-esteemèd courtesy.

CHAPTER LIX. அதி. ௫௯.

ஒற்றாடல்.—DETECTIVES.

581. ஒற்று முரைசான்ற நூலு மிவையிரண்டுந்
தெற்றென்க மன்னவன் கண் (௧)

These two: the code renowned, and spies,
In these let king confide as eyes.

582. எல்லார்க்கு மெல்லா நிகழ்பவை யெஞ்ஞான்றும்
வல்லறிதல் வேந்தன் றொழில் (௨)

Each day, of every subject every deed,
'Tis duty of the king to learn with speed.

583. ஒற்றினா னொற்றிப் பொருடெரியா மன்னவன்
கொற்றங் கொளக்கிடந்த தில் (௩)

By spies who spies, not weighing things they bring,
Nothing can victory give to that unwary king.

584. வினைசெய்வார் தஞ்சுற்றம் வேண்டாதா ரென்றாங்
கனைவரையு மாராய்வ தொற்று (௪)

His officers, his friends, his enemies,
All these who watch are trusty spies.

585. கடாஅ வுருவொடு கண்ணஞ்சா தியாண்டு
முகாஅமை வல்லதே யொற்று (௫)

Of unsuspected mien and all-unfearing eyes,
Who let no secret out, are trusty spies.

586. துறந்தார் படிவத்த ராகி
யிறந்தாராய்ந் தென்செயினுஞ் சோர்வில தொற்று (௬)

As monk or devotee, through every hindrance making way,
A spy, whate'er men do, must watchful mind display.

587. மறைந்தவை கேட்கவற் றாகி
யறிந்தவை யையப்பா டில்லதே யொற்று (௭)

A spy must search each hidden matter out,
And full report must render, free from doubt.

588. ஒற்றொற்றித் தந்த பொருளையு மற்றுமோ
ரொற்றினா லொற்றிக் கொளல் (அ)

Spying by spies, the things they tell
To test by other spies is well.

589. ஒற்றொற் றுணராமை யாள்க வுடன்மூவர்
சொற்றொக்க தேறப் படும் (௯)

One spy must not another see: contrive it so;
And things by three confirmed as truth you know.

590. சிறப்பறிய வொற்றின்கட் செய்யற்க செய்யிற்
புறப்படுத்தா னாகு மறை (௰)

Reward not trusty spy in others' sight,
Or all the mystery will come to light.

CHAPTER LX. அதி. ௬0.

ஊக்கமுடைமை.—Energy.

591. உடைய ரெனப்படுவ தூக்க மஃதில்லா
ருடைய துடையரோ மற்று (௧)

'Tis energy gives men o'er that they own a true control;
They nothing own who own not energy of soul.

592. உள்ள முடைமை யுடைமை பொருளுடைமை
நில்லாது நீங்கி விடும் (௨)

The wealth of mind man owns a real worth imparts,
Material wealth man owns endures not, utterly departs.

593. ஆக்க மிழந்தேமென் றல்லாவா
ரூக்க மொருவந்தங் கைத்துடை யார் (௩

' Lost is our wealth,' they utter not this cry distressed,
The men of firm concentred energy of soul possessed.

594. ஆக்க மதர்வினாய்ச் செல்லு மசைவிலா
வூக்க முடையா னுழை (௪)

The man of energy of soul inflexible,
Good fortune seeks him out and comes a friend to dwell.

579. ஒறுத்;ளத் தனைய மலர்நீட்ட மாந்தர்தம்
பொ.ரளத் தனைய துயர்வு (ரு)

To smile .fing flood the rising lotus flower its stem unwinds;
Endurignity of men is measured by their minds.

596. உள்ளுவ தெல்லா முயர்வுள்ளன் மற்றது
தள்ளினுந் தள்ளாமை நீர்த்து (சா)

Whate'er you ponder, let your aim be lofty still,
Fate cannot hinder always, thwart you as it will.

597. சிதைவிடத் தொல்கா ருரவோர்
புதையம்பிற் பட்டுப்பா டூன்றுங் களிறு (எ)

The men of lofty mind quail not in ruin's fateful hour,
The elephant retains his dignity mid arrows' deadly shower.

598. உள்ள மிலாதவ ரெய்தா ருலகத்து
வள்ளிய மென்னுஞ் செருக்கு (அ)

The soulless man can never gain
Th' ennobling sense of power with men.

599. பரியது கூர்ங்கோட்ட தாயினும் யானை
வெரூஉம் புலிதாக் குறின் (கூ)

Huge bulk of elephant with pointed tusk all armed,
When tiger threatens shrinks away alarmed!

600. உரமொருவற் குள்ள வெறுக்கை யஃதில்லார்
மரமக்க ளாதலே வேறு (ம)

Firmness of soul in man is real excellence;
Others are trees, their human form a mere pretence.

CHAPTER LXI. அதி. சுக.

மடியின்மை.—Unsluggishness.

601. குடியென்னுங் குன்றா விளக்க
மடியென்னு மாசூரக் கெடும் (க)

Of household dignity the lustre beaming bright,
Flickers and dies when sluggish foulness dims its light.

602. மடியை மடியா வொழுகல்
குடியைக் குடியாக வேண்டு பவர் (உ)

Let indolence, the death of effort, die,
If you 'd uphold your household's dignity.

603. மடிமடிக்கொண் டொழுகும் பேதை பிறந்த
குடிமடியுந் தன்னினு முந்து (௩)

Who fosters indolence within his breast, the silly elf!
The house from which he springs shall perish ere himself.

604. குடிமடிந்து குற்றம் பெருகு
மடிமடிந்து மாண்ட வுஞற்றி லவர்க்கு (௪)

His family decays, and faults unheeded thrive,
Who, sunk in sloth, for noble objects doth not strive.

605. நெடுநீர் மறவி மடிதுயி னான்குங்
கெடுநீரார் காமக் கலன் (௫)

Delay, oblivion, sloth, and sleep: these four
Are pleasure-boat to bear the doomed to ruin's shore.

606. படியுடையார் பற்றமைந்தக் கண்ணு
மடியுடையார் மாண்பய னெய்த லரிது (௬)

Though lords of earth unearned possessions gain,
The slothful ones no yield of good obtain.

607. இடிபுரிந் தெள்ளுஞ்சொற் கேட்பர்
மடிபுரிந்து மாண்ட வுஞற்றி லவர் (௭)

Who hug their sloth, nor noble works attempt,
Shall hear reproofs and words of just contempt.

608. மடிமை குடிமைக்கட் டங்கிற்றன் னொன்னார்க்
கடிமை புகுத்தி விடும் (௮)

If sloth a dwelling find mid noble family,
Bondsmen to them that hate them shall they be.

609. குடியாண்மை யுள்வந்த குற்ற மொருவன்
மடியாண்மை மாற்றக் கெடும் (௯)

Who changes slothful habits saves
Himself from all that household rule depraves.

610. மடியிலா மன்னவ னெய்து
மடியளந்தான் றாஅய தெல்லா மொருங்கு (௰)

The king whose life from sluggishness is rid,
Shall rule o'er all by foot of mighty god bestrid.

CHAPTER LXII. அதி. ௬௨.

ஆள்வினையுடைமை.—MANLY EFFORT.

611. அருமை யுடைத்தென் றசாவாமை வேண்டும்
பெருமை முயற்சி தரும் (௧)

Say not, '''Tis hard,' in weak, desponding hour,
For strenuous effort gives prevailing power.

612. வினைக்கண் வினைகெட லோம்பல்
வினைக்குறை தீர்ந்தாரிற் றீர்ந்தன் றுலகு (௨)

In action be thou 'ware of act's defeat;
The world leaves those who work leave incomplete!

613. தாளாண்மை யென்னுந் தகைமைக்கட் டங்கிற்றே
வேளாண்மை யென்னுஞ் செருக்கு (௩)

In strenuous effort doth reside
The power of helping others: noble pride!

614. தாளாண்மை யில்லாதான் வேளாண்மை பேடிகை
வேளாண்மை போலக் கெடும் (௪)

Beneficent intent in men by whom no strenuous work is wrought,
Like battle-axe in sexless being's hand availeth nought.

615. இன்பம் விழையான் வினைவிழைவான் றன்கேளிர்
துன்பந் துடைத்தூன்றுந் தூண் (௫)

Whose heart delighteth not in pleasure, but in action finds delight,
He wipes away his kinsmen's grief and stands the pillar of their might.

616. முயற்சி திருவினை யாக்கு
முயற்றின்மை யின்மை புகுத்தி விடும் (௬)

Effort brings fortune's sure increase,
Its absence brings to nothingness.

617. மடியுளாண் மாமுகடி யென்ப
மடியிலான் றாளுளா டாமரை யினாள் (௭)

In sluggishness is seen misfortune's lurid form, the wise declare;
Where man unslothful toils, she of the lotus flower is there!

618. பொறியின்மை யார்க்கும் பழியன்
றறிவறிந் தாள்வினை யின்மை பழி (௮)

'Tis no reproach though unpropitious fate should ban;
But not to do man's work is foul disgrace to man!

619. தெய்வத்தா னாகா தெனினு முயற்சிதன்
மெய்வருத்தக் கூலி தரும் (௯)

Though fate divine should make your labour vain;
Effort its labour's sure reward will gain.

620. ஊழையு முப்பக்கங் காண்ப ருலைவின்றித்
தாழா துஞற்று பவர் (௰)

Who strive with undismayed, unfaltering mind,
At length shall leave opposing fate behind.

CHAPTER LXIII. அதி. ௬௩.

இடுக்கணழியாமை.—Hopefulness in Trouble.

621. இடுக்கண் வருங்கா னகுக வதனை
யடுத்தூர்வ தஃதொப்ப தில் (௧)

Smile, with patient, hopeful heart, in troublous hour;
Meet and so vanquish grief; nothing hath equal power.

622. வெள்ளத் தனைய விடும்பை யறிவுடையா
னுள்ளத்தி னுள்ளக் கெடும் (௨)

Though sorrow, like a flood, comes rolling on,
When wise man's mind regards it,—it is gone!

623. இடும்பைக் கிடும்பை படுப்ப
ரிடும்பைக் கிடும்பைப் படாஅ தவர் (௩)

Who griefs confront with meek, ungrieving heart,
From them griefs, put to grief, depart.

624. மடுத்தவா யெல்லாம் பகடன்னா னுற்ற
விடுக்க ணிடர்ப்பா டுடைத்து (௪)

Like bullock struggle on through each obstructed way;
From such an one will troubles, troubled, roll away.

625. அடுக்கி வரினு மழிவிலா னுற்ற
விடுக்க ணிடுக்கட் படும் (௫)

When griefs press on, but fail to crush the patient heart,
Then griefs defeated, put to grief, depart.

626. அற்றேமென் றல்லற் படுபவோ
பெற்றேமென் றோம்புத றேற்றா தவர் (௬)

Who boasted not of wealth, nor gave it all their heart,
Will not bemoan the loss, when prosperous days depart.

627. இலக்க முடம்பிடும்பைக் கென்று
கலக்கத்தைக் கையாறாக் கொள்ளாதா மேல் (எ)

'Man's frame is sorrow's targe,' the noble mind reflects,
Nor meets with troubled mind the sorrows it expects.

628. இன்பம் விழையா னிடும்பை யியல்பென்பான்
றுன்ப முறுத லிலன் (அ)

He seeks not joy. to sorrow man is born, he knows;
Such man will walk unharmed by touch of human woes.

629. இன்பத்து ளின்பம் விழையாதான்
றுன்பத்து டுன்ப முறுத லிலன் (கூ)

Mid joys he yields not heart to joys' control,
Mid sorrows, sorrow cannot touch his soul.

630. இன்னாமை யின்ப மெனக்கொளி னாகுந்தன்
னொன்னார் விழையுஞ் சிறப்பு (௰)

Who pain as pleasure takes, he shall acquire
The bliss to which his foes in vain aspire.

அரசியன் முற்றிற்று.

THE END OF THE SECTION ON 'ROYALTY.'

§ 2.—MINISTERS OF STATE. அமைச்சியல்.

CHAPTER LXIV. அதி. சுச.

அமைச்சு.—The Office of Minister of State.

631. கருவியுங் காலமுஞ் செய்கையுஞ் செய்யு
மருவினையு மாண்ட தமைச்சு (க)

A minister is he who grasps, with wisdom large,
Means, time, work's mode, and functions rare he must discharge.

632. வன்கண் குடிகாத்தல் கற்றறித லாள்வினையோ
டைந்துடன் மாண்ட தமைச்சு (உ)

A minister must greatness own of guardian power, determined mind,
Learn'd wisdom, manly effort with the former five combined.

633. பிரித்தலும் பேணிக் கொளலும் பிரிந்தார்ப்
பொருத்தலும் வல்ல தமைச்சு (௩)

A minister is he whose power can foes divide,
Attach more firmly friends, of severed ones can heal the breaches wide.

634. தெரிதலுந் தேர்ந்து செயலு
மொருதலையாச் சொல்லலும் வல்ல தமைச்சு (௪)

A minister has power to see the methods help afford,
To ponder long, then utter calm conclusive word.

635. அறனறிந் தான்றமைந்த சொல்லானெஞ் ஞான்றுந்
திறனறிந்தான் றேர்ச்சித் துணை (௫)

The man who virtue knows, has use of wise and pleasant words,
With plans for every season apt, in counsel aid affords.

636. மதிநுட்ப நூலோ டுடையார்க்
கதிநுட்பம் யாவுள முன்னிற்பவை (௬)

When native subtilty combines with sound scholastic lore,
'Tis subtilty surpassing all, which nothing stands before.

637. செயற்கை யறிந்தக் கடைத்து முலகத்
தியற்கை யறிந்து செயல் (௭)

Though knowing all that books can teach, 'tis truest tact
To follow common sense of men in act.

638. அறிகொன் றறியா னெனினு
முறுதி யுழையிருந்தான் கூறல் கடன் (அ)

'Tis duty of the man in place aloud to say
The very truth, though unwise king may cast his words away.

639. பழுதெண்ணு மந்திரியிற் பக்கத்துட் டெவ்வோ
ரெழுபது கோடி தலை (௯)

A minister who by king's side plots evil things
Worse woes than countless foemen brings.

640. முறைப்படச் சூழ்ந்து முடிவிலவே செய்வர்
திறப்பா டிலாஅ தவர் (௰)

For gain of end desired just counsel nought avails
To minister, when tact in execution fails.

CHAPTER LXV. அதி. ௬௫.

சொல்வன்மை.—Power in Speech.

641. நாநல மென்னு நலனுடைமை யந்நலம்
யாநலத் துள்ளதூஉ மன்று (க)

A tongue that rightly speaks the right is greatest gain,
It stands alone midst goodly things that men obtain.

642. ஆக்கமுங் கேடு மதனால் வருதலாற்
காத்தோம்பல் சொல்லின்கட் சோர்வு (உ)

Since gain and loss in life on speech depend,
From careless slip in speech thyself defend.

643. கேட்டார்ப் பிணிக்குந் தகையவாய்க் கேளாரும்
வேட்ப மொழிவதாஞ் சொல் (௩)

'Tis speech that spell-bound holds the listening ear,
While those who have not heard desire to hear.

644. திறனறிந்து சொல்லுக சொல்லை
யறனும் பொருளு மதனினூஉங் கில் (ச)

Speak words adapted well to various hearers' state;
No higher virtue lives, no gain more surely great.

645. சொல்லுக சொல்லைப் பிறிதோர்சொ லச்சொல்லை
வெல்லுஞ்சொ லின்மை யறிந்து (ரு)

Speak out your speech, when once 'tis past dispute
That none can utter speech that shall your speech refute.

646. வேட்பத்தாஞ் சொல்லிப் பிறர்சொற் பயன்கோடன்
மாட்சியின் மாசற்றார் கோள் (௬)

Charming each hearer's ear, of others' words to seize the sense,
Is method wise of men of spotless excellence.

647. சொலல்வல்லன் சோர்வில னஞ்சா னவனை
இகல்வெல்லல் யார்க்கு மரிது (௭)

Mighty in word, of unforgetful mind, of fearless speech,
'Tis hard for hostile power such man to overreach.

648. விரைந்து தொழில்கேட்கு ஞால
நிரந்தினிது சொல்லுதல் வல்லார்ப் பெறின் (௮)

Swiftly the listening world will gather round,
When men of mighty speech the weighty theme propound.

649. பலசொல்லக் காமுறுவர் மன்றமாசற்ற
சிலசொல்ல றேற்றா தவர் (௯)

Who have not skill ten faultless words to utter plain,
Their tongues will itch with thousand words men's ears to pain.

650. இணருழ்த்து நாறா மலரனையர் கற்ற
துணர விரித்துரையா தார் (௰)

Like scentless flower in blooming garland bound
Are men who can't their lore acquired to others' ears expound.

CHAPTER LXVI. அதி. ௬௬.

வினைத்தூய்மை.—PURITY IN ACTION.

651. துணைநல மாக்கந் தரூஉம்
வினைநலம் வேண்டிய வெல்லாந் தரும் (௧)

The good external help confers is worldly gain;
By action good men every needed gift obtain.

652. என்று மொருவுதல் வேண்டும் புகழொடு
நன்றி பயவா வினை (௨)

From action evermore thyself restrain
Of glory and of good that yields no gain.

653. ஓஒதல் வேண்டு மொளிமாழ்குஞ் செய்வினை
யாஅது மென்னு மவர் (௩)

Who tell themselves that nobler things shall yet be won,
All deeds that dim the light of glory must they shun.

654. இடுக்கட் படினு மிளிவந்த செய்யார்
நடுக்கற்ற காட்சி யவர் (ச)

Though troubles press, no shameful deed they do,
Whose eyes the ever-during vision view.

655. எற்றென் றிரங்குவ செய்யற்க செய்வானேன்
மற்றன்ன செய்யாமை நன்று (ரு)

Do nought that soul repenting must deplore,
If thou hast sinned, 'tis well if thou dost sin no more.

656. ஈன்றாள் பசிகாண்பா னாயினுஞ் செய்யற்க
சான்றோர் பழிக்கும் வினை (சா)

Though her that bore thee hung'ring thou behold, no deed
Do thou, that men of perfect soul have crime decreed.

657. பழிமலைந் தெய்திய வாக்கத்திற் சான்றோர்
கழிநல் குரவே தலை (எ)

Than store of wealth guilt-laden souls obtain,
The sorest poverty of perfect soul is richer gain.

658. கடிந்த கடிந்தொரார் செய்தார்க் கவைதா
முடிந்தாலும் பீழை தரும் (அ)

To those who hate reproof and do forbidden thing,
What prospers now, in after days shall anguish bring.

659. அழக்கொண்ட வெல்லா மழப்போ
மிழப்பினும் பிற்பயக்கு நற்பா லவை (கூ)

What 's gained through tears with tears shall go;
From loss good deeds entail harvests of blessings grow.

660. சலத்தாற் பொருள்செய்தே மார்த்தல் பசுமட்
கலத்துணீர் பெய்திரீஇ யற்று (ய)

In pot of clay unburnt he water pours and would retain,
Who seeks by wrong the realm in wealth and safety to maintain.

CHAPTER LXVII. அதி. சுஎ.

வினைத்திட்பம்.—Power in Action.

661. வினைத்திட்ப மென்ப தொருவன்
மனத்திட்ப மற்றைய வெல்லாம் பிற (க)

What men call 'power in action' know for 'power of mind';
Externe to man all other aids you find.

662. ஊறொரா லுற்றபி னொல்காமை யிவ்விரண்டி
னாறென்ப ராய்ந்தவர் கோள் (௨)

'Each hindrance shun,' 'unyielding onward press, if obstacle be there,'
These two define your way, so those that search out truth declare.

663. கடைக்கொட்கச் செய்தக்க தாண்மை
யிடைக்கொட்கி னெற்றா விழுமந் தரும் (௩)

Man's fitting work is known but by success achieved;
In midst the plan revealed brings ruin ne'er to be retrieved.

664. சொல்லுதல் யார்க்கு மெளிய வரியவாஞ்
சொல்லிய வண்ணஞ் செயல் (௪)

Easy to every man the speech that shows the way;
Hard thing to shape one's life by words they say!

665. வீறெய்தி மாண்டார் வினைத்திட்பம் வேந்தன்க
ணூறெய்தி யுள்ளப் படும் (௫)

The power in act of men renowned and great,
With king acceptance finds and fame through all the state.

666. எண்ணிய வெண்ணியாங் கெய்துப
வெண்ணியார் திண்ணிய ராகப் பெறின் (௬)

Whate'er men think, ev'n as they think, may men obtain,
If those who think can steadfastness of will retain.

667. உருவுகண் டெள்ளாமை வேண்டு
முருள்பெருந்தேர்க் கச்சாணி யன்னா ருடைத்து (௭)

Despise not men of modest bearing;
Look not at form, but what men are:
For some there live, high functions sharing,
Like linch-pin of the mighty car!

668. கலங்காது கண்ட வினைக்கட்
டுளங்காது தூக்கங் கடிந்து செயல் (௮)

What clearly eye discerns as right, with steadfast will,
And mind unslumbering, that should man fulfil.

669. துன்ப முறவரினுஞ் செய்க துணிவாற்றி
யின்பம் பயக்கும் வினை (௯)

Though toil and trouble face thee, firm resolve hold fast,
And do the deeds that pleasure yield at last.

670. எனைத்திட்ப மெய்தியக் கண்ணும்
வினைத்திட்பம் வேண்டாரை வேண்டா துலகு (௰)

The world desires not men of every power possessed,
Who power in act desire not,—crown of all the rest.

CHAPTER LXVIII. அதி. சுஅ.

வினைசெயல்வகை.—The Method of Acting.

671\. சூழ்ச்சி முடிவு துணிவெய்த லத்துணிவு
தாழ்ச்சியுட் டங்குத றீது (க)

Resolve is counsel's end. If resolutions halt
In weak delays, still unfulfilled, 'tis grievous fault.

672\. தூங்குக தூங்கிச் செயற்பால
தூங்கற்க தூங்காது செய்யும் வினை (உ)

Slumber when sleepy work 's in hand: beware
Thou slumber not when action calls for sleepless care!

673\. ஒல்லும்வா யெல்லாம் வினைநன்றே யொல்லாக்காற்
செல்லும்வாய் நோக்கிச் செயல் (ங)

When way is clear, prompt let your action be;
When not, watch till some open path you see.

674\. வினைபகை யென்றிரண்டி னெச்ச
நினையுங்காற் றீயெச்சம் போலத் தெறும் (ச)

With work or foe, when you neglect some little thing,
If you reflect, like smouldering fire, 'twill ruin bring.

675\. பொருள்கருவி காலம் வினையிடனொ டைந்து
மிருடீர வெண்ணிச் செயல் (ரு)

Treasure and instrument and time and deed and place of act:
These five, till every doubt remove, think o'er with care exact.

676\. முடிவு மிடையூறு முற்றியாங் கெய்தும்
படுபயனும் பார்த்துச் செயல் (சா)

Accomplishment, the hindrances, large profits won
By effort: these compare,—then let the work be done!

677\. செய்வினை செய்வான் செயன்முறை
யவ்வினை யுள்ளறிவ னுள்ளங் கொளல (எ)

Who would succeed must thus begin: first let him ask
The thoughts of them who throughly know the task.

678\. வினையான் வினையாக்கிக் கோட
னனைகவுள் யானையால் யானையார்த் தற்று (அ)

By one thing done you reach a second work's accomplishment;
So furious elephant to snare its fellow brute is sent.

679. நட்டார்க்கு நல்ல செயலின் விரைந்ததே
யொட்டாரை யொட்டிக் கொளல் (௯)

Than kindly acts to friends more urgent thing to do,
Is making foes to cling as friends attached to you.

680. உறைசிறியா ருண்ணடுங்க லஞ்சிக்
குறைபெறிற் கொள்வர் பெரியார்ப் பணிந்து (௰)

The men of lesser realm, fearing the people's inward dread,
Accepting granted terms, to mightier ruler bow the head.

CHAPTER LXIX. அதி. ௬௯.

தூது.—The Envoy.

681. அன்புடைமை யான்ற குடிப்பிறத்தல் வேந்தவாம்
பண்புடைமை தூதுரைப்பான் பண்பு (௧)

Benevolence, high birth, the courtesy kings love :—
These qualities the envoy of a king approve.

682. அன்பறி வாராய்ந்த சொல்வன்மை தூதுரைப்பார்க்
கின்றி யமையாத மூன்று (௨)

Love, knowledge, power of chosen words, three things,
Should he possess who speaks the words of kings.

683. நூலாரு ணூல்வல்ல னாகுதல்
வேலாருள் வென்றி வினையுரைப்பான் பண்பு (௩)

Mighty in lore amongst the learned must he be,
Midst jav'lin-bearing kings who speaks the words of victory.

684. அறிவுரு வாராய்ந்த கல்வியிம் மூன்றன்
செறிவுடையான் செல்க வினைக்கு (௪)

Sense, goodly grace, and knowledge exquisite,
Who hath these three for envoy's task is fit.

685. தொகச்சொல்லித் தூவாத நீக்கி
நகச்சொல்லி நன்றி பயப்பதாந் தூது (௫)

In terms concise, avoiding wrathful speech, who utters pleasant word,
An envoy he who gains advantage for his lord.

686. கற்றுக்கண் ணஞ்சான் செலச்சொல்லிக் காலத்தாற்
றக்க தறிவதாந் தூது (௬)

An envoy meet is he, well-learned, of fearless eye,
Who speaks right home, prepared for each emergency.

687. கடனறிந்து காலங் கருதி
யிடனறிந் தெண்ணி யுரைப்பான் றலை (எ)

He is the best who knows what 's due, the time considered well,
The place selects, then ponders long ere he his errand tell.

688. தூய்மை துணைமை துணிவுடைமை யிம்மூன்றின்
வாய்மை வழியுரைப்பான் பண்பு (அ)

Integrity, resources, soul determined, truthfulness;
Who rightly speaks his message must these marks possess.

689. விடுமாற்றம் வேந்தர்க் குரைப்பான்
வடுமாற்றம் வாய்சோரா வன்க ணவன் (கூ)

His faltering lips must utter no unworthy thing,
Who stands, with steady eye, to speak the mandates of his king.

690. இறுதி பயப்பினு மெஞ்சா திறைவற்
குறுதி பயப்பதாந் தூது (ய)

Death to the faithful one his embassy may bring;
The envoy gains assured advantage for his king.

CHAPTER LXX. அதி. எய.

மன்னரைச் சேர்ந்தொழுகல்.—Conduct in the Presence of the King.

691. அகலா தணுகாது தீக்காய்வார் போல்க
விகல்வேந்தர்ச் சேர்ந்தொழுகு வார் (க)

Who warm them at the fire draw not too near, nor keep too much aloof;
Thus let them act who dwell beneath of warlike kings the palace-roof.

692. மன்னர் விழைப விழையாமை மன்னரான்
மன்னிய வாக்கந் தரும் (உ)

To those who prize not state that kings are wont to prize,
The king himself abundant wealth supplies.

693. போற்றி னரியவை போற்றல் கடுத்தபின்
றேற்றுதல் யார்க்கு மரிது (ங)

Who would walk warily, let him of greater faults beware;
To clear suspicions once aroused is an achievement rare.

694. செவிச்சொல்லுஞ் சேர்ந்த நகையு
மவித்தொழுக லான்ற பெரியா ரகத்து (ச)

All whispered words and interchange of smiles repress,
In presence of the men who kingly power possess.

695. எப்பொருளு மோரார் தொடரார்மற்
றப்பொருளை விட்டக்காற் கேட்க மறை (ரு)

Seek not, ask not, the secret of the king to hear;
But if he lets the matter forth, give ear!

696. குறிப்பறிந்து காலங் கருதி
வெறுப்பில வேண்டுப வேட்பச் சொலல் (சா)

Knowing the signs, waiting for fitting time, with courteous care,
Things not displeasing, needful things, declare.

697. வேட்பன சொல்லி வினையில வெஞ்ஞான்றுங்
கேட்பினுஞ் சொல்லா விடல் (எ)

Speak pleasant things, but never utter idle word;
Not though by monarch's ears with pleasure heard.

698. இளைய ரினமுறைய ரென்றிகழார் நின்ற
வொளியோ டொழுகப் படும் (அ)

Say not, 'He 's young, my kinsman,' despising thus your king;
But reverence the glory kingly state doth bring.

699. கொளப்பட்டே மென்றெண்ணிக் கொள்ளாத செய்யார்
துளக்கற்ற காட்சி யவர் (கூ)

'We 've gained his grace, boots nought what graceless acts we do.'
So deem not sages who the changeless vision view.

700. பழைய மெனக்கருதிப் பண்பல்ல செய்யுங்
கெழுதகைமை கேடு தரும் (ய)

Who think 'We 're ancient friends,' and do unseemly things;
To these familiarity sure ruin brings.

CHAPTER LXXI. அதி. எக.

குறிப்பறிதல்.—The Knowledge of Indications.

701. கூறாமை நோக்கிக் குறிப்பறிவா னெஞ்ஞான்று
மாறாநீர் வையக் கணி (க)

Who knows the sign, and reads unuttered thought, the gem is he
Of earth round traversed by the changeless sea.

702. ஐயப் படாஅ தகத்த துணர்வானைத்
தெய்வத்தோ டொப்பக் கொளல் (உ)

Undoubting, who the minds of men can scan,
As deity regard that gifted man.

703. குறிப்பிற் குறிப்புணர் வாரை
யுறுப்பினுள் யாது கொடுத்துங் கொளல் (௩)

Who by the sign the signs interprets plain,
Give any member up his aid to gain.

704. குறித்தது கூறாமைக் கொள்வாரோ டேனை
யுறுப்போ ரனையரால் வேறு (௪)

Who reads what 's shown by signs, though words unspoken be,
In form may seem as other men, in function nobler far is he.

705. குறிப்பிற் குறிப்புணரா வாயி
னுறுப்பினு ளென்ன பயத்தவோ கண் (௫)

By sign who knows not signs to comprehend, what gain,
'Mid all his members, from his eyes does he obtain?

706. அடுத்தது காட்டும் பளிங்குபோ னெஞ்சங்
கடுத்தது காட்டு முகம் (௬)

As forms around in crystal mirrored clear we find,
The face will show what 's throbbing in the mind.

707. முகத்தின் முதுக்குறைந்த துண்டோ
வுவப்பினுங் காயினுந் தான்முந் துறும் (௭)

Than speaking countenance hath aught more prescient skill?
Rejoice or burn with rage, 'tis the first herald still!

708. முகநோக்கி நிற்க வமையு
மகநோக்கி யுற்ற துணர்வார்ப் பெறின் (௮)

To see the face is quite enough, in presence brought,
When men can look within and know the lurking thought.

709. பகைமையுங் கேண்மையுங் கண்ணுரைக்குங் கண்ணின்
வகைமை யுணர்வார்ப் பெறின் (௯)

The eye speaks out the hate or friendly soul of man;
To those who know the eye's swift varying moods to scan.

710. நுண்ணிய மென்பா ரளக்குங்கோல் காணுங்காற்
கண்ணல்ல தில்லை பிற (௰)

The men of keen discerning soul no other test apply
(When you their secret ask) than man's revealing eye.

CHAPTER LXXII. அதி. எஉ.

அவையறிதல்.—The Knowledge of the Council Chamber.

711. அவையறிந் தாராய்ந்து சொல்லுக சொல்லின
தொகையறிந்த தூய்மை யவர் (க)

Men pure in heart, who know of words the varied force,
Should to their audience known adapt their well-arranged discourse.

712. இடைதெரிந்து நன்குணர்ந்து சொல்லுக சொல்லி
னடைதெரிந்த நன்மை யவர் (உ)

Good men to whom the arts of eloquence are known,
Should seek occasion meet, and say what well they 've made their own.

713. அவையறியார் சொல்லன்மேற் கொள்பவர் சொல்லின்
வகையறியார் வல்லதூஉ மில் (ங)

Unversed in councils, who essays to speak,
Knows not the way of suasive words,—and all is weak.

714. ஒளியார்முன் னொள்ளிய ராதல்
வெளியார்முன் வான்சுதை வண்ணங் கொளல் (ச)

Before the bright ones shine as doth the light!
Before the dull ones be as purest stucco white!

715. நன்றென் றவற்றுள்ளு நன்றே முதுவருண்
முந்து கிளவாச் செறிவு (ரு)

Midst all good things the best is modest grace,
That speaks not first before the elders' face.

716. ஆற்றி னிலைதளர்ந் தற்றே வியன்புல
மேற்றுணர்வார் முன்ன ரிழுக்கு (சு)

As in the way one tottering falls, is slip before
The men whose minds are filled with varied lore.

717. கற்றறிந்தார் கல்வி விளங்குங் கசடறச்
சொற்றெரிதல் வல்லா ரகத்து (எ)

The learning of the learned sage shines bright
To those whose faultless skill can value it aright.

718. உணர்வ துடையார்முற் சொல்லல்
வளர்வதன் பாத்தியு ணீர்சொரிந் தற்று (அ)

To speak where understanding hearers you obtain,
Is sprinkling water on the fields of growing grain!

719. புல்லவையுட் பொச்சாந்துஞ் சொல்லற்க
நல்லவையு ணன்குசெலச் சொல்லு வார் (கூ)

In councils of the good, who speak good things with penetrating power,
In councils of the mean, let them say nought, e'en in oblivious hour.

720. அங்கணத்து ளுக்க வமிழ்தற்றாற்
றங்கணத்த ரல்லார்முற் கோட்டி கொளல் (௰)

Ambrosia in the sewer spilt, is word
Spoken in presence of the alien herd.

CHAPTER LXXIII. அதி. எ௩.

அவையஞ்சாமை.—NOT TO DREAD THE COUNCIL.

721. வகையறிந்து வல்லவை வாய்சோரார் சொல்லின்
றொகையறிந்த தூய்மை யவர் (க)

Men, pure in heart, who know of words the varied force,
The mighty council's moods discern, nor fail in their discourse.

722. கற்றாருட் கற்றா ரெனப்படுவர்
கற்றார்முற் கற்ற செலச்சொல்லு வார் (உ)

Who what they 've learned, in penetrating words have learned to say,
Before the learn'd, among the learn'd most learn'd are they.

723. பகையகத்துச் சாவா ரெளிய ரரிய
ரவையகத் தஞ்சா தவர் (௩)

Many encountering death in face of foe will hold their ground;
Who speak undaunted in the council hall are rarely found.

724. கற்றார்முற் கற்ற செலச்சொல்லித் தாங்கற்ற
மிக்காருண் மிக்க கொளல் (௪)

What you have learned, in penetrating words speak out before
The learn'd; but learn what men more learn'd can teach you more.

725. ஆற்றி னளவறிந்து கற்க வவையஞ்சா
மாற்றங் கொடுத்தற் பொருட்டு (௫)

By rule, to dialectic art your mind apply,
That in the council fearless you may make an apt reply.

726. வாளோடென் வன்கண்ண ரல்லார்க்கு
நூலோடென் னுண்ணவை யஞ்சு பவர்க்கு (௬)

To those who lack the hero's eye what can the sword avail?
Or science what, to those before the council keen who quail?

727. பகையகத்துப் பேடிகை யொள்வா
ளவையகத் தஞ்சு மவன்கற்ற நூல் (௭)

As shining sword before the foe which 'sexless being' bears,
Is science learned by him the council's face who fears.

728. பல்லவை கற்றும் பயமிலரே
நல்லவையு ணன்கு செலச்சொல்லா தார் (அ)

Though many things they 've learned, yet useless are they all,
To men who cannot well and strongly speak in council hall.

729. கல்லா தவரிற் கடையென்ப கற்றறிந்து
நல்லா ரவையஞ்சு வார் (கூ)

Who, though they 've learned, before the council of the good men quake,
Than men unlearn'd a lower place must take.

730. உளரெனினு மில்லாரோ டொப்பர்
களனஞ்சிக் கற்ற செலச்சொல்லா தார் (ய)

Who what they 've learned, in penetrating words know not to say,
The council fearing, though they live, as dead are they.

அமைச்சியன் முற்றியது.

THE END OF THE SECTION ON 'MINISTERS OF STATE.'

§ 3. THE ESSENTIALS OF A STATE. அங்கவியல்.

CHAPTER LXXIV. அதி. எச.

நாடு.—THE LAND.

731. தள்ளா விளையுளுந் தக்காருந் தாழ்விலாச்
செல்வருஞ் சேர்வது நாடு (க)

Where spreads fertility unfailing, where resides a band
Of virtuous men, and those of ample wealth, call that a '*land*.'

732. பெரும்பொருளாற் பெட்டக்க தாகி
யருங்கேட்டா லாற்ற விளைவது நாடு (உ)

That is a '*land*' which men desire for wealth 's abundant share,
Yielding rich increase, where calamities are rare.

733. பொறையொருங்கு மேல்வருங்காற் றாங்கி யிறைவற்
கிறையொருங்கு நேர்வது நாடு (ங)

When burthens press, it bears ; yet, with unfailing hand,
To king due tribute pays : that is the '*land*.'

734. உறுபசியு மோவாப் பிணியுஞ்
செறுபகையுஞ் சேரா தியல்வது நாடு (ச)

That is a '*land*' whose peaceful annals know,
Nor famine fierce, nor wasting plague, nor ravage of the foe.

735. பல்குழுவும் பாழ்செய்யு முட்பகையும் வேந்தலைக்குங்
கொல்குறும்பு மில்லது நாடு (ரு)

From factions free, and desolating civil strife, and band
Of lurking murderers that king afflict, that is the '*land*.'

736. கேடறியா கெட்ட விடத்தும் வளங்குன்றா
நாடென்ப நாட்டிற் றலை (சா)

Chief of all *lands* is that, where nought disturbs its peace ;
Or, if invaders come, still yields its rich increase.

737. இருபுனலும் வாய்ந்த மலையும்
வருபுனலும் வல்லரணு நாட்டிற் குறுப்பு (எ)

Waters from rains and springs, a mountain near, and waters thence ;
These make a *land*, with fortress' sure defence.

738. பிணியின்மை செல்வம் விளைவின்ப மேம
மணியென்ப நாட்டிற்கிவ் வைந்து (௮)

A country's jewels are these five: unfailing health,
Fertility, and joy, a sure defence, and wealth.

739. நாடென்ப நாடா வளத்தன
நாடல்ல நாட வளந்தரு நாடு (௯)

That is a *land* that yields increase unsought,
That is no *land* whose gifts with toil are bought.

740. ஆங்கமை வெய்தியக் கண்ணும் பயமின்றே
வேந்தமை வில்லாத நாடு (௰)

Though blest with all these varied gifts' increase,
A *land* gains nought that is not with its king at peace.

CHAPTER LXXV. அதி. ௭௫.

அரண்.—The Fortification.

741. ஆற்று பவர்க்கு மரண்பொரு ளஞ்சித்தற்
போற்று பவர்க்கும் பொருள் (௧)

A *fort* is wealth to those who act against their foes;
Is wealth to them who, fearing, guard themselves from woes.

742. மணிநீரு மண்ணு மலையு
மணிநிழற் காடு முடைய தரண் (௨)

A *fort* is that which owns a fount of waters crystal clear,
An open space, a hill, and shade of beauteous forest near.

743. உயர்வகலந் திண்மை யருமை யிந்நான்கி
னமைவர ணென்றுரைக்கு நூல் (௩)

Height, breadth, strength, difficult access:
Science declares a *fort* must these possess.

744. சிறுகாப்பிற் பேரிடத்த தாகி
யுறுபகை யூக்க மழிப்ப தரண் (௪)

A *fort* must need but slight defence, yet ample be,
Defying all the foeman's energy.

745. கொளற்கரிதாய்க் கொண்டகூழ்த் தாகி யகத்தார்
நிலைக்கெளிதா நீர தரண் (௫)

Impregnable, containing ample stores of food,
A *fort*, for those within, must be a warlike station good.

746. எல்லாப் பொருளு முடைத்தா யிடத்துதவு
நல்லா ளுடைய தரண் (௬)

A *fort*, with all munitions amply stored,
In time of need should good reserves afford.

747. முற்றியு முற்றா தெறிந்து மறைப்படுத்தும்
பற்றற் கரிய தரண் (௭)

A *fort* should be impregnable to foes who gird it round,
Or aim there darts from far, or mine beneath the ground.

748. முற்றாற்றி முற்றி யவரையும்
பற்றாற்றிப் பற்றியார் வெல்வ தரண் (௮)

Howe'er the circling foe may strive access to win,
A *fort* should give the victory to those who guard within.

749. முனைமுகத்து மாற்றலர் சாய
வினைமுகத்து வீறெய்தி மாண்ட தரண் (௯)

At outset of the strife a *fort* should foes dismay;
And greatness gain by deeds in every glorious day.

750. எனைமாட்சித் தாகியக் கண்ணும்
வினைமாட்சி யில்லார்க ணில்ல தரண் (௰)

Howe'er majestic castled walls may rise,
To craven souls no fortress strength supplies.

CHAPTER LXXVI. அதி. ௭௬.

பொருள்செயல்வகை.—WAY OF ACCUMULATING WEALTH.

751. பொருளல் லவரைப் பொருளாகச் செய்யும்
பொருளல்ல தில்லை பொருள் (௧)

Nothing exists, save wealth, that can
Change man of nought to worthy man.

752. இல்லாரை யெல்லாரு மெள்ளுவர்
செல்வரை யெல்லாருஞ் செய்வர் சிறப்பு (௨)

Those who have nought all will despise;
All raise the wealthy to the skies.

753. பொருளென்னும் பொய்யா விளக்க
மிருளறுக்கு மெண்ணிய தேயத்துச் சென்று (௩)

Wealth, the lamp unfailing, speeds to every land,
Dispersing darkness at its lord's command.

754. அறனீனு மின்பமு மீனுந்
திறனறிந்து தீதின்றி வந்த பொருள் (௪)

Their wealth, who blameless means can use aright,
Is source of virtue and of choice delight.

755. அருளொடு மன்பொடும் வாராப்
பொருளாக்கம் புல்லார் புரள விடல் (௫)

Wealth gained by loss of love and grace,
Let man cast off from his embrace.

756. உறுபொருளு முல்கு பொருளுந்தன் னொன்னார்த்
தெறுபொருளும் வேந்தன் பொருள் (௬)

Wealth that falls to him as heir, wealth from the kingdom's dues,
The spoils of slaughtered foes: these are the royal revenues.

757. அருளென்னு மன்பீன் குழவி
பொருளென்னுஞ் செல்வச் செவிலியா லுண்டு (௭)

'Tis love that kindliness as offspring bears;
And wealth as bounteous nurse the infant rears.

758. குன்றேறி யானைப்போர் கண்டற்றாற்
றன்கைத்தொன் றுண்டாகச் செய்வான் வினை (௮)

As one to view the strife of elephants who takes his stand,
On hill he 's climbed, is he who works with money in his hand.

759. செய்க பொருளைச் செறுநர் செருக்கறுக்கு
மெஃகதனிற் கூரிய தில் (௯)

Make money! Foeman's insolence o'ergrown
To lop away no keener steel is known.

760. ஒண்பொருள் காழ்ப்ப வியற்றியார்க்
கெண்பொரு ளேனை யிரண்டு மொருங்கு (௰)

Who plenteous store of glorious wealth have gained,
By them the other two are easily obtained.

CHAPTER LXXVII. அதி. எஎ.

படைமாட்சி.—The Excellence of an Army.

761. உறுப்பமைந் தூறஞ்சா வெல்படை வேந்தன்
வெறுக்கையு ளெல்லாந் தலை (௧)

A conquering *host*, complete in all its limbs, that fears no wound,
Mid treasures of the king is chiefest found.

762. உலைவிடத் தூறஞ்சா வன்கண்
டொலைவிடத்துத் தொல்படைக் கல்லா லரிது (௨)

In adverse hour, to face undaunted might of conquering foe,
Is bravery that only veteran *host* can show.

763. ஒலித்தக்கா லென்னா முவரி
யெலிப்பகை நாக முயிர்ப்பக் கெடும் (௩)

Though, like the sea, the angry mice send forth their battle cry;
What then? The dragon breathes upon them, and they die!

764. அழிவின் றறைபோகா தாகி
வழிவந்த வன்க ணதுவே படை (௪)

That is a *host*, by no defeats, by no desertions shamed,
For old hereditary courage famed.

765. கூற்றுடன்று மேல்வரினுங் கூடி யெதிர்நிற்கு
மாற்ற லதுவே படை (௫)

That is a '*host*' that joins its ranks, and mightily withstands,
Though death with sudden wrath should fall upon its bands.

766. மறமான மாண்ட வழிச்செலவு தேற்ற
மெனநான்கே யேமம் படைக்கு (௬)

Valour with honour, sure advance in glory's path, with confidence:
To warlike host these four are sure defence.

767. தார்தாங்கிச் செல்வது தானை தலைவந்த
போர்தாங்குந் தன்மை யறிந்து (௭)

A valiant army bears the onslaught, onward goes,
Well taught with marshalled ranks to meet their coming foes.

768. அடற்றகையு மாற்றலு மில்லெனினுந் தானை
படைத்தகையாற் பாடு பெறும் (௮)

Though not in war offensive or defensive skilled;
An army gains applause when well equipped and drilled.

769. சிறுமையுஞ் செல்லாத் துனியும்
வறுமையு மில்லாயின் வெல்லும் படை (௯)

Where weakness, clinging fear and poverty
Are not, the host will gain the victory.

770. நிலைமக்கள் சால வுடைத் தெனினுந் தானை
தலைமக்க ளில்வழி யில் (௰)

Though men abound, all ready for the war,
No army is where no fit leaders are.

CHAPTER LXXVIII. அதி. எஅ.

படைச்செருக்கு.—MILITARY SPIRIT.

771. என்னைமுன் னில்லன்மின் றெவ்விர் பலரென்னை
முன்னின்று கன்னின் றவர் (௧)

Ye foes! stand not before my lord! for many a one
Who did my lord withstand, now stands in stone!

772. கான முயலெய்த வம்பினில்
யானை பிழைத்தவே லேந்த லினிது (௨)

Who aims at elephant, though dart should fail, has greater praise
Than he who woodland hare with wingèd arrow slays.

773. பேராண்மை யென்ப தறுகணொன் றுற்றக்கா
லூராண்மை மற்றத னெஃகு (௩)

Fierceness in hour of strife heroic greatness shows;
Its edge is kindness to our suffering foes.

774. கைவேல் களிற்றொடு போக்கி வருபவன்
மெய்வேல் பறியா நகும் (௪)

At elephant he hurls the dart in hand; for weapon pressed,
He laughs and plucks the javelin from his wounded breast.

775. விழித்தகண் வேல்கொண் டெறிய
வழித்திமைப்பி னொட்டன்றோ வன்கண் ணவர்க்கு (௫)

To hero fearless must it not defeat appear,
If he but wink his eye when foeman hurls his spear.

776. விழுப்புண் படாதநா ளெல்லாம்
வழுக்கினுள் வைக்குந்தன் னாளை யெடுத்து (௬)

The heroes, counting up their days, set down as vain
Each day when they no glorious wound sustain.

777. சுழலு மிசைவேண்டி வேண்டா வுயிரார்
கழல்யாப்புக் காரிகை நீர்த்து (௭)

Who seek for world-wide fame, regardless of their life,
The glorious clasp adorns, sign of heroic strife.

778. உறினுயி ரஞ்சா மறவ ரிறைவன்
செறினுஞ்சீர் குன்ற லிலர் (௮)

Fearless they rush where'er 'the tide of battle rolls';
The king's reproof damps not the ardour of their eager souls.

779. இழைத்த திகவாமைச் சாவாரை யாரே
பிழைத்த தொறுக்கிற் பவர் (௯)

Who says they err, and visits them with scorn,
Who die and faithful guard the vow they 've sworn?

780. புரந்தார்கண் ணீர்மல்கச் சாகிற்பிற் சாக்கா
டிரந்துகோட் டக்க துடைத்து (௰)

If monarch's eyes o'erflow with tears for hero slain,
Who would not beg such boon of glorious death to gain?

CHAPTER LXXIX. அதி. ௭௯.

நட்பு.—Friendship.

781. செயற்கரிய யாவுள நட்பி னதுபோல்
வினைக்கரிய யாவுள காப்பு (௧)

What so hard for men to gain as friendship true?
What so sure defence 'gainst all that foe can do?

782. நிறைநீர நீரவர் கேண்மை
பிறைமதிப் பின்னீர பேதையார் நட்பு (௨)

Friendship with men fulfilled of good
Waxes like the crescent moon;
Friendship with men of foolish mood,
Like the full orb, waneth soon.

783. நவிறொறு நூனயம் போலும்
பயிறொறும் பண்புடை யாளர் தொடர்பு (௩)

Learned scroll the more you ponder,
Sweeter grows the mental food;
So the heart by use grows fonder,
Bound in friendship with the good.

784. நகுதற் பொருட்டன்று நட்டன்
மிகுதிக்கண் மேற்சென் றிடித்தற் பொருட்டு (௪)

Not for laughter only friendship all the pleasant day,
But for strokes of sharp reproving, when from right you stray.

785. புணர்ச்சி பழகுதல் வேண்டா
வுணர்ச்சிதா னட்பாங் கிழமை தரும் (௫)

Not association constant, not affection's token bind;
'Tis the unison of feeling friends unites of kindred mind.

786. முகநக நட்பது நட்பன்று நெஞ்சத்
தகநக நட்பது நட்பு (௬)

Not the face's smile of welcome shows the friend sincere,
But the heart's rejoicing gladness when the friend is near.

787. அழிவி னவைநீக்கி யாறுய்த்
தழிவின்க ணல்ல லுழப்பதா நட்பு (௭)

Friendship from ruin saves, in way of virtue keeps;
In troublous time, it weeps with him who weeps.

788. உடுக்கை யிழந்தவன் கைபோல வாங்கே
யிடுக்கண் களைவதா நட்பு (௮)

As hand of him whose vesture slips away,
Friendship at once the coming grief will stay.

789. நட்பிற்கு வீற்றிருக்கை யாதெனிற்
கொட்பின்றி யொல்லும்வா யூன்று நிலை (௯)

And where is friendship's royal seat? In stable mind,
Where friend in every time of need support may find.

790. இனைய ரிவரெமக் கின்னம்யா மென்று
புனையினும் புல்லென்னு நட்பு (௰)

Mean is the friendship that men blazon forth,
'He's thus to me,' and 'such to him my worth.'

CHAPTER LXXX. அதி. ௮௰.

நட்பாராய்தல்.—Investigation in forming Friendships.

791. நாடாது நட்டலிற் கேடில்லை நட்டபின்
வீடில்லை நட்பாள் பவர்க்கு (௧)

To make an untried man your friend is ruin sure;
For friendship formed unbroken must endure.

792. ஆய்ந்தாய்ந்து கொள்ளாதான் கேண்மை கடைமுறை
தான்சாந் துயரந் தரும் (௨)

Alliance with the man you have not proved and proved again,
In length of days will give you mortal pain.

793. குணனுங் குடிமையுங் குற்றமுங் குன்றா
வினனு மறிந்தியாக்க நட்பு (௩)

Temper, descent, defects, associations free
From blame: know these, then let the man be friend to thee.

794. குடிப்பிறந்து தன்கட் பழிநாணு வானைக்
கொடுத்துங் கொளல்வேண்டு நட்பு (௪)

Who, born of noble race, from guilt would shrink with shame,
Pay any price, so you as friend that man may claim.

795. அழச்சொல்லி யல்ல திடித்து
வழக்கறிய வல்லார்நட் பாய்ந்து கொளல் (௫)

Make them your chosen friends whose words repentance move,
With power prescription's path to show, while evil they reprove.

796. கேட்டினு முண்டோ ருறுதி கிளைஞரை
நீட்டி யளப்பதோர் கோல் (௬)

Ruin itself one blessing lends:
'Tis staff that measures out one's friends.

797. ஊதிய மென்ப தொருவற்குப்
பேதையார் கேண்மை யொரீஇ விடல் (௭)

'Tis gain to any man, the sages say,
Friendship of fools to put away.

798. உள்ளற்க வுள்ளஞ் சிறுகுவ
கொள்ளற்க வல்லற்க ணாற்றறுப்பார் நட்பு (௮)

Think not the thoughts that dwarf the soul; nor take
For friends the men who friends in time of grief forsake.

799. கெடுங்காலைக் கைவிடுவார் கேண்மை
யடுங்காலை யுள்ளினு முள்ளஞ் சுடும் (௯)

Of friends deserting us on ruin's brink,
'Tis torture e'en in life's last hour to think.

800. மருவுக மாசற்றார் கேண்மையொன் றீத்து
மொருவுக வொப்பிலார் நட்பு (௰)

Cling to the friendship of the spotless ones; whate'er you pay,
Renounce alliance with the men of evil way.

CHAPTER LXXXI. அதி. அக.

பழைமை.—Familiarity.

801. பழைமை யெனப்படுவ தியாதெனின் யாதுங்
கிழமையைக் கீழ்ந்திடா நட்பு (௧)

Familiarity is friendship's silent pact,
That puts restraint on no familiar act.

802. நட்பிற் குறுப்புக் கெழுதகைமை மற்றதற்
குப்பாதல் சான்றோர் கடன் (௨)

Familiar freedom friendship's very frame supplies;
To be its savour sweet is duty of the wise.

803. பழகிய நட்பெவன் செய்யுங்
கெழுதகைமை செய்தாங் கமையாக் கடை (௩)

When to familiar acts men kind response refuse,
What fruit from ancient friendship's use?

804. விழைதகையான் வேண்டி யிருப்பர்
கெழுதகையாற் கேளாது நட்டார் செயின் (௪)

When friends unbidden do familiar acts with loving heart,
Friends take the kindly deed in friendly part.

805. பேதைமை யொன்றோ பெருங்கிழமை யென்றுணர்க
நோதக்க நட்டார் செயின் (௫)

Not folly merely, but familiar carelessness,
Esteem it, when your friends cause you distress.

806. எல்லைக்க ணின்றார் துறவார் தொலைவிடத்துந்
தொல்லைக்க ணின்றார் தொடர்பு (௬)

Who stand within the bounds quit not, though loss impends,
Association with the old familiar friends.

807. அழிவந்த செய்யினு மன்பறா ரன்பின்
வழிவந்த கேண்மை யவர் (௭)

True friends, well versed in loving ways,
Cease not to love, when friend their love betrays.

808. கேளிழுக்கங் கேளாக் கெழுதகைமை வல்லார்க்கு
நாளிழுக்க நட்டார் செயின் (௮)

In strength of friendship rare of friend's disgrace who will not hear,
The day his friend offends will day of grace to him appear.

809. கெடாஅ வழிவந்த கேண்மையார் கேண்மை
விடாஅர் விழையு முலகு (௯)

Friendship of old and faithful friends,
Who ne'er forsake, the world commends.

810. விழையார் விழையப் படுப
பழையார்கட் பண்பிற் றலைப்பிரியா தார் (௰)

Ill-wishers even wish them well, who guard,
For ancient friends, their wonted kind regard.

CHAPTER LXXXII. அதி. அஉ.

தீநட்பு.—Evil Friendship.

811. பருகுவார் போலினும் பண்பிலார் கேண்மை
பெருகலிற் குன்ற லினிது (க)

Though evil men should all-absorbing friendship show,
Their love had better die away than grow.

812. உறினட் டறினொரூஉ மொப்பிலார் கேண்மை
பெறினு மிழப்பினு மென் (உ)

What though you gain or lose friendship of men of alien heart,
Who when you thrive are friends, and when you fail depart?

813. உறுவது சீர்தூக்கு நட்பும்
பெறுவது கொள்வாருங் கள்வரு நேர் (ங)

These are alike: the friends who ponder friendship's gain,
Those who accept whate'er you give, and all the plundering train.

814. அமரகத் தாற்றறுக்குங் கல்லாமா வன்னார்
தமரிற் றனிமை தலை (ச)

A steed untrained will leave you in the tug of war;
Than friends like that to dwell alone is better far.

815. செய்தேமஞ் சாராச் சிறியவர் புன்கேண்மை
யெய்தலி னெய்தாமை நன்று (ரு)

'Tis better not to gain than gain the friendship profitless
Of men of little minds, whose succour fails when dangers press.

816. பேதை பெருங்கெழீஇ நட்பி னறிவுடையா
ரேதின்மை கோடி யுறும் (எ)

Better ten million times incur the wise man's hate,
Than form with foolish men a friendship intimate.

817. நகைவகைய ராகிய நட்பிற்
பகைவராற் பத்தடுத்த கோடி யுறும் (எ)

From foes ten million fold a greater good you gain,
Than friendship yields that's formed with laughers vain.

818. ஒல்லுங் கரும முடற்றுபவர் கேண்மை
சொல்லாடார் சோர விடல் (அ)

Those men who make a grievous toil of what they do
On your behalf, their friendship silently eschew.

819. கனவினு மின்னாது மன்னோ
வினைவேறு சொல்வேறு பட்டார் தொடர்பு (௯)

E'en in a dream the intercourse is bitterness
With men whose deeds are other than their words profess.

820. எனைத்துங் குறுகுத லோம்பன்
மனைக்கெழீஇ மன்றிற் பழிப்பார் தொடர்பு (௰)

In anywise maintain not intercourse with those,
Who in the house are friends, in hall are slandering foes.

CHAPTER LXXXIII. அதி. ௮௩.

கூடாநட்பு.—UNREAL FRIENDSHIP.

821. சீரிடங் காணி னெறிதற்குப் பட்டடை
நேரா நிரந்தவர் நட்பு (௧)

Anvil where thou shalt smitten be, when men occasion find,
Is friendship's form without consenting mind.

822. இனம்போன் றினமல்லார் கேண்மை மகளிர்
மனம்போல வேறு படும் (௨)

Friendship of those who seem our kin, but are not really kind,
Will change from hour to hour like woman's mind.

823. பலநல்ல கற்றக் கடைத்து
மனநல்ல ராகுதன் மாணார்க் கரிது (௩)

To heartfelt goodness men ignoble hardly may attain,
Although abundant stores of goodly lore they gain.

824. முகத்தி னினிய நகாஅ
வகத்தின்னா வஞ்சரை யஞ்சப் படும் (௪)

'Tis fitting you should dread dissemblers' guile,
Whose hearts are bitter while their faces smile.

825. மனத்தி னமையா தவரை
யெனைத்தொன்றுஞ் சொல்லினாற் றேறற்பாற் றன்று (௫)

When minds are not in unison, 'tis never just,
In any words men speak to put your trust.

826. நட்டார்போ னல்லவை சொல்லினு
மொட்டார்சொ லொல்லை யுணரப் படும் (௬)

Though many goodly words they speak in friendly tone,
The words of foes will speedily be known.

827\. சொல்வணக்க மொன்னார்கட் கொள்ளற்க
வில்வணக்கந் தீங்கு குறித்தமை யான் (எ)

To pliant speech from hostile lips give thou no ear;
'Tis pliant bow that shows the deadly peril near!

828\. தொழுதகை யுள்ளும் படையொடுங்கு மொன்னா
ரழுத கண்ணீரு மனைத்து (அ)

In hands that worship weapon often hidden lies;
Such are the tears that fall from foeman's eyes.

829\. மிகச்செய்து தம்மெள்ளு வாரை
நகச்செய்து நட்பினுட் சாப்புல்லற் பாற்று (கூ)

'Tis just, when men make much of you, and then despise,
To make them smile, and slay in friendship's guise.

830\. பகைநட்பாங் காலம் வருங்கான் முகநட்
டகநட் பொரீஇ விடல் (௰)

When time shall come that foes as friends appear,
Then thou, to hide a hostile heart, a smiling face may'st wear.

CHAPTER LXXXIV. அதி. அச.

பேதைமை.—Folly.

831\. பேதைமை யென்பதொன் றியாதெனி
னேதங்கொண் டூதியம் போக விடல் (க)

What one thing merits folly's special name?
Letting gain go, loss for one's own to claim!

832\. பேதைமையு ளெல்லாம் பேதைமை
காதன்மை கையல்ல தன்கட் செயல் (உ)

'Mid follies chiefest folly is to fix your love
On deeds which to your station unbefitting prove.

833\. நாணாமை நாடாமை நாரின்மை யாதொன்றும்
பேணாமை பேதை தொழில் (ங)

Ashamed of nothing, searching nothing out, of loveless heart,
Nought cherishing, 'tis thus the fool will play his part.

834\. ஓதி யுணர்ந்தும் பிறர்க்குரைத்துந் தானடங்காப்
பேதையிற் பேதையா ரில் (ச)

The sacred law he reads and learns, to other men expounds,—
Himself obeys not: where can greater fool be found?

835. ஒருமை செயலாற்றும் பேதை
யெழுமையுந் தான்புக் கழுந்து மளறு (ரு)

The fool will merit hell in one brief life on earth,
In which he entering sinks through sevenfold round of birth.

836. பொய்படு மொன்றோ புனைபூணுங்
கையறியாப் பேதை வினைமேற் கொளின் (சா)

When fool some task attempts with uninstructed pains,
It fails; nor that alone, himself he binds with chains.

837. ஏதிலா ரார்த் தமர்பசிப்பர்
பேதை பெருஞ்செல்வ முற்றக் கடை (எ)

When fools are blessed with fortune's bounteous store,
Their foes feed full, their friends are prey to hunger sore.

838. மைய லொருவன் களித்தற்றாற் பேதைதன்
கையொன் றுடைமை பெறின் (அ)

When folly's hand grasps wealth's increase, 'twill be
As when a madman raves in drunken glee.

839. பெரிதினிது பேதையார் கேண்மை
பிரிவின்கட் பீழை தருவதொன் றில் (கூ)

Friendship of fools is very pleasant thing;
Parting with them will leave behind no sting.

840. கழாஅக்கால் பள்ளியுள் வைத்தற்றாற் சான்றோர்
குழாஅத்துப் பேதை புகல் (ய)

Like him who seeks his couch with unwashed feet,
Is fool whose foot intrudes where wise men meet.

CHAPTER LXXXV. அதி. அரு.

புல்லறிவாண்மை.—Ignorance.

841. அறிவின்மை யின்மையு ளின்மை
பிறிதின்மை யின்மையா வையா துலகு (க)

Want of knowledge, 'mid all wants the sorest want we deem;
Want of other things the world will not as want esteem.

842. அறிவிலா னெஞ்சுவந் தீதல்
பிறிதியாது மில்லை பெறுவான் றவம் (உ)

The gift of foolish man, with willing heart bestowed, is nought
But blessing by receiver's penance bought.

843. அறிவிலார் தாந்தம்மைப் பீழிக்கும் பீழை
செறுவார்க்குஞ் செய்த லரிது (௩)

With keener anguish foolish men their own hearts wring,
Than aught that even malice of their foes can bring.

844. வெண்மை யெனப்படுவ தியாதெனி
னொண்மை யுடையம்யா மென்னுஞ் செருக்கு (௪)

What is stupidity? The arrogance that cries,
'Behold, we claim the glory of the wise.'

845. கல்லாத மேற்கொண் டொழுகல் கசடற
வல்லதூஉ மையந் தரும் (௫)

If men what they have never learned assume to know,
Upon their real learning's power a doubt 'twill throw.

846. அற்ற மறைத்தலோ புல்லறிவு தம்வயிற்
குற்ற மறையா வழி (௬)

Fools are they who their nakedness conceal,
And yet their faults unveiled reveal.

847. அருமறை சோரு மறிவிலான் செய்யும்
பெருமிறை தானே தனக்கு (௭)

From out his soul who lets the mystic teachings die,
Entails upon himself abiding misery.

848. ஏவவுஞ் செய்கலான் றான்றேறா னவ்வுயிர்
போஒ மளவுமோர் நோய் (௮)

Advised, he heeds not; of himself knows nothing wise;
This man's whole life is all one plague until he dies.

849. காணாதாற் காட்டுவான் றான்காணான்
காணாதான் கண்டானாந் தான்கண்ட வாறு (௯)

That man is blind to eyes that will not see who knowledge shows;—
The blind man still in his blind fashion knows.

850. உலகத்தா ருண்டென்ப தில்லென்பான் வையத்
தலகையா வைக்கப் படும் (௰)

Who what the world affirms as false proclaim,
O'er all the earth receive a demon's name.

CHAPTER LXXXVI. அதி. ௮௬.

இகல்.—Hostility.

851. இகலென்ப வெல்லா வுயிர்க்கும்
பகலென்னும் பண்பின்மை பாரிக்கு நோய் (௧)

Hostility disunion's plague will bring,
That evil quality, to every living thing.

852. பகல்கருதிப் பற்றா செயினு
மிகல்கருதி யின்னாசெய் யாமை தலை (௨)

Though men disunion plan, and do thee much despite,
'Tis best no enmity to plan, nor evil deeds requite.

853. இகலென்னு மெவ்வநோய் நீக்கிற்
றவலில்லாத் தாவில் விளக்கந் தரும் (௩)

If enmity, that grievous plague, you shun,
Endless undying praises shall be won.

854. இன்பத்து ளின்பம் பயக்கு மிகலென்னுந்
துன்பத்து டுன்பங் கெடின் (௪)

Joy of joys abundant grows,
When malice dies, that woe of woes.

855. இகலெதிர் சாய்ந்தொழுக வல்லாரை யாரே
மிகலூக்குந் தன்மை யவர் (௫)

If men from enmity can keep their spirits free,
Who over them shall gain the victory?

856. இகலின் மிகலினி தென்பவன் வாழ்க்கை
தவலுங் கெடலு நணித்து (௬)

The life of those who cherished enmity hold dear,
To grievous fault and utter death is near.

857. மிகன்மேவு மெய்ப்பொருள் காணா
ரிகன்மேவு மின்னா வறிவி னவர் (௭)

The very truth that greatness gives their eyes can never see,
Who only know to work men woe, fulfilled of enmity.

858. இகலிற் கெதிர்சாய்த லாக்க மதனை
மிகலூக்கி னூக்குமாங் கேடு (௮)

'Tis gain to turn the soul from enmity;
Ruin reigns where this hath mastery.

859. இகல்காணா னாக்கம் வருங்கா லதனை
மிகல்காணுங் கேடு தரற்கு (௯)

Men think not hostile thought in fortune's favouring hour,
They cherish enmity when in misfortune's power.

860. இகலானா மின்னாத வெல்லா
நகலானா நன்னய மென்னுஞ் செருக்கு (ம)

From enmity do all afflictive evils flow;
But friendliness doth wealth of kindly good bestow.

CHAPTER LXXXVII. அதி. அஎ.

பகைமாட்சி.—The Might of Hatred.

861. வலியார்க்கு மாறேற்ற லோம்புக வோம்பா
மெலியார்மேன் மேக பகை (க)

With stronger than thyself, turn from the strife away;
With weaker shun not, rather court the fray.

862. அன்பில னான்ற துணையிலன் றான்றுவ்வா
னென்பரியு மேதிலான் றுப்பு (உ)

No kinsman's love, no strength of friends has he;
How can he bear his foeman's enmity?

863. அஞ்சு மறியா னமைவில னீகலான்
றஞ்ச மெளியன் பகைக்கு (ங)

A craven thing! knows nought, accords with none, gives nought away;
To wrath of any foe he falls an easy prey.

864. நீங்கான் வெகுளி நிறையில னெஞ்ஞான்றும்
யாங்கணும் யார்க்கு மெளிது (ச)

His wrath still blazes, every secret told; each day
This man 's in every place to every foe an easy prey.

865. வழிநோக்கான் வாய்ப்பன செய்யான்
பழிநோக்கான் பண்பிலன் பற்றார்க் கினிது (ரு)

No way of right he scans, no precepts bind, no crimes affright,
No grace of good he owns; such man 's his foes' delight.

866. காணாச் சினத்தான் கழிபெருங் காமத்தான்
பேணாமை பேணப் படும் (சா)

Blind in his rage, his lustful passions rage and swell;
If such a man mislikes you, like it well.

867. கொடுத்துங் கொளல்வேண்டு மன்ற
வடுத்திருந்து மாணாத செய்வான் பகை (௭)

Unseemly are his deeds, yet, proffering aid, the man draws nigh;
His hate—'tis cheap at any price—be sure to buy!

868. குணனிலனாய்க் குற்றம் பலவாயின் மாற்றார்க்
கினனிலனா மேமாப் புடைத்து (௮)

No gracious gifts he owns, faults many cloud his fame;
His foes rejoice, for none with him will kindred claim.

869. செறுவர்க்குச் சேணிகவா வின்ப
மறிவிலா வஞ்சும் பகைவர்ப் பெறின் (௯)

The joy of victory is never far removed from those
Who 've luck to meet with ignorant and timid foes.

870. கல்லான் வெகுளுஞ் சிறுபொரு ளெஞ்ஞான்று
மொல்லானை யொல்லா தொளி (௰)

The task of angry war with men unlearned in virtue's lore
Who will not meet, glory shall meet him never more.

CHAPTER LXXXVIII. அதி. அஅ.

பகைத்திறந்தெரில்.—Knowing the Quality of Hate.

871. பகையென்னும் பண்பி லதனை யொருவ
னகையேயும் வேண்டற்பாற் றன்று (௧)

For Hate, that ill-conditioned thing, not e'en in jest,
Let any evil longing rule your breast.

872. வில்லே ருழவர் பகைகொளினுங் கொள்ளற்க
சொல்லே ருழவர் பகை (௨)

Although you hate incur of those whose ploughs are bows,
Make not the men whose ploughs are words your foes!

873. ஏமுற் றவரினு மேழை தமியனாய்ப்
பல்லார் பகைகொள் பவன் (௩)

Than men of mind diseased, a wretch more utterly forlorn,
Is he who stands alone, object of many foeman's scorn.

874. பகைநட்பாக் கொண்டொழுகும் பண்புடை யாளன்
றகைமைக்கட் டங்கிற் றுலகு (௪)

The world secure on his dexterity depends,
Whose worthy rule can change his foes to friends.

875. தன்றுணை யின்றாற் பகையிரண்டாற் றானொருவ
னின்றுணையாக் கொள்கவற்றி னொன்று (ரு)

Without ally, who fights with twofold enemy o'ermatched,
Must render one of these a friend attached.

876. தேறினுந் தேறா விடினு மழிவின்கட்
டேறான் பகாஅன் விடல் (சா)

Whether you trust or not, in time of sore distress,
Questions of diff'rence or agreement cease to press.

877. நோவற்க நொந்த தறியார்க்கு
மேவற்க மென்மை பகைவ ரகத்து (எ)

To those who know them not, complain not of your woes;
Nor to your foeman's eyes infirmities disclose.

878. வகையறிந்து தற்செய்து தற்காப்ப மாயும்
பகைவர்கட் பட்ட செருக்கு (அ)

Know thou the way, then do thy part, thyself defend;
Thus shall the pride of those that hate thee have an end.

879. இளைதாக முண்மரங் கொல்க
களையுநர் கைக்கொல்லுங் காழ்த்த விடத்து (கூ)

Destroy the thorn, while tender point can work thee no offence;
Matured by time, 'twill pierce the hand that plucks it thence.

880. உயிர்ப்ப வுளரல்லர் மன்ற
செயிர்ப்பவர் செம்மல் சிதைக்கலா தார் (ω)

But breathe upon them, and they surely die,
Who fail to tame the pride of angry enemy.

CHAPTER LXXXIX. அதி. அகூ.

உட்பகை.—Enmity within.

881. நிழனீரு மின்னாத வின்னா
தமர்நீரு மின்னாவா மின்னா செயின் (க)

Water and shade, if they unwholesome prove, will bring you pain;
And qualities of friends, who treacherous act, will be your bane.

882. வாள்போல் பகைவரை யஞ்சற்க வஞ்சுக
கேள்போல் பகைவர் தொடர்பு (உ)

Dread not the foes that as drawn swords appear;
Friendship of foes, who seem like kinsmen, fear!

883. உட்பகை யஞ்சித்தற் காக்க வுலைவிடத்து
மட்பகையின் மாணத் தெறும் (௩)

Of hidden hate beware, and guard thy life ;
In troublous time 'twill deeper wound than potter's knife.

884. மனமாணா வுட்பகை தோன்றி
னினமாணா வேதம் பலவுந் தரும் (௪)

If secret enmities arise that minds pervert,
Then even kin unkind will work thee grievous hurt.

885. உறன்முறையா னுட்பகை தோன்றி
னிறன்முறையா னேதம் பலவுந் தரும் (௫)

Amid one's relatives if hidden hate arise,
'Twill hurt inflict in deadly wise.

886. ஒன்றாமை யொன்றியார் கட்படி னெஞ்ஞான்றும்
பொன்றாமை யொன்ற லரிது (௬)

If discord finds a place midst those who dwelt at one before,
'Tis ever hard to keep destruction from the door.

887. செப்பின் புணர்ச்சிபோற் கூடினுங் கூடாதே
யுட்பகை யுற்ற குடி (௭)

As casket with its cover, though in one they live alway,
No union to the house where hate concealed hath sway.

888. அரம்பொருத பொன்போலத் தேயு
முரம்பொரு துட்பகை யுற்ற குடி (௮)

As gold with which the file contends is worn away,
So strength of house declines where hate concealed hath sway.

889. எட்பக வன்ன சிறுமைத்தே யாயினு
முட்பகை யுள்ளதாங் கேடு (௯)

Though slight as shred of 'sesame' seed it be,
Destruction lurks in hidden enmity.

890. உடம்பாடி லாதவர் வாழ்க்கை
குடங்கருட் பாம்போ டுடனுறைந் தற்று (௰)

Domestic life with those who don't agree,
Is dwelling in a shed with snake for company.

CHAPTER XC. அதி. ௯0.

பெரியாரைப்பிழையாமை.—NOT OFFENDING THE GREAT.

891. ஆற்றுவா ராற்ற லிகழாமை
போற்றுவார் போற்றலு ளெல்லாந் தலை (௧)

The chiefest care of those who guard themselves from ill,
Is not to slight the powers of those who work their mighty will.

892. பெரியாரைப் பேணா தொழுகிற்
பெரியாராற் பேரா விடும்பை தரும் (௨)

If men will lead their lives reckless of great men's will,
Such life, through great men's powers, will bring perpetual ill.

893. கெடல்வேண்டிற் கேளாது செய்க
வடல்வேண்டி னாற்று பவர்க ணிழுக்கு (௩)

Who ruin covet, let them shut their ears, and do despite
To those who, where they list, to ruin have the might.

894. கூற்றத்தைக் கையால் விளித்தற்றா
லாற்றுவார்க் காற்றாதா ரின்னா செயல் (௪)

When powerless men 'gainst men of power will evil deeds essay,
'Tis beck'ning with the hand for Death to seize them for its prey.

895. யாண்டுசென் றியாண்டு முளராகார் வெந்துப்பின்
வேந்து செறப்பட் டவர் (௫)

Who dare the fiery wrath of monarchs dread,
Where'er they flee, are numbered with the dead.

896. எரியாற் சுடப்படினு முய்வுண்டா முய்யார்
பெரியார்ப் பிழைத் தொழுகு வார் (௬)

Though in the conflagration caught, he may escape from thence;
He 'scapes not who in life to great ones gives offence.

897. வகைமாண்ட வாழ்க்கையும் வான்பொருளு மென்னாந்
தகைமாண்ட தக்கார் செறின் (௭)

Though every royal gift, and stores of wealth your life should crown,
What are they, if the worthy men of mighty virtue frown?

898. குன்றன்னார் குன்ற மதிப்பிற் குடியொடு
நின்றன்னார் மாய்வர் நிலத்து (௮)

If they, whose virtues like a mountain rise, are light esteemed;
They die from earth who, with their households, ever-during seemed.

899. ஏந்திய கொள்கையார் சீறி னிடைமுரிந்து
வேந்தனும் வேந்து கெடும் (௯)

When blazes forth the wrath of men of lofty fame,
Kings even fall from high estate and perish in the flame.

900. இறந்தமைந்த சார்புடைய ராயினு முய்யார்
சிறந்தமைந்த சீரார் செறின் (௰)

Though all-surpassing wealth of aid they boast,
If men in glorious virtue great are wrath, they 're lost.

CHAPTER XCI. அதி. ௯௧.

பெண்வழிச்சேறல்.—Being led by Women.

901. மனைவிழைவார் மாண்பயனெய்தார்
வினைவிழைவார் வேண்டாப் பொருளு மது (௧)

Who give their soul to love of wife acquire not nobler gain;
Who give their soul to strenuous deeds such meaner joys disdain.

902. பேணாது பெண்விழைவா னாக்கம் பெரியதோர்
நாணாக நாணுத் தரும் (௨)

Who gives himself to love of wife, careless of noble name,
His wealth will clothe him with o'erwhelming shame.

903. இல்லாள்கட் டாழ்ந்த வியல்பின்மை யெஞ்ஞான்று
நல்லாரு ணாணுத் தரும் (௩)

Who to his wife submits, his strange, unmanly mood
Will daily bring him shame among the good.

904. மனையாளை யஞ்சு மறுமையி லாளன்
வினையாண்மை வீறெய்த லின்று (௪)

No glory crowns e'en manly actions wrought
By him who dreads his wife, nor gives the other world a thought.

905. இல்லாளை யஞ்சுவா னஞ்சுமற் றெஞ்ஞான்று
நல்லார்க்கு நல்ல செயல் (௫)

Who quakes before his wife will ever tremble too,
Good deeds to men of good deserts to do.

906. இமையாரின் வாழினும் பாடிலரே யில்லா
ளமையார்தோ ளஞ்சு பவர் (௬)

Though, like the demi-gods, in bliss they dwell secure from harm,
Those have no dignity who fear the housewife's slender arm.

907. பெண்ணேவல் செய்தொழுகு மாண்மையி னாணுடைப்
பெண்ணே பெருமை யுடைத்து (௭)

The dignity of modest womanhood excels
His manliness, obedient to a woman's law who dwells.

908. நட்டார் குறைமுடியார் நன்றாற்றார் நன்னுதலாட்
பெட்டாங் கொழுகு பவர் (௮)

Who to the will of her with beauteous brow their lives conform,
Aid not their friends in need, nor acts of charity perform.

909. அறவினையு மான்ற பொருளும்
பிறவினையும் பெண்ணேவல் செய்வார்க ணில் (௯)

No virtuous deed, no seemly wealth, no pleasure, rests
With them who live obedient to their wives' behests.

910. எண்சேர்ந்த நெஞ்சத் திடனுடையார்க் கெஞ்ஞான்றும்
பெண்சேர்ந்தாம் பேதைமை யில் (௰)

Where pleasures of the mind, that dwell in realms of thought, abound,
Folly, that springs from overweening woman's love, is never found.

CHAPTER XCII. அதி. ௯௨.

வரைவின்மகளிர்.—WANTON WOMEN.

911. அன்பின் விழையார் பொருள்விழையு மாய்தொடியா
ரின்சொ லிழுக்குத் தரும் (௧)

Those that choice armlets wear, who seek not thee with love,
But seek thy wealth, their pleasant words will ruin prove.

912. பயன்றூக்கிப் பண்புரைக்கும் பண்பின் மகளிர்
நயன்றூக்கி நள்ளா விடல் (௨)

Who weigh the gain, and utter virtuous words with vicious heart,
Weighing such women's worth, from their society depart.

913. பொருட்பெண்டிர் பொய்ம்மை முயக்க
மிருட்டறையி லேதில் பிணந்தழீஇ யற்று (௩)

As one in darkened room, some stranger corpse inarms,
Is he who seeks delight in mercenary women's charms.

914. பொருட்பொருளார் புன்னலந் தோயா
ரருட்பொரு ளாயு மறிவி னவர் (௪)

Their worthless charms, whose only weal is wealth of gain,
From touch of these the wise, who seek the wealth of grace, abstain.

915. பொதுநலத்தார் புன்னலந் தோயார்
மதிநலத்தின் மாண்ட வறிவி னவர் (ரு)

From contact with their worthless charms, whose charms to all are free,
The men with sense of good and lofty wisdom blest will flee.

916. தந்நலம் பாரிப்பார் தோயார் தகைசெருக்கிப்
புன்னலம் பாரிப்பார் தோள் (சா)

From touch of those who worthless charms, with wanton arts, display,
The men who would their own true good maintain will turn away.

917. நிறைநெஞ்ச மில்லவர் தோய்வர்
பிறநெஞ்சிற் பேணிப் புணர்பவர் தோள் (எ)

Who cherish alien thoughts while folding in their feigned embrace,
These none approach save those devoid of virtue's grace.

918. ஆயு மறிவின ரல்லார்க் கணங்கென்ப
மாய மகளிர் முயக்கு (அ)

As demoness who lures to ruin, woman's treacherous love
To men devoid of wisdom's searching power will prove.

919. வரைவிலா மாணிழையார் மென்றோள்
புரையிலாப் பூரியர்க ளாழு மளறு (கூ)

The wanton's tender arm, with gleaming jewels decked,
Is hell, where sink degraded souls of men abject.

920. இருமனப் பெண்டிருங் கள்ளுங் கவறுந்
திருநீக்கப் பட்டார் தொடர்பு (ம)

Women of double minds, strong drink, and dice: to these giv'n o'er
Are those on whom the light of Fortune shines no more.

CHAPTER XCIII. அதி. கூங.

கள்ளுண்ணாமை.—NOT DRINKING PALM-WINE.

921. உட்கப் படாஅ ரொளியிழப்ப ரெஞ்ஞான்றுங்
கட்காதல் கொண்டொழுகு வார் (க)

Who love the palm's intoxicating juice, each day,
No rev'rence they command, their glory fades away.

922. உண்ணற்க கள்ளை யுணிலுண்க சான்றோரா
லெண்ணப் படவேண்டா தார் (உ)

Drink not inebriating draught. Let him count well the cost
Who drinks. By drinking, all good men's esteem is lost.

923. ஈன்றாண் முகத்தேயு மின்னாதா லென்மற்றுச்
சான்றோர் முகத்துக் களி (௩)

The drunkard's joy is sorrow to his mother's eyes;
What must it be in presence of the truly wise?

924. நாணென்னு நல்லாள் புறங்கொடுக்குங் கள்ளென்னும்
பேணாப் பெருங்குற்றத் தார்க்கு (௪)

Shame, goodly maid, will turn her back for aye on them
Who sin the drunkard's grievous sin, that all condemn.

925. கையறி யாமை யுடைத்தே பொருள்கொடுத்து
மெய்யறி யாமை கொளல் (௫)

With gift of goods who self-oblivion buys,
Is ignorant of all that man should prize.

926. துஞ்சினார் செத்தாரின் வேறல்ல ரெஞ்ஞான்று
நஞ்சுண்பார் கள்ளுண் பவர் (௬)

Sleepers are as the dead, no otherwise they seem;
Who drink intoxicating draughts, they poison quaff, we deem.

927. உள்ளொற்றி யுள்ளூர் நகப்படுவ ரெஞ்ஞான்றுங்
கள்ளொற்றிக் கண்சாய் பவர் (௭)

Who turn aside to drink, and droop their heavy eye,
Shall be their townsmen's jest, when they the fault espy.

928. களித்தறியே னென்பது கைவிடுக நெஞ்சத்
தொளித்ததூஉ மாங்கே மிகும் (௮)

No more in secret drink, and then deny thy hidden fraud;
What in thy mind lies hid shall soon be known abroad.

929. களித்தானைக் காரணங் காட்டுதல் கீழ்நீர்க்
குளித்தானைத் தீத்துரீஇ யற்று (௯)

Like him who, lamp in hand, would seek one sunk beneath the wave,
Is he who strives to sober drunken man with reasonings grave.

930. கள்ளுண்ணாப் போழ்திற் களித்தானைக் காணுங்கா
லுள்ளான்கொ லுண்டதன் சோர்வு (௰)

When one, in sober interval, a drunken man espies,
Does he not think, 'Such is my folly in my revelries'?

CHAPTER XCIV. அதி. கூச.

சூது.—GAMING.

931. வேண்டற்க வென்றிடினுஞ் சூதினை வென்றதூஉந்
தூண்டிற்பொன் மீன்விழுங்கி யற்று (க)

Seek not the gamester's play; though you should win,
Your gain is as the baited hook the fish takes in.

932. ஒன்றெய்தி நூறிழக்குஞ் சூதர்க்கு முண்டாங்கொ
னன்றெய்தி வாழ்வதோ ராறு (உ)

Is there for gamblers, too, that gaining one a hundred lose, some way
That they may good obtain, and see a prosperous day?

933. உருளாய மோவாது கூறிற்
பொருளாயம் போஒய்ப் புறமே படும் (ங)

If prince unceasing speak of nought but play,
Treasure and revenue will pass from him away.

934. சிறுமை பலசெய்து சீரழிக்குஞ் சூதின்
வறுமை தருவதொன் றில் (ச)

Gaming brings many woes, and ruins fair renown;
Nothing to want brings men so surely down.

935. கவறுங் கழகமுங் கையுந் தருக்கி
யிவறியா ரில்லாகி யார் (ரு)

The dice, and gaming-hall, and gamester's art, they eager sought,
Thirsting for gain—the men in other days who came to nought.

936. அகடாரா ரல்ல லுழப்பர் சூதென்னு
முகடியான் மூடப்பட் டார் (சா)

Gambling 's Misfortune's other name: o'er whom she casts her veil,
They suffer grievous want, and sorrows sore bewail.

937. பழகிய செல்வமும் பண்புங் கெடுக்குங்
கழகத்துக் காலை புகின் (எ)

Ancestral wealth and noble fame to ruin haste,
If men in gambler's halls their precious moments waste.

938. பொருள்கெடுத்துப் பொய்மேற் கொளீஇ
யருள்கெடுத் தல்ல லுழப்பிக்குஞ் சூது (அ)

Gambling wastes wealth, to falsehood bends the soul; it drives away
All grace, and leaves the man to utter misery a prey.

939. உடைசெல்வ மூணொளி கல்வியென் றைந்து
மடையாவா மாயங் கொளின் (௯)

Clothes, wealth, food, praise, and learning, all depart
From him on gambler's gain who sets his heart.

940. இழத்தொறூஉங் காதலிக்குஞ் சூதேபோற் றுன்ப
முழத்தொறூஉங் காதற் றுயிர் (௰)

Howe'er he lose, the gambler's heart is ever in the play;
E'en so the soul, despite its griefs, would live on earth alway.

CHAPTER XCV. அதி. ௯௫.

மருந்து.—MEDICINE.

941. மிகினுங் குறையினு நோய்செய்யு நூலோர்
வளிமுதலா வெண்ணிய மூன்று (௧)

The learned books count three, with wind as first; of these,
As any one prevail, or fail, 'twill cause disease.

942. மருந்தென வேண்டாவாம் யாக்கைக்
கருந்திய தற்றது போற்றி யுணின் (௨)

No need of medicine to heal your body's pain,
If, what you ate before digested well, you eat again.

943. அற்றா லளவறிந் துண்க வஃதுடம்பு
பெற்றா னெடிதுய்க்கு மாறு (௩)

Who has a body gained may long the gift retain,
If, food digested well, in measure due he eat again.

944. அற்ற தறிந்து கடைப்பிடித்து மாறல்ல
துய்க்க துவரப் பசித்து (௪)

Knowing the food digested well, when hunger prompteth thee,
With constant care, the viands choose that well agree.

945. மாறுபா டில்லாத வுண்டி மறுத்துண்ணி
னூறுபா டில்லை யுயிர்க்கு (௫)

With self-denial take the well-selected meal;
So shall thy frame no sudden sickness feel.

946. இழிவறிந் துண்பான்க ணின்பம்போ னிற்குங்
கழிபே ரிரையான்க ணோய் (௭)

On modest temperance as pleasures pure,
So pain attends the greedy epicure.

947. தீயள வன்றித் தெரியான் பெரிதுண்ணி
னோயள வின்றிப் படும் (௭)

Who largely feeds, nor measure of the fire within maintains,
That thoughtless man shall feel unmeasured pains.

948. நோய்நாடி நோய்முத னாடி யதுதணிக்கும்
வாய்நாடி வாய்ப்பச் செயல் (௮)

Disease, its cause, what may abate the ill:
Let leech examine these, then use his skill.

949. உற்றா னளவும் பிணியளவுங் காலமுங்
கற்றான் கருதிச் செயல் (௯)

The habitudes of patient and disease, the crises of the ill:
These must the learned leech think over well, then use his skill.

950. உற்றவன் றீர்ப்பான் மருந்துழைச் செல்வானென்
றப்பானாற் கூற்றே மருந்து (௰)

For patient, leech, and remedies, and him who waits by patient's side,
The art of medicine must fourfold code of laws provide.

அங்கவியல் முற்றிற்று.

THE END OF THE SECTION ON 'THE ESSENTIALS OF A STATE.'

§ 4. APPENDIX. ஒழிபியல்.

CHAPTER XCVI. அதி. ௯௬.

குடிமை.—NOBILITY.

951. இற்பிறந்தார் கண்ணல்ல தில்லை யியல்பாகச்
செப்பமு நாணு மொருங்கு (௧)

Save in the scions of a noble house, you never find
Instinctive sense of right and virtuous shame combined.

952. ஒழுக்கமும் வாய்மையு நாணுமிம் மூன்று
மிழுக்கார் குடிப்பிறந் தார் (௨)

In these three things the men of noble birth fail not:
In virtuous deed, and truthful word, and chastened thought.

953. நகையீகை யின்சொ லிகழாமை நான்கும்
வகையென்ப வாய்மைக் குடிக்கு (௩)

The smile, the gift, the pleasant word, unfailing courtesy:
These are the signs, they say, of true nobility.

954. அடுக்கிய கோடி பெறினுங்
குடிப்பிறந்தார் குன்றுவ செய்த லிலர் (௪)

Millions on millions piled would never win
The men of noble race to soul-degrading sin.

955. வழங்குவ துள்வீழ்ந்தக் கண்ணும்
பழங்குடி பண்பிற் றலைப்பிரித லின்று (௫)

Though stores for charity should fail within, the ancient race
Will never lose its old ancestral grace.

956. சலம்பற்றிச் சால்பில செய்யார்மா சற்ற
குலம்பற்றி வாழ்துமென் பார் (௬)

Whose minds are set to live as fits their sire's unspotted fame,
Stooping to low deceit, commit no deeds that gender shame.

957. குடிப்பிறந்தார் கண்விளங்குங் குற்றம் விசும்பின்
மதிக்கண் மறுப்போ லுயர்ந்து (௭)

The faults of men of noble race are seen by every eye,
As spots on her bright orb that walks sublime the evening sky.

958. நலத்தின்க ணாரின்மை தோன்றி னவனைக்
குலத்தின்க ணையப் படும் (௮)

If lack of love appear in those who bear some goodly name,
'Twill make men doubt the ancestry they claim.

959. நிலத்திற் கிடந்தமை கால்காட்டுங் காட்டுங்
குலத்திற் பிறந்தார்வாய்ச் சொல் (௯)

Of soil the plants that spring thereout will show the worth;
The words they speak declare the men of noble birth.

960. நலம்வேண்டி னாணுடைமை வேண்டுங்
குலம்வேண்டின் வேண்டுக யார்க்கும் பணிவு (௰)

Who seek for good the grace of virtuous shame must know;
Who seek for noble name to all must reverence show.

CHAPTER XCVII. அதி. ௯௭.

மானம்.—HONOUR.

961. இன்றி யமையாச் சிறப்பின வாயினுங்
குன்ற வருப விடல் (௧)

Though linked to splendours man no otherwise may gain,
Reject each act that may thine honour's clearness stain.

962. சீரினுஞ் சீரல்ல செய்யாரே சீரொடு
பேராண்மை வேண்டு பவர் (௨)

Who seek with glory to combine honour's untarnished fame,
Do no inglorious deeds, though men accord them glory's name.

963. பெருக்கத்து வேண்டும் பணிதல் சிறிய
சுருக்கத்து வேண்டு முயர்வு (௩)

Bow down thy soul, with increase blest, in happy hour;
Lift up thy heart, when stript of all by fortune's power.

964. தலையி னிழிந்த மயிரனையர் மாந்தர்
நிலையி னிழிந்தக் கடை (௪)

Like hairs from off the head that fall to earth,
When fall'n from high estate are men of noble birth.

965. குன்றி னனையாருங் குன்றுவர் குன்றுவ
குன்றி யனைய செயின் (௫)

If meanness, slight as 'abrus' grain, by men be wrought,
Though like a hill their high estate, they sink to nought.

966. புகழின்றாற் புத்தேணாட் டுய்யாதா லென்மற்
றிகழ்வார்பின் சென்று நிலை (௬)

It yields no praise, nor to the land of gods throws wide the gate:
Why follow men who scorn, and at their bidding wait?

967. ஒட்டார்பின் சென்றொருவன் வாழ்தலி னந்நிலையே
கெட்டா னெனப்படுத னன்று (௭)

Better 'twere said, 'He 's perished!' than to gain
The means to live, following in foeman's train.

968. மருந்தோமற் றூனோம்பும் வாழ்க்கை
பெருந்தகைமை பீடழிய வந்த விடத்து (௮)

When high estate has lost its pride of honour meet,
Is life, that nurses this poor flesh, as nectar sweet?

969. மயிர்நீப்பின் வாழாக் கவரிமா வன்னா
ருயிர்நீப்பர் மானம் வரின் (௯)

Like the wild ox that, of its tuft bereft, will pine away,
Are those who, of their honour shorn, will quit the light of day.

970. இளிவரின் வாழாத மானா முடையா
ரொளிதொழு தேத்து முலகு (௰)

Who, when dishonour comes, refuse to live, their honoured memory
Will live in worship and applause of all the world for aye!

CHAPTER XCVIII. அதி. ௯௮.

பெருமை.—Greatness.

971. ஒளியொருவற் குள்ள வெறுக்கை
யிளியொருவற் கஃதிறந்து வாழ்து மெனல் (௧)

The light of life is mental energy; disgrace is his
Who says, 'I 'll lead a happy life devoid of this.'

972. பிறப்பொக்கு மெல்லா வுயிர்க்குஞ்
சிறப்பொவ்வா செய்தொழில் வேற்றுமை யான் (௨)

All men that live are one in circumstance of birth;
Diversities of works give each his special worth.

973. மேலிருந்து மேலல்லார் மேலல்லர்
கீழிருந்துங் கீழல்லார் கீழல் லவர் (௩)

The men of lofty line, whose souls are mean, are never great;
The men of lowly birth, when high of soul, are not of low estate.

974. ஒருமை மகளிரே போலப்
பெருமையுந் தன்னைத்தான் கொண்டொழுகி னுண்டு (௪)

Like single-hearted women, greatness too,
Exists while to itself itself is true.

975. பெருமை யுடையவ ராற்றுவா ராற்றி
னருமை யுடைய செயல் (௫)

The man endowed with greatness true,
Rare deeds in perfect wise will do.

976. சிறியா ருணர்ச்சியு ளில்லைப்
பெரியாரைப் பேணிக்கொள் வேமென்னு நோக்கு (௬)

'As votaries of the truly great we will ourselves enroll,'
Is thought that enters not the mind of men of little soul.

977. இறப்பே புரிந்த தொழிற்றாஞ்
சிறப்புந்தான் சீரல் லவர்கட் படின் (௭)

Whene'er distinction lights on some unworthy head,
Then deeds of haughty insolence are bred.

978. பணியுமா மென்றும் பெருமை சிறுமை
யணியுமாந் தன்னை வியந்து (௮)

Greatness humbly bends, but littleness always
Spreads out its plumes, and loads itself with praise.

979. பெருமை பெருமித மின்மை
சிறுமை பெருமித மூர்ந்து விடல் (௯)

Greatness is absence of conceit; meanness, we deem,
Riding on car of vanity supreme.

980. அற்ற மறைக்கும் பெருமை சிறுமைதான்
குற்றமே கூறி விடும் (௰)

Greatness will hide a neighbour's shame;
Meanness his faults to all the world proclaim.

CHAPTER XCIX. அதி. ௯௯.

சான்றாண்மை.—PERFECTNESS.

981. கடனென்ப நல்லவை யெல்லாங்
கடனறிந்து சான்றாண்மை மேற்கொள் பவர்க்கு (௧)

All goodly things are duties to the men, they say,
Who set themselves to walk in virtue's perfect way.

982. குணநலஞ் சான்றோர் நலனே பிறநல
மெந்நலத் துள்ளதூஉ மன்று (௨)

The good of inward excellence they claim,
The perfect men; all other good is only good in name.

983. அன்புநா ணொப்புரவு கண்ணோட்டம் வாய்மையொ
டைந்துசால் பூன்றிய தூண் (௩)

Love, modesty, beneficence, benignant grace,
With truth, are pillars five of perfect virtue's resting-place.

984. கொல்லா நலத்தது நோன்மை பிறர்தீமை
சொல்லா நலத்தது சால்பு (௪)

The type of 'penitence' is virtuous good that nothing slays;
To speak no ill of other men is perfect virtue's praise.

985. ஆற்றுவா ராற்றல் பணித லதுசான்றோர்
மாற்றாரை மாற்றும் படை (௫)

Submission is the might of men of mighty acts; the sage
With that same weapon stills his foeman's rage.

986. சால்பிற்குக் கட்டளை யாதெனிற்
தோல்வி துலையல்லார் கண்ணுங் கொளல் (௬)

What is perfection's test? The equal mind,
To bear repulse from even meaner men resigned.

987. இன்னாசெய் தார்க்கு மினியவே செய்யாக்கா
லென்ன பயத்ததோ சால்பு (௭)

What fruit doth your perfection yield you, say!
Unless to men who work you ill you good repay?

988. இன்மை யொருவற் கிளிவன்று சால்பென்னுந்
திண்மை யுண்டாகப் பெறின் (௮)

To soul with perfect virtue's strength endued,
Brings no disgrace the lack of every earthly good.

989. ஊழி பெயரினுந் தாம்பெயரார் சான்றாண்மைக்
காழி யெனப்படு வார் (௯)

Call them of perfect virtue's sea the shore,
Who, though the fates should fail, fail not for evermore.

990. சான்றவர் சான்றாண்மை குன்றி னிருநிலந்
தாங்காது மன்னோ பொறை (௰)

The mighty earth its burthen to sustain must cease,
If perfect virtue of the perfect men decrease.

CHAPTER C. அதி. ௧00.

பண்புடைமை.—Courtesy.

991. எண்பதத்தா லெய்த லெளிதென்ப யார்மாட்டும்
பண்புடைமை யென்னும் வழக்கு (௧)

Who easy access give to every man, they say,
Of kindly courtesy will learn with ease the way.

992. அன்புடைமை யான்ற குடிப்பிறத்த லிவ்விரண்டும்
பண்புடைமை யென்னும் வழக்கு (௨)

Benevolence and high-born dignity,
These two are beaten paths of courtesy.

993. உறுப்பொத்தன் மக்களொப் பன்றால்
வெறுத்தக்க பண்பொத்த லொப்பதா மொப்பு (௩)

Men are not one because their members seem alike to outward view;
Similitude of kindred quality makes likeness true.

994. நயனொடு நன்றி புரிந்த
பயனுடையார் பண்புபா ராட்டு முலகு (௪)

Of men of fruitful life, who kindly benefits dispense,
The world unites to praise the 'noble excellence.'

995. நகையுள்ளு மின்னா திகழ்ச்சி
பகையுள்ளும் பண்புள பாடறிவார் மாட்டு (௫)

Contempt is evil though in sport. They who man's nature know,
E'en in their wrath, a courteous mind will show.

996. பண்புடையார் பட்டுண் டுலக மதுவின்றேல்
மண்புக்கு மாய்வது மன் (௬)

The world abides; for 'worthy' men its weight sustain.
Were it not so, 'twould fall to dust again.

997. அரம்போலுங் கூர்மைய ரேனு
மரம்போல்வர் மக்கட்பண் பில்லா தவர் (௭)

Though sharp their wit as file, as blocks they must remain,
Whose souls are void of 'courtesy humane.'

998. நண்பாற்றா ராகி நயமில செய்வார்க்கும்
பண்பாற்றா ராதல் கடை (௮)

Though men with all unfriendly acts and wrongs assail,
'Tis uttermost disgrace in 'courtesy' to fail.

999. நகல்வல்ல ரல்லார்க்கு மாயிரு ஞாலம்
பகலும்பாற் பட்டன் றிருள் (௯)

To him who knows not how to smile in kindly mirth,
Darkness in daytime broods o'er all the vast and mighty earth.

1000. பண்பிலான் பெற்ற பெருஞ்செல்வ
நன்பால் கலந்தீமை யாற்றிரிந் தற்று (௰)

Like sweet milk soured because in filthy vessel poured,
Is ample wealth in churlish man's unopened coffers stored.

CHAPTER CI. அதி. ௧௦௧.

நன்றியில்செல்வம்.—Wealth without Benefaction.

1001. வைத்தான்வாய் சான்ற பெரும்பொரு ளஃதுண்ணான்
செத்தான் செயக்கிடந்த தில் (௧)

Who fills his house with ample store, enjoying none,
Is dead. Nought with the useless heap is done.

1002. பொருளானா மெல்லாமென் றீயா திவறு
மருளானா மாணாப் பிறப்பு (௨)

Who giving nought, opines from wealth all blessing springs,
Degraded birth that doting miser's folly brings.

1003. ஈட்ட மிவறி யிசைவேண்டா வாடவர்
தோற்ற நிலக்குப் பொறை (௩)

Who lust to heap up wealth, but glory hold not dear,
It burthens earth when on the stage of being they appear.

1004. எச்சமென் றென்னெண்ணுங் கொல்லோ வொருவரா
னச்சப் படாஅ தவன் (௪)

Whom no one loves, when he shall pass away,
What doth he look to leave behind, I pray?

1005. கொடுப்பதூஉந் துய்ப்பதூஉ மில்லார்க்
கடுக்கிய கோடியுண் டாயினு மில் (௫)

Amid accumulated millions they are poor,
Who nothing give and nought enjoy of all they store.

1006. ஏதம் பெருஞ்செல்வந் தான்றுவ்வான் றக்கார்க்கொன்
றீத லியல்பிலா தான் (௬)

Their ample wealth is misery to men of churlish heart,
Who nought themselves enjoy, and nought to worthy men impart.

1007. அற்றார்க்கொன் றாற்றாதான் செல்வ மிகநலம்
பெற்றா டமியண்மூத் தற்று (எ)

Like woman fair in lonelihood who aged grows,
Is wealth of him on needy men who nought bestows.

1008. நச்சப் படாதவன் செல்வ நடுவூரு
ணச்சு மரம்பழுத் தற்று (அ)

When he whom no man loves exults in great prosperity,
'Tis as when fruits in midmost of the town some poisonous tree.

1009. அன்பொரீஇத் தற்செற் றறநோக்கா தீட்டிய
வொண்பொருள் கொள்வார் பிறர் (கூ)

Who love abandon, self afflict, and virtue's way forsake
To heap up glittering wealth, their hoards shall others take.

1010. சீருடைச் செல்வர் சிறுதுனி
மாரி வறங்கூர்ந் தனைய துடைத்து (ய)

'Tis as when rain-cloud in the heaven grows dry,
When generous wealthy man endures brief poverty.

CHAPTER CII. அதி. க0உ.

நாணுடைமை.—SHAME.

1011. கருமத்தா னாணுத னாணுத்
திருநுத னல்லவர் நாணுப் பிற (க)

To shrink abashed from evil deed is 'generous shame';
Other is that of bright-browed ones of virtuous fame.

1012. ஊணுடை யெச்ச முயிர்க்கெல்லாம் வேறல்ல
நாணுடைமை மாந்தர் சிறப்பு (உ)

Food, clothes, and other things alike all beings own;
By sense of shame the excellence of men is known.

1013. ஊனைக் குறித்த வுயிரெல்லா
நாணென்னு நன்மை குறித்தது சால்பு (ங)

All spirits homes of flesh as habitation claim,
And perfect virtue ever dwells with shame.

1014. அணியன்றோ நாணுடைமை சான்றோர்க் கஃதின்றேற்
பிணியன்றோ பீடு நடை (ச)

And is not shame an ornament to men of dignity?
Without it step of stately pride is piteous thing to see.

1015. பிறர்பழியுந் தம்பழியு நாணுவார் நாணுக்
குறைபதி யென்னு முலகு (௫)

As home of virtuous shame by all the world the men are known,
Who feel ashamed for others' guilt as for their own.

1016. நாண்வேலி கொள்ளாது மன்னோ வியன்ஞாலம்
பேணலர் மேலா யவர் (௬)

Unless the hedge of shame inviolate remain,
For men of lofty soul the earth's vast realms no charms retain.

1017. நாணா லுயிரைத் துறப்ப ருயிர்பொருட்டா
னாண்டுறவார் நாணாள் பவர் (௭)

The men of modest soul for shame would life an offering make,
But ne'er abandon virtuous shame for life's dear sake.

1018. பிறர்நாணத் தக்கது தானாணா னாயி
னறநாணத் தக்க துடைத்து (௮)

Thou know'st no shame, while all around ashamed must be:
Virtue will shrink away ashamed of thee!

1019. குலஞ்சுடுங் கொள்கை பிழைப்பி
னலஞ்சுடு நாணின்மை நின்றக் கடை (௯)

'Twill race consume if right observance fail;
'Twill every good consume if shamelessness prevail.

1020. நாணகத் தில்லா ரியக்க மரப்பாவை
நாணா லுயிர்மருட்டி யற்று (௰)

'Tis as with strings a wooden puppet apes life's functions, when
Those void of shame within hold intercourse with men.

CHAPTER CIII. அதி. ௧௦௩.

குடிசெயல்வகை.—The Way of Maintaining the Family.

1021. கருமஞ் செயவொருவன் கைதூவே னென்னும்
பெருமையிற் பீடுடைய தில் (௧)

Who says 'I 'll do my work, nor slack my hand,'
His greatness, clothed with dignity supreme, shall stand.

1022. ஆள்வினையு மான்ற வறிவு மெனவிரண்டி
னீள்வினையா னீளுங் குடி (௨)

The manly act and knowledge full, when these combine
In deed prolonged, then lengthens out the race's line.

1023. குடிசெய்வ லென்னு மொருவற்குத் தெய்வ
மடிதற்றுத் தான்முந் துறும் (௩)

'I 'll make my race renowned,' if man shall say,
With vest succinct the goddess leads the way.

1024. சூழாமற் றானே முடிவெய்துந் தங்குடியைத்
தாழா துஞற்று பவர்க்கு (௪)

Who labours for his race with unremitting pain,
Without a thought, spontaneously, his end will gain.

1025. குற்ற மிலனாய்க் குடிசெய்து வாழ்வானைச்
சுற்றமாச் சுற்று முலகு (௫)

With blameless life who seeks to build his race's fame,
The world shall circle him, and kindred claim.

1026. நல்லாண்மை யென்ப தொருவற்குத் தான்பிறந்த
வில்லாண்மை யாக்கிக் கொளல் (௬)

Of virtuous manliness the world accords the praise
To him who gives his powers, the house from which he sprang to raise.

1027. அமரகத்து வன்கண்ணர் போலத்
தமரகத்து மாற்றுவார் மேற்றே பொறை (௭)

The fearless hero bears the brunt amid the warrior throng;
Amid his kindred so the burthen rests upon the strong.

1028. குடிசெய்வார்க் கில்லைப் பருவ
மடிசெய்து மானங் கருதக் கெடும் (௮)

Wait for no season, when you would your house uprear;
'Twill perish, if you wait supine, or hold your honour dear.

1029. இடும்பைக்கே கொள்கலங் கொல்லோ
குடும்பத்தைக் குற்ற மறைப்பா னுடம்பு (௯)

Is not his body vase that various sorrows fill,
Who would his household screen from every ill?

1030. இடுக்கண் கால்கொன் றிடவீழு
மடுத்தூன்று நல்லா ளிலாத குடி (௰)

When trouble the foundation saps the house must fall,
If no strong hand be nigh to prop the tottering wall.

CHAPTER CIV. அதி. ௧௦௪.

உழவு.—Agriculture.

1031. சுழன்றுமேர்ப் பின்ன துலக மதனா
லுழந்து முழவே தலை (௧)

Howe'er they roam, the world must follow still the plougher's team;
Though toilsome, culture of the ground as noblest toil esteem.

1032. உழுவா ருலகத்தார்க் காணியஃ தாற்றா
தெழுவாரை யெல்லாம் பொறுத்து (௨)

The ploughers are the linch-pin of the world; they bear
Them up who other works perform, too weak its toils to share.

1033. உழுதுண்டு வாழ்வாரே வாழ்வார்மற் றெல்லாந்
தொழுதுண்டு பின்செல் பவர் (௩)

Who ploughing eat their food, they truly live;
The rest to others bend subservient, eating what they give.

1034. பலகுடை நீழலுந் தங்குடைக்கீழ்க் காண்ப
ரலகுடை நீழ லவர் (௪)

O'er many a land they'll see their monarch reign,
Whose fields are shaded by the waving grain.

1035. இரவா ரிரப்பார்க் கொன்றீவர்
கரவாது கைசெய் தூண்மாலை யவர் (௫)

They nothing ask from others, but to askers give,
Who raise with their own hands the food on which they live.

1036. உழவினார் கைம்மடங்கி னில்லை
விழைவதூஉம் விட்டேமென் பார்க்கு நிலை (௬)

For those who've left what all men love no place is found,
When they with folded hands remain who till the ground.

1037. தொடிப்புழுதி கஃசா வுணக்கிற்
பிடித்தெருவும் வேண்டாது சாலப் படும் (௭)

Reduce your soil to that dry state
When ounce is quarter-ounce's weight;
Without one handful of manure,
Abundant crops you thus secure.

1038. ஏரினு நன்றா லெருவிடுதல் கட்டபி
னீரினு நன்றதன் காப்பு (௮)

To cast manure is better than to plough;
Weed well; to guard is more than watering now.

1039. செல்லான் கிழவ னிருப்பி னிலம்புலந்
இல்லாளி னூடி விடும் (௯)

When master from the field aloof hath stood;
Then land will sulk, like wife in angry mood.

1040. இலமென் றசைஇ யிருப்பாரைக் காணி
னிலமென்னு நல்லா ணகும் (௰)

The earth, that kindly dame, will laugh to see,
Men seated idle pleading poverty.

CHAPTER CV. அதி. ௧0௫.

நல்குரவு.—Poverty.

1041. இன்மையி னின்னாத தியாதெனி னின்மையி
னின்மையே யின்னா தது (௧)

You ask what sharper pain than poverty is known;
Nothing pains more than poverty, save poverty alone.

1042. இன்மை யெனவொரு பாவி மறுமையு
மிம்மையு மின்றி வரும் (௨)

Malefactor matchless! poverty destroys
This world's and the next world's joys.

1043. தொல்வரவுந் தோலுங் கெடுக்குந் தொகையாக
நல்குர வென்னு நசை (௩)

Importunate desire, which poverty men name,
Destroys both old descent and goodly fame.

1044. இற்பிறந்தார் கண்ணேயு மின்மை யிளிவந்த
சொற்பிறக்குஞ் சோர்வு தரும் (௪)

From penury will spring, 'mid even those of noble race,
Oblivion that gives birth to words that bring disgrace.

1045. நல்குர வென்னு மிடும்பையுட்
பல்குரைத் துன்பங்கள் சென்று படும் (௫)

From poverty, that grievous woe,
Attendant sorrows plenteous grow.

1046. நற்பொரு ணன்குணர்ந்து சொல்லினு நல்கூர்ந்தார்
சொற்பொருள் சோர்வு படும் (௬)

Though deepest sense, well understood, the poor man's words convey,
Their sense from memory of mankind will fade away.

1047. அறஞ்சாரா நல்குர வீன்ற தாயானும்
பிறன்போல நோக்கப் படும் (௭)

From indigence devoid of virtue's grace,
The mother e'en that bare, estranged, will turn her face.

1048. இன்றும் வருவது கொல்லோ நெருநலுங்
கொன்றது போலு நிரப்பு (௮)

And will it come to day as yesterday,
The grief of want that eats my soul away ?

1049. நெருப்பினுட் டுஞ்சலு மாகு
நிரப்பினுள் யாதொன்றுங் கண்பா டரிது (௯)

Amid the flames sleep may men's eyelids close,
In poverty the eye knows no repose.

1050. துப்புர வில்லார் துவரத் துறவாமை
யுப்பிற்குங் காடிக்குங் கூற்று (௰)

Unless the destitute will utterly themselves deny,
They cause their neighbour's salt and vinegar to die.

CHAPTER CVI. அதி. ௧௦௬.

இரவு.—Mendicancy.

1051. இரக்க விரத்தக்கார்க் காணிற்
கரப்பி னவர்பழி தம்பழி யன்று (௧)

When those you find from whom 'tis meet to ask,—for aid apply ;
Theirs is the sin, not yours, if they the gift deny.

1052. இன்ப மொருவற் கிரத்த லிரந்தவை
துன்ப முறுஅ வரின் (௨)

Even to ask an alms may pleasure give,
If what you ask without annoyance you receive.

1053. கரப்பிலா நெஞ்சிற் கடனறிவார் முன்னின்
றிரப்புமோ ரேஎ ருடைத்து (௩)

The men who nought deny, but know what's due, before their face
To stand as suppliants affords especial grace.

1054. இரத்தலு மீதலே போலுங்
கரத்தல் கனவிலுந் தேற்றாதார் மாட்டு (௪)

Like giving alms, may even asking pleasant seem,
From men who of denial never even dream.

1055. கரப்பிலார் வையகத் துண்மையாற் கண்ணின்
றிரப்பவர் மேற்கொள் வது (௫)

Because on earth the men exist, who never say them nay,
Men bear to stand before their eyes for help to pray.

1056. கரப்பிடும்பை யில்லாரைக் காணி
னிரப்பிடும்பை யெல்லா மொருங்கு கெடும் (௬)

If those you find from evil of 'denial' free,
At once all plague of poverty will flee.

1057. இகழ்ந்தெள்ளா தீவாரைக் காணின்
மகிழ்ந்துள்ள முள்ளு ளுவப்ப துடைத்து (௭)

If men are found who give and no harsh words of scorn employ,
The minds of askers, through and through, will thrill with joy.

1058. இரப்பாரை யில்லாயி னீர்ங்கண்மா ஞால
மரப்பாவை சென்றுவந் தற்று (௮)

If askers cease, the mighty earth, where cooling fountains flow,
Will be a stage where wooden puppets come and go.

1059. ஈவார்க ணென்னுண்டாந் தோற்ற மிரந்துகொண்
மேவா ரிலாஅக் கடை (௯)

What glory will there be to men of generous soul,
When none are found to love the askers' *rôle*?

1060. இரப்பான் வெகுளாமை வேண்டு
நிரப்பிடும்பை தானேயுஞ் சாலுங் கரி (௰)

Askers refused from wrath must stand aloof;
The plague of poverty itself is ample proof.

CHAPTER CVII. அதி. ௧௦௭.

இரவச்சம்.—THE DREAD OF MENDICANCY.

1061. கரவா துவந்தீயுங் கண்ணன்னார் கண்ணு
மிரவாமை கோடி யுறும் (௧)

Ten million-fold 'tis greater gain, asking no alms to live,
Even from those, like eyes in worth, who nought concealing gladly give.

1062. இரந்து முயிர்வாழ்தல் வேண்டிற்
பரந்து கெடுக வுலகியற்றி யான் (௨)

If he that shaped the world desires that men should begging go,
Through life's long course, let him a wanderer be and perish so.

1063. இன்மை யிடும்பை யிரந்துதீர் வாமென்னும்
வன்மையின் வன்பாட் டதில் (௩)

Nothing is harder than the hardness that will say,
'The plague of penury by asking alms we 'll drive away.'

1064. இடமெல்லாங் கொள்ளாத் தகைத்தே
யிடமில்லாக் காலு மிரவொல்லாச் சால்பு (௪)

Who ne'er consent to beg in utmost need, their worth
Has excellence of greatness that transcends the earth.

1065. தெண்ணீ ரடுபுற்கை யாயினுந் தாடந்த
துண்ணலி னூங்கினிய தில் (௫)

Nothing is sweeter than to taste the toil-won cheer,
Though mess of pottage as tasteless as the water clear.

1066. ஆவிற்கு நீரென் றிரப்பினு
நாவிற் கிரவி னிளிவந்த தில் (௬)

E'en if a draught of water for a cow you ask,
Nought's so distasteful to the tongue as begger's task.

1067. இரப்ப னிரப்பாரை யெல்லா மிரப்பிற்
கரப்பா ரிரவன்மி னென்று (௭)

One thing I beg of beggars all, 'If beg ye may,
Of those who hide their wealth, beg not, I pray.'

1068. இரவென்னு மேமாப்பி றோணி
கரவென்னும் பார்தாக்கப் பக்கு விடும் (௮)

The fragile bark of beggary
Wrecked on denial's rock will lie.

1069. இரவுள்ள வுள்ள முருகுங்
கரவுள்ள வுள்ளதூஉ மின்றிக் கெடும் (௯)

The heart will melt away at thought of beggary;
With thought of stern repulse 'twill perish utterly.

1070. கரப்பவர்க் கியாங்கொளிக்குங் கொல்லோ
விரப்பவர் சொல்லாடப் போஒ முயிர் (௰)

E'en as he asks, the shamefaced asker dies;
Where shall his spirit hide who help denies?

CHAPTER CVIII. அதி. கoஅ.

கயமை.—BASENESS.

1071. மக்களே போல்வர் கயவ ரவரன்ன
ஒப்பாரி யான்கண் டதில் (க)

The base resemble men in outward form, I ween;
But counterpart exact to them I 've never seen.

1072. நன்றறி வாரிற் கயவர் திருவுடையர்
நெஞ்சத் தவல மிலர் (உ)

Than those of grateful heart the base must luckier be,
Their minds from every anxious thought are free!

1073. தேவ ரனையர் கயவ ரவருந்தா
மேவன செய்தொழுக லான் (ங)

The base are as the gods; they too
Do ever what they list to do!

1074. அகப்பட்டி யாவாரைக் காணி னவரின்
மிகப்பட்டுச் செம்மாக்குங் கீழ் (ச)

When base men those behold of conduct vile,
They straight surpass them, and exulting smile.

1075. அச்சமே கீழ்கள தாசார
மெச்ச மவாவுண்டே லுண்டாஞ் சிறிது (ரு)

Fear is the base man's virtue; if that fail,
Intense desire some little may avail.

1076. அறைபறை யன்னர் கயவர்தாங் கேட்ட
மறைபிறர்க் குய்த்துரைக்க லான் (சா)

The base are like the beaten drum; for, when they hear,
They sound the secret out in every neighbour's ear.

1077. ஈர்ங்கை விதிரார் கயவர் கொடிறுடைக்குங்
கூன்கைய ரல்லா தவர்க்கு (எ)

From off their moistened hands no clinging grain they shake,
Unless to those with clenched fist their jaws who break.

1078. சொல்லப் பயன்படுவர் சான்றோர் கரும்புபோற்
கொல்லப் பயன்படுங் கீழ் (அ)

The good to those will profit yield fair words who use;
The base, like sugar-cane, will profit those who bruise.

1079. உடுப்பதூஉ முண்பதூஉங் காணிற் பிறர்மேல்
வடுக்காண வற்றாகுங் கீழ் (௯)

If neighbours clothed and fed he see, the base
Is mighty man some hidden fault to trace?

1080. எற்றிற் குரியர் கயவரொன் றுற்றக்கால்
விற்றற் குரியர் விரைந்து (௰)

For what is base man fit, if griefs assail?
Himself to offer, there and then, for sale!

ஒழிபியன்முற்றும்.

THE END OF THE APPENDIX.

பொருட்பான்முற்றிற்று.

THE END OF BOOK II. ON WEALTH.

BOOK III.—LOVE.

BOOK III.—LOVE. காமத்துப்பால்.

§ 1.—THE GANDHARVA MARRIAGE. களவியல்.

CHAPTER CIX. அதி. க0கூ.

தகையணங்குறுத்தல்.—MENTAL DISTURBANCE CAUSED BY THE BEAUTY OF THE PRINCESS.

1081. அணங்குகொ லாய்மயில் கொல்லோ
கனங்குழை மாதர்கொன் மாலுமென் னெஞ்சு (க)

Goddess? or peafowl rare?
She whose ears rich jewels wear,
Is she a maid of human kind?
All wildered is my mind!

1082. நோக்கினா ணோக்கெதிர் நோக்குத
றாக்கணங்கு தானைக்கொண் டன்ன துடைத்து (உ)

She of the beaming eyes,
To my rash look her glance replies,
As if the matchless goddess' hand
Led forth an armèd band.

1083. பண்டறியேன் கூற்றென் பதனை யினியறிந்தேன்
பெண்டகையாற் பேரமர்க் கட்டு (௩)

Death's form I formerly
Knew not; but now 'tis plain to me:
He comes in lovely maiden's guise,
With soul-subduing eyes.

1084. கண்டா ருயிருண்ணுந் தோற்றத்தாற்
பெண்டகைப் பேதைக் கமர்த்தன கண் (௪)

In sweet simplicity,
A woman's gracious form hath she;
But yet those eyes, that drink my life,
Are with the form at strife!

1085. கூற்றமோ கண்ணோ பிணையோ மடவர
ணோக்கமிம் மூன்று முடைத்து (௫)

The light that on me gleams,
Is it death's dart? or eye's bright beams?
Or fawn's shy glance? All three appear
In form of maiden here.

1086. கொடும்புருவங் கோடா மறைப்பி
னடுங்கஞர் செய்யல மன்னிவள் கண் (௬)

If cruel eye-brow's bow,
Unbent, would veil those glances now;
The shafts that wound this trembling heart
Her eyes no more would dart.

1087. கடாஅக் களிற்றின்மேற் கட்படா மாதர்
படாஅ முலைமேற் றுகில் (௭)

As veil o'er angry eyes
Of raging elephant that lies,
The silken cincture's folds invest
This maiden's panting breast.

1088. ஒண்ணுதற் கோஒ வுடைந்ததே ஞாட்பினு
ணண்ணாரு முட்குமென் பீடு (௮)

Ah! woe is me! my might,
That awed my foemen in the fight,
By lustre of that beaming brow
Borne down, lies broken now!

1089. பிணையேர் மடநோக்கு நாணு முடையாட்
கணியெவனோ வேதில தந்து (௯)

Like tender fawn's her eye;
Clothed on is she with modesty;
What added beauty can be lent
By alien ornament?

1090. உண்டார்க ணல்ல தடுநறாக் காமம்போற்
கண்டார் மகிழ்செய்த லின்று (௰)

The palm-tree's fragrant wine,
To those who taste yields joys divine;
But love hath rare felicity
For those that only see!

CHAPTER CX. அதி. கக0.

குறிப்பறிதல்.—Recognition of the Signs (of Mutual Love).

1091. இருநோக் கிவளுண்க ணுள்ள
தொருநோக்கு நோய்நோக்கொன் றந்நோய் மருந்து (க)

A double witchery have glances of her liquid eye;
One glance is glance that brings me pain; the other heals again.

1092. கண்களவு கொள்ளுஞ் சிறுநோக்கங் காமத்திற்
செம்பாக மன்று பெரிது (உ)

The furtive glance, that gleams one instant bright,
Is more than half of love's supreme delight.

1093. நோக்கினா ணோக்கி யிறைஞ்சினா ளஃதவள்
யாப்பினு ளட்டிய நீர் (௩)

She looked, and looking drooped her head:
On springing shoot of love 'tis water shed!

1094. யானோக்குங் காலை நிலனோக்கு நோக்காக்காற்
றானோக்கி மெல்ல நகும் (௪)

I look on her: her eyes are on the ground the while;
I look away: she looks on me with timid smile.

1095. குறிக்கொண்டு நோக்காமை யல்லா லொருகண்
சிறக்கணித்தாள் போல நகும் (௫)

She seemed to see me not; but yet the maid
Her love, by smiling side-long glance, betrayed.

1096. உறாஅ தவர்போற் சொலினுஞ்
செறாஅர்சொ லொல்லை யுணரப் படும் (௬)

Though with their lips affection they disown,
Yet, when they hate us not, 'tis quickly known.

1097. செறாஅச் சிறுசொல்லுஞ் செற்றார்போ னோக்கு
முறாஅர்போன் றுற்றார் குறிப்பு (௭)

The slighting words that anger feign, while eyes their love reveal,
Are signs of those that love, but would their love conceal.

1098. அசையியற் குண்டாண்டோ ரேஎர்யா னோக்கப்
பசையினள் பைய நகும் (௮)

I gaze, the tender maid relents the while;
And, oh the matchless grace of that soft smile!

1099. ஏதிலார் போலப் பொதுநோக்கு நோக்குதல்
காதலார் கண்ணே யுள (௯)

The look indifferent, that would its love disguise,
Is only read aright by lovers' eyes.

1100. கண்ணொடு கண்ணிணை நோக்கொக்கின் வாய்ச்சொற்க
ளென்ன பயனு மில (௰)

When eye to answering eye reveals the tale of love,
All words that lips can say must useless prove.

CHAPTER CXI. அதி. ௧௧௧.

புணர்ச்சிமகிழ்தல்.—Rejoicing in the Embrace.

1101. கண்டுகேட் டுண்டுயிர்த் துற்றறியு மைம்புலனு
மொண்டொடி கண்ணே யுள (௧)

All joys that senses five—sight, hearing, taste, smell, touch—can give,
In this resplendent armlet-bearing damsel live!

1102. பிணிக்கு மருந்து பிறம
னணியிழை தன்னோய்க்குத் தானே மருந்து (௨)

Disease and medicine antagonists we surely see;
This maid, to pain she gives, herself is remedy.

1103. தாம்வீழ்வார் மென்றோட் டுயிலி னினிதுகொ
றாமரைக் கண்ணா னுலகு (௩)

Than rest in her soft arms to whom the soul is giv'n,
Is any sweeter joy in his, the Lotus-eyed-one's heaven?

1104. நீங்கிற் றெறூஉங் குறுகுங்காற் றண்ணென்னுந்
தீயாண்டுப் பெற்றா ளிவள் (௪)

Withdraw, it burns; approach, it soothes the pain;
Whence did the maid this wondrous fire obtain?

1105. வேட்ட பொழுதி னவையவை போலுமே
தோட்டார் கதுப்பினா டோள் (௫)

In her embrace, whose locks with flowery wreaths are bound,
Each varied form of joy the soul can wish is found.

1106. உறுதோ றுயிர்தளிர்ப்பத் தீண்டலாற் பேதைக்
கமிழ்தி னியன்றன தோள் (௬)

Ambrosia are the simple maiden's arms; when I attain
Their touch, my withered life puts forth its buds again!

1107. தம்மி லிருந்து தமதுபாத் துண்டற்றா
லம்மா வரிவை முயக்கு (எ)

As when one eats from household store, with kindly grace
Sharing his meal: such is this golden maid's embrace.

1108. வீழு மிருவர்க் கினிதே வளியிடை
போழப் படாஅ முயக்கு (அ)

Sweet is the strict embrace of those whom fond affection binds,
Where no dissevering breath of discord entrance finds.

1109. ஊட லுணர்தல் புணர்த லிவைகாமங்
கூடியார் பெற்ற பயன் (கூ)

The jealous variance, the healing of the strife, reunion gained:
These are the fruits from wedded love obtained.

1110. அறிதோ றறியாமை கண்டற்றாற் காமஞ்
செறிதோறுஞ் சேயிழை மாட்டு (ய)

The more men learn, the more their lack of learning they detect;
'Tis so when I approach the maid with gleaming jewels decked.

CHAPTER CXII. அதி. கக௨.

நலம்புனைந்துரைத்தல்.—The Praise of her Beauty.

1111. நன்னீரை வாழி யனிச்சமே நின்னினு
மென்னீரள் யாம்வீழ் பவள் (க)

O flower of the sensitive plant! than thee
More tender 's the maiden beloved by me.

1112. மலர்காணின் மையாத்தி நெஞ்சே யிவள்கண்
பலர்காணும் பூவொக்கு மென்று (உ)

You deemed, as you saw the flowers, her eyes were as flowers, my soul,
That many may see; it was surely some folly that over you stole!

1113. முறிமேனி முத்த முறுவல்
வெறிநாற்றம் வேலுண்கண் வேய்த்தோ ளவட்கு (ங)

As tender shoot her frame; teeth, pearls; around her odours blend;
Darts are the eyes of her whose shoulders like the *bambû* bend.

1114. காணிற் குவளை கவிழ்ந்து நிலனோக்கு
மாணிழைகண் ணொவ்வே மென்று (ச)

The lotus, seeing her, with head demiss, the ground would eye,
And say, 'With eyes of her, rich gems who wears, we cannot vie.'

1115. அனிச்சப்பூக் கால்களையாள் பெய்தா ணுசுப்பிற்கு
நல்ல படாஅ பறை (ரு)

The flowers of the sensitive plant as a girdle around her she placed ;
The stems she forgot to nip off ; they 'll weigh down the delicate waist.

1116. மதியு மடந்தை முகனு மறியாப்
பதியிற் கலங்கிய மீன் (சு)

The stars perplexed are rushing wildly from their spheres ;
For like another moon this maiden's face appears.

1117. அறுவாய் நிறைந்த வவிர்மதிக்குப் போல
மறுவுண்டோ மாதர் முகத்து (எ)

In moon, that waxing waning shines, as spots appear,
Are any spots discerned in face of maiden here ?

1118. மாதர் முகம்போ லொளிவிட வல்லையேற்
காதலை வாழி மதி (அ)

Farewell, O moon ! If that thine orb could shine
Bright as her face, thou shouldst be love of mine.

1119. மலரன்ன கண்ணாண் முகமொத்தி யாயிற்
பலர்காணத் தோன்றன் மதி (கூ)

If as her face, whose eyes are flowers, thou wouldst have charms for me,
Shine for my eyes alone, O moon, shine not for all to see !

1120. அனிச்சமு மன்னத்தின் றூவியு மாத
ரடிக்கு நெருஞ்சிப் பழம் (ய)

The flower of the sensitive plant, and the down on the swan's white breast,
As the thorn are harsh, by the delicate feet of this maiden pressed.

CHAPTER CXIII. அதி. ககங.

காதற்சிறப்புரைத்தல்.—DECLARATION OF LOVE'S SPECIAL EXCELLENCE.

I.—He.

1121. பாலொடு தேன்கலந் தற்றே பணிமொழி
வாலெயி றூறிய நீர் (க)

The dew on her white teeth, whose voice is soft and low,
Is as when milk and honey mingled flow.

1122. உடம்போ டுயிரிடை யென்னமற் றன்ன
மடந்தையோ டெம்மிடை நட்பு (உ)

Between this maid and me the friendship kind
Is as the bonds that soul and body bind.

1123. கருமணியிற் பாவாய் நீபோதா யாம்வீழுந்
திருநுதற் கில்லை யிடம் (௩)

For her with beauteous brow, the maid I love, there place is none;
To give her image room, O pupil of mine eye, begone!

1124. வாழ்த லுயிர்க்கன்ன ளாயிழை
சாத லதற்கன்ன ணீங்கு மிடத்து (௪)

Life is she to my very soul when she draws nigh;
Dissevered from the maid with jewels rare, I die!

1125. உள்ளுவன் மன்யான் மறப்பின் மறப்பறியே
னொள்ளமர்க் கண்ணாள் குணம் (௫)

I might recall, if I could once forget; but from my heart
Her charms fade not, whose eyes gleam like the warrior's dart.

II.—She.

1126. கண்ணுள்ளிற் போகா ரிமைப்பிற் பருவரார்
நுண்ணியரெங் காத லவர் (௬)

My loved one's subtle form departs not from my eyes;
I wink them not, lest I should pain him where he lies.

1127. கண்ணுள்ளார் காத லவராகக்
கண்ணு மெழுதேங் கரப்பாக் கறிந்து (௭)

My love doth ever in my eyes reside;
I stain them not, fearing his form to hide.

1128. நெஞ்சத்தார் காத லவராக வெய்துண்ட
வஞ்சுதும் வேபாக் கறிந்து (௮)

Within my heart my lover dwells; from food I turn
That smacks of heat, lest he should feel it burn.

1129. இமைப்பிற் கரப்பாக் கறிவ
லனைத்திற்கே யேதில ரென்னுமிவ் வூர் (௯)

I fear his form to hide, nor close my eyes:
'Her love estranged is gone!' the village cries.

1130. உவந்துறைவ ருள்ளத்து ளென்று
மிகந்துறைவ ரேதில ரென்னுமிவ் வூர் (௰)

Rejoicing in my very soul he ever lies;
'Her love estranged is gone far off!' the village cries.

CHAPTER CXIV. அதி. ௧௧௪.

நாணுத்துறவுரைத்தல்.—The Abandonment of Reserve.

[This Chapter has its special difficulties, see Notes. I give a literal rendering.]

I.—He.

1131. காம முழந்து வருந்தினார்க்
கேம மடலல்ல தில்லை வலி (௧)

To those who 've proved love's joy, and now afflicted mourn,
Except the helpful '*horse of palm*,' no other strength remains.

1132. நோனா வுடம்பு முயிரு மடலேறு
நாணினை நீக்கி நிறுத்து (௨)

My body and my soul, that can no more endure,
Will lay reserve aside, and mount the '*horse of palm*.'

1133. நாணொடு நல்லாண்மை பண்டுடையே னின்றுடையேன்
காமுற்ற ரேறு மடல் (௩)

I once retained reserve and seemly manliness;
To-day I nought possess but lovers' '*horse of palm*.'

1134. காமக் கடும்புன லுய்க்குமே
நாணொடு நல்லாண்மை யென்னும் புணை (௪)

Love's rushing tide will sweep away the raft
Of seemly manliness and shame combined.

1135. தொடலைக் குறுந்தொடி தந்தாண்
மடலொடு மாலை யுழக்குந் துயர் (௫)

The maid that slender armlets wears, like flowers entwined,
Has brought me '*horse of palm*,' and pangs of eventide!

1136. மடலூர்தல் யாமத்து முள்ளுவேன் மன்ற
படலொல்லாப் பேதைக்கென் கண் (௬)

Of climbing 'horse of palm' in midnight hour, I think;
My eyes know no repose for that same simple maid.

1137. கடலன்ன காம முழந்து
மடலேறாப் பெண்ணிற் பெருந்தக்க தில் (௭)

There 's nought of greater worth than woman's long-enduring soul,
Who, vexed by love like ocean waves, climbs not the '*horse of palm*.'

II.—She.

1138. நிறையரியர் மன்னளிய ரென்னாது காம
மறையிறந்து மன்று படும் (௮)

In virtue hard to move, yet very tender, too, are we;
Love deems not so, would rend the veil, and court publicity!

1139. அறிகிலா ரெல்லாரு மென்றே யென்காம
மறுகின் மறுகு மருண்டு (௯)

'There's no one knows my heart,' so says my love,
And thus, in public ways, perturbed will rove.

1140. யாங்கண்ணிற் காண நகுப வறிவில்லார்
யாம்பட்ட தாம்படா வாறு (௰)

Before my eyes the foolish make a mock of me,
Because they ne'er endured the pangs I now must drie.

CHAPTER CXV. அதி. ககரு.

அலரறிவுறுத்தல்.—The Announcement of the Rumour.

[See note to last Chapter.]

I.—He.

1141. அலரெழ வாருயிர் நிற்கு மதனைப்
பலரறியார் பாக்கியத் தால் (க)

By this same rumour's rise, my precious life stands fast;
Good fortune grant the many know this not!

1142. மலரன்ன கண்ணா ளருமை யறியா
தலரெமக் கீந்ததிவ் வூர் (௨)

The village hath to us this rumour giv'n, that makes her mine;
Unweeting all the rareness of the maid with flower-like eyne.

1143. உறாஅதோ வூரறிந்த கௌவை யதனைப்
பெறாஅது பெற்றன்ன நீர்த்து (௩)

The rumour spread within the town, is it not gain to me?
It is as though that were obtained that may not be.

1144. கவ்வையாற் கவ்விது காம மதுவின்றேற்
றவ்வென்னுந் தன்மை யிழந்து (௪)

The rumour rising makes my love to rise;
My love would lose its power and languish otherwise.

1145. களித்தொறுங் கள்ளுண்டல் வேட்டற்றாற் காமம்
வெளிப்படுந் தோறு மினிது (௫)

The more man drinks, the more he ever drunk would be;
The more my love's revealed, the sweeter 'tis to me!

II.—She.

1146. கண்டது மன்னு மொருநா ளலர்மன்னுந்
திங்களைப் பாம்புகொண் டற்று (௬)

I saw him but one single day: rumour spreads soon
As darkness, when the dragon seizes on the moon.

1147. ஊரவர் கௌவை யெருவாக வன்னைசொன்
னீராக நீளுமிந் நோய் (௭)

My anguish grows apace: the town's report
Manures it; my mother's word doth water it.

1148. நெய்யா லெரிநுதுப்பே மென்றற்றாற்
கௌவையாற் காம நுதுப்பே மெனல் (௮)

With butter-oil extinguish fire! 'Twill prove
Harder by scandal to extinguish love.

1149. அலர்நாண வொல்வதோ வஞ்சலோம் பென்றார்
பலர்நாண நீத்தக் கடை (௯)

When he who said 'Fear not!' hath left me blamed,
While many shrink, can I from rumour hide ashamed?

1150. தாம்வேண்டி னல்குவர் காதலர்
யாம்வேண்டுங் கௌவை யெடுக்குமிவ் வூர் (௰)

If we desire, who loves will grant what we require;
This town sends forth the rumour we desire!

களவியன் முற்றிற்று.

END OF THE SECTION ON 'THE GANDHARVA MARRIAGE.'

§ 2. WEDDED LOVE. கற்பியல்.

CHAPTER CXVI. அதி. ககசு.

பிரிவாற்றாமை.—SEPARATION UNENDURABLE.

1151. செல்லாமை யுண்டே லெனக்குரை மற்றுநின்
வல்வரவு வாழ்வார்க் குரை (க)

If you will say, 'I leave thee not,' then tell me so;
Of quick return tell those that can survive this woe.

1152. இன்க ணுடைத்தவர் பார்வல் பிரிவஞ்சும்
புன்க ணுடைத்தாற் புணர்வு (உ)

It once was perfect joy to look upon his face;
But now the fear of parting saddens each embrace.

1153. அரிதரோ தேற்ற மறிவுடையார் கண்ணும்
பிரிவோ ரிடத்துண்மை யான் (ங)

To trust henceforth is hard, if ever he depart,
E'en he, who knows his promise and my breaking heart.

1154. அளித்தஞ்ச லென்றவர் நீப்பிற்
றெளித்தசொற் றேறியார்க் குண்டோ தவறு (ச)

If he depart, who fondly said, 'Fear not,' what blame 's incurred
By those who trusted to his reassuring word?

1155. ஓம்பி னமைந்தார் பிரிவோம்பன் மற்றவர்
நீங்கி னரிதாற் புணர்வு (ரு)

If you would guard my life, from going him restrain
Who fills my life! If he depart, hardly we meet again.

1156. பிரிவுரைக்கும் வன்கண்ண ராயி
னரிதவர் நல்குவ ரென்னு நசை (சு)

To cherish longing hope that he should ever gracious be,
Is hard, when he could stand, and of departure speak to me.

1157. துறைவன் றுறந்தமை தூற்றுகொன் முன்கை
யிறையிறவா நின்ற வளை (எ)

The bracelet slipping from my wrist announced before
Departure of the Prince that rules the ocean shore.

1158. இன்னா தினனிலூர் வாழ்த லதனினு
மின்னா தினியார்ப் பிரிவு (அ)

'Tis sad to sojourn in the town where no kind kinsmen dwell;
'Tis sadder still to bid a friend beloved farewell.

1159. தொடிற்சுடி னல்லது காமநோய் போல
விடிற்சுட லாற்றுமோ தீ (கூ)

Fire burns the hands that touch; but smart of love
Will burn in hearts that far away remove.

1160. அரிதாற்றி யல்லனோய் நீக்கிப்
பிரிவாற்றிப் பின்னிருந்து வாழ்வார் பலர் (௰)

Sorrow's sadness meek sustaining,
Driving sore distress away,
Separation uncomplaining
Many bear the livelong day!

CHAPTER CXVII. அதி. கக௭.

படர்மெலிந்திரங்கல்.—COMPLAININGS.

1161. மறைப்பேன்மன் யானிஃதோ நோயை
யிறைப்பவர்க் கூற்றுநீர் போல மிகும் (க)

I would my pain conceal, but see! it surging swells,
As streams to those that draw from ever-springing wells.

1162. கரத்தலு மாற்றே னிந்நோயை நோய்செய்தார்க்
குரைத்தலு நாணுத் தரும் (உ)

I cannot hide this pain of mine, yet shame restrains
When I would tell it out to him who caused my pains.

1163. காமமு நாணு முயிர்காவாத் தூங்குமென்
னோனா வுடம்பி னகத்து (ங)

My soul, like porter's pole, within my wearied frame,
Sustains a two-fold burthen poised, of love and shame.

1164. காமக் கடன்மன்னு முண்டே யதுநீந்து
மேமப் புணைமன்னு மில் (ச)

A sea of love, 'tis true, I see stretched out before,
But not the trusty bark that wafts to yonder shore.

1165. துப்பி னெவனாவர் மற்கொ லுயர்வரவு
நட்பினு ளாற்று பவர் (ரு)

Who work us woe in friendship's trustful hour,
What will they prove when angry tempests lower?

1166. இன்பங் கடன்மற்றுக் காம மஃதடுங்காற்
றுன்ப மதனிற் பெரிது (௬)

A happy love's a sea of joy; but mightier sorrows roll
From unpropitious love athwart the troubled soul.

1167. காமக் கடும்புன லீந்திக் கரைகாணேன்
யாமத்தும் யானே யுளேன் (௭)

I swim the cruel tide of love, and can no shore descry,
In watches of the night, too, 'mid the waters, only I!

1168. மன்னுயி ரெல்லாந் துயிற்றி யளித்திரா
வென்னல்ல தில்லை துணை (௮)

All living souls in slumber soft she steeps;
But me alone kind night for her companion keeps!

1169. கொடியார் கொடுமையிற் றாங்கொடிய விந்நா
ணெடிய கழியு மிரா (௯)

More cruel than the cruelty of him, the cruel one,
In these sad times are lengthening hours of night I watch alone.

1170. உள்ளம்போன் றுள்வழிச் செல்கிற்பின்
வெள்ளநீர் நீந்தல மன்னோவென் கண் (௰)

When eye of mine would as my soul go forth to him,
It knows not how through floods of its own tears to swim.

CHAPTER CXVIII. அதி. ௧௧௮.

கண்விதுப்பழிதல்.—Eyes consumed with Grief.

1171. கண்டாங் கலுழ்வ தெவன்கொலோ
தண்டாநோய் தாங்காட்ட யாங்கண் டது (௧)

They showed me him, and then my endless pain
I saw: why then should weeping eyes complain?

1172. தெரிந்துணரா நோக்கிய வுண்கண்
பரிந்துணராப் பைத லுழப்ப தெவன் (௨)

How glancing eyes, that rash unweeting looked that day,
With sorrow measureless are wasting now away!

1173. கதுமெனத் தாநோக்கித் தாமே கலுழு
மிதுநகத் தக்க துடைத்து (௩)

The eyes that threw such eager glances round erewhile
Are weeping now. Such folly surely claims a smile!

1174. பெயலாற்று நீருலந்த வுண்க
ணுயலாற்று வுய்வினோ யென்க ணிறுத்து (௪)
Those eyes have wept till all the fount of tears is dry,
That brought upon me pain that knows no remedy.

1175. படலாற்றுப் பைத லுழக்குங்
கடலாற்றுக் காமநோய் செய்தவென் கண் (௫)
The eye that wrought me more than sea could hold of woes,
Is suffering pangs that banish all repose.

1176. ஓஒ வினிதே யெமக்கிந்நோய் செய்தகண்
டாஅ மிதற்பட் டது (௬)
Oho! how sweet a thing to see! the eye
That wrought this pain, in the same gulf doth lie.

1177. உழந்துழந் துண்ணீ ரறுக
விழைந்திழைந்து வேண்டி யவர்க்கண்ட கண் (௭)
Aching, aching, let those exhaust their stream,
That melting, melting, that day gazed on him.

1178. பேணாது பெட்டா ருளர்மன்னோ மற்றவர்க்
காணா தமைவில கண் (௮)
Who loved me once, unloving now doth here remain;
Not seeing him, my eye no rest can gain.

1179. வாராக்காற் றுஞ்சா வரிற்றுஞ்சா வாயிடை
யாரஞ ருற்றன கண் (௯)
When he comes not, all slumber flies; no sleep when he is there;
Thus every way my eyes have troubles hard to bear.

1180. மறைபெற லூரார்க் கரிதன்றா லெம்போ
லறைபறை கண்ணா ரகத்து (௰)
It is not hard for all the town the knowledge to obtain,
When eyes, as mine, like beaten tambours, make the mystery plain.

CHAPTER CXIX. அதி. ௱௰௯.

பசப்புறுபருவரல்.—The Pallid Hue.

1181. நயந்தவர்க்கு நல்காமை நேர்ந்தேன்
பசந்தவென் பண்பியார்க் குரைக்கோ பிற (௧)
I willed my lover absent should remain;
Of pining's sickly hue to whom shall I complain?

1182. அவர்தந்தா ரென்னுந் தகையா
லிவர்தந்தென் மேனிமே லூரும் பசப்பு (௨)

'He gave': this sickly hue thus proudly speaks,
Then climbs, and all my frame its chariot makes.

1183. சாயலு நாணு மவர்கொண்டார் கைம்மாறா
நோயும் பசலையுந் தந்து (௩)

Of comeliness and shame he me bereft,
While pain and sickly hue, in recompense, he left.

1184. உள்ளுவன் மன்யா னுரைப்ப தவர்திறமாற்
கள்ளம் பிறவோ பசப்பு (௪)

I meditate his words, his worth is theme of all I say,
This sickly hue is false that would my trust betray.

1185. உவக்காணெங் காதலர் செல்வா
ரிவக்காணென் மேனி பசப்பூர் வது (௫)

My lover there went forth to roam;
This pallor of my frame usurps his place at home.

1186. விளக்கற்றம் பார்க்கு மிருளேபோற் கொண்கன்
முயக்கற்றம் பார்க்கும் பசப்பு (௬)

As darkness waits till lamp expires, to fill the place,
This pallor waits till I enjoy no more my lord's embrace.

1187. புல்லிக் கிடந்தேன் புடைபெயர்ந்தே னவ்வளவி
லள்ளிக்கொள் வற்றே பசப்பு (௭)

I lay in his embrace, I turned unwittingly;
Forthwith this hue, as you might grasp it, came on me.

1188. பசந்தா ளிவளென்ப தல்லா லிவளைத்
துறந்தா ரவரென்பா ரில் (௮)

On me, because I pine, they cast a slur;
But no one says, 'He first deserted her.'

1189. பசக்கமற் பட்டாங்கென் மேனி
நயப்பித்தார் நன்னிலைய ராவ ரெனின் (௯)

Well! let my frame, as now, be sicklied o'er with pain,
If he who won my heart's consent, in good estate remain!

1190. பசப்பெனப் பேர்பெறுத னன்றே
நயப்பித்தார் நல்காமை தூற்றா ரெனின் (௰)

'Tis well, though men deride me for my sickly hue of pain;
If they from calling him unkind, who won my love, refrain.

CHAPTER CXX. அதி. ௧௨௧.

தனிப்படர்மிகுதி.—The Solitary Anguish.

1191. தாம்வீழ்வார் தம்வீழப் பெற்றவர் பெற்றாரே
காமத்துக் காழில் கனி (௧)

The bliss to be beloved by those they love who gains,
Of love the stoneless, luscious fruit obtains.

1192. வாழ்வார்க்கு வானம் பயந்தற்றால்
வீழ்வார்க்கு வீழ்வா ரளிக்கு மளி (௨)

As heaven on living men showers blessings from above,
Is tender grace by lovers shown to those they love.

1193. வீழுநர் வீழப் படுவார்க் கமையுமே
வாழுந மென்னுஞ் செருக்கு (௩)

Who love and are beloved, to them alone
Belongs the boast, 'We 've made life's very joys our own.'

1194. வீழப் படுவார் கெழீஇயலர் தாம்வீழ்வார்
வீழப் படாஅ ரெனின் (௪)

Those well-beloved will luckless prove,
Unless beloved by those they love.

1195. நாங்காதல் கொண்டார் நமக்கெவன் செய்பவோ
தாங்காதல் கொள்ளாக் கடை (௫)

From him I love to me what gain can be,
Unless, as I love him, he loveth me?

1196. ஒருதலையா னின்னாது காமங்காப் போல
விருதலை யானு மினிது (௬)

Love on one side is bad; like balanced load
By porter borne, love on both sides is good.

1197. பருவரலும் பைதலுங் காணான்கொல் காம
னொருவர்க ணின்றொழுகு வான் (௭)

While Kâman rushes straight at me alone,
Is all my pain and wasting grief unknown?

1198. வீழ்வாரி னின்சொற் பெறாஅ துலகத்து
வாழ்வாரின் வன்கணா ரில் (௮)

Who hear from lover's lips no pleasant word from day to day,
Yet in the world live out their life,—no braver souls than they!

1199. நசைஇயார் நல்கா ரெனினு மவர்மாட்
டிசையு மினிய செவிக்கு (௯)

Though he my heart desires no grace accords to me,
Yet every accent of his voice is melody.

1200. உறாஅர்க் குறுநோ யுரைப்பாய் கடலைச்
செறாஅஅய் வாழிய நெஞ்சு (௰)

Tell him thy pain that loves not thee?
Farewell, my soul, fill up the sea!

CHAPTER CXXI. அதி. ௧௨௧.

நினைந்தவர்புலம்பல்.—Sad Memories.

I.—He.

1201. உள்ளினுந் தீராப் பெருமகிழ் செய்தலாற்
கள்ளினுங் காம மினிது (௧)

From thought of her unfailing gladness springs,
Sweeter than palm-tree wine the joy love brings.

1202. எனைத்தொன் றினிதேகாண் காமந்தான் வீழ்வார்
நினைப்ப வருவதொன் றில் (௨)

How great is love! Behold its sweetness past belief!
Think on the lover, and the spirit knows no grief.

II.—She.

1203. நினைப்பவர் போன்று நினையார்கொ றும்மல்
சினைப்பது போன்று கெடும் (௩)

A fit of sneezing threatened, but it passed away:
He seemed to think of me, but do his fancies stray?

1204. யாமு முளேங்கொ லவர்நெஞ்சத் தெந்நெஞ்சத்
தோஒ வுளரே யவர் (௪)

Have I a place within his heart?
From mine, alas! he never doth depart.

1205. தந்நெஞ்சத் தெம்மைக் கடிகொண்டார் நாணார்கொ
லெந்நெஞ்சத் தோவா வரல் (௫)

Me from his heart he jealously excludes:
Hath he no shame who ceaseless on my heart intrudes?

1206. மற்றியா னென்னுளேன் மன்னோ வவரொடியா
னுற்றநா ளுள்ள வுளேன் (௬)

How live I yet? I live to ponder o'er
The days of bliss with him that are no more.

1207. மறப்பி னெவனாவன் மற்கொல்
மறப்பறியே னுள்ளினு முள்ளஞ் சுடும் (௭)

If I remembered not, what were I then? And yet,
The fiery smart of what my spirit knows not to forget!

1208. எனைத்து நினைப்பினுங் காயா
ரனைத்தன்றோ காதலர் செய்யுஞ் சிறப்பு (௮)

My frequent thought no wrath excites. Is it not so?
This honour doth my love on me bestow.

1209. விளியுமெ னின்னுயிர் வேறல்ல மென்பா
ரளியின்மை யாற்ற நினைந்து (௯)

Dear life departs, when his ungracious deeds I ponder o'er,
Who said erewhile, 'We 're one for evermore.'

1210. விடாஅது சென்றாரைக் கண்ணினாற் காணப்
படாஅதி வாழி மதி (௰)

Set not, so may'st thou prosper, moon! that eyes may see
My love who went away, but ever bides with me.

CHAPTER CXXII. அதி. ௧௨௨.

கனவுநிலையுரைத்தல்.—The Visions of the Night.

1211. காதலர் தூதொடு வந்த கனவினுக்
கியாதுசெய் வேன்கொல் விருந்து (௧)

It came and brought to me, that nightly vision rare,
A message from my love,—what feast shall I prepare?

1212. கயலுண்கண் யானிரப்பத் துஞ்சிற் கலந்தார்க்
குயலுண்மை சாற்றுவேன் மன் (௨)

If my dark, carp-like eye will close in sleep, as I implore,
The tale of my long-suffering life I'll tell my loved one o'er.

1213. நனவினா னல்கா தவரைக்
கனவினாற் காண்டலி னுண்டென் னுயிர் (௩)

Him, who in waking hour no kindness shows,
In dreams I see: and so my lifetime goes!

1214. கனவினா னுண்டாகுங் காமம்
நனவினா னல்காரை நாடித் தரற்கு (௪)

Some pleasure I enjoy when him who loves not me
In waking hours, the vision searches out and makes me see.

1215. நனவினாற் கண்டதூஉ மாங்கே
கனவுந்தான் கண்ட பொழுதே யினிது (௫)

As what I then beheld in waking hour was sweet,
So pleasant dreams in hour of sleep my spirit greet.

1216. நனவென வொன்றில்லை யாயிற்
கனவினாற் காதலர் நீங்கலர் மன் (௬)

And if there were no waking hour, my love
In dreams would never from my side remove.

1217. நனவினா னல்காக் கொடியார்
கனவினா னென்னெம்மைப் பீழிப் பது (௭)

The cruel one, in waking hour, who all ungracious seems,
Why should he thus torment my soul in nightly dreams?

1218. துஞ்சுங்காற் றோண்மேல ராகி விழிக்குங்கா
னெஞ்சத்த ராவர் விரைந்து (௮)

And when I sleep he holds my form embraced;
And when I wake to fill my heart makes haste!

1219. நனவினா னல்காரை நோவர்
கனவினாற் காதலர்க் காணா தவர் (௯)

In dreams who ne'er their lover's form perceive,
For those in waking hours who show no love will grieve.

1220. நனவினா னந்நீத்தா ரென்பர்
கனவினாற் காணார்கொ லிவ்வூ ரவர் (௰)

They say, that he in waking hours has left me lone;
In dreams they surely see him not,—these people of the town!

CHAPTER CXXIII. அதி. ௧௨௩.

பொழுதுகண்டிரங்கல்.—LAMENTATIONS AT EVENTIDE.

1221. மாலையோ வல்லை மணந்தா ருயிருண்ணும்
வேலைநீ வாழி பொழுது (௧)

Thou art not evening, but a spear that doth devour
The souls of brides: farewell, thou evening hour!

1222. புன்கண்ணை வாழி மருண்மாலை யெங்கேள்போல்
வன்கண்ண தோநின் றுணை (௨)

Thine eye is sad; Hail, doubtful hour of eventide!
Of cruel eye, as is my spouse, is too thy bride?

1223. பனியரும்பிப் பைதல்கொண் மாலை
துனியரும்பித் துன்பம் வளர வரும் (௩)

With buds of chilly dew wan evening's shade enclose;
My anguish buds apace, and all my sorrow grows.

1224. காதல ரில்வழி மாலை கொலைக்களத்
தேதிலர் போல வரும் (௪)

When absent is my love, the evening hour descends,
As when an alien host to field of battle wends.

1225. காலைக்குச் செய்தநன் றென்கொ லெவன்கொல்யான்
மாலைக்குச் செய்த பகை (௫)

O morn, how have I won thy grace? thou bring'st relief!
O eve, why art thou foe? thou dost renew my grief.

1226. மாலைநோய் செய்தன் மணந்தா ரகலாத
காலை யறிந்த திலேன் (௬)

The pangs that evening brings I never knew,
Till he, my wedded spouse, from me withdrew.

1227. காலை யரும்பிப் பகலெல்லாம் போதாகி
மாலை மலருமிந் நோய் (௭)

My grief at morn a bud, all day an opening flower,
Full-blown expands in evening hour.

1228. அழல்போலு மாலைக்குத் தூதாகி யாயன்
குழல்போலுங் கொல்லும் படை (௮)

The shepherd's pipe is like a murderous weapon, to my ear,
For it proclaims the hour of ev'ning's fiery anguish near.

1229. பதிமருண்டு பைத லுழக்கு
மதிமருண்டு மாலை படர்தரும் போழ்து (௯)

If evening's shades, that darken all my soul, extend;
From this afflicted town will sound of grief ascend.

1230. பொருண்மாலை யாளரை யுள்ளி
மருண்மாலை மாயுமென் மாயா வுயிர் (௰)

This darkening eve, my darkling soul must perish utterly;
Remembering him who seeks for wealth, but seeks not me.

CHAPTER CXXIV. அதி. கஉச.

உறுப்பு நலனழிதல்.—Wasting away.

I.—She.

1231. சிறுமை நமக்கொழியச் சேட்சென்றா ருள்ளி
நறுமலர் நாணின கண் (க)

Thine eyes grown dim are now ashamed the fragrant flow'rs to see,
Thinking on him, who wand'ring far, leaves us in misery.

1232. நயந்தவர் நல்காமை சொல்லுவ போலும்
பசந்து பனிவாருங் கண் (உ)

The eye, with sorrow wan, all wet with dew of tears,
As witness of the lover's lack of love appears.

1233. தணந்தமை சால வறிவிப்ப போலு
மணந்தநாள் வீங்கிய தோள் (ங)

These withered arms, desertion's pangs abundantly display,
That swelled with joy on that glad nuptial day.

1234. பணைநீங்கிப் பைந்தொடி சோருந்
துணைநீங்கித் தொல்கவின் வாடிய தோள் (ச)

When lover went, then faded all their wonted charms,
And armlets' golden round slips off from these poor wasted arms.

1235. கொடியார் கொடுமை யுரைக்குந்
தொடியொடு தொல்கவின் வாடிய தோள் (ரு)

These wasted arms, the bracelet with their wonted beauty gone,
The cruelty declare of that most cruel one.

1236. தொடியொடு தோணெகிழ நோவ லவரைக்
கொடியரெனக் கூற னொந்து (சா)

I grieve, 'tis pain to me to hear him cruel chid,
Because the armlet from my wasted arm has slid.

1237. பாடு பெறுதியோ நெஞ்சே கொடியார்க்கென்
வாடுதோட் பூச லுரைத்து (எ)

My heart! say ought of glory wilt thou gain,
If to that cruel one thou of thy wasted arms complain?

II.—He.

1238. முயங்கிய கைகளை யூக்கப்
பசந்தது பைந்தொடிப் பேதை நுதல் (அ)

One day the fervent pressure of embracing arms I checked,
Grew wan the forehead of the maid with golden armlet decked.

1239. முயக்கிடைத் தண்வளி போழப்
பசப்புற்ற பேதை பெருமழைக் கண் (௯)

As we embraced a breath of wind found entrance there;
The maid's large liquid eyes were dimmed with care.

1240. கண்ணின் பசப்போ பருவர லெய்தின்றே
யொண்ணுதல் செய்தது கண்டு (௰)

The dimness of her eye felt sorrow now,
Beholding what was done by that bright brow.

CHAPTER CXXV. அதி. ௧௨௫.

நெஞ்சொடு கிளத்தல்.—Soliloquy.

1241. நினைத்தொன்று சொல்லாயோ நெஞ்சே
யெனைத்தொன்று மெவ்வநோய் தீர்க்கு மருந்து (௧)

My heart, canst thou not thinking of some med'cine tell,
Not any one, to drive away this grief incurable?

1242. காத லவரில ராகநீ நோவது
பேதைமை வாழியென் னெஞ்சு (௨)

Since he loves not, thy smart
Is folly, fare thee well, my heart!

1243. இருந்துள்ளி யென்பரித னெஞ்சே
பரிந்துள்ளல் பைதனோய் செய்தார்க ணில் (௩)

What comes of sitting here in pining thought, O heart? He knows
No pitying thought, the cause of all these wasting woes.

1244. கண்ணுங் கொளச்சேறி நெஞ்சே யிவையென்னைத்
தின்னு மவர்க்காண லுற்று (௪)

O rid me of these eyes, my heart; for they,
Longing to see him, wear my life away.

1245. செற்றா ரெனக்கை விடலுண்டோ நெஞ்சே யா
முற்றா லுறாஅ தவர் (௫)

O heart, as a foe, can I abandon utterly
Him who, though I long for him, longs not for me?

1246. கலந்துணர்த்துங் காதலர்க் கண்டாற்
புலந்துணராய் பொய்க்காய்வு காய்திஎன் னெஞ்சு (௬)

My heart, false is the fire that burns; thou canst not wrath maintain,
If thou thy love behold, embracing, soothing all thy pain.

1247. காமம் விடுவொன்றோ நாண்விடு நன்னெஞ்சே
யானோ பொறேனிவ் விரண்டு (௭)

Or bid thy love, or bid thy shame depart;
For me, I cannot bear them both, my worthy heart!

1248. பரிந்தவர் நல்காரென் றேங்கிப்
பிரிந்தவர் பின்செல்வாய் பேதையென் னெஞ்சு (௮)

Thou art befooled, my heart, thou followest him who flees from thee;
And still thou yearning criest: 'He will nor pity show nor love to me.'

1249. உள்ளத்தார் காத லவராக
வுள்ளிநீ யாருழைச் சேறியென் னெஞ்சு (௯)

My heart! my lover lives within my mind;
Roaming, whom dost thou think to find?

1250. துன்னாத் துறந்தாரை நெஞ்சத் துடையேமா
வின்னு மிழத்துங் கவின் (௰)

If I should keep in mind the man who utterly renounces me,
My soul must suffer further loss of dignity.

CHAPTER CXXVI. அதி. ௧௨௬.

நிறையழிதல்.—Reserve overcome.

1251. காமக் கணிச்சி யுடைக்கு நிறையென்னு
நாணுத்தாழ் வீழ்த்த கதவு (௧)

The princess has long repressed her feelings. She resolves to implore his return, and says:

Of womanly reserve love's axe breaks through the door,
Barred by the bolt of shame before.

1252. காம மெனவொன்றோ கண்ணின்றென் னெஞ்சத்தை
யாமத்து மாளுந் தொழில் (௨)

What men call love is the one thing of merciless power;
It gives my soul no rest, e'en in the midnight hour.

1253. மறைப்பேன்மற் காமத்தை யானோ
குறிப்பின்றித் தும்மல்போற் றோன்றி விடும் (௩)

I would my love conceal, but like a sneeze
It shows itself, and gives no warning sign.

1254. நிறையுடையே னென்பேன்மன் யானோவென் காம
மறையிறந்து மன்று படும் (௪)

In womanly reserve I deemed myself beyond assail;
But love will come abroad, and casts away the veil.

1255. செற்றார்பின் செல்லாப் பெருந்தகைமை காமநோ
யுற்றா ரறிவதொன் றன்று (௫)

The dignity that seeks not him who acts as foe,
Is the one thing that loving heart can never know.

1256. செற்றவர் பின்சேறல் வேண்டி யளித்தரோ
வெற்றென்னை யுற்ற துயர் (௬)

My grief how full of grace, I pray you see!
It seeks to follow him that hateth me.

1257. நாணென வொன்றோ வறியலங் காமத்தாற்
பேணியார் பெட்ப செயின் (௭)

No sense of shame my gladdened mind shall prove,
When he returns my longing heart to bless with love.

1258. பன்மாயக் கள்வன் பணிமொழி
யன்றோநம் பெண்மை யுடைக்கும் படை (௮)

The words of that deceiver, versed in every wily art,
Are instruments that break through every guard of woman's heart!

1259. புலப்ப லெனச்சென்றேன் புல்லினே னெஞ்சங்
கலத்த லுறுவது கண்டு (௯)

'I'll shun his greeting'; saying thus with pride away I went:
I held him in my arms, for straight I felt my heart relent.

1260. நிணந்தீயி லிட்டன்ன நெஞ்சினார்க் குண்டோ
புணர்ந்தூடி நிற்பே மெனல் (௰)

'We'll stand aloof and then embrace': is this for them to say,
Whose hearts are as the fat that in the blaze dissolves away?

CHAPTER CXXVII. அதி. ௧௨௭.

அவர்வயின்விதும்பல்.—Mutual Desire.

I.—She.

1261. வாளற்றுப் புற்கென்ற கண்ணு மவர்சென்ற
நாளொற்றித் தேய்ந்த விரல் (௧)

My eyes have lost their brightness, sight is dimmed, my fingers worn,
With noting on the wall the days since I was left forlorn.

1262. இலங்கிழா யின்று மறப்பினென் றோண்மேற்
கலங்கழியுங் காரிகை நீத்து (௨)

O thou with gleaming jewels decked, could I forget for this one day,
Henceforth these bracelets from my arms will slip, my beauty worn away.

1263. உரனசைஇ யுள்ளந் துணையாகச் சென்றார்
வரனசைஇ யின்னு முளேன் (௩)

On victory intent,
His mind sole company he went;
And I yet life sustain,
And long to see his face again!

1264. கூடிய காமம் பிரிந்தார் வரவுள்ளிக்
கோடுகொ டேறுமென் னெஞ்சு (௪)

'He comes again, who left my side, and I shall taste love's joy,'—
My heart with rapture swells, when thoughts like these my mind employ.

1265. காண்கமற் கொண்கனைக் கண்ணாரக் கண்டபி
னீங்குமென் மென்றோட் பசப்பு (௫)

O let me see my spouse again and sate these longing eyes!
That instant from my wasted frame all pallor flies.

1266. வருகமற் கொண்க னொருநாட்
பருகுவன் பைதனோ யெல்லாங் கெட (௬)

O let my spouse but come again to me one day!
I 'll drink that nectar: wasting grief shall flee away.

1267. புலப்பேன்கொல் புல்லுவேன் கொல்லோ
கலப்பேன்கொல் கண்ணன்ன கேளிர் வரின் (௭)

Shall I draw back, or yield myself, or shall both mingled be,
When he returns, my spouse, dear as these eyes to me.

II.—He.

1268. வினைகலந்து வென்றீக வேந்தன்
மனைகலந்து மாலை யயர்கம் விருந்து (௮)

O would my king would fight, o'ercome, divide the spoil;
At home, to-night, the banquet spread should crown the toil.

1269. ஒருநா ளெழுநாள்போற் செல்லுஞ்சேட் சென்றார்
வருநாள்வைத் தேங்கு பவர்க்கு (௯)

One day will seem like seven, to those who watch and yearn
For that glad day when wanderers from afar return.

1270. பெறினென்னாம் பெற்றக்கா லென்னா
முறினென்னா முள்ள முடைந்துக்கக் கால் (௰)

What 's my return, the meeting hour, the wished-for greeting worth,
If she heart-broken lie, with all her life poured forth?

CHAPTER CXXVIII. அதி. கஉ௮.

குறிப்பறிவுறுத்தல்.—THE READING OF THE SIGNS.

1271. கரப்பினுங் கையிகந் தொல்லாநின் னுண்க
ணுரைக்க லுறுவதொன் றுண்டு (க)

She cannot hide her dread of his departure.
He *reads the sign*, and says:

Thou hid'st it, yet thine eye, disdaining all restraint,
Something, I know not what, would utter of complaint.

1272. கண்ணிறைந்த காரிகைக் காம்பேர்தோட் பேதைக்குப்
பெண்ணிறைந்த நீர்மை பெரிது (உ)

The simple one whose beauty fills mine eye, whose shoulders curve
Like *bambū* stem, hath all a woman's modest sweet reserve.

1273. மணியிற் றிகழ்தரு நூல்போன் மடந்தை
யணியிற் றிகழ்வதொன் றுண்டு (௩)

As through the crystal beads is seen the thread on which they 're strung,
So in her beauty gleams some thought that cannot find a tongue.

1274. முகைமொக்கு ளுள்ளது நாற்றம்போற் பேதை
நகைமொக்கு ளுள்ளதொன் றுண்டு (௪)

As fragrance in the opening bud, some secret lies
Concealed in budding smile of this dear damsel's eyes.

1275. செறிதொடி செய்திறந்த கள்ள
முறுதுயர் தீர்க்கு மருந்தொன் றுடைத்து (௫)

The secret wiles of her with thronging armlets decked,
Are medicines by which my rising grief is checked.

1276. பெரிதாற்றிப் பெட்பக் கலத்த
லரிதாற்றி யன்பின்மை சூழ்வ துடைத்து (௬)

He cannot hide the sadness he feels as he departs.
She *reads the sign*, and says:

While lovingly embracing me, his heart is only grieved:
It makes me think that I again shall live of love bereaved.

1277. தண்ணந் துறைவன் றணந்தமை நம்மினு
முன்ன முணர்ந்த வளை (௭)

My severance from the lord of this cool shore,
My very armlets told me long before.

1278. நெருநற்றுச் சென்றாரெங் காதலர் யாமு
மெழுநாளே மேனி பசந்து (௮)

My loved one left me, was it yesterday?
Days seven my pallid body wastes away!

1279. தொடிநோக்கி மென்றோளு நோக்கி
யடிநோக்கி யஃதாண் டவள்செய் தது (௯)

She would join him, but shrinks from proposing it.
Her companion *reads the sign*, and says:

She viewed her tender arms, she viewed the armlets from them slid;
She viewed her feet: all this the lady did.

1280. பெண்ணினாற் பெண்மை யுடைத்தென்ப
கண்ணினாற் காமநோய் சொல்லி யிரவு (௰)

He is overcome.

To show by eye the pain of love, and for relief to pray,
Is womanhood's most womanly device, men say.

CHAPTER CXXIX. அதி. ௧௨௯.

புணர்ச்சிவிதும்பல்.—Desire for Reunion.

1281. உள்ளக் களித்தலுங் காண மகிழ்தலுங்
கள்ளுக்கில் காமத்திற் குண்டு (௧)

She answers the question—Why are you not angry with him who, unmindful of you, is preparing for departure:

Gladness at the thought, rejoicing at the sight,
Not palm-tree wine, but love, yields such delight.

1282. தினைத்துணையு மூடாமை வேண்டும்
பனைத்துணையுங் காம நிறைய வரின் (௨)

When as palmyra tall, fulness of perfect love we gain,
Distrust can find no place small as the millet grain.

1283. பேணாது பெட்பவே செய்யினுங் கொண்கனைக்
காணா தமையல கண் (௩)

Although, his will his only law, he lightly value me,
My heart knows no repose unless my lord I see.

1284. ஊடற்கட் சென்றேன்மற் றோழி யதுமறந்து
கூடற்கட் சென்றதென் னெஞ்சு (௪)

My friend, I went prepared to show a cool disdain;
My heart, forgetting all, could not its love restrain.

1285. எழுதுங்காற் கோல்காணாக் கண்ணேபோற் கொண்கன்
பழிகாணேன் கண்ட விடத்து (௫)

The eye sees not the rod that paints it; nor can I
See any fault, when I behold my husband nigh.

1286. காணுங்காற் காணேன் றவறாய
காணாக்காற் காணேன் றவறல் லவை (சு)

When him I see, to all his faults I'm blind;
But when I see him not, nothing but faults I find.

1287. உய்த்த லறிந்து புனல்பாய் பவரேபோற்
பொய்த்த லறிந்தேன் புலந்து (எ)

As those of rescue sure, who plunge into the stream,
So did I anger feign, though it must falsehood seem?

1288. இளித்தக்க வின்னா செயினுங்
களித்தார்க்குக் கள்ளற்றே கள்வநின் மார்பு (அ)

Though shameful ill it works, dear is the palm-tree wine
To drunkards; traitor, so to me that breast of thine!

1289. மலரினு மெல்லிது காமஞ்
சிலரதன் செவ்வி தலைப்படு வார் (கூ)

He muses:

Love is tender as an opening flower. In season due
To gain its perfect bliss is rapture known to few.

1290. கண்ணிற் றுனித்தே கலங்கினாள் புல்லுத
லென்னினுந் தான்விதுப் புற்று (ம)

Her eye, as I drew nigh one day, with anger shone;
By love o'erpowered, her tenderness surpassed my own.

[Comp. 1284.]

CHAPTER CXXX. அதி. க௱௩௰.

நெஞ்சொடுபுலத்தல்.—Expostulation with Oneself.

1291. அவர்நெஞ் சவர்க்காதல் கண்டு
மெவனெஞ்சே நீயெமக் காகா தது (க)

You see his heart is his alone:
O heart, why not be all my own?

1292. உறாஅ தவர்க்கண்ட கண்ணு மவரைச்
செறாஅரெனச் சேறியென் னெஞ்சு (உ)

'Tis plain, my heart, that he 's estranged from thee;
Why go to him as though he were not enemy?

1293. கெட்டார்க்கு நட்டாரில் லென்பதோ நெஞ்சேநீ
பெட்டாங் கவர்பின் செலல் (௩)

'The ruined have no friends,' they say; and so, my heart,
To follow him, at thy desire, from me thou dost depart.

1294. இனியன்ன நின்னோடு சூழ்வார்யார் நெஞ்சே
துனிசெய்து துவ்வாய்காண் மற்று (௪)

'See, thou first show offended pride, and then submit,' I bade;
Henceforth such council who will share with thee, my heart?

1295. பெறாஅமை யஞ்சும் பெறிற்பிரி வஞ்சு
மறாஅ விடும்பைத் தென் னெஞ்சு (௫)

I fear I shall not gain, I fear to lose him when I gain;
And thus my heart endures unceasing pain.

1296. தனியே யிருந்து நினைத்தக்கா லென்னைத்
தினிய விருந்ததென் னெஞ்சு (௬)

My heart consumes me when I ponder lone,
And all my lover's cruelty bemoan.

1297. நாணு மறந்தே னவர்மறக் கல்லாவென்
மாணு மடநெஞ்சிற் பட்டு (௭)

Fall'n neath the sway of this ignoble foolish heart,
Which will not him forget, I have forgotten shame.

1298. எள்ளி னிளிவா மென்றெண்ணி யவர்திற
முள்ளு முயிர்க்காத னெஞ்சு (௮)

If I contemn him, then disgrace awaits me evermore;
My soul that seeks to live his virtues numbers o'er.

1299. துன்பத்திற் கியாரே துணையாவார் தாமுடைய
நெஞ்சந் துணையல் வழி (௯)

And who will aid me in my hour of grief,
If my own heart comes not to my relief?

1300. தஞ்சந் தமரல்ல ரேதிலார் தாமுடைய
நெஞ்சந் தமரல் வழி (௰)

A trifle is unfriendliness by aliens shown,
When our own heart itself is not our own!

CHAPTER CXXXI. அதி. ககூக.

புலவி.—POUTING.

1301. புல்லா திராஅப் புலத்தை யவருறு
மல்லனோய் காண்கஞ் சிறிது (க)

Be still reserved, decline his proferred love;
A little while his sore distress we'll prove.

1302. உப்பமைந் தற்றாற் புலவி யதுசிறிது
மிக்கற்றா னீள விடல் (உ)

A cool reserve is like the salt that seasons well the mess,
Too long maintained, 'tis like the salt's excess.

1303. அலந்தாரை யல்லனோய் செய்தற்றாற் றம்மைப்
புலந்தாரைப் புல்லா விடல் (ஙூ)

'Tis heaping griefs on those whose hearts are grieved;
To leave the grieving one without a fond embrace.

1304. ஊடி யவரை யுணர்த்தாமை
வாடிய வள்ளி முதலரிந் தற்று (ச)

To use no kind conciliating art when lover grieves,
Is cutting out the root of tender winding plant that droops.

1305. நலத்தகை நல்லவர்க் கேஎர்
புலத்தகை பூவன்ன கண்ணா ரகத்து (ரு)

Even to men of good and worthy mind, the petulance
Of wives with flowery eyes lacks not a lovely grace.

1306. துனியும் புலவியு மில்லாயிற் காமங்
கனியுங் கருக்காயு மற்று (சா)

Love without hatred is as ripened fruit;
Without some lesser strife, fruit immature.

1307. ஊடலி னுண்டாங்கோர் துன்பம் புணர்வது
நீடுவ தன்றுகொ லென்று (எ)

A lovers' quarrel brings its pain, when mind afraid
Asks doubtful, 'Will reunion sweet be long delayed?'

1308. நோத லெவன்மற்று நொந்தாரென் றஃதறியுங்
காதல ரில்லா வழி (அ)

What good can grieving do, when none who love
Are there to know the grief thy soul endures?

1309. நீரு நிழல தினிதே புலவியும்
வீழுநர் கண்ணே யினிது (௯)

Water is pleasant in the cooling shade ;
So coolness for a time with those we love.

1310. ஊட லுணங்க விடுவாரோ டென்னெஞ்சங்
கூடுவே மென்ப தவா (௰)

Of her who leaves me thus in variance languishing,
To think within my heart with love is fond desire.

CHAPTER CXXXII. அதி. கஙஉ.

புலவிநுணுக்கம்.—Feigned Anger.

I.—She.

1311. பெண்ணியலா ரெல்லாருங் கண்ணிற் பொதுவுண்பர்
நண்ணேன் பரத்தநின் மார்பு (க)

From thy regard all womankind
Enjoys an equal grace ;
O thou of wandering fickle mind,
I shrink from thine embrace !

1312. ஊடி யிருந்தேமாத் தும்மினர் யாந்தம்மை
நீடுவாழ் கென்பாக் கறிந்து (உ)

One day we silent sulked ; he sneezed :
The reason well I knew ;
He thought that I, to speak well pleased,
Would say, 'Long life to you !'

II.—He.

1313. கோட்டுப்பூச் சூடினுங் காயு மொருத்தியைக்
காட்டிய சூடினீ ரென்று (ங)

I wreathed with flowers one day my brow,
The angry tempest lowers ;
She cries, 'Pray, for what woman now
Do you put on your flowers ?

1314. யாரினுங் காதலமென் றேனா வூடினாள்
யாரினும் யாரினு மென்று (ச)

'I love you more than all beside,'
'Twas thus I gently spoke ;
'What *all*, what *all* ?' she instant cried,
And all her anger woke.

1315. இம்மைப் பிறப்பிற் பிரியல னென்றேனாக்
கண்ணிறை நீர்கொண் டனள் (ரு)

‘While *here* I live, I leave you not,’
I said to calm her fears.
She cried, ‘*There*, then, I read your thought’;
And straight dissolved in tears.

1316. உள்ளினே னென்றேன்மற் றென்மறந்தீ ரென்றென்னைப்
புல்லாள் புலத்தக் கனள் (சு)

‘Each day I called to mind your charms.’
‘O, then, you had forgot,’
She cried, and then her opened arms,
Forthwith embraced me not.

1317. வழுத்தினா டும்மினே னாகவழித்
தழுதாள் யாருள்ளித் தும்மினீ ரென்று (எ)

She hailed me when I sneezed one day;
But straight with anger seized,
She cried, ‘Who was the woman, pray,
Thinking of whom you sneezed?’

1318. தும்முச் செறுப்ப வழுதா ணுமருள்ள
லெம்மை மறைத்திரோ வென்று (அ)

And so next time I checked my sneeze;
She forthwith wept and cried,
(That woman difficult to please,)
‘Your thoughts from me you hide.’

1319. தன்னை யுணர்த்தினுங் காயும் பிறர்க்குநீ
ரிந்நீர ராகுதி ரென்று (கூ)

I then began to soothe and coax,
To calm her jealous mind;
‘I see,’ quoth she, ‘to other folks
How you are wondrous kind.’

1320. நினைத்திருந்து நோக்கினுங் காயு
மனைத்துநீர் யாருள்ளி நோக்கினீ ரென்று (ய)

I silent sat, but thought the more,
And gazed on her. Then she
Cried out, ‘While thus you eye me o'er,
Tell me whose form you see.’

CHAPTER CXXXIII. அதி. ௧௩௩.

ஊடலுவகை.—The Pleasures of 'Temporary Variance.'

I.—She, in answer to the question, Why do you pout?

1321. இல்லை தவறவர்க் காயினு மூடுதல்
வல்ல தவரளிக்கு மாறு (௧)

Although there be no fault in him, the sweetness of his love
Hath power in me a fretful jealousy to move.

1322. ஊடலிற் றோன்றுஞ் சிறுதுனி நல்லளி
வாடினும் பாடு பெறும் (௨)

My 'anger feigned' gives but a little pain;
And when affection droops, it makes it bloom again.

1323. புலத்தலிற் புத்தேணா டுண்டோ
நிலத்தொடு நீரியைந் தன்னா ரகத்து (௩)

Is there a bliss in any world more utterly divine,
Than 'coyness' gives, when hearts as earth and water join?

1324. புல்லி விடாஅப் புலவியுட் டோன்றுமென்
னுள்ள முடைக்கும் படை (௪)

Within the 'anger feigned,' that close love's tie doth bind,
A weapon lurks, which quite breaks down my mind.

II.—He consoles himself, since reconciliation makes amends.

1325. தவறில ராயினுந் தாம்வீழ்வார் மென்றோ
ளகறலி னாங்கொன் றுடைத்து (௫)

Though free from fault, from loved one's tender arms
To be estranged awhile hath its own special charms.

1326. உணலினு முண்ட தறலினிது காமம்
புணர்தலி னூட லினிது (௬)

'Tis sweeter to digest your food than 'tis to eat;
In love, than union's self is anger feigned more sweet.

1327. ஊடலிற் றோற்றவர் வென்றா ரதுமன்னுங்
கூடலிற் காணப் படும் (௭)

In lovers' quarrels, 'tis the one that first gives way,
That in re-union's joy is seen to win the day.

1328. ஊடிப் பெறுகுவங் கொல்லோ நுதல்வியர்ப்பக்
கூடலிற் றோன்றிய வுப்பு (௮)

And shall we ever more the sweetness know of that embrace
With dewy brow; to which 'feigned anger' lent its piquant grace.

1329. ஊடுக மன்னோ வொளியிழை யாமிரப்ப
நீடுக மன்னோ விரா (௯)

Let her, whose jewels brightly shine, aversion feign!
That I may still plead on, O night, prolong thy reign!

1330. ஊடுதல் காமத்திற் கின்ப மதற்கின்பங்
கூடி முயங்கப் பெறின் (௰)

A 'feigned aversion' coy to pleasure gives a zest;
The pleasure's crowned when breast is clasped to breast.

கற்பியன் முற்றும்.

THE END OF THE SECTION ON 'WEDDED LOVE.

காமத்துப்பான் முற்றும்.

THE END OF BOOK III. ON LOVE.

THE END OF THE KURRAL.

திருக்குறண் முற்றிற்று

NOTES.

CHAPTER I.

ALL Tamiḻ compositions must begin with an invocation. Here the invocation is a whole decade, and forms a main topic of the work—its creed.

The following is a summary of this chapter, according to the Commentary:—

I.—1. God is first in the world.

II.—2. The end of learning is the worship of the only Wise.

[This also satisfies the condition that an author should state in the beginning of a book the *benefit* to be gained by its study.]

III.—The benefits of true devotion:

3. The devout worshipper shaḻl enjoy prolonged felicity in some higher sphere;

4. He shall be delivered from all evil;

5. He shall escape from the results of action, good and bad;

6. He shall enjoy prolonged felicity in this world.

IV.—The evil results of ungodliness:

7. The undevout man has no relief from heart-sorrow;

8. He has no aid in the midst of the sea of evil;

9. His whole existence is null and void.

V.—The devout and undevout contrasted:

10. These shall escape from endless transmigrations: those shall not.

Verse 1. Comp. *Bhagavatgîtâ*, x. 33, *aksharâṇâm akaro'smi*: 'inter elementa sum littera A.' பகவன்=S. *bhagavân*, occurs in *Manu*, I. 6, with *swayambhu*, 'self-existent,' as its attribute. ஆதி implies this. The masc. term. brings out the Personality of the Deity, which கடவுள் does not.

Ellis translates:

'As ranked in every alphabet the first,
The self-same vowel stands, so in all worlds
Th' eternal God is chief.'

Beschi: 'Literae omnes principium habent literam A:
Mundus principium habet numen primordiale.'

Graul: 'A als Erstes haben alle Buchstaben;
Den Urseligen als Erstes hat die Welt.'

In the *Nannûl*, I. 73, 76, it is said that அ is first of letters by 'eminence and affinity'; and the explanation given is that it is 'mere sound, நாதமாத்திரையாய், and the first sound uttered by infants when they are born. It is produced by the mere opening of the mouth and expiration. All other vowels are modifications of it; it is the first cause of all others.' The Com. says that, from the visible world comes the knowledge of the invisible God, and this by intuition, not by any artificial means. He seems to interpret the latter clause thus: 'the idea of the Supreme is the first impression the world produces in the reflecting mind.'

2. 'The purely wise One.' This வாலு = S. *paramârthatas.* [Comp. Wilson's *Vishṇu Purâṇa*, bk. I. ch. ii. p. 8.] His knowledge is of the actual truth, not tinged by any medium of transmission, immediately His own.

Ellis: 'What is the fruit that human knowledge gives,
If at the feet of Him who is pure knowledge
Due reverence be not paid?'

Beschi: 'Plurima didicisse quid, amice, proderit, nisi verearis bonos ejus pedes, qui puram scientiam habet; *i.e.* sc. *ab omni errore defaecatum.*'

3. The Jain deity *Arugan* is represented as standing on a lotus flower. Perhaps the main idea here is the Omnipresence of the Deity (Psa. cxxxix.). It is a poet—a true poet—that speaks, and he seems to say: 'It is the foot-fall of God that makes His creation rejoice and put forth its flowers, as It rests on each "spirit's folded bloom."'

'Above the earth' may be 'on the earth'; the Tamiḻ admits of either. Beschi says: 'Qui adhaerent venerabilibus pedibus illius qui supra flores graditur in loco terrae superiori diu vivet; id est, qui veretur eum qui floribus venustatem tribuit in caelo aeternum beabitur.'

Graul interprets: 'Supra terram diu vivent (antequam novam suscipient migrationem).' Each has read something into the text. The most ancient Tamiḻ commentator says: 'Without decay in the world of relinquishment, above all worlds, he shall flourish.'

Ellis translates, or paraphrases and adapts, the whole couplet thus:—

> 'They who adore His sacred feet, whose grace
> Gladdens with sudden thrill the fervent heart,
> High o'er the earth shall soar to endless joy.'

There is an inconsistency in the Tamil poet's conception of the invisible world, much the same as that which meets us in Vergil's Sixth Æneid. The 'Pythagorean' philosophy of transmigration 'is a sublime one, and well adapted for poetry; but it is quite incompatible with the conception that pervades the rest of the description of the lower (upper) world.' See Conington's *Introduction.*

Nor must we expect consistency and firm treatment of such subjects in a 'seeker after truth'—a poet, too. The poet wanders 'in shadowy thoroughfares of thought,' and tells us of his visions as they appear. There is a mania for classification, as if human souls—and especially the souls of true poets, to whom God has given the 'vision and the faculty divine'—could all be arranged in *genus* and *species* like so many shells!

Our poet seizes upon each form and phrase that has anything of truth and beauty; but the life he breathes into it is his own: the harp may be the old one of 'ten strings'; the song is a 'new song.'

4. *Lit.* 'Sorrow never assails those who have drawn nigh to the foot of Him who is free from desire and aversion.'

He desires not, for there is no want to be supplied. He has no aversion, for nothing can enter the sphere of His Being that troubles.

If from his Christian friends the sage had obtained any knowledge of the life of Christ, we might imagine him referring to her who chose the 'better part' sitting at the Master's feet; and to that other (if indeed another) who would have touched His feet; and to the many who found help and healing there.

Ellis: 'To Him, whom no affection moves, nor hate,
Those constant in obedience, from all ill
In this world and the next are free.'

The Com. says: 'The sorrows of birth.' These are threefold: (1) from oneself; (2) from others; (3) from God.

Beschi: 'Qui adhaeserit pedibus illius in quo cupiditas et aversio locum non habent, perpetuo ab hujus mundi malis immunis erit.'

5. Ellis: 'Those who delight with fervent mind to praise
The true and only Lord of heav'n and earth,
No false ideas of right and wrong can cloud.'

Beschi: 'Mala opera cum bonis mixta qua inducit falsa rerum apprehensio, non adhaerebunt ei, qui cupiscit laudem cum vera Dei notione connexam; *i.e.* qui veram habet Dei notionem plurimas falsas idaeas corriget, ex quibus mala opera sequi solent.'

Every form of Hindû faith—orthodox and unorthodox—regards action as evil. The word *môksha*, and its equivalent Tamiḻ *viḍu*, and the specially Buddhist *nirvâṇa*, point to the same thing, though with characteristic differences.

We, too, regarding life as a probation, contemplating the coming judgment to be passed upon all actions, 'whether they be good, or whether they be evil,' feeling how we see all things, duties among the rest, as 'through a glass darkly,' and anticipating the time when we hope we shall see 'the King in His beauty, and behold the land of far-off places'—we, I say, can understand that the poet may have risen in thought above the mere technicalities of any of the systems, into the heart of which his poet's eye penetrated.

Two kinds of action, *good deeds* and *evil deeds.*

'*Darkness*,' for they are the results of *ignorance*: all action is blind.

True, since men define God and praise Him erroneously. The devout are 'those who desire the praise'—who with hearty desire offer praise—'which is connected with reality.' This may mean *true notions of God*, or 'a true and sincere mind.' It is the 'worship in spirit and in truth' of a greater Master.

6. Ellis: 'Those who pursue the path of His true law,
Who is of sensual organs void, in Heav'n
Shall dwell in never-ending bliss.'

Beschi: 'Qui non aberrat a recto et errori non obnoxio tramite, *i.e.* doctrinâ illius, qui caret quinque iis affectibus, qui quinque sensuum viâ in animum irrepere solent, aeternum beatus erit.'

The five organs of sense. Comp. 7.

The Jain deity Arugan, called *çinêndra*='Lord of wrath,' may be referred to. It may be 'who has extinguished them *in himself*' (see 25); or, 'who extinguishes them in others': 'whose grace extinguishes in *others* the fires of sensual passion.'

7. The phrase-epithet 'to whom none is like,' relates, as Ellis says (as do all others in this Chap.), to the ஆதிபகவன் of the first couplet: 'the Eternal, Adorable One, whom no symbol can express and no form design.'

Horace, *Odes*, Book I. xii. 18:

'Nec viget quidquam simile aut secundum.'

Comp. Aeschy. *Agam.* 163–66:

> Οὐκ ἔχω προσεικάσαι πάντ' ἐπισταθμώμενος
> Πλὴν Διὸς, εἰ τὸ μάταν ἀπὸ φροντίδος ἄχθος
> Χρὴ βαλεῖν ἐτητύμως.

Ellis: 'The anxious mind against corroding thought
No refuge hath, save at the sacred feet
Of Him to whom no refuge is.'

Beschi: 'Non adhaeseris pedibus illius, qui sibi similem non habet, difficile erit animi anxietatem sedare.'

Ellis says rightly *similem* should be *similitudinem.*

8. Ellis: 'Hard is the transit of this sea of vice,
Save by that Being's gracious aid, who is
Himself a sea of virtue.'

Beschi: 'Nisi adhaeseris pedibus illius, qui mare virtutum est, difficile erit aliud mare, quod extra illum est (nempe hoc miserum pelagus) trajicere.'

The word ஆழி *âṛi*, 'sea,' is also translated 'circle': 'ocean mirrours rounded large.' The idea may be here the 'whole round of existence.' Moore's poem is quite in the spirit of South Indian poetry:

> 'Poor wanderers of a stormy day
> From wave to wave we 're driven.'

Comp. Dante, *Paradiso*, I.:

> 'Per lo gran mar dell' essere.'

The periphrasis for God here is especially fine: அறவாழியந்தணன் '*arravâṛiyantaṇan*'=

> 'Virtue's sea, the fair and loving one.'

It seems to be a near approach to the Christian annonncement, 'God is Love'; and then 'drawing near to His feet' must mean a lowly love of Him.

Thus Tiruvaḷḷuvar founds his system on Love. In speaking of the householder, he insists (Ch. VIII.) on heartfelt affection as the very life of man. The ascetic, too, must have a benevolent love of all men (Ch. XXV.) as the foundation of all. The poet approaches the subject of man's duty in many ways:

> 'But love is the fountain of all.'

9. Ellis: 'Of virtue void, as is the palsied sense,
The head must be, that bows not at His feet,
Whose eight-fold attributes pervade the world.'

Beschi: 'Nullius est emolumentum caput non venerans Deum; non secus ac sensus suum objectum non percipiens. (Caput non venerans Deum, perinde est ut oculus caecus.)'

It is impossible to decide what 'eight qualities' or attributes the poet refers to. The Com. says: (1) self-existence; (2) essential purity; (3) intuitive wisdom; (4) infinite intelligence; (5) essential freedom from all bonds; (6) infinite grace; (7) omnipotence; (8) infinite enjoyment.

It is significant, as Ellis remarks, that every Hindû enumeration omits justice as one of the attributes of God.

It has not been noticed that eight 'qualities' of the Supreme have been in some way mentioned or referred to by the poet in the eight preceding couplets. I conclude that these may be the eight to which he now refers. They are: (1) eternity (at least *a parte ante*); (2) wisdom; (3) omnipresence; (4) happiness; (5) power (the King); (6) purity; (7) immateriality; (8) love.

10. Ellis: 'Of those who swim the wide extended sea
Of mortal birth, none ever can escape,
But those who to the feet of God adhere.'

Beschi: 'Hoc vastum miseriarum pelagus in quo nati sumus in illud natantes non trajicient, nisi qui Dei pedibus adhaeserint.'

Here we have the doctrine of the metempsychosis:

'Eternal process moving on,
From state to state the spirit walks.'

The end is absorption into the Divine Essence. This seems, here, at least, to be the poet's 'further bank,' to which he attains after swimming over the 'sea of birth.' Our English poet's instinct is truer:—

'That each, who seems a separate whole,
Should move his rounds, and fusing all
The skirts of self again, should fall
Remerging in the general soul,
Is faith as vague as all unsweet;
Eternal form shall still divide
The eternal soul from all beside;
And I shall know him when we meet.'

In Memoriam, XLXI.

The epithets applied to God in Ch. I. are various. These are:—

(i.) 'The eternal (first) adorable one'; ஆதி பகவன்.

(ii.) 'He who hath pure knowledge'; வால் அறிவன்.

(iii.) 'He who hath moved (as a breath of air) over the flower (of the expanded soul)'; மலர்மிசை ஏகினன்.

(iv.) 'He to whom is neither desire nor aversion' [qy. Lucretius: '*Deos secure agere aevom*']; வேண்டுதல் வேண்டாமை இலான்.

(v.) and (x.) 'The Lord'; இறைவன.

(vi.) 'He who has destroyed the gates of the five senses' [? 'without parts or passions']; பொறி வாயில் ஐந்தவித்தான்.

(vii.) 'He to whom no likeness is' ['*nec viget quidquam simile aut secundum*']; தனக்குவமை இல்லாதான்.

(viii.) 'The ocean of virtue, beautiful and gracious one'; அறவாழி அந்தணன்.

(ix.) 'He who possesses eight attributes.'

The eclectic poet has selected, I suppose, the choicest epithets existing in the language, and several which admit of being explained in various senses.

There is—and the poet intended this—ample room for men of many systems to import into these verses, under the guise of commentaries, their own dogmas. The ten great Tamiḻ commentators, belonging to as many systems, have done this with much ingenuity.

Ellis sees in them an enlightened and sublime monotheism. To Beschi they were exponents of the Christian theology; and, without doubt, Christian influences most affected him.

The Jains, delighted with his skilful appropriation of one or two beautiful terms from their writings, claim him as their own.

It may be allowable to say that we see in Tiruvaḷḷuvar a noble, truth-loving, and devout man, *feeling in the darkness after God, if haply he might find Him.*

The language in which alone the poet expresses the mental attitude of the true worshipper is worthy of all consideration. In 2–10 the same idea is expressed—that of drawing near to, or worshipping at, the foot of God, the idea being that of profoundest, most loving, clinging humility.

CHAPTER II.

It seems strange to European readers that the introductory chapter on God should be followed by one on Rain. This is very usual, however, in Tamiḻ compositions, the idea being (as the Com. says) that neither virtue, wealth, nor pleasure could exist without rain. The connection is seen in Acts xiv. 17: 'Nevertheless He left not Himself without a witness, in that He did good, *and gave us rain from heaven,* and fruitful seasons, filling our hearts with food and gladness.' In *Bhagavatgîtâ*, III. 14, it is said: 'All things which have life are produced from bread which they eat; bread is produced from rain; rain from divine worship, and divine worship from good works.' [Tam. trans. III. 9.]

The word *vân* or *viṇ* (which in Tamiḻ signifies 'sky,' 'rain') may be a corruption of *varuṇa*, 'the investing sky' in the old Aryan mythology.

11. Ellis: 'As by abundant rain the world subsists,
Life's sole elixir in this fluid know.'

Beschi: 'Cum pluvia indeficienter pluens faciat mundum subsistere, putandum est eam orbi esse vitale pharmacum. Mundi subsistantia est hominum vitae, quae sine pluviâ servari nequit.'

The idea of this couplet is an obvious one: 'rain gives life to all creation, revives the dying vegetation, restores life to what seems dead.' Anyone who has seen an Indian district suffering from drought, and noted the instantaneous change in the aspect of all living things when the long-expected rain has fallen, will understand the poet's feeling: 'rain is the elixir of immortality to the whole earth.' (See Ellis.)

12. 'It slakes men's thirst, and it causes food to spring from the earth.'

Beschi: 'Pluvia non modo pluit ut comedentibus varia alimenta subministret, sed etiam ut ipsa comedentibus alimentum est. Pluviam namque aquam bibimus.'

13. Ellis: 'When clouds, deceiving hope, withhold their stores,
Around the sea-girt earth gaunt famine stalks.'

Beschi: 'Si pluvia sistendo, spem fallat; fames in mundo sistens vexabit vastam hanc terram quam mare alluit.'

Lit. 'If the cloud standing (in the sky) deceive (by not falling in rain to the earth), hunger will afflict, standing in the midst of the wide-spread earth, though (this earth is) surrounded by an expanse of waters.'

The clouds charged with moisture stand over the hills, big with the promise of fertilizing showers. If they remain there, and do not fulfil their promise, the earth, though surrounded by vast oceans of water, must fall a prey to all the miseries of famine.

During the disastrous droughts in 1880, each day heavy clouds collected and hung over the Maisûr province; but strong winds from the west arose and bore them away in the direction of the sea, leaving the broad fields dry and parched, and abandoning multitudes to misery and death by famine. Those who have seen something like this can understand the force of this couplet.

In the *Nâlaḍi* (269) the poet thus applies the idea of this sad waste of rain:—

'While in th' unripened ear the golden grain is parched,
The heavens with lightnings gleaming pour their treasures forth
Upon the sea! When silly men gain ample wealth,
So are their liberal gifts bestowed!'

பொன்னிறச் செந்நெற் பொதியொடு பீள்வாட
மின்னொளிர் வானங் கடலுள்ளுங் கான்றுகுக்கும்;
வெண்மை யுடையார் விழுச்செல்வம் எய்தியக்கால்
வண்மையும் அன்ன தகைத்து

As in *As you like it*:

'Thou mak'st a testament,
As worldlings do, giving thy sum of more
To that which had too much.'

14. Agriculture is the great employment of the Tamiḻ people; it ceases when rains fail. Comp. Ch. CIV.

Ellis: 'The fruitful toil of men and steers must cease,
If cease the flow of waters from the clouds.'

Beschi: 'Neque agricolae bobus arabunt terram si minuatur subsidium aquae, quam dat pluvia.'

15. *Lit.* 'That which will ruin; that which will uplift, becoming a help to the ruined: all is rain.'
The destructive violence of tropical storms, and the life-giving effects of the first burst of the monsoons in India, are referred to here.

Ellis: 'It spreads destruction round; its genial aid
Again revives, restores all it destroys;
Such is the power of rain.'

Beschi: 'Miseros facere, et quos miseros fecit, iisdem favendo, iterum sublevare, id omne potest pluvia.'

16. Beschi: 'Nisi pluvia a nubibus ceciderit, tunc haud facile esset cernere viventis herbae colorem.'

17. Com.: 'Rain is necessary to the sea too, which itself is the source of the rain.'
Beschi: 'Et ipsum spatiosum mare suam conditionem minuet, si nubes illud minuendo illi aquam non dederint.'

18. 'Without rain no produce; without produce no worship.'
Beschi: Et ipsis Deis, *qui coelum exsiccant* in hac terrâ non persolventur festivae solennitates et sacrificia.'

19. Beschi: 'Non poterunt in hoc spatioso orbe morari eleemosina et poenitentia, si pluvia desit.'

20. Beschi: 'Sine pluviâ celsitudinem nequit quis obtinere, nec poterit quis qualiscunque ille sit (quantumvis celsus sit) absque pluviâ obtinere ejusdem conservationem; si pluvia desit, ob famam quae inde sequitur nec divitiae, nec deliciae, nec scientiae acquiri possunt, et si acquisitae fuerint, non possunt servari.'

The Com. thus analyses the chapter :—

I. 1–7. Rain is the cause of the affairs of the world going on their wonted way.

II. 8–10. Rain is the cause of the continued existence of *virtue, wealth,* and *pleasure* on earth.

CHAPTER III.

WITH this compare Ch. XXV.–XXXVII., where the whole subject of Asceticism is dealt with. It is evident that our author did not—at least, exclusively—contemplate in this chapter a Jain saint, as has been supposed. In Jain works this latter is (1) 'lord of the world.' (This might seem to be pointed to in couplet 5.) He is (2) 'free from bodily and ceremonial acts'; (3) 'omniscient'; (4) 'supreme lord'; (5) 'god of gods'; (6) 'one who has crossed over the world' (*tîrthan-kâra*); (7) 'possessor of a spiritual nature, free from investing sources of error'; (8) 'one entitled to the homage of gods and of men'; (9) 'victor over all human infirmities.' (See Wilson's *Hindû Sects*, p. 187.)

But a Jain saint could not have 'wrath,' as in couplet 9; nor is couplet 5 quite consistent with Jain doctrines, though the poet may refer to a current story, without accepting it. Nowhere is the eclecticism of Tiruvaḷḷuvar more conspicuous than in this chapter. Every system has its ascetics, and self-denial is everywhere mighty. There is much here which may be compared with the teaching of the Christian Scriptures, and we can fancy in the Tamiḻ verses an echo of such words as these: 'Yet have I set my king upon my holy hill'; 'Kiss the Son lest He be angry, and ye perish from the way, when His wrath is kindled but a little'; 'I have overcome the world'; 'This is the victory which overcometh the world, even your faith'; 'He that doeth the will of God abideth for ever.' Comp. also Rev. ii. 26, 27; vi. 17.

The poet's knowledge and experience would extend to the Christian establishments in Mayilâpûr, to the Buddhist works in the Vihâra Rath of Mahâmallaipura (Foulkes in *Ind. Ant.* vol. vii. p. 7); to Daṇḍis and Tridaṇḍis, Yôgis—probably to the Mâdhavâchâris—with their adaptations of Christian doctrines and institutions; and to the Jain monasteries. These had different institutions (*oṛukkam*) and reverenced different sacred books (*panuval*); while all appealing to a mysterious 'word' or scripture (*marrai-moṛi*). The worth and power of the whole is summed up in couplet 30.

Com. analysis:—

I. 1-3. The greatness of the 'renounced' exceeds all other greatness.

II. 4–7. The sources of this greatness: (i.) restraint of senses (4, 5); (ii.) ascetic practices [S. *yôga*], (6); (iii.) true knowledge (7). [Ch. xxxvi.]

III. 8, 9. The might of their words.

IV. 10. Their gracious disposition. [Ch. xxv.]

21. Ellis: 'A strict adherence to the rule professed,
Than do all other virtues, the devout
Exalteth more; this every code ordains.'

Beschi: 'Nulla ex scientiis dubitat concupiscere ut omnium maximum decus religiosorum a suo instituto non aberrantium.'

The Com. says: 'A strict adherence to the proper rule is true devotion (renunciation). By thus adhering to the rules of their respective *castes*, or positions, virtue increases; by increase of virtue sin is worn away; by wearing away of sin ignorance departs; by departure of ignorance the perception of the difference between things temporal and things eternal is gained, and with it a disgust at the transient pleasures of this world and the next, and a feeling of the affliction of successive births is conceived; thence comes an eager desire for *vîḍu* (release); thence comes abandonment of fruitless effort, which is cause of births, with the practice of meditation (*yôga*); from this true knowledge proceeds; the external bond, which is "mine," and the internal bond, which is "I," are loosed, and these two bonds are renounced with abhorrence.' [Ch. xxxv.–xxxvii.]

22. Ellis: 'To count the virtues holy men attain,
Were as to count the ghosts that from this world
Have taken flight.'

Beschi: 'Si numeres religiosorum decora perinde erit, ac si numeres mortuos ab initio mundi ad hunc diem.'

23. The two ways of 'renewed birth' and 'deliverance.'

Beschi: 'Considerando hujus et alterius vitae varias qualitates in mundo, celsissimum decus illorum, qui in hâc vitâ ornantur virtute religiosorum propriâ.'

24. Here, in somewhat obscure language, is set forth the idea of the development in the 'better world' of the virtuous soul. It is a seed which, planted in that better soil, shall grow and yield immortal fruit. The mixture of metaphor is remarkable. Comp. *Nâlaḍi*, 183:

'See ye sow seed whose yield in other world survives;
From earth's bewilderment and meanness free your lives;
Stand in your lot as wise men should; the changing hue
Of things shall causeless fade, and many things be new.'

மறுமைக்கு வித்து மயலின்றிச் செய்து,
சிறுமைப் படாதேநீர் வாழ்மின் ;
அறிஞராய்
நின்றுழி நின்றே ; நிறம்வேறுங் காரணம்
இன்றிப் பலவும் உள !

Ellis : ‘ As the hook rules the elephant, so he
In wisdom firm his sensual organs rules,
Who hopes to flourish in the soil of heaven.’

Beschi : ‘ Qui harpagone, qui dicitur animi robur, suos quinque sensus fraenat, semen est pro agro qui dicitur coelum [*i.e.* qui utitur ad suorum sensuum fraenationem animi robore, sicuti harpagone utimur ad fraenandos elephantes, semen est in terrâ custoditum, ut suo tempore in coeli agro seratur ; hoc est, coelum assequatur].’

25. The story of the curse pronounced on Indra by the ascetic, referred to in this couplet, may be read by the Tamiḷ scholar in Kamban's *Râmâyaṇam, Bâla-Kâṇḍam*, xth *Paḍalam*, *Agaliyaippaḍalam*, 72, &c., where the beauty of the verse contrasts with the uncouthness of the story.

Ellis : ‘ Let Indren say, the king who all controls
Within the expanse of heav'n, how great his power,
Who his five senses in subjection holds.’

Beschi : ‘ Decus illius qui quinque affectus ex quinque sensibus emanantes extinxit (*i.e.* mortificavit), pro se habet testimonium Indirenis coelitum regis.’

26. The Com. says the *difficult things* are powers acquired by the *yôgi*, something like those which so-called ‘spiritualists’ claim. I suppose the poet means the harder conquest of self and attainment of virtue.

Beschi : ‘ Sublimes tantum homines difficilia (*uti est sui fraenatio*) operantur ; infimi homines ardua operari nequeunt.’

27. Comp. *Nâlaḍi*, 59 :
‘ Who undisturbed, in “ way of right ordained,” has might
To guard and guide desires and lusts that entrance find
By sense-gates five, called “ body, mouth, eye, nose, and ear ”—
Unfailing he “ release ” shall gain.’

மெய்வாய்கண் மூக்குச் செவியெனப் பேர்பெற்ற
ஐவாய வேட்கை அவாவினைக்
கைவாய்
கலங்காமற் காத்துய்க்கும் ஆற்றல் உடையான்
விலங்காது வீடு பெறும்

The five. See 6, 25, 343, 361–70.

The Com. enters into a long explanation of the *sânkhya* doctrine regarding the five, a knowledge of which puts the whole world into the power of the ascetic. All this is quite foreign to the poet's object.

Ellis has a long discussion of this couplet. He says: 'The simple meaning of the author in this verse is, that, as it is by the senses only that the mind can derive knowledge, human knowledge of all kinds must be connected with (or must be according to the *way of*), the objects of sense here enumerated; he, therefore, who has a clear understanding of them, of their powers and effects, is alone complete in knowledge. Such is the contemplative sage, who, having reduced his sensual organs to entire subjection, must, beyond all others, have acquired a more perfect comprehension of the senses and their operations.'

Beschi's translation is: 'Qui quinque illa, nempe, saporem, lucem, quantitatem, sonum et odorem, cum eorum proprietatibus ac relationibus attente considèrat, totum in se mundum habet (*i.e.* mundum totum in se comprehendit, cum nil sensibile sit in mundo quod in illis quinque non contineatur.'

He adds: 'Exaltat hic religiosos ob contemplationem, quam mortificationi jungunt, quaque ex rerum naturalium attenta consideratione veri notitiam assequendo ad Deum facilius diriguntur.'

Ellis: 'Taste, light, touch, sound, and smell, if these be known
And with them all connected, of the world
The whole is known.'

28. Their words of benediction or of malediction are fulfilled.

Beschi: 'Decus hominum indeficientia verba habentium (nempe, religiosorum) ostendit spiritualis doctrina, quam in terrâ docent (ait, verba religiosorum non deficere, quia cui benedicunt felix est; cui maledicunt, indubitanter infelix invadit).'

29. Com.: 'Their excellence is a hill, for it is exalted and immoveable.'

Beschi: 'Neque per unam temporis instans (?) facile erit retardare effectus maledictionum illius qui virtutum montem ascendens in culmine perseverat.'

30. For the epithet *Anthaṇar* see 8. It is applied to God, and to Brâhmans also. There is (Graul thinks) a hit at these latter, who relied more on birth than on 'fair and loving' grace of character.

The poet shows how men are to deserve a title which is given to the Supreme Himself.

Beschi: 'Religiosi vocantur *andaner* (quod est *pulchrè ornati*) qui ornati incedunt affabilitate, quae omnibus pulchra est.'

CHAPTER IV.

THIS is the special introduction to Book I. The invocation, the praise of rain, and the declaration of the virtues of 'the renouncers,' introduce the whole work.

God's grace, rain which alone renders life on earth possible, and the existence of saintly sages, are as the postulates of his system.

He now asserts the value of virtue, or *arram*. The word, as Ellis says, has 'great latitude of meaning.' It denotes:

(i.) VIRTUE in general.

(ii.) *Right* as opposed to wrong.

(iii.) *Religious righteousness* and *merit* accruing from religious acts.

(iv.) *Positive rights*, as defined by law and custom, and their maintenance: *justice*.

(v.) *Charity* in the abstract, and *charitable acts*.

(vi.) The *goddess* or *guardian genius of virtue* (verse 77).

It is divided (taken in meaning i.) into *The virtue of the householder* (Ch. v.–xxiv.) and *The virtue of the ascetic* (Ch. xxv.–xxxvii.).

As to the teaching of this chapter, comp. the *Gîtâ* (Ch. xviii.). Action is not to be forsaken. Ascetics are great; but in the performance of virtuous deeds men obtain their highest enjoyments and merit the greatest rewards. This chapter contains a loftier moral than any Hindû composition—at least, of earlier date. Ch. iv. of the *Nâlaḍi* bears the same title.

The following is the Com. analysis of the chapter:—

I. 1. No strength like that which virtue gives.

II. 2. Ruin from its neglect.

III. 3. The way it must be cultivated.

IV. 4, 5. Its true nature.

V. 6–8. It affords unfailing assistance in other life if practised in this life.

VI. 9. It brings present rewards.

VII. What to do and what to shun.

31. The Com. thinks 'final release' and the temporary pleasures of *svarga* are meant.

Beschi says: 'Quodnam est homini emolumentum virtute majus, quae et eternam et temporalem felicitatem parit.' Ariel: 'Grandeur et félicité.' Graul: 'Glorie—glück.'

Ellis: 'What more doth profit man than virtue doth,
By which felicity is given, and whence
Eternal bliss ensues?'

32. Ellis: 'No greater gain than virtue canst thou know,
Than virtue to forget no greater loss.'

Beschi: 'Virtute majus emolumentum non est, nec majus damnum ejus oblivione.'

33. Com.: 'With the mind, by thinking good thoughts; with the mouth, by speaking good words; with the body, by doing good acts.' [Eccles. ix. 10.]

Beschi: 'Quocunque potes modo virtuosa opera sine intermissione, in omni occasione quae se offerat, operari debes.'

34. Com.: 'Sound—made to attract the notice of others.' [Matt. vi. 2; v. 8.] Comp. *Gîtâ*, XVI. 1.

Ellis: 'That which is spotless purity preserves
The mind in real virtue; all besides
Is evanescent sound.'

Beschi: 'Ex immunitate a culpâ in animo metienda est virtus, caetera omnia conditionem habent strepitus.'

35. *Gîtâ*, XVI. 21. Comp. Ch. XVII., XXXVII., XXXI., X.

Beschi: 'Virtutis proprietas est non errare in his quatuor, nempe, invidiâ, cupiditate, irâ et malis verbis.'

36. Com.: 'When the body dies virtue will join itself to the soul and accompany it into another body.'

It is the belief of nearly all Hindûs that *a man's good and evil deeds determine the state into which he passes at death, and accompany him into that new state, and influence his character and fortunes therein.*

This is 'destiny,' or ஊழ் *ûṛ* (which means simply 'antiquity'—the 'old things' which have not passed away); and Tiruvaḷḷuvar, in Ch. XXXVIII. [*q.v.*], teaches that this presides over all action; yet, in a sense, as we shall see, man is yet man, and 'master of his fate.'

It is only when a human body is reached in the round of births, that the 'virtue' whose fruit is 'final release' can be practised; hence this mortal life is the time for prompt virtuous effort.

I add three verses, selected from many beautiful ones of similar import, out of the *Nâlaḍi*, where procrastination is on this ground deprecated:

(36) 'This day? That day? What day? O question not the time.
Bethink thee death behind thee waiting ever stands?
Put from you every evil thing; with all your powers
Embrace the virtue sages teach.'

இன்றுகொல், அன்றுகொல், என்றுகொல், என்னாது
பின்றையே நின்றது கூற்றம்என் றெண்ணி,
ஒருவுமின் தீயவை, ஒல்லும் வகையான்
மருவுமின் மாண்டார் அறம்!

(34) ‘As gain from mortal frame now reached—so hard to reach—
With all thy might lay hold of virtue's lasting good.
As juice from cane expressed 'twill after be thine aid,
When body goes like refuse flung away.’

அரும்பெறல் யாக்கையைப் பெற்ற பயத்தாற்
பெரும்பயனும் ஆற்றவே கொள்க!
கரும்பூர்ந்த
சாறுபோற் சாலவும் பின்னுதவி, மற்றதன்
கோதுபோற் போகும் உடம்பு.

(19) ‘Say not “In after time we 'll virtue learn; we 're young.’
While wealth is yours, conceal it not; do virtuous deeds.
When evil tempests rage, not ripened fruit alone,
But unripe fruit's fair promise falls.’

‘மற்றறிவா நல்வினை யாமிளையம்’ என்னாது
கைத்துண்டாம் போழ்தே கரவா தறஞ்செய்மின.
முற்றி இருந்த கனிஒழியத் தீவளியா
னற்காய் உதிர்தலும் உண்டு.

Ellis: ‘Refer not virtue to another day;
Receive her now, and at thy dying hour
She 'll prove thy never-dying friend.’

Beschi: ‘Ad mortis horam non differendo virtutem instanter operare, dum moriens illa tibi comes immortalis erit.’

37. This seems to mean that their respective positions are the result of deeds—good or evil—done in a former birth. The Jews seem to have had such a notion. [S. John ix. 2.]

Beschi: ‘Quonam modo se gerat virtus, ne multum scruteris, illud enim clarè videre poteris, in eo qui per bajulos in lectica defertur.’

He adds: ‘It may be explained, “You need not doubt about the way of virtue: as the bearers do not desert the man they carry, so virtue is the immortal companion of the virtuous man.”’

But he prefers this: ‘Don't say the way of virtue is like that of bearers, who can only bear you to the grave, and must leave you there.’

38. ‘Virtue prevents a man from passing through other forms of being’: procures him ‘release.’

Comp. Browning, *Old Pictures in Florence*, XXI.:

‘There 's a fancy some lean to and others hate—
That, when this life is ended, begins
New work for the soul in another state,
Where it strives and gets weary, loses and wins:

Where the strong and the weak, this world's congeries,
  Repeat in large what they practised in small,
Through life after life in unlimited series;
  Only the scale 's to be changed, that 's all.

* * * * *

  'Yet I hardly know . . . .
Why, the child grown man, you burn the rod,
  The uses of labour are surely done;
There remaineth a rest for the people of God:
  And I have had trouble enough, for one.'

Beschi: 'Si nullam diem sine virtuosis operibus abire sinas, illa erunt veluti lapis occludens viam miserae vitae quae mortem sequitur.'

39. Nothing but virtue can give real enjoyment.

Ellis: 'Pleasure from virtue springs; from all but this
  No real virtue e'er ensues, nor praise.'

Beschi: 'A virtute venit dulcedo, caetera omnia, nec dulcia, nec laudabilia sunt.'

40. This seems to suppose a natural sense of right and wrong in human minds.

In Hindû minds this sense is supposed to be affected by 'destiny' (note on 36), but, on the whole, is a safe guide. [Comp. 293.] The poet believes in Natural Conscience.

Ellis: 'Know that is virtue which each ought to do;
  What each should shun is vice.'

Beschi: 'Virtus est quam quisque sectari debet, vitium quod cuique vitandum.'

CHAPTER V.

THE title is explained by the Com. மனையாளோடு கூடிவாழ்தலினது சிறப்பு 'the excellence of living in union with a wife.'

Com. analysis:—

I. 1, 2. In domestic life lies the power of bestowing all benefits.
II. 3–5. The way in which the householder fulfils virtue.
III. 6–9. Its fruits of virtue and excellence.
IV. 10. Its crown in the future life.

The difference between the *Kurraḷ* and the *Nâlaḍi* is nowhere more evident than in the way in which this subject is treated. The *Nâlaḍi* discourages and mocks at marriage. Comp. 56, 364.

'Though wife possess no excellence and bear no child,
'Tis hard to rid one of the marriage bond. For this,
Since he who weds puts sorrow on, in olden days
The learned men made *marriage* synonym of *dread*.'

[A play on கடி, which means, among many other things, 'marriage' and 'dread.']

மாண்ட குணத்தொடு மக்கட்பே றில்லெனினும்,
பூண்டான் கழித்தற் கருமையால்,
பூண்ட
மிடிஎன்னுங் காரணத்தின் மேன்முறைக் கண்ணே
கடிஎன்றார் கற்றறிந் தார்

'He hears that *marriage* is another name for *dread*,
Yet dreads it not! The fearful marriage drum gives him
No sense! To dwell bewildered mid domestic joys
Is fault that merits stoning, say the wise.'

கடிஎனக் கேட்டுங் கடியான்; வெடிபட
ஆர்ப்பது கேட்டும் அதுதெளியான்;
போத்தும்ஓர்
இற்கொண் டினிதிரூஉம் ஏமுறுதல் என்பவே
கற்கொண் டெறியுந் தவறு!

Indeed, 1–60 of these quatrains are intended to exalt asceticism at the expense of domestic life. The tone of the *Nâlaḍi* is morbidly ascetic, while the *Kurraḷ*, as we should expect from the tradition of its author's life (see Intro. pp. x., xi., and the notes to next chapter), heartily praises, and exhibits in the most attractive light every human and social virtue. Ch. xxxv. gives the other side of the question.

41. Ellis: 'He for domestic virtues is esteemed,
Who, firm in virtue's path, the virtuous aids
In life's three orders found.'

Beschi: 'Conjugatus debet esse auxiliator in viâ virtutis triplici hominum generi, qui virtuti addicti sunt.'

The *three* are the பிரமசாரி or 'student'; the வானப்பிரஸ்தன் or 'eremite,' 'the dweller in the wilderness'; and the சந்நியாசி 'the absolute ascetic.' The householder (கிரகஸ்தன்) is the fourth. Manu has given a full exposition of the duties of each of these states. The Jains have only two classes, and thus the poet was not a teacher of their system. Manu, iii. 78.

The householder is a *help* (துணை) to them, by assisting them with food, medicine, and other things, relieving them from hunger, pain, and cold (Com.).

நல்லாறு refers to the idea of Ch. XIV.

42. Ellis: 'Domestic virtue is to him ascribed
Whose care befriends the pious and the poor,
And aids departed souls.'

Beschi: 'Praetera conjugatus auxiliari debet iis qui omnibus renunciarunt, pauperibus, et animabus defunctorum, qui apud se obierint.'

To the dead the householder is a help by performance of funeral rites, especially the sprinkling with water (நீர்க்கடன்). Manu, iii. 80.

The Hindûs, in common with the ancient nations of Europe, attach great importance to this. [Hor. *Odes*, I. xxvii. 30–34.] 'Confucianism inculcates the worship of the dead as a part of filial piety.' (Legge.)

43. Ellis: 'Thine ancestors deceased, thy God, thy guest,
Thy relatives, thyself; these cherished, know
Of life the five great duties are fulfilled.'

Beschi: 'Insuper praecipuum conjugati debitum est virtutem exercere in hos quinque, nempe, in majores vita defunctos, in Deum, in hospites, in consanguineos, et in se ipsum, in modo superius dicto.'

This is almost a translation of Manu, iii. 72. The *feriae novemdiales*, the *feralia*, or *parentalia* of the Romans, and the offerings to the Manes attest the universality of the sentiment.

The தென்புலத்தார் 'those who have their dwelling in the south,' the Manes. Manu, iii. 91.

Pitṛibhôbalisêshantu sarvam dakshiṇatô harêt, 'with his face towards the south.' The *pitṛis* are the dwellers in the south. (See Wilson's *Vishṇu Purâṇa*, p. 320 *note.*) They include collectively a man's ancestors. Their 'path' is among the asterisms, south of the line of the goat, and north of *Agastya* or Canopus.

The duties of the Tamiḻ householder, as contemplated by the poet, are of no trivial or degrading character. What Manu enjoins on the Brâhman householder Tiruvaḷḷuvar takes for granted as the duty of all, but with a wider interpretation than would be put upon the precepts by any modern Hindû sect. The *Smṛiti* or traditional usage, and the *Dharmaçâstras*, especially Manu, which is a *résumé* of the *Smṛiti*, are the foundations of the law laid down by the poet. (Barth, *Religions of India*, p. 53.)

44. Beschi: 'In conjugio quod morem habeat partiendi cum caeteris cibum, cum peccati timore acquisitum, progeniei defectus nunquam erit.'

No merit could be gained by sharing with others what had been obtained by injustice, says the Com.; but the text says simply 'shunning guilt,' and this may mean the guilt of inhospitality. Dr. Graul's German is more exact: 'Hütet sich ein Hauswesen vor Unrecht und giebt gern von seiner Nahrung, so wird's an Nachkommenschaft nie fehlen.'

Comp. Manu, iii. 118.

45. Ellis : 'If love and virtue be thy constant guests,
Domestic life is blest, and finds in these
Its object and reward.'

Beschi : 'Si conjugium possideat amorem inter conjuges mutuum, et virtutum exercitum, hoc et conjugii debitum erit, et ejusdem emolumentum.'

Love is the essence, quality, perfect grace (பண்பு), and virtue the profit, crown, reward (பயன்) of wedlock.

46. Wanting in MS. of Beschi, and not given by Ellis. The Poet here distinctly declares the sufficiency and superiority of household life. The tone of *Nâlaḍi* is far different.

Thus, again and again, in energetic but sad verse, they urge :—

(53) 'The chief of men in quiet thought discern how house,
And youth, and beauty's grace, and high estate, and wealth,
And strength—all pass away ; and thus to save themselves
Prolonging not the time, they all renounce.'

(54) 'Though wretched men afflictions suffer many a day,
One day's delight they eagerly desire. The men
Of wisdom calm and full, *in pleasure's core see pain,*
And quit the pleasant household paths.'

(55) 'Spent is my youth in vain. E'en now diseases wait,
And death will come. O soul ! be bold ; wrangle no more
With me, but rise ! Wilt thou not go where virtue's path
Both thou and I may gain ?'

(60) 'Though wretched men behold afflictions urge and press,
Renunciation is not in their thoughts. Delight
They eagerly desire. The great in every joy
Behold its pain, and seek it not.'

[(54) and (60) seem two versions of one original.]

47. Beschi : 'Qui in conjugio vivit, cum virtute conjugii propria, omnes qui mundo renunciarunt excellit ; quia difficilius est inter mundi illecebras quam extra illas virtuosum esse.'

The idea in this and in 46, *mutatis mutandis,* is almost that of Keble :

'We need not bid, for cloistered cell,
Our neighbour and our work farewell ;
The trivial round, the common task,
Will furnish all we need to ask.'

'In nature's way' (இயல்பினான்) :

'And I could wish my days to be
Bound each to each by natural piety.'—Wordsworth.

48. Ellis: 'He who from virtue swerves not, but her path
To others shows, gained in domestic life,
More merit hath than the recluse can boast.'

Beschi: 'Conjugium quod caeteros ad virtutem promovendo â suâ virtute numquam aberrat, habet quemdam poenitentiae speciem, quae eos poenitentes superat.'

Manu, iii. 78: 'Because men of the three (other) orders are daily supported by the householder alone with knowledge and food, therefore the householder (is) of the chief order.'

49. Beschi: 'Quae autonomasticè dicitur virtus est conjugium; illa verò nempe virtus renunciandi mundo, et ipsa aestimabilis erit, si non sit in eâ quod caeteri censurare possint.' He adds, 'Si legatur இன்று யின் erit idem.'

Tiruvaḷḷuvar hints at the notorious hypocrisy and scandalous lives of many professed ascetics, who, as Sannyâsis, Jogis, Fakîrs, &c., have ever been, and are, the bane of India.

Comp. Ch. XXVIII.

50. Ellis: 'Who in domestic joys thus lives on earth,
May with the gods, heaven's denizens, be ranked.'

Beschi: 'Qui modo dicto conjugatus vixit in terrâ, adscribendus erit inter numina, quae in coelo vivunt.'

The Com. says, 'he will certainly be born again as a god.'

CHAPTER VI.

Ellis renders துணை 'protection'; and thinks வாழ்க்கைத்துணை= 'she to whose safeguard domestic happiness is entrusted.' It means, 'she by whose assistance.' See துணை.

51. Ellis: 'To every household duty fitly trained,
The wife should to her husband be in all
A help-mate meet.'

Beschi: 'Uxor debet habere virtutem conjugio debitam, et debet viam sui conjugis calcare; *i.e.* suo conjugi in omnibus obedire.'

Here பண்பு='duty,' *virtus*; it means 'all that befits her station.' The Com. says, it includes (1) qualities, such as reverence to ascetics, hospitality, kindness to the poor, &c.; (2) acts, such as due provision for household needs, skill in cookery, attention to the duties of her station, &c.

Beschi translates வளம் by 'via.' It means வரவு 'income.' The Com. 'she who adapts her expenditure to her husband's income.'

52. Ellis: 'The wife maintains the glory of the house;
All other glory, if she fail in this,
As if it were not, is.'

Beschi: 'Si in uxore desit praerogativa conjugii propria, nempe fides conjugalis, quotcumque alias praerogativas habeat, perinde est ac si non haberet.'

53. Ellis: 'What is deficient with a virtuous wife?
If in the wife defect, then what is all
This world can give?'

Beschi: 'Si uxor dictam conditionem habeat, quid tibi deerit? Si uxor non fuerit virtuosa quid possidebis?'

Manu, ix. 26.

54. Ellis: 'Than virtuous woman what more excellent,
Who, firm in mind, her wedded faith maintains?'

Beschi: 'Quid est quod dici debeat praestantius muliere, si obtinuerit ut sibi insit robur, quod dicitur fides conjugalis?'

55. Beschi: 'Mulier quae speciale Diis obsequium non praestet sed suo conjugi obsequendo fidem ei servet, statim ac imperabit coelo ut pluviam det, pluvia cadet.'

'Even the gods obey her,' says the Com.

56. Beschi: 'Mulier in sui custodiâ, in mariti amore, in laude servandâ numquam remissa omnes excellit.'

57. Beschi: 'Custodia quam faciunt obseratae januae quid proderit? Praecipua custodia debet esse ea qua uxor suum honorem custodiat.'

Manu, ix. 12. See *Nâl.* (362) on the uselessness of restraint to a shameless woman.

'Though compassed round as though with faultless guard of swords,
When once they freedom gain, 'tis but a little time
Ere they are stained with every fault; and long the time
Those women, soft of speech, spurn every law of right.'

58. Ellis: 'Women all happiness from wedded love
Derive, and by it blest foretaste on earth
The joys of heaven.'

Beschi: Si mulier obtinuerit talem, conjugem qui dici possit, quod eam obtinuerit (quod non fit, nisi illa fidem servet suo conjugi) obtinebit magnam gloriam in mundo ubi Deae regnant.' He regards புத்தேளிர் as fem.

The meaning turns upon the ellipsis with பெறில். The Com. says வணங்குவது (or வழிபாடு) is understood: 'attain to the due reverencing of.'

Ellis supplies ஈண்டு 'in this world': 'If women obtain one who has obtained them in marriage, they shall here obtain the joys of the divine world.' I prefer Beschi's: 'if she really gain him by being his true spouse.' So, in effect, Graul.

59. Ellis: 'Before their scornful foes,
Bold as a lion those dare never walk,
Whose fame is sullied by their wives' base deeds.'

Beschi: 'Qui non habet uxorem quae laudem satagat, non poterit uti leo magnanime incedere coram suis hostibus.'

In Beschi's MS. the text of this chapter is not given, but in his interpretation he has 'இல்லி pro இல், uxor.' For this word there is no authority. He seems to have read: புகழ்புரிந்த இல்லியில்லோர் ஏர். புரிந்து for புரிந்த, or final அ is elided.

The history of the poet's wife Vâçugi illustrates this chapter. (Intro. p. xi.) It is not improbable that the verses may have given rise to the legends.

60. Beschi: 'Magnum emolumentum esse dicunt sapientes, uxorem conjugati fide praeditam, quod verò illi majus ornamentum addit, ajunt esse bonorum gnatorum procreationem.'

This couplet prepares the way for the next chapter. With என்ப understand அறிவுடையோர்.

மங்கலம் [S.] is the one word for any auspicious event, and is especially used of everything connected with marriage.

The following from Vêmana, who in Telugu ranks with our Tamiḻ bard, has a touch of nature that makes all the world kin (II. 202):

'Is *wealth* to wife or husband *wealth?*
Wealth of sons on earth is best.
'Tis wealth of wealth to live and side by side grow old.'

Vêmana enjoys the advantage of matchless rhythm and flexibility; but, as an artist, not less than as a teacher, he is far inferior to Tiruvaḻḻuvar.

The Com.'s analysis of this chapter is:

I. 1. The two special gifts of a wife: tact and economy.
II. 2, 3. They ensure the welfare of the house.
III. 4. The excellence of chastity.
IV. 5. Its power.
V. 6. Her prudent, guarded life.
VI. 7. The good housewife's praise.
VII. 8. The reward in the world to come.
VIII. 9. Evil resulting from lack of wifely virtues.
IX. 10. An ornament of domestic life. A link between this chapter and the next.

The following from the *Nâlaḍi* illustrate this and the foregoing chapter:—

(361) 'The mansion meets the clouds. Around a stately band
Of warders watch. There glisten gems as lamps. What then?
Where owner has not wife of dainty excellence,
The house within is desert hard to be explored.'

(363) '*Death* is the wife that stands and dares her spouse to strike!
Disease is she who kitchen enters not betimes!
Demon domestic she who cooks and gives no alms!
Thēse three are *swords* to slay their lords!'

(381) 'Though women live for rarest gift of chastity
As Ayirâṇi famed, absence of men who stand
Enamoured of their charms is help in way of good
To those of fragrant brow who guard themselves.'

[Ayirâṇi, the virtuous wife of Indra.]

(382) 'When in the straitened time, one pot of water set
On hearth, she c̣ooks,—if relatives arrive enough
The sea to drain, each seemly duty well fulfils
The soft-voiced dame, the glory of her home.'

(383) 'On every side the narrow dwelling open lies,
On every part the rain drips down; yet, if the dame
Have noble gifts, by townsfolk praised for modest worth,
Call such a housewife's blest abode a home.'

(384) 'Sweet to the eye, adorned in way that lover loves,
Enforces awe, her virtue shames the village folk,
Submiss, in fitting place is stern, but sweet relents;
Call such a soft-voiced dame *a wife.*'

All Tamiḷ poets regard it as an accomplishment in a woman to know how and when to assume an offended air (ஊடு. புல. பிணங்கு) and when to lay it aside (உணரு).

The idea is that of Terence:

'Amantium irae amoris integratio est.'

Comp. Ch. cxxxi.

(386) 'Like learned scroll to him of understanding heart
Is glorious wealth to men adorned with liberal grace;
Like javelin keen in dauntless hero's hand is gift
Of beauty gained by her of modest mind.'

CHAPTER VII.

THE title is 'the procreation of sons': but some parts of the chapter refer to children in general.

The Com.'s analysis is:

I. 1. The distinguished excellence of the gain of children.
II. 2, 3. The benefit obtained in the next world.
III. 4–6. Benefits obtained in this world.
IV. 7. The father's duty.
V. 8. The joy of the world.
VI. 9. The mother's delight.
VII. 10. The son's duty.

61. Beschi: 'Inter bona quae quis obtinere hic potest, ego nullum aliud scio, quod adeo jucundum sit, uti procreasse filios qui sapientes evaserint.'

Ellis: 'Of all the world calls good, no good exists
Like that which wise and virtuous offspring give;
I know no greater good.'

The Com. says: 'This verse refers to sons only, for daughters cannot be described as அறிவறிந்த: can never be *learned*.'

Everything depends upon a man's having a son to maintain the household fire, to discharge the duties of hospitality, and to perform the ceremonies which secure the welfare of the departed. A man must have a son or adopt one.

The S. *putra*='deliverer from hell.' Of this புதல்வன் is probably a corruption. A man who dies without a son must suffer in one of the hells prepared for such ill-fated persons. The sentiment is very powerful amongst all classes of men in India.

62. Beschi: 'Neque post mortem te mala tangent si genueris filios qui indolem habeant quae malum de se rumorem non edat; *i.e.* si filios incensurabiles habueris, etiam post mortem ex iis emolumentum capies; nam illi suis orationibus, eleemosynis ac jejuniis, tibi suffragabunt. [Est inter gentiles hujus regionis mos jejunandi in quolibet plenilunio animabus genitorum decessorum.]' This is at the *Amâvâsi*.

The *seven* births are: (1) gods, (2) men, (3) quadrupeds, (4) birds, (5) reptiles, (6) fish, and (7) things without motion: தேவர்மனிதர்விலங்கு பறவை ஊர்வனநீர்வாழ்வனதாவரம்.

63. Beschi: 'Sapientes suos filios suos fructus vocabunt, quia eorum qualitas ex ipsorum, nempe parentum, operibus pendet. [Hic versus fundatur in persuasione quae inter gentiles communis est, quod ob bona

opera parentum boni filii; et ob mala mali nascantur; ob quam persuasionem solent plurimi ante quam uxor filium pariat, toto eo tempore quo gravida est, aliquod genus poenitentiae exercere, ut bonos filios ex partu assequantur.]'

Ellis: 'Children are offspring called, and justly so,
For from their parents' deeds, or good or ill,
Their disposition springs.'

Not so the Com. தம் புதல்வரைத் தம்பொருள் என்றுசொல்லுவர்: ஏனெனில் பிள்ளைதேடிய பொருள் பிதாவிற்குவரும் 'Man's children are his wealth, for the wealth the children acquire is for the father'; *i.e.* they employ it in performing acts of piety for the benefit of their deceased parent: thus, *children constitute the only possession or wealth that aids man after death.*

I have translated it literally, preserving the ambiguity.

64. Beschi: 'Cibus infantium manibus versatus eorum parenti dulcior est ipsâ Ambrosiâ.'

65. Beschi: 'Filium corpus tangere tactui dulce, et ipsorum verba audire, parentibus auribus jucundum est.'

Ellis: 'Sweet the sensation to the parent's breast,
His child's soft touch imparts; 'tis real bliss
Which others hear of, fathers only know.'

66. Beschi: 'Fistulam et citharam dulces vocabunt, qui non audierunt suorum infantium imperfecta verba; *i.e.* infantes balbutientes audire, parentibus dulcius esse, quam fistulae and citharae sonum.'

Ellis: 'Sweet is the pipe and sweet the lute they say,
They who have never heard their children's tongues
In infant prattle lisp.'

67. Beschi: 'Favor quem pater debet filio praestare est facere ut ille in sapientium coetu primum locum habeat; *i.e.* ita illum instruere ut inter sapientes primo loco dignus sit.'

68. Beschi: 'Omnibus hominibus in hâc vastâ terrâ existentibus, dulce est habero filios, qui se sapientiores sint.'

The Com. says: 'The wòrld will rejoice more than the parent when children are wise!' This seems a slip. Comp. *Nâl.*

(197) 'If *banyan's* trunk be eaten by the gnawing ant,
Its offshoot bears it up, like buttress; even so
When in the sire decay appears, the son he gained
Shall hide it straight, and weakness is no more.'

69. Beschi: 'Mater qui audit suum filium sapientem vocari, magis gaudet quam gavisa fuit cum illum peperit.'

The Com. says: 'The mother must hear of her son's proficiency, being *naturally incapable of judging for herself.*'

70. Beschi: 'Filius quam retributionem dabit patri, causare debet verba quae dicant, istius pater quânam arduâ poenitentiâ talem filium obtinuit?—[Sensus est, retributionem a filiis patri dandam esse, ita procedere ut qui eum viderint, illius patrem, valdè felicem dicant, quod illum obtinuerit.]'

Ellis: 'When men shall say, "By what infliction hard
In penance borne gained he this child?" the word
Requiteth all a father's pains.'

Many pilgrimages are performed in India, as they have been in other lands, and many vows are made at various shrines, by childless parents. At *Tirupati* or *Tiru-vĕngaḍam* is a renowned temple where this boon is sought. Hindû stories abound in which penance has extorted from the gods the gift of male offspring.

CHAPTER VIII.

The Com.'s analysis is:—

I. 1. The reality of love. [Sympathy.]

II. 2–6. Its excellence.

III. 7–10. The evils of an absence of it.

'அன்பு is the affection a man feels for wife, children, and all connected with him. Its fruit is the pleasant discharge of all household duties, and benevolence towards all living beings: இல்லறம் இனிது நடத்தலும் பிறவுயிர்களின்மேல் அருள்பிறத்தலும் அன்பின் பயன்.' This அருள் alone is to be cultivated by ascetics. See Ch. xxv.

71. 'Estne etiam amori sera? qua occultentur amantium oculi pluviam lachrymarum dabunt. [Sensus est, amorem occultari non posse, quia lachrymae aut alius affectus in vultu amantis apparens occultum amorem detegit.]'

Ellis: 'What bolt can love restrain? what veil conceal?
One tear-drop in the eye of those thou lov'st
Will draw a flood from thine.'

72. 'Qui amorem non habent omnia possident sibi; qui amorem habent, et ipsum corpus possident caeteris.'

73. 'Sapientes dicent viam, seu causam, cur humanus spiritus corpori amicabiliter uniatur esse amorem, quo inter se junguntur. [Sensus est,

quod sicuti in naturali amore quo corpus et spiritus se invicem prosequuntur, ita amicabiliter uniuntur, ut corpus spiritum et spiritus corpus foveat, ita qui amorem habent debent sibi invicem praesto esse.]'

74. 'Tuus amor in caeteros in iis tui desiderium causabit, illud vero pariet tibi incomprehensibile decus, quod est omnium amicitia.'

75. 'Sapientes ajunt viam qua conjugati dulcem hic vitam ducendo aeternam felicitatem assequentur, esse inter se junctos esse mutuum amorem obtinendo.'

76. 'Aliquid dicunt amorem ad virtutis exercitium prodesse, sed errant quia ille ipse ad peccatum avertendum prodest (quod usu venit cum quis ei a quo injuriam accepit benefecerit, nam tunc praeter bonum quod illi fit avertitur etiam malum odii et caetera mala quae inde sequuntur, unde infertur quod amor non modo virtutis exercitium promovet sed etiam ea quae virtuti contraria sunt avertit).'

So the Com., in effect, says, 'Love conquers evil.'

But Ellis: 'The ignorant say that love is virtue's friend;
But know that love the wicked aideth more.'

He explains: 'Virtue requires no external assistance, being all-sufficient to herself; to vice, however degraded and despised, the consoling protection of love or friendship is most beneficial.'

Dr. Graul says: 'Amorem clementiae adjutorem dicunt imperiti: etiam irae (in amicis corrigendis) adjutor est.' This is hardly a translation.

See Oldenburg's *Life of Buddha*.

77. 'Sicuti sol adurit quod non est corpus vivum, ita Deus destruet id quod amorem non habet.'

He renders என்பு by 'corpus,' interpolating 'vivum.'

The idea is, that as insects are melted away by the sun's heat, as Hindus imagine, so the deity that presides over virtue consumes those who have no affection.

78. 'Vita conjugalis, quae in animo amorem non habet, perinde est ac si in siccâ terrâ sicca arbor revivesceret.'

Ellis: 'As in a barren soil a sapless tree,
So flourish those in wedded bliss, whose souls
Know not the sweets of love.'

79. 'Ei, qui caret amore, quod est animi membrum, caetera omnia corporis membra quid proderunt ad vitam conjugalem?'

Ellis: 'What though the body each perfection own,
If in the breast, the beauty of the mind,
Sweet love exist not?'

80. 'Quod amoris viam tenet, hoc est, quod amorem habet, vivum corpus est; ii qui eo carent corpus habent ex ossibus pelle co-opertis

conflatum (*i.e.* praeter hoc quod habeant apparentiam seu figuram corporis, in iis vita non residet, quia in iis non deprehenditur, quod est homini vivo naturale, nempe amare).'

Ellis: 'That breast alone contains a living soul,
Which love inspires; void of this genial warmth,
'Tis bone o'erlaid with skin.'

CHAPTER IX.

Beschi: *Hospitalitas.*

COM.'s analysis:—

I. 1, 2. Its special excellence.
II. 3–5. Its benefits in this life.
III. 6. In the other life.
IV. 7. In both.
V. 8, 9. Evils of its neglect.
VI. 10. It must be exercised with cheerfulness.

'Hospitality' here is not entertainment of friends, but the affording of food and shelter to wayfarers, mendicants, and ascetics. In v. 43 five classes of duties are mentioned: to *manes, gods, guests, relatives* and *self.* The first and second are to invisible beings, while the fourth and fifth involve no exercise of charity; the third, then, is treated of here as a work of அன்பு. It can only be exercised where the householder and his wife live in harmony. Hence its place in this work. It has now degenerated into the feeding of promiscuous multitudes in various charitable foundations.

81. 'Quare quis posthabitis silvis in urbem sedem figendo, et fortunae bona quaerendo et custodiendo conjugium exercet, nisi causâ praestandi favorem hospitibus, eos affectuose tractando?'

Ellis: 'To honour guests with hospitable rite,
Domestic life and all its various joys
To man was given.'

82. 'Hospite excluso, quidquam, etiam si sit vitale pharmacum solus si comedas, id non est laude dignum.'

83. 'Qui continenter affectuosè excipit ad se venientes hospites, non videbit suum conjugium a paupertate ruinam pati.'

84. 'Lacscimi (*sic*) Dea felicitatis laeto animo sedem figet in ejus domo, qui laeto vultu hospites affectuosè excipit.'

Ellis: 'He who with smiles receives a virtuous guest,
Shall see prosperity, with joyful mind,
Make his abode her home.'

85. 'Numquid opus erit, ut seratur ager illius qui hospitem bene tractando, si quid supersit, comedit?'

86. 'Qui venientes hospites affectuosè excipiendo, deinceps venturos hospites cum desiderio praestolatur, coelitibus valde gratus hospes erit.'

Comp. Ovid, *Met.* viii. 620–724:

'Cura pii dis sunt, et qui coluere, coluntur.'

Ellis: 'He who, while one rejoiceth in his cheer,
Awaits with anxious mind a coming guest,
Will be a welcome guest to gods.'

87. 'Nihil est de quo dici possit: hanc mensuram habet fructus hospitalitatis: fructûs sacrificii, quod est hospitalitas, mensura est mensura hospitis.'

He explains it thus: not the amount of your aid, but the necessities of the guest, measure the merit of your kindness. The Com. more naturally refers it to the worthiness (தகுதி) of the guest.

See வேள்வி.

88. 'Qui dicunt se dimississe desiderium multo labore quaerendi et custodiendi fortunae bona, non obtinebunt fructum sacrificii, quod fit hospitem bene tractando.'

This would seem to have no meaning.

89. 'Stultitia non custodiens (*i.e.* despiciens), hospitalitatem, quae idem est ac paupertas inter divitias, in insipientibus reperitur.'

Even wise men have their follies; this is not one of them.

90. 'Naribus admotus macescit flos *anicciam* dictus; hospes macescet si eum aspiciens vultum ab eo averteris.'

A guest is more sensitive than the அனிச்சம் flower.

Ellis: 'As that sweet flower which droops its head and dies,
When once its fragrant odour is inhaled,
From an averted face so shrinks the guest.'

Some take விருந்து here by metonomy for 'banquet': *the feast loses its charm* where its giver lacks courtesy. The beautiful word முகமலர்ச்சி is used for 'cheerfulness.' Comp. Heb. xiii. 2; Rom. xii. 13; S. Luke xiv. 12–14.

CHAPTER X.

Beschi : *Dulcia verba loqui : Affabilitas.* Ellis : 'Courtesy or affability.' Ch. c. may be compared.

Com.'s analysis :—

I. 1. What are pleasant words ?
II. 2, 3. More excellent than even charity.
III. 4, 5. Their benefit in this world.
IV. 6. In the next.
V. 7, 8. In both.
VI. 9, 10. Evil of harsh words.

This is essential to hospitality, so follows it.

91. 'Non nisi dulcia erunt verba, quae ore profert, qui nôrit virtutis conditionem, ex amore compactam, et ab omni fraude alienum. [Sensus est, virtuosos affabiles esse.]'

Ellis : 'Fair are the words of those, but void of guile,
Who know that sterner virtue should be joined
To mild affection.'

92. 'Si valeas esse dulcium verborum locutor, laeto cum vultu, id tibi melius erit quam laeto animo tua largiri.'

Ellis : 'Though bounty may rejoice the heart, yet words
Of courtesy, which dress the face in smiles,
Will more avail.'

This is within the reach even of the poor.

93. 'Si laeto vultu et hilari obtutu ex intimo pectoris eruta dulcia verba loquaris, illa sane virtus erit.'

In the *Ethics* of Aristotle, Book IV. chap. vi., the courtesy in speech here inculcated is said to be the mean between the habit of the disputatious and surly (δυσέριδες, δύσκολοι) and the (ἄρεσκος, κόλαξ) assentor or flatterer. It has no name in Greek, though it is said to be nearest to *φιλία*, and is called so in Book II. chap. vii. In Tamiḷ பண்பு expresses the general character. (Ch. c.)

94. 'Paupertas, quae maestitiam affert, non erit ei, qui cum omnibus dulcia et laetitiam afferentia verba loquitur.'

95. 'Esse humilem et dulcia loquentem, verum est cujusvis ornamentum : caetera omnia praeter hoc non sunt ornamenta.'

Ellis : 'The grace of fair humility, the grace
Of courteous words, do all far more adorn
Than do all other ornament.'

96. 'Si verba investigando caeteris bonum causantia, dulcia semper loquaris, vitia minuentur, virtus crescet.'

97. 'Verba quae junctam habent conditionem creandi, caeteris emolumentum, et gaudium pro hac vitâ et virtutem pro aliâ vitâ profituram tibi parient.'

98. 'Dulcia et a proximi malo sejuncta verba et in hac vitâ, et post mortem gaudium causabunt.'

99. 'Qui recte novit dulcia verba dulcedinem parere, cur quaeso aspera verba loquitur?'

Ellis: 'O, wherefore useth he discourteous words,
Who knows full well the sweets of courteous speech?'

100. 'Cum bona praesto sunt, mala verba loqui perinde est ac acerba poma comedere, cum praesto sunt matura.'

Ellis: 'Discourteous speech when courteous may be used,
Is like the sickly appetite which culls
Fruit immature, leaving the ripe untouched.'

The careful use of honorifics is much neglected by foreigners in their intercourse with Orientals, although courtesy costs little and goes far! [Comp. Tamiḷ Handbook, Pt. II. p. 104.]

CHAPTER XI.

Beschi: *Grati animi virtus.*

Com.'s analysis:—

I. 1–3. The infinite value of benefits (1) unmerited, (2) seasonable (3) disinterested.

II. 4, 5. Due estimation of benefits by the wise.

III. 6, 7. Gratitude enjoined.

IV. 8. Benefit *v.* injury.

V. 9. How memory of wrongs is to be effaced.

VI. 10. Evil of ingratitude.

The title is written often *செய்ந்நன்றி.* Beschi and Ellis do not double the *ந்*, nor is there any rule requiring it. செய் is வினைத் தொகை.

101. 'Ei qui tibi praesto fuit, quin tu illi profueris, etiam si coelum et terram dederis, par pari referre difficile sit.'

Ellis: 'Though earth and heaven could in return be given,
A benefit received when none was due
They would not recompense.'

The construction is difficult: 'It is hard, impossible (அரிது), to make the gift of earth and heaven an equal return (வையகமும் வானகமும் மாற்றல்) for the help (உதவிக்கு) which one has rendered you (செய்த) when you have done him no previous assistance (செய்யாமல்).'

செய்யாமல்=செய்யாதிருக்க. This is the emphatic word. The *spontaneity* of the favour gives it its value.

102. 'Opportune collatum beneficium, quamvis parvum sit, mundo ipso majus erit.'

As in 101 and 103, the first word is the emphatic one. A *timely* benefit is of infinite value. 'A friend in need is a friend indeed.' காலத்தினல் is உருபுமயக்கம்: III. Gr. 135*, 4th case for 7th.

103. 'Fructus beneficii sine retributionis ponderatione collati, si ponderetur ipso pelago major erit.'

தூக்கா in Beschi. The first phrase is the important one: *disinterested* kindness is of inestimable value.

104. 'Quamvis milii grano parem favorem praestiteris, qui illius fructum noscunt, illum palmae arbori parem judicabunt.'

105. 'Beneficium non est dimetiendum a mensura favoris praestiti, sed a magnitudine illius, qui beneficium accepit.' (Comp. 87.)

Ellis: 'The exalted mind no benefit esteems
By mere return repaid, but by the scale
Of its own greatness measures each.'

106. 'Noli oblivisci amicitiae inculpabilium vivorum; noli rejicere amicitiam eorum, qui in adversitate sunt tibi baculus.'

So அவ்வை in ஆத்திசூடி has நன்றிமறவேல், *forget no benefit conferred.*

Since our Eastern fellow-subjects have often been accused (I think, unjustly) of ingratitude, a quotation from Vêmana is added (v. 514; comp. v. 262):

'Forget the faults of others;
But, Vêma, ne'er on earth forget a benefit conferred.'

107. 'Gratus homo etiam post mortem recordabitur amoris, quo quis in eo haerentem afflictionem abstersit.'

Beschi reads விழுமம்='afflictio, dolor': and not விழும் அம் as Com. Comp. *Nál.* 356:—

'The hill-man thinks upon the beauty of his hills;
The farmer thinks upon the fruits his fields have borne;
The good think on the boon by worthy men bestowed;
The base men's thoughts are centred all in self.'

There is a v.r. வைதனை for தான் வைத்தே: 'the base remember only how they abused him.'

108. 'Bonum non est oblivisci beneficii accepti; sed quod maleficium est eo ipso die, quo tibi fit, ex memoria delere optimum est.'

109. 'Gratus homo, qui unum tantum ab aliquo beneficium receperit, si deinde ab hoc afficiatur malo, quod sit par homicidio, in memoriam revocando illud unum beneficium, maleficii accepti memoriam delebit.'

Ellis: 'To one small favour though there may succeed
Deadly offence; the grateful from the mind will rase
For that all memory of this.'

Comp. *Nâl.* 357:

'The good attach themselves to those who do one act
Of kindness, and forgive a hundred wrongs that
Rise. The base receive seven hundred benefits,—
One wrong will turn them all to ill!'

110. 'Qualemcunque virtutem caedentibus, id est, quocunque crimen patrantibus ad remissionem via invenietur, sed ad illam via non invenietur hominibus, qui acceptum beneficium caedunt (*i.e.* pro bono malum reddunt).'

Ellis: 'Though every virtue by his hand expire,
Yet may he live; but by the stroke he dies
When murdered gratitude before him falls.'

CHAPTER XII.

Beschi: *Equitas.*

Com.'s analysis:—

I. 1. Its excellence.
II. 2, 3. It yields lasting prosperity; its transgression can only yield prosperity that ruins.
III. 4. How the just and unjust are discerned.
IV. 5-7. Ruin the true result of injustice.
V. 8, 9. In council a just mind to be preserved.
VI. 10. In trade to regard others' interests as your own.

It is to be exercised in the treatment of (1) foes, (2) strangers, (3) friends. [பகைவர், அயலர், நட்பினர்.]

This is not political justice. See Ch. LV.–LVII.

The virtue here inculcated is *probity, fairness.* The poet passes from the sphere of the family, where domestic affection reigns, to the world, in which the householder is to learn to treat all men with equity. The standard of this is shown in 120, where the trader is to regard *all men's interest as his own.* This alone secures the welfare of himself, and of his family.

This virtuous habit is called :—

(1) தகுதி (δίκη, δικαιοσύνη, ἐπιείκεια [Ar. *Eth.* V. x.]), 'fitness, what is due': தகவு. Those who possess it are தக்கார். Those without it are தகவிலர்.

(2) செப்பம் (ὀρθότης). This is defined in 119: 'unswerving rectitude in word and mind.'

(3) கோடாமை: 'like the evenly-poised balance, inclined to neither side,' 118.

(4) நடுவுநிலைமை 'impartial justice.' நடு, நடுவு, 113, 116, 117.

111. 'Est quaedam virtus aequitas dicta, quae tunc optima erit si valuerit procedere servando suam proprietatem in complexu amicorum, inimicorum, et extraneorum, seu indifferentium, qui nec amici nec inimici sunt.'

Ellis: 'That virtue which in all relations holds
Unchangeably its nature, that alone
Deserves the name of justice.'

This is almost the idea of Theognis (Aris. *Eth.* V. i. 15):

ἐν δὲ δικαιοσύνῃ συλλήβδην πᾶσ' ἀρετὴ ἔνι.

Aristotle says: αὔτη μὲν οὖν ἡ δικαιοσύνη ἀρετὴ μέν ἐστι τελεία, ἀλλ' οὐχ ἁπλῶς ἀλλὰ πρὸς ἕτερον.

112. 'Divitiae cumulatae ab eo, qui aequitatem possidet, sine destructione vigorem, id est, consistentiam habebunt, etiam in ejus progenitis.'

Ellis: 'By justice do the just their wealth uphold,
And confirmation, strong as virtue's self,
Bequeath their heirs.'

113. 'Divitias aequitatem transgrediendo partas, licet bonum tibi offerant, eo ipso die (quo tibi obveniunt) abjiciendo desere.'

114. 'Aequus ne, an aequitate carens, quis fuerit ex ejus progenitis dignoscetur.'

Ellis: 'Unerringly the just and unjust shows
The state in which their progeny is found.'

115. 'Emolumenti et damni gressum in aequo pectore non torqueri sapientium ornamentum est.'

The MS. is not clear, and the interpretation is strange. It is thus :— கேடு= *damnum*; பெருக்கம் = *emolumentum*; இல்லல் = *gressus* (?); அலம்=அமைவு=*conformity* (?); கோடுதல்=*torqueri*.

'அலநெஞ்சம்=pectus quod se accomodat alteri, *i.e.* se rationi conformat.' நெஞ்சத்து=நெஞ்சில். B. adds: 'Emolumenti gressus est exoriri ex peccato, torquetur amborum gressus quando quis ex aequitate sibi *damnum* ne immineat timet, aut ex iniquitate sibi *emolumentum* proventurum sperat.'

The Com. says: 'Loss and gain come from actions done in a former

28

state (அவற்றுக்குக் காரணம் பழவினையே); so the wise should not be diverted by them from right action.'

Graul says: 'Unheil und Heil kommt nicht für nichts.'

I think the idea is: 'Joy and sorrow are common to men; a wise man does not allow himself to be influenced too much by hopes or fears.'

116. 'Si quis ex corde (*i.e.* volens ac sciens) justitiam deserendo, aequum quod non est fecerit, sciat id idem esse ac dicere, volo meam ruinam.'

117. 'Damnum illius qui, ut aequitas fiat, in virtute sistit (hoc est, aequitatis virtutem constanter servat), sapientes damnum non aestimant.'

118. 'Ad instar librae, quae aequalitatem faciendo quod justum est librat, conformando se rationi in unam ex partibus non propendere, sapientium ornamentum est.'

Ellis: 'It is the glory of the just to stand
Like the adjusted balance duly poised,
Nor swerve to either side.'

119. 'In verbis tortuositate carere (*i.e.* proferre verba a ratione non deflectentia) aequitas est; si obtinueris, ut animus constanter tortuositate careat (*i.e.* si constantem animi ab aequitate inflexibilitatem obtinueris).'

120. 'Illi qui lucrandi officio incumbunt, valde lucrosum officium exercebunt, si aliorum bonum ita procuraverint, uti suum procurant.'

CHAPTER XIII.

Beschi: *Sensuum fraenatio.* Graul: *Continentia, Selbstzucht.*
Ellis: Subjection, restraint.

COM.'s analysis:—

I. 1–5. Its excellence.
II. 6. Control of body: காயம்.
III. 7–9. Restraint of tongue: வாக்கு.
IV. 10. Government of mind: மனம்.

This seems best expressed by σωφροσύνη.

121. 'Sensuum fraenatio ad coelites conducit, eorum relaxatio ad inferos.'

Ellis: 'To intercourse with gods
Forbearance leads; but passion unrestrained
Its victims, plunged in darkness, leaves.'

Comp. *Nâl.* 74:
'Who know what should be known, and rule themselves thereby;
Who fear what should be feared; who use all faculties
To bless the world; whose nature joys in all good gains;
For ever free from woes are they!'

122. 'Ut pretiosum quid fraenationem sensuum custodi, nam nullum est homini emolumentum eâ majus.'

காக்க an optative.

123. 'Si fraenationis scientiam discendo in virtutis viâ te continere valueris, id tibi apud eos qui fraenationis notitiam habent, magnum decus pariet.'

செறிவு=*compressio.*

124. 'Montium celsitudine valde major est celsitudo illius qui a suo statu non aberrando suos sensus fraenat.'

125. 'Omnibus bona est (*i.e.* utilis est) submissio; sed inter eos, qui sublimes ac divites sunt, valde sublimium opum conditionem habet.'

Ellis: 'Though self-control be excellent in all,
It most befits the envied state of those
That fortune smiles upon.'

126. 'Si in hac vitâ ad instar testitudinis quinque sua membra comprimentis, tuos quinque sensus comprimi feceris, etiam post mortem tibi celsitudinem affert; ob id enim in coelo beaberis.'

Bhag. Gîtâ, ii. 58.

127. 'Etsi omnia non custodias, linguam custodi; nisi custodieris, in verbis errando minimè fies.'

Ellis: 'Though unrestrained all else, restrain thy tongue;
For those degraded by licentious speech
Will rue their tongue's offence.'

128. 'Ex malorum verborum prosectione proximo unum tantum malum sequatur (nempe dehonoratio), ei tamen qui illa proferendi indolem habet, facit haec ut caetera bona quae habet, bona non sunt.'

But he adds that the literal sense is better: '*Divitias proximo damnosis verbis acquisitas male cedere, pessumire.*'

129. 'Vulnus quod alteri infligas ignis adustione, in animo delebitur; non delebitur vulnus linguae adustione inflictum.'

Ellis: 'The wound may heal, though from a burning brand,
And be forgotten; but the wound ne'er heals
A burning tongue inflicts.'

Comp. *Nâl.* 63, *words that burn*:

'Who opes his mouth and speaks unguarded words, his words
Will ceaseless burn his soul. The wise who ceaseless hear
And ponder well and calmly, never in their wrath
Give utterance to words of fire.'

130. 'Deus ipse conspicatum accurret pulchritudinem illius, qui scientias cum didicerit, iram fraenando suum animum intra virtutis viam continere valuerit.'

CHAPTER XIV.

Beschi: *Bene moratum esse.*
'Decorous life according to the laws of caste and order.'
Graul: *Sitte.*

Com.'s analysis:—

I. 1, 2. Its excellence.
II. 3–7. Good from its observance, evils from its neglect.
III. 8. Its consequences.
IV. 9, 10. Summary of '*decorum*' in word and deed.

The S. word is आचार *âchâra*, 'prescription.' Without self-restraint it is impossible, hence the order of subjects.

Comp. Barth, *Religions of India*, pp. 267, 268. Custom or மாறல் governs the world.

131. 'Cum boni mores homini celsitudinem afferant, boni mores plus quam vita ipsa sunt cautè custodiendi.'

132. 'Omni labore et conatu morum bonitatem custodi, nam si caetera omnia attentè et studiosè inspicias, nil praeter illam invenies quod tibi majus auxilium affere possit.'

133. 'Morum rectitudo etiam vilium prosapiam nobilitat; si mores a rectitudine deficiant, etiam nobilium prosapiam vilescere facient.'

This seems to say that to be strict in the performance of your assigned duty is true nobility. Comp. *Bhag. Gitâ*, iii. 35, xviii. 47.

Here धर्म=ஒழுக்கம். See Graul, *in loco*. In India the men of lowest caste are as tenacious of their dignity and privilege as the highest. The one thing is strong regard to ஆசாரம், ஒழுக்கம், குலத்தர்மம்.

134. 'Si Brachman obliviscatur eorum, quae didicit, ea iterum discere poterit; si vero in morum bonitate deficiat, ejus prosapia destruetur, id est abjectus evadet.'

135. 'Sicuti invidiam habentibus non fit opum incrementum, ita morum bonitate carentibus non fit celsitudo.'

136. 'In morum integritate non relaxantur sapientes, sciendo passuros se esse damnum abjectionis (*i.e.* se minimi esse faciendos).'

137. 'Ex morum integritate celsitudinem assequentur, ex morum integritatis defectu homines intolerabile vituperium referent.'

138. 'Virtutis semina sunt boni mores: mali mores omni tempore malum parient.'

139. 'Morum integritatem possidenti non convenit mala verba, licet indeliberatè suo ore proferre.'

140. 'Qui, multa postquam didicerint, sapientum moribus suos conformare nesciunt igorantes dicendi.'

CHAPTER XV.

Beschi: *Alienam uxorem non concupiscere.*

Com.'s analysis:—

I. 1–6. The evils of coveting another's wife.

II. 7–10. The virtue of not doing so.

The terms for a neighbour's wife are பிறனில், பிறனியலாள், பிறன்மனை, பிறற்குரியாள், பிறன்வரையாள், பிறன்பொருளாள். Add to these in *Nâlaḍi*, பிறன்றாரம், ஏதின்மனையாள், வம்பலன்பெண்.

Comp. *Nâl.* Ch. IX., பிறர்மனைநயவாமை, 81–87.

141. 'Stultitia, quae morem habet concupiscendi mulierem alterius propriam non reperietur in eo qui in orbe virtutem et divitias novit.'

Comp. *Nâl.* 81:

'The fear it brings is great. Its joy is brief. Each day
If 'tis divulged, death threatens by the King's decree.
And ever 'tis a deed that ends in pains of hell.
O shamefaced men, desire not neighbour's wife!'

142. 'Inter omnes, qui extra virtutem manent (*i.e.* qui vitia sectantur), non est stultior illo, qui in alterius domo sistit (*i.e.* alienam uxorem concupiscit).'

The Com. says, 'Fools, because they not only sacrifice virtue and wealth as other libertines; but, through fear of detection, lose even the pleasure they sought.'

143. 'Qui procedit concupiscendo malum cum uxore illius qui ei fidit, procul dubio non differt a mortuis.'

144. 'Quantumcunque magnitudinem habeas, quid tibi proderit, si nec tantum, quantum *milii* granum (*i.e.* nec minimum) considerando, alienam uxorem adeas.'

145. 'Qui peccandi facilitate allectus in aliena uxore honestatis limites transilierit, nunquam moriturum (*i.e.* nunquam desiturum) vituperium referet.'

எய்தும் for எய்துவான். The third person in உம் is one of the oldest forms in the language (see Intro. p. xx. § 7), and is used for both ஆண்பால் and பெண்பால். [Comp. 50, 69.]

146. 'Ab eo, qui in aliena conjuge honestatis limites praeterierit, inseparabilia sunt haec quatuor, nempe odium, peccatum, metus et infamia.'

இகவா is neg. adv. part. § 121=இகவாமல்.

Comp. *Nâl.* 82:

'Virtue, praise, friendship, greatness, all these four draw not
Anigh the men who covet neighbour's wife. Hatred,
Disgrace, and sin with fear, these four possessions dire,
Abide with men who covet neighbour's wife.'

147. 'Ille dicetur juxta virtutis proprietatem conjugatus vivere, qui non desiderat corpus mulieris quae est alterius propria.'

அறனியலான் (*Nannûl*, 297)=together with what is true virtue, in an essentially virtuous manner.

148. 'Magnanimitas non respiciendi (*i.e.* non concupiscendi), alienam uxorem magno in viro et virtus et sublime decus est.'

ஒன்றோ. Beschi: 'solumne?' Com. says ஓ is எண்ணிடைச்சொல். *Râmânuja* has ஒன்றுதானே, as Beschi. Graul thinks it is emphatic, but this is not Tamiḻ idiom.

149. 'Si quaeras quisnam sit in hoc maris habitaculo (*i.e.* in hoc orbe terraqueo), qui boni sit proprietarius (*i.e.* jus habeat ad bonum assequendum; est ille qui se non miscet corpori mulieris alterius propriae.'

150. 'Quamvis virtutem *non metiens* (*i.e.* virtuti *non se conformans*), ei contraria facias, semper tamen tibi bonum erit non concupiscere mulierem quae est intra alterius limites (*i.e.* alieni est juris).'

Graul: 'Sich Tugend nicht aneignend'; but in note he says, 'not wedding.' The meaning seems to be 'not making virtue his limit, so as not to transgress.'

CHAPTER XVI.

Beschi: *Patientia.*

Com.'s analysis:—

I. 1–4. Its excellence.
II. 5–8. Bearing with evil deeds.
III. 9, 10. Bearing with evil words.

150. 'Sufferre eos, qui te despiciunt, instar terrae, quae sustinet eos, qui eam calcant, praestans est virtus.'

152. 'Injuria quae tibi fit, quocumque tempore (i.e. *etiam cum id ulcisci possis*) [so also Com.] patienter toleranda est, sed isto melius erit illius omnino oblivisci.'

Comp. *Nâl.* 65:

'The young man's self-restraint is self-restraint. The gift
Of him who owns no stores of wealth is gift indeed.
When man has means and might to punish every fault,
If he forbear, call him the patient man.'

153. 'Sicuti inter miserias ea est praestantior miseria, quae hospitem non excipit, ita inter decora illud est praestantius decus, quod insipientium culpas sufferet ?'

This is called எடுத்துக்காட்டுவமையணி: 'As to cease to entertain guests is the lowest depths of poverty, so to bear with foolish men the highest virtue.' (III. Gr. 204.)

154. 'Si tuum honorem a te inseparabilem optas, procedendum tibi est cautè patientiam custodiendo.'

155. 'Sapientes non aestimant ut quid pretiosum impatientes; aestimant verò ut aurum patientes, eos cautè custodiendo (*i.e.* cavendo, ne quid indecorum iis fiat).'

156. 'Qui de injuria sibi illata ulciscuntur, unius diei gaudium referent, qui verò eam patienter sufferunt, usque ad mortem laudabuntur.'

157. 'Quamvis tuus proximus tibi injustum quid fecerit optimum tibi erit nil facere contrarium virtuti, commiserans illum ob damnum quod in altera vita ei paratum est.'

Comp. *Nâl.* 221, 223:

'When those to whom as good with strong desire we clung,
Prove otherwise; keep the sad secret undivulged!
The growing grain hath husk; the water hath its foam;
And flowers have outer sheath of leaves.'

'Lord of the lofty hilly land, where hum the bees
Through all the flowery Gôngu glade! Though friends should work
Ills passing thought, to bear is only thing that 's meet:
Patience of one is friendship of the twain.'

158. 'Eos qui ob animi elationem faciunt quod nimium (*i.e.* injustum) est, tu tuâ aequinimitate victos dimitte.'

The verse seems to embody the idea of S. Paul's injunction, 'Be not overcome of evil, but overcome evil with good.'—Rom. xii. 21.

159. 'Ipsis qui omnibus renunciarunt, majorem munditionem (*i.e.* splendorem seu perfectionem) habebunt conjugati, qui patienter suf-

ferunt mala verba quae ore proferunt qui limites transiliunt (*i.e.* qui nimis elati sunt).'

160. 'Qui poenitentiam agunt jejunando magni quidem fient, sed posteriores iis qui aliorum injuriosa verba patienter sufferunt.'

Comp. *Nâl.* 58 :

'To bear with those that speak despiteful words; yea, more,
To say, "Ah, will they sink in other world to hell,
The place of fire, as fruit of their despiteful words,"
And grieve, is duty of the perfect men.'

CHAPTER XVII.

Beschi: *Invidiâ non Affici.*

THE last Chapter treated of *பொறை* or *பொறுமை*, while the common word for envy is *பொறாமை* 'the not enduring.'

Com.'s analysis :—

I. 1, 2. Its absence is excellent.
II. 3–8. The evils of this temper.
III. 9, 10. Contrasted in effects.

161. 'Proprietatem non habendi invidiam in suo pectore viam cuíque esse ad celsitudinem assequendam, quisque secum statuat.'

The order is much inverted: 'Let (any) one (*ஒருவன்*) esteem (*கொள்க*) the quality which is free from envy in its soul (*தன்—வியல்பு*) as the way of decorum (*ஒழுக்காறுக*).' See 131, where *ஒழுக்கம்* is to be cherished more than life.

162. 'Si valueris erga omnes (*i.e.* etiam erga hostes), ab invidiâ immunis esse, hoc inter omnia decora par non habebit.'

163. 'Qui aliorum emolumentum non desiderando, illud iis invidet, dicetur nolle emolumentum à virtute profluens.'

164. 'Ex invidiâ malum alteri non inferunt sapientes sciendo damnum quod ob id experientur (propriè, quod patienter in illa mala via).'

165. 'Invidus, quamvis omnes suos hostes destruat, ruinam patietur, quia ad eum destruendum ipsa sua invidia satis superque est.'

166. 'Ejus qui invidis oculis aspicit ea, quae caeteris dantur, familia ad vestitûs ac cibi inopiam redigetur.'

167. 'Dea felicitatis invido irata, suae sorori, (quae est dea miseriae) eum prodet.'

168. 'Crudelis illa, quae dicitur invidia, hujus mundi felicitatem destruit, et postremò ad inferos perducit.'

169. 'Invidi hominis felicitas, et recti hominis infelicitas attentè considerandа est.'

Prosperity cannot proceed from envy, nor ruin from its opposite. If, then, an envious man be prosperous, or an unenvious person suffer loss, the wise will ponder the mystery. Com. says, 'old deeds' are the cause. The idea is expanded in Psa. lxxiii.

170. 'Nemo per invidiam dives evasit;
Nemo ob invidiae carentiam evasit pauper.'

CHAPTER XVIII.

Beschi: *Non inhiare alienis bonis.*

Com.'s analysis:—

I. 1–7. Evils of coveting other men's goods.
II. 8, 9. Excellence of not coveting.
III. 10. The two contrasted.

171. 'Si, sine ullo jure, alienis bonis inhiaveris, id tibi et familiae destructionem, et varia eo ipso tempore detrimenta causabit.'

172. 'Qui injusti vocari erubescunt, ob desiderium emolumenti, quod aliena bona afferunt, non faciunt quid, quod aequi censurare possint.'

173. 'Ob desiderium instantanei gaudii, quod affert alienorum bonorum possessio, virtuti contraria non facit, qui alia (nempe in aeternum duratura) gaudia desiderat.'

174. 'Qui sensus devictos, et ab omni deceptione immunem scientiam habent, aliena non concupiscent, neque in suae paupertatis remedium.'

175. 'Quidnam tibi proderit acutum et vasta eruditione praeditum ingenium, si aliena concupiscendo, apud omnes stulta opereris.'

176. 'Qui ob desiderium charitatem erga proximos exercendi, statum conjugalem, qui via est ad illis subveniendum, amplexus est, aliena concupiscendo, solâ fraudulentorum ad illa assequenda mediorum investigatione, suum propositum destruet (quia fraus omnis charitati adversatur).'

177. 'Noli appetere emolumentum aliena concupiscendo partum, quia dum illud fructicaverit, difficile erit, ut ex illo bonum fructum referas.'

178. 'Si quaeras quidnam sit unde tua felicitas immunita consistere possit, opus est ut non concupiscas quae alius concupiscit fortunae bona.'

179. 'Dea felicitatis apud eos, qui scientiam habent non concupiscen-

tem aliena bona, ex eo quod noscant, id esse virtuti consentaneum, sedem figet, sciens illum locum suae mantione consonum esse.'

180. 'Si non praevidendo mala, quae inde sequuntur, aliena concupiscas, id tibi ruinam pariet; elevatus verò animus, quo tale desiderium a te distinueris, tibi decus pariet.'

CHAPTER XIX.

Beschi: *Non detrahere.*

COM.'s analysis:—

I. 1. Benefit of the virtue of abstaining from backbiting.

II. 2-4. Detraction a cruel evil.

III. 5-9. Faults resulting from it.

181. 'Quamvis nec virtutem sectaris, et ei contraria facias, semper tamen tibi decorosum erit dici, quod detrahere nescis.'

182. 'Virtutem exterminando vitia sectari malum est, sed eo pejus erit proximo praesenti fictam laetitiam ostendere et absenti detrahere.'

183. 'Ad assequendum fructum de quo virtutis scientia loquitur melius est mori, quam vivere proximo absenti detrahendo et praesenti falsam amicitiam ostendendo.'

184. 'Quamvis aliquis coram te sine ulla commiseratione asperrima in te verba proferat, tu noli unquam post ejus tergum verba loqui quae futurum non respicient (*i.e.* quae non attendant ad mala quae inde sequentur).'

185. 'Detractor, qui virtutem laudat, quod ex corde id non faciat, dignosci potest, ex vili officio detrahendi, cui se manciparit.'

186. 'Si tu alicujus vitium manifestaveris, ille inter omnia tua vitia, ex quae majora sunt seligendo manifestabit.'

தன்=உடைய 'the chief faults, culled out, of him who . . .'

187. 'Detractores, nescientes laetis verbis amicitiam fovere, suis odiosis verbis et ipsos sibi amicitiâ junctos a se alienabunt.'

188. 'Qui indolem habent detrahendi ipsis suis amicis, quid, quaeso, facient suis inimicis?'

189. 'Nonne ex mero virtutis motivo tellus sustinet eos, qui proximo detrahendi vile munus exercent?'

190. 'Si quisque eo modo, quo censurat inimicorum vitia censuraret suum detrahendi vitium, esset ne inter homines detractionis malum?'

CHAPTER XX.

Beschi : *Otiosa verba non loqui.*

Com.'s analysis :—

I. 1–6. The evil of using idle words.
II. 7–9. The virtue of eschewing them.
III. 10. What to speak, and what not to speak.

191. 'Qui audientibus stomacum causando inutilia loquitur ab omnibus contemnetur.'

Beschi reads எல்லாராலும், which destroys metre. It is வே. தொ. (§ 270).

192. 'Coram multis vana loqui pejus est, quam amico injuriam facere.'

193. 'In utilia verba quae diffuse profers, te fatuum praedicant.'

194. 'Si in coetu infructuosos ac vanos sermones institueris, nec laetitiâ audientes afficies, et probi nomen amittes.'

He reads நன்மையுணீங்கும்='ex probitate alienabuntur.' Comp. *Nâl.* 71 :—

'Lord of the pleasant land, where down the mountains cool
The streams as garlands fall! with fools no converse hold.
The fool will speak all words that hurt. As best you can
To slip away from him is good.'

195. 'Si praestans vir futilia loquatur, statim suam magnitudinem atque aestimationem amittet.'

196. 'Eum qui in futilibus sermonibus tempus terit, hominem ne vocato, hominum scoriam voca.'

197. 'Praestanti viro non adeo nocet irrationabilia loqui, uti nocet loqui futilia.'

198. 'Qui ingenio pollent difficilia quaeque perscrutante, verba, quae notabilem fructum non habeant, proferre non audent.'

199. 'Qui ab erroribus defaecatum et perfectam scientiam habent, neque per oblivionem infructuosa loquuntur.'

200. 'Ex quae loqui vis, ea quae alicujus momenti sunt, loquere; ea quae nullius momenti sunt, silentio involve.'

CHAPTER XXI.

Beschi: *Peccati metus.*

COM.'s analysis:—

I. 1–3. Evil deeds to be dreaded.

II. 4–9. Evil done to others brings evil on oneself.

III. 10. He who does no evil, suffers none.

201. 'Qui peccata patrarunt peccatum non timent, qui vero probi sunt valde timent peccati fascinum.'

202. 'Cum ignis quandoque bonum, peccatum vero semper malum afferat, plusquam ignem peccatum time.'

203. 'Inter omnes scientias eam praestantissimam dicent, quae etiam cum occasio se affert faciendi hostibus quidquam quod peccaminosum sit, scit ab eo abstinere.'

204. 'Neque per oblivionem aliorum damnum excogites; si enim excogitaveris, excogitantis ruinam Deus excogitabit.'

205. 'Etiam nullum aliud tuae ruinae remedium adsit, peccare noli; si peccaveris, nec novas divitias assequeris, et caetera, quae ante possidebas, amittes.'

206. 'Qui non vult a malis perimi, nolit ipse caeteris malum facere.'

207. 'A quovis potenti hoste evadere poteris; qui est peccatum perpetuô te insequendo, tandem te perimet.'

208. 'Peccatoris ruina ab eo inseparabilis est, non secus ac umbra à corpore.'

209. 'Si teipsum amas, nil quod malum sit, quantumvis minimum, facere audeas.'

210. 'Si dixeris, quod quis a rectâ viâ aberrendo malum facere non audet, scito quod ille difficulter ruinam patietur.'

CHAPTER XXII.

Beschi: *Munificum esse cum iis, cum quibus mundi mos id postulat, puta cum templis, cum pauperibus, cum propinquis, cum amicis, cum hospitibus.* A.: *Bienfaisance éclairée.* Drew: The knowing and discharging of those acts of benevolence, which are approved by the world.

COM.'s analysis:—

I. 1–3. The excellence of due beneficence.

II. 4. Neglect is death.

III. 5–7. Wealth is thus of value.

IV. 8, 9. Poverty should not hinder it.

V. 10. Real loss cannot accrue from it.

Com.: 'He has spoken of evils from which mind, tongue, and body are to be guarded, now he speaks of good things to be done.'

211. 'Sicuti pluvia suo tempore non desinit pluere, licet nullum a terrâ retributionem ferat, ita non debet munificentia omitti, etiamsi nulla sit retributio.'

212. 'Omnia quae quis suâ industriâ cumulat, ad quid ei dantur, nisi ut munificus sit cum iis, cum quibus mos id postulat?'

213. 'Neque in coelo, neque in hac terrâ, facile erit adipisci bonum quod majus sit munificentiâ in eos, in quos par est eam exercere.'

214. 'Qui in munificentiâ morem servat vivus dicendus est; caeteri, licet vivant, inter mortuos sunt recensendi.'

215. 'Divitiae illius, qui erga eos, quos mundi mos postulat, munificentiam exercet, simile sunt lacui aquâ pleno juxta oppidum.'

216. 'Divitiae, si possideantur ab eo, qui munificentiam exercere gestit, perinde se habet, ac si arbor fructifera in medio oppidi fructibus referta sit.'

217. 'Divitiae illius, qui habet praestans illud decus munificentiam exercendi, similes erunt arbori medicinali, quae sit omnibus obvia.'

218. 'Qui scientiam habent gnaram obligationis, quam quisque habet morem servandi, etiam cum divitiis carent, munificentiam totaliter non deserunt, sed pro viribus illam exercent.'

219. 'Munificum virum pauperem evadere non adeo illum vexat, uti displicentia, quam habet, quod nequeat exercere munificentiam ut aequum est.'

220. 'Si ex munificentiâ inopiam gigni dixeris, ego dicam talem inopiam adeo pretiosam esse, ut quovis pretio emi debeat, etiamsi te ipsum vendere opus sit.'

CHAPTER XXIII.

Beschi: *Eleemosinae largitio.*

ஈகை is the S. दान தானம். The Com. says: 'The last chapter refers to this world; this to the next world. There charity is inculcated as due to a man's position, here as necessary to the obtaining of *vîdu*.' ஈகை 'act of giving'; ஈவு 'gift'; § 143.

221. 'Iis qui omnino pauperes sunt, aliquid largiri virtuosa largitio erit, nam caeterae omnes largitiones conditionem habent retributionis; quia vel factae in retributionem, vel ob spem retributionis.'

The real nature of charity: it seeks no return.

222. 'Quamvis tibi suadeant optimam ad coelum viam esse divitias cumulare, semper malum puta; quamvis tibi suadeant sua erogantibus aditum in coelo non esse, tu semper id optumum puta.'

எனினும்='though it were possible for them to say this, which it is not.'

223. 'Pauperi stipem petenti, non profitendo abjectum illum verbum, "nil habeo," statim stipem erogare, vivorum nobilium conditio est.'

Since உள is plural, we must supply உம் twice: உரையாமையும் ஈதலும் (Intro. p. xviii. *e*).

224. 'Malum est a mendico rogari quousque ejus vultum laetum aspexeris.'

The use of படு is noteworthy.

225. 'Decus est poenitentium famem tolerare, sed hoc inferius est decore eorum, qui caeterorum fami consulunt.'

'Charitas perfectior est poenitentiâ.'

226. 'Qui pauperum fami consulit, aliquid erogando, hoc non amittit; sed in manu pauperis deponit, deinceps sibi profuturum.'

227. 'Difficile est ut pessimus morbus famis aggrediatur eum qui didicit suum cibum cum caeteris partiri.'

ஊண் from உண். Intro. p. xxiv. § 8.

228. 'Immisericors ille, qui suas divitias caeteris non elargitas in morte amittere, quam caeteris distribuere mavult, nonne ignorare videtur quale gaudium afferat caeteros suis largitionibus laetificare?'

229. 'Plusquam ipsum mendicandi officium indecorum sane est sua, usque ad fastidium, sine socio (*i.e.* exclusis pauperibus) comedere?'

230. 'Morte pejus nullum est malum; sed ubi largitio non jungitur, bonum erit mori (quia cessat terrae illud inutile pondus).'

அது+உம் 'even that'=அதுவும், but அளபெடை takes the place of வ்.

CHAPTER XXIV.

Beschi: *Laus*, i.e. *laudabiliter vivere*. G.: *Ruhm*.

'Renown.' The word புகழ்='praise, fame, glory.' A.: *Honneur*.

THE Com. says it is 'the reward that comes to the householder in this life, who obeys the precepts contained in the foregoing chapters. It is chiefly bestowed on those who give. Hence its place after the chapter on *giving*.'

I. The special excellence of it (3).

1. Man's greatest gain on earth.

2. The theme of those who talk—not of poets only. His name becomes a 'household world.'

3. Spontaneously—by the world's consent—it ever rises.

II. The excellence of those who gain it (2).

4. They gain in both worlds.

5. They turn all to gain.

III. The inferiority of those who gain it not (4).

6. Their life a failure.

7. They bring reproach on themselves.

8. A good name is the best thing he can leave behind. This he forfeits.

9. They bring a curse on the earth: mere cumberers of the ground.

IV. The contrast: living and dead (1).

10. Fame is life: its absence, death.

The picture of the life of the virtuous Tamil householder, as drawn (in Ch. v.–xxiv.) by the Pariah weaver-priest of Mayilâpûr a thousand years ago, is, it will be admitted, a very attractive one; and there is reason to believe that the villages of the Karnatic still contain many worthy householders whose life is governed by the rules here prescribed.

231. 'Ita vive ut munifici laudem assequaris, nam nihil est homini quod in hac vitâ magis profectum sit.'

232. 'Quidquid homines dixerint, vera laus in eum cadet qui pauperibus necessaria largitur'; *or*, 'Quotquot poetae intexunt laudes omnes in eum cadent, qui pauperibus aliquid largitur.'

233. 'Unam si excipias laudem, nil aliud est in mundo quod immortale sit.'

234. 'Si intra terrae fines immortalem assequaris laudem, mundus deorum suos cives non curabit; *i.e.* suorum civium oblitus in te oculos convertet.'

235. 'Damnum emolumento esse, et mortem vitam esse, non facile invenies, nisi apud magica prodigia monstrantes.'

He explains: 'Glory is like magic, which exhibits gain in loss and death in life; for it makes poor men happy, and causes the dead to live in the memory of men.'

236. 'Si nascaris, cum dotibus laudabilibus nascere, qui has non habent, melius est si non nascantur, quam si nascantur?'

237 (240). 'Dedecus est homini non assequi id per quod non toti morimur, sed pars nostri in terris remanet, nempe laudem.'

[237 and 240 are interchanged in Beschi.]

238. 'Terra quae sustinet homines laude carentes suam foecunditatem in sterilitatem vertet.'

239. 'Qui sine notâ vivunt, ii sunt vivi; qui sine laude vivunt, ii sunt mortui.'

240 (237). 'Qui absque laude vivit, si a caeteris despiciatur, cur de illis queritur, de se ipso queri debet.'

CHAPTER XXV.

Beschi: '*Virtutes religiosorum,*

i.e. de virtutibus eorum propriis, qui omnibus renunciarunt, ne affectus ad aliquod sensibile impedimento sit ad aeternam gloriam assequendam.'

அருள்='amor proximi, seu commiseratio in illum.' 1 Cor. xiii.

This is the beginning of the section of துறவறம், or 'the virtue of renunciation': ascetic virtue. The praises of ascetics have already been celebrated in Ch. III. This section is divided into two parts—

Ch. XXV.–XXXIII., விரதம் [S. *vrata*], 'religious observances;'
Ch. XXXIV.–XXXVII., ஞானம் 'wisdom';

to which is added a chapter on ஊழ் 'fate, destiny.'

I feel a doubt as to the authority for the divisions and titles throughout the work.

அருள் is defined by Com. as 'the tenderness (கருணை) which, without any association or connection with them, naturally is felt for all that live.' What அன்பு 'special affection' (Ch. VIII.) is to the householder, that அருள் 'general tender regard' is to the ascetic.

Com.'s analysis:—

I. Its special excellence (2).
 1. It belongs only to the good.
 2. It is the outcome of all teaching.

II. It removes affliction in both worlds (3).
 3. Gracious men escape the 'evil world.'
 4. It saves from vice.
 5. The testimony of universal experience.

III. The evils of the absence of 'grace' (4).
 6. Oblivion of higher things.
 7. No future bliss.
 8. Irreparable loss.
 9. No virtue without it.

IV. How to cultivate it (1).
 10. Put yourself in their place.

The ‘methods,’ ஆறு, in 242, are said by Com. to be :—(1) காட்சி ‘perception by the senses’; (2) அனுமானம் ‘inference’; and (3) ஆகமம் ‘authority.’ This differs somewhat from the Nyâya. See *Tarka-saṅgraha*, p. 40.

241. ‘Inter omnes felicitates, illa est praestans felicitas quae derivatur ex *amore proximi*; nam quae derivatur ex divitiis vilibus etiam vilibus hominibus communis est.’

Ellis: ‘The highest felicity is that which proceeds from *universal benevolence*; the felicity proceeding from wealth is enjoyed even by the vilest of mankind.’

242. ‘Mature omnia considerando proximi amorem assequi cura; nam si consideres omnes diversas sectas, quae inter homines vigent, videbis hunc ab omnibus tanquum socium admitti.’

Ellis: ‘On due consideration it will be found, that all sects maintain that the aid of charity is necessary to obtain felicity; reflect carefully, therefore, and cherish the benevolent affections.’

243. ‘Qui in suo pectore proximi amorem fovent, non intrabunt in mundum afflictionis, ubi tenebrae regnant.’

Ellis: ‘They enter not the world, where darkness reigns
And where affliction howls, whose bosoms glow
With love for all their kind.’

244. ‘Qui homines in mundo existentes a malis defendendo erga ipsos *charitatem* fovent, his, ex unanimi sapientum voce, nil est, unde sibi malum timere possint.’

Ellis: ‘Those who in their hearts cherish charity towards all existent beings, they truly say, need not fear any mischief to themselves.’

245. ‘Quod iis, qui *erga proximum amorem* servant, nullum malum obveniat, testis est vasta haec terra, in quâ venti spirant (quae nescit exemplum in contrarium).’

Ellis: ‘Witnesses the mighty earth, where'er the winds
Send forth their blasts, that evil cannot reach
The charitable man.’

246. ‘Sapientes dicent, illos qui *amorem proximi* a se alienando, contraria faciendo procedunt, oblitos esse malorum, in quae incidunt, qui a virtute deficiunt.’

247. ‘Eodem modo quo divitiis carentes frui nequeunt hujus mundi gaudiis, *amore proximi* carentes frui nequeunt alterius mundi gloriâ.’

Ellis: ‘The other world (*i.e.* its joys) belongeth not to those who are devoid of *charity*, as this world belongeth not to those who are devoid of wealth.’

248. ‘Qui divitias amiserunt poterunt aliquando florescere uti prius;

qui vero *amorem proximi* dimisit, difficile est ut iterum vere virtuosus sit.'

Ellis: 'Those now devoid of wealth may hereafter flourish in happiness; but those devoid of *charity* cannot be free from offence.'

249. 'Virtutes omnes, quas exercet, qui *amore proximi* caret, si bene consideres, perinde se habent ac Dei notitia in mente capto.'

He adds: 'Both things are impossible.'

Ellis: 'As the comprehension of the true God, without clearness of understanding is impossible; so, also, is the practice of virtue without *charity*.'

250. 'Dum in proximum qui te debilior est, absque pietate inveheris, memento, qualis tu sis, quum coram caeteris te potentioribus adstas.'

Ellis: 'Imagine thyself before those more powerful than thou art, when about to treat harshly those more weak than thyself.'

CHAPTER XXVI.

Beschi: *Abstinentia a carnibus.*

251. 'Qui ut sua caro pinguescat, alienas carnes comedit quinam eum viventibus lenitatem et clementiam exercere dicetur?'

252. 'Sicuti qui suas divitias custodire nescit, illarum possessionem non habet (quia illas amittet); ita qui carnes comedit, lenitatis possessionem non habet.'

253. 'In quonam differt animus illius, qui ob solum gustum carnes viventium comedit, ab animo illius qui ob solum gustum arma capit ad viventium necem? (Nil inter se differunt, cum uterque ad illorum necem dirigatur.)'

254. 'Si quaeras quid sit lenitas, quid ejus contrarium, scito esse haec duo, nempe viventia non mactare, et ea mactare; quapropter virtuosa esse nequit illorum carnium comestio.'

255. 'Ab abstinentiâ a carnibus viventium vita servatur, quapropter eos qui viventium carnes comedunt, infernus iterum non evomet (*i.e.* diu in inferno cruciabuntur).'

256. 'Si dicas non mactari in mundo viventia ad finem comestionis, jam nullus erit, qui carnes ob pretium det.'

This points to the controversy between the Buddhists and the Jains. The former might not slay, but might eat the slain. The latter, with more consistency, were forbidden to eat or slay. Comp. Manu, v. 51.

257. 'Illi quibus cadavera nauseam causant, qui poterunt sine stomacho carnibus vesci, si considerent eas ex alterius viventis cadavere refectas esse?'

Here B. takes புண்='cadaver,' as though it were பிணம்.

258. 'Qui scientiam habent ab omni deceptione immunem non vescentur carnibus, quae non sunt nisi cadavera.'

259. 'Melius est non comedere carnes damnificando alicujus viventis vitam, quam mille victimas immolare butyrum fundendo super illas.'

260. 'Eum qui viventes non mactat, et carnes respuit, viventia omnia junctis manibus venerabuntur.'

CHAPTER XXVII.

Beschi: *Poenitentia.*

261. 'Ex vitae austeritate provenientia incommoda patienter ferre ac ne caeteris molestiam aut dolorem afferat, sui depressionem et mortificationem aequo animo tolerare, duo sunt, quae poenitentiae formam constituunt.'

262. 'Iis qui supradictam poenitentiam possident, praeter meritum, quod illis obvenit, poenitentiae quoque virtus oritur; qui vero supradictam poenitentiam non habent infructuosè in poenitentiae virtute acquirendâ laborant.'

263. '*Sub praetextu subveniendi Religiosis nonne caeteri obliti videntur poenitentiae, quam agere debent?*' B. adds: 'Sensus est, falsum esse, quod plurimi putant, Poenitentiae virtutem propriam esse status religiosi, non vero conjugalis, et sufficere si conjugatus Religioso succurrat, ut in suo statu poenitenti vivat, nam poenitentia est cuilibet statui necessaria.'

Dr. Graul more exactly translates: '*Ceteri studiosi poenitentibus subveniendi—num forte poenitentiae obliti sunt?*' This seems to be correct. But in his German version he says: 'Die Andern, den Andern beizuspringen willens, haben wohl der Busse vergessen'; and explains substantially as F. Beschi. The Com. says the meaning is 'Penitence is more than gifts.' The sense seems to be, 'The householder, though he perform no penance himself, is not unmindful of it; since he supplies to penitents the means by which they live to perform their penitential acts; and so he shares in the reward and merit of those acts.' Comp. 41, 46, and the whole scope of Ch. v.

264. 'Virtutis hostium destructio, et virtutis fautorum cumulatio, si bene consideres, per poenitentiam obtinentur.'

B. read ஒன்னாரை; but says the metre requires ஒன்னார், which is the text of the Madras editions.

265. 'Cum per illum obtinere possis omnia, quae in futuro seculo cupis bona, poenitentiam in hoc mundo exercere debes.'

266. 'Qui poenitentiam agunt sibi emolumentum parant; caeteri qui, concupiscentiae laqueis irretiti, eam non agunt, damnum sibi parant.'

Comp. *Nâl.* 51 :—

'As when lamp enters darkness flies, so sin stands not
Before man's penitence. As when in lamp the oil
Wastes, darkness rushes in, so evil takes its place
Where deeds of virtue cease.'

267. 'Sicuti aurum in igne lucidum evadit, ita corporis afflictatio poenitentium animum nitidum reddit.'

268. Beschi: '*Eum qui perfectam sui animi possessionem obtinuit, caeteri mortales, qui tale decus not habent, venerabuntur*'; adding, '*perfecte* autem *suum animum possidet,* qui eum non dividit cum concupiscentiis suis, à quibus per poenitentiam emancipaverit sese.'

Hè explains தானற by *perfectè.* The *Vêdânta* philosophy would interpret தானற by அகங்காரமற 'so that the *I*, the sense of *self* may cease.'

Comp. M. Arnold :—

'We see all sights from pole to pole,
And glance, and rush, and bustle by,
And never once possess our soul,
Before we die.'

269. 'Qui poenitentiae decus obtinuerunt, et ipsius "Yamnis" qui deus est mortis, poterunt manus effugere (hoc est, immortales evadere).'

270. 'Causa cur plurimi verâ virtute careant, est quia poenitentiam agunt pauci, plurimi eum non agunt.'

CHAPTER XXVIII.

Beschi: *Hipocrisis*; i.e. *virtutis species, cui animus non jungitur, sed exterius tantum demonstratur.* A.: *Feinte moralité.*

271. 'Eum, qui animo fraudulento virtutem quâ caret exterius fingit, quinque elementa, quae ejus corpori mixta sunt, interius deridebunt.'

The Sanskrit *Tarka Saṅgraha* (Ballantyne), p. 3, gives nine categories: 'earth, water, light, air, ether, time, place, soul and mind.'

Beschi interprets: 'Hippocrita ab ipsâ suâ conscientiâ (qui per elementa sibi admixta designatur) quae suae fictionis testis est, deridebatur.'

A.: '*Les cinq éléments (de son être).*'

272. 'Talem virtutis speciem fingas, quae coelum ipsum aequet;—quid tibi proderit, si tuae cum conscientiae testimonio pravus fueris?'

273. 'Virtutis larva, quam in exteriori habitu prae se fert qui virtute vacuus suis concupiscentiis habenas laxat, est sicuti larva bovis, qui tigridi pelle coopertus segetes depascitur.'

274. 'Poenitentiam fingendo poenitentiae dissona facere, perinde est ac venatoris officium, qui post arbustum se celando, aves decipit.'

275. 'Ficta virtus eorum qui se dicunt affectibus orbos, ut magnifiunt, multa ac talia damna affert, ut dicere cogantur, eheu! quid feci.'

276. 'Nemo est in mundo inclementior (vel saevior) iis, qui interius affectibus non renuntiando, sed exterius quasi affectibus orbos se praebendo vivunt, decipiendo eos, a quibus vitae subsidia extorquent.'

277. 'Aliqui sunt in mundo, quid quoad exteriorem habitum spectati similes videntur semini குன்றிமணி dicto; in interiore verò statu, nigriores sunt apice ejusdem seminis?'

278. 'Multi homines interiorem animi nequitiam lavacris aliisque actionibus exterioribus virtutem redolentibus celando procedunt.'

279. 'Sagitta quamvis recta sit crudelis est; cithara licet tortuosa dulcis est (idque ob affectus quos causant); eodem prorsus modo homines non sun aestimandi ex aspectu, sęd ex operum qualitate.'

280. 'Nec capitis rasio nec longa caesaries opus tibi erit, si abstinueris ab iis, quae sapientes reprobant.'

This alludes to the diverse practices of Çaivas, of whom the *Paṇḍârams* shave the head, and the *Tambirâns*, with Yôgis in general, allow the hair to grow.

The poet's idea as to the standard of moral excellence is that of Aristotle (*Ethics*, II. vi. 15, Sir A. Grant's ed., vol. i. p. 499) who speaks of *ἀρετὴ* (அறம்) as *ὡρισμένη λόγῳ καὶ ὡς ἂν ὁ φρόνιμος ὁρίσειεν*, 'determined by a standard according as the *thoughtful man* would determine.' Sir A. Grant adds: 'The *thoughtful man* stands as the representative of the absolute reason of man, manifested in the individual consciousness.' The *φρόνιμος* in the குறள் is variously named as *கற்றவன்*, *அறிந்தவன்*, *சான்றவன்*, and collectively உலகு.

Comp. 140, 280, Ch. XLIII.

CHAPTER XXIX.

Beschi: *Nullum defraudare.*

281. 'Qui dicitur coelestem gloriam sine contemptu assequi desiderans, cavere debet, ne caeteros in aliquo, quantulum cunque illud sit, defraudet.'

282. 'Cum ipsa peccandi intentio peccatum sit, noli unquam dicere, seu cogitare dicendo, aliena bona per fraudem rapiam.'

283. 'Fraude partum emolumentum, quasi limites transgrediendo ruinam afferet.'

284. 'Aliquem defraudandi cupiditas, quamvis dum nascitur parva quaedam culpa videatur, cum tamen fructificat, immortalia damna affert.'

285. 'In iis qui obtutum figunt (*i.e.* animum intendunt) in vile officium defraudandi caeteros, reperiri nequit possessio amoris erga proximum necessarii cuique qui statum religiosum intendit.'

286. 'Qui nimiam cupiditatem habent caeteros defraudendi non possunt procedere conformiter perfectioni in quâ sistunt.'

287. 'Tenebrosum consilium defraudandi caeteros non invenitur in eo qui ambit decus ex justitiâ proveniens.'

288. 'Sicuti ab eorum animo, qui justitiam servare sciunt, inseparabilis est virtus; ita ab eo, qui aliena rapere didicit, inseparabilis est fraus.'

289. 'Eo ipso tempore in quo mensuram non servant, sibi ruinam parant ii, qui nil aliud scire videntur nisi aliena rapiendi officium?'

290. 'Qui proximum defraudant incerti sunt de vitâ temporali; qui verò neminem defraudant certi sunt etiam de eternâ.'

CHAPTER XXX.

Beschi: *Oris integritas.* Com.: மெய்யினதுதன்மை.

291. 'Si quaeras, quid sit quod dicitur oris integritas, scito esse non loqui nisi talia, quae nullum in se malum contineant.'

292. 'Et ipsum loqui falsa in oris integritate locum habebit, sine culpâ proximo bonum afferat.' He adds: 'Sermo est *de falsitate sine mendacio prolatâ.*'

'S. Paul's position appears to be that the duty of truth-speaking is an offshoot of the ordinary relations of man to man, and that it is a consequence of men being members one of another. The ground for the duty is the relation of charity in which we stand to each other, of the unity, moral and social, by which we are connected with each other. Eph. iv. 25.' Compare the whole passage, pp. 155–160, in Mozley's *Ruling Ideas in Early Ages.*

293. 'Noli unquam sciens ac prudens mentiri quia post prolatum mendacium tuamet te conscientia vexabit.'

தன்னெஞ்சறிவது is nom. of respect. 'Lie not in rĕgard to that of which thy mind is conscious.'

294. 'Si in loquendo nunquam contra tuam mentem ieris (processeris) in mente sapientum omnia possidebis decora.'

295. 'Si animum habeas a quovis mendacio refugientem, et os huic animo conformiter loquens, ipsos poenitentes, atque eleemosinarios superabis.'

He adds: 'It is easier to afflict the body and to give alms than to guard oneself from every falsehood.'

296. 'Nil est ita laudabile uti oris integritas, cum per ipsum sine labore ac molestiâ adipisci possis bonum quod tibi afferrent caeterae virtutes omnes.'

But comp. 323.

297. 'Si constanter oris integritatem servaveris, bonum est caeteras virtutes exercere.'

Beschi thinks பொய்யாமை=(1) oris integritatem; (2) constanter. In செய்யாமைசெய்யாமை he sees a double negative='non facere omissionem.' The absence of truthfulness would invalidate every virtue: 'First secure truth, and then do not omit the practice of any virtue.' The repetition (அடுக்கு, III. Gram. 200) is for emphasis.

298. 'Corporis munditiem parit aqua, animi munditiem parit oris integritas.'

299. 'Non omnis splendor proprius est sapientis splendor; proprius ejus splendor est in oris integritate splendere.'

A.: '*C'est la lumière (d'une bouche) qui ne ment pas.*'

300. 'In omnibus scientiis, quas veridicas ego novi, nil est quod superat veracitatis decus.'

CHAPTER XXXI.

Beschi : *Non irasci.*

THE commonest word for this, the S. *கோபம்*, is not found in the *குறள்.* We have *வெகுளி*, *சினம்*, *கதம்*, *q.v.*

301. 'Si irasci caveas in eum, qui id meretur, dici poteris irae fraenator; nam in eum, qui id non meretur, quid si irascaris, quid si non irascaris?'

செல் gives another idea: 'Where your anger can make itself felt.' I see no reference to merit.

302. 'Insuper irasci in te potentiores malum est; sed multo pejus erit irasci in tibi inferiores.'

In one case you hurt yourself, in the other both your foe and yourself.

303. 'Cum ex eo semper tibi malum obveniat, noli alicui irasci, sive te major sit, sive minor, sive aequalis.'

யார்மாட்டும் includes *வலியார்*, *எளியார்* and *ஒப்பார்*.

304. 'Est ne hostis tam noxius uti interior hic hostis nempe ira, quae vultûs laetitiam et cordis serenitatem destruit?'

305. 'Si teipsum a malis defendere cupis, ab irâ cave, nam nisi caveris, tu amet ira te cruciabit.'

306. 'Irae ignis non modo eos, in quibus gignitur, adierit; sed etiam tabulam securitatis quam in hoc miseriarum pelago habent, nempe consanguineos, et amicos absumit.'

307. 'Ejus qui iram sibi proficuam putando eam sibi comitem adsciscit, ruina ita infallibilis est uti infallibilis est ictus manu terram percutientis.'

308. 'Etiam ei, qui tibi tale malum fecit, ut aequet splendorem plurium ignium simul junctorum, si possibile tibi erit, non irasci optimum erit?'

309. 'Si quis neque irascendi cogitationem in corde admiserit, omnia quae cogitaverit bona simul obtinebit.'

310. 'In ira exorbitantes sunt mortuis similes; qui iram fraenant, similes sunt iis, qui in coelo felicitur vivunt.'

CHAPTER XXXII.

Beschi: *Nemini malefacere.*

[I have refrained from references to the Holy Scriptures, which the reader can readily supply.]

311. 'Inculpatorum virorum conditio est nemini malum facere, etiam si inde talem felicitatem obtenturi sint, quae ipsis celsitudinem pariat.'

Com. says: 'Neither for your own profit, nor from malice, nor from heedlessness.'

செல்வம் is interpreted to be the 'mystic powers' which a *yogi* acquires. The obvious meaning is 'wealth which confers distinction.'

312. 'Inculpatorum virorum conditio est, etiam si quis ex odio ipsis malefaciat ei malum non referre.'

313. 'Et ipsis hostibus non sunt facienda mala; nam postquam illa feceris, tibi inevitabile damnum afferent.'

செய்யாமை=செய்யாமல் used abs.='even when you have done no wrong to them.'

314. 'Tibi malum facientes plectendi optimus modus est, beneficium ipsis faciendo pudore affectos eos dimittere.'

This is in effect the saying ascribed to Buddha: 'Enmity never comes to an end through enmity here below; it come to an end by non-enmity.' (Oldenberg's *Buddha*, p. 293.) See the story of Long-grief and Long-life. Comp. *Dhamma-pada*, 222, 223, translated by F. Max Müller.

315. 'Quid tibi spirituales ac divinae scientiae proderunt, si alienum malum perinde ac proprium cavere nescias?'

316. 'Quod tu nosti malum essĕ, ne concupiscas alteri facere.'

317. 'Quovis tempore, cuicumque, quantulum-cumque illud sit, volens ac prudens, malum [ne facias] cavere optimum est.'

[The rest of the Chapter and verses to 326 (inclusive) are missing in the India House MS. of Beschi's *Kuṛṛaḷ*.]

CHAPTER XXXIII.

Beschi: *Non occidere.*

1–6. In Beschi missing.

This chapter inculcates the virtue of अहिंसा *ahiṁsâ*, or 'respect for all that has life.' The Com. says this subject is treated last because this virtue is the highest. Manu, v. 43 *seq.*, x. 63, xi. 23.

322. பல்லுயிர் 'the manifold life of other creatures.'—Drew. It is

not only abstinence from animal food that is inculcated, but cherishing (ஓம்புதல்) all the inferior creation.

All the negative commands, obedience to which confers on man 'the five-fold uprightness,' are reiterated by Tiruvaḷḷuvar, though not in order. (See Oldenberg's *Buddha*, p. 290.)

These are—

1. To kill no living thing: கொல்லாமை.
2. Not to lay hands on another's property: கள்ளாமை. Ch. XXIX.
3. Not to touch another's wife: பிறனில்விழையாமை. Ch. XV.
4. Not to speak what is untrue: வாய்மை. Ch. XXX.
5. Not to drink intoxicating drinks: கள்ளுண்ணாமை. Ch. XCIII.

324. It requires care to avoid injury to living beings. Hence சூழ்= 'study.'

325. 'Permanence.' Dreading a continuance of this embodied existence, and renouncing all in order to gain வீடு. Comp. Ch. XXXV.

327. 'Quamvis tua ipsius vita a te separatur, tu noli facere malum separans alterius dulcem vitam.'

A man may not kill, even in self-defence. The reasoning in *Bhag. Gîtâ*, ii. is adverse to this.

328. 'Quamvis et bonum et magna felicitas sequatur ex viventium occisione (uti contingit in victimarum immolatione), tamen sapientes abhorrent ab emolumento proprio aliorum nece comparato.'

Even sacrifices are forbidden.

329. 'Qui munere funguntur necandi viventia, minimae notae sunt in aestimatione eorum qui talis officii vilitatem agnoscunt.'

Sacrificing priests, and soldiers, are not to be honoured.

330. 'Non desunt, qui videntes aliquem obesa membra prae se ferentem, et valdè infelicem vitam ducentem, dicant eum alicujus necis reum esse.'

Comp. *Nâl.* 122, 123:

'Their legs in iron bound, as slaves to alien lords,
They 'll till the black and barren soil, who snared and kept
In cages partridges and quails, that dwell in wilds
Where beetles hum amid the flowers.'

'Who loved in other time on crabs to feed, and broke
Their joints, what time the guilt of olden deeds comes home,
Like fire their palms shall glow, their fingers rot away,
When direful leprosy's fierce pangs arise.'

CHAPTER XXXIV.

Beschi: *Mundanarum rerum instabilitas.*

Com.: Only by knowledge of this does a man learn to relax his hold on visible things, and so attain to the துறவு of the next chapter.

Analysis:—

I. 1. Ignorance of it is folly.
II. 2, 3. Instability of prosperity.
III. 4–10. Time hurries us away.
Decay and death.
Life's brevity.
Body's instability.

The teaching of the four chapters (xxxiv.–xxxvii.) to which commentators (but not the poet) give the title ஞானம், is much the same as that of the following extract:—

'The separated condition of the soul, which is the cause of mental error (மருள்), is also the cause of moral evil. Ignorant of its true nature, the soul attaches itself to objects unworthy of it (பேதைமை). Every act which it performs to gratify this attachment (பற்று), entangles it deeper in the perishable world; and, as it is itself imperishable, it is condemned to a perpetual series of changes (பிறப்பு). Once dragged into the *saṁsâra*, into the vortex of life, it passes from one existence into another, without respite and without rest. This is the twofold doctrine of the *Karma*, *i.e.* the act (வினை) by which the soul determines its own destiny (ஊழ்); and of the *Punarbhava*, *i.e.* the successive rebirths in which it undergoes it.' (Barth, pp. 77, 78.)

331. 'Quod caducum est stabile esse opinari inscitia est religioso valdè noxia.'

Comp. *Nâl.* 52:

'The chief of men reflect on change, disease, old age,
And death, and do their needful work. The endless round
Of sevenfold science, lore of stars, who raving teach,
Are maddest of the foolish throng.'

332. 'Divitiarum adventus est uti adventus spectatorum ad publicum ludum; abeunt vero eodem modo, quo dissolvitur spectatorum coetus absoluto ludo.'

Drew says: 'the one is by slow degrees; the other is rapid—in a moment.'

333. 'Divitiae instabilis conditionis sunt, quapropter si eas obtineas statim iis utere; ad virtutum exercitium, quae unicè stabilem tibi fructum affere possunt.'

334. 'Quod a nobis dies dicitur ostendit se tanquam temporis men-

suram quamdam; sed illum ritè percipientibus, non est nisi gladius vitam secans.'

335. 'Antequam linguae loquela desit, et singultus guttur intercipiat, bona opera festinanter operare.'

See *Nál.* 332 ('Rusticus expectat,' &c.):

'In the great sea to bathe they went, but cried, "We 'll wait
Till all its roar is still, then bathe." Such is their worth
Who say, "We 'll practise virtue and be wise when all
Our household toils and cares have end." '

336. 'Frequentissimum in hoc mundo est dici de aliquo, quod heri exstitit, et hodie non est.'

Comp. *Nál.* 27–29:

'Like bubble that, when rain falls, oftentimes appears
And disappears, is this our frame. The steadfast wise
Resolve to rid themselves of this perplexity.
In the wide world, who can compare with these?

'Those who have gained this well-knit frame should seize the gain
The body yields. For, like a cloud upon the hills
That casts its shadow, nor abides, but thence departs,
The body leaves no trace behind.

'The body's transient state is as the dew-drop hangs
On grassy tufts. This very hour do virtuous deeds!
*E'en now he stood, he sat, he fell, while friends bewailed
He died*; such is man's history!'

337. 'Qui nec sciunt an per unum instans victuri sint, innumera mente moliuntur futuro tempore agenda.'

Comp. *Nál.* 359 (vain dreams):

'To-day, at once, a little hence, our joys are crowned!
And so men think, and tell their friends with hearts full glad;
But soon their eager minds are changed; and many men
Have faded like a lotus' leaf!'

338. 'Aviis ovum deserendo volans symbolum est unionis animae cum corpore.'

Comp. *Nál.* 30:

'Unasked men come, as kinsmen in the home appear,
Then silent go. As silently the bird deserts
The tree where nest remains, and go far off, so these
Leave but the body to their friends.'

339. 'Generatio et interitus sunt veluti somnus et vigilia.'

340. 'Si anima tanquam hospes in corpore moratur, nonne certum est corpus non esse propriam animae domum.'

CHAPTER XXXV.

Beschi: *Omnibus mundanis rebus renunciare, atque ab iis affectum divellere.*

The second chapter of the *Gîtâ* should be compared with this.

Com.'s analysis :—

I. 1–4. Relinquishment of all external bonds: புறப்பற்று.
II. 5. Of internal bonds: அகப்பற்று.
III. 6. Reward of renouncing both.
IV. 7. Sorrows to those who renounce not.
V. 8, 9. Both combined.
VI. 10. The means.

341. 'Qui ab omnibus mundanis rebus se disjungit, non experietur afflictiones, quae ob iis proveniunt.'

The repetition gives emphasis.

342. 'Si desideras frui gaudiis, quae in hâc etiam vitâ omnium renunciatio affert, citô renuntia, ut illis diu frui possis.'

Comp. *Nâl.* 11:

'"Hoar age will come," thus think the men of knowledge good,
And have from earliest years all ties renounced. Who joy
In youth, unstable, never free from fault, with pain
Leaning upon a staff, erewhile will rise.'

343. 'Qui ad caelum anhelant, opus est ut eodem tempore, et suos sensus mortificent, et omnia quae possidunt, relinquant.'

ஐந்து பொறிகளுக்குரிமையாகிய ஐந்துபுலன்கள். Comp. பொறி in Vocab.

344. 'Perfecti poenitentis est nihil possidere; alicujus enim boni temporalis possessio, cum caussa sit, ut animus illaqueetur, poenitentiam quoque destruet.'

All possessions must be abandoned.

345. 'Si nostrum corpus intolerabile pondus est nos retardans ne ad coelum festinemur, quid quaeso erit, si supra hoc pondus adjecerimus pondus affectuum ad caetera nobis extrinseca?'

346. 'Qui a se removet fascinum, quo amor proprius, et amor eorum quae possidemus nos fascinat, gloriam assequetur quam ipsorum caelicolarum plurimi adepti non sunt.'

அகங்காரம் and மம்மதை (*ahankâra*, *mammatâ*) are continually denounced. The one asserts the reality of self, and the other thinks external things are its own.

வீடு is beyond the various 'heavens' assigned to Çiva, Brahma, &c.

347. Qui nunquam deserunt affectum bonorum sentibilium, nunquam desinent ab iis cruciari.'

348. 'Qui perfectè omnibus renunciant, aeternam beatitatem obtinent; caeteri omnes, a suorum affectuum rete illaqueati, et a suis desideriis fascinati, a caelo distinebuntur.'

தலைப்பட்டார்: the past tense denoting certainty. See *Nâl.* 331:

'The turtle's murderers have put it in the pot,
Set fire beneath; it sports, unconscious of its fate.
Such is their worth who joy entangled in life's *net*,
While death, the mighty slayer, waits to seize.'

349. 'Si affectus omnes obtruncaveris, ab alterius vitae suppliciis liber evadens, ad caelum festinabis; si secus feceris, ab aeternâ beitate diu distentus, variis cruciatibus obnoxius eris.'

My version varies.

350. 'Dei amorem tenaciter prehende, et ut sensibilium amorem extinguas, illum ipsum Dei amorem quotidie tenacius prehendere, atque augere stude.'

Beschi quotes S. Augustine: 'Crescente charitate decrescit cupiditas.'

CHAPTER XXXVI.

Beschi: *Verum assequi conari.*

351. 'Fascinatio quâ quis sibi suadet, verum esse, quod verum non est, infelix vitae genus in altero mundo causabit.'

352. 'Tenebris (nempe infernalibus), amotis, suavitas (*i.e.* beatitas nempe aeterna) obveniet illi, qui a fascinatione liberam et puram ab erroribus scientiam acquisivit.'

353. 'Qui omne dubium a se alienando, verum assequi conatur, quamvis in terrâ existat, caelo valdè proximus erit.'

354. 'Quid tibi proderit scientia omnium quae quinque sensibus objiciuntur, si veri scientiam non assequaris.'

355. 'Veri assecutio in eo consistit, ut cujuscunque rei, cujusvis conditionis sit, non quas primo obtutui objiciuntur, sed proprias ac veras ejusdem qualitates, causas et effectus assequaris.'

It seems that the poet must mean, *to see God in everything is true knowledge.* He (*or* it) is the மெய்பொருள் or தத்துவம்.

The teaching of the *Chândogya upanishad*, vi. 15: तद् त्वं असि 'thou art it,' on which the Tamiḷ sectarian poets have written volumes, is that which the poet has adopted; but it is somewhat vaguely expressed, and there is a manifest avoiding of Sanskrit formulas. He so teaches the doctrine of the Upanishads as to avoid anything that could mark him as a follower of any sectarian teacher. Comp. 423.

356. 'Qui in hoc mundo apud sapientes discendo veri Dei notitiam assequuntur, viam ingredientur, quae non est iterum in mundum illos ductura.'

357. 'Si tua mens attentè omnia considerando verum Deum assequatur, procul dubio noli cogitare quod aeternam vitam non sis assequuturus.'

358. 'Veri assecutio illa est quae talem obtinet veri Dei notionem, ut fugando inscitiam, quae post mortem miseram vitam causat, ad aeternam beatitatem perducat.'

359. 'Si assequendo veram notionem illius, qui rebus omnibus adhaeret (nempe Dei), ita vivas ut in te omnino pereat mundanis rebus adhaesio, tibi non adhaerebunt mala, quae adhaererent, si illam vivendi rationem infringeres.'

360. 'A malis omnino immunis non eris, nisi illorum trium, nempe, cupidatis, aversionis, et veri ignoratiae ipsum quoque nomen in te extinguatur.'

See *Bhag. Gîtâ*, ii. 62, 63. The Tamil scholar will derive much information (together with a little wholesome mental discipline), from a study of the பஞ்சதசப்பிரகரணம்.

CHAPTER XXXVII.

Beschi: *A sensibilibus ipsa quoque desideria divellere.*

361. 'Desiderium sensibilium a sapientibus vocatur semen, quod omnibus nullo unquam tempore desituram infelicem vitam post mortem parit.'

362. 'Si aliquid desiderare vis, desidera a te abigere infelicitatem, quae post mortem sequitur: id vero non assequeris, nisi desiderando omnium desideriorum carentiam.'

363. 'Immunitas ab omni sensibilium desiderio adeo magna felicitas est, ut in hoc mundo et in altero similem non habeat.'

364. 'Omni desiderio carere ab omni labe immunitatem parit; illud verò assequeris, si verum assequi studueris.'

365. 'Ab omni malo immunes dicentur ii qui omne desiderium abegerunt; caeteri, licet aliqua hujus mundi mala effugiant, ab alterius vitae malis immunes non erunt.'

366. 'Religiosi propria virtus est cavere a desideriis sensibilium, quae homines decipiunt illaqueantque.'

367. 'Desideriis carentes omni malo carebunt; si desideria adsint, nulla licèt sit alia caussa, mala indesinentia incessenter venient.'

368. 'Si desideriis, quae inter omnia mala pessima mala sunt, extinxeris, in hâc quoque vitâ indesinentem felicitatem assequeris.'

369. 'Si desideria superando extinxeris, eâ ipsâ, quam cogitas, viâ opera assequeris, quae tibi ab omnibus malis immunitatem afferant.'

370. 'Si a te elongaveris desideria, quae insatiabilis conditionis sunt, eo ipso instanti meritum assequeris ad id quod immutabilis conditionis est (nempe ad beatitatem).'

CHAPTER XXXVIII.

Beschi: *Divinorum Decretorum irrefragabilitas.* ஊழ்=பழமை.

Beschi prefixes to the chapter: 'Caput unicum et ab anterioribus materiis avulsum.'

371. 'Si divitias lucrandi statutum tempus adveniat, statim industriosus evades; si illas amittendi tempus adveniat, statim ad laborandum piger, et ad divitias servandas ineptus evades.'

Ellis has given a version of seven couplets in this chapter.

'By the decreed effect of the works of former births, industry is excited and wealth accrues; and by the same, indolence prevails and wealth departs.'

372. 'Quamvis valde solers quis sit, si ei divitias amittendi statutum tempus adveniat, statim insipiens evadit; quamvis valde insipiens quis sit, si divitias lucrandi statutum tempus advenerit, solers evadit.'

373. 'Licèt quis multas ac subtiles scientias suâ ingenii subtilitate didicerit, insipientia quam affert divitias amittendi statutum tempus, ejus ingenii subtilitatem superabit.'

Ellis: 'Although he have obtained various and profound learning, his natural disposition will overcome his knowledge.'

See *Nál.* 108 (Infatuation, result of deeds in a former birth):

'Not ignorant are they; but, though what man should know
They know, yet deeds that bring guilt to their souls they do.—
Lord of the wide sea's pleasant shore, where breezes breathe
The lily's fragrance round!—*This comes from former deeds.*'

374. 'Duplex in mundo proprietas, nempe divitem esse et sapientem; valde latam differentiam patiuntur; nam aliâ viâ quis dives evadit; aliâ sapiens.'

375. 'Si divitias lucrandi statutum tempus advenerit, omnes ad felicitatem et divitias assequendas ineptae occasiones opportunae et aptae evadent; si illud non advenerit, omnes lucrandi opportunitates ineptae evadent.'

376. 'Quod ex divino statuto non habet conditionem ut sit tuum, tuum non erit, quamvis multum labores in eo custodiendo; quod ex divino statuto tuum est, etiamsi illud procul a te projicias, a te procul non ibit.'

Hitop. Intro. 28, 29.

Ellis: 'That which is not by nature theirs, no labour can obtain; and that which is, though they reject it, will not quit them.' See *Nâl.* 101:

'Though you send forth the tender calf midst many cows,
It hath unerring skill its mother to find out;
Deeds of old days have even so the power to search
Him out to whom their fruit pertains.'

377. 'Etiamsi immensas divitias cumulaveris, non erit tibi possibile iis frui supra mensuram quam Déus tibi praefinivit.'

Ellis: 'Those who have accumulated millions can enjoy nothing but what the apportioner has apportioned to them.'

As B. says in the note given below, this couplet changes the whole aspect of the chapter. This idea of the *Personal* Apportioner—Judge, Administrator of the World,—'Who by His Providence governs all things,' is to be noted.

378. 'Etiamsi, qui pauperrimi sunt, non concipient propositum renunciandi omnibus, nisi Deus avertat impedimenta quae adesse statuit.'

379. 'Si scis quod tu cupis fieri non posse, nisi cum ad id praefinitum tempus advenerit, quando illud non fit, quare quaeso tristaris.'

Ellis: 'Why should those who see that good only happens in the destined season of prosperity be grieved in the season of adversity?'

380. 'Quidquid excogitaveris ut divina decreta retardes, illa semper tuas industrias omnes praeibunt; quid in mundo divinis decretis potentius.'

Ellis: 'What is more powerful than the destined effect of former works? It anticipates even thy thoughts while considering how to avoid it.' *Hitop.* Intro. 33.

NOTE BY B.

'Non me latet vocem ஊழ், cui ego *divinorum decretorum* significationem tribuo, ab aliis usurpari pro பழவினை quod significat *opera antiquitus facta*, neque ignoro eosdem humanarum rerum vices tribuere operibus antiquitus factis, sive bonis, sive malis, pro effectuum diversitate; dicunt enim, virum probum pauperem esse, ob peccata quae antiquitus patravit (sive antequam nasceretur in alia generatione, uti Tamulenses stulte putant, sive postquam natus est, in adolescentiâ vel pueritiâ), quaeque adhuc non luit ferendo supplicium iis debitum; virum vero improbum felicem esse, ob virtutes quas antiquitus exercuit, et pro

32

quibus, adhuc praemium iis debitum non retulit; atque, eodem modo virum industrium ac indefesse laborantem pro divitiis acquirendis nil acquirere in poenam peccatorum veterum; virum vero omnino ineptum atque pigrum sine ullo labore divitem evadere in praemium veterum virtutum; ita ut quidquid vulgus malam fortunam, aut bonam fortunam appellat, id ipsi refundant in opera antiquitus facta. In hoc vero capitulo dictam vocem melius explicari et proprius significare *divina decreta*, patet, tum ex serie tota sententiarum in hoc capitulo contentarum, tum ex illo versu speciatim—

வகுத்தான் வகுத்த வகையல்லாற் கோடி
தொகுத்தார்க்குந் துய்க்க வரிது,

in quo ne per somnium quidem Auctor meminit operum antiquitus factorum, sed solum divini statuti, quod nemo praeterire potest: et quamvis detur quod opera antiquitus facta suum locum habeant in humanarum rerum vicibus, quarum causam ignoramus, cum tamen dicta opera antiquitus facta, sive bona, sive mala, hic et nunc, et non antea neque postea suum sortiri effectum, sive bonum, sive malum, non dependeat, nisi a divinâ voluntate, quae statuit tempus in quo alicujus virtus praemiari, peccatum puniri debeat; cumque omnis vis operum antiquitus factorum ad *divinorum decretorum* virtuti praemium, peccato poenam statuentium irrefragabilitatem reducatur, recte voci ஊழ் *divinorum decretorum* significatio tributa est; eo vel magis, quod vox ஊழ் ex suâ naturâ nil significat nisi *antiquum quid*, quod aeque, competit operibus antiquitus factis, quorum vim nunc quis experitur, ac divino statuto decernenti, ut dicta opera nunc suam vim exerceant, nam nil est divinis decretis antiquius.'

CHAPTER XXXIX.

Beschi: *Regis magnitudo.*

This chapter speaks of the king; but in the following chapters, though the title is அரசியல், the verses apply to men in general.

381. 'Qui validum exercitum, copiam subditorum, auri vim, rectos consiliarios, vicinorum regum foedus, et fortem arcem (quae sex sunt regi necessaria) possidet, caeteros inter reges erit veluti inter caetera animantia leo.'

Manu, vi. 160.

382. 'Proprium regum est, in his quatuor, nempe imperturbabilitate, liberalitate, prudentiâ, et animi robore nunquam deficere.'

383. 'Ab eo qui terram gubernat, dissociabilia sunt ista tria, nempe in suo munere sollicitudo, ejusdem peritia, et animi firmitas.'

384. 'Rex debet a virtute nunquam aberrando, et vitiosum quod est a

suo regno eliminando, sublimem animum a generositate non aberrantem possidere.'

385. 'Rex talis sit ut valeat divitias cumulare, cumulatas absque detrimento in suo thesauro congerere, congestas ne ab hostibus rapiantur custodire, custoditas pro virtutis exercitio, pro aerarii incremento, et magnificâ sui sustentatione prudenter distribuere.'

This is Manu, vii. 99, 100.

386. 'Orbis regem qui suis subditis facile se praebeat visendum, iisque dura non loquatur verba, laudibus extollet.'

387. 'Regibus qui suavibus verbis et regali munificentiâ subditos amanter defendere valeat, hic orbis suis laudibus tantus erit quantum ipsi cogitaverint (*i.e.* ob laudes, quas in orbe referent, dicti reges tot regnis dominabuntur, quot ipsi voluerint).'

388. 'Rex qui justitiam servando subditorum defensionem curat, aestimabitur tanquam hominum Deus.'

389. 'Totus orbis habitationem figet sub throno regis qui indolem habet sufferentem verba suorum consiliariorum, utut auribus amara sint.'

390. 'Rex qui liberalitatem amorem in subditos, justitiam, et suorum subditorum curam habet, erit regum coetui splendor.'

[Manu, vii. may with advantage be compared throughout.]

CHAPTER XL.

Beschi: *Scientia sui muneris regi necessaria.*

THE distinction between கல்வி [see கல்] 'learning' and அறிவு (Ch. XLIII.) must be observed. The poet does not use the S. *ñânam.* From கல்வி '*the study of books,*' and கேள்வி '*oral instruction,*' comes அறிவு.

391. 'Quod discendum est, perfectè disce; postquam didiceris, ad normam praeceptorum, quae didicisti, permane.'

392. 'Illae duae scientiae quarum unam arithmeticam, alteram scribendi et legendi artem appellant, homini sunt duo veluti oculi.'

So Avvai says: எண்ணெழுத்திகழேல், 'despise not *number* and *letter.*' *Hitop.* Intro. 12.

393. 'Illi oculos habere dici possunt, qui scientias didicerunt; qui verò nil didicerunt, non oculos, sed duo in fronte ulcera habere dicendi.

394. 'Doctorum vivorum officium in eo consistit, ut ita inculpabiliter vivant, ut omnes laeto animo eos sibi superiores profiteantur; adeo suaviter caeteros ad virtutem incitent, ut qui eorum meminerint, de eorumdem absentiâ tristentur.'

395. 'Qui ante magistros humiliter stant ad finem discendi, perinde ac pauper ante divitem, sublimes evadent; qui dictae humilitati non consentiendo nil discunt, semper infimi erunt.'

396. ‘Sicuti in puteo, ad mensuram quâ arena extrahitur, aqua surgit; ita in hominibus, ad mensuram quâ discunt, scientia crescit.’

397. ‘Si docto viro quaelibet mundi provincia sua provincia est, quaelibet urbs patria est, cur, quaeso, plurimi usque ad mortem indocti vivere malunt?’

This is the only example of ஏந்திசைச் செப்பல், Intro. p. xxviii.

398. ‘Scientia quam quis in hoc mundo assequitur, etiam in alio mundo ei proficua erit, quia adjumento est ad beatitatem assequendam.’

399. ‘Docti viri, videntes, ex scientiâ et sibi et mundo dulcedinem pari, magis magisque scire desiderant.’

400. ‘Incorruptibiles et sublimes divitiae sunt scientiae, non verò aurum et caetera quae quis possidet.’

Comp. *Nâl.* 135 (discriminating study):

> கல்வி கரையில; கற்பவர் நாள்சில;
> மெல்ல நினைக்கிற் பிணிபல; தெள்ளிதின்
> ஆராய்ந் தமைவுடைய கற்பவே, நீரொழியப்
> பாலுண் குருகிற் றெரிந்து.

> ‘Learning’s a shoreless sea; the learner’s days are few;
> Think calmly. Lo, diseases many wait around!
> With clear discrimination learn what’s meet for you,
> Like swan that leaves the water, drinks the milk.’

குருகு=any bird, here the *haṁsa,* that can drink the milk, and leave the water mingled with it. இல்=‘like.’

CHAPTER XLI.

Beschi: *Ignorantia, a rege vitanda.*

401. ‘Absque scientiâ necessariâ in coetu doctorum loqui, perinde est ac in tabulâ nullis lineis obsignatâ globum projiciendo ludere.’

402. ‘Qui sine debitâ scientiâ in coetu loqui affectat, perinde se habet, ac qui affectat corpus mulieris cui ubera desunt.’

The construction is ambiguous. Make கல்லாதர்ன=கல்லாதவனுடைய, and இல்லாதாள் also the 6th case. பெண்=பெண்மையை. Supply ஒருவன். ‘For anyone to desire to listen to an unlearned man’s words, would be like desiring, &c.’

403. ‘Etiam qui penitus indocti sunt, valde docti evadent, si continere se poterint quin ante doctos loquantur.’

பெறின்: ‘if they only could gain the grace of modest self-effacement!’

404. ‘Ei, qui nihil didicit, quantumvis magnum ingenium sit, illud a sapientibus nihili fit.’

405. 'Qui cum indoctus sit, se doctum praesumit, si ante doctos loqui contigerit, dictam praesumptionem amittet.'

406. 'Indocti viri hoc tantum habent, quod dicuntur in mundo existere; caeterum sterili agro similes sunt.'

'They have the measurement of living beings.' In common speech மாத்திரம்='only.' Beschi reads மாத்திரையல்லால்='hoc tantum praeter.'

407. 'Qui decus non habet res subtiliter inquirendi, et latam eruditionem non possideat, ejus decora omnia, ex luto affabre elaboratae et pulchrè ornatae statuae decora imitantur.'

408. 'Pejus est indoctos viros esse divites quam sapientes esse pauperes.'

409. 'Qui indocti sunt, quamvis nobili loco nati, nunquam possidebunt decus par decori eorum, qui licèt infimi sint, docti tamen sunt.'

பாடு 'in respect to dignity.' பாடு is nom. of 'respect.' See 293.

410. 'Quantum distat inter hominem et brutum, tantum distat inter doctum et indoctum.'

In the comparison there is an inversion. It should be—

as *Brutes* : *men* : : *unlearned* : learned men.

But the order is விலங்கு, மக்கள், கற்றார், ஏனையவர். This is called மயக்கநிரனிறைப்பொருள்கோள்=*confused arrangement.*

CHAPTER XLII.

Beschi : *Doctos inter homines versando ab iis discere.*

The word கேள்வி reminds us that teaching in Ancient India was always oral. The learner must attach himself to a குரு or ஆசிரியன். The *Nannûl*, 26–46, will illustrate this chapter.

Comp. S. *çru, çruti, çrâvana. Avvai* says கேள்விமுயல் 'Give diligence to hearing.'

411. 'Divitiae, quae per aures, id est per doctorum conversationem acquiruntur, praecipuae divitiae dici debent, cum sint caeteris omnibus divitiis praestantiores.'

412. 'Si auribus suus cibus desit, tunc et ventri aliquem cibum dare oportebit.'

413. 'Qui doctorum conversationem, quae est veluti aurium cibus quaeritant, terrigenae licèt sint, pares erunt caelicolis, qui sacrificiorum odore pascuntur.'

414. 'Quamvis indoctus omnino sis, doctorum sermones audi, id enim in adversitatibus baculus tibi erit, cui innitaris, quin animo decidas.

415. 'Verba eorum qui bene morati, ac docti sunt, ab indoctis audita

idem istis emolumentum afferunt, quod affert baculus in lubrico loco gradienti.'

416. 'Quantulumcunque sit quod doctus profert scitu dignum libenter audi; nam licèt id minimum quid videatur, deinde magnum tibi decus afferet.'

417. 'Vitiose quamvis didiceris, si tamen praeter attentum in discendo studium, frequentem etiam cum doctis collationem habueris, talis evades, ut possis sine erroris notâ loqui.'

418. 'Aures in quas penetrare non possunt doctorum vivorum colloquia, quamvis sonum audiant, ejusdem conditionis sunt ac aures surdae.'

419. 'Qui cum doctis viris versando subtilem rerum notitiam non assequuntur difficile est ut submisse loquantur.'

The கேள்வியர்=S. *Çrâvaka.* The Sâvaka of the Buddhist books.

420. 'Ii qui non nórunt auribus gratum cibum, et solum noscunt quid ori sit gratum, quid ingratum, quodnam erit orbi emolumentum si vixerint, quodnam erit orbi damnum si moriantur?'

Beschi says 'puto legendum உணருமாக்கள்'; but why?

CHAPTER XLIII.

Beschi: *Prudentia.*

THIS is φρονήσις and σοφία. The inimitable practical wisdom of the author is especially seen in these chapters.

421. 'Prudentia quoddam armorum genus est ad mala avertenda, et arx est ab ipsis hostibus inexpugnabilis, quia ipsis inaccessibilis.'

422. 'Prudentiae proprium est non sinere ut voluntas feratur quo suapte naturâ fertur, sed attentè considerando objectum a voluntate concupitum, bonum ne an malum sit, a malo eam revocare et ad bonum impellere.'

423. 'Prudentiae debitum est, ea quidquid audieris ex cujus vis ore audieris, illius veram significationem percipere.'

Comp., however, 355.

424. 'Prudentiae debitum est, ea quae loquitur quamvis captu difficilia audientibus facilia reddere, et ea quae caeteri loquantur, quamvis subtilia sint percipere.'

425. 'Prudentium est cum sapientibus amicitiam inire, sed in eâ non sequi conditionem quorundam florum, qui aperiuntur, et postea clauduntur (*h.e.* post contractam amicitiam eam dimittere).'

Comp. *Nâl.* 215.

426. 'Prudentis regis debitum est eo modo vivere, quo vivit orbis, cum eo se conformando.'

427. 'Prudentes quod futurum est antequam eveniat noscunt, imprudentes vero futura priusquam eveniant percipere nesciunt.'

428. 'Stultorum est non metuere quae metuenda sunt, prudentium est timere, ubi timendum est.'

429. 'Ei qui prudentiam habet praevisa mala praecavendi iis occurrendo, nullum venturum est malum quod illum consternat.'

430. 'Prudentes in prudentiâ omnia bona possident, imprudentes quid possident, nil omnino possident.'

CHAPTER XLIV.

Beschi: *Vitia abigere.*

THE Com. says, 'Only the wise discern and correct their own faults, hence this chapter follows that on அறிவுடைமை.'

431. 'Felicitas ejus regis qui de suâ felicitate non fit ebrius, nec effraenam iram, nec luxuriam sectatur, sublimis conditionis est.'

The six faults enumerated in this verse and the next are (1) arrogance, (2) wrath, (3) lust, (4) avarice, (5) overweening pride, and (6) unseemly mirth. This last is also explained as indiscriminating kindness.

432. 'Nimia auri cupiditas, aequum transiliens magnitudo (*i.e.* superbia), et non bona vultûs laetitia (*i.e.* omnes etiam sontes laeto vultu aspicere), vitia sunt a rege vitanda.'

433. 'Quamvis milii grano par culpa sit, eam palmae arbori parem judicabunt qui a vitiis abhorrent.'

434. 'Cum vitium hostis sit valde exitialis, vitium cave, intuendo emolumentum, quod ex hac cautelâ referes.'

435. 'Felicitas regis qui vitia non praecavet, destruetur perinde ac palearum fasciculus ante ignem.'

436. 'Felicitas regis, qui ab nimiam auri cupiditatem, illud non impendit in ea, quae opus fuerint, diu durare non poterit quin destruatur.'

437. 'Si rex à se vitia abigendo deinde subditorum vitia insequatur, quidnam ultra erit, quod tanquam vitiosum cavere debeat?'

438. 'Nimia cupiditas, quo nomine vocatur nimius auri amor, qui illud impendere non sinit, cum oportet, caetera vitia ita superat, ut prae illa nil sit, quod tam deforme videatur.'

439. 'Quovis tempore (*h.e.* etiam eo tempore, quo magnus es), noli te extollere; ea quae utilitatem non afferunt, noli concupiscere.'

Comp. *Nál.* 340.

440. 'Si rex iis, quae in deliciis habet, ita frui valeat ut sua in illa propensio non percipiatur, inutilis evadet omnis hostium scientia (*i.e.* hostes non poterunt nosse, quid ipsi carum sit, nec media adhibere ad illud prohibendum).'

A king should at least avoid the appearance of evil; and if he indulge himself, let it be secretly.

CHAPTER XLV.

Beschi: *Magnos sibi viros associare.*

Com.: 'The getting assistance of superior men as ministers and spiritual guides: அமைச்சர் and புரோகிதர்.'

Among Eastern sovereigns Akbar was famous for the men he gathered around him, as were his contemporaries Queen Elizabeth and Henri Quatre. [See Pope's *Text-book of Indian History*, 3rd. Ed. pp. 101, 102.]

441. 'Rex eos, qui virtutes exercere sciunt, ac maturam prudentiam habent, attentè illorum celsitudinem considerando, et modos, quibus eos sibi amicos reddat investigando sibi associet.'

திறனறிந்து is variously taken. திறன்=' *their worth*,' or 'the *methods* by which their friendship may be secured.'

442. 'Regno advenientia mala abigendi, et ne in posterum adveniant praecavendi indolem habentes rex amicos habere debet.'

Com.: 'Evils come from gods (droughts, excessive rains, winds, fire, disease: மழையின்மை, மிகுமழை, காற்று, தீ, பிணி); or from men (enemies, thieves, kindred, servants: பகைவர், கள்வர், சுற்றத்தார், தொழில்செய்வோர்). To remove the former, சாந்திகள் (atonements) must be used. For the latter, the four methods (சாமபேததானதண்டங்கள்) of pacification, disruption, gift, and punishment must be used.' See *Panchatantra*.

443. 'Inter omnia difficilia difficillimum est magnos viros, amicè illos tractando, suos facere.'

444. 'Regem cum iis, qui se majores sunt, ita procedere ut suos reddat, est quid quâlibet potentiâ validius.'

445. 'Cum boni ac prudentes ministri regi instar oculorum sint, quibus ad rectè procedendum dirigatur, quos tales attentâ consideratione deprehenderit, rex sibi associet.'

சூழ் 'use circumspection.'

446. 'Nullum est malum quod hostes inferre possint regi, qui procedere valeat uti proborum ministrorum amicum decet.'

447. ‘Quisnam valeat ruinam inferre regi, qui eos sibi adsciscit socios, qui non dubitent, cum opus fuerit, eum arguere.’

448. ‘Rex cujus custodia iis caret qui eum arguere audeant, quamvis nullus sit hostis, qui ejus ruinam moliatur, ex se destruetur.’

இல் and அல் havo many peculiarities. H.B. § 202. Here இல் governs 2nd case, and is the neg. mode of a verb itself signifying negation.

449. ‘Sicuti mercator, qui non habet capitale nil lucrari potest, ita rex carens sociis, qui illum arguendo substentent, stare nequit quin ruat.’

450. ‘Regi decies pejus est non curare amicitiam proborum ac prudentium hominum, quam multorum hostium in se odium procreare.’

CHAPTER XLVI.

Beschi: *Ab eorum qui infimae conditionis sunt, nempe improborum, atque adulatorum societati cavere.*

சிற்றினம்=‘little, *i.e.* low and mean association.’

451. ‘Magnus vir metuit infimorum societatem, infimi viri proprium est ejusmodi homines tanquam consanguineos sibi associare.’

Comp. *Nâl.* 171 (good and bad associations):

அறியாப் பருவத் தடங்காரோ டொன்றி
நெறியல்ல செய்தொழுகி யவ்வும்
நெறியறிந்த
நற்சார்வு சாரக் கெடுமே வெயின்முறுகப்
பிற்பனிப் பற்றுவிட் டாங்கு

‘In youth unwise, though men with lawless ones consort,
And walk in ways of sin; yet, if they join the band
That knows the righteous path, their faults shall melt away
As dew from off the grass when sunbeams scorch.’

பெருமை, சிறுமை, abstract for concrete.

452. ‘Sicuti aqua ob terrae, per quam transit, qualitatem alia fit, et terrae qualitatem induit, ita hominum ingenium induit qualitates eorum quibuscum degunt.’

453. ‘Intellectus nascitur ex propriâ hominis naturâ cujusque animo insitâ; sed aliquem talem aut talem dici id ex societorum qualitate provenit.’

‘Noscitur a sociis.’

454. ‘Specialia quaedam judicia videntur esse cuique naturalia; sed non proveniunt nisi ex societate.’

455. 'Societatis munditiem tanquam forcipem habendo, mentis et operis munditiem conservabis.'

B. says தூவு='forceps.' But qy. See தூ.

456. 'Qui animum habet à culpâ depuratum bonos filios procreabit: qui societatem habet a vitiis depuratum, non procreabit actiones quae bonae non sint.'

457. 'Animi bonitas hominibus in mundo existentibus felicitatem affert: sociorum bonitas ad omne laudum genus assequendum prodest.'

458. 'Magna licèt sit animi bonitas, cordato tamen viro sociorum bonitas fructuosior erit.'

459. 'Aeterna beatitas ob uniuscujusque animi probitatem obvenit; attamen in eâ assequendâ sociorum bonitas maximam partem habet.'

'Bonitas sociorum servat ac promovet animi probitatem.'

460. 'Nil est quod majus emolumentum afferat, quàm bona societas: nil quod magis noxium sit quàm mala societas.'

Comp. *Nâl.* 171–180.

CHAPTER XLVII.

Beschi: *Non nisi post maturam considerationem agere.*

Com.: 'This would result from Ch. xlv., xlvi. He who avoids low company, and has worthy counsellors, will act after due deliberation.'

461. 'Rex facinus ullum non debet aggredi, nisi prius maturè consideravit, quid ad illum conficiendum impendendum sit, quinam effectus ex eo proveniat, et quidnam emolumenti dicti effectus allaturi sint.'

462. 'Ei, qui et selectos consiliarios adhibendo, et maturè considerando operatur, nullum facinus difficile erit.'

463. 'Prudens vir non aggreditur facinus, quod ob spem lucri caussa sit amittendi sortem principalem.'

464. 'Incertum finem habens facinus non incipit, qui metuit aliorum subsannationem, si fortè illud non conficiat, aut malum exitum habeat.'

465. 'Regem in hostem ferri quin prius maturè consideraverit non solum aliqua sed omnia, neque confusè sed clarè, idem erit ac hostem fortiorem reddere in loco, quem occupat.'

466. 'Non modo facere, quod faciendum non est, sed etiam non facere quod faciendum est, ruinam affert.'

467. 'Non nisi post maturam reflexionem aliquod facinus aggredi statuas, nam non levis culpa erit illud aggredi dicendo, postea considerabo.'

468. 'Quantumcumque pro aliquâ re conficiendâ labores, ni laborares in maturâ consideratione viarum, quae ad illam perficiendam

conducunt, et si multi coeuntes tuus labor ne incassum eat cavere conentur, inutilis erit.'

469. 'Etiamsi ad quid perficiendum omnia bene feceris, tamen inter illa error obveniet, nisi cujusque indolem noscendo, eidem te accomodando rem gesseris.'

470. 'Si rex suo statui indecora fecerit, mundus illa non probabit; propterea non omnia quae proficua sunt, sed ea tantum, quae mundus non contemnat, media eligere debet ad quid perficiendum.'

தம்மொடு, ellipsis of *நிலை(மை)*: *தம் நிலையொடு பொருந்தாத*= 'what is inconsistent with his (the king's) position.'

CHAPTER XLVIII.

Beschi: *Suam cum hostis potentiâ comparare, ac caetera, quae ipse et hostis habent media, quantum valeant, ponderare.* [He reads வலிவறிதல் as though from வலிவு.]

471. 'Rex antequam in hostem agat, ponderare debet vigorem actionum, quas ipse et hostis facere possunt, suam et hostis potentiam, nec non robur auxiliorum quae ipse et hostis habent.'

472. 'Nil erit inassequibile iis, qui perscrutando quid sibi possibile sit, caeteraque, quae scire oportet sciendo, iisque omni contentione animum applicando, in hostem ferantur.'

473. 'Multi suam invalidam potentiam non considerantes, animi elevatione ducti, se potentiores aggrediendo, ante finem destructi perierunt.'

உடை either from v. 'be broken,' வி. தொ.='which will be broken, is weak'; or from n. 'possession,' in which case it strengthens *தம்*= 'their possession.'

474. 'Qui nec vicinis regibus morem gerendo procedit, nec se metiri scit, et iis, qui sibi morem gerunt elatum se praebet, festinè ruinam patietur.'

475. 'Etiam axis currûs, qui plumis oneratus sit, effringetur, si nimium oneres, ita ut plumae vim currûs superent.'

'The last straw that breaks the camel's back.'

476. 'Qui usque ad rami apicem ascendit, si ad apicem transiliendum animum elevet, illa animi elevatio ei vitae finem adducet.'

477. 'Largiri pecuniam considerando ejus mensuram, via est quae ad divitiarum conservationem ducit.'

478. 'Quamvis mensura viae per quam pecunia venit angusta sit, nullum erit detrimentum, dummodo via per quam abit, non sit latior.'

479. 'Felicitas ejus, qui vixit non considerando mensuram suorum reddituum, fingendo se existere, et revera non existendo, evanescendo peribit.'

480. 'Si rex munificentiam ostentare velit, quae non ponderet limites divitiarum quas habet, brevi tempore ejus operum limites breviabuntur.'

CHAPTER XLIX.

Beschi: *Facinori aggrediendo opportunum tempus noscere.*

481. 'Cornix cuculum, à quo nocturno tempore vincitur, diurno tempore vincit: regibus ad hostes vincendos, necessaria est temporis opportunitas.'

எடுத்துக்காட்டுவமை, or simile. III. Gram. 204.

482. 'Procedere accomodando se temporis opportunitati est funis alligans regi felicitatem, ut numquam ab eo discedat.'

483. 'Si rex necessariis cum instrumentis ad finem assequendum, opportunum ad id tempus noscendo operetur, eritne qùidquam ei difficile?'

484. 'Quamvis totum orbem subjugare cogites, id assequeris, si ad id opportunum tempus, et locum seligendo opereris.'

485. 'Reges qui cogitant orbem subjugare, quamvis indubitanter sibi subditum iri videatur, non agunt quidquam priusquam opportunum tempus adveniat.'

486. 'Regem animo elevatum, expectando opportunum tempus, nil agere, eandem nobilem conditionem habet, quam in pugnâ (*dum manus miscere non convenit*), retrocedere, ut validius pugnatur.'

He reads தகா='unfit,' for தகர் 'a ram.'

Ariel: 'L'abstention de qui est énergetique a la mérite de faire place au bond du bélier luttant.'

487. 'Rex, qui prudens sit, statim ac ab hostibus injuriam acceperit, non manifestat exterius iram, sed etiam intus fovet, opportunum tempus expectando.'

Graul: 'Ein kluger König grollt nicht sogleich "Hui, hui!"
Nach aussen hin,—nein innerlich—die Zeit ersehend.'

488. 'Si hostem videris ad quem subjugandum opportunum tempus deest, eum suffer: nam cum ejus ruinae, tempus opportunum videris, infra tuum caput decidet.'

Drew: 'If a king meets his enemy, let him show him all respect, until the time for his destruction is come; when that is come, his head will be easily brought low.'

Graul: 'So kommt sein Haupt herab.'

489. 'Dum assecutus fueris quod est obtentu difficillimum, nempe temporis opportunitatem, eo ipso temporis momento aggredere ea quae prius aggredi difficile erat.'

490. 'Ardeam imitare tempore quo immota manet, et eamdem imitare quae rostro piscem ferit, statim ac opportunum tempus advenerit.'

Graul: 'Den Reiger nimm zur Regel zur Wartezeit!
Zur rechten Zeit sein Zufahren.'

CHAPTER L.

Beschi: *In proelio locum sibi faventem, et hosti noxium seligere.*

491. 'Antequam videris locum aptum ad hostis obsidionem, noli quidquam aggredi; noli hostem contemnere.'

492. 'Etiam iis, qui cum odio in hostem multam potentiam conjunctam habent, favor arcis propinquae in proelio multa afferet emolumenta.'

493. 'Etiam ii qui viribus carent, vires acquirendo hostem subjicient, si eligendo locum sibi faventem, loci favore se tuendo, in hostem proelientur.'

494. 'Si rex non se approximet hosti, nisi in loco sibi favente, hostis qui venerat cum spe illum vincendi, eam spem amittet.'

495. 'Crocodillus in profundâ aquâ omnes vincet, omnes eum vincent si ex aquâ egrediatur.'

496. 'Magnus currus, qui in rotis vim habet pedibus parem, in mari non currit, et navis, quae in mari currit, in terrâ non currit.'

497. 'Si in hostem feratis omnia considerando, et faventem tibi locum eligendo, nullus tibi auxiliator necessarius erit praeterquam timoris expulsio.'

498. 'Si qui parvum habet exercitum ad locum sibi faventem eum ducat, utut magno cum exercitu advenientium hostium fiducia infringatur.'

499. 'Valde arduum est aggredi homines in suâ propriâ statione degentes, licet arcem non habeant, nec in militandi arte magnum nomen.'

500. 'Elephas, qui faciem habet penetrantem lanceatorum aciem, et non pavet suum frenatorem, in luto ubi pedes penetrent, a quavis vulpe necatur.'

The sense of வேலாண்முகத்தகளிறு is doubtful.

The Com. says முகம் is by meton. for கொம்பு, *tusk*: 'tusks that impale armed men.'

It seems to mean 'a face mighty as a host of javelin-bearers.'

Drew: 'Warrior-faced.'

CHAPTER LI.

Beschi: *In ministrorum electione de ipsorum aptitudine se certificare.*

501. 'Dum quis ad ministerium eligitur, debet rex indubitanter certificari post maturum examen quasnam inclinationes habeat circa haec quatuor, nempe *virtutem*, *divitias*, *mulieres*, et *vitae amittendae metum*.'

The candidate for office must be tested as to his strength of virtue, and power to resist temptations of avarice, lust, and fear.

502. 'Qui nobili genere natus; vitiis infensus, infamiam metuit, ac vilia facere erubescit, indubitanter eligendus est.'

Birth, unstained character, sensitive honour, and conscientious virtue are needed in a Minister.

503. 'Etiam in iis, qui difficiles scientias didicerunt, et nullum habent ex supradictis defectibus, si attentè consideratur, difficile est non inveniri ignorantiam.'

None are quite perfect.

504. 'Rex ministerium eligendo, bonas ac malas qualitates considerando, et inter illas praesertim praeponderantem maturè examinando, juxta id quae praeponderat, eum aptum vel ineptum judicet.'

Take the best.

505. 'Lapis Lydius, quo dignoscitur, sitne quis magnus an vilis, sunt cujusque actiones.'

Ariel: 'La pierre de touche pour la grandeur ou la bassesse, c'est l'œuvre de l'une et de l'autre.'

506. 'Cave ne eligas, qui nil habent; quia hujusmodi homines, cum adhaesiones non habeant, culpas non erubescunt admittere.'

Needy adventurers.

507. 'Eligere ad ministerium eos, qui quae scienda sunt ignorant, ob specialem affectum, seu propensionem in illos, caussa erit in quamvis stultitiam ineundi.'

Ruin from partiality and prejudice in the selection.

508. 'Eligere ad ministerium ignotos, quin maturè considerentur eorum indoles, damna afferet ab ipsâ regis posteritate inseparabilia.'

No untried stranger to be chosen.

509. 'Sine maturâ discussione, quemvis eligere noli; et postquam eligendum maturè consideraveris de ejus qualitatibus quas certo bonas nosti, noli suspicionem sine caussâ admittere.'

Slow in choice, generous in confidence.

510. 'Electio sine consideratione, et suspicio circa eum, quum probe noscendo rex elegerit, irreparabile damnum afferunt.'

Manu, vii. 141.

CHAPTER LII.

Beschi: *Quomodo debeat rex eos, quos elegit, ad officii exercitium adhibere.*

THIS refers to the allotment of offices and tasks among those whom the king has, according to Ch. LI., chosen: employment and promotion.

511. 'Ille ad sublimia munia eligendus est, qui bona et mala considerans, indolem habet non gaudentem nisi de bonis, hoc est, honestis mediis.'

512. 'Ille ministerium exerceat, qui regis aerarium augendo ejusque felicitatem procurando, aerario ac felicitati obvenientia impedimenta maturè praevenire sciat.'

513. 'Ille ad ministerium indubitanter adhibendus est, qui regem amet, qui sciat quae sui muneris sunt, qui in deliberando animo non vacillet, qui divitias et voluptates non affectet, ita ut nil ex his quatuor desit.'

நன்கு may be taken as noun or adv.

514. 'Plurimi qui in quovis modo considerati indubitantem ad ministerium apti apparent, in agendo alii evadunt, ac apparebant.'

515. 'Magni momenti facinora injungenda sunt iis, qui opportuna media eligere sciendo, iisque obvenientia impedimenta sufferando, ad finem illa perducere valeant, non vero aliis hac qualitate carentibus, quamvis regi sint cari.'

Comp. 159. இன் is a சாரியை : செய்+கு+இன்+பான்+கு.

516. 'Rex agentis indolem et actionis qualitatem maturè considerando, si haec et illam cum temporis opportunitate conjungi viderit, eam illi injungat.'

517. 'Actionem intentam, instrumenta ad eam perficiendam necessaria, et personam, quae ad eam conficiendam eligitur, maturè considerando, si noveris eam actionem ab eo, iis cum instrumentis perfici posse, et actionem et instrumenta in ejus manu relinque.'

518. 'Postquam rex alicujus aptitudinem ad actionem intentam

maturè consideraverit, debet illum ad eam perficiendam aptum facere, (*h.e.*, ei suppeditando instrumenta, quibus perficere illam valeat).'

519. 'Felicitas deseret regem qui aegre fert, quod secum familiariter se gerat minister, qui semper est in ministerio occupatus, illumque officium tanquam proprium possidet.'

520. 'Si regii ministri recti sint, omnia rectè procedent, ideo reges quotidie suorum ministrorum actiones attentè explorare debent.'

CHAPTER LIII.

Beschi: *Consanguineos complecti,* i.e. *facere ne a rege divellantur.* Drew: 'On kindness to relatives.' Graul: *Die Angehorigen umfassen.*

THIS refers to the kingly 'circle' (சுற்றம்), the ring of courtiers, intimate friends, the unofficial society of the palace, and in this, the Royal family, often large. In Indian history the king's foes have been often *of his own household.*

521. 'Etiam cum pauper evaseris, antiquam felicitatem eoque tempore accepta beneficia commemorare non nisi consanguinei solent.'

The பாராட்டுதல் is in a series of acts; thus உள is plural.

Ariel says curiously: 'C'est au sein de la famille qu'existe, sans intérêt quelconque, le culte du passé.'

522. 'Si rex consanguineos sortiatur, a quibus indesinenter ametur, hi regi felicitatem afferent numquam pullulare desinentem; quia si consanguinei nunquam a rege divellantur, nova semper germina procreabunt, quae regis tutelam et felicitatem augebunt.'

523. 'Felicitas regis, qui non habet mensuram commixtionis (*supple,* cum consanguineis), similis est lacui aquâ repleto sine profunditate et sine aggere: [quia sicuti hujus modi lacus, quamvis aquâ repletur, cum illum detinere nequeat, statim exsiccatur; ita rex, qui non metitur consanguineos eâdem mensurâ quâ se metitur, sed eos ut extraneos tractat, quamvis aliquam diu felix sit, a felicitate deseretur; quia à consanguineis, qui regis tutela sunt, derelinquetur].'

524. 'Fructus, quem rex percipere debet ex divitiis sibi obvenientibus est, ita se gerere cum suis consanguineis, ut ab iis semper ambiatur (eos nempe participes faciendo suarum divitiarum).'

525. 'Si rex quae consanguineis opus est, liberaliter dare, iisque sese affabilem praebere valeat, à confertâ consanguineorum turbâ circumdabitur.'

526. 'In magno hoc terrarum orbe nemo plures consanguineos habet quam ille, qui liberalis est, et iram non servat.'

527. 'Cornix inventum cibum non occultando, sed caeteras convo-

cando comedit ; similem conditionem habentes, habebunt etiam emolumentum, quo cornix fruitur.'

528. 'Si rex non omnes aequaliter respiciat, sed ad unius cujusque qualitatem attendat, hanc in eo praerogativam aspiciendo plures apud eum mantionem facient.'

529. 'Consanguineorum, qui regem deseruerunt, amicitiam iterum ut conciliet, satis erit tollere caussam, ob quam discordes abierunt.'

530. 'Eum, qui sine caussâ regem deserit, cum ob aliquam caussam redit, rex prudens admittere in suum consortium debet.'

CHAPTER LIV.

Beschi: *Non esse in regimine desidiosum.*

பொச்சாவாமை=மறவாமை. It is the *Apramâda* of the Dhammapada. See the trans. of this by F. Max Müller, p. 9. 'The absence of that giddiness or thoughtlessness which characterizes the state of mind of worldly people.'

531. 'Ex nimiâ gaudiorum et deliciorum exuberantiâ, animi relaxatio magis regi nocet, quam nimia ira.'

Drew: 'The thoughtlessness which springs from the intoxication of great joy.'

532. 'Regi desidia, atque oblivio ejus laudem destruet, non secus ac quotidie mendicando ventrem replere scientiam destruit.'

533. 'Regi desidioso modus non est laudem assequendi, in hoc omnis generis scientifici, qui in mundo sunt, conveniunt.'

534. 'Meticulosis arx non suffragatur: ita sane desidiosis eorum felicitas nihil prodest.'

535. 'Venientia non carendo desidiosus qui vivit, cum illa obvenerint, facient ut suum errorem doleat.'

536. 'Si rex erga omnes, quovis tempore, sine intermissione solertiter se gerendi indolem sortiatur, nullum erit bonum huic simile.'

537. 'Nil eorum, quae ardua sunt, inassequibile erit, se omnia solicito animo cautè feceris.'

538. 'Quae regem laudabilem faciunt caveat ne omittat; nam omissionem contemnentibus neque post mortem bonum obveniet.'

Rather, 'what (wise men) have (ever) praised.' If these words and teachings have failed to impress them now, even successive births in seven worlds would not avail.

539. 'Cum rex suae felicitatis ebrius desidiâ corripitur, meminerit eorum qui ob suam desidiam miserè perierunt.'

Ariel's is neat: 'Songez a ceux qui perdirent dans l'*insouciance*, quand vous vous laisserez enivrer dans les délices.'

540. 'Facile erit omnia, quae intenduntur assequi, si mens semper intenta sit in iis, quae assequi cogitarit.'

Ariel: 'Une pensée est facile à réaliser, si l'on s'attache itérativement à penser à cette pensée.'

CHAPTER LV.

Beschi: *Recti sceptri conditio*; i.e. *justitia*. Ellis: 'The uprightness of the sceptre.' (Manu, vii. 102, 103.)

541. 'Equitatis conditio est subditorum culpas considerando absque nimiâ indulgentiâ, erga omne personarum genus integritatem affectando, et à legibus statuta supplicia considerando, his et non majoribus illas castigare.'

Ellis: 'Carefully considering the facts, without yielding to feelings of compassion, acting with integrity towards all, and deciding according to law: so to act is to administer justice.'

542. 'Quamvis mundus totus pluviam intuendo vivat, subditi tamen nonnisi regis justitiam intuendo vivunt.'

Ariel: 'Grâce à la pluie le monde entier prospère;
Grâce au sceptre du prince prospère un peuple.'

543. 'Etiam divinarum legum et virtutum caussâ fuit regum justitia.'

Ellis: 'The sceptre of a king (*i.e.* the administration of justice) was the cause of the practice of virtue, and of the observance of the law of the sacred teachers.'

544. 'Totus orbis complectitur pedes regis, qui subditos amando, justitiam exercet, eumque vastissimae ditionis regem efficiet.'

Ellis: 'The whole world embraceth the feet of the monarch of extended dominion, who, in administering justice (*lit.* in directing his sceptre), embraceth all his subjects.'

545. 'In regno regis, qui suum sceptrum ad debitum locum dirigit (hoc est justitiae legibus conformat), opportunam pluviam felix messis sequetur.'

Comp. ver. 55.

Ellis: 'In the country of which the sovereign duly administereth justice (*lit.* directeth his sceptre to the right place), both the rain falleth in its season, and the harvest is abundant.'

546. 'Non lancea (*i.e.* non arma bellica) regi victoriam tribuunt, sed ejus sceptrum; si tortuosum illud non sit (*i.e.* si rex justus sit).'

Ellis: 'It is not the lance which giveth victory to a king, but his sceptre (the symbol of justice) if it never deviate from right.'

547. 'Rex defendit totum orbem. Regem verò defendit aequitas, si nunquam ei contraria faciat.'

Ellis: 'A king defendeth the whole world; and justice (if strictly administered), defendeth the king.'

548. 'Rex, qui nec affabilitatis decus habet, nec justitiae leges considerat, neque quod aequum est facit, ob vituperio dignum hujusmodi statum, ipsemet se destruet, quin hostes opus sint ad eum destruendum.'

549. 'Regi, qui subditos ab exteris hostibus defendendo, eorumque sollicitam curam gerendo, ipsorum crimina plectit, id vitio verti non debet: est ejus officium.'

550. 'Homicidas, eisque similes facinorosos cum rex plectit, perinde facit, ac qui inter segetes nascentia lollia evellit.'

Ellis: 'The act of the king in punishing those guilty of murder resembleth the weeding of green corn.' Manu, vii. 10.

CHAPTER LVI.

Beschi: *Sceptri Tortuositas;* i.e. *injusta gubernatio.*
Ellis: 'The obliquity of the sceptre.'

551. 'Eo, qui homicidae officium exercet, crudelior est rex, qui exercet officium vexandi subditos, et aequìtati contraria faciendo procedit.'

552. 'Eum qui sceptrum obtinet, praeter consueta tributa, subditorum bona petere, perinde est àc latronem armatum viatori dicere: da tuam pecuniam.'

Ariel: '"Donne" dit le (brigand) appuyé sur sa lance:
Ainsi mendie le (roi) appuyé sur son sceptre.'

553. 'Regis, qui quotidie subditorum facinora inquirendo, eos juxta leges non punit, regnum quotidie majorem in ruinam verget.'

Ellis: 'If a king enquiring day by day administer not justice, day by day will his kingdom fall to ruin.' Manu, vii. 16, &c.

554. 'Rex, qui tortuosum sceptrum obtinet non considerando justitiae leges, et adeptum aurum et (qui novum daturi sunt), subditos simul amittet.'

Ellis: 'The king who inconsiderately neglecteth the administration of justice, will lose both his wealth and his subjects.'

555. 'Lacrimae quas subditi fundunt tolerando impares vexationem quam à rege patiuntur, limae sunt quae eo ipso die regis felicitatem minuunt.'

Ellis: 'The tears of those who suffer from the injustice of the prince are files by which his felicity is worn away.'

556. 'Regis perpetuatio fit à sceptri rectitudine; haec si desit, quaecunque sit regi laus, perpetua non erit.'

Ellis: 'From the uprightness of the sceptre (from their justice) princes obtain immortal renown; if deficient in this respect the glory of princes cannot last.'

557. 'Qualis est pluviae carentia respectu terrae, talis est clementiae carentia in rege respectu suorum subditorum.'

558. 'Ei, qui regi injusto subditus est, praestat pauperem esse quam divitem.'

Ellis: 'It is worse than poverty, to be subject to the sceptre (sway) of an unjust prince.'

559. 'Si rex à justiciâ deflectendo operetur, pluvia ab ejus regno deflectendo, coelum pluere non sinet.'

560. 'Si qui subditorum servator est, eos non tutetur, in ejus regno vaccae lac non dabunt, et Brachmanes sua munia deserent.'

CHAPTER LVII.

Beschi: *Subditos non terrificare.*
Ariel: *Eloignement de causer la terreur.*
Drew: 'Against acting with cruelty: against *a reign of terror.*'

This is closely allied to the subject of the last chapter: that regards injustice, this specially forbids harshness.

561. 'Rex absque passione subditorum culpas examinare, et ne iterum eas committant, aequâ, et non majori, paenâ castigare debet.'

562. 'Reges, qui diu duraturam felicitatem à se inseparabilem cupiunt, debent in plectendis subditis cum magna irâ manum extollere, sed leniter percutere.' Manu, vii. 140.

Ariel: 'Poursuivez rudement et frappez mollement,
Si vous désirez l'ininterruption d'une longue prospérité.'

563. 'Si rex tortuosum sceptrum obtineat, subditisque terrifica faciat, procul dubio festinè ruinam patietur.'

564. 'Rex, de quo fama est, quod sit subditis terrificus, aevi diminutionem patiendo, festinè peribit.'

565. 'Quantumcunque magna sit felicitas regis, qui subditis difficilem aurem praebet, eosque terrifico vultu aspicit, perinde erit ac si daemon aspexerit (*i.e.* evanescet).'

What the daemon has looked on, is said to be useless.

566. 'Regis dura subditis verba loquentis, clementiâque carentis, quantumcunque magna felicitas, quin diu duret, eo ipso tempore destruetur.'

567. 'Dura verba, et aequum transiliens mulcta, sunt veluti lima quae minuit in rege fortitudinem quâ hostes vincat.'

568. 'Regis, qui ministris negotia committendo, cum iis ea non considerat, si dum male succedunt iis irascatur, felicitas minuetur (quia ab iis, qui eum juvare possunt, deseretur).'

569. 'Rex, qui sibi non construxerit arcem antequam ab hoste aggrediatur, ad hujus adventum timore correptus, statim corruet.'

Drew says 'a defence in the love of his subjects.'

570. 'Plus aequo rigidus rex nonnisi regni leges ignorantibus adhaeret: sed quodnam est praeter hoc hominum genus quod orbi gravius? Nil sane.'

But he explains பிணிக்கும் by 'sibi sociat.'

CHAPTER LVIII.

Beschi: *Clementia.*

This Ch. insists on the same subject; but states positively what the last inculcates negatively. Here benignity, the reverse of harshness, is enjoined.

571. 'Hic mundus non subsistit, nisi quia in regibus invenitur valde pulchra indoles, quae dicitur clementia.'

572. 'Propter clementiam viget mundi cursus (si quidem sine mutuâ sufferentiâ necnon mutuâ charitate in subveniendo egenis, qui effectus clementiae sunt, mundus non subsisteret): quid ergo praestat esse in mundo, qui clementiâ carent, nisi ut terrae grave pondus afferant?'

573. 'Musicalia instrumenta quid juvant, nisi musicas voces edant; eodem modo oculi quid juvant, nisi clementiam habeant?'

Graul: 'Das Auge soll gleichsam das ganze Thun des Menschen harmonisch accompagniren. Ein huldloses Auge bei dem besten Thun ist wie disharmonische Musik bei dem besten Gesange.'

574. 'Quamvis in fronte adesse videantur, quid prosunt oculi, qui aequum non transiliente carentiâ carent?'

575. 'Oculorum propria pulchritudo est clementia: si ista non adsit, non oculi, sed foramina vocandi sunt?'

576. 'Terrâ infixis arboribus similes sunt ii, quibus quamvis oculi in fronte infixi sint, clementiâ carent.'

577. 'Qui clementiâ carent, orbi sunt; qui orbi non sunt, nec clementiâ carent.'

578. 'Ii, qui clementiam exercere valent, quin justitiae legibus derogatur, quandem proprietatem habent in hunc orbem. [Sensus est: *quod orbis regimen iis debetur, qui cum justitiâ clementiam sociare valent.*]'

579. 'Etiam in eos, qui iram concitandi conditionem habent (*h.e.* etiam in reos), clementer se habendo, iis ignoscere optima qualitas est.'

580. 'Qui, etiamsi videant sibi venenum porrigi, illud sumant, nec irritentur, clementiae inhiant ab omnibus celebrandae.'

CHAPTER LIX.

Beschi: *Exploratoris officium.* Ariel: *Espionnage.*
Graul: *Auskundschaftung.*

Spies, or scouts. The Com. says: 'Enemies, strangers, and friends alike must be watched.' Manu, vii. 122, 153, 154.

581. '*Exploratores* habere, et regni jura callere, certus esto: quod regi sunt instar duorum oculorum: [quia per exploratores scit, qui subditi aut hostes agunt: per leges scit, quid cum iis agendum].'

582. 'Regis officium est (*i.e.* regis interest) quotidie omnia, quae ab omnibus fiunt, statim scire.'

583. 'Regi, qui nescit, quanti intersit per *exploratores* omnia scire, nulla ad hostes vincendos patet via.'

584. 'Ministros regis, ejus conjunctos, ejus hostes, hos omnes, attentè inspicere debet *explorator.*'

585. 'Qui habitum (seu figuram) sumendo, quae exploratis suspicionem non afferat, quamvis ab iis dignoscatur, sine timore quaelibet tormenta potius patiatur quam se prodat, ille sane optimus erit explorator.'

586. 'Religiosorum, aut peregrinantium personam simulando, impenetrabilia loca penetrando, omnia attentè explorando, quoquomodo torquatur, titubare non debet *explorator.*'

587. 'Hostiam secreta audire ut valeat nitendo, ea quae scivit, sine dubitatione referre debet *explorator.*'

588. 'Quae *explorator* explorando rettulit secreta, iterum *per alium exploratorem* exploranda sunt.'

589. 'Rex *plures* habeat *exploratores*, sed ita ut unus de alio nesciat, omnesque ad explorandum mittat: si omnium verba consentiant, de exploratis securus erit.'

590. 'Exploratori ne quid speciale feceris, quod caeteri sciant; nam si feceris, statim publicum fiet officium, quod ille secretè exercebat.'

CHAPTER LX.

Beschi: *Animositas.* Ariel: *Force d'âme.* Graul: *Geistes-starke.*

THE etymology suggests 'elevation of mind.'—See Vocab.

591. 'Qui *animum* habent, propriè dici potest, quod quid possideant; qui animo carent, quod possident, non possident (quia suam propter inertiam illud amittent).'

592. '*Animum,* qui ab homine inauferabilis est, possidere, verè divitem facit; nam divitiarum possessio neque constans est, et possessorem relinquit.'

593. 'Qui animo decidere nescit, etiamsi divitias amittat, non affligitur; quia iterum eas acquirendi remedium habet, nempe *animositatem.*'

594. 'Divitiae ipsae viam percunctando apud illum accurrent, qui constantem *animositatem* habet.'

595. 'Flores, qui in aquâ nascuntur, crescunt tantum quantum aqua crescit; eodem modo hominum celsitudo crescet ad mensuram *animositatis.*'

The lotus in the tank, with its long, flexible, winding stem is always on the surface, rising or falling with the depth of the water, unaffected by any vicissitude. So 'Man is man and master of his fate.'

Robinson's is neat:

'The water's depth 's the lily's length :
The height of man 's his mental strength.'

Comp. *Nâl.* 245.

'Though by the briny sea, sweet waters spring; by hill,
Bitter with salt the waters gush. Thus as their race
Are not the men,—Lord of the dashing sea's cool shore!—
The men are as their minds!'

596. 'Quidquid (rex) cogitet, sublimia semper cogitet, quod si illa non successerint, saltem cogitatus ille *animositatis* conditionem habebit, ac proinde regem sublimem faciet.'

597. 'Si damna obveniant animo non decidunt *animosi* viri, sicut elephas, licèt à sagittarum fasce feriatur, non retrocedit.'

598. '*Animo* carens (rex) nunquam obtinebit hanc gloriam, ut dicere possit: ego in hoc mundo potens sum.'

599. 'Quamvis magnitudine atque acutis dentibus superior sit, elephas timidus fiet si a tigre invadatur.'

600. 'Animus ratiocinii sedes est; qui ergo animum non habet, non pro homine, sed pro quâdam arboris specie hominis figurâ praeditae, habendus est.'

CHAPTER LXI.

Beschi: *Solertia*, h.e. *impigrum esse.*

601. 'Nobilitatis splendor, qui in familiâ nunquam defecit, *pigritiae* tenebris si locum dederit [adhaeserit, irrepserit], tenebrescendo extinguetur.'

Here மாசு=तामस. See *Sânkhya Kârikâ*, xxv., xxxvi. (H. H. Wilson's ed.) Comp. *Gitâ*, xiv.

602. 'Stude ut pigritia in te extinguatur, si tuam familiam nobilitare desideras.'

Graul: 'Wer will dass sein Stamm stämmig werde,
Der wandle so, dass die Lässigkeit von ihm lasse.'

603. 'Insipientis illius, qui quam vitare debet *pigritiam* sibi adoptaverit, nobilitati in quâ natus est, finis obveniet omnes ejus in contrarium conatus praeveniendo.'

604. 'Prosapiae splendor extinguetur, plurimaque insurgent damna in iis, qui nec *pigritiam* vitant, neque assiduum laborandi exercitium habent.'

605. 'Procrastinatio, oblivio, *segnities*, somnus: quatuor haec ornamenta sunt, quibus se exornare avent ii, qui suae ruinae student.'

See கலன் and நீர். There seems to be a double meaning, or இவேலை. கெடுநீரார்='those pertaining to the waters of destruction,' or 'those whose fate is destruction.' Comp. *Gitâ*, xiv. 8.

606. 'Etiamsi omnium potentissimi regis divitiae, eos insectentur (hoc est absque ullo labore iis obveniant) difficilimum est, ut ex iis magnam utilitatem percipiant qui *pigri* sunt.'

607. 'Eorum qui bona concilia dandi officium exercent, reprehensiones quin mussitet audire cogetur, qui *segnitiei* amore captus, laudabile assiduè laborandi exercitum non habet.'

608. 'Si rex in suâ familiâ *segnitiei* locum dederit, haec efficiet ut suis hostibus servus evadet; quia quum iis resistendi vim non habeat, iis obtemperare oportebit.'

609. 'Quisque in suâ familiâ oborta damna reparabit, si se à *segnitie* sectandâ averteret.'

610. 'Impiger rex sine intermissione assequetur totam terram, quam caeteri reges nonnisi suis pedibus dimetiendo assecuti sunt (*i.e.* absque morâ dominus evadet regnorum, qui caeteri reges nonnisi multo labore, ac tempore adepti sunt).'

This may refer to Viṣhṇu, who was said to have measured the universe with three steps.

CHAPTER LXII.

Beschi : *Assiduè laborare.*

ஆள்வினை may be '*the work of a man*' : ஆளுக்குரிய வினை, or ஆளும் வினை (வி. தொ.) '*the work which rules, exerts itself.*'

611. '*Assiduus labor* magnum cuique spiritum dabit, qui affectet non decidere animo, quum quid difficile videtur.'

He makes சாவாமை='animum non despondere,' and reads அருமை யுடைத்தென்று ; but is evidently at a loss.

612. 'Quum quid incoeperis, cave ne illud destruas non perficiendo ; ii enim qui ad finem perducunt quod in actione deest, nunquam sapientûm aestimationem amittent.'

The idea is, 'Nothing succeeds like success.'

613. 'Plurimis liberaliter largiendi gloria nonnisi in assiduè laborente indole residet ; (quia qui assiduè non laborant, nec quid largiantur habent).'

614. 'Sicuti timidi alicujus brachium quemvis ferire velit, ensem vibrare nescit ; is qui assiduè non laborat, quamvis liberalis esse velit, ob suam paupertatem liberalitatem exercere non poterit.'

Comp. 727.

615. 'Qui non delicias sed laboriosam vitam optat, hic sanè suae familiae fulcrum erit, eam ab omni damno liberare valens.'

616. 'Assiduus labor divitias affert ; assidui laboris defectus nonnisi paupertatem inducit.'

617. 'Apud pigros residere infelicitatis Deam, quam *Mûdêvi* vocant, in impigri assiduo labore Deam felicitatis, quam *Lakshmî* vocant, suam sedem figere, aiunt sapientes.'

தாமரையினாள்=Padmâ=Lakshmî, 'goddess of good fortune.' See Dowson's *Class. Dict. of Hindu Myth.*, *sub voce.* முதேவி='ancient goddess' ; S. *Mahāmāyā.*

618. 'Non est vitio vertendum alicui, si minus sapiens sit ; sed ei qui quid utile sit, et quâ viâ assequi possit optimè sciendo, segnitie victo illud omittere magnum est vitium.'

So Ariel : '*Le manque de sens à nul n'est reprochable.*' See பொறி.

619. 'Quamvis ob contrarium fatum non assequaris id quod tuo labore assequi intendis, nihilominus tuus labor nunquam tibi non afferet salarium tui corporis fatigationi debitum (*i.e.* nunquam omnino incassum ibit).'

In this and the following couplet Tiruv. strongly asserts that 'man is master of his fate.' This is hardly consistent with Ch. XXXVIII.

620. 'Ipsum removeri fatum videbunt, qui animo non deficientes, sine intermissione assiduè laborant.'

CHAPTER LXIII.

Beschi: *In adversis non turbari.* Ariel: *Impassibilité dans le malheur.* Drew: 'Against losing energy in difficulty.' Com.: இடுக்கண் (துன்பம்) வந்துழி (வந்தபோது) அதற்குமனங்கலங்காமை.

621. 'Cum adversitas venerit, laetus te ostende; nam nullum aliud est medium utilius quam cum eâ associatum incederas.'

Beschi quotes a passage in illustration from Seneca: 'Adversa adversis adversa non sunt, sed aversis; nempe si ab adversitate fugias, et ob ejus adventum tristeris, adversitas erit; si neque tristeris, neque ob ejus adventum a tuo itinere dimovearis, sed una cum illâ coeptum iter confeceris, *adversitas* non erit.'

Com. says: ஊர்வது ஆகிய அது. Supply உத்தமம்: 'that is the best: nothing can compare with that.'

622. 'Pelago ipsi pares adversitates, si tales aestimes quales sapientibus videntur, adversitates non erunt.'

The meaning is: 'Troubles are imaginary; try to grasp them in thought, and they vanish.' The Vêdânta regards all as delusion: ponder this, and sorrow disappears. *Gîtâ*, xviii. 70–74.

623. 'Qui ex adversitate non affligitur, ipsi adversitati afflictionem causabit.'

624. 'Qui bovi similis est (*h.e.* qui bovem imitatur), per cuncta salebrosa loca, quin desistat, carrum trahentem, hic adversitatibus quoddam genus adversitatis est.'

625. 'Plurimae adversitates, aliae aliis supervenientes, licet obviam fiant; ab eo, qui suam constantiam non deseret, adversitatem patiendo, victas manus dabunt.'

626. 'Num afflictionem patietur, si pauper fiat, qui cum dives est, extollere se nescit.'

627. 'Sapientes propter adversa non turbantur, scientes propriam esse humani corporis conditionem scopum esse adversitatis ictibus.'

628. 'Qui delicias non quaerit, et secum statuit, prospera cum adversis mixta habere, naturalem esse hujus mundi conditionem, in adversis animo non corruet.'

629. 'Qui inter prospera de prosperitate non gaudet, nec inter adversa de adversitate tristabitur.'

630. 'In rege cujus actionibus adversitates obveniunt, eas tamquam favores aestimare, quia gloriosiorem reddunt actionem, quam iis superatis conficere debet, praerogativa est ab ipsis suis hostibus valde aestimabilis.'

PARS II.

Beschi: அங்கவியல்=*Status regii proprietates.*
அமைச்சியல்=*De conciliariorum proprietibus.*

CHAPTER LXIV.

De ministro regis. Manu, vii. 58 *et seq.*

631. 'Regius Minister in agendo, ad id necessaria instrumenta, tempus, agendi modum, necnon actionis difficultates in praeveniendo eximius esse debet.'

Ariel translates மாண்டது '*font la grandeur d'un . . .*'; Graul: 'haec esse eximia,' 'dass ist Ministerschaft, wenn . . . vortrefflich sind.'

632. 'Cum quinque supradictis qualitatibus debet insuper regius minister in animi firmitate, in amore erga subditos, in juris peritiâ, et in indefesse laborando eximius esse.'

The கருவி or சாதனங்கள் in 631 are twofold: money and men—சேனை, பொருள் (Ch. LXXVI., LXXVII.). Thus there are five.

633. 'Inter regis hostes in regem confoederatos discidium inducere, regis amicos ac fautores ne amicitiam deserant amicè tractare, et qui regem deseruerunt ut iterum regi foederentur obtinere, qui valet, optimus Minister est.'

634. 'Negotia maturè considerare, ad ea conficienda, quae magis apta sunt media adhibere, et ita loqui ut omnes in suam sententiam trahat, qui valet, optimus Minister erit.'

635. 'Insuper Minister debet plenè imbutus esse notitiâ virtutum regi convenientium, affabilem se praebere, callere modum agendi diversum pro temporum diversitate, ac ingenii subtilitatem habere.'

636. 'Iis, qui cum naturali ingenii subtilitate scientias quoque acquisitas habeant, quidnam est utut subtilissimum, imperceptibile.'

637. 'Etiamsi agendi modum ex scientiis didiceris, attamen mundi mores discendo, juxta illos age.'

638. 'Quamvis rex nec gnaris obaudiat, et ipse nescius est, tamen apud ipsum Ministri officium exercens obligationem habet eum hortandi, ne agat, quae agenda non sunt.'

639. 'Melius est regi a septuaginta millionibus hostium oppugnari, quam Ministrum habere contrarium.'

The other reading is கோடி யுறும் (as in 1061)='will be 700 millionfold great.'

640. 'Quamvis Minister, quae agenda sunt, eo quo decet modo, maturè consideret, nunquam tamen ea perficiet, si dexteritatem pariter non habeat.'

Tact must accompany *caution.*

CHAPTER LXV.

Beschi: *Verborum efficacia*, i.e. *suadendi vim habens locutio.*

This amplifies 633–35.

641. 'Linguae bonitas (hoc est verborum vis suasiva), in sapientûm aestimatione Ministrum bonum facit, nam hujusmodi bonitas caeteras omnes bonitates antecellit.'

642. 'Cum ex Ministri verbis summum regi bonum, ac summum oriri possit malum, debet Minister in suis verbis valdè circumspectus esse.'

643. 'Ministri verba talia esse debent, ut amicos in amicitiâ magisque confirment, et in adversariis amicitiae desiderium creent.'

Graul says அவாய்=அவாவி; but தகைய ஆய்(ஆகி) is better.

644. 'Minister in loquendo respectum habeat ad statum, seu conditionem eorum, quibus cum loquitur; nam nil est quod sit hoc virtuti magis consonum, nil quod majus emolumentum afferat.'

Speech to be adapted to the audience.

645. 'Minister verbum non proferat nisi postquam sciverit (seu noverit), nullum aliud esse verbum quod suum verbum vincere possit.'

646. 'Qui in praeclaro Ministri officio perfectus est, is loqui debet ita, ut cum desiderio audiatur; cum verò caeteri loquuntur, non ad eorum loquendi modum, sed ad negotium quod afferunt, animum intendere.'

647. 'Eum qui in loquendo suasivam vim habet, oblivioni obnoxius non est, nec auditorium timet, quisnam in oppositione vincere poterit? Nemo sanè.'

648. 'Orbis celeriter se subjiciet illis, si in loquendo ordinatè ac suaviter loqui valentes habuerit.'

649. 'Asiaticè loqui affectant, qui purè et laconicè loqui nesciunt.'

650. 'Qui quod didicerunt clarè et perspicuè caeteris communicare nesciunt, similes sunt floribus, qui ramo adhaerent, sed odorem non reddunt.'

CHAPTER LXVI.

Beschi: *Puritas actionum.*

Not good words only, but pure actions are necessary.

651. 'Bonum auxiliatorem habere, temporale modo emolumentum dabit; sed puritas actionum, cum temporali emolumento, virtutem quoque, eique subsequens in coelo premium dabit.'

652. 'Semper vitandae sunt actiones, qui nec agenti laudem nec caeteris bonum afferunt.'

653. ‘Vitare omnino debet laudem destruentes actiones, qui in mundo praeclarus esse vult.’

ஆ து ம் : this is an obsolete form. Comp. Tel. *Avu* | *du* | *mu*. The mid. particle து=Tel. *du*. (Intro. p. xxi.)

654. ‘Neque ut aliquod damnum effugiant, indecora faciunt qui firmam mentem habet.’

The use of காட்சி by Tiruv., with its various epithets, must be studied. It is more than the ‘poet's vision and faculty divine’; being the intuitive knowledge of invisible things given to the pure alone. The following verse (cii.) of the நீதிநெறிவிளக்கம் * beautifully illustrates this significant word :—

ஐயந் திரிபின்ற ளந்துத்தி யிற்றெளிந்து
மெய்யுணர்ச்சிக் கண்விழிப்பத் தூங்குவார் தம்முளே
காண்பதே காட்சி ; கனவு நனவாகப்
பூண்பதே தீர்ந்த பொருள்.

‘Nought doubting, wav'ring not, sages explore till all grows clear
By reason's aid ; with eye of apprehension true op'd wide,
They sleep, and see the *vision* clear. In that pure mystic light
When waking life arrays itself, 'tis being's perfect gain.’

How far Tiruv. and the gnomic bards of Southern India can be classed as votaries of any sect, or *darṣana*, may be seen by an examination of the *Sarva-darçana-saṅgraha* by Professors Cowell and Gough. Especially the *Árhata* (or *Jain*) system, while presenting some analogies, is evidently very different from that of the author of the Kurraḷ.

655. ‘Aut noli facere unquam id, de quo postea conquerendum tibi sit ; aut si aliquando feceris, querelas omitte.’

656. ‘Etiamsi tuam matrem fame mori videris, noli facere quod a sapientibus viturabile sit.’

657. ‘Sapientibus melius est summam paupertatem pati, quam divites fieri collum subdendo sapientûm vituperio (*i.e.* vituperio dignis actionibus).’

Comp. *Nâl.* 275.

658. ‘Qui aliquid vituperabile non vituperando inconsideratè fecerit, quamvis illud ad finem perducat, postea tamen afflictionem patietur.’

Beschi : ஓரா=‘ sine consideratione.’ ஓரார்=ஒருவாதவராக=‘ not shunning.’

659. ‘Quod cum (*exterorum*) luctu (*i.e.* caeteros opprimendo) cumulaveris, cum (*tuo*) luctu peribit ; si vero propter justitiam aliquod damnum patiaris, postea multa tibi afferet bona.’

* The very complete edition of this exquisite work, issued by H. Stokes, Esq., should be in the hands of every Tamil student.

660. 'Per nefas divitias cumulando regem in solio firmare velle, idem est ac velle firmum reddere ex crudâ argillâ fictum vas aquam ei infundendo.'

But இருத்தி is not 'making firm,' but 'putting, keeping.'

Graul: '*in neuen Erdkrug Wasser und wahren wollen.*'

CHAPTER LXVII.

Beschi: *Firmitas in agenda.*

661. 'Quod facit actionum firmitatem est animi firmitas; caetera omnia ad id non prosunt.'

662. 'Perfecti ministri conditio est inter haec duo viam tenere, ut neque aggrediatur ea, quibus insuperabilem obicem venturum praevidet, et si obex advenerit non retrocedat.'

663. 'Fortis in agendo minister, quod in hostem intentat, ita exsequi debet, ut nonnisi finis actionis hosti notus sit, quod si ante finem hosti innotuerit diu lugendam afflictionem patietur.'

664. 'Regulas agendi dare, seu praescribere, omnibus facile est; sed difficillimum est juxta praescriptas regulas agere.'

This idea has been expressed in most languages. This couplet seems to be a translation of the çlôka in *Hitopadeça*, III. 107. The comparison will illustrate the relative powers of the languages, and the merit of a *Kurraḷ* couplet as compared with a Sanskrit çlôka.

परोपदेशे पाण्डित्यं सर्व्वेषां सुकरं नृणाम्
धर्म्मे स्वीयमनुष्ठानं कस्यचित् तु महात्मनः

B. says ஊன்று='*refluentia.*' See Lex.

665. 'Eorum, qui praecelsum ministri officium obtinendo clari sunt, in gens firmitas quum redundet in regem, ab ipso magni fiet.'

666. 'Omnia quae intentaverint, eo quo cogitaverunt modo obtinebunt ii, qui cum consideratione agendi firmitatem quoque possident.'

667. 'Despicabilis licèt figurae sit, noli quemquam despicere; sunt enim qui similes sunt axe magni currus, firmanti clavo.'

Ariel: 'À la vue de l'apparence il ne faut pas dédaigner; il est de (gens) tels que la cheville d'essieu d'un grand char qui roule.'

668. 'Actio quam, maturè considerando, faciendam esse perspexisti, sine titubatione, procrastinationem vitando, perficienda est.'

669. 'Quamvis plurimo labore, et animi contentione conficiendum sit,

animi firmitatem sustentando perfice opus, quod postea magnam tibi dulcedinem pariet.'

670. 'Caeteras omnes firmitatas licet obtineas; si tamen animi firmitatem non aveas, a sapientibus non magni fies.'

CHAPTER LXVIII.

Beschi: *Modus agendi.* Graul: *Die Art des Handelns.*

671. 'Maturè considerandum, quousque certitudo oriatur, quod ad finem opus perduci possit; talem autem certitudinem habens opus crastinum differre magnus error erit.'

672. 'In iis quae moram exigunt, moratus sis; in eis verò quae moram non sufferunt, moratus ne sis.'

673. 'Quotiescunque vires suppetunt, in hostem agere debes; si viribus inferior sis, aliquam viam excogitando opereris (sensus est, *ubi vires desunt astutiâ utendum*).'

674. 'Inchoatae et non perfectae actiones, inchoatum et non perfectum bellum; si ritè consideres, easdem (quia semper malum subsequetur), consequentias habere nosces.'

In the Com., Beschi says தீ='*ignis reliquae*'; but in this rendering he makes தீ=தீமை.

Ariel: 'Comme une reste de feu.'

675. 'Quid impendendum? quae adsint instrumenta? aptum ne sit tempus? quasnam actiones facere possit? opportunus an faveat locus? haec quinque sine allucinatione considerando, ad aliquem actionem procedendum.'

676. 'Antequam aliquid aggrediaris,—"ad id perficiendum, quanto labore opus sit?—quaenam impedimenta obvenire possint?—his superatis, et re ad finem perductâ, quodnam emolumentum sit obventurum?"—aequâ lance vibrando, agere debes.'

677. 'Praeterea ab opus perficere volente haec servanda lex est, ut ab iis notitiam acquirat qui opere in illo praxim habent.'

678. 'Ex unâ actione feliciter confectâ gradus est faciendus ad aliam similem actionem, non secus ac per domesticum elephantem alii elephantes capientur.'

679. 'Expedit citius hostium fautores sibi amicos reddere, quam amicos gratificare.'

680. 'Minister regis, qui exiguum habet regnum, timens ostendere panicum quo capietur metum, si fortè à fortiori oppugnetur, si se

vincere poterit, non debet inique ferre aliquam depressionem, quae fortiori assequendo, sibi proveniat.'

This is a perplexing couplet: 'Kings of small states, fearing the inward weakness of their own people, must pay homage to greater rulers in order to obtain the needful assistance: it is no disgrace to seek the friendship and protection of mightier states.'

CHAPTER LXIX.

Beschi: *Legatio*, i.e. *legati officium.*

THE character of the accomplished ambassador, or resident at a foreign court, is admirably drawn.

681. 'Legati dotes esse debent sequentes; nimirum ut sit (suis consanguineis) benè affectus; ut sit optimo loco natus; ut regis personam affectare sciat.'

பண்பு=குணம்='quality,' especially good quality, intrinsic excellence.

அன்பு, here 'a benevolent mind.'

682 (683 in B.). 'Amor (in regem), quae regi convenientia sunt probe scire, et in loquendo consideratio et verborum efficacia: tres sunt qualitates quae nonnisi in legatis reperiuntur.'

அன்பு, here 'special attachment to the king.'

683 (684 in B.). 'Inter regia jura callentes versando, in dictâ scientiâ valde peritus esse debet; qui inter armatos reges suis verbis suo regi victoriam obtinendi officium sustinent, nempe legatus.'

684 (682 in B.). 'Ingenii sublimitas, venerabilis aut amabilis praesentia, magno studio ac praxi comparata scientia: qui horum trium unionem habet, ad legati officium prodeat.'

685. 'Si plurima sint proferenda, ordinatè ac concisè id faciendo; si displicentia sint repraesentanda ab odium concitantibus verbis abstinendo; amicabilibus verbis id faciendo, suo regi emolumentum procurare debet legatus.'

686. 'Necessariam scientiam habendo, si torvis oculis aspiciatur metum non ostendendo, rem ita ut ab audiente bene intelligatur exponendo, si tempus sibi non faveat, quamnam tunc industriam adhibere debeat, scire debet legatus.'

687. 'Quomodo se gerere debeat noscendo, ad alloquendum regem tempus aptum et locum opportunum procurando, omnia cum maturâ consideratione faciendo, legationem qui absolvit optimus legatus erit.'

688. 'Illibatos mores, aulicorum favorem, et intrepidum animum, et cum his tribus in loquendo sinceritatem possidere boni legati conditio est.'

689. 'Qui verba à suo rege prolata ad alios reges ferendi officio funguntur, debent ita intrepidè loqui, ut nunquam ob metum aliquod ex suo ore effluat verbum, quod suo regi indecorum sit.'

690. 'Qui etiamsi sibi damnum imminere videat, nil timendo apud caeteros reges suo regi exaltationem, non depressionem afferentia verba proferre valet, optimus legatus est.'

Beschi reads அஞ்சாது 'unfearing' for எஞ்சாது 'unfailing.'

CHAPTER LXX.

Beschi: *Quomodo legatus cum regibus versari debeat.* So also Graul; but the subject seems to be more general: conduct in a court, courtiership, the way of pleasing a king. Ariel: *Conduite auprès des princes.*

691. 'Nec prope nec procul, non secus ac qui ad ignem calefit, cum exteris regibus versandum.'

இகல்வேந்தர் is not 'exteris regibus,' surely. Ariel: '*rois puissants.*' Neither making himself too prominent, nor relegating himself to obscurity.

692. 'Non appetere quae reges tanquam sibi propria appetunt, via est assequendi ab ipsis regibus diu permansura emolumenta.'

It is not safe to seem to be the King's rival.

693. 'Si cautus esse vis, cave ab iis, quae difficulter tolerantur; nam postquam regum animum aversum senseris, difficile erit illum benevolum reddere.'

694. 'Coram regibus cave ne quidquam secretè cum alio confabuleris, aut alium intuendo mutuum risum edas, quia haec et similia suspicionem inducunt.'

695. 'Quidquid rex alicui secretè loquatur, neque ut audias aurem admoveas, neque quid dixerit statim interroges, neque cures illud secretum scire, nisi quum ille tibi sponte patefecerit.'

696. 'Regis intentum percipere studens, ad ei loquendum opportunum tempus eligendo, sive odiosa, sive grata sint, quae loqui debes, ita loquaris ut gratè audiaris.'

697. 'Grata loquendo futilia nunquam loquaris, licet alii coram te ac rege loquantur.'

698. 'Quamvis rex aetate tibi inferior sit, et in eo consanguinitatis gradu, ut tibi reverentiam debeat, ne istam praesumas, sed procede attendendo ad supremam quam gerit dignitatem.'

699. 'Qui sanam mentem habent, quamvis se videant a rege, plurimi fieri, nunquam audent ea facere quae regi non placent.'

700. 'In regis familiaritate veteranus licet sis, cave ruinam afferet.'

CHAPTER LXXI.

Beschi: *Regis intentum percipere, quin illud rex patefaciat.*
Graul: *Mentem percipere. Die Absicht merken.*

The tact required alike by envoy and by courtier, that reads the countenance, takes note of the subtlest indications of the ruler's will.

701. 'Qui, quin rex loquatur, ab ejus vultu ejus intentum percipere valet, huic mundo, quae nunquam siccatur aquâ circumfuso, ornamentum erit.'

702. 'Eos, qui valent sine dubitatione alicujus intima penetrare, diis similes aestima.'

703. 'Eum, qui ex eo, quod in suo interiori experitur aliorum interiora noscere valet, etiam ei dando aliquid ex iis, quae regium statum conficiunt membris, debet rex ad servitium suum attrahere.'

A king should even sacrifice an *aṅgam* (அங்கம், உறுப்பு) of his state to win such a servant. These 'essential members' are இரதகஜதுரகபதாதிகள்=தேர்கரிபரிகாலாட்கள்='chariots, elephants, horses, and foot-soldiers.'

704. 'Ab iis qui alicujus intimum animum, quin ab isto patefiet, penetrare valent, caeteri (qui id nequeunt) multum diversi sunt, quamvis quoad membra similes sint.'

உறுப்பு nom. of respect: 'as regards members.'

705. 'Si ex similibus quae in se videt signis, caeterorum intima penetrare nesciant, quamnam quaeso supra caetera membra specialitatem habebunt oculi?'

706. 'Sicuti speculum repraesentat quidquid ei objicitur, ita vultus repraesentat quae in pectore latet iram!'

707. 'Quid est ad intima dignoscenda aptius, quam vultus, si quidem statim ac in animo laetitia oritur, aut ira, ipse caeteris praenuntiat?'

708. 'Si sit, qui suum animum intuendo quidni his vel illis affectibus expertus scrutari valeat: huic ut caeterorum animum noscat sufficit, si eorum vultum intuendo insistat.'

709. 'Internum odium et amicitiam oculi manifestabunt iis qui sciri valent diversos oculorum motus pro affectuum diversitate.'

710. 'Etsi acutissimus quis sit, ad animum dimetiendum, nulla ei suppetet melior ulna quam oculi.'

CHAPTER LXXII.

Beschi: *Auditorium* (G. *coetum*) *discernere.*

A MINISTER must know the tone and temper of the council before whom he must discuss affairs of state.

711. 'Doctum auditorium si habeat, maturè considerando loqui debet, qui verborum selectionem et linguae puritatem possidet.'

712. 'Loco in quo loquitur se accomodando nonnisi doctè loquatur, qui in verborum qualitate discernendâ peritiam habet.'

713. 'Qui auditorium non discernendo in publico loquendi cacoethem habent, nec loqui sciunt, neque ad quidquam valent.'

714. 'Coram doctis doctè loquaris, coram albis (*h.e.* nesciis) albi stipitis colorem indue.'

He makes *சுதை*='*stipes.*' But?

Graul: '*Vor gelehrten rede man gelehrt, vor Ungelehrten ungelehrt.*'

715. 'Inter omnes bonas qualitates optima est in seniorum coetu non esse primum ad loquendum.'

716. 'Coram doctis latam eruditionem ostendere cupiens insciè loqui, idem est ac religiosum statum profitendo ab eo desciscere.'

717. 'Doctrina eorum qui scientiarum studio incubuerunt, in coetu eorum qui sine errore et consideratè loquendi peritiam habent, innotescet.'

718. 'Coram doctis loqui idem est ac crescentium florum areolis aquam infundere.'

When a man finds 'fit audience,' his words distil as the fertilizing dew. There may be the idea of gain to the speaker: *docendo discitur.*

719. 'Qui coram doctis subtilia quaeque cum laude loquuntur, ea neque per oblivionem coram nesciis loquantur.'

720. 'Noli subtilia loqui inter eos qui infra tuum coetum sunt; nam id idem erit ac pretiosum pharmacum in luto projicere.'

CHAPTER LXXIII.

Beschi: *Coetum non timere.*

THE Minister requires nerve and courage, to face the council, often packed, full of favourites, intriguers, and time-servers. Comp. the Book of Daniel.

721. 'Qui verborum selectu gaudentem sermonis puritatem habet, coetuum diversitatem noscendo, ob docti coetûs metum errare non debet.'

722. 'A doctis docti dicentur, qui inter doctos absque metu et confusione quae didicerint, aliis communicare sciunt.'

723. 'Plurimi sunt qui in proelio mori non timent; pauci sunt qui in coetu doctorum loqui non timeant.'

724. 'Quae tu didicisti, ita inter doctos loquere, ut et ii discere possint; quae tu non didicisti, ab iis qui plus quam tu didicerunt, disce.'

725. 'Ita disce ut viae quae ad scientiam ducit limites omnes attingas; ut sine timore ad quamcumque interrogationem in eâ materiâ responsum dare queas.'

அளவு = ἡ διαλεκτική.

726. 'Sicuti nil prodest ensis in ejus manu qui timidus est, ita nil prodest scientia ei qui doctum coetum pavet.'

727. 'Scientia ejus qui doctum coetum timet, similis est ensi quem in proelio vibrat timida manus.'

'Timida manus' euphemistically for பேடிகை, q.v.

728. 'Plurima quamvis didicerunt nullum exinde fructum capient, qui inter doctos doctè et clarè loqui nesciunt.'

729. 'Eos qui scientias didicerunt sed prae auditorum metu ea patefacere nesciunt, pejores esse iis qui non didicerunt, sapientes ajunt.'

730. 'Qui, quae didicerunt ob metum clarè patefacere nesciunt, quamvis vivi sint, tanti aestimantur, quanti fiunt mortui.'

PARS III.

De membris, quae regium statum conflant.

CHAPTER LXXIV.

Beschi: *Ditio, seu regnum.* Graul: *Territorium.*

THERE are no addresses to kings or wealthy landowners in the *Kurraḷ*, such as give a peculiar charm to many of the quatrains in the *Nâlaḍi*. In 1277 only, the princess speaks of her beloved as 'lord of the cool shore.' In *Nâl.* the king is addressed as 'நாட' *lord of the land.* In the South a landed proprietor, even of the humblest class, is a நாடான். The country has a sea-board, and chains of hills, with forests, and streams flowing down to irrigate the fields below. *Nâl.* 10, 71, 142, 146, 161, 166, 186, 194, 211, 212, &c.

In the நாட்டுப்படலம், or chapter describing the Tamiḷ land, in Kamban's *Râmâyaṇam*, and in the *Naishaḍam*, the poets have exhausted the resources of the language in elaborate descriptions of the நாடு. Comp. Manu, vii. 69.

731. 'Illud est (optimum) *regnum*, quod in se continet indefessos agricultores, virtuosos viros, et indeficientem pecuniam habentes.'

732. '(Optimum) est *regnum*, in quo talis sit rerum abundantia ut à caeteris regnicolis ibi desideretur incolatus, expers sit infirmitatibus et animalculis, quae ruinam segetibus afferant, et copiosum a segete fructum percipiat.'

733. '*Regnum* adeo opulentum esse debet, ut tempore famis sustentare etiam possit eos, qui a caeteris regnis illuc confugiunt, et tempore belli possit unâ vice solvere regi tantum tributum, quod per multas vices annuatim solvitur.'

734. 'Boni *regni* qualitas esse debet egestati obnoxium non esse, insalubre non esse, nec hostium incursionibus expositum esse.'

735. 'In bono *regno* non debent inveniri seditiosi coetus, intestini hostes, regem affligentia homicidia.'

In குறும்பு there may be a reference to the *Kurrambar* (Marravar), wild, predatory bands; but I think it simply means *lawlessness and plundering in general.*

736. 'Inter regna optimum dicetur quod neque frequenter ruinam pati videmus; et, si ruinam patiatur, statim illam copioso agrorum fructu reparet.'

737. 'Puteorum et lacuum aqua, fructuosi montes, flumina, et inexpugnabilis regia, membra sunt, quae optimum regnum conflant.'

The limits of the Tamiḻ country, as assigned by the *Nannûl*, சிறப்புப்பாயிரம், 8, 9, are:

(குணகடல் குமரி குடகம் வேங்கடம்
எனுநான் கெல்லையின் இருந்தமிழ்க் கடலுள்)

The eastern sea, Cape Kumari, Kuḍagam (Coorg), and Vêṅgaḍam (Tripety).

This 'Tamiḻ-land' has rain; springs that send their waters down the hills; a fine chain of hills as its western frontier, down which flow the Pâlârru, the Pennârru, the Kâvêrî, the Vaigai, and the Tâmbarapûrṇî, with many tributaries; and mountain heights which a little effort can convert into strong places of defence.

738. 'Salubritatem, acres divites incolas, copiosum agrorum fructum, vitam suaviter ducendi facilitatem, nec non securitatem ab hostibus: ornamenta quae bonum regnum efficiunt haec quinque dicunt sapientes.'

739. 'Illud *regni* nomen meretur, in quo annona facilè invenitur; regni nomen non meretur, si annonam multo labore investigare opus sit.'

740. 'Quamvis omnia, quae superius dicta sunt, in regno reperiantur, nil prosunt, si pariter in eo non inveniatur unio inter regem et subditos.'

CHAPTER LXXV.

Beschi: *Arces.*

Though not as important in the history of Southern India as in the annals of Sivaji and his Mahrattas, forts of considerable celebrity existed in the Carnatic, and are still to be seen in all stages of dilapidation. The pages of Orme's narrative abound in illustrations of the importance of these in South India. Comp. Manu, vii. 71–76.

741. 'Et iis, qui hostem offendere volunt, maximo praesidio sunt arces; it iis, qui timendo ab hoste se defendere volunt, optimum sunt asylum.'

Necessary both for offensive and defensive wars.

742. 'Arx debet habere aquam, uti gemmae (incorruptibilem), spatiosum campum, montem arduum, confertum sed ordinatum nemus, ut fortis dici possit.'

Compare the descriptions of Hill-forts in Captain Grant Duff's *History of the Mahrattas.*

743. 'Quod murorum altitudinem, spatii latitudinem, bellicorum instrumentorum copiam, et loci inaccessibilitatem, junctim possidet, arcem vocat bellica scientia.'

744. 'Quamvis parva sit tamen talis esse debet arx, ut in fortitudine magnas aequiparando, ad eam expugnandum advenientem hostem animo decidere faciat.'

745. 'Arx talis conditionis esse debet, ut sit expugnatu difficilis, commeatu referta sit, et qui eam custodiunt facile possint in ejus defensione consistere.'

746. 'Arx non solum debet iis omnibus, quae ad vigilum subsistentiam opus sunt, abundare, sed insuper habere debet bonos milites, qui in loco ei praesto sint (nempe eam defendant).'

747. 'Arx talis esse debet, ut difficilis expugnatu sit, sive per obsidionem, sive per aggressionem, sive per proditionem.'

Beschi says: அறைப்படுத்து='divisiones inducere.'

748. 'Arx talis esse debet ut qui illam defendunt, eam non deserendo, ex illa obsidione, eam vallantes vincere possint.'

749. 'Arx ejusmodi esse debet, ut in ipso aggressionis initio, ejus

defensorum in proeliando superioritatem videntes, animum despondendo hostes terga vertant.'

750. 'Quascunque ex supradictis excellentias arx habeat, idem est ac si non haberet, si eam qui defendunt in pugnando excellentes non sint.'

CHAPTER LXXVI.

Beschi: *Modus aerarium regium ditandi.* Ariel: *Manière d'acquerir la fortune.*

751. 'Nulla res ei rei similis, quae facit esse aliquid, eos qui nihil sunt.'

A play upon the different uses of the word பொருள்.

Ariel: 'Pour faire quelque chose de celui qui n'est rien, il est rien que la Fortune.'

752. 'Pecuniâ qui carent a cunctis despiciuntur; divitiis qui affluunt a cunctis honorantur.'

Comp. *Nâl.* 281, 283, 284:

'Though rags he wrap around his loins, a dozen coins
Or so, will gain the wretch respect 'mid many men!
The man devoid of wealth, though born of noble race,
Is viler than the lifeless corpse!'

'When on the high hill's crags the Kândaḷ blooms no more,
The crimson-spotted beetle tribe seek not its boughs.—
Lord of the glades where from the crofts they parrots scare,—
The pauper has no friends.'
(இலாஅஅர்க் கில்லைத் தமர்.)

'When wealth is there, like crows around the fallen corpse
Obsequious myriads gather round. When wealth is gone,
As wheels the beetle's flight,—no one in all the world
Will ask, "Is 't well with you?"'

753. 'Splendor divitiarum nunquam deficientum ad quod tibi libet regnum perveniens tuorum hostium tenebrosum odium affugabit.'

Simply, 'Money will help you in any region of the earth.' This reminds us of the favourite saying of Nero (Suet. Nero, cap. xi.), τὸ τεχνίον πᾶσα γαῖα τρέφει: *artificem omnis alit terra.* Comp. 397.

754. 'Divitiae, quas quis honestè cumulat modum sciens eas procurandi, et virtutes exercendi occasionem, et inde subsequentes felicitates illi parient.'

755. 'Abhorrendum est et contemnendum divitias cumulare quae non obveniant cum clementiâ (regis in subditos) et amore (subditorum in regem).'

756. 'Divitiae, quae regii juris sunt, quae sponte obveniunt, quae ex vectigalium tributis colliguntur, et quae hostes destruendo reportantur.'

His text and com. have உலகு, but this the metre forbids.

This is the only couplet that alludes to royal revenues; the other nine are quite general.

757. 'Clementia (regis in subditos) quae filia est amoris subditorum in regem nutriri debet a divite nutrice, quae dicitur pecunia.'

He who has nothing can bestow nothing on others.

758. '(Reges) tractatus inire unde sibi absque labore pecunia proveniat, perinde est ac ex eminenti loco elephantum pugnam spectare.'

He looks down in safety upon the combatants. He can, moreover, hire others to fight his battles.

759. 'Divitias cumula, nam non est illis validior ensis, qui hostium audaciam infringat.'

760. 'Divitiis justè et honestè cumulatis affluenti faciles evadent caeterae duae res, (nempe virtus et gaudium).'

The three topics of the book are 'Virtue, Wealth, and Enjoyment.' Intro. p. vii.

CHAPTER LXXVII.

Beschi: *Quae possidere debet exercitus decora.* Graul: *Heeresherrlichkeit.* Ariel: *Grandeur militaire.*

761. 'Inter omnes regias felicitates primaria esse debet talem habere exercitum, qui omnia quibus construitur habeat membra; et imperterritus hostem in proelio vincere valeat.'

The அங்கம் or உறுப்பு of an army is fourfold: இரதகசதுரகபதாதிகள். To these are added banners, musical instruments, &c.

762. 'Etiam si viribus inferior evasit, intrepidam in proeliando constantiam exhibere non nisi in veteranâ militiâ reperitur.'

763. 'Quid faciet murium multitudo, qui ipsum mare cum suo strepitu aequent? Si ipsorum hostis coluber sibilum edat, omnes peribunt.'

764. 'Ille verò exercitus dicitur, in quo reperitur nativa generositas, quae nec sui destructionem, nec sui divisionem patitur.'

765. 'Exercitus talis esse debet fortitudinis, ut milites etiamsi videant sibi mortem imminere, ad illi resistendum conflagrent.'

766. 'Quatuor sunt quae exercitum servant, militum fortitudo, honoris tenacitas, antiquorum fortium aemulatio, et in ducem fidelis obedientia.'

767. 'Exercitus callendo modum sustinendi primae aciei invasionem, et prohibendo equitatum, ne in se ruat, debet ipsum hostem invadere.'

768. 'Si exercitui nec animositas ad hostem caedendum, nec robur eum sustentandum insit, debet saltem in numero, ordine et apparatu talis esse, ut solo ejus aspectu hostes terrificet.'

769. 'Ut hostis hosti vincendo par sit, abesse ab eo debent desertiones quibus exercitus minuitur, effeminatio quae proeliandi indesinens taedium causat, et paupertas quae milites reddit tristes.'

770. 'Quamvis in exercitu multi fortesque sint milites, si tamen desinit duces, quibus subordinentur, perinde est ac si non essent.'

Ariel: 'Fut-elle pleine d'hommes résolus, une armée, si elle n'a des chefs, n'existe.'

CHAPTER LXXVIII.

Beschi: *Spiritus martialis.* Ariel: *Enthousiasme militaire.*
Graul: *Heeres-selbstgefühl.*

The author understood the feelings of a soldier. Madras Sepoys have, by their bravery, illustrated these two chapters. They need good leaders, 770.

771. 'Verba sunt ducis a proelio revertentis, qui refert quod sui milites, quos in arcis muro relinquerat, cum ipse in adversas acies rueret, clamabant hostem hortando, ne ante ducem suum consisterent, si vivere vellent: *ante me* (*i.e.* ante nostrum ducem) *consistere nolite! quidam fortes non ante me* (*i.e.* post meum tergum), *in arcis muro stantes* (dicebant).'

Either என்+ஐ='my leader': or என்னை='me.' This is a doubtful couplet.

Ariel: '*Devant moi ne demeurez, ennemis! Bien (d'autres) qui demeuraient devant moi, demeurent sous la pierre.*' A European turn of thought.

772. 'Gloriosius est manu gestare lanceam, qui irrito jactu in elephante in campo proeliante missa fuit, quam sagittam jactam in leporem in nemore quamvis illico eum confixerit.' See *Nāl.* 152.

773. 'Martialem in hostem ferociam sapientes magnanimitatem appellant; sed cum victis clementer se habere magnanimitatis apicem esse dicunt.'

Comp. Verg. *Aen.* vi. 853: 'Parcere subjectis et debellare superbos.'

774. ‘Martialem spiritum habens, postquam in proelio cum elephante lanceas omnes quas manu gestabat consumpserat, ad continuendum proelium alias quaerens, lanceam ab hoste suo corpore infixam videns, summâ cum laetitiâ eam eripiet jaculabitque.’

775. ‘Si in hostem feroci vultu ruens, cum ille te in armis impetit, priorem destruendo trepidum vultum ostenderis, nonne locum erit dare hosti ad te destruendum?’

776. ‘Martialis vir quum suos dies numerat, infructuosè transactos inter dies computabit omnes eos dies in quibus speciale ac notabile aliquod vulnus non retulit.’

777. ‘Catena quam cruri alligant ii, qui ut immortale nomen referant vitam spernunt, valde pulchrum ipsis est ornamentum.’

வேண்டாவுயிரார். A kind of Bahu-vrîhi compound. See Monier-Williams, *Sans. Gram.* 767.

Among the Mahrattas a hero so distinguished was called *Phâkre.* (See my *Ind. Hist.* § 97.)

778. ‘Cum martialis furor eos qui pro gloriâ mori non timent invadit, etiam si a duce revocentur, suam indolem non minuunt (*i.e.* proeliari non desinunt), donec hostem subjiciant.’

779. ‘Quisnam vituperare audeat eos, qui ne suum propositum transiliant, generosè quamvis in hoste ruant, in bello moriuntur?’

(Comp. my *Ind. Hist.* p. 86, 3rd. ed.)

780. ‘Mori extra domum (*i.e.* in proelio), sed ita ut rex plurimas ob tuam mortem lacrimas fundat, adeo pretiosum est, ut similis mors quocunque pretio emenda sit, etiamsi ad id mendicare oporteat.’

CHAPTER LXXIX.

Beschi: *Amicitia.*

The subject of friendship is treated in five chapters. These have no especial reference to kings. Comp. *Nâl.* xxii.

781. ‘Quid est tam factu difficile uti amicitia? sed quid est quod hac validius te defendat ab hostibus, cum iis impenetrabilis arx illa sit?’

Perhaps *alliances,* as necessary to a king, are primarily intended.

782. ‘Amicitia sapientûm novam lunam imitatur, qui in dies crescit; stultorum verò amicitia lunam plenam imitatur, quae quotidie decrescit.’

Ellis: ‘The friendship of the wise is like the moon in its increase;
The friendship of fools like the moon in its decrease.’

783. ‘Inter probos amicos quaevis collocutio novum gaudium affert;

sicuti scientias discentibus, quaevis nova notio novam dulcedinem affert.'

Ellis : 'As the pleasures of learning increase by constant application;
So the friendship of the worthy increaseth by constant intercourse.'

784. 'Amicitia non instituitur ad jocandum et ridendum, sed ut amicus amici errata videns, in eum feratur eumque corripiat.'

785. 'Ad amicitiam nec eodem in loco esse, nec jugiter conversari opus est, sed mentis ac indolis similitudo amicitiae causandae satis est.'

Ariel : '*C'est la (communauté de) pensée qui lui donne son mérite.*'

786. 'Amicitia quae solam vultûs laetitiam prae se fert, vera non est; illa vera est, quae cordis et animi laetitiam secum fert.'

Ellis: 'True friendship is not that which dimpleth the face with smiles, but that which maketh the heart rejoice.'

787. 'Ab amico ea quae perniciem afferunt removere, eum per virtutis semitas manuducere, et si quid infortunium accidat, quod removeri nequeat, illud unâ cum amico portare, amicitiae proprium est.'

Ellis: 'Friendship should repel all injuries, should take the lead in the path of virtue; and, in unavoidable misfortune, should share the adversity it causeth.'

788. 'Amicitiae proprium est amico in infortuniis praesto esse eâ celeritate, qua manus accurrit ad vestem quae dilabitur, ne in coetu nudus appareas.'

789. 'Si quaeras, ubinam sit amicitiae sedes regia, dicam ibi esse ubi sine tergiversatione, quovis tempore quolibet modo amici virtus et fortuna subtentantur ne decidant.'

790. 'Ejus qui quantum ab àmico ametur, et quantum ipse eum amet computat, quamvis ornatus amore nulla differentia appareat, ridicula tamen amicitia est (quia vera amicitia in amore limites non habet).'

Ellis: 'Vain is the fragile friendship, however specious, which saith, "Even as they are to us, so will we be to them."'

இன்னம், Intro. p. xxiii.

CHAPTER LXXX.

Beschi: *Quocum amicitiam ineas, attentè considerandum.*
Graul: *Prüfung in der Freundschaft.*

THIS and the following chapters (LXXX.–LXXXIII.) may be compared with *Nâl.* 211-240.

791. 'Cum post initam amicitiam difficilis sit separatio, iis qui amicitias ineunt, nil adeo periculosum est, quam sine consideratione amicitiam inire.'

Ellis: 'Nothing is more hurtful than friendship inconsiderately formed; for after it hath once been contracted, it is difficult for those sincerely united in friendship to separate.' *Nâl.* 220.

792. 'Amicitia cum aliquo inita, diu multumque non considerando ejus indolem et actiones, in finem tibi talem, ut vitam auferre valeat poenam afferet.' *Nâl.* 224.

793. 'Noli cum aliquo amicitiam inire, nisi postquam noveris ejus indolem, prosapiam, vitia et consanguineos defectu carentes.'

Ellis: 'Friendship should be contracted only after having ascertained the disposition, lineage, and faults of the party, and that his connections are honourable.' *Nâl.* 212.

For the v. யா comp. *Nâl.* 214:

'Though side by side for many days men dwell, when souls
Cling not, not few days even men in friendship cling.
And who lets go attachment's well-knit ties, though those
To whom his soul is knit dwell many days afar?'

794. 'Ejus amicitiam qui, honestâ prosapiâ ortus, culpam in se admittere erubescit, etiam si pretium dare opus sit, emere debes.'

795. 'Ei qui scire valet, quid juxta proborum morem agendum sit, et, quum amicus quid mori contrarium agere cogitat, ea ei dicere, quae ab eo fletum eliciant, si vero gesserit, cum corripere ne iterum faciat, maturè considerando, hujusmodi amicitiae emolumentum, amicus fias.'

Comp. *Nâl.* 73, 222, 225:

'Lord of the swelling sea's cool shore, where in each flower
Bright insects hum! Are words severe from loving lips
Harder to bear, if duly their result you scan,
Than pleasant words that strangers speak?'

If, though they dam it up, the fresh flood burst its bonds,
They straight imprison it again, nor feel aggrieved;
For by the precious stream they live: when friends offend
Men bear with those whose friendship's dear.'

'Though those, from whom you may not part, do grievous things,
O golden maid! you still must cherish chosen friends;—
The fire destroys men's wealth and happy homes, yet there
'Tis sought and kindled every day.'

796. 'Ad amicos seligendos in ipsâ infelicitate documentum invenies, quaedam enim mensura infelicitas est, quae superabundanter amicos dimetitur.' *Nâl.* 283, 284, 290, 337.

797. 'Stultorum amicitiam relinquere, ab iis se distinendo, non damnum sed lucrum puta.'

Ellis: 'To separate from the society of fools is the most profitable thing a man can do.'

798. 'Noli mente versari, quae animum despondere faciant; noli amicitiam inire cum eo, qui in adversis amicum deserit.'

Ellis: 'Ponder not on what depresseth the mind, and form not friendship with those who forsake their friends in adversity.'

799. 'Amicitiam ejus, qui te in adversis deseruit, etiamsi dum infelicitas te maximè vexat mente revolvas, haec recordatio, magisquam ipsa infelicitas, te affliget.'

Graul: 'Der Gedanke an treulose Freundschaft verliert
Selbst im Angesichte der Todesnoth seinen Stachel nicht,'

800. 'Inculpabilium virorum amicitiam compara; eorum qui probis se non conformant amicitiam desere, etiamsi aliquid dare opus sit, ut ab iis te liberes.'

CHAPTER LXXXI.

Beschi: *Ab antiquo tempore continuata familiaritas.*

The idea of the chapter is, the kindly indulgence due to old and tried friends.

Ariel translates பழைமை in the title 'vieille amitié,' and in ver. 801, 'l'intimité.'

801. 'Si quaeras, quidnam sit vetusta familiaritas, est amicitia quae in amico non prohibet ullum actum ex iis, quae amicorum intimorum sunt proprii, neque ob illos indignatur [tales actus sunt sine reverentiâ conversari, uti bonis amici tamquam propriis, aliqua facere ad amicum spectantia, eo inconsulto, et similia].'

802. 'Amicorum, qui sunt amicitiae veluti membra, adeoque inter se unum quid sunt, quamdam nimiam familiaritatem non dedignari prudentium conditio est.'

Ellis: 'The prudent bear complacently even the undue familiarity of those friends, with whom they are as intimately united in friendship as the limbs with the body.'

803. 'Quidnam erit in vetustâ amicitiâ emolumentum, si non valeat displicentiam non ostendere de iis, quae amicus cum nimiâ familiaritate facit?'

804. 'Si amicus ob intimam familiaritatem, amico inconsulto, quidquam ad eum spectans fecerit, sapientes id aeque ferent ob optabilem quamdam proprietatem quam id secum fert.'

'Nimium amorem denotat.'

So Shelley, 'Familiar acts are beautiful through love.'

805. 'Si amicus quid fecerit, quod tibi displiceat, scito id fecisse aut ex judicii defectu, aut ex nimia familiaritate.'

Ellis: 'If thy friends do anything to offend thee, consider it the effect either of thoughtlessness, or of too great familiarity.'

806. 'Qui in amicitiâ constans est, non deserit ejus amicitiam, qui nunquam a vetustâ familiaritate aberravit, etiamsi in aliquâ occasione aliquod ei damnum afferat.'

Ellis: 'Those constant in friendship will not forsake the society of those, who from old time have been faithful to them, even when they are injured by the connexion.'

807. 'Qui ab amore ortam vetustam familiaritatem habent, nunquam amorem minuunt, etiamsi amicus quid fecerit unde ipsis damnum obveniat.'

808. 'Iis qui scire valent amicitiae indolem, quae non audit (seu non curat) amici culpam, fortunatus est dies, in quo amicus culpam admiserit [quia in eo elucescet magis ejus amor, libenter condonando eam culpam].'

Ellis: 'Those confirmed in the knowledge of the true nature of friendship listen not to the faults of their friends, although daily guilty of them.'

809. 'Totus mundus optabit amicum habere eum, qui nunquam deserit amicitiam illorum, qui in vetustâ familiaritate nunquam decreverunt, quamvis ipsi displicentia faciant.'*

810. 'Qui nescit antiquam conditionem mutare erga vetustos amicos, etiamsi quid culpabile fecerint, ejus amicitiam ipsi hostes desiderabunt.'

Ellis: 'Even their enemies will desire the love of those, who on account of ancient friendship, separate not from their friends, however culpable they may be.'

CHAPTER LXXXII.

Beschi: *Damnosa amicitia.* Graul: *Amicitia cum malis.*

811. 'Melius est decrescere quam crescere in amicitiâ eorum qui bonâ indole carent, licèt in tui amore ita ebrii videantur, uti qui vinum biberunt.'

812. 'Eorum qui uniformitatem non servantes, in affluentiâ tibi amici sunt, in inopiâ te deserunt, amicitiam si obtineas quid boni; si perdas, quid mali tibi erit?'

Ellis: 'Of what consequence is it whether the friendship of the incon-

* Comp. *Dionysii Catonis disticha, de moribus*, iv. 41 (Amstel. 1754):—

'Damnaris nunquam, post longum tempus amicum.
Mutavit mores; sed pignora prima memento.'

These disticha, 145 in number, more resemble the Kurral than anything else I have found. Comp. the following (iv. 19) with 400:—

'Disce aliquid; nam quum subito fortuna recessit,
Ars remanet, vitamque hominis non deserit unquam.'

stant, who attach themselves to thee in prosperity, but forsake thee in adversity, be gained or lost?'

813. 'Amicus, qui amat ad mensuram sui emolumenti; meretrix, quae amat pretium, non pretium dantem; et latro, qui unice suum lucrum respicit: nil inter se differunt.'

Ellis: 'The friend who considereth only his advantage is on a level with mercenary harlots and robbers.'

814. 'Melius est omni amico cavere, quam amicum qui stultam indolem habet, ei similem qui in pugnâ se auxiliaturum promittit, sed quum pugnandum est fugit.'

Instead of *மா* he reads *மரவு*; but this is against metre: *மரவன்னுர்* (*புளிமாங்காய்*) would require a *நேர்* in the beginning of the next foot. (Intro. p. xxvii. § VI.)

815. 'Melius est non obtinere quam obtinere amicitiam vilium illorum qui in pugnâ arcem deserunt, quam sibi construxerant.'

816. 'Decies centies millies majus bonum affert odium sapientûm, quam summa amicitia stultorum.'

Ellis: 'Ten million of times better is the enmity of the wise, than the most devoted attachment of fools.'

817. 'Deceis centies millies majora tibi bona obvenient ab ipsis hostibus, quam ex amicitiâ illorum, qui amicum deridere solent.'

818. 'Ab ejus generis amicis, qui non perficiunt quod coeperunt, nec valedicendo, longe recede.'

819. 'Neque somniando optare debes amicitiam ejus, cujus alia sunt verba, alia sunt opera.'

Ellis: 'It is unpleasant even to dream of the friendship of those whose words and whose deeds are at variance.'

820. 'Nec minimum tibi approximare sine, qui domi se tibi amicum ostendit, foris vero tibi detrahit.'

CHAPTER LXXXIII.

Beschi: *Amicitia simulata, seu quae non est conjuncta cum animo.*
Ellis: 'On improper friendship.' Graul: *Heuchel-Freundschaft.*

COMP. *Nâl.* 231–240.

821. 'Amicitia eorum qui se amicos praebent, ut datâ occasione amicum securius laedant, similis est incudi quae ferrum sustentat, ut fortius malleo percutiatur.'

Ellis: 'The friendship of those who dissemble attachment, while they seek occasion to betray thee, is like an anvil (which supports the metal while the hammer beats it).'

822. 'Non fidendum amicitiae eorum, qui quum sint animo extranei se familiares ostendunt; uti non fidendum est amori mulieris.'

823. 'Qui hostes sunt, quamvis plures egregias artes didicerint, difficile est ut ad veram amicitiam transeant.'

824. 'Cavere oportet ab iis, qui intus odium tegunt, sed in vultu laetitiam et risum ostendunt.'

Ellis: 'Mischief should be feared from the deceitful, whose countenances are pleasant, but their hearts filled with malice.'

825. 'Qui interius amorem non habent, eorum dulcibus verbis nec minimum fidendum est.'

826. 'Hostium verba statim dignoscuntur quamvis valde bona verba, uti verus amicus loquatur.'

Ellis: 'Although they assume the courteous address of friends, the words of foes will soon be known for what they are.'

827. 'Qui intestinum odium fovet, si humilia et amica verba loquatur, non est ei fidendum; exemplo arcûs, qui dum inclinatur, non nisi damnum illius erga quem inclinatur intendit.'

828. 'Hostes dum amoris in signum lachrymas fundunt similes sunt iis, qui subjectionem aut venerationem fingunt, ut arma occultent, quibus alicujus vitae insidiantur.'

[Comp. my *Ind. Hist.*, p. 165, 3rd ed.]

829. 'Rex cum iis hostibus qui exterius nimiam amicitiam ostendunt, sed intus odium fovent, et ipse tali amicitiâ utens, laetum vultum ostendendo cum iis ad eos interficiendos jungi debet (nam fraudem fraude repellere, aequum est).'

830. 'Quando venerit tempus in quo qui hostes sunt amicos se fingunt, tunc et tu in vultu amicitiam ostendendo, interius illorum amicitiam aversari debes.'

Ellis: 'When the time arrives for enmity to become amity, let your countenance be friendly; but carefully recede from such friendship.'

CHAPTER LXXXIV.

Beschi: *Insipientia.*

THE Com. regards these chapters, to XCIV., as pointing out those whose friendship is to be shunned. Comp. *Nál.* 331–340.

831. 'Est quid, quod *insipientia* dicitur; si quaeras, quidnam sit, est ea quae damnosa sunt sectari, quae verò utilia rejicere.'

832. 'Insipientia quae omnes insipientias vincit, est id studiosè

sectari, quod neque in hoc neque in altero mundo profuturum est, quia inordinatum est.'

833. 'Culpam non erubescere, futura non considerare, sine affabilitate rusticè loqui, et suum honorem, doctrinam, ac familiae splendorem non custodire, sunt insipientis officia.'

834. 'Quisnam erit eo insipientior, qui ad se domandum convenientes scientias discendo, quantum id prosit noscendo, et caeteris ad id conducentia consilia dando, se tamen domare nescit.'

835. 'Insipiens capax est sibi in hoc mundo parandi infernum in quo post mortem demergatur.'

In another place Beschi says, as to எழுபிறப்பு, 'et revera si bene consideretur, *non sunt nisi diversi modi animam torquendi ob peccata patrata*, atque ab iis eam purgandi, si purgabilia sunt.'

836. 'Cum ad id par non sit, aliquod facinus perficiendum suscipiens insipiens; aut id non perficiet, aut illaqueabitur.'

837. 'Si insipienti divitiae affluant, eas ita distribuet ut hostes ventrem repleant, amici fame pereant.'

838. 'Si insipienti divitiae obvenerint perinde erit, ac si qui vertiginem patitur, vinum bibendo ebrius quoque fiat [*insania duplicabitur*].'

839. 'Valde dulcis est quam insipientes inter se conflant amicitia,—quia cum separantur, nullam afflictionem patiuntur.'

Irony. மாறுபடுபுகழணி. III. Gram. 210.

840. 'Si insipiens in sapientûm coetum pedem inferat, perinde est ac si quis lutulentis pedibus pretiosum peristroma calcet [*hic peristroma, ille coetum conspurcat*].'

CHAPTER LXXXV.

Beschi: *Inscitia.*

Comp. *Nâl.* 321–330.

841. 'Inter omnes defectus, scientiae defectus maximus est defectus, nam si caetera omnia desint, id à scientibus non reputatur defectus.'

842. 'Si inscio caeteris aliquid largiendi voluntas obvenerit, ad id agendum nulla alia est caussa, quam fortuna illius qui recipit.'

843. 'Inscitiâ praeditum nec ipsi ejus hostes poterunt tot afflictionibus affligere, quod ipsemet sibi causat.'

844. 'Si quaeras, quid sit totalis inscitia, est quaedam stulta persuasio, quâ quis quum nil aut parum sciat, omnia tamen se scire putat.'

845. 'Qui de iis quae nescit loqui praesumit, etiam quum de iis loquitur de quibus sine errore loqui potest, dubitandi locum dabit.'

846. 'Ad quid inscius sua verenda contegit, si tegere nescit culpas quas in se videt.'

847. 'Inscius qui alicujus momenti secretum servare nescit, ipsemet sibi valde magnum damnum creat.'

848. 'Qui nil facit, quod caeteri ei faciendum insinuant, neque ipse ex se scit, quid sibi conveniat facere, est morbus mundum quousque vixerit, insectans.'

849. 'Si inscio, quum quid facere ignorat, modum id faciendi quis monstret, ipse inscius reputabitur; ille verò, qui ignorat, sciens aestimabitur, eo modo quo quum nil sciat, omnia se scire putat.'

850. 'Qui negat quod sapientes affirmant, habendus est uti daemon qui terram lustrat ut hominibus illudat.'

Com. thinks that the existence of God, of a future life and retribution, are the things which the common sense of the world affirms; and that he who would rob men of these beliefs is as a demon.

CHAPTER LXXXVI.

Beschi: *Animi aversio, vel oppositio.*

851. 'Animi aversio est quidam morbus qui in omnes diffundi facit malam illam qualitatem, quae divisio appellatur (h.e. *socialitatem destruens morbus*).'

852. 'Si quis a te dividi volens, hostilitatem ostenderit, quum tamen animum non avertendo illi malum si non faceris, optimum erit.'

853. 'Si ex animo molestissimum morbum, qui aversio dicitur abjeceris, absque ullâ unquam diminutione nunquam desituram gloriam adipisceris.'

854. 'Si in te destruxeris malorum maximum, quod est aversio, omnibus gaudiis majus gaudium obtinebis.'

855. 'Qui quum animi aversio sese objicit, eam declinando procedere valent, quisnam est, qui ad eos destruendos animum adjicere possit?'

856. 'Qui gloriosum putat eos a quibus aversus est superare, aut humiliare, ejus felicitas ut minuatur et omnino destruatur, nonnisi unico momento indiget.'

857. 'Caeteras scientias praecellentem veri scientiam non assequitur (non percipit) qui adeo insanâ mente praeditus est, ut aversioni manus det.'

858. 'Aversionem declinare emolumentum affert; si verò animum adjicias ad ejus cui aversus es humiliationem, infelicitas ad te aggrediendum animum concipiet.'

859. 'Quamvis emolumentum ex aversione obventurum sit, aversionem

non cogitat; quamvis damnum obventurum sit, aversionem magis magisque fovet animus humanus.' (860 in B.)

The disposition to hate shows that the man is marked out for misfortune: 'Quem Deus perdere vult, prius dementat.'

860. 'Ex animi aversione omnia mala proveniunt, animi autem adhaesio secum fert gloriam omnes laetificandi.' (This is 859 in B.)

CHAPTER LXXXVII.

Beschi: *Odium prudens.* 'Might in enmity.'

861. 'Rex caveat hostibus adversari se potentioribus: non cavendum, immo curandum iis adversari quum infirmiores sunt.'

With the strong, guard against accepting dissension.
With the weak, guarding not against (it), court enmity.

மாறு is a weaker word than பகை: you must not willingly accept a difference with the strong, though forced upon you; you may court even enmity with the weak. ஏற்றல் is opposed to மேவல்.

The rhythm is ஒழுகிசை; almost ஏந்திசை. The எதுகை is the best. Intro. p. xxvi. The figure அந்தாதி (III. Gram. 199). There is also வேற்றுமையணி (III. Gram. 206). The fourth case is used in பகை (III. Gram. 60). The optatives (III. Gram. 85). (ஒம்பா, III. Gram. 90.)

862. 'Si quis consanguineos non amando eos à se distineat, auxiliares non habeat, neque ipse vires habeat, quâ ratione infringetur ejus hostium odium?'

The loveless one, the man devoid of strong allies, the man himself indigent,—how can he cut down the foemen's strength?

For changes of த் into ற், see III. Gram. 38.

The advice is two edged: 'If this is your picture, do not hope to prevail; if your foe is such, you may confidently attack him.'

863. 'Qui non metuenda metuit, quae scienda sunt nescit, cum caeteris sociabilis non est, neque quidquam suis largitur, valde facilis est suis hostibus (i.e. *faciliter ab iis subjugatur*).'

The fearful, the ignorant, the unconciliating, the illiberal—
Is an utterly easy (prey) to his enemies.

அஞ்சும்=அஞ்சும் மனிதன். The rhythm is தூங்கிசை.

864. 'Qui nec occultare, nec secretum custodire scit, quovis tempore, quovis in loco, cuivis hosti, superatu facilis est.'

One who ceases not from wrath, has no self-command—
Always, everywhere, and to all, is an easy (prey).

865. 'Qui nec jura discit, neque iis conformitèr agit, neque curat si

vituperetur, neque bonam indolem habet: huic adversari valde jucundum est (*i.e.* facile, ejus hostibus).'

He who regards not prescription, he who does not actions suitable,
He who regards not guilt, he who is without innate goodness—is a pleasure to his enemies.

866. 'Desiderabile est odium fovere (seu adversari) ei, qui caecam iram sequitur, et valde luxuriosus est.'

867. 'Etiam si quid dare debeas, emendum est odium illius, qui in suis actionibus, quum fini appropinquant, eas pessum ire facit.'

868. 'Qui nullam bonam indolem (seu qualitatem) habet, si plurima habeat vitia, et socios (seu auxiliatores) non habeat, suis hostibus magnam laetitiam affert.'

869. 'Qui meticulosus est, neque callet strategemata quibus virium defectum suppleat, hunc si adversarius sortiatur, suis hostibus longo tempore non desituram laetitiam afferet.'

870. 'Nunquam gloriam assequetur, qui quotidie animum non adjicit huic facillimae rei, qualis est adversari iis, qui justitiae lèges ignorant.'

CHAPTER LXXXVIII.

Beschi: *Juxta hostium diversitatem diversè se gerere cum illis.*

871. 'In eo, quod dicitur odium, indiscretionem neque per jocum affectare debes.'

872. 'Si malum est in te concitare gladiatoris odium, pessimum est in te concitare regii ministri odium.'

873. 'Eo, qui vertigine laborat, insipientior est, qui solus quum sit, multorum odium in se concitat.'

874. 'Totus se mundus subdet magnitudini ejus regis, qui indolem habeat sibi conciliandi amicitiam suorum hostium.'

875. 'Qui solus est auxiliatorem non habens, et duos hostes habeat, unum ex his dulciter pacificando sibi confoederare debet.'

876. 'Si aliquem hostem pacaveris, sive non pacaveris, quum tibi aliunde ruina obvenerit, neque cum illo foedus in eas, neque illum rejicias (tanquam hostem).'

877. 'Iis, qui tuam afflictionem non ignorant, noli eam manifestare coram tuis hostibus noli unquam tuam debilitatem prodere.'

878. 'Si res gerendi modum discendo tu ipse eas perfeceris, quin aliis illas committas, teque ipsum semper caveris, laetitia quam de tuâ debilitate hostes conceperant peribit.'

879. 'Spinosam arborem quum parva est explanta; nam postquam creverit, ipsa nocebit manui eam explantare volentis.'

880. 'Si rex, opportunitatem habens deprimendi audaciam sui adversarii, eam despiciendo, id non fecerit, non erit, ubique in mundo ut diu vivat.'

Beschi reads அல்ல for அல்லர்.

CHAPTER LXXXIX.

Beschi: *Inimicitia occulta.*

881. 'Amici sunt ejusdem conditionis ac umbra et aqua, quibus cum voluptate utimur, quum persaepe damnum afferant ob aliquam qualitatem nobis ignotam, amicos etiam peramanter excipimus, quum interius et occulte hostes nobis sint.'

For இன்று he reads இன்ன = 'ad instar.'

Water and shade are most useful and pleasant; but may prove hurtful: so friendships.

882. 'Noli ita metuere hostes (*gladio*) evaginato similes, uti metuere debes hostes, qui se amicos ostendunt.'

883. 'Ab hoste occulto semper metuendo cave; ni caveris, in occasione tibi adversâ te pejus diffindet, quam figuli paxillus argillam findit.'

884. 'Si in te oriatur internum odium erga consanguineos, quod probum animum dedecet, illud tibi plurima et indecorosa damna causabit.'

885. 'Si rex in consanguineos internum odium foveat, illud ei plurima ruinam afferentia mala causabit.'

886. 'Si ii qui cum rege unum sunt, nempe consanguinei, internum odium fovent, huic quovis tempore, etiam quum potens est, difficile erit suam perditionem declinare.'

887. 'Familia in quâ interna odia regnant, quamvis exterius unionem obtendat, interius tamen divisa est, non secus ac capsula, quae videtur unum lignum esse, sed revera ex duobus lignis constat.'

888. 'Familia in quâ interna odia vigent, ex animorum contrietate pugnâ teritur non secus ac teritur ferrum cum limâ pugnans.'

889. 'Quamvis internum odium sit adeo exiguum, uti divisio quae apparet in semine sesamae nihilominus semper noxium erit.'

'The little rift within the lute!'

890. 'Vita illorum, qui in eadem domo viventes interno se odio prosequuntur, similis est vitae illius qui in parvâ domunculâ simul cum serpente vitam ducat.'

CHAPTER XC.

Beschi: *Magnos viros, puta sacerdotes, religiosos, hisque similes laedere.*

891. ' Qui sibi cavet ne à malis opprimatur, nullam meliorem cautionem adhibebit, quam cavendo ne despiceat magnitudinem eorum, qui (vel ob dignitatem, vel ob spiritualitatem, vel ob scientiam, vel ob dexteritatem venerandi sunt, vel) capaces sunt quidquid intentant perficiendi.'

892. ' Si magnos viros non verendo processeris, id per ipsosmet tibi nunquam desiturum damnum causabit.'

893. ' Si cupis tuam ruinam, justitiae legibus auditum ne praebe; si cupis tuam internecionem majoribus injuriam facito.'

894. ' Debilior aut inferior quum sis, noli potentioribus aut superioribus injuriam facere, quia id idem erit ac manu vocare deum mortis, ut te impetat suâ falce.'

895. ' Rex qui ab alio rege potentiore invaditur, ubinam gentium tutus erit? Nullibi mortem effugiet.'

896. ' Quamvis igne cremeris vivere poteris; nullo modo vivent qui majoribus injuriam faciunt.'

897. ' Ob membrorum, quae regnum constituunt praestantiam insigne licèt regnum obtineas, plurimisque divitiis affluas, quid tibi proderunt, si insignes in virtute viri tibi irascantur.'

898. ' Si iis qui ob virtutûm celsitudinem monti sunt similes defectum venerationis exhibeant, etiam ii, qui in mundo videntur cum suâ familiâ diuturnam stabilitatem habituri, peribunt.'

Ascetics are குன்றன்னோர், ' like hills,' in elevation; and also, they stand unmoved in shine and storm.

899. ' Si qui sublimi virtute pollet irascatur, et ipse deorum rex Dêvendiran (in suis verendis figuram amittendo !) damnum sentiet.'

In Beschi, 898. He reads வேந்தமைவேந்து, ' King of Kings= Indra.' Nahusha (Manu, vii. 41) had obtained sovreignty of the three worlds, but, for an intentional insult to Agastya, was changed into a serpent. B. has in mind 25. See note on 25.

900. ' Etiam ii, qui nimiam potentiam habent, cum vitâ non evadent, si ipsis, ii qui singularibus virtutibus praediti sunt, irascantur.'

CHAPTER XCI.

Beschi: *Non sinere se ab uxore regi.* Graul: *Den Weg der Frau gehen.*

EASTERN kings have often done great injustice to worthy councillors. Their courts are often disturbed by intrigues which have their origin in the *zenâna.* Hence this chapter naturally follows the last. It also connects itself with 'enmity': for nothing generates such deadly hate.

901. 'Qui nimis uxorii sunt nec virtutem consequentur, nec fortunae bona; qui enim ad haec acquirenda incumbunt, veluti maximum impedimentum uxoriam delectationem despiciunt.'

The idea of polygamy is not suggested,—and is, in fact, rendered impossible by the tenor of Ch. IV., &c.; yet it found place among the Râjas whom Tiruvaḷḷuvar contemplates. The practical value of the chapter is thus evident.

902. 'Felicitas illius, qui sui virilitatis oblitus nimium uxori deditus est, quum magnum dedecus afferat, valdè indecora est.'

903. 'In uxore viro se subjicientis conditionis defectus efficiet, ut quoties ejus vir ante probos viros appareat erubefiat.'

Ariel: 'Manquer de personalité en se soumettant à une épouse donne toujours honte parmi les sages.'

904. 'Qui uxorem suam timet, et pro alterâ vitâ virtute vacuus erit, et in hâc vitâ etiamsi in familiâ augendâ virilitatem ostendat, haec a nemine celebrabitur.'

905. 'Qui uxorem timet, timebit etiam quovis tempore probis viris benefacere.'

906. 'Quamvis (destructis omnibus tuis hostibus) ex pace fruaris, quam Beati fruuntur, nunquam vir dici potèris, si tuae uxoris manus, quae arundinis *mûnghil* dictae nitorem equant, pertimesces.'

Comp. Catullus, li.:—

'Ille mi par esse deo videtur,
. . . . . .
Otium et reges prius et beatas
Perdidit urbes.'

This is not to be taken literally; yet, I think, there is possibly a play on words. She might speak 'bambûs,' though she used none.

907. 'Valde aestimabilior erit verecunda muliercula, quam magnus vir, qui uxori se subdit.'

908. 'Qui juxta voluntatem uxoris in agendo procedit, neque amicorum necessitatibus succurret, neque sibi pro alterâ vitâ bona cumulabit.'

909. 'Neque virtutes, nec bene partae divitiae, neque caeterae actiones quibus hujus vitae gaudia comparare possit, locum habent in eo, qui suae uxori subditus est.'

In the enjoyment of இன்பம் he forgets அறம் and பொருள். (Intro. p. vii.)

910. 'Insipientia se suae uxori subdendi nunquam invenietur in illo, qui negotiis animum applicat, iis que partâ felicitate fruitur.'

The emphatic directness of this chapter is noteworthy. Many native states have perished through the effeminacy here so forcibly denounced.

CHAPTER XCII.

Beschi: *Mulier quae in suo corpore tradendo limites non habet,* i.e. *meretrix.* Graul: *Freche Dirnen.* Ariel: *Femmes sans retenue.*

THIS points to a still more frequent cause of ruin. Comp. *Nâl.* 371–80.

911. 'Valde noxium est seduci a dulcibus verbis mulieris, quae te non desiderat ex tui amore, sed tuam pecuniam desiderat.'

912. 'Sapientes bene ponderando dulcedinem quâ meretrix tui amorem non habens, ex emolumenti amore amantia verba profert, ab eâ fugere debent tanquam ab hoste.'

913. 'Meretrix, in suis fallacibus amplexibus, perinde se habet, ac si qui mercede conductus ad sepulturam ut deferat, cadaver extranei alicujus hominis amplectitur.'

This seems quite wrong. Com. also is far-fetched and obscure, imagining a scavenger carrying a corpse. Far better is Graul: 'Wer sich mit einer feilen Dirne abgiebt, der giebt sich mit einem Leichnam ab, denn sie giebt eben nur ihren Leib hin—ohne alle Seele.' So also Ariel.

914. 'Vilem gustum ab eâ illatum, quae unicè optat tuam pecuniam propriam facere, non tangunt qui attentè considerare valent veri amoris proprietatem.'

Alb. Tib. iii. 49: 'Heu heu divitibus video gaudere puellas.'

915. 'Qui in prudentiâ et sapientiâ excellunt, non tangunt vilem gustum ab illis illatum, quae communem amorem habent (*i.e.* omnibus pecuniam dantibus amorem ostendunt).'

916. 'Qui suam laudam per orbem diffundunt, non tangunt corpus earum, quae venustatem et laetitiam ostendendo vilem sui corporis usum in omnes, qui pecuniam dant, diffundunt.'

917. 'Corpus earum quae aliud quam coeuntem animo affectando

(nempe pecuniam) coeunt, ii solum tangunt qui vili animo praediti sunt.'

918. 'Sapientes fallaces meretricis amplexus vocant pestem illorum qui non habent adeò sanam mentem, ut valeant considerare illarum deceptionem.'

A kind of *Lamia*.

919. 'Delicata cutis meretricum, quae limites non habent, sed omnibus pecuniam dantibus se tradunt, infernus est in quo merguntur viles atque infimae notae homines.'

Beschi translates தோல் for தோள்: yet his text is right.

920. 'Meretrices, inebrians liquor, et ludus, nonnisi cum iis a quibus felicitas recessit, amicitiam ineunt.'

See Ch. XCIII., XCIV.

CHAPTER XCIII.

Beschi: *Abstinere ab inebriantibus.*

ANOTHER enemy to the state of kings.

கள் = S. *surâ*; but is restricted in use to *toddy*, the fermented juice of the பனை, *Borassus flabelliformis.*

In Kamban's Tamil version of the Râmâyaṇam, I. *Kândam*, xviii. *Paḍalam*, entitled உண்டாட்டுப்படலம், or 'The drinking revels,' the poet describes, with evident sympathy, in sixty-seven quatrains, the wild Bacchanalian orgies in which King Daçarathan, his wives and all his court—all drunk together, it would seem—indulge for a week in a palm-tree grove on their journey to Mithilâ.

921. 'Reges qui semper dediti sunt potationi liquorum inebriantium, nec ab hostibus metuentur, et partas laudes omnes omittent.'

922. 'Nemo inebriantia bibat; si quis bibere velit, ille bibat, qui non curat a sapientibus aestimari.'

923. 'Si ebrietas et ipsis tuae matris oculis turpis videtur, qualis videbitur oculis sapientûm.'

924. 'Mulier quae dicitur verecundia dorsum vertet iis, qui non cavent ab maximo hoc vitio potandi inebriantia.'

925. 'Nonne quid sit opprobrium ignorari videtur, qui pretio sui oblivionem emit.'

926. 'Qui dormiunt, quamdiu dormiunt mortuis sunt similes; qui vero inebriantia bibunt, quovis tempore, sunt similes iis qui venenum sumpserunt.'

927. 'Qui semper inebriationi dediti, dum bibunt a caeterorum oculis se abscondunt, non evitabunt subsannationem suorum concivium quibus secreta potatio ab ebrietate manifesta sit.'

928. 'Desine dicere quod non bibere soleas, nam tua culpa in tuo pectore abscondita, statim ac bibisti, se prodet.'

929. 'Ebrium velle rationibus ad bonam frugem reducere, idem est ac cum lucernâ quaerere velle eum qui subtus aquam est.'

930. 'Qui se inebriare solet, dum ebrius non est, et alium ebrium videt, nonne considerat qualis sua fuerit deformitas cum ebrius fuit?'

CHAPTER XCIV.

Beschi: *Ludus.*

Gambling and disease are both hindrances.

Com. Analysis :—

I. 1–5. It brings loss.
II. 6–9. It entails many degradations.
III. 10. Hard to cure.

931. 'Noli ludum appetere, quamvis tibi victoriam det; quia sicuti piscis hamum deglutiens decipitur, ita ludus victoriam veluti hamum extendendo, tuam pecuniam omnem surripiendo te fallet.'

See நைடதம், சூதாடுபடலம், உஉ :—

எள்ளுக சூதினை, இகலி வென்றதூஉங்
கள்ள மேற்கொடு வலைகரந்துவேட்டுவர்
உள்ளுற வமைத்திடு முணவை யோர்கிலாப்
புள்ளின மருந்தின போலும், என்பவே!

'Gaming despise! Ev'n when you strive and overcome,
'Tis as when fowler, mind on fraudful scheme intent,
His net conceals, and places dainty food within,
And winged tribes unweeting haste to eat,' they cried.

The whole passage, 11–28, is a commentary on this chapter.

932. 'Est ne in ludo, ubi si semel vincas, centies perdes, via ad virtutum et deliciarum consequutionum?'

933. 'Si rex semper in ore habeat lucrum ludo partum (*i.e.* si incessanter ludat), in aerario congesta pecunia, et ex tributis congerenda, ipsum destituens ad hostes perveniet.'

934. 'Nil est quod paupertatem inducat, uti ludus, qui et varias angustias affert, et felicitatem destruit.'

935. ['Reges, qui aleam, et ludi locum, et ludendi exercitium, magno cum gaudio, nimium sectati fuere, esse desierunt.']

So especially the Pâṇḍavas, and Naḷa. See Dowson's *Classical Dict.* 'Çakuni' is synonymous with 'cheat.' Manu forbids dice, iv. 74.

936. 'Nunquam ventrem implebunt, ac miseriam patientur, qui ab infelicitatis deâ, cui nomen ludus, occupati sunt.'

937. 'Si tempus in ludo teras, et ab atavis haereditate acceptam felicitatem, et bonas animi quas habes conditiones amittes.'

Manu repeatedly forbids gambling. In II. 179, it is associated with 'disputes.' So *Avvai* says: சூதும் வாதும் வேதனைசெய்யும 'gaming and disputation bring distress.'

938. 'Ludus ludentis pecuniam destruendo, et eum mendaciis addictum faciendo, virtuosas largitiones amandando, et in hâc et in alterâ vitâ miseriam affert.'

In Manu again, gambling and prize-fighting are classed together as things a king should exclude from his kingdom, ix. 221–28.

939. 'Qui ludo deditus est, nunquam assequetur haec quinque, nempe divitias, felicitatem, lautem cibum, laudem et scientiam.'

940. 'Sicuti quamvis valde afflictus quis vivat, semper vivere desiderat, ita qui ludo deditus est, quamvis saepissime perdat, semper ludere desiderat.'

The climate and the conditions of Eastern court life have always predisposed Oriental kings to this exciting pursuit; hence stories of rulers ruined by gambling are many; and denunciations of the vice abound, the vehemence of which shows the greatness of the evil.

CHAPTER XCV.

Beschi: *Medicina.*

Diseases, according to C., are partly from deeds done in a former birth (Manu, xi. 48), and so are fated (378); partly from mistakes in diet and other things. These last only are here contemplated.

The Hindû idea is closely connected with that of heredity, which is justly regarded as so important in these days. [Comp. S. John ix. 2.]

941. 'Sive excessum sive diminutionem patiantur, tria illa, quae medicinae professores enumerant, nempe melancolia, bilis et phlegma, aegritudinem afferent.'

942. 'Corpori nulla erit necessaria medicina, si cautè servaveris cibi mensuram, quam tibi proficuam expertus es in comedendo.'

943. 'Cibum sume servando mensuram diminutionis quam proficuam expertus es; quia iis qui corpus obtinuerunt (*i.e.* morti obnoxii sunt) haec est via ad diu vivendum.'

944. 'Quam tibi praefixisti, neque comedas ea, quae dissontiam habent vel inter se, vel cum tuo corpore, vel cum tempore.'

945. 'Nulla erit homini aegritudo, si comedat ea, quae diversitatem (seu dissontiam quam supra diximus) non habeant, et fraenet desiderium plus aequo comedendi.'

946. 'Sicuti bona valetudo semper erit ei qui comedit, servando diminutionem sibi necessariam; ita aegritudines nunquam destituent eum qui excessivè comedit.'

947. 'Qui non considerando quid ferre possit sui stomachi calor, cibum qui calorem excedat sumpserit, innumeras aegritudines patietur.'

948. 'Medicus debet considerare aegritudinis qualitatem, ejus originem (seu caussam), et hanc ablegandi viam, et debet remedium applicare, quod ex circumstantiis inefficax non evadat.'

949. 'Qui medicam artem callet (quum eam in praxin redigit), debet remedia applicare attendendo ad aegri qualitatem, ad aegritudinis statum, et ad tempus in quo medetur.'

950. 'Medicina ut efficax sit, quatuor pati debet divisiones; nempe, qualitates aegri, medici, remedii, et remedium praeparantis.'

PARS IV.

Proprietates intermissae; i.e. *appendix, in quâ agitur de iis, quae in tribus praecedentibus partibus non continentur.*

CHAPTER XCVI.

Beschi: *Prosapiae nobilitas.* Ariel: *Noblesse.*

COMP. *Nāl.* 141–50.

Com.'s analysis:—

I. 1–3. Its nature.

II. 4–6. Nothing unworthy.

III. 7, 8. Disgrace of derogation.

IV. 9, 10. Essentials: truth and humanity.

951. 'Non nisi in nobili loco natis, tamquam sui generis propriae, aequitas et erubescentia reperiuntur.'

952. 'Nobili loco nati nunquam deficiunt in his tribus, nempe in procedendo conformiter suo statui, in sinceritate locutionis, et in erubescendo de his quae mundus reprobat.'

953. 'Sapientes asserunt esse partes proprias eorum, qui verè nobiles sunt, vultûs hilaritatem, manûs largitatem, oris affabilitatem, et neminem despicere.'

954. 'Nobili loco nati, etiamsi multos nummorum milliones lucrari possint, numquam talia facient unde suo generi decus minuatur.'

955. 'Quamvis pristinae opes minuantur, qui ex antiquâ familiâ oriuntur, nunquam a suâ magnificâ conditione degenerant.'

956. 'Vitia eorum qui sublimi loco nati sunt, non secus ac in aere lunae maculae; quum luna sublimis exstat, omnibus patent, adeòque magisquam ab iis cavere debent.'

957. 'Qui omni defectu carenti prosapiae conformiter vivere vult, etiamsi paupertati prematur, non faciet quid sibi indecorum.'

958. 'Nobili loco licèt natus, si affabilitatem non prae se fert, de suae prosapiae nobilitate dubitationem inducet.'

959. 'Sicuti germina quae producit, soli qualitatem indicant; ita verba quae loquuntur, prosapiae qualitatem in hominibus ostendunt.'

960. 'Si laudem optas, erubescentia tibi necessaria est, quae te ab omnibus quae vituperabilia sunt distrahat; si prosapiae nobilitatem servare optas, omnibus te submittere affecta.'

CHAPTER XCVII.

Beschi: *Honoris tenacitas.* Graul: *Honestas.* Ariel: *Dignité.*

THIS is the first essential of Nobility. It must suffer no disgrace. Rather voluntary death than dishonour. Suicide seems sanctioned.

Comp. *Nál.* 291–300.

961. 'Etiamsi quid faciendo maximum emolumentum, quod aliâ viâ obtineri nequit, obtineas, noli illud facere, si tale sit, unde honor tuus minuatur.'

962. 'Quantumvis laudabilia feceris, nil facere debes, quod vituperabile sit, si tuam laudem et honorem servare desideras.'

963. 'Quando divitiis affluis, necessaria tibi est animi submissio erga caeteros; quando paupertate angustiaris, necessaria tibi est animi elevatio, ne ob paupertatem vile quid facias.'

964. 'Nobiles viri si à suo honoroso statu decidant, similes sunt capillis qui e capite deciderunt.'

965. 'Etiam ii, qui ita sublimes sunt, ut monti pares videantur, infimi evadent, si suum honorem minuens quid fecerint, licèt id parvo semini குன்றி dicto aequale sit (*i.e.* si vel minimum quid sit).'

Comp. 277.

966. 'Si neque ad laudem assequendam, nec ad coelitûm regnum te

ducendum prodest, ad quid quaeso permanes in eos sectando, qui te contemnant (nempe indecora faciendo).'

967. 'Melius est dici quod quia indecorum quid facere noluisti, in illo ipso momento periisti, quàm opipare vivere, eundo post eos qui te vituperent.'

அந்நிலையே 'there and then,—not leaving his proper position.'

968. 'Si sublimi loco natus suum robur (nempe honorem) amiserit, corpus cum vitâ servare eritne suo malo remedium?'

969. 'Sublimi loco nati similes animali கவரி dicto, quod statim moritur, si vel unus ex pilis illi auferatur: si vita cum honore contendat, vitam abjiciant, ne honorem amittant.'

970. 'Mundus laudibus efferet ejus gloriam, qui honorem ita servavit, ut in occasione indecorum quid faciendi, vitam honori postposuerit.'

CHAPTER XCVIII.

Beschi: *(Vera) magnitudo.*

Greatness of mind. Conduct worthy of a man's name and station.

971. 'Verus cujusque splendor est animi elevatio (nempe ad ardua conspirare); sine hâc sibi qui praetigit vitam ducere, indecoram ducet vitam.'

972. 'Cunctis hominibus aequalis est ortus, diversitas inter ipsos nonnisi ex officiorum diversitate manat.'

973. 'Quamvis sublimi loco natus sis, aut sublimi munere fungeris, nisi sublimia habeas opera, sublimis non eris; infimo loco natus, si infima non habeat opera, infimus non erit.'

974. 'Sicuti in muliere honos non persistet, nisi illa, unicam habens voluntatem, cautè illum custodiat; ita magnitudo non persistet nisi in eo qui illam custodierit, cavendo ab iis, qui vilia sunt.'

975. 'Qui verâ magnitudine praediti sunt, non modo ardua audere, sed et ea debito modo (*h.e.* honestis mediis) perficere debent.'

976. 'Intuitus procedendi cum veneratione erga majores ita magnorum vivorum est proprius, ut ne in cogitationem quidem incidat infimorum.'

977. 'Si dotes, quas magnus vir habet, in eo reperiantur, qui magnis viris aequalem conditionem non habet, ad superbiam et caeterorum depressionem ei inservient.'

978. 'Qui verè magnus est, semper (*i.e.* sive pauper, sive dives sit) humilis est; qui vilis est, etiamsi dives non sit, ex se sibi ornamentum facit, caeteris se praeferendo.'

979. ‘Magni viri conditio est non inflari; vilis viri conditio est usque ad excessum inflari.’

980. ‘Proprium est magnorum vivorum occultare (*i.e.* excusare), quae caeteris indecora sunt; vilium proprietas est, nescire loqui nisi de aliorum vitiis.’

Comp. Ch. XIX.

CHAPTER XCIX.

Beschi: *Omnes probitatis conditiones (seu qualitates) possidere.*
Graul: *Vollkommenheit; perfectio.*

FULNESS of excellence (சால்): τελειότης.

This noble chapter might be illustrated by quotations from all quarters.

981. ‘Sapientes asserunt eum qui praetigit probum esse velle, probitatis debitum sciendo, ad omnes bonas qualitates possidendas obligari.’ [‘ =Bonum ex integrâ caussâ.’]

Comp. ‘*Integer* vitae, scelerisque purus.’

982. ‘Bonum virum bonae qualitates faciunt; caetera omnia qualiscunque bonitatis sint, probum non faciunt.’

983. ‘Columnae, quae probitatem sustentant, sunt haec quinque: amor in omnes, culpam erubescere, egenis succurere, clementiam habere, et sincerum esse in loquendo.’

984. ‘Poenitentium decus est non interficere viventia; proborum decus est non loqui de caeterorum defectibus.’

985. ‘Religiosorum decus est demissio: his armis probus vir hostes suos superabit.’

986. ‘Si quaeras quinam sit Lydius lapis probitatem explorans, dicam esse, si sciat non modo se potentioribus, sed etiam iis qui sibi inferiores sunt victas dare manus.’

987. ‘Ad quid utilis erit probitas, si nesciat etiam malè meritis benefacere?’

988. ‘Viro, qui possederit robur, quod dicitur probitas, non erit dedecus esse pauperem.’

989. ‘Qui non mutantur, etiamsi tempus mutetur (*h.e.* qui nec paupertatis tempore probitatem destituunt) probitatis litus vocabuntur.

But compare ஊழி.

990. ‘Si probi probitatem non sustentando, ab illâ deficiant, tunc nec infernus suum pondus sustentare poterit.’

He reads இருணிலம்=இருள்நிலம்.

CHAPTER C.

Beschi : *Bona indoles : ingenuitas.*

Graul : *Boni mores ; gute Art.* Ariel : *Courtoisie.*

THIS is the crown of perfectness : a mingling of unaffected kindness with consummate tact. See Ch. VIII., XXV. It is from பண் (*vide sub loco*) 'harmony' ; and harmonizes all things, while it is the result of a happy and harmonious combination of good qualities.

991. 'Sapientes aiunt facile esse cuivis assequi optimam semitam quae dicitur *ingenuitas*, facilem se atque affabilem praebendo.'

992. 'Amor in omnes et prosapiae nobilitas duo sunt, quae ad ingenuitatem viam sternunt.'

993. 'Quoniam per membrorum similitudinem non fit hominis cum probro homine similitudo; superest ut fiat per similitudinem indolis, quae patitur reformationem, quam membra non patiuntur.'

வெறுத்தக்க='quae reformari potest': as though from வேறு. See Concordance, *sub voce.*

This hints that குடிப்பிறத்தல் is not mere purity of caste or family.

994. 'Mundus laudibus efferet ejus indolem, qui justitiae et virtutis cupidum emolumentum possidet (*h.e.* qui justitiam et virtutem sectando sibi emolumentum comparavit).'

995. 'Ingenuitatis naturam scientibus, neque per jocum permittitur subsannare vel ipsos suos hostes.'

Ariel. 'Le dedain en plaisanterie mème, est mal pour qui connaît l'importance de la courtoisie envers un ennemi mème.'

996. 'Ideo mundi mos adhuc perdurat, quia incidit in bonae indolis homines; nam si ita non esset, jam intus terram abiens periisset.'

Courtesy enables the world's work to get done.

997. 'Qui hominum propriam indolem non habent, quamvis limae acumini parem ingenii, subtilitatem possideant, arboribus similes dicendi sunt.'

Against those who say sharp unpleasant things.

998. 'Dedecus est ab humanitate deficere etiam cum iis, qui ex odio tibi malefecerint.'

Courtesy towards opponents.

999. 'Qui nesciunt cum caeteris amicabiliter vivere, his diurna etiam lux tenebrae sunt.'

Malvolio ?

1000. 'Divitiae, quae malae indolis homini obveniunt, malae evadunt; non secus ac bonum lac malum evadit, si in malum vas infundatur.'

A discourteous wealthy man is like sour milk.

CHAPTER CI.

Beschi: *Divitiae infructuosae,* i.e. *Avaritia.*
Graul: *Opulentia inutilis.*

This is the reverse of the picture presented in Ch. xxiii. It is a very favourite topic with Tamiḷ poets. Comp. *Nâl.* 261–70, 276, 296, 328.

1001. 'Qui amplam domum divitiis replet, iisque non fruitur, vivus licet sit, respectu divitiarum jam mortuus est, cum ei nulla circa illis actio supersit.'

Comp. 214.

1002. 'Ex eo, quod divitias obtinendo, omnia bona obtinere poteris, illas cumulare, sed posteâ in stultitiâ incidere ita illas affectandi, ut nil caeteris largiaris, haud bonum post mortem tibi statum causabit.'

1003. 'Homines, qui solam divitiarum cumulationem affectando, laudem ex largitione profluentem non affectant, ad quid nascuntur, nisi ut terrae pondus augeant.'

1004. 'Qui nil largiendo, a nemine desiderari se facit, quid quaeso relinquere meditatur, quod post mortem remansurum sibi sit?'

1005. 'Ei, qui nec divitiis fruitur, nec caeteris eas largitur, quamvis multi divitiarum milliones sint, idem erit ac si non essent.'

1006. 'Ei, qui nec ipse fruitur, nec iis, quibus largiri debent, divitias largiendi indolem habet, quid remanent, nisi pura afflictio et labor in iis cumulandis atque servandis?'

1007. 'Divitiae illius, qui egentibus eas non largitur, sed frustra sub clavi putrescere sinit, eâ sunt commiseratione dignae, quâ mulier praeclarae formae, quae usque ad senium innupta manere cogitur.'

1008. 'Illum, qui ob suam avaritiam à nullo desideratur, divitiis plenum esse, perinde est ac arborem venenosam in medio urbis pulcherrimis fructibus onustam esse.'

Comp. 216, 217.

1009. 'Divitiis illius, qui neque ex amore parentibus aut amicis subvenit, et ipse fame perit, nec eleemosinae virtutem affectat, alii fruentur.'

1010. 'Si is, qui divitias cum laude possidet (*h.e.* laudabilitur elargitur), in aliquantam egestatem incidat, haec similis erit nubium siccitati (*i.e.* diuturna non erit).'

CHAPTER CII.

Beschi: *Erubescentia.* Graul: *Pudor.* Αἰδώς.

The idea is much that of conscience. Comp. Ch. xxi.

1011. 'Erubescere de indecoris actionibus est *virilis erubescentia;* de caeteris erubescere est *erubescentia muliebris.*'

1012. 'Comestio et reliquae corporis passiones (puta somnus, pulchritudo, etc.), sunt homini cum belluis communia: *erubescentia* est quae hominem a belluis specificat.'

1013. 'Omnia viventia corpus respiciunt uti vitae sustentaculum; probitas *erubescentiam* respicit uti suum sustentaculum.'

பிறப்பு 'embodiment,' according to the Vêdânta, is an evil. வீடு 'relinquishment' of all corporeal bonds is to be sought. Here the idea is, 'Souls require bodies here, so virtue requires a sense of shame.'

1014. 'Nonne probis ornamentum est *verecundia?* Haec si desit, nonne morbus est inflatum incedere?'

1015. 'Illum, qui de caeterorum perinde ac de suo vituperia erubescit, *erubescentiae* regiam vocabunt sapientes.'

1016. 'Sublimes homines vastam hanc terram ideo non magni faciunt, quia intra *erubescentiae* sepem non se cohibet.'

1017. 'Qui *erubescentiam* possident, propter hanc vitae renunciabunt; nunquam verò propter vitam *erubescentiae* renunciabunt.'

1018. 'Si tu non *erubescis* facere, quae caeteri audire aut videre *erubescunt*; virtus, quod ejus assecla dicaris, *erubescet.*'

1019. 'Si tuo statui non convenientia facias, tuae tantum prosapiae dedecus afferes; si vero permanenter sine *erubescentiâ* vixeris, omnia quae in te sunt bona pessum ibunt.'

1020. 'Qui interius *erubescentiâ* carent, quamvis inter homines degant, similes sunt pupae, quae funiculis agitata oculos fallit vivam se ostendendo.'

CHAPTER CIII.

Beschi: *Modus familiam exaltandi.* Ariel: *Manière de servir sa famille.*

1021. 'Nullum est majus decus quam illud dicere valentis, "ego nunquam ab industriâ cesso, ut familiam exaltem."'

1022. 'Assiduâ contentione illius qui haec duo, nempe industriam et rerum experientiam possidet, familia dilatabitur.'

1023. 'Ei qui ad suae familiae dilatationem assiduè laborare sibi proposuit, Deus Ipse lumbos praecingens, ad laborandum comes accurret.'

An idea familiar to all races.

1024. 'Qui impigrè et assiduè laborat, ne familia detrimentum capiat, non opus est, ut consideret quonam modo id assequetur, nam ipsamet quam adhibet industria propositum perficiet.'

Comp. 594.

1025. 'Eum, qui inculpatam vitam ducens, ad suam familiam exaltandam laborat, totus mundus, ei se consanguineum profitendo, vallabit.'

See the play on words, சுற்றம், சுற்றும் 'the circle of kindred will encircle.'

1026. 'Virilem animum ei inesse dicetur, qui sibi familiae in quâ natus est gubernationem assumit, ad eam exaltandam.'

1027. 'Sicuti in campo, quamvis multi proelientur, iis laus defertur, qui forti animo proelium sustinuerunt; ita quamvis familiam multi confient, illi laus danda, qui familiae pondus sustinet.'

Comp. 777.

A man must not shrink from homely duties. There is heroism here also. Duty makes 'drudgery divine.'

1028. 'Qui familiam exaltare vult, nullam respicere debet temporis importunitatem; quodsi gloriosis cogitationibus locum dando piger evadat, familia in ruinam verget.'

See பருவம்.

He must make his own *opportunities*; also he must be instant 'in *season* and out of *season*.'

1029. 'Amara ne an dulcis dicenda est vita illius, qui suo assiduo labore suos felices reddi videt?'

The poet seems to say, 'Is it not so, that all sufferings must be endured by him?' Yet comparing Ch. v., we should feel sure he rather felt with the reverend Father, that the bread-winner must be content to bear the burthen: 'The labour we delight in physicks pain.'

1030. 'Familiae arbor, cum paupertas ejus radices caedere conatur, procul dubio decidet, nisi industriosus homo, ei humeros supponendo, illam sustentet.'

CHAPTER CIV.

Beschi: *Agricultura.*

This is the main support of the family. Hence the sequence.

Cultivation is the work of the *Vaiçya*, and is said to be degrading to Brâhmans: Manu, i. 90; iii. 64, 165; x. 83, 84, 116.

1031. 'Cum totus mundus quantumvis circumeat, tandem ad agricultores recurrere debeat, dicendum quod inter caetera munia principem locum habeat laboriosa agricultura.'

1032. 'Agricultura licet parvi fiat, tamen quum sustentet caeteros omnes, qui hoc officium negligunt, eandem habet vim in mundo quam clavus axem firmans in curru, quo ablato cursus omnis deficit.'

Not much esteemed, yet indispensable.

1033. 'Qui agros colendo victum sibi comparat, suam vitam vivere dicendus; nam caeteri omnes, qui serviendo vivunt, ab aliis pendent ut vivant.'

Comp. *Nâl.* 365 (The three modes of life):—

தலையே தவமுயன்று வாழ்தல்; ஒருவர்க்
கிடையே இனியார்கட் டங்கல்;
கடையே
புணராதென் றெண்ணிப் பொருணசையாற் றம்மை
உணரார்பின் சென்று நிலை!

'The best is life in penitential practice spent;
The middle course to live with dear ones round. The worst
With restless thought desiring wealth, subservient
To follow those who understand us not.'

1034. 'Qui frumentum possidentes eo egentibus umbraculum sunt, videbunt sub umbraculo sui reges concurrere gentes, quae sub variorum regum umbraculo manent.'

1035. 'Qui proprium officium habent comedendi quod suus labor in agriculturâ peperit, nec mendicationi obnoxius erit, et ipse mendicantibus nil abscondendo necessaria suppeditabit.'

The poet would not approve of imported rice.

1036. 'Si agricultorum manus a labore desistat, jam nec poenitentiam iis, qui dicunt se renunciasse omnibus, quae caeteri appetunt, exercendi locus erit.'

1037. 'Si terrae unciam iterum iterumque arando ita exsiccari facias, ut ad quartam unciae partem reducatur, nec tantum fimi, quantum manus capere potest necessarium erit, ut ager fructificet.'

This and the following seem to be rustic saws, such as occur in Vergil's *Georgics*.

1038. 'Agro magis proficit fimi projectio, quam aratio et postquam segetes mundaveris; aquae irrigatio non tam fructuosa erit, quam illarum defensio (ab avibus et latronibus).'

1039. 'Si agri dominus quotidie illum non visitando procul absit; ager ei irascens uti mulier diu a viro derelicta, adhaesionem negabit (*i.e.* fructum optatum non dabit).'

Comp. Ch. CXXXI., CXXXII.

1040. 'Mulier, quae terra dicitur, si viderit aliquem qui ob pigritiam agros non colat, et de paupertate doleat, illum subsannabit.'

CHAPTER CV.

Beschi: *Paupertas.*

THERE is a certain intensity about this chapter which seems to indicate personal experience of the evils of poverty. Comp. *Nál.* 281, 283, 285.

1041. 'Si quaeras, quodnam sit malum paupertate majus, dicam paupertate pejorem solam esse paupertatem.'

Comp. *Nál.* 285:

'Lord of the pleasant land of clustered hills whose crags
By sounding waterfalls are washed!—Their race is nought,
Their manly prowess nought; their learning rare is nought;
When men are held in poverty's embrace.'

பிறந்த குலமாயும், பேராண்மை மாயும்,
சிறந்ததங் கல்வியு் மாயும்;—
கறங்கருவி
கன்மேற் கழூஉங் கணமலை நன்னாட!—
இன்மை தழுவப்பட் டார்க்கு

1042. 'Malefactor ille qui dicitur paupertas, et hujus et alterius vitae gaudia homini surripit.'

Personification. Poverty deprives a man of the means of enjoyment in this life, and of securing happiness in the next world by liberal alms-giving.

1043. 'Affectus erga paupertatem, et quam quis suis facinoribus acquisivit amplitudinem famamque junctim destruet.'

1044. 'Paupertas talem affert vilitatem, et cum contemptu loqui faciat etiam de iis, qui sublimi loco nati sunt.'

1045. 'In uno malo paupertatis multa ac diversa mala coadunantur.'

1046. 'Pauper quamvis optimas quasque scientias perfectè callens doctissimè loquatur, ejus tamen verbis fructus deerit.'

Comp. *Nál.* 115.

1047. 'Paupertas virtuti non amica, quia impedit illius exercitium; et facit ut quis suam ipsam matrem tanquam extraneam respiciat.' (?)

Comp. *Nál.* 290.

1048. 'Numquid et hodie veniet paupertas, quae heri quasi me interemit?'

1049. 'Ipso in igne (aut amuleti aut praestigiae ope) somnus capi potest, at in paupertate nec minimum oculos claudendi locus est.'

1050. 'Qui nil habendo quod comedant, neque totaliter gulam abnegando, ventrem implere volunt, sunt daemones, qui aliorum cibos infestant.'

காடி = the sour, stale 'conjee-water,' or rice-gruel, which is the beggar's portion. If beggars will not be so considerate as to renounce the world and die, 'tis death to the stores of those who must feed them! The poet says this bitterly: 'So are the poor regarded.'

CHAPTER CVI.

Beschi: *Mendicatio.*

In this and the following chapter there seems to be no reference to the 'religious' beggars, Fakirs and others, that infest Indian towns and villages: he contemplates those who are suffering misfortune.

1051. 'Eleemosinam pete ab iis, quos eam dare posse noveris; si negaverint, illis, non tibi, vitio tribuetur.'

1052. 'Dulce est mendicare, si quod petitur, absque poenâ veniat.'

If a man's self-respect is not wounded.

1053. 'Mendico, qui scit ab eis petere, qui debitum sciunt non fallacis et avari animi, sua mendicatio quandem habet dulcedinem.'

1054. 'Si non petas, nisi ab iis, que neque per somnium negare sciunt, quod mendicus petit, hujusmodi mendicatio cum ipsâ largitione quandam similitudinem habet.'

1055. 'Cur aliorum oculis se sistendo mendicat pauper, nisi quia sunt in mundo qui negare nesciunt quod caeteris deest?'

1056. 'Si tales inveneris, qui non habeant malam indolem sua pauperibus occultandi (ac negandi), paupertatis mala omnia finem habebunt.'

Were kindly liberality the rule, poverty would no longer be an evil.

1057. 'Si tales inveniantur, qui nec despiciendo, nec erubescentiam causando, sua dent egeno, hic inveniat unde animus suus intus et intimè laetificetur.'

1058. 'Si in mundo non essent, qui mendicarent, quid aliud essent, nisi tot pupae ligneae sine vitâ ambulantes ?'

1059. 'Quaenam esset laus iis qui nunc sua largiuntur, si deesset qui aliena mendicandi officium exerceret ?'

1060. 'Si mendicus quod petit non inveniet, neganti non debet irasci, quia ipsa sua paupertas satis illi testificatur.'

This is ambiguous. It seems to mean: 'Be not angry with and reproach the man who refuses to relieve you: your sufferings are a sufficient evidence against him.'

CHAPTER CVII.

Beschi: *Mendicatio vitanda.* Graul: *Scheu vor Betteln.*

Comp. *Nâl.* 301–10.

The last chapter sanctions a modest medicancy, in time of necessity. This denounces it as a profession.

1061. 'Centies millies melius est tuo labore paupertati occurrere quam mendicare etiam ab iis, qui tibi cari sunt ut oculi, et sine ullâ occultatione tibi necessaria daturi sint.'

Comp. *Nâl.* 287 (Beggary) :—

'O thou whose teeth in sharpness vie with jasmine buds !—
Man's attributes of goodness all are lost, at once,—
With mind's acuteness gained from wisdom's ample store,—
When sharp distress of beggary assails.'

நீர்மையே யன்றி நிரம்ப எழுந்தகம்
கூர்மையும் எல்லாம் ஒருங்கிழப்பர் ;—
கூர்மையின்
முல்லை அலைக்கும் எயிற்றாய் !—நிரப்பென்னும்
அல்லல் அடையப்பட் டார்.

1062. 'Si hominibus ad vitam sustentandum ab eo qui orbem condidit, indicta fuit mendicatio, talis illi ruina (seu damnum) obveniat, ut hoc fecisse poeniteat.'

The idea is 'Brahmâ, the creator, never made men to be beggars. It cannot be a part of religion.'

1063. 'Non est in mundo pectus adeo ferreum, uti pectus illius qui suae paupertati succurrere sibi proponit, non suo labore sed mendicatione.'

1064. 'Magnanimitas, quae etiam in extremâ penuriâ non se inducit ad mendicandum, sed suo sibi labore consulit, adeò magnum decus habet, ut mundi totius limites transiliat.'

1065. 'Nil est dulcius quam comedere quod sibi suus labor peperit, etiamsi jusculum sit adeô rarum, ut aqua clara videatur.'

1066. 'Nulla est linguae vilior vox quam quae aliquid mendicat, etiamsi nihil aliud petat quam puram aquam ad consulendum ejus vitae qui siti perit.'

He says ஆவிற்கு='vitae necessariam!'

1067. 'Mendicare volo ab ipsis medicantibus; sed quid ab iis petam? Petam, ut si mendicare volunt, non mendicent ab iis, qui sua pauperibus occultant.'

1068. 'Indecora navis mendicatio dicta, quam quis conscendit, ut egestatis mare trajiciat; si in scopulum qui negatio dicitur inciderit, diffringetur.'

1069. 'Mendici animus dum suam paupertatem cogitat, prae dolore liquescit; sed quum ei negatur quod petit, prae pudore adeò magnâ poenâ afficitur, ut paupertatis dolorem absorbeat.'

1070. 'Ubinam, quaeso, se abscondit vita illius, qui sua negat, dum videt mendicum adeò flebiles voces emittere, ut prae pudore mori videatur?'

CHAPTER CVIII.

Beschi: *Vilium hominum conditio.* Graul: *Gemeinheit.*
Ariel: *Infamie.*

The connection is not clear.

Comp. *Nāl.* 351–60 (Wealth without heart):—

'Though in the water born, and green its hue appear,
The *Neṭṭi's* pith no moisture knows; so in the world
Are men of amplest wealth whose hearts are hard as stones
Upon the rocky mountain fell!'

நீருட் பிறந்து நிறம்பசிய தாயினும்,
ஈரங் கிடையகத் தில்லாகும்;
ஓரும்
நிறைப்பெருஞ் செல்வத்து நின்றக் கடைத்தும்,
அறைப்பெருங் கல்லன்னார் உடைத்து.

Neṭṭi (நெட்டி, சடை, கிடை) = 'aischynomene.'

1071. 'Viles sunt similes hominibus,—neque ego quidquam vidi homini adeô simile!'

He takes it: 'They really look very like men; but are not so.'

1072. 'Viles feliciores sunt sapientibus, quum nullum animi afflictionem patiantur.'

Irony. III. Gram. 210. Destitute of feeling and sympathy.

1073. 'Diis ipsis similes sunt viles homines, quum et ipsi, uti Divi, omnia juxta suam voluntatem faciant.'

Irony. Entirely given up to arrogance and self-will.

1074. 'Viles, si quem videant, qui juxta morem eorum qui non in urbe, sed in pago degunt, paucis contenti parcè vivant, statim se majores aestimando valdè inflati incedunt.'

He makes *அகப்பட்டியார்*='qui ad pagorum morem vivunt!'

Their ambition is to surpass the wicked in their wickedness.

1075. 'Vilium est semper timere (regis, aut nobilium, vexationem); praeter hoc siquid concupiscunt, nonnisi id unde aut nullum aut parvum emolumentum obveniat, concupiscere sciunt.' (?)

Governed entirely by fear or selfishness.

1076. 'Similes tympano pulsato sunt viles, quia secretum eorum auribus commissum statim ad caeterorum aures deferunt.'

Cannot keep a secret.

1077. 'Viles homines iis, qui manum non curvant ad eorum comam succutiendam, etiamsi ita fit ut grana succutiant, quae humidae manui adhaerent, post orizae comestionem, non dabunt.'

They grudge another any good, even when it costs them nothing.

1078. 'Sublimes homines statim ac quis suam necessitatem exponit, necessaria dabunt; vilia sua non dabunt, nisi torqueantur, uti torquetur arundo saccarea, ut suum liquorem fundat.'

Cowardly bullies. Comp. *Nál.* 355.

1079. 'Si vilis homo videat aliorum vestes ac cibum meliores esse quam suum cibum ac vestes, capax est invenire defectus quamvis defectu careant (ob invidiam).'

Envy a proof of worthlessness.

1080. 'Quodnam est officium proprium vilium? omnes despicere; sed quantamvis parvam ob angustiam, statim currere ad se vendendum ac caeteris mancipandum.'

In any distress, craven-hearted, slavish.

BOOK III.

CHAPTER CIX.

Comp. Intro. p. xii., xiii.

THESE last chapters must be considered as an Eastern romance not fully told, but indicated in a number of beautiful verses, which leave much to the imagination of the reader, and the ingenuity of the interpreter. The verses are deserving of study, but such commentaries as I have seen are simply disgusting, and utterly misrepresent the writer. Taken as they are, these chapters are worthy of Theocritus, and much less open to objection than parts of his writings. Like the verses of Bhartṛihari and other Sanskrit writers, these Kurraḷs 'merely portray isolated situations, without any connection as a whole.' *

On the Gandharva marriage, see Ellis, p. 156, &c. The following verse from the *Tolkâppiyam*, பொருளதிகாரம் will suffice :—

'Fearless, when maids with golden jewels decked, and youths
Meet, see and love, they call it still *Gandharva* marriage-bond.
Thus once the pairs of these, of blameless vision fair, who tuned
The lute, all gold and radiant, used to join.'

அதிர்ப்பில், பைம்பூணுரும், ஆடவருந், தம்முள்
எதிர்ப் பட்டுக் கண்டியைதல், என்ப
கதிர்ப்பொன்யாழ்
முந்திருவர் கண்ட முனிவறு தண்காட்சிக்
கந்திருவர் கண்ட கலப்பு

Comp. Manu, iii. 20, 21, 32.

The drama of Çakuntalâ will illustrate the general idea of the verses. See Monier-William's edition, 1876, p. 127.

1081. The prince sees the princess in the grove, and doubts.

Ariel: 'L'indication des personages de ce petit drame lyrique ne se trouve pas dans le texte.'

1082–89. He sees her to be human, and describes the impression her beauty makes upon him.

1090. He sees love in her glance.

* Weber, *Hist. of Indian Lit.*, p. 210. Trübner & Co., 1882

CHAPTER CX.

HERE Com. says there are three present, the prince who observes the princess, the princess who stealthily observes the prince, and the handmaiden who observes them both. It would seem as if all the couplets were his.

CHAPTER CXI.

Graul: *Freude über die Verbindung.*

HE is the sole speaker.

CHAPTER CXII.

HE is still the sole speaker. Much of this greatly resembles Çakuntalâ.

CHAPTER CXIII.

Graul: *Die ausserordentliche Liebe sagen.*
Ariel: *Exaltation de la passion.*

HERE seem to be two speakers. They are separated, and soliloquize.

CHAPTER CXIV.

THERE is no way for their reunion, but to acknowledge the marriage, and obtain its confirmation by parents and friends.

To effect this the lover, bestriding a palmyra stem for a horse (மடல், மடன்மா), is carried into the village in the night, and aloud bewails his separation from his bride, avows the union, proclaims his love, and defies all rivals. This is done with doleful love-ditties; and hence is called புலம்பல்=‘*wailing.*’

This is ‘abandonment of reserve,’ or shame, or concealment; the town or village is full of the ‘rumour,’ which is ended by a homely, unromantic wedding, more conventional, but not, according to ancient Hindû laws and sentiments, more binding and lawful than the romantic Gandharva union.

1131, &c. The only way, as suspicion is aroused, is to claim my bride.

1138. She dreads, yet desires, the publicity which will sanction and renew their union.

CHAPTER CXV.

THIS is the day of excitement, after the public announcement. It seems that we have two soliloquies, in which the bridegroom and the bride express their anxiety; while satisfied that all the hubbub will in time subside, and their nuptials be sanctioned.

CHAPTER CXVI.

THE public marriage has taken place; and now the poet makes the incidents of married life the theme of 17 chapters. These are mainly three:—

(1) Separation (necessary, and, it would seem, sometimes unnecessary). Ch. CXVI.–CXXX.

(2) Petulant, capricious, feigned anger; ஊடல், புலவி. Ch. CXXXI.

(3) Jealousy, Ch. CXXXII.

The Com. distinguishes here and elsewhere the words of the husband and his companion, and of the wife and her maid; and the native grammarians in the third part of grammar, called பொருளதிகாரம் ‘Chapter on Topics,’ lay down rules for each sentiment and situation. *Tantum ad nauseam profuse exponunt*, says Beschi.

These rules are founded on the usage of the poets, and nothing is gained by employing them to explain our author. Each couplet must tell its own story. It must be remembered that the Hindû lady was not supposed to possess any resources, in times of separation, such as education gives.

1151. He announces his departure and promises speedy return. She says, 'I cannot survive the separation.'

The whole chapter I take as spoken by her.

CHAPTER CXVII.

Still her words. It seems as if jealousy mingles with sorrow. Is his absence not in some degree voluntary? Can she bring herself to send a messenger to beg him to return?

CHAPTER CXVIII.

Her words. The eyes are dim with watching and weeping.

CHAPTER CXIX.

Her words. The yellow sickly hue of pining anguish. Comp. *Nál.* 393:

கம்மஞ்செய் மாக்கள் கருவி ஒடுக்கிய
மம்மர்கொண் மாலை மலராய்ந்து பூத்தொடுப்பாள்,
கைம்மாலை யிட்டுக் கலுழ்ந்தா டுணையில்லார்க்
கிம்மாலை என்செய்வ தென்று.

'At wildering eventide, when workmen all put by
Their tools, she culled choice flowers and wove a garland gay
Then from her hands let fall, and wailed, "What can this wreath
Avail to me who weep alone?"'

CHAPTER CXX.

Her words. The agony of suspense.

CHAPTER CXXI.

His thoughts and hers, while severed.

1203. Comp. Catullus, xlv. Acme and Septumius. Also 1317, 1318.

CHAPTERS CXXII., CXXIII.

She speaks throughout.

This last chapter seems to me full of beauty. Comp. *Nâl.* 397, where there is much pathos.

'When those who read the palm-leaf scrolls had ceased,
In eve's dim light, she thought of absent spouse and wept;
And weeping pluckt the flowers from out her wreath, and brushed
The odorous sandal from her lovely breast.'

ஓலைக் கணக்கர் ஒலியடங்கு புன்செக்கர்
மாலைப் பொழுதின் மணந்தார் பிரிவுள்ளி
மாலை பரிந்திட் டழுதாள் ; வனமுலைமேற்
கோலஞ்செய் சாந்தந் திமிர்ந்து.

CHAPTER CXXIV.

Eyes are dimmed and arms wasted. The brow is a sickly yellow.

1231–37. She or her companion speaks.

1238. His soliloquy.

1239. Comp. 1108.

1240. Ariel: 'Oh! ces yeux pâlis ont eu de la peine, voyant ce que faisait le front brillant.'

The bright brow is sicklied over with yellow now (1238), and eye must weep for this!

CHAPTERS CXXV., CXXVI.

She strives to reason herself into composure; but loses all self-control, and speaks of nothing but of seeing him again.

CHAPTER CXXVII.

The time of his return draws near. It would seem as if these words were uttered on the morning of the day when the King permits him to return.

There is a ring of the old song about it: 'And are ye sure the news is true?' &c.

1270. The natural anxiety of one to whom it seems too much joy to return, and find all well.

CHAPTER CXXVIII.

Another absence is contemplated.

CHAPTER CXXIX.

Reconciliation after some lovers' quarrel.

CHAPTER CXXX.

She soliloquizes, 1291–98.

He utters 1299, 1300.

So says Com. Each tries to cherish unyielding resentment in the mind; but nature is too strong.

CHAPTER CXXXI.

Gr. *Schmollen.*

1301–4. She pouts.
1305–10. He ponders her perversity.

CHAPTER CXXXII.

'Refined petulance.' Sulking when ingenuity must be used to find a pretext. The Prince might have taken the poet's words as his motto (Sex. Propertius, iv. 2) : 'Stant mihi cum dominâ proelia dura meâ.'

LEXICON AND CONCORDANCE

TO THE

KURRAḶ AND NÂLAḌI.

[The Concordance to K. *is complete*; that to N. partial. § refers to the Tamil Handbook.]

அ

அ, அகரம். **1.** 'the first letter,' 1 (H.B. Intro. p. 16). **2.** A demonstrative: 'that' (§ 25; comp. இ, உ and எ), 225, 247, 254, 350, 355, 370, 411, 423, 426, 475, 489, 641, 671, 677, 695, 848, 950, 967, 1091. Prefixed to nouns it doubles the initial consonant. See அவன், &c., அவ்வது, அனை, அன்ன, அன்று.

அஃகு (§ 62), 'diminish, grow refined' [S. *aç*; Lat. *ac-us*]. அஃகியகன்றவறிவு '*minute* and comprehensive,' 175. அஃகாமை 'undiminishing permanence,' 178, Nâl. 12.

அகடு 'the belly,' 936 [அகம்]; 'the centre,' Nâl. 2.

அகம் (Opp. புறம் and to முகம்). [In Nigaṇḍu, அக மன மனையே பாவ மகலிட முள்ளுமாமே. 1, மனம் (अहम् 'I'); 2, மனை; 3, பாவம்(अघ); 4, அகலிடம்; 5, உள். Add 6, depth, the earth (जगत्); 7, a tree (S. अग); 8, grain, அஃகம்.] **1.** 'Place,' in comp. வையகம், வானகம், q.v., 101, 547, 1055, Nâl. 80. இல்லகம் 'house,' Nâl. 361. **2.** 'Mind, internal being,' 93, 277, 298, 708, 830. Also அகன், 84, 92. நெஞ்சத்தகம் 'the innermost soul, heart and soul,' 786. அகத்து inf. base, used with n. as a prep. phrase = 'in the midst of,' 194, 694, 717, 723, 727, 814, 877, 1027, 1163, 1180, 1305, 1323; 'in the mind,' 'within,' 78, 271, 329, 824, 1024; 'inner,' 79. அகத்தது 'what is in the mind,' 702. அகத்தார் 'in-dwellers,' 745, Nâl. 31. அகப்பட்டி 'sin,' 1074. [See பட்டி].

அகரம். See அ, **1.**

அகல்(லு) (§ 70, as வெல்) 'expand, grow wide; recede.'

I. v. intr. (1) வினைத்தொகை. அகல்விசும்பு 'the spacious firmament,' 25. (2) வினைப்பெயர் (§ 148), Nâl. 151, 354, 371. அகறல் for அகல்தல்=அகலல் 'a receding from,' 1325. (3) past. rel. part. and n. (§ 74, 87). அகன்ற contr. ஆன்ற, q.v. அஃகியகன்றவறிவு, 175 [அஃகு]. அகன்றார் 'men who have grown great,' 170. (4) neg. (§ 121). அகலாது (opp. to அணுகாது) 'not withdrawing too far,' 691. அகலாக்கடை 'when (it) does not enlarge itself,' 478. அக

லாதகாலே 'ere (he) went away,' 1226.

II. அகற்று (v. causal., § 160, ii. *g*). அகற்றும் '(it) will enlarge,' 372.

III. அகலம் (noun, § 190), 'expansion, roominess, breadth.' By met. 'a broad breast,' Nâl. 389, 392.

அகழ் (§ 57) 'dig into.' அகழ்வார், 151 (§ 87).

அக்கு 'fire' [S. *agni*], Nâl. 123.

அங்கை=அகங்கை 'the palm of the hand.' Nâl. 122.

அங்கணம் 'a gutter, sewer' [S. *aṅgaṇa*], 720, Nâl. 175.

அசாவாமை [from v. அசாவு (§ 62), from அசா='languor'], 'absence of languor, energy,' 611, Nâl. 201.

அசை (§ 57) 'waver, shake, move; grow feeble.'

I. (வினைத்தொகை). அசையியல் 'she of flexible form,' 1098.

II. (part., § 77) அசைஇ=அசைந்து. Instead of ந்த் we have அளபெடை. அசை இயிருப்பார் 'those who sit feebly trembling,' 1040.

III. அசைவு (v. noun, § 190), 'agitation, a yielding to indolence, weariness, failure.' அசைவின்மை 'unwearied effort,' 371. [Opp. to சோம்பல் or மடி wh.=அசைவு.] அசைவில்லாவூக்கம் 'unwavering energy,' 594.

அச்சம். See அஞ்சு.

அச்சு 'an axle' [S. *akshi*], 475. அச்சாணி 'the pin of the axle, linch-pin,' 667.

அஞர் [S. *aghas*; Lat. *ang-*], 'severe pain, agony,' 1086, 1179.

அஞ்சு (§ 62), 'dread.' [Comp. S. *yaj*; Gr. ἅζ-.] [Syn. உடகு, நாணு.] அஞ்சும் (§ 72)='it will dread, shrink from,' 451, 863, 905, 1295 (அஞ்சுமவன்=அஞ்சுபவன்), 727, Nâl. 297. அஞ்சும் (§ 74), 'those who dread,' 869, 1152, 904, 244. அஞ்சுதும் (III. Gr. 81), 'we will fear,' 1128. அஞ்சா (III. Gr. 90), 'not fearing,' 725; 500=அஞ்சாத, 761, 762, 778. அஞ்சுவான் (§ 87), 'he who will dread,' 905, 729. அஞ்சுபவர் 'those who will dread,' 464, 906, 726. அஞ்சான் (§ 121), 'the fearless,' 647, 686. அஞ்சுக (§ 140), 'fear!' 882. அஞ்சுமின், Nâl. 172. அஞ்சற்க (III. Gr. 92), 'fear not!' 882. அஞ்சல் 'fear, fearing,' 1149, 428. அஞ்சல் (III. Gr. 92) 'fear not!' 1154. அஞ்சி (§ 77), 'having feared,' 680, 44, 325, 883, 730, 741, Nâl. 74, 87, 88, 256, 297, 396. அஞ்சப்படும் (§ 92), 'should be feared,' 202, 824 [படு], Nâl. 89. அஞ்சுவது 'what (men) shall fear, respect,' 428, 366, Nâl. 74. அஞ்சாமை (§ 154), 'the not fearing,' 428, 382, 497. அவையஞ்சாமை, Ch. LXXIII. அஞ்சாது, 585. அஞ்சார் (§ 110), 'they dread not,' 201. அஞ்சுவர் 'they will dread,' 201. அஞ்சாதவர் 'those who dread not,' 723. அச்சம் (§ 190), 'dread' [in the stem அஞ்சு, the nasal ஞ் is merely a euphonic insertion, as *n* in *tango*; the root is AJ. In forming a noun, the stem is changed to ACH (ச்ச் being a clumsy way of expressing the S. च): the *media* to the *tenuis*. See Table in H.B. Intro. p. 10], 1075, 146, 501, 534, Nâl. 81, 82, 83, 84, 145, 299. Ch. XXI. தீவினையச்சம் 'dread of evil action,' Nâl. Ch. XIII. Ch. CVII. இரவச்சம் 'dread of mendicancy,' Nâl. Ch. XXXI.

அட-ங்கு, அட-க்கு (§ 62, 162), [Comp. S. *adha*], 'submit, restrain.' [See note to அஞ்சு. ங் is a euphonic insertion. The intrans. has the *media*, G and the trans. the *tenuis* K.] அடங்கியான் (§ 87), 'he who has restrained himself,' 124, Nâl. 74. அடங்க, 123, Nâl. 397. அடங்காமை (§ 154), 121. [Opp. அடக்கம்.] அடங்கல் (§ 148), 130. அடங்கா (§ 121), 834, Nâl. 171. அடக்கல் (§ 148), 126, Nâl. 196, 351. அடக்கம் (§ 190), '(self)-restraint,' 121, 122, Nâl. 65. அடக்கமுடைமை Ch. XIII. அடக்கி, Nâl. 105.

அடி (§ 64), 'strike.' Nâl. 279. [Comp. S. *adhas.*] n. 'foot' =தாள், 3, 4, 10, 544, 610, 1120, 1279; 'the footsteps,' 208, Nâl. 62, 391, 388. அடிமை 'servitude,' 608.

அடு. I. (§ 56, II.), 'destroy, defeat, torment (boil, cook)'; intr. 'die.' அடுமுரண் 'victorious might,' 567. அடல் 'destruction,' 893; 'vexation,' 206; 'conquest,' 343. அடற்றகை 'bravery,' 768. அட்டு, Nâl. 382. அடுப 'will defeat with slaughter,' 493. அடும் 'will destroy, defeat,' 207, 495, 500. அடுங்காலை 'in the hour of death,' 799; 'cooking time,' Nâl. 68; 'when it torments,' 1166. அடு 'boiled,' 1065, 1090, Nâl. 363. அட்டில் 'a cook-room,' Nâl. 363.

II. (§ 64) 'approach, accumulate, attack.' அடுத்து, 621, 867, 1030. அடுத்தது 'that which has approached (it),' 706. பத்தடுத்த 'ten-fold,' 450, 817.

அடுக்கு (§ 62), 'heap up, accumulate.' [Comp. அடு, II.] அடுக்கிய (சுற்றம்) 'heaps of clients,' 526, 1005. அடுக்கிவரினும் 'though they come in shoals,' 625.

அடை (§ 57), 'draw near,' Nâl. 123. அடையாவாம் 'will not draw near,' 939; (§ 64) 'close up, shut in.' அடைக்கும் 'that which will close up,' 38, 71.

அட்டு (§ 62), 'pour.' அட்டியநீர் 'water poured forth,' 1093.

அணங்கு (from அண). 1. A goddess, 1081. தாக்கணங்கு 'Lakshmî,' 'the overpowering goddess,' 1082. 2. 'Destruction (as from fascination of a Lamia),' 918. 3. 'Fear,' 'fascination.' தகையணங்குறுத்தல், Ch. CIX. அணங்கரா 'Râgu: the serpent that swallows the moon,' Nâl. 241.

அணி (n.) 'ornament,' 95, 115, 118, 701, 738, 1014, 1089, 1273. அணிகலம், 575 (கலன்). (v. § 57) அணியும் 'will adorn, trick itself out,' 978. அணிநிழற்காடு 'a forest with beauteous shade,' 742. அணியிழை, *see* இழை.

அணு-கு (§ 62) 'approach.' அணுகாது 'not approaching,' 691.

அண்ணு (§ 64), 'open the mouth, as in ejecting.' [அண்ணம் 'palate.'] அண்ணுத்தல், 255.

அதர் 'way,' 594.

அதி [S.] 'exceedingly.'

அதிர் (ரு § 57), 'tremble.' அதிர 'causing to shake with fear,' 429.

அது, இது 'it, that, this.' (See அ, இ, எ. Comp. அவன்.) அது is written also அஃது.

Sing.—C. I.: அது, 45, 36, 74, 231, 362, 364, 165, 332, 477, 533, 536, 546, 781, 596, 901, 985, 996, 1144, 1164, 1302, Nâl. 276; இது, 37, 1173, 1327. அதூஉம் 'even that,' 230. அஃது, 38, 49, 76, 80, 162, 170, 132, 220, 226, 236, 242, 262, 414, 427, 363, 368, 459, 476, 556, 572, 591, 600, 943, 971, 1001, 1014, 1032, 1093, 1166, 1279. C. II.: அதனை (அது by வே. தொ.), 32, 152, 262, 495, 517, 621, 858, 859, 948, 1284, 1141, 1143, 1164, Nâl. 276; இதனை, 517. C. III.: அதனால் (ன்), 303, 642, 1031; இதனால், 517. C. IV.: அதற்கு, 391, 518, 802, 1124, 1330. C. V.: அதனின், 122, 152, 302, 341, 644, 759, 1158, 1166. C. VI.: அதன்,

60, 323, 490, 1289; இதன், 1176; அதன்கண், 472.

PLUR. — C. I.: அவை, 658; இவை, 581, 1109, 1244. C. II.: அவையவை 'each one (imaginable) thing,' 1105. C. V.: அவற்றின், 875. C. VII.: அவற்றுள், 61, 504. அவ்வது 'each mode,' 426.

அந்தணன். **1.** The Supreme Being, 8. கடவுள். **2.** Ascetics (in pl.), 30. அறவோர் (evidently from அம்=செம்+தண்மை). **3.** Sages, 543. பெரியோர்.

அந்தம் [S.; in comp.] ஒருவந்தம்=ஏகாந்தம் 'mental concentration,' 593; 'utterly,' 563.

அமரர் (S.) 'immortals,' 121.

அமர். I. (§ 57), [Comp. அமை], 'acquiesce in,' 'join,' 'harmonize with,' 'be complaisant,' 'join battle,' Nâl. 383. அமர்ந்த வழக்கு, 75, 'harmonious combination.' அகனமர்ந்து, முகனமர்ந்து 'with complaisant heart, face,' 92, 93, 84, Nâl. I. அமராமை 'dissatisfaction,' 529.

II. n. (as போர் from பொரு) 'battle,' 814, 1027, 1083, 1125.

III. v. அமர்த்தனகண் 'have been at variance with' (§ 64), 1084.

அமிழ்தம், அமிழ்து 'ambrosia' [S. *amrita*], 702; applied to rain, 11; to food handled by one's children, 64; to the touch of the beloved, 1106. [This word is variously spelt, அமிர்தம், அமுதம், அமுது. மருந்து is a corruption of it, 968. In 82 சாவா மருந்து is given as its equivalent.]

அமை (§ 57), 'be composed,' 'satisfied,' 'fit.' [Comp. அமர், சம்மதி.] அமையாது 'goes not on its way,' 20. அமைகலாவாறு 'discontent,' 219. அமையல 'know no content,' 1283. அமைந்து (=பொருந்தி), 474, 118, 761, 340. அமைவர் 'they will rest content,' 580. அமைந்தக்கண்ணும், 606. அமையாக்கடை, 803. அமைந்தசொல், 635; 'abounding,' 900. அமையும் 'will suffice, be fitting,' 708, 298, 1193. அமைவு 'quiet,' contentment,' 'union,' 740, 743, 1178. அமையாதவரை 'those with whom you are not in complete accord,' 825. உப்பமைந்தற்று 'as when (it) is sufficiently salt,' 1302. அமைந்தார் 'my beloved,' 1155. அமைவிலன் 'one of inharmonious disposition,' 863. இன்றியமையாத 'indispensable,' 682; 'not to be obtained otherwise,' 961; =வெய் 'bambû,' 906 [from its smoothness ?].

அமைச்சு [S. *amātya*; syn. மந்திரி], 'the office of a chief minister of state,' or 'the minister' himself. Ch. LXIV., 631, 632, 633, 634, 381. அமைச்சியல், the part from Ch. LXIV. to LXXIII.

அம். **1.** (=நீர்), 'a tear.' விழுமம் 'the tear that falls,' 107. [Cp. however விழுமம்.] **2.** (=அழகு 'beauty,' 1107. In comp. அந்தணன், q.v., Nâl. 151. **3.** விகுதி, used in forming nouns, as ஆக்கம். **4.** Term. of 1st pers. pl. of verbs, for com. ஓம். See இல்ம்.

அம்பு 'arrow,' 597, 772.

அயர் 'do, perform, celebrate' (connected with something joyous), 1268. அயர்கம்=செய்யக்கடவோம். [III. Gr. 85, வியங்கோள், பன்மை. Comp. காண்கம், 1301.]

அரங்கு [S. *ranga*], 'a square, chess-board with squares,' 401.

அரசு 'king, kingdom, kingly rule.' [S. *râjan*.] [Syn. மன்னன், வேந்தன, வேந்து, இறை.] அரசர் 'kings,' 381. அரசியல், Ch. XXXIX.-LXIII.

அரண் 'fort,' 381, 421, 492, 534, 737, 741-750. Ch. LXXV.

அரம் 'a file,' 567, 888.

அரி (§ 57), 'nip off.' அரிந்தற்று 'is like the nipping off,' 1304. [அற்று.]

அரிவை (=மாது), 'a beautiful damsel,' 1107.

அருந்து (§ 62), 'eat.' அருந்தியது 'what one has eaten,' 942.

அரும்பு (§ 62). [See அரு= 'tender.'] அரும்பி 'having appeared as a tender blossom,' 1223, 1227. [Here அரும்பு= 'tender blossom'; போது = 'fully - formed bud'; மலர்= 'the full-blown flower.']

அருப்பு (for அரும்பு, by வலித்தல், III. Gr. 41) = 'flower-bud.' அருப்பறு 'whose bud falls not,' 522.

அருள் 'benevolence.' [அர் + உள். So பொருள், இருள், மருள். Comp. அன்பு].
176, 285, 755, 757, 938, Nâl. 20, 27, 321. அருளுடைமை, Ch. xxv. அருட்செல்வம், 241. அருட்பொருள், 914. அருளாளு (see ஆள்), 242, 244, 245, 251, 252. அருள்சேர்ந்த 'which is the abode of grace,' 243. அருளாதான் (from அருளு § 121) = அருளாதவன் 'he who performs no gracious acts,' 249. அருளல்லது 'that which is devoid of grace,' 254.

அர், அரு, அரி, அரும், ஆர் (§ 184) 'rare, difficult.' [Comp. S. √ara. See அருள், அரும்பு, அரிவை.] அரு 'difficult to do,' 483, 631; 'rare, precious,' 847. அரும் 'difficult,' 462, 565; with கேடன் 'one whose ruin can hardly be effected,' 210, 732; 'hard to comprehend,' 198. அரிது, pred. with ஆம் ex. or und. 177, 7, 8, 29, 503, 693, 419, 443, 377, 886, 101, 213, 227, 235; with or without ஏ, 248, 1155, 1156, 419, 1153, 823, 843, 1180, 1049, 647, 499, 606, 16; (obj. or sub.) 1160, 745, 1276, 762. அரியது 'hard to attain,' 489, 747 (in dat.). அரிய 'difficult to effect,' 26, 489, 503, 537, 664, 781 (opposed to எளிய). அரியர் (நிறையரியர்) 'hard to assail,' 1138; 'hard to find,' 723. அரியவை 'serious, hard to pardon,' 443, 693. ஆர் with உயிர் 'the precious life,' 73, 1141; 'terrible,' 1179; with இருள் 'thick, gross darkness,' 121. அரு-மை 'difficulty,' 611, 975; 'rare value,' 1142; 'of approach,' 743 (comp. 1138).

அலகு 'grains of *paddy*, food, corn,' 1034.

அலகை 'a daemon' (பேய்), 850.

அலவன் 'a crab,' Nâl. 123.

அலர் = மலர் 'a full - blown flower'; hence, 'a wide-spread rumour.' கௌவை, 1141, 1142, 1146, 1149. அலரறிவுறுத்தல், Ch. cxv.

அலை 'oppression, affliction,' 551; (§ 64) 'afflict,' 753.

அல்லல் (§ 148; =துன்பம்), 'privation, affliction.' (1) Simply, 245, 798 (7th case). (2) Comp. with நோய் 'the pain of privation,' 1160, 1301, 1303 [with அலந்தார்]; (3) with உழ and உழப்பி, 936, 938; (4) with படு and படுத்து, 379, 555, 626, 460.

அல (§ 66), 'suffer privation, perish.' அலந்தார் (87), 1303. அல்லாவார் 'they are not disquieted,' 593. An irreg. form; perhaps for அலாதவர் ஆவார் (§ 121).

அல் [comp. இல், § 44], a root denoting the non-existence of a quality or attribute. அல் (Intro. p. § 4 (2) b). அல்லிடத்து 'where (or when) it is not so'=அல்லாத, 301. அல்வழி, 1299, 1300. This root takes inflections as a குறிப்புவினை (§ 184). அல்லன், 3rd sing. masc., 'he who is not —,' 386.

அல்லர், 3rd pl. com., 143, 926, 880, 973, 1300. அல்லவர், 973, 977, 751. அல்லார், 973, 720, 726, 822, 918, 986, 999, 419; with noun und., 266. அல்லாதவர் [a double neg., § 124 (5)], 1077. அல்லது or அன்று, 3rd s. neut., (1) as part. noun, 795, 254, 108, 379, 825, 1051, 618, 1180, 784. (2) as finite verb [this is then contracted into அன்று], 105, 370, 982, 988, 1092, 993, 1255, 82, 786, 438, 871, 549, 546, 641. (3) as particle='otherwise, but, except,' 1090, 1131, 231, 570, 951, 751, 710 (§ 202), 491, 1159. என்னல்லது 'save myself,' 1168. அன்ரே 'is it not so?' 1208, 1258, 775, 1014. அன்றே 'is it not so?' 555. அன்றுகொல் '(or) will it not?' 1307. அல்ல, 3rd pl. neut., (1) part., 61, with பிற: 'other things which are not —,' 289. களவல்லமற்றைய 'other things which are not fraud.' (2) [where no name of quality is expressed, we may understand அறம் or பொருள்: thus, அல்லவை = 'sins, evils, unreal things'], as noun: 'things which are not —,' 157, 962, 466, 337, 116, 182, 246, 274, 551, 384, 1286, 150, 173, 289, 700, 944, 164, 376, 96, 351. (3) as finite verb: '(they) are not —,' 95, 115, 299, 400. அல்லை, 2nd sing., 'thou art not —,' 1221. அல்லம, 1st pl., 'we are not —,' 1209. அல்லால், with வீழின் 'unless,' 16; with noun, 1095, 'besides, but, except,' 1188, 406, 233, 377, 497, Nâl. 105; with a dat. 'save to these,' 7, 235, 515, 762. Equiv. to அல்லது and அல்லாமல்; perhaps a kind of subjunctive: 'if it is not.' அன்றி 'without, the attribute not existing.' வினையெச்சம் of non-existent verb அன்று [§ 62, 77], 437. அன்மை [abs. noun அல்+மை, § 184], 'the absence, non-existence of anything,' with oblique case, 162; in comp. 172; with noun und. 185.

அவம், S. 'vanity, nothingness.'

அவலம் [S. *a+bala*], 'sympathetic sorrow,' 1072.

அவன் (see அ, இ, எ), 'he, that man, this man.' அவள், இவள் 'she, that woman, this woman.' [Comp. அது.] 63, 70 (ellipsis of 6th case), 517, 1182, 1204, 1155, 1156, 1321, 109, 790, 1152, 1154 (ellipsis of 2nd case), 1178, 1244, 65, 314, 506, 1051, 1188, 1301, 1297, 1298, 1291, 1183, 1184, 1261. அவன்கண் (7th case), 517. அவருள், 125. அவர்பின், 1293. அவர்க்கு, 1321. இவள், அவள், 1188, 1086, 1093, 1091, 1104, 1112. இவளை, 1188. அவனை, 518, 547, 647, 958. அவனின், 526. அவரின் (5th case), 1074. அவரை, 1292, 1236. அவரோடு, 1206. அவர்மாட்டு, 1199. அவரவர் 'each one's,' 114, 469. அவர்வயின் விதும்பல், Ch. CXXVII.

அவா 'desire'=ஆசை, 35, 361–370, 1075, 1310. அவாவறுத்தல், Ch. XXXVII. அவாவின்மை 'indifference,' 364, 513.

அவாவு (§ 62), 'desire.' அவாம் (=அவாவும், § 74), 'which (the world, the king) will desire,' 215, 681. அவாய் (=அவாவி) 'having desired,' 643.

அவி [S. *havis*]. **1.** நெய் 'melted butter,' 259. **2.** வேள்வி 'a sacrifice,' 413.

அவி (§ 57), 'be extinguished, die.' அவியினும்=அவிந்தாலும் 'if (they) die,' 420; (§ 64) 'extinguish, destroy, quench, repress.' அவித்து 'having repressed,' 694. அவித்தான்=அவித்தவன், 6, 25.

அவிர் (§ 60, III.), 'glisten' (வினைத்தொ, III. Gr. 153), 1117.

அவை. **1.** See under அது. **2.** சபை 'an assembly' [from S. *sabhâ*; so அரா, அர, அரவம for சர்ப்பம்], 711, 713, 725, 727; 332, 'an assembly of dancers.' [Syn. கோட்டி, களன், அவையம் a variation of அவை with சாரி யை, அம்], 67. அவையறிதல், Ch. LXXII., 'Knowing the (methods) of the assembly of councillors.' அவையஞ்சாமை, Ch. LXXIII., 'Not dreading the assembly.' புல்லவை, 719, 'The assembly of the mean.' நல்லவை, 719, 'The assembly of the good,' 728. நல்லாரவை, 729. வல்லவை, 721, 'The assembly of those mighty in learning,' நுண்ண வை, 726, 'The assembly of the men of subtle learning.'

அவ்வி [ஔவி]. அவ்வியம் [or ஔவியம்], 'envy.' அழுக்காறு, பொறாமை, 169. அவ்வியநெஞ் சத்தான் 'the man of envious soul.' அவ்வி (§ 64), அவ்வித்து 'having been envious of,' 167.

அள (§ 66), 'measure,' Nâl. 103. அளந்தான் (=அளந்தவன், III. Gr. 41), 'he who measured,' 610. அளக்கும் 'which will measure,' 710. அளப்பது 'that which will measure,' 796. அளவு. **1.** =அளவைநூல்='logic and dialectics,' 725. **2.** 'Measure, due (just *or* defined) measure *or* limit'; 'justitia quae suâ quidlibet mensurâ metitur,' B., 283, 286, 287, 288, 289, 474, 477, 478, 479, 574, 943, 947, 949. **3.** As adv. காணுமளவும் 'until,' 224, 848. அவ்வளவில் 'at that exact moment,' 1187.

அளபெடை (அளபு = அளவு) occurs in (III. Gr. 14) :—v. 2, ஆ becomes ஆ அ, 14, 653, 1301; v. 182, அழீஇ=அழித்து; v. 12, உ is first lengthened: ஊஉ, 15, 460, 461; v. 31, ஊ becomes ஊ உ, 32; v. 653, ஓருவு becomes ஓஒ, 797, 929; தழுவி becomes தழீஇ, 544, 425, 913; v. 1040, அசைஇ=அசைந்து, 91. Comp. Nâl. 6, 201.

அளாவு (§ 64), அளை (§ 57), 'mingle, mix up,' 64; and with reduplication. அளவளா (வில் லாதான்) 'he who does not mix on terms of intimacy,' 523. அளைஇ = அளைந்து 'having mingled with tenderness,' 91.

அளறு 'mire, hell' [comp. அழு, ஆழ, அள: the idea is 'depth'], 255, 835, 919.

அளி (§ 64), அளிக்கல், 387, 'defend.' அளித்து 'having shown affection,' 1154, 1168, 1256. அளிக்குமளி, 'the love, lovingly shown,' 1192, 1321. (noun, =அருள், அன்பு), 'kindness,' 390, 557, 1192, 1209, 1321. அளியர் 'full of tenderness,' 1138.

அள்ளு 'take in handfuls.' அள் ளிக்கொள்வற்றே, 1187.

அழல் 'a glowing fire,' 1228. [தீ, நெருப்பு, தழல்] (? from அழி). அழகு 'beauty,' Nâl. 131. Not in K., where எழில், ஏர் are found, which, perhaps, have the same root.

அழி (§ 57), 'perish, 498, Nâl. 105; (§ 64) 'destroy.' அழி (வி. தொ.), அழிபசி 'hunger that destroys,' 226 (III. Gr. 153). அழிவந்த 'ruinous things,' 807 (வரு, comp. 968). அழிய, 968. அழிதல். கண்விதுப்பழிதல், Ch. CXVIII., 'being consumed, wasting away.' [Comp. Psa. xxxi. 9.] உறுப்புநலனழிதல், Ch. CXXIV. நிறையழிதல், Ch. CXXVI., 'reserve overcome.' அழிக்கல் 'destruction,' 421. அழிவு 'despair,' 625; 'ruin, defeat,' 764, 787, 876. அழியாமை, Ch. LXIII. இடுக்கணழியாமை 'not despairing in adversity,' Ch. LXIII. அழித்து 'having wrought destruction,' 359; 'having abated the keenness of its glance,'

775; 'having changed it, destroyed its effect,' 1317. அழீஇ (III. Gr. 86), 182, =அழித்து (see அளபெடை). அழிவது 'expenditure, what will be expended,' 461. அழிப்பது 'that which will destroy,' 744. அழிக்கும் 'which will destroy,' 934.

அழு 'weep' (§ 60). [Comp. S. *aśru*. அலறு seems another form.] அழுத 'wept,' 555, 828. அழ 'with weeping, at the cost of tears,' 659; 'so as to draw tears,' 659. அழுதாள் 'she wept,' 1317, 1318.

அழுகு (§ 62), 'rot away,' Nâl. 123.

அழுக்காறு 'envy' (=அவ்வியம் பொறாமை). The deriv. is அழுக்கு 'foulness,' and ஆறு 'way.' The three verbs under are formed by a poetic license. அழுக்காறு, 35, 135, 161, 162, 164, 165, 167, 168. அழுக்காறு (§ 62); அழுக்காறாமை 'absence of envy,' Ch. XVII. அழுக்கறு (§ 64); அழுக்கறுப்பான் 'he who will be envious,' 163, 166. அழுக்கறு (56, II.); அழுக்கற்று 'having envied,' 170.

அழுந்து 'will sink down,' 835. (Connected with ஆழ்.)

அறம். See *Notes*, p. 186. (1) One of the four objects of study and pursuit (S. *dharma*). (2) It is the general subject of Ch. I.–XXXVIII. அறப்பால். (3.) It is divided into இல்லறம், Ch. V.–XXIV., 'The virtue of the house;' and துறவறம், Ch. XXV.–XXXVIII., 'The virtue of renunciation.' 76, 543, 32, 31, 35, 36, 39, 181, 183, 185, 93, 96, 501, 23, 141, 296, 297, 249, 288, 1047, 1009, 1018. (=அறக்கடவுள்), 77, 130, 204, personification. அறன் [நன்னூல், 122], Ch. IV., 34, 40, 45, 48, 49, 441, 189, 182, 179, 384, 147, 148, 150, 644, 754, 173, 635, 366. அறனல்ல 'vices, vicious acts,' 157. அறன்கடை 'the outside of virtue=vice,' 142. (See கடை.) அறவாழி 'the round sea of virtue,' 8. அறவினை 'virtuous action,' 33, 321, 909. அறத்தாறு 'the way of virtue,' 37, 46. அறனாக்கம் 'the increase, wealth of virtue,' 163. அறவோர் 'virtuous persons,' 30.

அறி (§ 57), 'know (as result of study), be wise, be able.' [Syn. தெரி 'perceive'; தேறு 'perceive clearly' (strengthened form of தெரி); உணரு (உள்) 'understand and feel.' Often combined with கல், of which it is the result. Comp. 396. Connected with அறு, ஆறு, அறம். Ellis says, 'In Tamil the more frequent acceptations of அறிஞர் the *learned*, and அறியார் the *ignorant*, are the *virtuous* and the *vicious*.

I. Root (வினைத்தொகை). அறி-தோறு (see தோறு), 'whenever one obtains some new gain of knowledge,' 1110. தானறி குற்றம் 'a fault of which one is conscious, a wilful fault,' 272. அறி - கொன்று 'having murdered (set at nought) the lessons of wisdom,' 638. கடனறிகாட்சி யவர் 'those whose mental vision perceives duty,' 218 [comp. 981].

II. Past tense, part. adv., and adj., and nouns (§ 77, 74, 87). [With அறிவு, 123, &c.] அறி-ந்து 123, 136, 164, 179, 441, 469, 472, 483, 477, 479, 493, 494, 515; 'having known, knowing,' 635, 637, 644, 645, 687, 696, 711, 721, 725, 729, 754, 767, 793, 878, 943, 944, 946, 947, 981, 1127, 1128, 1287, 1312. அறி-ந்த 'which has known, knows,' 637, 711, 721, 1143. அறி-ந்தவை 'things that have been ascertained,' 587, அறி-ந்தேன் 'I have known, I know, *novi*,' 1083. அறி-ந்தான்-

அறிந்தார் (=அறிந்தவர்), 288, 399, 635, 717. அறி-வது, 293, 472, 686, 1255.

III. Fut. tense, part., and nouns. (Intro. xxi.) அறி-வல் (=அறிவேன், III. Gr. 81), 'I shall know, I know,' 1129. அறி-வாம் (=அறிவோம், III. Gr. 77), 'we will know,' 36. அறி-வார் 'they will know,' 427. அறிவான், ஆர் 'those who (will) know,' 318, 428, 677, 701, 995, 1053, 1072. அறி-யும் 'that will know,' 1308.

IV. Inf. and verb. noun (§ 168, 148). அறி-ய 'to know, so as to know, in order to know,' 590, 795. அறி-தல் 'the knowing, knowledge of,' 582. குறிப்பறிதல், Ch. LXXI., CX. வலியறிதல், Ch. XLVIII. செய்(ந்)நன்றியறிதல், Ch. XI. காலமறிதல், Ch. XLIX. ஒப்புரவறிதல், Ch. XXII. இடனறிதல், Ch. L. அவையறிதல், Ch. LXXII. கற்றறிதல் (கற்று), 'the faculty of learning,' 632.

V. Optative (§ 140). அறி-க '(he) should know,' 116, 210. (Intro. xx.)

VI. Negative (§ 110, 121). அறி-யேன் 'I know not, cannot,' 928, 1083, 1125, 1207. அறி-யலம் 'we know not,' 1257 (=அறியோம்). (யாம்) அறிவதில்லை 'we know not' (§ 114), 61. அறிவிலா 'which is devoid of knowledge,' 869. அறியான், ஆர் (n.), 'they who know not,' 76, 337, 473, 474, 638, 713, 863, 877. அறியார் (fin. v.), 'they know not,' 228, 1141, Nâl. 108. அறியாது 'not knowing,' 1142. அறியா (=அறியாமல்), 1116. அறியா 'that knows not,' 736, 836. Poetic, அறிகல்லாதவர் (கு inserted + அல்லாதவர்) 'men without knowledge,' 427; அறிகிலார் 'they know not' (கு ins. +இலார்); அறிந்ததிலேன் 'I knew not,' 1226, *lit.* 'I was not that which knew.'

VII. Nouns. அறிவு 'knowledge,' (§ 190*a*), 123, 175, 203, 315, 355, 358, 372, 373, 382, 396, 421–426, 452, 454, 513, 532, 682, 684, 1022. அறிவுடைமை, Ch. XLIII. 68. புல்லறிவாண்மை, Ch. LXXXV. 287, 331. அலரறிவுறுத்தல், Ch. CXV. குறிப்பறிவுறுத்தல், Ch. CXXVIII. அறிவாளன், 215 [ஆளன்]. அறிவுடையார் (உடை), 179, 404, 427, 430, 441, 463, 622, 816, 1153. (§ 184) அறிவினர், 918; அறிவிஞர், 198, 429; அறிவினவர், 914, 915, 857. (இல்) அறிவி(ல்)லார், 427, 430; அறிவிலாதார், 140. அறிவறியார், 507; அறிவறிந்த, 61, 123, 618 [அறிவு used as acc. of cognate signif.], Nâl. 108. அறியாமை (§ 154), 'ignorance,' 440, 925, 1110.

VIII. Causal (§ 160, I. *b*). அறிவிப்ப 'they will cause to be known' (= அறிவிப்பன), 1233.

அறு. I. அறு, adj. (see ஆறு), 'six,' Nâl. 1.

II. அறு (§ 56, II.), 'be cut off, cease, be digested.' அற்றேம் (III. Gr. 79), 'we are deprived of, free from,' 88, 275 [comp. 505], 626. அற்றார் (§ 87), 'those who are without, freed from,' 503; = 'less' in compounds, 311, 312, 646, 106, 800. 'The destitute,' 226, 248, 365, 506, 1007. அற்றான், 350. அற்றவர் 'those set free,' 365. அற்ற, 654, 649, 699, 956. அற்ற கண்ணே 'where (bonds) have been severed,' 349, 521; 'where all support has failed.' அற்றது 'that which is freed, carried off, digested,' 365, 942, 944. அற்று, 1261. அறு [வினைத்தொகை], 199, 352='less,' 1117. அற= 'thoroughly, absolutely, so as to be free from all conditions,' 268, 391, 465, 845, 717, 184; 'without.' (இடை)யறாது 'fails not,' 369. அறாஅ, 1295. அறின் (opp. to உறின்), 'if it is not,'

812. அறல் 'digestion.' அற்ருல் 'if it digest easily,' 943.

III. அறு (§ 64), 'cut off.' அறுக்கல், 345. அறுத்தல், Ch. XXXVII. அறுக்கும, 349, 814 [see ஆறு], 753, 759. அறுப்பான், 346, 'he who will free himself from,' 798, 163 [see அழுக்கு]. அறுப்பில், 367. அறுக 'let them consume away,' 1177. அரு 'unfailing,' 522. அருர் 'cease not (to love),' 807.

IV. (Intro. xxiv.) அறை 'chamber (cut off); a mine,' 747, 764, 913. அற்றம் (=அழிவு) 'destruction,' 434, 421; 'cessation,' 1186; 'shame,' 980, 846.

அறை (§ 57), 'beat (as a drum),' 1076. [வினைத்தொகை], 1180. அறைந்தான் '(of) him who has struck,' 307.

அற்கு (§ 64; = நிலே), 'endure.' அற்கா 'not enduring' (§ 121), 333. அற்குப 'things that will endure' (III. Gr. 95), 333. [ப added to a root forms an aoristic part. noun plur. neut.]

அனிச்சம், an imaginary (?) flower, the poet's commonplace for anything peculiarly delicate or sensitive, 90, 1111, 1115, 1120.

அன் (see அ), 'such.' [Comp. அனே. The difference is that between *talis* and *tantus*. அன் is 'such in quality,' அனே 'such in magnitude or number.'] அன்ஞர், 1061, 814; நின்றன்ஞர் for நின்ற அன்ஞர் (see அற்று), 'they who are as,' 898, 969. அன்னர், 1076, 1323. அன்ஞன் 'he is as,' 624. அன்னள் 'she is as,' 1124. அன்னது 'that which is as,' 565, 1082 [comp. அற்று]. அன்ன (1) for அன்னது, or rel. part. in agreement with ஒப்பாரி, 1071, 296, 889, 308, 363, 527, 109; கொன்றன்ன (கொன்று, comp. அற்று), 1142, 1143, 1260, 655, 1305, 1119, 1137. (2) 'things that are so,' 279, 1122, 1294, Nâl. 101, 104.

அன். 1. As 'சாரியை' or *inserted particle*; கற்றது+அன்+ஆல், 2. 2. As 'விகுதி' or termination forming a masc. noun sing. அறிவு+அன்=அறிவன், 2.

அனே 'such.' See அ. [Comp. இனே and எனே; and அன், which has nearly the same force. These forms all belong to the குறிப்புவினே, Intro. p. xxii. 10. They govern a gen. oblique case, மரத்தனேயர், விலங்கோடனேயர். அனேயது 'it is (such) as,' 595 [comp. அற்று]. அனேத்தும், 'all over,' 1320. அனேத்து 'it is thus (much),' 34, 387, 394, 828, 1208. அனேத்திலர் 'are not of this much, of equal value,' 409. (1) pred. அனேயர் 'they are (such) as,' 595, Nâl. 104; (2) rel. part., 622; (3) noun, 965, 964, 410, 406, 310, 576 [comp. அன்ஞர்], 1073, 650, 704. அனேயார் 'those who are as —,' 965. அனேவரையும் 'all sorts of persons,' 584. அனேத்தானும், 'thus much even,' 416. கண்டனேயர் 'as those whom (one) has seen.' (கண்டு for கண்ட; comp. நின்றன்ஞர் and அற்று.) அனேத்திற்கே 'to such an extent,' 1129. தொட்டனேத்து, கற்றனேத்து 'in proportion as,' 396.

அன்பு 'affection,' 513. அன்புடைமை, Ch. VIII., 862, 911, 992, 1009, 45, 71–80, 681, 682, 285, 807, 1276, 757. [Comp. அருள், காமம், நட்பு, கேண்மை, ஆர்வம்.]

அன்று (see அ), 'that day, tomorrow,' 36; with ஏ, 108; 'that very day,' 113. [Comp. இன்று, என்று.]

அன்னம் [S. *hañça*], 'swan,' 1120.

அன்னே 'mother': தாய், 1147.

அற்று 'like, it is like, it is such

as.' [Comp. எற்று. See அன், அன்னது, அன்+து=அற்று.] **1.** It is added to past adv. part. where we should expect rel. part. (Intro. xxiv. § 10.) கவர்ந்தற்று 'it is like grasping at,' 22, 100, 78, 401, 402, 208, 274, 338, 215, 216, 1007, 1008, 452, 1058, 931, 678, 758, 1302, 1303, 1304, 838, 913, 1020, 1107, 1110, 890, 332, 1192, 1121, 1145, 1146, 307, 1148, 718, 894. **2.** It is added to nouns (inf. base), மரத்தற்று, 217, 332. **3.** It is added to nouns, simply, 1306, 261; almost redundant, 720, 407, 415, 1288. அள்ளிக் கொள்வற்றே, 1187 (கொள்வு= கொள்வது). **4.** Corr. to எற்று 'such as is . . . so is.' அற்றாக 'so,' 365.

ஆ

ஆ is a demonstrative, a stronger form of அ. See ஆங்கு, ஆண்டு.

ஆ. **1.** 'Ox, cow,' 560, 1066, Nâl. 101, 115, 118. **2.** See under ஆகு.

ஆகுலம் (=ஆரவாரம்) [S. *âkula*], 'confusion, turbulence,' 34.

ஆ, ஆகு (§ 58, 136–140), ஆக்கு (§ 64). ஆகு (root used in வி. தொ.), 371, 478. ஆ, ஆக= 'when,' 1312, 1315, 1317; ='as,' 850, 841, 874, 1163, 104, 117, 122, 433, 434, 424, 443, 444, 445, 507, 751, 1263, 1147; ='while, is,' 82, 278, 1127, 1128; ='to be,' 666, 92; adverbial, 119, 357, 1043. ஆகல், 372; =ஆ in 371, 'favouring fate.' ஆதல் 34, 95, 285, 219, 374, 419, 714, 801, 998, 600, 1291 [as optative mood we must suppose ellipsis of வேண்டும்.] ஆகுதல், 683, 823. ஆய், ஆகி, form. adv., 543, 479, 15, 17, 586, 587, 998, 51, 217, 868, 133, 461, 446, 529, 744, 745, 764, 910, 1218, 1227, 1228, 630, 476. ஆம், ஆகும், 375, 368, 590, 1002, 379, 993, 897, 868, 978, 146, 573, 138, 175, 858, 889, 397, 436, 449, 939, 556, 685, 763, 1298, 1270, 942, 1079, 93, 94, 125, 205, 134, 144, 860, 113, 328, 456, 459, 492, 787, 788, 1049, 514, 320, 433, 344, 452. ஆகுதிர் 'you are,' 1319. ஆத்தி 'thou didst become,' 1112. ஆதும் 'we shall prosper,'=ஆவோம், 653. ஆகிய, 283, 270, 329, 750, 817. ஆயிடை 'therefore,' 1179. ஆய, 2, 12. ஆயது 'what has become,' 12. ஆயார் 'those who have been,' 106. ஆயவர் 'those who are,' 1016. ஆவது 'what will accrue,' 283, 427, 461; ஆகுவது, 315. ஆவர் 'they will be, become,' 1165, 1189, 1218, 1207. ஆவார் 'those (that) will become,' 1074, 1299. ஆயின் 'if (it become),' 44, 45, 52, 49, 209, 868, 1156, 1306, 566, 1018, 1119, 1216. ஆனல் 'if (be),' 53. ஆயினும், ஆனும் 'although, whatsoever,' 355, 478, 656, 889, 900, 599, 52, 127, 144, 458, 961, 128, 397, 317, 416, 1321, 1325, 1065, 404, 409, 414, 705. Neg. forms:—ஆகாதது, 1291; ஆகாதாகி, 128; ஆகாது, 619; ஆகாவாம், 376; ஆகா, 421, 456. With உண்டு, இல் and அல்:— உளராகார், 895; இலராக, 1242; உண்டாயினும், 1005; உண்டாக, 54, 988; உள்ளதாம், 889; உண்டாம், 110, 896, 1059; உள்ளவாக, 100; உள்ளதாகும், 454; உண்டாயின, 128; இல்லாகி, 479; அல்லாவார், 593; இல்லாகியார்; இலவாம், 91; இல்லாகும், 368, 94; இல்லாயின், 49, 52, 769, 1058; ஆகாதவில்லை, 'nothing which may not come about,' 537. ஆக்கி 'having caused to become,' 678, 1026. ஆக்கல் 'a causing to prosper,' 264. ஆக்கும், 616.

ஆக்கம் (opp. to கேடு), 'increase, wealth, prosperity,' 31, 32, 112, 113, 122, 135, 163, 169, 177, 183,

283, 328, 457, 463, 492, 522, 526, 562, 593, 594, 642, 651, 657, 692, 755, 858, 859, 902.

ஆங்கு [comp. இங்கே, அங்கே, எங்கே, and ஆ, யாங்கு]. **1.** 'So,' 252, 740, 'as above'; ஆங்கு 'with such persons,' 474, 534, 279, 803. **2.** 'As,' 532, 666, 1189; பட்டாங்கு 'as it suffers,' 247, 265, 279, 561, 908; ஒத்தாங்கு, 561; ஆங்கனைவரையும் 'and all such persons,' 584; 'closing and summing-up,' 43; 'as is fit,' 50. **3.** மற்றாங்கே 'again,' 15, 16. **4.** ஆங்கே 'as it is, at once,' 179, 171, 289, 333, 487, 566, 788, 1307, 928, 1215; 'when,' 676, 1325.

ஆசு = மாசு 'stain,' 503.

ஆசாரம் [S. *âchâra*], 1075; 'propriety of conduct, rule of life:' ஒழுக்கம்.

ஆசை [S. *âçâ*], 'desire,' 266.

ஆடு (§ 62), 'move, play' [comp. ஆள்]. ஆடியற்றே 'like playing'; see அற்று. சொல்லாட 'use words,' 405, 1070. சொல்லாடார் 'they speak not, interchange no words,' 818. ஆடவர் = மக்கள் 'men,' 1003 [comp. ஆள், ஆண்]. ஆடல் = ஆளுதல் 'employment'; Ch. LII. தெரிந்துவினையாடல். நட்பாடல் 'the *exercise* of friendship,' 187. ஒற்றாடல் 'the *use* of detectives.' நீராடி 'swimming,' 278.

அட்டு (§ 62). பாராட்டும், 994, 521 (see பார்). பாராட்டுவான், 196. (வி. தொ.) கூத்தாட்டவை 'the assembly of dancers.'

ஆட்சி. See ஆள்.

ஆணி 'a nail' [S. *âṇi*], 667, 1032.

ஆண்டு (see ஆ), 'there,' 363, 1098. [Comp. யாண்டு, ஈண்டு.]

ஆண்மை. See ஆள்.

ஆதி [S.]. ஆதிபகவன் 1. ஆதியாய் 'source,' 543.

ஆமை 'tortoise,' 126.

ஆறு. I. 'Six,' 381. (§ 172.) அறு. அறுதொழிலோர் 'the men of six works,' 560, Nâl. 1.

II. ஆறு (§ 62), 'grow cool, heal up.' ஆறும், 129. ஆறுதே, 129.

III. (See அறு, *cut.*) ஆறு 'a way,' 37, 43, 161, 219, 465, 478, 787, 849, 1321, 397, 932, 943, 662, Nâl. 97. ஆற்றின் 'in the (right) way,' 468, 975, 130, 46, 123, 176, 48, 716, 725, 477, Nâl. 103; with நல், 41, 222, 242, 324. ஆறு = படி, 1140. In comp. see அழுக்காறு, இழுக்காறு, 164; ஒழுக்காறு, 161; கையாறு, 627; ஆற்றறுக்கும் 'forsake,' 814, 798; ஆற்றான், 367.

IV. ஆற்று (§ 62). (1) 'do,' 'be strong'; (2) 'endure, undergo, bear.' [Comp. காப்பாற்று (see காப்பு)]. ஆற்றல், 469, 287, 891, 985, 225, 765, 25, 269, 768. ஆற்று, 469, 1174, 1175. ஆற்றுதழுத, 555, 1032. ஆற்றார், 493, 998, 286, 908. ஆற்றேன், 1162. ஆற்றி, 493, 515, 568, 669, 212, 1160, 1276, 748. ஆற்றின், 525, 46, 126, 234, 297, 38. ஆற்றுபவர் 'those who wage offensive war,' 741, 893, 1165. (v. and n.) ஆற்றுவார் 'the men of active energy,' 1027, 891, 894, 985, 975 130, 225. ஆற்றுதான், 1007, 894. (p. and f.v.) ஆற்றும், 67, 70, 189, 211, 1159, 579, 835. ஆற்றுமை, Ch. CXVI. பிரிவாற்றுமை. ஆற்ற (= மிக), 64, 367, 732, 1209.

ஆள் (§ 56, III.), 'govern, act, employ.' [Comp. ஆடு.] ஆள் 'a person; servant, slave,' 1030, 746. வேலாள், 500, Nâl. 122. ஆண்டவள், 'a lady,' 1279. ஆள்வினை, Ch. LXII.; = 'முயற்சி,' 618, 632, 1022. ஆள்க 'manage!' 589, 242; 'exercise,' 'rege, *i.e.* tibi associa,' B. ஆள்பவர், 1017, 383, 791. ஆள்வார், 447, 244, 245; in comp. மாலையாளர், 1230; மறுமையிலாளன், 904;

அறிவாளன், 215; பண்புடையாளர், 783. ஆளப்படும் 'will be employed,' 511. ஆளும் 'will exercise,' 251, 1252. ஆண்மை, 663, 907. தாளாண்மை, 613, 614; நல்லாண்மை, 1026, 1133, 1134; இல்லாண்மை, 1026. வேளாண்மை, 613, 81, 212; புல்லறிவாண்மை, 287, 331, Ch. LXXXV. வாளாண்மை, 614; ஒப்புரவாண்மை, 480. குடியாண்மை, 609; பேராண்மை, 773, 148, 962. மடியாண்மை, 609; ஊராண்மை, 773; வினையாண்மை, 904. சான்றாண்மை, Ch. XCIX., 981, 989, 990. ஆட்சி, 252, comp. பொருளாட்சி, அருளாட்சி.

ஆயம் [S. *âya*], 'gain.' ஆதாயம், 933.

ஆயன் 'a herdsman,' 1228.

ஆயிரம் 'a thousand' [S. *sahasra*], 259.

ஆர் (see அரு; the idea seems to be 'excellence, fulness'). ஆர்வம், 74, '=ஆசை, or the quality which excites it.' ஆர்வலர், 71, '=அன்புடையவர்.' ஆர், அமையார்தோள் 'shoulder like a bambû,' 906. ஆர் (§ 57), 'fill.' ஆரா 'insatiable,' 370. ஆர 'to be satisfied, filled,' 837. அகடாரார் 'they fill not their bellies,' 936. தோட்டார்கதப்பு, 1105. கண்ணாரக்கண்டபின், 1265. ஆர் (§ 64), 'bind.' ஆர்க்குங்கயிறு, 482; Nâl. 122, 'bind; hum.' யானையார்த்தற்று, 678.

ஆல். 1. 993. (அசை) 'redundant,' 216, 217, 397, 894, 875, 1155, 758, 838, 1145, 1148, 923, 840, 1152, 1180, 1184, 1192; with அன்று, அற்று, ஆம், 1038, 966. 2. Sign of third case, 2. 3. For ஆனல், 704 (so B. in 397, 'if it be so').

ஆழ் 'deep.' ஆழி (=கடல்), 8 (fig.). (=கரை), 989 (fig.). ஆழ் (§ 57). காலாழ்களர் 'mire in which the foot sinks,' 500. ஆழுமளறு 'the hell in which they sink down,' 919.

ஆன் for அவன், 3. ஏகினான்= ஏகினவன்.

ஆன்ற [='அகன்ற' (see அகல்), or from சான்ற (see சால்) as அவை from சபை], 'full, perfect, complete,' 416 (பெருமை), 681, 922 (குடி), 694 (பெரியார்), 1022 (அறிவு). ஆன்றமைந்த, 635 (சொல்), 909 (பொருள்), 862 (துணை), 148 (ஒழுக்கு), Nâl. 106. ஆன்றோர் 'the gods, the perfect ones, those of good fulfilled,' 413.

ஆய் (§ 57), 'examine.' Oftener written ஆராய் (with ஆர் 'fully'). நட்பாராய்தல், Ch. LXXX. ஆராய்வது 'explore, search out,' 584. ஆராய்ந்து, 586, 711. ஆராய்ந்த சொல்வன்மை, 682; கல்வி, 684. ஆராய்வான், 512. ஆய்ந்து, 517. ஆய்ந்தாய்ந்து, 792. நட்பாய்ந்து கொள்ளல், 795. ஆய்ந்தவர், 662. 'Exquisite, *recherché*,' ஆய்தொடியார், 911. ஆய்மயில், 1081. ஆயிழை, 1124. ஆயும், 914, 918. (அறிவினவர்), 198.

இ

இ demonstrative. [Comp. அ, எ, இவன், இங்கே, இன், இனை.] Before nouns, 247, 382, 383, 392, 336, 98, 513, 571, 578, 738, 662, 743, 952, 992, 1042, 1085, 1129, 1130, 1142, 1162, 1227, 1247, 1220, 1315, 1319, 1169. இஃதோ 'Lo!' 1161.

இக (§ 66), 'pass beyond the bounds of.' [Comp. இற; S. *i*.] இகந்துறைவர் 'he dwells apart, afar,' 1130. இகந்த 'unrestrainable,' 567; (with கை) 'immoderate,' 113. இகவாமை 'not transgressing,' 779. இகவா 'do not pass away from,' 146, 869.

இகல் 'hostility.' [From இக B. *animi aversio.* மாறுபாடு.] (Nig. இகல்பகைவலிபோர்வலி மையுத்தம்.] Ch. LXXXVI. 851–860, 647, 481, 'பகைவர்.' இகல் வேந்தர் 'warlike kings,' 691.

இகழ் (§ 57), 'despise, scorn.' [Opp. புகழ் and மகிழ். Comp. with என்.] இகழ்ந்தார், 538. இகழார், 698. இகழ்ச்சி, 539, 995, 'scorn' [comp. வசை]. இகழ்ந்து, 1057. இகழாமை 'the absence of a scornful spirit,' 891, 953. இகழ்வார், 966, 59, 151, 237, Nâl. 117.

இசை = புகழ். [Opp. to வசை. Comp. இயை.], 231, 238, 239, 240; 'praise,' 777; 'renown,' 1003; 'word, speech,' 1199. As verb, Nâl. 111; 'suit, fit,' 152.

இடம், இடன் (இடை). **1.** 'Place,' 1064, 1123; 'room,' 422, Nâl. 116. **2.** 'Fitting place,' 484, 491, 493, 494, 497, 498, 675, 687; with சீர், 821. இடனறிதல் 'knowledge of the right place, Ch. L. **3.** 'Ease, prosperity.' இடனிற் பருவத்தும், 'when in straightened circumstances,' 218, 1064. இடத்தது 'what possesses space,' 744. இடத்த 'things that take the place of,' 292. இடத்து inflex. base used adv., 'when' or 'where'; 'in the nick of time,' 746; with பெ. எச். 879, 968, 1124, 302, 490, 1285, 736; with வி. தொ. 301, 302; with num. ஒரிடத்து, 1153; sign of 7th case, 806, 883, 597, 762.

இடர் 'affliction.' [Comp. இடும்பை, இடுக்கண். ✓ இடி. S. *dur.*] இடர்ப்பாடு, 624 (பாடு).

இடி (§ 64), 'thunder, reprove with earnestness,' 447, 448, 784, 795. — D. 'a forcible word,' 607.

இடு (§ 68), 'give.' [Comp. S. *dâ.* கொடு, தரு, ஈ.] இடு 'give!' 552. இடல், 85. இட்டன்ன 'as though (it) were thrown into,' 1260. இடினும் [aux. strengthening meaning], 931 (§ 263). இடா, 801. இட, 1030.

இடுக்கண் [see கண். Comp. இட்டு, இடர், இடும்பை. S. *dukh*; syn. துன்பம், இன்னாமை], 'narrowness, straitened circumstances, affliction,' Ch. LXIII. இடுக்கணழியாமை 'not despairing in adversity,' 621, 624, 625, 654, 788, 1030.

இடும்பை 'pain, evil,' 138, 508, 622, 623, 627, 628, 1045, 1056, 1060, 1063, 1295. It is used for இடுக்கண். இடும்பை is rather an effect of இடுக்கண். Nâl. 107.

இடை (seems another form of இடம்), 'position, middle,' 663, 1108. **1.** இடைமுரிந்து, 899, 'fall from high estate,' explained by 473, இடைக்கண்முரி. **2.** இடையறு 'fail,' 369. இடையூறு 'hindrance' (உறு), 676. [Râm. I. XXIII. 5. . . . இடை இங்குளதிடையூறெனநடவான் 'He stopped, saying there is here in the way a *hindrance* (a bad omen).'] **3.** இடைதெரி 'discern the fitting place and time,' 712. **4.** Sign of 7th case (§ 251), 37, 338, 1122, 2239. ஆயிடை 'because' = ஆகியவிடத்தில், 1179.

இட்டு 'smallness,' 478. இட்டிது 'small, narrow.'

இணர் 'a cluster,' 308, 360.

இணை 'a pair.'

இந்திரன் [S.] 'Indra,' 25.

இமை (§ 64), 'wink, close the eyes,' 1129, 775, 1126. இமையார் (§ 121), 'the heavenly ones, who do not close their eyes,' 906; Nâl. 146, 'twinkle, glisten,' 361. [குருமணி யிமைக்குநீள்கூலம் 'The long shore where the bright pearls *twinkle.*' இழைவிளக்கு நின்றிமைப்பின் 'Though jewels *sparkle* like lamps standing there.']

இம்மை. See இ and மை.

இயக்கம் 'motion,' 1020. (✓ இய.)

இயல் (n.). 1. 'Nature.' 'One whose nature is —,' 1098; 'natural course,' 572. பெண்ணியலார் 'women,' 1311. பிறனியலாள் 'she who belongs to another,' 147. அறனியலான் 'one who has made virtue his very own,' 147. 2. (56, III.), 'proceed, be, come about in a natural way.' இயல்பால (வி. தொ.), 'things which will become one's own,' 342. இயன்றது 'that which has proceeded naturally,' 35. இயல்வது 'what naturally is so,' 734. இயன்றன 'they naturally are,' 1106. இயற்று (v. caus. § 62), 'make *or* bring about' (§ 161). இயற்றியான் 'the Creator,' 1062. இயற்றியார் 'those who have made, acquired,' 760. இயற்றல் 'acquisition.' இயல்பு (strengthened form of இயல்), 'nature,' 41, 47, 161, 333, 344, 382, 452, 545, 628, 903, 951, 1006. இயற்கை 'natural course,' 370, 374, 637. 3. 'A section.'

இயை [Comp. S. *yā*] (§ 57), combine, 'join, harmonize.' [Comp. இசை, எய்து.] இயைந்து 'having been joined with, possessed of,' 576. இயைந்த composed of,' 576; 'joined (with),' 73, 489, 1323. இயையின் 'if (it) attach itself,' 522. இயையாக்கடை 'when (it) cannot be,' 230. இயைபு 'harmony,' 573.

இர (§ 66), 'beg, excite, compassion.' [Used with கர.] இரந்து 'having begged,' 780, 1059, 1063. இரந்தும் 'though they beg,' 1062. இரவார் 'they beg not,' 1035. இரப்பார் 'suppliants,' 1035, 1058, 232, 1060, 1067. இரபபவா், 1055, 1070, Nâl. 307. (யா)னிரப்ப 'that I may ask,' 1212, 1329. இரக்கப்படுதல் 'the being asked from,' 224. இரந்தவர், 224. இரத்தல் 'begging,' 229, 1052, 1054. இரக்க ! 'beg thou,' 1051. இரத்தக்கார் 'people from whom it is meet to ask,' 1051. இரந்தவை 'what he has asked,' 1052. இரப்பு = இரவு, 1053. இரவாமை 'refraining from mendicancy,' 1061. இரப்பினும் 'though you beg,' 1066. இரப்பின் 'if you beg,' 1067. இரவன்மின் 'beg not,' 1067. இரப்பன்=(இரப்பேன்) 'I pray,' 1067. இர-வு (§ 190, *a*), 'begging,' 552. Ch. CVI., 'mendicancy,' 1064, 1066, 1069, 1280. இரவச்சம், Ch. CVII., 'the dread of mendicancy,' Nâl. 301. இரங்கு (§ 62), 'feel sorrow, compassion.' இரங்கிவிடும் 'will be sorry for,' 535. இரங்குவ 'which (you) will be sorry for,' 655. இரங்கல், Ch. CXXIII. 'heaviness at eventide.' படர்மெலிந்திரங்கல், Ch. CXVII. 'wasting and weeping.'

இரு. 1. adj. form of இரண்டு 'two.' (§ 172.) 5, 374, 737, 620, 1091, 1196. இரண்டு 'two,' 19, 392, 393, 402, 581, 875, 760, 662, 992, 1022, 1247. இருமை 'both states *or* worlds—this and the next,' 23. இருவர் 'two persons,' 1108. Another form of இரு is ஈர், not found in Kurraḷ. 2. adj. 'great, strong,' 990, 999 (in reference to earth). 3. (v.) 'be, remain, sit.' (§ 60.) [S. *as*, in meaning.] It occurs as auxiliary (§ 79), as well as in its primary meaning. இருக்க, 403. இருப்ப, 67, 100. இருக்கை, 789. இராஅ=இருந்கு, 1301. இருந்து, 81, 530, 1160, 1243, 1296, 1320, 867; with இல், a sign of 5th case, 1107. இருந்தது, 'it was,' 1296. இருந்தான், 638. இருந்தேம், 1312. இருந்த, 340. இருந்தும் 'though (they) are,' 973. இருப்பர் 'they will be,' 485, 804. இருப்பான், 86, 1040. இருப்பின், 1039. இரீஇ =இருத்தி, from இருத்து (§ 62, causal. § 161), 'place, put, cause to be.'

இருள் 'darkness.' [√ இர் + a pluralising particle, the Telugu *lu*. Comp. பொருள், அருள், and many others.] 5, 121, 243, 352, 675, 753, 999, 1186. இருட்டு, adj. 'dark,' 913. இரும்பு 'iron,' Nâl. 122.

இரா [from S. *râtri*], 'night,' 1168, 1169, 1329.

இரை 'food, fodder,' 946. பேரிரையான் 'a glutton.'

இலக்கம் 'target, mark,' 627. [S. *laksha*.]

இலங்கு (§ 64), 'shine.' [S. *laksh*.] இலங்குநூல் (வி. தொ.) 'resplendent science,' 410. இலங்கிழாய்! 'thou with glistening jewels!' 1262. [See இழை.]

இல். I. 'In,' sign of 7th case, or local ablative, 1322, 1327, 1328.

II. (n.) 'a house; housewife;' (in comp.), 'family or clan'; as ஆகுபெயர் for இல்லறம் (in some compounds). **1.** = மனை 'house,' 84 (7th case), Nâl. 383. இல்லம் = இல், Nâl. 361. அட்டில் 'cook-house,' Nâl. 363. **2.** Meton. = மனைவி 'housewife,' 59, 144, Nâl. 83. **3.** Derivatives. இல்-லவள், 53 (bis). இல்லவாள், 52, 903, 905, 906, 1039, Nâl. 1, 86, 383. [= மனையாள், பொருளாள், 141.] **4.** Compounds :—இல்-லறம் 'virtue in domestic life.' This is the title of the first portion of the குறள், Ch. v.-XXIV. இல்-லாண்மை 'family management,' 1026 [see ஆள்]. இல்-லிறப்பான் (= இல்லாளிடத்து வரம்புகடந்து செல்லுவோன்) 'he who by transgression draws near to (his neighbour's) wife,' 145, 146 (§ 88 = இறப்பவன்). இல்பிறந்தார், 951 [= குடி, 952; குலம் 956], 'those born of noble family, the scions of a noble house,' 1044. இல்-வாழ்க்கை 'the life of domestic virtue,' Ch. v. 45-49. இல்-வாழ்வான் (= இல்லறத்தோடுகூடி வாழ்பவன்) 'the man who lives a life of domestic virtue,' 41, 42, 147. இல்-வாழ்வதெல்லாம் 'the whole of domestic life,' 81. பிறனில்-விழையாமை, Ch. xv. 'The not desiring another's wife.'

III. 'Not.' This root, sig. 'in,' curiously expresses non-existence (§ 44. Comp. அல்). [Seems to govern an accusative in some places; but perhaps it is ஏ emphatic changed to ஐ, 448.] **1.** இல். The root is used for '(it, they, there) is (are) not,' = இல்லை, 44, 233, 52, 276, 909, 910, 583, 1063, 1065, 577, 621, 839, 363, 170, 1243, 222, 141, 142, 287, 285, 462, 538, 850, 460, 244, 934, 770, 302, 1005, 1001. Forms a neg. யாங்கண்டதில் 'we have not seen,' 1071, 1066, 446. **2.** இல்லை is probably a corruption, இல் + ஏ emphatic, 363, 170, 570, 456, 469, 478, 534, 533, 230, 231, 336, 243, 245, 252, 945, 32, 537, 751, 59, 247, 135, 791, 162, 842, 976, 87, 110, 710, 1028, 1036, 449, 951, 300, 296, 122, 1123, 1131, 1321. அறிவதில்லை 'we know not,' 61. **3.** இல் is used by வினைத்தொகை [Intro. p. xvii. § 4, *b*.] for இல்லாத, 770, 'when (or where) it is not,' 9, 400, 912, 1068, 853, 174, 194, 196. **4.** As conjugated appellative. (1) இலன் (1st pers. sing.), 'I am destitute,' 223 [வறியேன், நான் தரித்திரன்], 205; (2) இலம் (1st pers. plur.), 'we are destitute,' 174, 1040 [வறியேம், நாந் தரித்திரர்]; (3) 3rd pers. m. f. n. sing. plur. இல்லான், இலான், 135, 847, 4, 617, 625, 842, 1000, 407. இலன், 34, 205, 341, 566, 628, 629, 862-8, 193. இலாள் 'she who is without —,' 56, 1194, 499, 506, 1325, 270, 906, 1129, 1130. இலர், 577, 365, 114, 1242, 954, 430, 1072, 778, 499; opposed to உடையர்.

இலார், 170, 449, 430, 80, 800, 811, 812, 236, 72, 1055, 843, 449, 427, 572, generally with a noun; sometimes absolutely= *destitute*; sometimes as a predicate. இல்லார், 431, 591, 378, 600, 1050, 1056, 1005, 750, 752, 730, 368, 247, 395, 1020. இலோர், 59. இலவர், இல்லவர் 577, 79, 917. இலது, இல்லது 'that which is not, *or* without'; sometimes =இல்லை, 750, 53, 77, 119, 586, 587, 750, 425, 735, 871. இனறு [Comp. இன்று], 354, 740, 966, 1252, 875, 83, 340, 955, 904, 1090. இன்றேல் 'if — is wanting,' 575, 1014, 1144, 996, 556, 573. இல, இல்ல '(they) are not.' Ch. xx. பயனில 'things without profit,' 191–197, 640, 4, 9, 39, 1100. நயமில 'things not right,' 998, 956, 91. (4) Compounded:—இல்லாயின் 'if (it) is not,' 52, 1058, 49, 1306, 769. இலாளன் (see ஆள்). இல்லல்ல 'are not things which have no real existence,' 115. இல்லாகி 'having come to nought,' 479. இல்லெனினும் 'though it were non-existent,' 222, 768. இல்லாகியார் 'those who came to nought,' 935. இல்லாகும் 'it will not exist,' 368. இலானும் 'though there be none,' 448. செய்தலிலர் 'are men who (will) not do,' 954 (=செய்யார்). காதலவரிலர் (for அவர் காதலிலர்), 1242. கற்றிலன்=கல்லாதவன், 414. 5. With double neg.: இல்லாது, இல்லாதியங்கு 'as it exists not to —,' 247. இ(ல்)லாத, 198, 448, 'who suffer lack of' (with 2nd case), 412, 573, 574, 740, 945, 161, 1030. இ(ல்)லா, 239, 853, 200, 869, 1053, 1059, 594, 919, 610, 731, 1064, 78, 1308. இ(ல்)லாதான், 7, 523, 614, 1006. இல்லாதாள் 'she who is without —,' 40[illegible]. இல்லாதவர், இலாதவர், 997, 35[illegible], 890, 598, 640. இலாதார், 140. 6. இன்றி [as though from இன்று, இன்றினேன் (§ 64). Comp. அன்றி], 'without,' 523, 1253, 112, 166, 754, 1069, 789, 1042, 401, 529, 947. இன்று [வினையெச்சம், as from இன்றேன்] = இல்லாமல் 'without,' 20, 184, 764. இன்றியமையா 'which without (it) (otherwise) is not gained,' 961; 'essentially necessary,' 682. 7. இன்மை [இல்+மை. Comp. அன்மை]. (1) In comp. with a noun= *-lessness*, 577, 841, 119, 903, 616, 618, 557, 344, 979, 851, 320, 364, 513, 958, 371, 1209, 1276, 738, 833, 1019. மடியின்மை, Ch. LXI. 'activity.' (2) Absolutely, 'destitution,' 841, 1041, 1042, 1044, 616, 558, 1063, 988, 89 (opp. to உடைமை), 153, 503; B. '*egestas.*'

இவ-க்காண் 'lo, here!' 1185. [Comp. உவ, இ.]

இவர்தரு 'rise, climb.' [இவர் (§ 57) with தரு, q.v.] இவர்தந்து = இவர்ந்து 'having climbed.'

இவறு (§ 64), 'covet, lust after.' இவறல், 432. இவறியான் (§ 87), 437, 935. இவறும் (§ 74), 1002. இவறி, 1003. இவறன்மை 'covetousness.' [இவறல்+மை, § 74.]

இழ (§ 66), 'lose,' opp. பெறு. இழந்தவன், 788 (§). இழுக்குஞ்சூதர், 932, 228, 463 (§ 74). இழத்தொறூஉம், 940. [v. தொறும்]. இழந்து, 1144. இழவூழ் 'destiny entailing loss,' 372. இழந்தேம், 593. இழப்பர், 494, 921. இழக்கும் (=இழப்பான்), 554. இழப்பினும், 659, 812. இழத்தும் 'we shall lose,' 1250. [Old form=இழப்போம்.]

இழி (§ 57), 'slip, fall down, become vile.' இழிந்த, 964, 133; B. '*vilis.*' இழிவு 'diminution,' 946.

இழு-க்கு (§ 62), 'slip.' [Comp. இழி.] இழுக்கல் 'slipperiness,' 415. இழுக்கார், 952. இழுக்

கியான், 535. இழுக்காமை, 536. இழுக்கு 'a slip,' 893, 127, 164, 467, 716, 911. இழுக்கா(து), 35, 48, 384. இழுக்கம் 'ignominy,' 133, 808, 137, 136.

இழை (§ 64), 'determine, do carefully.' இழைத்துணர்ந்து 'with careful investigation,' 417. இறைத்திருந்தேண்ணி, 530. இழைத்ததிகவாமை 'what was resolved on,' 779, Nâl. 6. [இழைத்தநாள் எல்லை இகவா 'the days allotted to man pass not their bounds.' Comment. தமக்குவரைந்த. இழைத்ததிகவாமை 'not transgressing their fixed resolve.' Comment. சொல்லியசபதம். அமரர்களுக்கி டரிழைக்கு மசுரர் 'the Asuras who caused affliction to the immortals,' Râm. I. vi. 64.] n. 'a jewel'; by meton. 'a lady,' Nâl. 361. இழாய! (voc. case), 1262. இழை, 1102, 1110, 1114, 1124, 1329, with different epithet in each: அணி, ஆய், சே, ஒளி, மாண் இலங்கு. இழையார் 'those adorned with jewels,' 919. (§ 57), 'grow soft.' [Comp. இள.] இழைந்து, 1177.

இளி 'disgrace.' [Comp. இழி; opp. ஒளி.] இளி, 971, 970. இளிவந்த, 654, (வரு) 1044, 1066. இளித்தக்க 'disgraceful,' 1288. இளிவு, 1298, 988, 464.

இளை 'young.' [Comp. இழை, இள.] இளையர், 698. இளைது, 879. இளைமை, Nâl. (இளமை) 11, 17, 102. இளையம் (§ 184; Intro. xxiii.), 'we are young,' Nâl. 19.

இற (§ 66), 'pass away.' [Comp. இக.] இறந்து, 586. ('=புகுந்து') 'having passed over.' '=ஒழிந்து,' 971. '=கடந்து,' 283, 476, 531, 1138, 432, 1254. '=மிகுந்த' 'beyond bounds,' 900. இறவா நின்ற 'slipping off,' 1157. இறப்பு 'excess,' 977; 'injury,' 152, Nâl. 99, 38. செய்திறந்த, 1275. இறந்தார் 'those who have passed away,' 22, 42 இறந்தார் 'transgressors,' 159; 310, both meanings. இல்லிறப்பான் 'he who invades the sanctity of his neighbour's house,' 145, 146; B. '*Exorbitare, limites praeterire.*'

இறு (§ 68), 'break (int.),' 475. இறுவரை 'the time of ruin,' 488. இறுதி, 'முடிவு,' 476, 690.

இறல், 'அழிவு,' 180. [இறு.] இறன்முறையான் 'allied to ruin, ruinous,' 885.

இறைஞ்சு (§ 62), 'குனி.' இறைஞ்சினள் 'she hung down her head.'

இறை (§ 64), 'irrigate, draw water,' 1161.

இறை. **1.** 'அரசன்,' 432, 436, 547, 564, 778. **2.** 'நீதி,' 541. **3.** 'A joint,' 1157. **4.** 'Revenue,' 733. **5.** 'வருத்தம்,' 847. **6.** 'A god,' 388. இறைவன், 5, 10, 690, 733. இறைமாட்சி, Ch. xxxix.

இன். **1.** Sign of case and சாரியை or euphonic insertion. **2.** In comp. and deriv. from இல் as இன்மை. **3.** 'Pleasant, sweet,' 91–99, 224, 327, 387, 525, 911, 953. Chiefly in comp. with சொல் and உயிர். Used as வினைக்குறிப்பு (§ 184), Nâl. 146. இனிது 'it is sweet,' 93, 64, 66, 68, 181, 230, 648, 772, 839, 865, 866, 811, 1103, 1108, 1145, 1176, 1196, 1201, 1202, 1215, 1309, 1326. இனியது 'that which is sweet,' 1065. இனிய, 96, 100, 824, 987, 1199. இனியவைகூறல் 'kindly speech,' Ch. x. இனியார் 'dear ones,' 1158, Nâl. 365. இன்னு 'unpleasant,' (§ 121), 35, 109, 159, 160, 243, 308, 311, 312, 314, 316, 318, 319, 564, 565, 824, 852, 857, 881, 894, 987, 1288. இன்னுமை 'evil,' 318, 630. இன்னுது, 224, 408, 558, 819, 923, 995, 1158, 1196. இன்னுதது, 230, 1041. இன்னுத, 100, 313, 860, 881. இன்

பம் 'pleasure,' 39, 65, 98, 156, 228, 173, 352, 369, 501, 615, 628, 629, 630, 669, 738, 754, 854, 869, 946, 1052, 1166, 1330. இன்பு, 75, 94, 399. இன்கண், 1152. 4. 'Such.' [See இ and இனை. Comp. அன், இனை *talis, tantus.*] இன்னம் 'we are such,' 790. இன்னன் 'he is such,' 453.

இனம் 'kindred, affinity, company.' (இன்) Nâl. 171–180, 146, 306, 451–59, 460, 462, 568, 822, 884. சிற்றினஞ்சேராமை 'not joining with low persons,' Ch. XLVI. இனன், 793=இனம் 'one who is allied,' 868, 1158. இனத்தன் 'one who is allied,' 446.

இனை [comp. அனை, எனை, ஏனை]. இனையர் 'they are such, *tanti,*' 790. இனைத்துணைத்து 'it is of this value, measure,' 87.

இன்னும் 'yet, still,' 1250. [இ.]

இனி 'now, hereafter' [இ], 1083, 1294, Nâl. 29.

இன்று 'to-day' [comp. அன்று, என்று], 336, 1048, 1133, 1262, Nâl. 36.

ஈ

ஈண்டு 'here, in this world *or* birth,' 18, 23, 213, 265, 356, 363, 369. [Comp. ஆண்டு, யாண்டு strengthened dem. from இ.]

ஈண்டு (§ 62), int., ஈட்டு, (§ 160), tr., 'collect, accumulate.' ஈண்டிய, 417. ஈட்டிய, 1009. ஈட்டல் 'accumulation,' 385. ஈட்டம் 'wealth,' 1003, Nâl. 109.

ஈ (§ 57), 'give.' [Syn. கொடு, தரு.] ஈதல் 'giving,' 92, 222, 223, 230, 231, 842, 1006, 1054. ஈயப்படும் '(it) should be given.' ஈத்து (for ஈந்து by வலித்தல்), 228, 387, 800. ஈந்தது 'it has given,' 1142. ஈவது 'that which will give,' 221. ஈயும் 'that will give,' 1061. ஈவார் 'givers,' 232, 1057–59. ஈவர் 'they will give,' 1035. ஈக! 'let him give,' 477, 1268. ஈயாது 'not giving,' 1002. ஈகலான் 'one who gives not,' (அல்), 863. ஈகை 'a gift, giving,' Ch. XXIII., 221, 382, 953.

ஈரம். 1. 'Moisture,' 1077, 1058. 2. Hence=அன்பு 'benevolence, love,' 91.

ஈர் (§ 57), 'saw asunder,' 334. [இரு, ஈர் *two.*]

ஈர். See இரு.

ஈனு (§ 56, III.), 'yean.' [Comp. ஈ.] ஈன் (வே. தொ.), 757. ஈனும் '(it) will produce,' 31, 74, 180, 754; 'which will produce,' 311, 361. ஈன்ற 'which brought forth,' 69, 1047. ஈன்று 'having produced,' 97. ஈன்றல், 99. ஈன்பது, 165. ஈன்றாள் 'she who bare, a mother,' 656, 923.

உ

உ, a dem. letter. See உம்மை, உப்பக்கம், உவக்காண்.

உகு (§ 56, II.), 'spill, drip away.' உக்க 'spilt,' 720, 1270. உகாமை 'secresy, letting nothing ooze out,' 585.

உஞற்று (§ 62), 'use effort.' உஞற்றுபவர் 'those who make strenuous efforts,' 620, 1024; n. 'effort,' 604, 607. உஞற்றிலவர், reverse of the above.

உடலு (§ 56, III.), 'be fierce,' 765. உடற்று (§ 62), 'plague.' உடற்றுபவர் 'those who are angry *or* worry about,' 818. உடற்றும் 'will torment,' 13.

உடல் 'body,' 65, 253. (உட, உடன.)

உடம்பு (உடல்+பு), 'body' [யாக்கை], 80, 330, 338, 340, 345, 627, 943, 1029, 1122, 1132, 1163, Nâl. 37–40, 102.

உடன் 'together with, at once.' [உட; comp. தொடு.] A sign of 3rd case=ஓடு, ஒடு, (§ 239), 309, 589, 632, 890. உடம்பாடு (=உடன்பாடு), 'agreement' [படு].

உடு (§ 64), 'put on clothes.' உடுப்பது 'what one puts on, clothes,' 166, 1079. உடை 'garments,' 939, 1012. உடுக்கை 'dress,' 788.

உடை. **1.** See உடு. **2.** (§ 64), 'break' [comp. இடி, அடி]; (§ 57), 'be broken,' 473. [உடைத்தம்வலி: three interpretations are possible: உடை strengthens தம்='own'; or as தலைவனுதலையுடைய = 'having prevailing power'; or வி. தொ. of உடை (§ 57), 'which will be broken' = 'weak, fragile.' These are Graul's, the Com. and Beschi's respectively. Comp. Nâl. 368, and render 'their strength of possessions, their *resources*.'] உடைக்கும் 'which will break,' 1077, 1251, 1258, 1324. உடைந்தது 'has been broken,' 1088, 1270. **3.** 'Possession'; con. with உள் and ஒடு [a வினைக்குறிப்பு, § 184]. Its opposite is இல். It simply connects two nouns: 389, 415, 907, 1010, 1034. உடையேன் 'I (am) a possessor of,' 1133. உடையான், உடையன் 'he who is possessed,' 390, 486, 381. உடையார் abs. for 'possessors of wealth,' 395, 718; with nouns, 593, 594, 513, 519, 112, 622, 219, 502, 684, 165, 167, 526, 866, 577, 910, 970, 1153, 72, 994, 996, 404, 441, 413, 415, 430, 636, 606, 534, 135, 463, 427, 223, 262. உடையர், 591, 1072, 900, 393, 430, 95, 458. உடையவர், 139, 179, 285, 159, 975; opposed to இல்லாதவர். உடையாளர்=உடையார் [comp. ஆள்]. உடையாள், உடையள், 51, 1089. உடையது, 384, 591, 742, 746, 1021, 'that which (one) possesses.' உடைத்து 'it is possessed of' [it is often redundant and sometimes='it is'; always a predicate], 45, 48, 126, 112, 220, 221, 277, 336, 353, 398, 578, 565, 611, 667, 624, 770, 746, 907, 925, 1010, 1018, 1053, 1057, 1082, 1085, 1173, 1152, 1275, 1276, 1280, 1325.

உடைய (it often connects two nouns, and makes a kind of possessive case), 'things possessed of' [opp. to இல்], 41, 200, 975, 1299, 1300. உடையம் 'we possess,' 844. (Intro. xxiii.) உடையேம், 1250. உடைமை 'possession of property'; in comp. it is almost redundant; opp. இன்மை; 89, 228, 344, 558, 592, 641, 838. அடக்கமுடைமை, Ch. XIII. அருளுடைமை, Ch. XXV. அறிவுடைமை, Ch. XLIII., 68. அன்புடைமை, Ch. VIII. 681, 992. ஆர்வமுடைமை, 74. ஆள்வினையுடைமை, Ch. LXII. உள்ளமுடைமை, 592. ஊக்கமுடைமை, Ch. LX. ஒழுக்கமுடைமை, Ch. XIV., 133. துணிவுடைமை, 688, 383. நாணுடைமை, Ch. CII. 1012, 960. நிறையுடைமை, 154. பண்புடைமை, Ch. C., 991. பொருளுடைமை, 592. பொறையுடைமை, Ch. XVI., 154.

உட்கு (§ 62), 'stand in awe of, reverence, feel modest shame.' உட்கப்படாஅர், 921. உட்கும், 1088, Nâl. 102, 384.

உணக்கு 'dry'; உணங்கு 'grow dry, languish.' உணக்கின், 1037. உணங்க், 1310.

உணர் (§ 57), 'feel, understand, perceive, conceive.' [Comp. உள்.] மெய்யுணர்தல், Ch. XXXVI. உணரும் 'conceive of,' 331, 351. உணர்ந்தவை 'what (you) have felt,' 316. உணரா, 420, 705, 1172. உணராமை, 589 (உணராமல்). உணரின், 357. உணர்ந்தும், 417, 834. உணர்வின், 420. உணர்ந்த, 1277 = உணர்ந்தன. உணர்ந்து, 417, 516, 712, 1046, 359. உணர்க், 805. உணர, 650. உணரப்படும், 575, 826, 1096. உணர்வான், 702, 703, 708, 709, 716, 257, 334. உணர்வது, 718. உணர்தல் 'reconciliation,' 1109. உணராய், 1246. உணர்ச்சி 'perception,' 976, 453, 785. உணர்வு 'feeling,' 354, 420. உணர்த்து (§§ 62, 160), 'cause to understand, explain away misunderstandings.' உணர்த்துங்காதலர், 1246. உணர்த்தாமை, 1304. உணர்த்தினும், 1319.

உண் 'eat' (உள்) [ஊண்], used as = தின், மிசை. உண், 1091, 1172, 1212, 1174, 1113 [with கண். வி. தொ. 'the eye that eats, *absorbs* the pigment' = 'black'; but comp. 1084]. உண்பார், 926, 251, 946. உண்பவர், 926. உண்ணும், 527, 1084, 1221, 326. உண்டு 'having eaten,' 580, 1033, 1101, 322. உண்டது, 1326, 930. உண்டீர், Nâl. 18. உண்ணற்க, 922. உணில், 922, 942. உண்ணின், 945, 947. உண்க, 922, 943, Nâl. 2. கள்ளுண்ணாமை, Ch. xciii., 255, 257, 259. உண்ணாது, 160. உண்ணு, 930. உணஞர், 258, 1001, Nâl. 9. உண்டார், 1090, 253, Nâl. 1. உண்டற்று, 1107 (see அற்று). உணல், 229, 1326, 1065. உண்டல், 82, 1128, 1145. உண்ண, 255. உண்பது, 166, 1079. உண்டி 'food,' 945, Nâl. 1. உணவு, 412, 413. ஊண். ஊண்மாலையவர் 'food' (Intro. xxiii.), 1035, 44, 1012, 227, 939. உணி. ஊருணி, 215. ஊட்டு (§ 62), 'feed.' ஊட்டா, 378, Nâl. 1. (§ 160.)

உண்மை. See உள்.

உதவு (§ 62), 'help.' (பெ. எச.) உதவும், 746. உதவி 'assistance,' 70, 101, 103, 105. உப்பக்கம், 620 (உ), 'on that side, behind. [Comp. அ, இ, எ.] உவக்காண், 1185 (உ), 'there, behold.' (See இவக்காண்).

உப்பு 'salt, flavour, zest,' 802, 1050, 1302, 1328. [Comp. உவரி.]

உம். **1.** 'And, also,' 12, 15. **2.** 'Even,' 17, 18, 987, 995, 1069. **3.** In summing up, 581, 19. **4.** Converts inter. into universal, 20, 991. (§ 126.) **5.** In verbal forms = 'although,' 989. **6.** Forms 3rd pers. plur. fut. and fut. rel. part., 17, as என்னும, *passim*.

உயர் (§ 57), 'be high' [உய்]. வானுயர் தோற்றம (வி. தொ.), 272. உயர்ந்து, 957. உயர்ந்த, 233, 246. உயர்வு 'elevation, dignity,' 135, 595, 596, 743, 963.

உய் (§ 57), 'go off, avoid, escape, survive.' உயல், 1212, 40, 437, 1174. உயவர் 'may escape,' 207. உய்யார் 'they cannot escape,' 896, 900. உய்யா 'inevitable,' 313. உய்வு 'escape,' 896, 110, 1174.

உய் (§ 64), 'send off, *or* away; destroy, preserve.' உய்க்கும், 121, 1134, 943. உய்ப்பது, 422. உய்த்தல், 1287. உய்த்து, 1076, 376, 787, 168, 121, Nâl. 101. உயக்கிற் (பின்), 440. உய்யாது, 996.

உயிர் 'life, breath, soul' [உய் = emit], 78, 131, 183, 214, 244, 258, 259, 268, 318, 326, 327, 330, 334, 338, 340, 476, 501, 557, 778, 848, 940, 945, 969, 1017, 1020, 1062, 1070, 1106, 1122, 1124, 1132, 1163, 1213, 1230, 1298; 'a living being,' 30, 31, 122, 231, 260, 261, 361, 322, 392, 851, 972, 1012, 1013. ஆருயிர் 'dear life,' 73, 1141. இன்னுயிர் 'sweet life,' 327, 1209. மன்னுயிர் 'life, *or* living being that abides,' 68, 244, 268, 318, 457. மன்னுமுயிர், 190, 1168. உயிர்நிலை 'seat of life, body,' 80, 255, 290. வேண்டா வுயிரார் 'heroes who make light of their lives,' 777.

உயிர் (§ 64), 'smell, breathe.' உயிர்த்து 'having inhaled, so smelt,' 1101. உயிர்ப்ப 'when it will breathe; at the breath of its nostrils,' 763; 'for the purpose of breathing,' 880.

உரம், உரன் 'strength,' 24, 600, 888, 1263. [Comp. S. *uru*, *uras*.] உரவோர் 'the brave,' 136, 597.

உரை (§ 64), 'speak out, declare.' Imp. 1151. Noun, 'a word,' 581, 193. உரைத்து, 1237. உரைத்தும், 834. உரைக்கும் 'which (he) will utter,' 193, 564, 912, 1156; '(it) will say,' 709, 743, 1235. உரைப்பாய், 1200. உரைப்பான், ர், 189, 232, 681–9. உரைப்பது, 1184. உரைப்பவை, 232. உரையாதார், 650. உரைகோ 'shall I tell?' 1181. உரையாமை, 223. உரைக்கல் 'speaking,' 1076, 1271. காதற்சிறப்புரைத்தல், Ch. CXIII., 1162. நாணுத்துறவுரைத்தல், Ch. CXIV. நலம்புனைந்துரைத்தல், Ch. CXII.

உரி. உரிமை 'fitness,' 518, 578. உரியன் 'one fit for, master of anything,' 72, 149, 518, 1080. உரியாள் 'she who belongs to,' 149.

உரு 'form, type,' 261. [S. *rûpa*. Comp. எழில், உருபம், உருபு, உருவு, உரு.] உருவு 'form, shape, mien, beauty,' 585, 667, 684, Nâl. 101. உருவம், 273.

உருகு (§ 62), 'melt,' 1069. உள்ளமுருகும் 'the heart will melt.'

உருளு (§ 66, III.). உருள்பெருந்தேர் 'the huge rolling chariot' [வி. தொ.], 667, 933, 'gain got by the rolling dice.'

உல (§ 66), *or* உலரு (§ 57), 'be destroyed, fail, be dried up.' [S. ग्ल.] நீருலந்தகண் 'an eye that can weep no more,' 1174. (உலர்ந்த). (The spelling is doubtful.)

உலகம் [S. *lôka*]. [Comp. ஞாலம், வையம், மை.] **1.** 'The world,' 11, 13, 374, 996. **2.** 'People,' 117. **3.** 'A world,' 247, 346. **4.** 'The wise' (?), 280, 140, 426, 425.

உலகு. **1.** 'This world, course of things, universe,' 1, 20, 23, 27, 211, 336, 387, 389, 520, 542, 544, 571, 572, 578, 612, 874, 1062. **2.** 'A world,' 58, 234, 290, 1103. **3.** 'The people of the world,' 215, 256, 399, 470, 670, 809, 841, 994, 970, 1015, 1025. உலகத்தார், 1032, 850, 294. உலகத்து 'in *or* of the world,' 213, 233, 533, 598, 1198. மேலுலகம் 'the higher world,' 222. இன்னுவுலகம் 'the world of woe,' 243.

உலைவு 'irresolution, weakness,' 620, 883, 762. [Comp. அலை.]

உல்கு 'tax,' 756.

உவ (§ 66), 'rejoice.' [மகிழ்.] உவந்து 'joyously,' 842, 1061, 1130. உவப்ப 'so as to gladden,' 394. உவப்பினும் 'whether it rejoices,' 707. உவப்பது, 1057. உவக்கும், 69, 228. உவந்தார் (opp. ஒன்னார்), 264. உவகை, 304, 432, 531. ஊடலுவகை, Ch. CXXXIII.

உவமை [S.], 'comparison,' 7.

உவரி 'the (salt) sea,' 763. [Comp. உப்பு.]

உழ (§ 66); 'suffer.' It is used absolutely and with காமம், அல்லல் and பைதல் [comp. உணர]. உழக்கும், 1175, 1135, 1229. உழப்பது, 787, 1172. உழப்பா, 936. உழந்து, 1131, 1177, 1137. உழந்தும் 'though they suffer,' 1031. உழப்பிக்கும், 938 (§ 160).

உழு 'plough' (§ 60). உழாஅர்

'they plough not,' 14. உழவர் 'ploughers,' 14, 872. உழவார், 1032. உழவினார், 1036. உழவு 'ploughing, agriculture, Ch. CIV. 1031. உழுது, 1033.

உழை. 1. Sign of 7th case = இடத்து; qy. a form of உள், 594, 1249. 2. 'Place': உழைப்பிரிந்து, 530. உழையிருந்தான், 638. உழைச்செல்வான், 950.

உழி. 1. Sign of 7th case. (§ 251.) தீயுழி, 168. [Comp. உள், உழை.] 2. இடம், 415. வைப்புழி 'storehouse,' 226.

உள். [Comp. உடன், உண், உணர், உழை, உழி, உளி.] 1. Sign of case, 'within,' 13, 995, 890, 98, 1049, 50, 106, 126, 469, 718, 61, 1165, 495, 186, 715, 828, 703, 705, 1130, 153, 241; equal to gen. of thing distrib., 891, 411, 47, 89, 438, 444, with எல்லாம, making super.; see எல்லாம, 203, 1324, 715. கண்ணுள்ளில் 'from the inner part of (my) eye,' 1126. 2. Adverb, 129. உள்ளாறும 'will heal within, thoroughly,' 487, 927, 421. உள்ளழிக்கல், 677. 3. Noun, உள்ளுள், 1057. உளி (sign of 7th case), 545. 4. As a verb. root it is a குறிப்புவினை (§ 184). உள்வழி, 1170. உள்ளார், 1127. உளாள், 617. உளேன், 1167, 1206, 1263. உளேம், 1204. உண்பர், 1311. உள 'are, exist, have place,' 995, 574, 54, 380, 223, 241, 479, 483, 480, 521, 527, 636, 781, 1099, 1101. உளன், உளர் 'persons who are,' 895, 406, 336, 880, 294, 25, 1204, 1178. உ(ள்)ளது (opp. இல்லது), 'it exists, what exists, what is true, real,' with ஆம், 889, 572, 53, 235, 1274, 982, 255, 641, 357, 1069, 1091. உண்டு, 1098, 1281, 571, 190, 128, 996, 974, 89, 71, 315, 1245, 1260, 1164, 1307, 1323, 1271, 1273, 1274, 469, 707, 757, 796, 1117, 1154, 1213. உண்டாம், 896, 110, 932, 1075, 1214. உண்டாயினும், 1005. உள்ள 'which is within, internal,' 971, 600. உண்டாக 'that (it) may be,' 342; '*in tempore, festinanter, et in ipsa adolescentia*' (B.), 988, 54, 758. உண்டேல், 'if (it) exists,' 368, 1075, 1151. உண்மை 'the fact of the existence of (anything),' 1055, 571, 572, 1153. [The 7th case is made into an abstr. noun.] உண்மையறிவு 'one's real wisdom,' 373; 'reality, real method,' 1212. In comp. உட்பகை, Ch. LXXXIX., 883, 885, 887, 888, 889, 884, 735. உட்கொட்டம், 119. உள்ளுநர், 216. உண்ணடுங்கல், 680. உள்ளம் 'the mind,' 294, 592, 595, 598, 1207, 677, 357, 622, 798, 799, 1263, 438, 1170, 282, 309, 1057, 1130, 971, 1324, 1270, 1069. உள்ளத்தார், 1249. உள்ளு (§ 62), 'think, call to mind, remember,' '*recordari.*' [Comp. உணர்.] உள்ளுவது, 596. உள்ளல், 596, 282, 1318, 1243. உள்ளான், 930. உள்ள 'while (I) think of,' 1206, 357, 540, 622, 665, 109, 394, 1069, 1281. உள்ளினேன் 'I remembered,' 1316. உள்ளினும், 1207, 1201, 799. உள்ளான், 309. உள்ளுக, 539. உள்ளற்க, 798. உள்ளியது, 540. உள்ளி, 1264, 1230, 1317, 1320, 1249, 1231, 1243. உள்ளுவன், 1184, 1125. உள்ளுவர், 107. உள்ளுவேன், 1136. உள்ளிய, 309. உள்ளும், 1298. உள் forms nouns with prim. roots. [This is Tel. *lu*?] பொருள், கடவுள், அருள், இருள், மருள். வினையுள், 545.

உறங்கு (§ 62), 'sleep.' உறங்குவது (§ 88). உறங்கி (§ 77). 339.

உறை (§ 57), 'dwell, live.' [உறு, இரு.] உறைவர் 'he will dwell,' 1130. உறையும், 50, 84. உறைவது 'that which will dwell, the dwelling,' 426. உறைந்தற்று 'as (it) attends the steps,' 208,

890. உறை (வி. தொ.). உறைநிலம், 499. உறைபதி, 1015.

உறை n. 1. 'Life on earth,' 564. 2. 'Dwelling-place,' 680. 3. 'Seasons, rain,' 559. 4. 'Curdle, congeal.'

உறு (§ 1), 'feel, be': sometimes redundant, a pass. aux. An ellipsis often occurs; thence='gain, suffer, be great,' &c. As வி. தொ., 498, 734, 744, 756, 1106, 1200, 1275. உறுகண் 'trouble'; see கண், 261. உறல், 378, Nâl. 104. உறன்முறையான் 'a relative,' 885. உறுதல் 'the feeling of,' 402, 628, 629. With காம் and துன்பம்:— உறுவர் (with காம்), 399, 649; 'ascetics' (? உரவுர்), Nâl. 104. உறும், 539, (with மைந்து) 649, (with காம்) 380, (முந்து) 1023, 707, 816, 817. (கோடி) 1061, (with அல்லல்) 1301. உறுவது (with இன்பு) 'what (they) delight in,' 399, 813 (abs.). உற (with இன்பு), 390, (with துன்பம்) 699. முன்னுற 'beforehand,' 535. உறின் (with தாக்கு), 599, (abs.) 778, (opp. to அறின்) 812, (opp. to பெறின்) 1270. உற்று (with அன்பு), 75, (with காம்) 402, (abs.='felt') 1101, 1244, 1290. உற்றான், உற்றார், உற்றவன (with இன்பு), 75, 949, 950, 207, (with ஏம்) 873, 1097, (with காம்) 1133, (with காமநோய்) 1255. உற்ற, 261, 442, 624, 625, 662, 1206, 1239, 1256 (என்னே); (with கால், கடை) 372, 773, 837, 1080. உற்றது, 708. உற்றவை, 512. உற்றன 'they have endured,' 1179. உற்றல், 1245. Neg.:— உறாஅ, 1052 (= உறுத்தா ?). உறார், 1097. உறாதவர் 'unsympathetic persons,' 1096, 1245, 1290. உறாது 'is it (not) of good omen?' 1143. உறாமை, 442. உறவு (ved.), 510=ஐயம். [Comp. உரவு in ஒப்புரவு, &c.] உறுதி, 638, 690, 796. [Comp. உரம்.] ஊறு 'suffering; sense of touch,' 535, 662, 665, 761, 762, 27. [Comp. 1101; =உறுவது.] ஊறுபாடு, 945 (படு). இடையூறு 'hindrance,' 676. உறுத்து (§ 62), 'cause to feel.' உறாஉம்= உறுத்தும் 'which will affect with,' 94. உறுத்தல், Ch. IV., CIX., CXV., CXXVIII. It seems to mean 'declare' = உரைத்தல். உறுப்பு 'member, essential part,' Ch. CXXIV. உறுப்புநலனழிதல 'the wasting away of the frame.' புறத்துறுப்பு, அகத்துறுப்பு 'external and internal members,' 79, 703, 704, 705, 761, 802, 903.

ஊ

ஊங்கு, ஊங்கும் (§ 62), 'greater.' [Comp. ஓங்கு.] ='which will rise higher,' 31, 32, 122, 460, 644, 1065. ஊக்கு (§ 62), 'ascend, lift up, struggle up, strive, endeavour' = Lat. *nitor*. ஊக்கும், 855, 858. ஊக்க, 1238. ஊக்கி, 473. ஊக்கின், 476. ஊக்கார், 463. ஊக்காது, 253. ஊக்கம் (§ 190), 591, 593, 594, 382, 486, 498, 744. உக்கமுடைமை 'energy, strenuous effort,' Ch. LX.

ஊடு (§ 62), 'pout, sulk, feign aversion.' [புல, பிணங்கு, துனி.] ஊடி, 1039, 1260, 1312, 1328. ஊடுக, 1329. ஊடிஞள், 1314. ஊடல், ஊடுதல், 1321, 1330, 1109, 1322, 1326, 1327, 1307, 1310, 1284. ஊடலுவகை 'the pleasure derived from sulking,' Ch. CXXXIII. ஊடியவர், 1304. ஊடாமை, 1282.

ஊண், ஊட்டு. See உண்.

ஊதியம் 'gain,' 231, 449, 461, 797, 831. [Comp. ஆயம்.]

ஊர். 1. 'A town,' 216, 397, 927, 1008, 1129, 1142, 1143, 1150,

1158. ஊராண்மை 'humanity, magnanimity' [ஆள்], 773. ஊருணி 'a village *tank*, 215. ஊரார், ஊரவர் 'townsfolk,' 1147, 1180, 1220. **2.** (§ 57) 'creep, spread over, mount, rise above, ride on.' [Comp. ஏறு.] ஊரும், 1182. ஊர, 601. ஊர்தல், 1136. ஊர்ந்து, 979. ஊர்ந்தான் 'the rider in,' 37. ஊர்வது, 621, 1185.

ஊழ். **1.** 'Antiquity, destiny,' Ch. XXXVIII., Nâl. 101–110, 371, 372, 380, 620. [Comp. பழ.] ஊழி 'eternity, destiny,' 989. **2.** (§ 64), 'bloom.' ஊழ்த்தும் 'though it has bloomed,' 650 [பழு].

ஊறு. **1.** See உறு. **2.** (§ 62), 'gush forth; yield water.' ஊறும், 396. ஊறிய 'which has yielded water.' ஊற்றுநீர் 'water from a spring,' 1161 [ஊற்று].

ஊற்று. **1.** 'A spring,' 1161 [ஊறு]. **2.** 'A prop, staff,' 414, 415 [ஊன்று].

ஊன்று (§ 62), (1) 'lean upon'; (2) 'support' (int. and trans.). ஊன்றும், 597, 615, 789, 1030. ஊன்றிய, 983.

ஊன் 'flesh.' புலால் 'body,' 968; 'any organism,' 251–58, 1013.

எ

எ, an initial interrog. letter; often with உம். [§ 25, 126. Comp. அ, இ, and யா.] With nouns: 30, 110, 355, 361, 423, 491, 533, 695, 982. எவ்வது 'how?' 426. எங்ஙனம் 'how?' 251. எற்று 'what?' 275, 557, 655, 438, 1080. எஞ்ஞான்றும் 'always'; see ஞான்று. என் 'how?' 862, 1243, 1217. [Comp. இன், அன்.] 'Whatever,' 586, 430, 573, 1059; with கொல் 'what?' 2, 70, 211, 318, 1004, 812, 923; 'what?' 53, 301, 897, 144, 420, 1225, 1270, 175, 436, 726, 763, 1195, 1172; 'why?' 397, 1287, 966. என்ன (adj.), 987, 705, 1100, 1122. என்னைகொல், 188. எவன் 'why?'=ஏன, 379; (with கொல்) 99, 237, 1291, 1171; 'what'=என், 46, 57, 79, 272, 1308, 574, 803, 1225, 1207, 1165. எவனோ, 31, 1089. எனை= என்ன foll. by உம் 'whatever'; with nouns 'however much,' 52, 207, 209, 514, 670. [Comp. அனை, இனை.] எனைத்து, 1208, 820. எனை(த்துணை), 144, 750. எனைத்தானும், 317, 416. எனைத்தொன்றும், 209, 281, 300, 1202, 825, 1241. என்றும் 'always,' 978, 138, 152, 652, 536, 1130.

எஃகு 'weapon,' 759, 773.

எஞ்சு (§ 62), 'fail; remain, survive.' எஞ்சல், 44. எஞ்சாது, 690. எஞ்சாமை, 382, 497. எச்சம். **1.** 'Posterity,' 112, 114, 456, 238. **2.** 'Remnant,' 674, 1004. **3.** 'Et cetera,' 1012. **4.** 'As for the rest,' 1075.

எடு (§ 64), 'take up.' [Comp. எழு.] எடுப்பது 'what will restore,' 15. எடுத்து 'having summed up,' 776. எடுக்கும் 'will excite,' 1150.

எண். **1.** 'Eight,' 9. [எட்; S. *ashṭan.*] **2.** 'Number, arithmetic,' 392. [S. *gaṇa.*] **3.** (§ 62), 'count, think, reflect, design, esteem.' எண்சேர்ந்த 'thoughtful' [சேர்]. எண்ணும் 'will think, plan,' 639, 1004. எண்ணி, 22, 462, 467, 470, 497, 530, 666, 687, 699, 1298. எண்ணியார் 494, 666. எண்ணின், 264. எண்ண, 438, 922. எண்ணிய, 666, 753, 941. எண்ணுவம், 467. எண்ணுது, 180. எண்ணுத, 568. எண்ணம் 'design,' 494. **4.** See எள்.

எதிர் 'opposite, future, over

against.' எதிர்நோக்குதல் 'regard,' 1082. எதிர்நிற்கும், 765 [நில்]. எதிர்சாய்ந்து, 855, 859 [சாய்]. (§ 64) எதிர்ப்பு 'recompense,' 221. எதிரது 'what is future,' 429. எதிர்தா.

எயிறு 'tooth,' 1121.

எய் (§ 58), 'shoot an arrow.' எய்த, 772. எய்யாமை: com. says = வருந்தாமல் 'without trouble,' 296; B. thinks it= அறியாமை 'without your knowledge.'

எய்து (§ 62), 'obtain; fit, suit.' எய்தல், 265, 606, 671, 815, 904, 991, 489. எய்துவர், 137. எய்தாமை, 815. எய்தி, 665, 749, 932. எய்த 'so as to suit,' 516. எய்தின்று (= அடைந்தது), 1240. எய்தும், 75, 145, 309, 610, 676, 1024. எய்துப, 666. எய்திய, 354, 657, 670, 740. எய்தார், 598, 901. எய்தா, 137.

எரி 'fire,' 308, 435, 896, 1148 [தீ].

எரு 'manure,' 1037, 1038, 1147.

எலி 'a rat,' 763.

எல்லை 'limit,' 806.

எல்லாம் (§ 126), 'all, every, whole.' 1. In app. to a noun, 1, 33, 68, 79, 81, 212, 232, 238, 294, 375, 624, 268, 320, 321, 507, 542, 547; in any case, 1012, 1013, 1064, 1067, 1056, 1168, 1227, 1266, 673, 776, 582, 981, 860, 596, 1032. 2. Summing up: 'all these,' 15. 3. Noun: 'all things *or* persons; the whole,' 430, 309, 610, 343, 951, 659, 661, 1002, 1033, 72 (='wholly'); with மற்று, 39, 221. 4. With உள் making a superlative, 47, 142, 203, 322, 325, 411, 443, 444, 761, 832, 891. எல்லா, prefixed to noun, followed by உம், 361, 296, 299, 260, 457, 746, 851, 972. எல்லார் + உம், 582, 125, 191, 752, 1139, 1311.

எவ்வம் 'affliction,' 223, 853, 1241.

எவ்வது. See எ.

எள். 1. 'Rape-seed.' [Comp. இளா.] எட்பகவு 'a split in a grain of sesame,' 889. 2. 'Slight, easy'; used as வினைக்குறிப்பு. எண்பதத்தால 'by easiness of access,' 991, 548, 424. எண்பொருள், 760. எளிது '(it is) easy' [opp. அரிது], 991, 745, 540, 864, 145. எளிய, 664. எளியர், 723, 863, 386.

எள்ளு (§ 62), 'despise.' [Comp. இழு, இகழ்.] எள்ளின், 1298. எள்ள, 191. எள்ளற்க, 491. எள்ளும், 607. எள்ளுவார், 829, 752. எள்ளாமை, 667, 281. எள்ளாத, 470. எள்ளாது, 1057.

எழு (§ 57), 'rise.' [எறு; comp. √OR-.] எழுவாள் 'rise (from a seat),' 55. எழுதல் 'rise (in arms),' 465. எழுவார் 'rise (up to labour),' 1032. எழ 'rise (as a rumour),' 1141. எழிலி= 'மேகம்,' 17. எழில்='அழகு,' 407.

எழு-து (§ 62), 'write, paint.' எழுதேம் 'we paint not,' 1127. எழுதுங்கால் 'when (one) paints,' 1285. எழு-த்து 'letter; reading,' 392.

எழு, எழுபது, எழுமை. See ஏழு.

எறி (§ 57). எறிக 'let (them) strike,' 562. எறிந்தும் 'whether (they) hurl missiles,' 747. எறிய 'when hurling,' 775. எறிதற்கு 'for the purpose of striking,' 821.

எற்று (§ 62), 'destroy,' 663. எற்ரு 'unending.' எற்று, 1256. See எ.

எனை. See எ.

என். 1. See எ. 2. 'Say' (§ 70, 82). என்றேன், 1314, 1315, 1316. என்றார் 'he (who) said,' 1149. என்றது 'the saying,' 552. என்க 'say thou!'

with noun தெற்று, q.v. என [the use is remarkable]. **1.** 'To say,' 37; 'when — says,' 55, 69, 145, 1245, 1259, 1292, 630. **2.** With படு, q.v. **3.** 'Emphasizes and specializes a noun--is almost like an article, 111, 168, 316, 334, 942. It almost is= marks of quotation, 1236, 1252, 1257. **4.** Sums up='these,' 146, 1022, 766.

என்று 'having said' (see § 82, 83), 593, 626, 627, 1139, 1002, 1313–20, 174, 205, 611, 1067, 1112, 1114. **1.** 'As being,' 11, 307, 331, 351, 537. **2.** In summing up, as என= 'these,' 27, 43, 674, 939, 950. **3.** Serves to specialize a statement, and almost equal to quotation marks, 1307, 1308, 388, 575, 805, 699, 1298, 1248, 1154, 1004, 517, 1066. என்றவற்றுள் (7th case pl.), 715. என்றல் 'the saying, the fact,' 181. எனல், 282, 971, 1148, 1260. Imp. reg. and pos., 196. (Intro. p. xx.) என்னும் (§ 132), =appositive 'of'; joins two words, phrases, or even clauses, which are in apposition or very closely connected, 14, 1040, 790, 571, 369, 641, 306, 1013, 753, 336, 924, 936, 24, 29, 54, 70, 74, 180, 988, 223, 227, 991, 992, 287, 464, 844, 601, 790, 1251, 1043, 1045, 1068, 1182, 1156, 1134. 'It *or* which will say,' 1015, 1130, 1129, 1023, 1021, 976, 598, 1063, 346, 406, 438, 1193. என்பேன், 1254. என்பாக்கு (Intro. p. xxii.), 'which will say,' 1312. என்பர் 'they will say, will be called,' 88, 246, 336, 662, 1220. என்பான், ர், 1036, 41, 42, 47, 147, 163, 275, 281, 628, 850; 'he who will say, will be called' (§ 151), 365, 956; (pl.) என்போர், 30. என்பவர், 393, 856. என்னுமவர், 653 (irr. =என்பவர்). என்ப 'they will say,' 60, 63, 66, 73, 75, 76, 203, 238, 244, 361, 392, 483, 617, 729, 736, 738, 739, 773, 851, 981, 991, 918, 953, 1280. என்பது (an aoristic form of என்று, § 82), 87, 114, 116, 193, 210, 364, 467, 661, 797, 831, 850, 928, 1026, 1083, 1188, 1293. எனின் 'if you say, if,' 2, 19, 20, 178, 220, 254, 256, 210, 292, 309, 321, 324, 378, 546, 560, 789, 801, 831, 844, 986, 1041, 1189, 1190, 1194. எனினும் 'though you say, though,' 82, 102, 222, 328, 499, 619, 638, 730, 768, 770, 1199. என்னது (§ 121), 36. என forms verbs with the particles கதும், தவ்வு, தண் (q.v.), 1175, 1144. தண்ணென்னும் 'it will grow cool,' 1104.

என்பு=எலும்பு 'bone,' 72, 73, 77, 80.

என்றும். See எ and என்.

ஏ.

ஏ. See யா. **1.** An interrogative 447, 1299. **2.** Part. denoting emphasis and *certainty*, 9, 1064, 1309, 1283, 1240. **3.** Emph. and exclusive: 'that and that alone,' 25, 27, 242, 585, 587. **4.** Emph. and antithetic, 1, 39, 40, 240, 987. **5.** Added to nouns, with உம். நகையேயும் 'even in jest,' 871. கணமேயும் 'even for a moment,' 29. கண்ணேயும் 'even there,' 1044. தானேயும் 'even it alone,' 1060. **6.** Sign of 8th or voc. case, 1291, *passim*. **7.** For இ in inflexions: கூடுவேம், 1310, 1278, 1250. **8.** With போல், 1285.

ஏகு (§ 62), 'pass over,' 3. [Comp. இக; S. *êti.*] ஏகினான்=ஏகினவன் (§ 87), 2.

ஏக்கறு. See அறு. [ஏக்கு for ஏக்கம் from ஏங்கு.] ஏக்கற்றும் 'though they languish, bow humbly,' 395; '*humiliter discere*' (B.).

ஏங்கு (§ 62), 'languish, long for, yearn after,' 1248, 1269; ஏங்கி, ஏங்குபவர்.

ஏதம் 'disgrace,' 136, 164, 275, 432, 831, 884, 885, 1006. ஏதப் பாடு [படு], 464.

ஏதில் 'other, foreign, strange,' 913. [Prob. ஏது+இல்.] ஏதின்மை 'indifference, alienation,' 816. ஏதில 'extraneous things,' 440, 1089. ஏதிலான், ஏதிலர் 'strangers, enemies,' 188, 190, 440, 837, 862, 1099, 1129, 1130, 1224, 1300, Nâl. 122.

ஏத்து (§ 62), 'extol.' [ஏ='up.' ஏறு. Comp. முந்து, பிந்து.] ஏந்து (§ 62), 'rise; bear up.' ஏந்தல், 772. ஏந்திய 'lofty,' 899. ஏத்தும், 970.

ஏம், ஏமம், 873; with உறு='be mad; madness; security, safety.' [? S. *kshêma*.] ஏமப்புணை, 306, 1164. ஏமம் 'guard, defence,' 1131, 815, 766, 738. ஏமரா (=காவலற்ற), 448. [ஏம்+அா. ? வேம்+அரா 'a king like a fiery serpent.'] ஏமாப்பு 'safety; exaltation,' 112, 126, 398, 458, 459; '*decus, sublimitas*' (B.). ஏமாப்பிரேணி, 1068. [Comp. 306.]. ஏமார்த்தல் (ஏம்+ஆர்='bind'), 'guard,' 660. [Another reading is ஏமாற்றல் 'deception.']

ஏர். 1. 'A team, yoke of oxen and plough, ploughing,' 14, 1031, 872, 1038. 2. 'Like' (*as a team*), 1089, 1272. 3. 'Fitness, beauty,' 1053, 1098, 1305.

ஏல். 1.='ஆயின்' 'if,' 18, 1118. [ஆயில்.] அல்லனேல் 'if he is not,' 386. இன்றேல் '*sin minus*,' 996, 556, 573, 575, 1014, 1144. உண்டேல் 'if it exist,' 368. 2. 'Take, receive.' ஏற்று (§ 70, like கல்), 716.

ஏனும்=ஆயினும்=ஆனும், 997, 277, 430.

ஏனை 'other,' 392, 505, 704. [Comp. அனை, இனை, எனை.] ஏனைய, 268. ஏனையவர், 410. ஏனையிரண்டும் 'the other two.'

ஏவு (§ 62), 'stir up.' [Comp. ஏந்து. √ஏ.] ஏவல் (§ 148, 149), 'command, instigation,' 515, 907, 909. ஏவவும் (§ 168), 'even when . . . incite,' 848.

ஏறு. 1. 'A lion,' 59, 381. [Comp. எழு, உயரு, ஏவு, ஏந்து; √ஏ.] 2. (§ 62) 'Ascend.' ஏறினார் 'they (who) have climbed.' ஏறிநின்றார் 'they (who) have climbed and taken their stand,' 29, 758. ஏறும் 'will mount; swell,' 1132, 1133, 1264. ஏறா 'that mounts not,' 1137.

ஏழு (§ 172), 'seven.' எழு, 62, 107, 126, 398, 538, 835, 1278. [See மை.] எழுபது, 639.

ஏழை 'a wretch,' 873. [இழி. என்.]

ஐ.

ஐ. 1. 'Lord,' 771. 2. 'Doubt.' ஐயம், 353, 845. ஐயப்படு (see படு), 702, 958. ஐயப்பாடு 'doubt,' 587. ஐயுறவு (see உறு), 'suspicion,' 510. 3. 'Five,' (§ 172). ஐ 'perception by the *five* senses,' 354. ஐம், 43, 1101. ஐந்து, 6, 24, 25, 27, 126, 271, 343, 632, 675, 738, 939, 983. 4. Sign of 2nd case, 509, 702. 5. Replaces final ஆ of S. அவை =சபை=*sabhâ*. So in deriv. Comp. வாய்='place,' with வை. 6. Term. of 2nd sing. in verbal forms=ஆய் (§ 31). அல்லை='thou art not.' வேலை='thou art a dart,' 1221.

ஒ.

ஒ (§ 64), 'befit, resemble, agree,' 993. ஒத்து with ஆங்கு='as befits,' 561. ஒத்தது, 214. ஒத்தல், 993. ஒத்தி 'thou viest with,' 1119. ஒக்க 'be like!' 490. ஒக்கல் 'kindred,' 43. ஒக்கின் 'if it agree,' 1100. ஒக்கும் 'is the same,' 972. ஒப்ப 'equal to,' 702. ஒப்பர் 'they are alike,' 413. ஒப்பது 'what equals,' 162, 363; 'resembles,' 631, 993, 536. ஒப்பு, 993, 800, 812. ஒப்பிலார் 'unfitting persons.' ஒப்பாரி 'what corresponds' [term. ஆரி], 1071. ஒப்புரவு [comp. துப்புரவு], Ch. XXII. (see Notes), 213, 218, 220; with ஆண்மை, 480 [ஆள்]. ஒவ்வா 'is not the same,' 972. ஒவ்வேம், 1114.

ஒடு-ங்கு (§ 62), 'lie hidden.' [Comp. அடை.] ஒடுக்கம் 'reserve,' 486. ஒடுங்கும் 'will lie concealed,' 828.

ஒட்டு (§ 62), 'adhere to.' ஒட்ட 'in conformity with,' 140, 482. ஒட்டல் 'the attacking,' 499. ஒட்டி 'attaching to oneself,' 679. ஒட்டார் 'non-adherents, enemies,' 678, 826.

ஒட்பம் (from ஒள்), 'splendour, praise,' 404, 425.

ஒண். See ஒள்.

ஒரு (ஓர் and ஒன்று), 'one, the one, any,' 1091, 118, 119, 126, 168, 156, 248, 357, 397, 634, 974, 1042, 1095, 1146, 1196, 1266, 1269. [Comp. இரு, ஈர், இரண்டு.] ஒருவந்தம (அந்தம்), 563, 593. ஒருவன், 838, 95, 38, 40, 161, 181, 220, 226, 336, 366, 400, 405, 414, 454, 609, 600, 797, 971, 988, 967, 1004, 1021, 1023, 1026, 1052, 1197, 661, 397, 398, 871, 875. ஒருத்தி, 1313. ஒருங்கு 'at once,' 343, 554, 610, 733, 760, 951, 1056. ஓர், 24, 429, 465, 645, 704, 796, 848, 902, 1053, 1098, 1153, 1307. ஒன்று, 87, 109, 111, 831, 833, 836, 838, 839, 128, 221, 148, 155, 232, 233, 253, 323, 324, 334, 344, 380, 438, 758, 773, 800, 805, 875, 291, 462, 257, 259, 281, 300, 825, 932, 934, 1006, 1007, 1049, 1080, 1091, 1202, 1216, 1035, 1241, 1247, 1252, 1255, 1257, 1271–75. v. (§ 62). ஒன்றல் 'the existing,' 886. ஒன்றியார் 'those who are united,' 886. ஒன்றாமை 'disunion,' 886.

ஒருவு (§ 62), 'avoid, shun, renounce.' ஒரீஇ = ஒருவி, 116, 422, 797, 830, 1009. ஒருவுதல், 652; ஒரால், 153, 662. ஒருவுக 'shun!' 800. ஒரூஉம = ஒருவும், 812. ஒரார், 658.

ஒலி (§ 64), 'sound, make a noise,' 763. ஒலித்த.

ஒல்-கு (§ 62), 'relax, despond'; '*relaxari, suam proprietatem amittere*' (B.). ஒல்காமை, 662. ஒல்கார், 136, 218, 597.

ஒல்-லு (§ 62), 'be possible.' [Comp. இயல்.] ஒல்லும் '(which) is possible,' 33, 673, 789, 818. ஒல்வது, 1149. ஒல்வான் 'he who cannot manage,' 870. ஒல்லாது '(it) is not possible to,' 870, 559. ஒல்லா, 139, 673, 1064, 1136, 1271.

ஒல்லை 'swiftly' [cor. from ஒல்லே, ஒல்லென], 563, 564, 826, 1096.

ஒழி (§ 57, 64), 'cease; cause to cease, leave off.' ஒழிய (§ 170), 113, 240, 338, 1231, Nâl. 123. ஒழித்து 'having abandoned,' 280.

ஒழு-கு (§ 62), 'live, conduct oneself.' [Opp. இழு. Comp. வழு.] ஒழுகல், 30, 140, 286, 445, 482, 524, 602, 694, 845, 1073; மன்னரைச்சேர்ந்தொழுகல், Ch. LXX.; ஒழுகுதல், 444. ஒழுக, 111, 154, 446, 698, 855. ஒழுகும், 141, 278, 551, 563, 603, 874, 907. ஒழுகின், 294, 359, 892, 974. ஒழுகுவார், 143, 246, 326, 691, 896, 921, 1197; ஒழுகுபவர், 908. ஒழுகான், 474. ஒழு-க்கு (§ 62) = ஒழுகு. ஒழுக்கி, 48. ஒழுக்

கம் 'conduct, decorum' (=ஆசாரம்); '*rectitudo, ordo, supplemorum*' (B.). ஒழுக்கமுடைமை '*mores*, decorous conduct, conformity to the rule of life,' Ch. XIV. கூடாவொழுக்கம் 'unworthy conduct,' Ch. XXVIII. With நல் and தீ, 138='good and evil conduct'; with படிறு='faulty conduct, indecorum,' 271, 275, 6, 21, 131–39, 415, 952. ஒழுக்கு =ஒழுக்கம், 20, 148, 161.

ஒள் 'bright,' 727, 1125. ஒண், 760, 1009, 1088, 1101, 1240, Nâl. 102. ஒண்மை 'glory, brightness,' 844. ஒட்பம் [comp. இன்பம, துன்பம், நுட்பம்], 404, 425. ஒளி 'light, sense of sight; glory' [opp. இளி], 27, 267, 390, 556, 653, 698, 870, 921, 939, 970, 971, 1118, 1329. ஒளியார், ஒள்ளியர், ஒள்ளியவர், 487, 714.

ஒளி (§ 64), 'hide.' [Comp. ஒழி.] ஒளிக்கும் 'where will (he) hide himself?' 1070. ஒளித்தது 'what (he) has hidden,' 928.

ஒறு (§ 64), 'punish, blame, vex.' ஒறுக்கிற்பவர், 779. ஒறுத்தார், 155, 156. ஒறுப்பது, 561. ஒறுத்து, 579. ஒறுத்தல், 314, 550. ஒறகம் 'misery,' 414.

ஒற்று (§ 62), 'spy out, look out for, examine.' ஒற்றி 'having spied out,' 583, 588, 927; 'sought for,' 927; 'examined,' 1261. ஒற்று 'a spy, a detective,' 581–90. ஒற்றாடல் 'the employment of detectives,' Ch. LIX.

ஒன்றாமை. See ஒரு.

ஒன்று. See ஒரு.

ஒன்னார்=ஒன்றாதவர் 'foes,' 165, 264, 608, 630, 756, 827, 828. (See ஒரு.)

ஓ

ஓ. 1. An interrogative (§ 46), 483, 591, 705, 707, 968, 987, 1085, 1318, 1323; with அன்று, 1208; with கொல், 85, 1048, 1081, 1328; with மன், 1206, 1329. 2. An interjection, ஓஓ, 1088, 1176, 1204. (See அளபெடை.) 3. ஓவு (§ 62), 'cease.' [Commonly ஓய். Comp. ஒருவு.] ஓவா 'unceasing,' 734, 1205. ஓவாதே (§ 77), 'without intermission,' 33, 933. ஓஒதல் (=ஓவுதல் *or* ஒருவுதல்), 'desisting from,' 653. [அளபெடை.]

ஓசை 'sound,' 27. [=ஓதை. Comp. ஓது and இசை.]

ஓச்சு (§ 62), 'wield or sway as a sceptre, uplift in a threatening manner.' [? உயர்த்து. Comp. ஓங்கு.] கோலோச்சும், 544, 545. ஓச்சி, 562.

ஓடு (§ 62), 'run.' ஓடா (§ 110), 'it runs not,' 496. ஓடும் 'it will run,' 496. மருங்கோடி 'having transgressed, run to one side,' 210. [மருங்கு.] [With கண்:—the idea is of the 'benignant glance sent forth'; கண்ணோடாதவர், 576; கண்ணோடாது, 541; கண்ணோட, 578; கண்ணோடி, 579; கண்ணோட்டம், 983, 571–75, 577. Ch. LVIII.] ஓட்டு 'defeat,' 775 (=ஓட்டம், § 190).

ஓது (§ 62), ஓதி, 'recite, study the Vêdas,' 834. [S. *vad.*] ஒத்து (§ 190), 'the Vêdas, recitation,' 134.

ஓம்பு (§ 62), [comp. ஏம்], 'guard against; guard; attend to, watch over, cherish, care for.' [With கா 'keep watch and ward.'] அஞ்சலோம்பு (§ 27), 'fear not,' 1149. ஓம்பின் (§ 95), 'if you would keep in safety,' 1155. ஓம்பல் (§ 148), v.n. and opt. (really v.n. and வேண்டும் und.), 'the guarding against, warding off,' 1155, 612, 642, 820, 89, 43, 390. விருந்தோம்பல, Ch. IX., 'Hospitality—due attention to guests.' ஓம்புதல், 322, 626.

ஓம்பி (§ 77), 549, 81, 85, 86, 88, 132, 244. ஓம்பும் (§ 74), 968. ஓம்புக (§ 140), 'beware of,' 506, 861. ஓம்ப (§ 92), 'should be attended to.' [பல்.] ஓம்பா (§ 121), 'that does not sedulously attend to,' 89. (=ஓம்பாமல்) 'not guarding against or shunning,' 861. ஓம்புவான் (=ஓம்புபவன், § 88), 'he who attends to, cherishes,' 83, 84.

ஓரும், 40, 366, an expletive, supposed to be meaningless; perhaps from ஓர் 'consider,' and='mark well!' It is used by Tiruv. with each of two contrasted notions.'

ஓர். 1. (§ 64), 357, ஓர்த்து (§ 77), 'ponder, examine.' [Comp. ஆர்.] ஓர்ந்து (§ 57), 541. ஓரார் (§ 110), 695. ஓரா 'having investigated,' 548. [Comp. § 97, of the form செய்யா.] 2. See ஒரு.

ஔ.

ஔ. See அவ்.

க.

க°°சு, a quarter தொடி, 1037.

கசடு 'fault.' [√ கச = 'be bitter.' Seems to have the notion of '*bitter dregs.*'] கசடற 'faultlessly,' 391, 717, 845. [அற.]

கட. [Comp. கட்டு, கடு.] கடப்பாடு 'obligation, duty'=ஒப்புரவு, 211 [படு]; '*munificentia, largitio*' (B.). கடவுள் 'God,' title of Ch. I. கடவுள்வாழ்த்து. [Comp. அருள், பொருள்.] கடன் 'duty, moral obligation,' 218, 638, 687, 802, 981, 1053. கடல் 'sea, the wide sea,' 10, 17, 103, 496, 1137, 1164, 1166, 1175, 1200.

கடாம் 'the secretion of an elephant in rut.' கடாக்களிறு 'an elephant in rut,' 1087. [களிறு.]

கடி 'guard.' கடிகொண்டார் 'he has guarded (his heart against me).' (§ 57) 'guard against, reprehend, punish.' குற்றங்கடிதல், Ch. XLIV. கடிந்த, 658. கடிந்து, 658, 668.

கடு=கொடு, கடும், கடிய, கடுமை, with the idea of 'hardness, swiftness, severity.' [Comp. பெரு, அரு; also கொடு.] கடும் 'fierce,' 386, 566, 567, 570, 1134, 1167. கடியன் 'a cruel man,' 564. கடிது 'with severity,' 562. (§ 64) 'be harsh, angry, suspicious.' கடுத்தது 'the soul's anger,' 706. கடுத்தபின் 'after anger has arisen,' 693. கடாஅ 'not exciting distrust,' 585. (See அளபெடை.)

கடுகு (§ 62), 'hasten to an end.' கடுகி, 564. [கடு.]

கடை. [கடு.] 1. 'A limit, place.' (III. Gr. 63.) 2. 'Where *or* when,' with rel. part., 53, 230, 315, 372, 469, 478, 803, 837, 964, 1019, 1059, 1149, 1195. So also when கடை is inflected as வினைக். we have கடைத்தும்='although,'= *and when it is in the place that*, 637, 823. 3. 'The last, lowest place.' அறன்கடை 'outside of virtue,' பிறன்கடை 'neighbour's outer gate,' 142; '*porta exterior domui*, et hic significat *extra*' (B.), 328, 729, 998. கடைக்கொட்க 'so as to merit acceptance at last,' 663. கடைமுறை 'at last,' 792. கடையர் 'the lowest,' 395. கடைப்பிடி (§ 64), 'persevere, hold on till the end,' 944. [பிடி.]

கட்டளை [=கண்+தளை?], 'touchstone, test,' 505, 986.

கண். 1. 'Eye' [S. *akṣha*; see காண்], 107, 184, 392, 393, 445, 500, 573-77, 581, 585, 686, 705, 709, 710, 775, 927, 1061,

1084–86, 1091, 1092, 1095, 1100, 1126, 1127, 1140, 1136, 1170–79, 1210, 1212, 1231, 1232, 1239, 1240, 1261, 1265, 1267, 1272, 1280, 1283, 1285, 1290, 1311, 1315. கண்விதுப்பழிதல், Ch. CXVIII. கண்ணாள், 1119, 1125, 1142. கண்ணார், 1180, 1305. **2.** 'Kindliness, pity'; '*miseratio*,' (B.), 184. கண்ணற, 184, 566, 1252. கண்ணோட்டம், Ch. LVIII. 'favourably, kindly regard.' (See under ஓடு.) **3.** 'Place,' 52, 184 (?), 1055, 1058. யாங் கணும் 'everywhere' [யா], 864. It becomes = 'where *or* when,' 573, 574, 312, 349, 514, 521, 606, 740, 750, 955, 354, 670, 1292. **4.** Sign of 7th case, 579, 223, 216, 217, 874, 878, 951, 34, 89, 117, 146, 176, 141, 135, 241, 284, 285, 286, 408, 493, 521, 590, 517, 519, 503, 612, 613, 642, 668, 750, 784, 886, 806, 810, 832, 957, 958, 986, 1059, 1061, 1044, 1099, 1101, 1174, 1197, 1090, 1153, 1284, 1243, 1309. இடைக்கண் 'in the midst,' 473.

கட்டு, a வினைக்குறிப்பு (= கண் + து = 'it belongs to the place') which still remains as a sign of 7th case (§ 251), 27, 502, 513; = 'it is possessed of eyes,' 1083.

In compounds (see under அஞ்சு, ஓடு, உண், வல்):—

I. **1.** வன்கண் [வல்] = 'bravery,' 632, 762, 764. வன்கணார், வன்கணார், வன்கணவர், 1198, 1156, 726, 228, 689, 775, 1027. வன்கண்ணது 'what has cruel eyes,' 1222. **2.** தறுகண் 'ferocity' [தறு], 773. **3.** உறுகண் 'trouble' [உறு], 261. **4.** இன்கண் 'pleasure' [இன்], 1152. **5.** புன்கண் 'sadness' [புல்], 1152; புன்கண்ணது 'gloomy-eyed,' 1222. **6.** தாமரைக்கண்ணன், Brahmâ, 1103. **7.** இடுக்கண். (See இடு).

II. **1.** கண்பாடு 'sleep' [படு], 1049. **2.** கண்ணீர் 'tear' [நீர்], 555, 780, 828. [Comp. 107.] **3.** கட்படாம் 'a veil' [படாம்], 1087. **4.** கண்ணோடு [ஓடு]; கண்ணோட்டம் 'kindness.'

கண்டு. See காண்.

கணம் [S.]. **1.** 'An instant' [S. *kshana*], 29. **2.** 'A class' [S. *gaṇa*]. தங்கணத்தர் 'those of one's tribe,' 720.

கணிச்சி 'an axe,' 1251. [S. *khan.*]

கணை 'an arrow,' 279.

கதம் 'wrath,' 130.

கதவு 'a door,' 1251.

கதுப்பு 'woman's hair.' கதுப்பினாள், 1105.

கதுமென 'swiftly,' imitative word. (See என்.)

கந்து 'a stake, staff to lean on,' 507. [S. *skandha.*]

கயல் 'a fish: *Cyprianus L.*, carp,' 1212.

கயமை [√கய = இழ்] 'baseness,' Ch. CVIII. Nâl. Ch. XXXVI. கயவர், 1071–1080. [Opp. சான்றோர்.]

கயிறு 'rope,' 482.

கர (§ 66), 'conceal'; *hence* 'refuse to give.' [Comp. S. *kri*. Syn. மறை, ஒளி.] கரத்தல், 1054, 1162. கரப்பார், கரப்பவர், 1067, 1070. கரப்பாக்கு (§ 97), 'that it will hide,' 1127, 1129. கரப்பின், 1051. கரப்பினும், 1271. சரப்பு, 1053, 1055, 1056. கரவு, 1068, 1069; 'guile,' 288. கரவாது, 527, 1035, 1061.

கரு 'black,' 1123. [கரும், கரி, கார், கருமை. Comp. அர்.] கரியார் 'those who are black,' 277. கருக்காய் [S. கரு = 'germ'] = 'immature fruit,' 1306. [காய்.] கார் 'dark,' 287.

கருவி 'an instrument,' 421, 483, 537, 631, 675. [Comp. S. *kri*; கருமம்.]

கரி 'witness,' 25, 245, 1060. [Prob. from கரு. கரி is '*charcoal*.']

கருது (§ 62), 'think, devise,

ponder, aim at.' [Comp. எழு-தி.] கருத, 1028. கருதுப, 337. கருதுபவர், 485. கருதி, 285, 463, 484, 485, 687, 696, 700, 852, 949. கருதினும், 484.

கரும்பு 'sugar-cane,' 1078.

கரை. 1. (§ 57), 'call,' 527. 2. 'Shore,' 1167.

கருமம் [S. *karma*], 'work,' 266, 467, 505, 578, 818, 1011, 1021. In Nâl. கம்மம், 393.

கல (§ 66), tr. and int., 'mix, join battle, embrace, arrive at.' கலத்தல் 'embracing,' 1259, 1276. கலப்பேன் 'I shall combine (the two),' 1267. கலந்து, 1121, 1246, 1268. கலந்தார், 'my husband,' 1212. கலக்கம் 'affliction.' கலங்கு (§ 62, 160), 'be confused.' கலங்கினள், 1290. கலங்காது, 485, 668. கலங்கிய, 1116. கலம், 1. 'An ornament,' 1262; with நல், 60; with அணி, 575. 2. 'A vessel, pot,' 660, 1000, 1029. கலன் 'a vessel, ship,' 605, Nâl. 206, 12.

கலுழு (§ 60), 'weep,' 1171, 1173, Nâl. 393.

கல். 1. 'Stone,' 38, 505, 771. கன்று (§ 62), 'grow intense'; with காதல், 284, 286. 2. (§ 70), 'learn'; con. with அறி. [Comp. கேள்.] கல்வி (§ 190), Ch. XL., 383, 398, 400, 684, 717, 939. கற்க (§ 140), 391, 725. கற்றது (§ 87), 2, 650. கற்ற 'things learned,' 'who has learnt,' 391, 398, 722, 724, 727, 730, 823. கற்று (§ 77), 130, 356, 396, 399, 503, 632, 686, 717, 729. கற்றிலன், 414. கற்றும் (§ 100), 140, 728. கற்பவை (§ 88), 391. கற்பினும் (§ 100), 373. கற்றோர், கற்றார் (§ 87), 393, 395, 403, 410, 722, 724, 949. கல்லா, கல்லாத, 397, 405, 814, 845. கல்லாதவன், கல்லாதான், 393, 395, 402–9, 729. கல்லார், 140, 408, 570, 870. கல்லாமை, Ch. XLI.

கவர் 'grasp at,' 100. [கவர்ந்தற்று.]

கவரிமா [S.], 'the yak, *bos grunniens*,' 969. [மா = மான்.]

கவறு 'dice,' 920, 935.

கவலை 'anxiety,' 7.

கவிகை 'umbrella,' 389.

கவிழ் (§ 57), 'be overturned,' 1114.

கவுள் 'elephant's temples,' 678.

கவின் 'beauty,' 1234, 1235, 1250.

கவ்வை (= கௌவை), 'scandal, evil report,' 1143–48, 1150. கவ்விது 'is full of scandal,' 1144.

கழனி 'a field,' Nâl. 122.

கழகம் 'a gaming table,' 935, 937.

கழல் 'the foot-ring of honour given to a warrior,' 777.

கழி (§ 57), 'pass off or away, slip off, surpass, exceed.' [√ KAR.] = நீங்கு, செல்லு, கழலு, மிகு. '(if fated evils) shall pass away.' கழியும (= நீங்கும்) (§ 72), 'will slip off,' 378, 1169, 1262. கழிய நன்று (§ 41, 170), 'an exceedingly good thing,' 404.

கழி, root as adj. or adv. (§ 270 (5) and Intro. p. xvii.). கழி நல்குரவு '*extreme* poverty,' 657. கழிபேரிரையான் 'an *excessively* great eater,' 946. கழிபெருங் காரிகை '*exceedingly* great beauty,' 571. கழிபெருங்காமத்தான் 'a man of *exceeding* great lust,' 866.

கழுவு (§ 62), 'wash.' கழாஅ (§ 121), 'unwashed,' 840. (See அளபெடை.)

களம் 'a field,' 1224. [S. *khala*.]

களன் 'an assembly,' 730.

களர் 'sterile land, bog,' 406, 500.

கள் (ளு) 'use fraud'; 'pluck out, weed' (§ 70, like கேள்). [Comp. களை.] கட்டதனொடு, 550. கட்டபின், 1038. கள்வார், 290. கள்ளார், 290. கள்ளாமை, Ch. XXIX., 281. கள்வேம், 282.

காடு 'forest,' 742. [Comp. S. *kâshṭha.*]

காதல் 'desire, love,' 284, 440, 921, 1195, 1298. [Comp. காமம்.] காதற் சிறப்புணர்த்தல், Ch. CXIII. Dec. as குறிப்புவினை (Intro. p. xxii.) :—காதலம் (1 pl.), 'we love,' 1314; காதலை (2 sing.), 'thou (shalt be) desired,' 1118; காதலன் (3 sing.), 209; காதற்று (3 sing.), 940; காதலர், காதலார், காதலவர் (3 pers.), 'a lover,' 1150, 1208, 1099, 1185, 1211, 1216, 1219, 1224, 1246, 1278, 1308; காதல (3 pers.), 440; காதன்மை (§ 154), 507, 832. காதலி (§ 64), 940. காதலிக்கும் 'will incite desire' [' desire,' Nâl. 123].

காப்பு. See கா. (§ 190.)

காமம் 'desire, love, lust.' [S. *kâma.*] காமத்துப்பால் 'pleasure,' Ch. CIX.-CXXXIII. **1.** 'Lust,' 360. **2.** 'Love.' In Book III. it is the equivalent to இன்பம் : 1090, 1092, 1131, 1137, 1138, 1139, 1144, 1145, 1148, 1159, 1163, 1164, 1166, 1167, 1175, 1191, 1196, 1201, 1202, 1214, 1247, 1251–1257, 1264, 1281, 1282, 1289, 1306, 1326, 1330. காமக்கலன் 'a pleasure-boat,' 605. காம் (with உறு, *q.v.*), 399, 402, 649, 1133. காமத்தான், 866. காமநோய் 'the pains of love,' 1159, 1175, 1255, 1280. காமன் 'Cupid,' 1197, Nâl. 391–400.

காம்பு 'bambû,' 1272. [மூங்கில், வேய்.]

காய். **1.** 'Unripe fruit,' 100, 1306. [Comp. கச; பழம், கனி.] **2.** (§ 57), 'be hot, angry.' காயும் 'scorch,' 77; 'will not be angry,' 1313, 1319, 1320. காய்வார் 'those who warm themselves,' 691. காயினும் 'though (you) are angry,' 707. காயார் 'he is not angry,' 1208. காய்வு 'anger,' 1246. காய்தி 'thou art angry.'

கார். See கரு.

காரணம் [S.], 'cause, reason,' 270, 529, 530, 929.

காரிகை 'ornament,' 571, 777, 1262, 1272.

காவலன். See கா.

கால், காலம். (See Nâl. 122, 123.) **1.** 'Wheel,' 496, Nâl. 2. **2.** 'Foot,' 500, 840. **3.** 'Stalk,' 1115. **4.** 'Foundation,' 1030. **5.** 'Germ, shoot,' 959. **6.** காலம் ='time,' 102, 949, 631, 696, 516, 675, 686, 687, 830; 'right time, opportunity,' Ch. XLIX., 483, 484, 485, 487. [Syn. பொழுது, பருவம்.] கால், with rel. part. poss. and neg., 1080, 601, 503, 695, 489, 14, 379, 859, 36, 1094, 987, 127, 673, 674, 1218, 1296, 305, 710, 930, 1285, 1286, 830, 1166, 301, 763, 362, 1064, 1270, 733, 773, 1104, 1179. ஒருகால், 248.

காலை (1) [? for காலே] 'the morning' [opp. to மாலை], 1225, 1226, 1227, 937. (2) for கால், 'when,' 1094. (3) (=காலம்), 799.

காழ். **1.** 'Stone (of fruit),' 1191. **2.** (§ 64), 'grow strong, harden.' [கல்.] காழ்த்த, 879. காழ்ப்ப 'exceedingly,' 760; '*ita ut obdurescunt,* h.e. *persistentiam habeant*' (B.).

கானம் 'forest,' 772. [S. *kânana.* Comp. காடு.]

கிட (§ 66). கிடந்தேன் 'I lay.' கிடந்தது 'what has lain open,' 446, 583, 1001. கிடந்தமை 'what has lain in anything: its quality,' 959.

கிழ-மை 'essential quality, propriety,' 785, 801, 805. [Comp. கெழு.] கிழவன் 'proprietor,' 1039, Nâl. 101.

கிழக்கு = கீழ், 488.

கிள-த்தல் (§ 66), Ch. CXXV., 'soliloquy.' கிளவா 'that speaks not,' 715.

கிளைஞர் 'friends,' 796. [Comp. கிழ, கெழு.]

கீழ் 'under.' [Comp. கய, கிழ, கிழக்கு.] **1.** Adv., 929, 973. **2.** Case-ending, 389, 1034. **3.** Noun, 'a base man' (=கயவன், கடை), 1074, 1075, 1078, 1079. **4.** Verb (§ 57), 'depreciate,' 801, *கீழ்ந்து*. **5.** In comp. with *பிற* and *படு*, 409, 558. கீழ்மை, Nal. 341–50.

குடம்பம் [S.], 1029; (=குடி) 'family.' குடம்பை 'egg, nest, shell,' 338. குடங்கர் 'hut,' 890.

குடி [S.]. **1.** 'Family,' 171, 601–609, 887, 888, 898, 1022–28, 1030. குடிசெயல்வகை, Ch. CIII. **2.** 'Subjects,' 381, 390, 632, 542–49. **3.** 'Noble family' (=குலம்), 502, 681, 794, 952, 953, 954, 955, 957, 992. குடிமை, 133, 793; Ch. XCVI. '*prosapiae nobilitas*' (B.), Nâl. 141–50.

குடை 'umbrella,' 1034. [*கவிகை*.] Nâl. 3.

குணம் (=*பண்பு*) [S.] 'quality, attribute,' 982. *குணத்தான்*, 9; 'high quality,' 29, 1125. குணன் 'good quality,' 504, 793, 868.

குதி (§ 64). *குதித்தல்* 'escaping,' 269.

குத்து 'peck, strike,' 490.

குரை, an expletive, 1045.

குலம் 'family' (=குடி), 956–59, 960, 1019. குலன், 223.

குவளை 'water-lily,' 1114, Nâl. 236.

குளம் 'tank,' 523. குளி (§ 64), 'bathe, go under water.' குளித்தான், 929.

குழல் 'pipe,' 66, 1228.

குழ-வி 'a tender infant,' 757, Nâl. 101. [Comp. குழை.]

குழாம் 'an assembly,' 332, 840. குழுவு, 735.

குழை [குழ='tender']. **1.** (§ 57) 'Shrivel up, become sad.' குழையும், 90. **2.** 'An ear-ring,' 1081.

குறி (§ 64). குறி (வி. தொ.), 221; for *குறித்து*, 1095. *குறித்தது*, (pl.) *குறித்த* 'what depends on,' 1013; 'what is indicated,' 704. *குறித்தமை* 'the having intended,' 827. குறிப்பு 'sign, indication, meaning, intention,' 696, 701–5, 1097, 1253. *குறிப்பறிதல்*, Ch. LXXI., CX. *குறிப்பறிவுறுத்தல*, Ch. CXXVIII.

குறு 'small.' குறுந்தொடி, 1135. குறை 'defect,' 612, 680, 908. (§ 57) (*முதுக்*) *குறைந்தது* (see *முது*), 'what is wise,' 707. குறையினும் 'if it be deficient,' 941. குறுகு (§ 62), குறுகுதல் 'the approach,' 820. குறுகும் 'when it approaches,' 1104. குறும்பு 'rapine, the work of the *Kurrambar*,' 735. குன்று (§ 62), 'grow less.' குன்றுவர் (§ 72), 'will be brought low,' 965. குன்றும் 'will *diminish*,' 17, 239, 560. குன்றி (§ 74; =குன்றிய), 'diminished.' [Apoc. கடைக்குறை, III. Gr. 41.] குன்ரு (§ 121), 'of *undiminished* splendour, &c.,' 601, 736, 793. குன்றின் (§ 95), 'if it diminish,' 990. குன்றல் (§ 148), 'diminution,' 778, 811. [Opp. பெருகல்.] *குன்ற* (§ 168), 'to fail, slightingly detract from,' 134, 898, 961. குன்றுவ (§ 88), 'low things,' 954, 965. குன்று 'a hill' (from its conical shape), 758, 898, 965, 29. குன்றி (='the pointed') 'the *abrus precatorius*'; its seed is of an intense scarlet, with a jet-black point: 965, 277. குற்றம் 'fault, deficiency,' 171, 188, 190, 272, 433, 434, 436, 549, 502, 504, 604, 609, 793, 846, 868, 957, 980, 1025, 1029. *குற்றத்தவர்* 'faulty ones,' 924. *குற்றங்கடிதல்*, Ch. XLIV.

கூகை 'an owl,' 481.

கூத்து 'a dance,' 332.

கூடு (§ 62), 'assemble, come together, be possible, fit; join in an embrace.' கூடல் (§ 148). 'embracement,' 1284, 1327, 1328, கூடுவேம் (=கூடுவோம்), 1310. கூடி, 1330; 765 (='combining'). கூடிய (§ 74), 'the joy of love's embrace,' 1264. கூடியார் (§ 87), 'who are joined,' 1109. கூடி னும் 'though *they* unite,' 887. கூடாது 'it combines not.' கூடா, in comp.='inconsistent, feigned.' கூடாவொழுக்கம் 'indecorum,' Ch. XXVIII. கூடா நட்பு 'feigned friendship,' Ch. LXXXIII., Nâl. 231–40. With தலை: தலைக்கூடி 'meeting,' 394. With கை: கைகூடும 'it is possible,' 269, 284. [Comp. *Nannûl*, 176.] கூடு 'a cage,' 122.

கூம்பு, கூப்பு (§ 62, 160, *j.*), 'contract (oneself), shut up; bring together, fold.' கைகூப்பி 'having clasped, folded the hands,' 260. கூம்பல் 'contracting, folding up, as a flower,' 425. கூம்பும்பருவம் 'when it is the season for holding in,' 490, Nâl. 215.

கூர், கூரும் 'sharp.' (See அர்.) கூரியது 'what is sharp, effective,' 759. கூர்ங்=கூரும் 'sharp,' 599. கூர்மை, கூர்மையர் 'sharp, clever people,' 997. (§ 57) in compounds: this is common with அன்பு, &c., but only once in குறள்: வறங் கூர்ந்து 'having failed to yield rain,' 1010.

கூலி 'wages, reward,' 619.

கூழ். **1.** 'Provisions; boiled rice,' 64, 381. கூழ்த்தது 'provisioned,' 745, Nâl. 1, 2. **2.** 'Wealth,' 554. **3.** '(Growing) grain,' 550.

கூறு. **1.** (§ 62) 'Say, announce.' [Comp. Gr. κήρ and κηρύσσω.] கூறல், 100, 638, 1236. இனிய வைகூறல், Ch. X. கூற, 186. கூறும், 183. கூறுவான், 186. கூறி, 183, 980. கூறின், 22, 933. கூறாமை, 701, 704; '*non detrahere*' (B.). புறங்கூறாமை, Ch. XIX. கூறான், 181. [Comp. மீக்கூறும் 'extol,' 386.] **2.** 'A division,' 950. கூற்று 'it is of four parts' (=கூற்றது). கூற் று 'what is destined, death' (=கூற்றது), 326, 765, 1050, 1083. கூற்றம்=கூற்று, 269, 894, 1085, Nâl. 7.

கூன் 'bent.' கூன்கையர் 'men with fists doubled,' 1077.

கெடு. **1.** 'Destruction'=கெடுவு, கேடு, 117. **2.** (§ 68) 'Perish.' கெடுநீரார் 'those doomed to destruction' (வி. தொ.), 605. கெடல், 612, 856, 893. கெடு தல், 208. கெட, 359, 360, 1266. கெடுக 'let him perish,' 1062. கெடுவல் 'I shall perish,' 116. கெடின், 369, 854. கெடும், 109, 134, 166, 176, 283, 360, 435, 437, 448, 466, 474, 479, 480, 548, 553, 563–69, 601, 622, 763, 1028, 1056, 1069, 1203. கெடா, 809. கெட்டான், 967. கெட்டார், 15, 539, 1293. **3.** (§ 64) 'Destroy.' கெடுப்பது, 15. கெடுக்கும், 447, 937, 1043. கெடுப்பார், 448. கெடுத்து, 938.

கேடு (opp. to ஆக்கம், பெருக் கம், நத்தம்), 'destruction,' 32, 115, 165, 169, 204, 220, 235, 307, 400, 478, 642, 700, 732, 736, 791, 796. அருங்கேடன், 210 [comp. 732].

கெழு, கெழுவு. **1.** 'Intimacy.' [Comp. கிழ, கேண்மை.] With தகை and தகைமை 'intimacy,' 700, 802, 803, 804, 807. **2.** (§ 62) 'Be intimate, blessed.' கெழீஇ for கெழுவி (see அளபெடை)= 'showing friendship,' 820; for கெழுவிய 'intimate,' 806. கெ ழீஇயலர் 'are unblest,' 1194.

கேடு. See கெடு.

கேணி 'a well,' 396. [S. *khan, khâni.*]

கேள். **1.** 'Lover,' 1222 [comp. கிழ, கெழு]; 'intimate friend,' 808, 882. Pl. கேளிர், 187, 615, 1267. கேண்மை, 106, 441, 519, 709,

782, 792, 797, 799, 800, 807, 811, 812, 815, 818, 822, 839. **2.** (§ 70) 'Hear, ask.' கேட்டல், 65. கேட்டு, 1101. கேட்ட, 69, 1076. கேட்டார், 643. கேட்க, 414, 416, 587, 695. கேட்பர், 607. கேட்கும், 648. கேட்பி னும், 418, 423, 697. கேளா, 418, 808. கேளாது, 804, 893. கேளார், 643. கேளாதவர், 66. கேள்வி 'hearing, receiving instruction,' Ch. XLII., 413, 417, 418, 419.

கை. **1.** 'Hand' [? con. with செய்=செயி], 64, 260, 307, 727, 788, 828, 838, 879, 894, 935 (='business'), 1021, 1036, 1077, 1157, 1238. **2.** 'Measure,' 567, 1271. **3.** 'Propriety,' 832, 925. கைவிடு 'forsake' (see விடு), 799, 928, 1245. கையறி 'be sensible, skilful' (see அறி), 836, 925. கைப்பொருள் 'wealth,' 178, 371. கையாறு 'affliction,' 627. கைத்து 'wealth,' 593, 758. கைசெய் 'work with one's hands,' 1035. கைகூடு 'be possible,' 268, 484. கைம்மாறு 'equivalent,' 211, 1183. கை வேல் 'hand-javelin,' 774.

கைப்ப (=கசப்ப), 'so as to be bitter to,' 389. [கை, கச.]

கொக்கு 'heron,' 490.

கொடிறு 'jaw,' 1077.

கொடிது. See கொடு.

கொடு. **1.** கொடும், கொடிய, 'cruel.' [Comp. கடு.] கொடும், 1086. கொடிய, 1169. கொ டுங்கோன்மை 'tyranny,' Ch. LVI. கொடுமை 'cruelty,' 1169, 1235. கொடிது, 279, 551. கொடியர், 550, 1169, 1217, 1235, 1236, 1237. **2.** (§ 64), 'give.' [Comp. கொள், of which it seems to be a causal=கொள்+து; the verbs are correlative.] கொடுத் தல், 525, 725. கொடுத்து, 925. கொடுத்தும் 'though you pay a price for it,' 703, 794, 867. கொடுக்கும், 924. [Comp. புறம், *q.v.*]. கொடுப்பது, 166, 1005. கொடை 'a gift,' 390. கொடை யான், 526.

கொட்பு 'a reverse of fortune,' 789. [? கொள்.]

கொண்கன் 'a husband,' 1186, 1265, 1266, 1283, 1285. [கொள்; but comp. கொழு.]

கொழு-நன் 'a husband,' 55. [Comp. கொண்கன், and கேள்.]

கொம்பர் (=கொம்பு), 'branch,' 476.

கொல். **1.** A particle: interrogative, *nonne?* 189, 228, 1220, 930, 1157, 1197; *num?* 263, 1203, 1204, 1205, 1207, 932, 1307, 1103; with என், 2, 70, 1225; என்னை, 188; and ஓ, 211, 318; with எவன், 1225, 345, and ஓ, 1171, 99; with யாது, 1211; with எவன் and மன், 1207, 1165; with ஓ, 1081, 1328, 1048, 1004, 340, 1029, 1070. In an enumeration = 'whether . . . or . . .' கொல் . . . கொல்லோ . . . கொல், 1081. **2.** (§ 70), 'Kill.' கொல் (வி. தொ.), 'murderous,' 735. கொல்க 'destroy,' 879. கொல்ல 'crush,' 1078. கொல் லா, 984. கொல்லான், 260. கொல்லாமை, Ch. XXXIII. 321–326, 254. கொல்லும் 'hurt, kill,' 304, 305, 532, 879, 1228. கொன்ற, 110. கொன்றார், fig. 'murderers of,' 110. கொன்று (அறி) = 'rejecting,' 638; 'by murder,' 328; 'cut,' 1030. கொன்றன்ன 'as though one committed murder,' 109. கொன் றாங்கு 'as (it) has destroyed,' 532. கொன்றது 'what has crushed,' 1048. கொல்வி 'murderer' (personification), 306. கொலை 'killing,' 325, 329, 550, 551. கொலைக்களம் 'battlefield,' 1224. கொற்றம் 'victory,' 583. கோறல் for கொல் லுதல் (so சேறல்=செல்லுதல்), 254, 321.

கொள் (§ 56, III.), 'take, accept, buy, approve.' [Comp. கொடு.]

கொள் (கொண், வி. தொ, 1223, 1029. கொள்க, 161, 875. கொ ளல். **1.** 'Obtain, take, receive, esteem, buy,' 134, 222, 279, 443, 450, 504, 530, 677, 702, 703, 714, 724, 745, 794, 795, 867, 925, 986, 401, 720. **2.** 'Middle voice' (§ 106, 259), 442, 445, 588, 633, 679, 1026. கோடல் (=கொள்ளுதல்; comp. சேறல், கோறல்), 646, 678, Ch. XLV., Nâl. 101. கொ(ள்)ள, 583, 1244, 699. கொள்ளும், 1092. கோள் வேம், 976. கொளின், 630, 836, 939. கொளினும், 872. கொள் ளாது, 256, 470, 627, 1016. கொள்ளாதான், 792. கொள் ளாத, 470, 699. கொள்ளா, 1195, 1064. கொள்ளார் 'they accept not,' 404. கொளற்க, 798, 827, 872. கொண்டு 'being master of,' 974, 22, 326, 1082, 1095 (see குறி), 603, 775, 831, 845, 921, 1146, 551. With a noun='by means of': as sign of 4th case. கொண்டனள் 'she took,' 1315. கொண்ட, 659, 745. கொண்டவன், 307. கொண்டார், 551, 253, 1183, 1195, 1205. தற்கொண்டான் 'her husband,' 51, 56. [Comp. கொண்கன.] கொள்வர், 104, 433, 680. கொள்வார், 704, 813, 1009. கொள்வது (with மேல்), 262, 1055. கொள்வற்று, 1187 (=கொள்வதற்று). கொள்ப வன், 713, 981, 873. கொள்கை 'tenet, principle,' 899, 1019. கொட்க (=கொள்ள), 'so as to accept,' கொட்கின் (=கொள் ளின்), 'if (they) accept,' 663. Some say கொட்கு (§ 62), 'come to notice, whirl round.' (See கொட்பு.)

கோள் (=கொளல், கொள் கை). **1.** 'Faculty of perception,' 9. **2.** 'The taking,' 220, 780, 1059. **3.** 'Accepted principle of action,' 311, 312, 646, 662. கொளீஇ (மேல்), for கொளுவி, from கொளுவு (§ 62), a causal deriv. of கொள்='cause to obtain,' with other uses; 'giving falsehood the predominance,' 938. [Comp. 836, 845.]

N.B.—கொள் (§ 106) is used in குறள் (1) as a verb; (2) as auxiliary (§ 259); (3) with nouns it forms verbs: thus, காதற் கொள்='love'; (4) compounded with மேல் (*q.v.*), 'undertake, prevail'; (5) கொண்டு, as sign of 3rd case='by means of' (§ 239).

கோடி [S.], 'ten millions, crore,' 337, 377, 639, 816, 817, 954, 1005, 1061; 'the point of anything' [S. कोटि]. **1.** 10,000,000. **2.** 'A corner, nook.' அதிலொர் கோடி நீளம நந்தகோடி காதம் 'the length of one of its *recesses* was an infinitude of *millions* of Kádams.'

கோடு. **1.** 'Crookedness; a curve,' 279; 'tusk' (கோட்டது 'it is tusked'); 'branch,' கோட் டுப்பூ, 1313; 'bank,' 523, Nâl. 215. **2.** (v. § 62), 'bend, swerve, deflect, become unjust.' கோடி, 554, 559. கோடா, 1086. கோடாது, 520, 546. கோடாமை, 520, 115, 118. கோட்டம் 'perversion,' 119. கோடுகொடேறும் 'my bosom swells with joy.' [Prob. an imitative word, § 273.]

கோல் 'staff, rod, pencil, sceptre,' 118, 542–46, 552, 554, 558, 710, 796, 1285, 390. ஊற்றுக்கொல், 415. கோன்மை 'sway of the sceptre.' செங்கோன்மை, Ch. LV., 'just rule,' 556. கொடுங் கோன்மை, Ch. LVI., 'tyranny.' கடுங்கோல், 570. செங்கோல், 390. வெங்கோலன், 563.

கோட்டி [S. *gôshṭi*], 'assembly' [அவை], 401, 720; (with கொள ளல்) 'holding a conference with learned men.'

கோமான் [S.], 'king,' 25.

கௌவை 'scandalous report.' [அலர்.] See கவ்வை, 1143–48, 1150.

ச.

சகடக்கால் 'a bandy-wheel,' Nâl. 2. [Comp. சாகாடு.]

சமன் 'level,' 118. சமன்செய்து 'adjusting itself.'

சலம் 'evil,' 660, 956. [S. *chhala.*]

சா (§ 58), 'die.' [Comp. இற. விளி.] சாக்காடு 'death' [? 'the death-wilderness,' by met. for 'death'], 235, 339, 780. சாப்புல்லல் 'a deadly embrace,' 829. (See புல்லு.) சாம் (=சாகும்), 397, 792. சாதல், 183, 230, 1124. சாவார், 723, 779. சாகிற்பின் 'if (they) die,' 780. [சாகு + இன் + பின் 'If . . . die—then.' § 95.] சா வாமருந்து 'Ambrosia,' 82. [சாவாமைக்குக் காரணமாகிய மருந்து.] செத்தார், 214, 926, 1001.

சாகாடு 'a wagon,' 475. [Comp. சகட.]

சாய் (§ 57), 'lean, fall.' [Comp. சேர்.] சாய 'while they are defeated,' 749. கண்சாய்பவர் 'those whose eyes incline,' 927. எதிர்சாய் 'oppose, resist,' 855, 858. சாயல் 'beauty,' 1183.

சார் (§ 57), 'draw near to, be joined with.' [Comp. சேர், சாய், whose meanings it combines.] பின்சார 'afterwards.' சாரா (=சாராமல் and சாராத), 'void of,' 194, 815, 1047. சார் தரா (=சாரா), 'approaches not.' (See தரு.) சார்தரும் 'clinging to,' 359. சார்பு 'what one clings to, leans on: a support,' 76, 359, 449, 900. சார்வு, 15.

சால் (§ 170). சால 'to be full'; adv. 'very much, abundantly,' 475, 770, 1037, 1233. சாலும் (with கரி), 'sufficient witness,' 25, 1060. சான்ற 'full of, filling,' 56, 581, 1001. சான் றாண்மை [சால் + ஆள்: fulness of good and active exercise of it], 'real, perfect excellence,' Ch. XCIX., 981, 989, 990. சான்றோர், சான்றவர் 'the excellent,' 69, 115, 118, 148, 197, 299, 328, 458, 656, 657, 802, 840, 922, 923, 982, 985, 990, 1014, 1078. சால்பு 'complete excellence,' 105, 983–88, 956, 1013, 1064.

சாற்று (§ 62), சாற்றுவேன் 'I shall declare,' 1212.

சிகை 'a course of food,' Nâl. 1, 18. Explained by the Com. ஒருபிடிசோறு, கவளம் (in S. सिक्थः *siktha*).

சிதை (§ 57, 62), 'perish, destroy.' [S. *chhida* and கெடு.] சிதை-யாமல் 'without injury to,' 578. சிதை-க்கல்லாதார் 'those who cannot frustrate,' 880. [For form comp. 26, 863, 427 (1139), 219.] சிதை-வு 'ruin,' 112, 597.

சிமிழ் (§ 64), from noun='box, casket.' சிமிழ்த்தற்று 'like as if one caught,' 274.

சில, சிலர் 'few things *or* persons,' 649, 270, 1289. [Comp. சிறு.]

சிவிகை 'a litter,' 37.

சிவல் 'a partridge.'

சிற (§ 66), 'be distinguished.' [Comp. S. *shrî*; சீர்.] சிறந்த, 531, 900. சிறந்தான், 515. சிறப்பு 'anything distinguished; distinction, glory,' 18, 31, 58, 74, 75, 311, 358, 590, 630, 972, 977, 1012, 1208. சிறப்பின, 961. வான்சிறப்பு, Ch. II. காதற்சி றப்புரைத்தல், Ch. CXIII.

சிறக்கணித்தல். See சிறு.

சிறை 'fort, custody, defence,' 57, 499, 569.

சிறு, சின், சிறிய, சிற் 'little.' [Comp. சில, சுருக்கம்.] சிறு, 64, 498, 744, 1092, 870, 1010, 1322. சிறுமை, 98, 431, 451, 505, 769, 934, 978–80. சிறுமைத்து 'it is a little one,' 889; 'anything mean, servile.' சிற்றினம் 'low association,' 451. சிற்றினஞ்சே

ராமை, Ch. XLVI. சிற்றின்பம் 'sensual delight,' 173. சிறிது 'a little thing,' 102, 412, 1075, 1301, 1302. சிறிய 'little,' 963. சிறிய(ா)ர், சிறியவர், 26, 680, 815, 976. சிறுகு (§ 62), 'grow small.' சிறுகும் 'will dwindle,' 568. சிறுகுவ (Intro. p. xxii.), 'things which will degrade.' சிறக்கணி (§ 64), 'wink, *make the eye small.*' சிறக்கணித்தாள், 1095.

சினம் 'anger,' 301–10, 431, 568. [வெகுளி, கதம்.] சினத்தான் 'a wrathful person,' 866, Nâl. 61–70.

சினை (§ 64), 'bud.' [S. *jan.*] சினைப்பது 'what is produced,' 1203.

சீர் [S. *ṣrî*], 'prosperity, glory, worth.' See திரு, which is another form of the same Sanskrit word, 499, 778, 934, 962, 1010. [Comp. சிற.] சீரல்ல 'ignoble things,' 962. சீரார் 'worthy persons,' 900. சீரல்லவர் 'worthless persons,' 977. சீர்தூக்கு (§ 62), 'weigh,' 118, 813. சீர்மை 'glory,' 123, 195. சீர் (§ 62), சீரினும் 'flourish,' 962; சீரு (§ 64), சீர்த்தவிடத்தும் 'when things are favourable,' 490.

சீறு 'be angry.' [Comp. செறு.] சீறின் (§ 62), 899. (So செறின், 900.)

சுடரு (§ 62), 'shine.' [Comp. சுடு.] சுடரும், 267.

சுடு (§ 68), 'burn.' சுட, 896. சுடச்சுட 'as it hotly burns,' 267. சுடச்சுடரும், 267. சுட்ட, 129. சுடும் 'it will burn, destroy, torture,' 293, 306, 799, 1019, 1207. சுடின், சுடல், 1159.

சுதை 'lime,' 714. [Comp. சுண்ணம்.]

சும (§ 6). சமக்க 'endure, bear,' 488. [Comp. பொறு; S. *ksham.*]

சுருக்கம், சுருக்கத்து 'in adversity,' 963. [சிறு.]

சுரும்பு 'a beetle,' Nâl. 122.

சுவை 'taste,' 27, 253, 420, Nâl. 1.

சுழலு (§ 56, III.), 'whirl.' சுழலும் 'which will reach far and wide,' 777. சுழன்றும் 'though it wander,' 1031.

சுற்று (§ 62), 'surround.' [Comp. சூழ், சுழலு.] சுற்றும் 'will surround,' 1025. சுற்றப்படும், 524, 525. சுற்றம் 'those who are around, kindred, dependants,' 166, 451, 522, 524, 529, 584, 1025. சுற்றந்தழால், Ch. LIII. சுற்றத்தார் 'kindred,' 521.

சூது 'gambling,' Ch. XCIV. 931–940. [S. *dyutam.*] சூதர், 932.

சூழ் (§ 57), lit. *surround*: 'ponder, contrive.' [சுற்று.] சூழ், 176. சூழும், 204, 324. சூழின், 204. சூழினும் 'though you devise,' 380. சூழற்க 'compass not!' 204. சூழ்ந்து 445, 451, 461. சூழ்ந்தும், 640. சூழ்ந்தவன், 204. சூழ்வான், 325, 445, 1294. சூழ்வது 'what must be pondered,' 1276. சூழாது, 465, 554. சூழாமல், 1024. சூழ்ச்சி 'circumspection, deliberation,' 671.

சூடு (§ 62), 'put on, as a wreath.' சூடினும் 'if (I) put on,' 1313. சூடினீர் 'have you put on,' 1313. [Comp. ஆழ்.]

செ, செம், சே (see செய்). [Cp. அர்.] செம் 'right, kindly, true,' 91, 358, 390, 556, 1092, Ch. LV. செங்கோன்மை 'just government.' செந்தண்மை, 30. செப்பம் [செம்+பம், comp. இன்பம், துன்பம்], 'equity.' செவ்வி 'opportunity, fitting time,' 130, 565, 1289. ['*Pulchritudo*' (B.), 130, see Notes.] செவ்விது 'it is straight,' 279. செவ்வியான் 'the right-minded man,' 169. சே 'beautiful,' 1110.

செகு (§ 64). செகுத்து 'destroy,' 259.

செப்பம். See செ.

செப்பு 'a casket,' 887. [? சேர்ப்பு.]

செம்மல் [செ], 'pride,' 880. [செருக்கு.]

செம்மா (§ 64), 'be haughty,' 1074.

செய் (§ 58, 97), 'do, make, cause, acquire.' [Comp. S. *kri.*]

I. Root, வினைத்தொகை. [Intro. p. xvii. § 4 (*b*).] செய்தவம் 'asceticism that should be practised,' 265. செய்தக்க 'things fit for (one) to do,' 466, 663. செய்தொழில் 'the work (one) does,' 972. செய்வினை 'the deeds done; work, business,' 455, 463, 653, 677. செய்நன்றி 'a benefit conferred,' 110. (ந் is doubled in many editions; it need not be so.) செய்நன்றியறிதல் 'the recognition of benefits conferred; gratitude,' Ch. XI.

II. Inf. mood, செய்ய (§ 168); sometimes செய. செய '(for them) to do,' 446, 1001; 'in order to do,' 1021; 'if he does,' 466. செய்யப்படும் (§ 92), 'should be done,' 335. செய்யப்பட்டார் (படு) 'those on whom it is conferred,' 105.

III. Opt. செய்க (§ 140) 'thou shouldst do, acquire,' 36, 669, 759, 893; 'he should do,' 512.

IV. Verb. noun, செயல், செய்யல், செய்தல் (§ 148), 'the doing,' 67, 182, 192, 274, 316, 318, 375, 634, 664, 677, 679, 832, 835, 894, 905, 975, 843, 954, 1090, 1201, 1226. செயற்கரிய 'things hard to accomplish,' 26, 489, 781. செயல் (an opt. in use, with ellipsis of வேண்டும்), 'do thou!' 33, 333, 461, 489 [cp. 470, 538], 471, 516, 518, 668, 673, 675, 676, 948, 949. செயற்பால (பால்) 'what ought to be done,' 40, 437, 672. செய்தற்பொருட்டு (பொருள்) 'for the sake of doing,' 81, 212. தெரிந்துசெயல்வகை, Ch. XLVII. வினைசெயல்வகை, Ch. LXVIII. பொருள்செயல்வகை, Ch. LXXVI. குடிசெயல்வகை, Ch. CIII.

V. Past tense, part. and nouns (§ 74, 77, 87). செய்தார் 'those who have done,' 158, 208, 314, 320, 658, 987, 1162, 1243. செய்து, 118, 246, 314, 388, 551, 563, 660, 815, 829, 878, 907, 934, 1025, 1028, 1035, 1073, 1275. செய்தாங்கு [ஆங்கு], 289, 803. செய்தற்று [அற்று] 'is like doing,' 1303. செய்த 'that has (been) done,' 101, 102, 103, 109, 313, 1175, 1176, 1225. செய்தது 'that which hath done,' 1240, 1279. செய்தவக்கண்ணும் [வ inserted; கண்] '*even* when—has done,' 312.

VI. Fut. part. noun (§ 72, 74, 88). செய்வல் 'I will make,' 1023. செய்வேன், 1211. செய்வர், செய்வான், செய்வார். (1) '(they) will do,' 26, 266, 640, 752; (2) '(they) who will do,' 120, 266, 295, 462, 516, 520, 584, 677, 758, 867, 909, 998, 1028. செய்ப (= செய்வார்), 1195. செய்வது = 'that which will do, the acting,' 541. செய்யும். (1) 'it will do, cause,' 57, 79, 272, 574, 803, 847, 941; (2) 'which will do,' 219, 249, 545, 631, 672, 700, 751, 735, 1208.

VII. Cond. செயின், செய்யினும் (§ 95–97), 'if — do,' 116, 120, 175, 205, 319, 483, 484, 493, 494, 497, 537, 547, 559, 590, 804, 805, 808, 881, 965, 1257. செய்கிற்பான் 'he who will haply do,' 515. [கு + இன் inserted.] செய்வானேல் 'if he will do,' 655. [ஏல் = ஆகில்.] செயினும் (§ 100), 'though (you) do,' 104, 109, 150, 157, 181, 308, 586, 807, 852, 1283, 1288.

VIII. Neg. செயற்க 'do not!' [Intro. p. xx.], 205, 206, 327, 590, 655, 656. செய்யான்(ர்) (§ 110). (1) '(they) do not,' 164, 172, 173, 174, 210, 320, 654, 699, 956, 962; (2) 'he who does not,' 865. செய்யாது (§ 121).

(1) 'it does not,' 255; (2) 'not doing'=செய்யாமல், 219, 437, 538. செய்யாமல் 'not doing, though it has not been done,' 101. [Other reading செய்யாமை.] செய்யா 'that does not,' 548, 553, 558, 569, 987; 'not doing'=செய்யாமல், 203. With அல்:—செய்யல 'they do not,' 1086; செய்கலான் 'he does not,' 848; செய்கலாதார் 'they are persons who do not,' 26.

IX. Deriv. செய்கை (§ 143), 'the work,' 631. செய்யாமை (§ 154), 'the not doing,' 157, 261, 297, 311, 312, 313, 317, 466, 655, 852. இன்னுசெய்யாமை, Ch. XXXII. வெருவந்தசெய்யாமை, Ch. LVII. செயற்கை (opp. இயற்கை), 'artificial method of acting, theory,' 637.

செய்யவள், செய்யாள் [செ; S. *ṣrî*], 'Lakshmi.'

செயிர். 1. 'Desire, passion,' 258, 330, Nâl. 358. 2. (§ 64), 'Be wroth.' செயிர்ப்பவர் 'enemies,' 880.

செரு 'a battle,' 569. [Comp. செகு.]

செருக்கு, 180, 201, 346, 431, 598, 613, 759, 844, 860, 878, 1193; '*fascinum, est enim i.q.* மயக்கம்' (B.). படைச்செருக்கு 'greatness, conceit, spirit, infatuation,' Ch. LXXVIII. செருக்கி (as from verb, § 62), 'exulting in.'

செல் (§ 56, III.), 'go, proceed.' செல் (வி. தொ.) விருந்து 'the parting guest.' செல்லிடம் 'favourable circumstances *or* place,' 301, 302, 498. செலல் (பின்), 1293. செல 'go, prevail,' 422, 424, 686, 719, 722, 724, 728, 730. சென்று, 207, 335, 753, 784, 895, 966, 967, 1045, 1048. சென்ற, 422, 1261. சென்றேன், 1259, 1284. சென்றார், 1210, 1231, 1263, 1269, 1278. சென்றது, 1284. செல்லும், 33, 250, 594, 1269. செல்வார், 472, 1185. செல்வான், 950. செல்பவர் (பின்.), 1033. செல்வது, 767. செல்வாய், 1248. செல்கிற்பின், 1170. செலவு, 766. செல்க, 684. செல்லா, 302, 330, 561, 769, 1255. செல்லாது, 18, 326. செல்லாதது, 472. செல்லாமை, 1151. செல்லான், 1039. செல்வம் 'wealth, prosperity'; with விழு, பெரும், நெடும், பழகிய, 31, 125, 178, 216, 217, 241, 311, 332, 363, 375, 400, 411, 437, 524, 555, 565, 566, 738, 757, 837, 937, 939, 1000, 1006, 1007, 1008, Nâl. 261. நன்றியில்செல்வம், Ch. CI., Nâl. 261–70. செல்வநிலையாமை, Nâl. 1–10. செல்வர், 125, 472, 731, 752, 1010. சேறல் (=செல்லுதல்), 1256. பெண்வழிச்சேறல் 'uxoriousness,' Ch. XCI. சேறி (=செல்லுவாய்), 1249, 1292; (=செல்லு), 1244. Forms compounds with தலை, *q.v.*

செவி 'ear,' 65, 389, 411–18, 420, 694, 1199.

செவிலி 'nurse,' 757.

செறி (§ 56, I.; வி. தொ.), 'be close, near,' 1110, 1275. [சேர்.] செறிவு 'modest reserve, nearness,' 123, 684, 715; '*compressio, et metaphorice fraenatio*' (B.)

செறு (§ 62), 'be wroth.' [சீறு.] செறின், 897, 900. செறினும், 778.

செறு (§ 56, II.), 'hate, destroy.' [செகு.] திருச்செற்று 'destroying,' 168. நாச்செற்று 'paralysing the tongue,' 335. தற்செற்று 'mortifying, afflicting,' 1009. செறுவார் 'foes,' 203, 421, 843, 869. செறுநர், 488, 759. செருஅ 'not being hostile,' 1096. செருஅர் 'those not unfriendly,' 1096, 1292. செறுசொல் 'words that kill,' 1096. செறுபகை 'murderous hate,' 734. செற்றார் 'foes,' 313, 446, 1096, 1245, 1255, 1256. செறுப்ப (as from

செறு, § 64), 'suppress,' 1318. செறூஅஅய் (=செறுவாய்) 'thou wilt fill up,' 1200.

சே. See செ.

சேண் 'afar off,' 869, 1231, 1269.

சேர் (§ 60, as தீர்), 'draw near to, be intimately related to' [சார், செறி], 5 (வி. தொ. III. Gr. 153; opp. தீர்). So சேர்ந்த, 243, 492, 910 (with ஆம்+சேர்ந்து). சேர்ந்த, 694. சேர்ந்து, 691. மன்னரைச் சேர்ந்தொழுகல், 691. சேரின், 498. சேரும், 179. சேர்வது, 731. சேர்ந்தார், 3, 4, 7, 8, 306. சேரா, 5. சேராது, 734. சேராதார், 10. சேராமை, Ch. XLVI.

சேறல். See செல்.

சொரி (§ 57), 'sprinkle, scatter.' [S. *çru.*]

சொல். 1. 'Word, talk, speech' [உரை], 65, 97, 127, 819, 825, 826; 'a saying,' 70, 184, 200, 196, 198, 387, 642–46, 717, 721, 1046, 1096, 1097, 402, 607, 1147, 1154, 589, Nâl. 311. 2. 'Fame, (good) report,' 56, 1024, 453, வாய்ச்சொல், 91, 415, 959, 1100. இன்சொல், 387, 911, 91–99, 525, 1198, 35, 564, 953. புன்சொல், 189. வன்சொல், 99. செவிச் சொல், 694. தீச்சொல், 128. பயனில்சொல், 196 (198). பண்பில்சொல், 194. இன்னுச்சொல், 160, 159. கடுஞ்சொல்லன், 386, 566. மழலைச்சொல், 66. சொற்கோட்டம், 119. சொல்வணக்கம், 827. சொல்வன்மை, Ch. LXV., 647, 682. சொல்லாட, 1070, 405, 818. சொல்லேருழவர், 872. சொல்லான், சொல்லன், 635. சொல்லு (§ 70), 'speak.' [உரை, கூறு, கிளவு.] சொல்லுதல், 648, 664. சொ(ல்)லல், 139, 192, 291, 634, 647, 696, 713, 718. சொ(ல்)ல, 649, 1078. சொல்லுக, 195, 200, 644, 645, 711, 712. சொல்லி, 187, 424, 646, 685, 686, 697, 724, 795, 1280, Nâl. 312. சொல்லிய, 664. சொல்லின், 96, 195, 200, 711, 712. சொல்லினும், 184, 197, 826, 1046, 1096. சொல்லற்க, 184, 200, 719. சொல்லுவ 'things that will speak,' 1232. சொல்லுவான், 191, 719, 722. சொல்லும், 160, 185, 193. Neg. சொல்லாயோ (?), 1241. சொல்லா, 697, 984. சொல்லாது, 403. சொல்லான்(ர்), 198, 199, 417, 635. சொல்லாதார், 728, 730. சொல்லாமை, Ch. XX., 197. சொற்று=சொல்லினது, Nal. 313, 'belonging to words.'

சோகா (§ 62), சோகாப்பர் 'they will suffer anguish,' 127. [S. *çoka.*]

சோர் (§ 57), 'fail, faint, forget.' சோரும், 847, 1234. சோர, 818. சோரா, சோரார் (with வாய்), 'trip with the tongue,' 689, 721. சோர்வு 'oblivion, forgetfulness; *segnitia,*' 56, 405, 531, 586, 642, 647, 930, 1044, 1046. [Comp. பொச்சா.]

ஞ

ஞாட்பு 'battle-field,' 1088.

ஞாலம் 'the pendant globe of earth' (with epithets, *always* varied: மாயிரு, வியன், ஈர்ங் கண்மா, வளிவழங்குமல்லன் மா), 102, 141, 245, 484, 485, 557, 648, 999, 1016, 1058.

ஞானம் [S.] 'wisdom.' Not in K.; Nâl. 311.

ஞான்று (=நாள்), 'a day' (= 'a revolution'; see நாலு, ஞாலு.) [Comp. அன்று.] Only in phrase எஞ்ஞான்றும் (=என்றும்), 'all the days, always,' 44, 145, 317, 361, 439, 582, 635, 697, 701, 864, 870, 886, 903, 905, 910, 921, 926, 927, Nâl. 174. (See எ.)

த

தகர் 'ram,' 486.

தகு (§ 56, II., 117, 118), 'be fit, right.' Used often in compounds of which a verbal root is the first member: செய், கோள், and others. தக 'fitly,' 391. தகை 'fitness, excellence, beauty, appropriate quality'; '*conditio*' (B.), 916, 1182. விழைதகை, 804. பெண்டகை, 1084. கெழுதகை, 804. பெருந்தகை(யான்), 217, 968. நலத்தகை, 1305. புலத்தகை, 1305. படைத்தகை, 768. அடற்றகை, 768. தகையணங்குறுத்தல், Ch. CIX., 'pain arising from the beauty of the princess.' தகைமாண்ட, 897. தகைசான்ற, 56. தகைத்து 'it possesses the quality of,' 125, 486, 1064, Nâl. 101, 211. தகைய, 643, 418. தகைமை (=தகை), 874, 613. தகைமையவர், 447. பெருந்தகைமை, 1255. கெழுதகைமை, 700, 802, 803, 808. தகுதி 'justice, integrity,' 111, 158. தகவு 'worth,' 114. தக்க (§157), 51, 54, 466, 580, 805, 993; 1288. தக்காங்கு, 561. தக்கது, 220, 466, 663, 686, 732, 780, 1018, 1137, 1173. தக்கார், 114, 212, 446, 731, 897, 1006, 1051. தக்காள், 51. தக்கனள், 1316.

தங்கு (§ 62), 'abide, remain.' தங்கும், 389. தங்குதல், 671. தங்கி, 472. தங்கிற்று, 613, 874. தங்கின், 608. தங்கியான், 117. தங்கா, 19.

தஞ்சம 'utterly,' 863, 1300.

தடி (§ 57), தடிந்து 'diminishing,' 17.

தண (§ 56, I., 66), 'separate.' [தண்.] தணந்தமை 'separation,' 1233, 1277.

தணி 'abate.' தணிக்கும் (§ 64), 'will alleviate.' [தண், com. meanings of ஆறு, *heal* and *cool.*]

தண் 'cool; low,' 1239. தண்ணம் 'coolness,' 30, 1277. [Perhaps தண்+அம்='the prince of the shore of the cool sea.'] தண்ணென்னும் 'will become cold,' 1104. (See என்.) தண்பதம் 'low condition,' 548.

தண்டு (§ 62), 'be relieved.' [தண்.] தண்டாநோய் 'remediless suffering,' 1171.

தண்டம் [S.], 'punishment,' 567.

தந்தை 'father,' 67, 70, Nâl. 197. [தம்; the only words for *father* in K.]

தப்பு (§ 62), 'fail.' [Comp. தவு, தவறு.] தப்பா 'unfailing,' 217; '*omnibus obvia*' (B.).

தம், தமியன். See under தான்.

தரு. See தா.

தருக்கு (§ 62), தருக்கி 'exulting in,' 935.

தலை. **1.** 'Head,' 9, 16, 488, 964. **2.** 'What is chief,' 43, 47, 57, 151, 203, 295, 317, 322, 325, 411, 444, 579, 657, 687, 736, 761, 770, 814, 1031. ஒருதலை, இருதலை 'one side, both sides,' 1196. ஒருதலையா 'decidedly, absolutely,' 119, 357, 634. தலைமக்கள் 'leaders,' 770, Nâl. 216. தலைக்கூடு 'assemble, join,' 394. தலைச்செல்லு 'not that it may not make head,' 561. தலைப்படு 'attain to, gain, practise,' 88, 269, 348, 356, 1289. தலைவரு 'attack,' 767. தலைப்பெய் 'assemble,' 405. தலைப்பிரி 'separate,' 97, 258, 810, 955. Here தலை=தலம்='place.'

தவம் [S. *tapas*], 'austerity, penance,' Ch. XXIII., 19, 261–66, 274, 295, 842. [நோன்பு.]

தவறு 'fault, slip' [தவு], 469, 1154, 1286, 1321, 1325. [Comp. தப்பு.]

தவு (§ 62), தவாஅ 'unfailing,' 361, 367. தவாது 'not failing, ceasing,' 368. தவல் 'failure, cessation,' 853, 856. தவ்வென்

னும் 'it will fail.' (See என்.) தவ்வு=தவுவு 'failure.'

தவ்வை (from தவு), 'the goddess of misfortune': elder sister of good fortune, மூதேவி.

தழுவு (§ 62), 'embrace.' தழீஇயது=தழுவியது 'what it has embraced,' 425. தழீஇ=தழுவி 'embracing, loving,' 544, Nâl. 213. சுற்றந்தழால் (=தழுவுதல்) 'love of kindred and dependants,' Ch. LIII., Nâl. 201–10. தழீஇயற்று 'is as the embracing,' 913. (See அற்று.)

தளர் (§ 57), 'stagger.' நிலைதளர்ந்தற்று 'is like losing one's footing,' 716.

தளிர் (§ 64), 'shoot, bud.' தளிர்ப்ப 'so as to spring forth,' 1106. தளிர்த்தற்று 'as though it budded,' 78.

தள்ளு (§ 62), 'fail.' [Not used in K. in its com. sense of '*push.*'] தள்ளும் 'it will fail,' 290. தள்ளினும் 'though it fail,' 596. தள்ளாமை 'non-failure, success,' 596. தள்ளா 'unfailing,' 731. தள்ளாது 'it fails not,' 290.

தறு (§ 68), 'bind.' மடிதற்று 'having girt up the loins,' 1023. தறுகண் 'undaunted bravery,' 773. (See கண்.)

தன், தற். See தான்.

தனி. See தான்.

தன்மை 'quality,' 767, 1144. (See தான்.) தன்மைத்து, 355. தன்மையான், 511. தன்மையவர், 855.

தா, தரு (§ 70), 'give.' [S. *dâ.*] தரு, 1273. தரூஉம், 434. தரும், 71, 98, 138, 171, 183, 275, 284, 296, 313, 321, 370, 416, 457, 492, 507, 508, 510, 522, 611, 619, 651, 658, 663, 692, 700, 739, 785, 792, 845, 853, 884, 885, 892, 902, 903, 911, 1044, 1162, 1229. தந்து, 1089, 1183. தந்த, 212, 588. தந்தார், 1182. தந்தது, 1065. தந்தாள் 'she caused,' 1135. தரல், 131, 859, 1214. தரினும், 113. தருவது, 546, 839, 934. தருவார், 256. With சார் for சாரா we find சார்தரா; for சாரும், சார்தரும், 359; with திகழ, 1273; with படர், 1229.

தாக்கு (§ 64). தாக்க 'to strike against,' 1068. தாக்கற்கு 'for an assault,' 486. தாக்கு 'an attack,' 599. தாக்கணங்கு 'the goddess that attacks: Lakshmi.'

தாங்கு (§ 64), 'support.' [பொறு, சும.] தாங்கும் 'which will uphold, bear, sustain,' 151, 767. தாங்கி 'bearing,' 733, 767. தாங்காது, 990.

தாமரை [S.], 'lotus.' [மரை.] தாமரையினுள் 'she of the lotus: Lakshmi,' 617. தாமரைக்கண்ணன் 'the lotus-eyed one: Brahmâ,' 1103.

தாய் [தாவு], 'a mother,' 69, 1047, Nâl. 15, 101. [அன்னை.]

தார் 'van of an army,' 767; '*equitatus*' (B.).

தானை 'army,' 76, 77, 78, 770, 1082.

தாவு 'wasting,' 853; (§ 64), தாஅயது=தாவினது 'which has passed, stepped over,' 610.

தாழ் 'a bolt,' 71, 1251 [தாள்]; (§ 57), 'become low.' தாழாது 'unfailing,' 620, 1024. தாழ்ந்த 'in subjection to,' 903. தாழ்வு 'depression,' 117, 731. தாழ்ச்சி 'neglect of duty,' 671.

தாள். 1. 'Foot': அடி, 7, 8, 9 [comp. தாழ்]. 2. 'Effort,' 212, 1065 [முயற்சி]. தாளாண்மை 'persevering effort,' 613, 617, Nâl. 191–200.

தானம் [S. *dâna*], 'gift,' 19, 295; with தவம். [Comp. ஈகை.]

தான் 'self.' SING.—(i.) தான், 11, 17, 43, 82, 206, 209, 250, 251, 272, 424, 446, 451, 305, 318, 327, 380, 548, 540, 707, 792, 785, 515, 834, 835, 847, 848, 849, 862, 875,

974, 977, 980, 1006, 1023, 1024, 1026, 1060, 1094, 1102, 1215, 1290, 268, 1202. (ii.) தன்னை 'oneself,' 206, 209, 250, 305, 316, 974, 293, 1319, 439, 474, 978. (iii.) தனக்கு 'to —self,' 7, 847. (iv.) தன்னின் 'than oneself,' 250, 603 (with உம்). (v.) தன் 'its, her, one's own,' 17, 251, 69, 272, 318, 327, 387, 373, 161, 186, 116, 1102, 838, 268, 875, 630, 436, 535, 293, 244, 471, 608, 615. (vi.) தன்கண் 'in regard to oneself,' 794. PLUR.—(i.) தாம், 989, 1173, 1191, 1194, 1195, 158, 539, 319, 1103, 1076, 399, 1325, 1171, 1176, 1140, 1150, 843, 1169, 229, 646, 658. (ii.) தம்மை, 843, 151, 1312, 1303, 237. (iii.) தம்மொடு, 470. (iv.) தமக்கு, 72, 319. (v.) தம்மிலிருந்து, 1107. தம்மின் 'than themselves,' 68, 444. (vi.) தம் 'their own,' 63, 64, 66, 68, 1024, 595, 107, 237, 1191, 916, 158, 473, 539, 1015, 1051, 1205, 315, 584. தந்தம் 'each one's,' 63. தத்தம், 505. தமது 'what is their own,' 1107. தாமுடைய, 1299, 1300. (vii.) தம்வயின், 846.

தன் (தற்), for தன்னை, &c., in comp., 878, 883, 529, 1009, 51, 56, 157, 741, Nâl. 101. தமர் 'one's own people,' 1300, 529, 881, 837, 814, 443, 444, 1027. தம 'one's own (fate),' 376, 120. தமியன் 'one by himself, alone,' 873. தமியள் 'a female alone,' 1007. தமியர், 229. தனியே 'alone,' 1296. தனிமை 'loneliness,' 814. தனிப்படர்மிகுதி, Ch. cxx. 'The excess of *solitary* grief.' தனித்து 'alone,' 338.

திகழ் (§ 57), 'gleam.' திகழ்வது 'what gleams.' திகழ்தரும் 'which gleams.' (See தரு.)

திங்கள் 'the moon,' 1146. [Comp. திகழ்.]

திண் (திட்), 'strength.' திண்மை 'strength,' 54, 743, 988. திண்ணியர் 'men of strength,' 666. திட்பம் 'strength, firmness,' 661, 665, 670. வினைத்திட்பம் 'strength in action,' Ch. LXVII. திடன் 'firmness,' 910.

திரி (§ 57), 'turn, change.' முகந்திரிந்து 'with changed countenance,' 90. திரிந்தற்று 'as when it changes,' 452, 1000. [அற்று.] நிலையிற்றிரியாது 'remaining fixed,' 124, Nâl. 212.

திரு [S. *çrî*], 'prosperity, wealth, goddess of fortune,' 168, 179, 215, 374, 408, 482, 519, 568, 616, 920, 1072. [Comp. சீர்.] திருநுதல் an epithet of a woman: 'one on whose brow Lakshmi sits,' 1011, 1123.

திறம், திறன் 'worth, ability, method, opportunity,' 157 ('*aequitas, bonitas*,' B.), 179, 186 ('*quod majus est*,' B.), 441, 501, 635, 644, 754, 1184, 1298. திறப்பாடு. See படு. பகைத்திறந்தெரிதல், Ch. LXXXVIII.

தினை 'millet' (with துணை, and opposed to பனை), 104, 144, 433, 1282, Nâl. 105.

தின் (§ 56, III.), 'eat.' தினல் 'eating,' 254, 256. தின்னும், 1244. தினிய (=தின்ன), 1296. தின்பவர் 'eaters,' 252, Nâl. 211.

தீண்டு (§ 62), 'touch.' [Comp. [தொடு.] தீண்டல் 'the touching,' 65, 227, 1106. தீண்டா (§ 110), 'infect not.'

தீ. I. 'Evil.' Its opp. is நல். தீவினை, 201, 209, 210. தீவினையச்சம், Ch. XXI., Nâl. 121–30. தீநட்பு, Ch. LXXXII. தீது, 302, 182, 190, 671, 192, 222, 282, 422, 531, 754. தீயவை, தீய, 202, 203, 205, 208, 375, 139, 302, 303, 62. தீப்பால, 206, Nâl. 223. தீச்சொல், 128. தீவாழ்க்கை, 330. தீயொழுக்கம், 138. தீயினம், 460. தீப்பிணி, 227. தீங்கு 'evil,' 827. தீமை 'evil,' 984, 1000, 143, 291, 511. தீமைத்து, 450.

II. 'Fire,' 129, 202, 1159, 1260, 1104, 929, Nâl. 224, 225. தீயெச்சம் 'a smouldering fire,'

674. தீக்காய்வார் 'those who warm themselves at a fire,' 691. தீயுழி 'hell,' 168. தீயளவு 'the digestive power,' 947.

தீர் (§ 57, 64), 'free from, be freed from.' தீர் (opp. to சேர், 5.), 'free from,' 6, Nâl. 2. தீர 'absolutely—so as to be free from,' 348. தீரா 'that passes not away,' 1201, 508, 510. தீர்த்தல் 'relieve thou,' 226. தீர்ந்தார் 'men who have failed of, failed to do,' 612, 170. தீர்ந்தன்று (தீர்ந்தது), 'has abandoned,' 612. தீராமை=தீராமல் 'so that it fails not,' 482. தீர்ப்பான் 'the remover of disease,' 950. தீர்வாம் 'we shall get rid of,' 1063. தீர்க்கும் 'which will remove,' 1241, 1275. தீர்ந்த (as rel. part. and verb. noun), 'freed from, things devoid of,' 199, 292.

து, verb. root, 'enjoy' (§ 62); sometimes written துய், and துவ்வு.

I. துப்பார் (§ 88), '*those who will enjoy* food: eaters,' 12.

II. துவ்வான் (§ 110), '*he enjoys not* vigour,' 862; '*enjoys not* his wealth,' 1006. துவ்வாய் 'thou wilt not enjoy,' 1294. துவ்வாதவர் (§ 121), '*those who enjoy not* affluence, the poor,' 42. துவ்வாமை (§ 154), '*non-enjoyment*: poverty,' 94.

III. துப்பு (§ 190). **1.** 'Food which is *enjoyed*,' 12. [துப்பாக்கி, துப்பாயது]. **2.** '*Enjoyment*,' 12. துப்பாய (=இனிமையான) 'pleasant.' **3.** '*Enjoyment* of vigour; strength,' 862. வெந்துப்பு 'stern strength,' 895. **4.** 'Enmity; strength put forth against' (opp. to நட்பு), 1165. **5.** 'Aid; strength exerted for,' 106.

IV. துப்புரவு. [For form comp. ஒப்புரவு. உரவு seems to strengthen the meaning.] **1.** (as துப்பு, **1.**), 1050. **2.** (as துப்பு, **2.**), 378. **3.** (as துப்பு, **5.**), 'aid; supplying their needs,' 263.

துஞ்சு (§ 62), 'sleep.' [Comp. துயில், தூங்கு.] துஞ்சல் 'slumbering,' 1049. துஞ்சில் 'if it slumber,' 1212. துஞ்சும், 1218. துஞ்சா, 1179. துஞ்சினர் 'slumberers,' 926.

துடை (§ 64), 'wipe.' துடைத்து 'having wiped away,' 615. துடைத்தவர், 107.

துணி (§ 57), 'decide.' துணிக 'decide thou,' 467. துணிந்தபின் 'after having decided,' 467. துணிவு 'decision, conclusion,' 21, 533, 669, 671. துணிவுடைமை 'decision of character,' 383, 688.

துணை. I. 'Assistance,' 471, 497, 651, 1299, 862, 875, 41, 42, 76, 132, 414, 242, 460, 635, 36, 51. துணைமை, 688.

II. 'Companion,' 1168, 1222, 1263, 1234. பெரியாரைத்துணைக்கோடல், Ch. XLV. துணையார் 'companions, assistants,' 447. வாழ்க்கைத்துணைநலம், Ch. VI.

III. 'Similarity,' 310.

IV. 'அளவு,' 'until,' 156, 433, 22, 87, 104, 144, 397, 1282, Nâl. 105, 218.

தும்மு (§ 62), 'sneeze'; 'a sneeze,' 1318. தும்மல் 'sneezing,' 1203, 1253. தும்மினீர், 1317. தும்மினர், 1312. தும்மினள், 1317.

துயர் 'sorrow,' 1135, 1165, 1275; துயரம், 792. [S. *duh.* Comp. துக்கம்.]

துயில 'sleep,' 605, 1103. [Comp. துஞ்சு.] துயிற்று (§ 62), 'lull to sleep,' 1168.

துய் (§ 64), 'enjoy, eat.' [Comp. து.] துய்த்தல் 'enjoyment,' 377. துய்க்க, 944. துயப்பது 'enjoyment,' 1005.

துருவு (§ 62), 'seek for.' துரீஇயற்று (=துருவி), 'is like seeking for,' 929.

துலே 'balance.' [S. *tulâ.*] துலேயல்லார் 'those not one's equals,' 986.

துவர (inf. of துவரு 'be harsh'), 'much,' 944, 1050.

துளக்கு, துளங்கு (§ 62), 'move.' துளங்காது 'not wavering,' 668. துளக்கற்ற 'unwavering,' 699.

துளி 'a drop *of rain*,' 16, 557.

துற (§ 66), 'renounce (the world).' [Comp. தூரம்.] துறந்த, 342. துறந்தார், 22, 42, 159, 276, 310, 342, 348, 529, 586, 1188, 1250. துறப்பார், 378, 1017. துறவார், 276, 806, 1017. துறக்க, 342. துறவற்க, 106. துறவு 'renunciation,' Ch. XXXV., Nâl. 51–60. நாணுதுறவுரைத்தல், Ch. CXIV. துறந்தமை, 1157. துறவாமை, 1050, Nâl. 226.

துறைவன் 'Lord of the haven,' 1157, 1277. [துறை.]

துனி 'anger, sorrow, pain, poverty, fear,' 769, 1010, 1223, 1294, 1306, 1322 [comp. துன்-பம்]; (§ 64) 'sulking,' 1290.

துன்பம் 'affliction' [opp. இன்பம்; S. *dur*], 106, 267, 368, 369, 615, 628, 629, 940, 1045, 1052, 1223, 1299, 1307. துன்பு, with உறு, 94.

துன்னு (§ 62), 'approach.' துன்னி, 494. துன்னு, 1250. துன்னியார் 'friends,' 188, 494. துன்னற்க, 209. துன்னுமை, 316, Nâl. 226.

தூ. 1. 'Hostility,' 685. 2. 'A support' (தூண்), 455 ['forceps' (B.), but?]. 3. See தூய்.

தூக்கு (§ 62), 'lift up, weigh.' தூங்கு (§ 62), 'hang down,' allow to be in suspense, protract.' தூக்கி 'weighing,' 471, 912. தூக்கார் 'they weigh not,' 103. தூக்கின் 'if you weigh,' 103. தூக்கும் 'which will weigh,' 118, 813. தூக்கம் 'sleep,' 668. தூங்கும் 'which will hang,' 1163. தூங்கி 'allowing to be deferred,' 672. தூங்காது 'not delaying,' 672. தூங்கற்க 'do without hesitation,' 672. தூங்குக 'do with slowness,' 672. தூங்காமை 'not delaying,' 383.

தூண் 'pillar,' 615, 983.

தூண்டில் 'a fishing-hook,' 931.

தூது [S.] 'a message, embassy,' Ch. LXIX., 681, 682, 1211; 'an ambassador,' 685, 686, 690, 1228.

தூறு 'a stack.' வைத்தூறு 'a stack of straw,' 435.

தூய் = தூ 'purity.' தூய்மை 'purity,' 159, 298, 364, 455, 688, 711. வினைத்தூய்மை, Ch. LXVI. தூயார் 'pure ones,' 456, Nâl. 41–50.

தூவு (§ 62), 'let droop.' கைதூவேன, 'I will not relax my efforts,' 1021. தூவி 'down, feathers,' 1120.

தூற்று (§ 62), 'defame, spread a report.' தூற்றுகொல் 'doth it not proclaim,' 1157. தூற்றார் 'they noise abroad,' 1190. தூற்றும் 'which will bruit about,' 188.

தெய்வம் [S.] 'the divinity; gods, divine power,' 43, 45, 50, 55, 619, 702, 1023.

தெரி (§ 57), 'be clear, discriminate, select.' [Comp. தேர், தேறு, தெளி.] தெரிதல் 'discrimination,' 634, 717. பகைத்திறந்தெரிதல், Ch. LXXXVIII. தெரிவர், 329, 104. தெரிவான், 27. தெரியான், 947. தெரியா, 583. தெரியுங்கால் 'when you see clearly,' 503. தெரிந்து, 23, 132, 186, 501, 712, 1172. தெரிந்துசெயல்வகை, Ch. XLVII. தெரிந்துவினையாடல், Ch. LII. தெரிந்த, 462, 712.

தெருள் (§ 56, III.), 'know clearly.' [தெரி.] தெருளா

தான் 'he who sees not clearly,' 249.

தெவ்வு 'hatred.' தெவ்வர் 'enemies,' 639. தெவ்விர் 'ye foes,' 771.

தெள் 'clear.' தெளி [comp. தெரி, தெருள், தேர்] (§ 57), 'become clear, trust'; (§ 64), 'promise.' தெண்ணீர் 'clear water,' 1065. தெளிதல் 'confidence.' தெரிந்துதெளிதல் 'trust after due selection,' Ch. LI. தெளிந்தான் 'he (who) has trusted,' 508, 143; 'those whose minds are clear from guile,' 353; 'one in whom you have reposed confidence,' 510. தெளிவு 'clearness,' 464; 'confidence,' 502, 510, 513. தெள்ளியர் 'men of upright mind,' 374. தெள்ளித்தசொல் 'plighted word,' 1154, Nâl. 219.

தெறு (§ 56, II., as அறு), 'destroy.' தெறுபொருள் 'enemies' spoil,' 756. தெறல் 'destruction,' 264. தெறும் 'will destroy,' 674, 883, 1104.

தெற்றென்க 'certainly,' 581. (See என்; தெற்று='certainty.')

தென் [cor. of S. *dakshiṇa*], 'south,' 43. (See புலம்.)

தேயம் 'country.' [S. *deça.*] தேயத்து 'through the lands.'

தேய் (§ 57, 64), 'be worn away; wear away.' தேய 'while (it) is worn away,' 96. தேயும் 'will be worn away,' 888. தேயந்த 'they have been worn away,' 1261. தேய்க்கும் 'which will wear away,' 555, 567.

தேர் 'chariot,' 496, 667. [Qy. by metathesis from S. இரதம்.]

தேர் (§ 57), 'know, investigate thoroughly.' [Another form of தெரி. Comp. தேறு.] தேரின், 249. தேரினும், 132, 242; '*attentè inspicere*' (B.). தேர்ந்து, 441, 462, 541, 634. தேர்ந்த, 509. தேரான், 144 ('*supple peccati gravitatem*,' B.), 508, 510. தேராது, 509. தேர்ச்சி 'accurate knowledge,' 635.

தேவர் [S.], 'the gods,' 1073, Nâl. 112.

தேறு 'know thoroughly, so as to trust.' [Comp. தெளி, தெரி, தேர்.] தேற, 501, 589. தேறுதல் 'trusting,' 506, 507. தேறல், 825. தேறினும் . . . தேறு . . . தேறுன், 876, 848. தேறியார், 1154. தேறிய, 514. தேறற்க . . . தேறுக . . . தேறும், 509.

தேற்று (§ 62), caus. of தேறு, but used for it sometimes (§ 160). தேற்றுதவர் 'those who have not gained the knowledge to . . ., 187, 289, 626, 649, 1054. தேற்றுதல் 'inspiring confidence,' 693. தேற்றம் 'certainty, confidence,' 513, 766, 1153. [Comp. தெற்று.]

தேன் 'honey,' 1121.

தொகு (§ 64 and 56, II.), 'collect together, amass.' தொகுத்தார், 377. தொகுத்தவற்றுள் 'amidst all, collected together,' 322; (§ 87, 251), 'be summed up.' தொக 'concisely,' 685. தொக்க (=தொக்கவை), 'things in which *all the three* agree=the sum of their consenting testimony,' 589. தொக்கு (§ 77), 'having combined, together,' 545. தொகை 'the sum total,' 711, 1043.

தொடர் (§ 57), 'follow after, be connected with.' [தொடு, ஒடு, உடன்.] தொடரார், 695. தொடர்கை 'connection,' 450. தொடர்பு, 73, 782, 806, 819, 820, 882, 920. தொர்ப்பாடு 'connection,' 345, Nâl. 211.

தொடங்கு (§ 62), 'begin.' [தொடு.] தொடங்கார், 464. தொடங்கற்க, 491.

தொடு (§ 68), 'touch; dig.' [தோண்டு.] தொடின் 'if you touch,' 1159. தொட்டு 'having dug,' 396, Nâl. 2.

தொடலை 'a wreath,' 1135. [தொடு, § 64.]

தொடி. **1.** 'A bracelet,' and by met. 'a woman,' 911, 1101, 1135, 1234–38, 1275, 1279. (Without epithet four times; with epithet ஆய், செறி, குறுந், ஒண், பைந்; no epithet used twice.) **2.** 'An ounce,' 1037.

தொலை (§ 57, 64), 'perish, destroy.' தொலைவு 'destruction,' 762, 806.

தொல் 'ancient,' 762, 1043, 1234, 1235. தொல்லை 'antiquity,' 806, Nâl. 101, 166, 216.

தொழு (§ 60), 'worship, serve.' தொழும், 260, 268. தொழுது, 55, 970, 1033. தொழுத, 828. தொழாஅர், 2. தொழாஅள், 55. தொழில் 'work, duty, mark, affair,' 394, 428, 549, 560, 582, 648, 833, 972, 1252. தொழிற்று (Intro. p. xxiii.), 977. தொழு, தொழுநோய் 'leprosy' (? தொடர், Nâl. 123.)

தோடு 'wreath of flowers,' 1105. [தொடு.]

தோட்டி [S.], 'a goad,' 24.

தோணி 'a boat,' 1068.

தோய் (§ 57), 'touch, embrace.' தோயாதார், 149. தோயார், 914-16. தோய்வர், 917. தோய்வன்ன 'as though it enveloped,' 308. [தோய்வு + அன்ன.]

தோல். **1.** 'Skin,' 80, 273. **2.** 'Beauty,' 1043. **3.** (§ 70, as கல்), 'Suffer defeat.' [Opp. வெல்.] தோற்றவர் 'those who have been worsted,' 1329. தோல்வி defeat,' 986.

தோழி 'female companion,' 1284. [Comp. தோழம், fem. of தோழன்.]

தோள். **1.** 'Shoulder, arm, person,' 149 (*corpus*, B.), 906, 916, 917, 919, 1103, 1105, 1106, 1113, 1218, 1233, 1236, 1237, 1262, 1265, 1272, 1279, 1325. **2.** (§ 70, as கேள்) 'perforate.' தோட்கப்படாதசெவி 'the unopened ear,' 418. [Comp. தொளை.]

தோறு, தோறும், தொறும், 'every.' (1) With noun: நாடோறும் 'every day,' 520; நாடொறும், 553. (2) With v. root: நவிறொறும், பயிறொறும், 783; களித்தொறும், 1145; அறிதோறு, செறிதோறும், 1110; உறுதோறு, 1106. (3) With inf.: இழத்தொறூஉம், உழத்தொறூஉம், 940. (4) With fut. rel. part.: வெளிப்படுந்தோறு, 1145.

தோன்று (§ 62), 'appear.' தோன்றல், 236, 1119. தோன்றும், 371, 1322, 1324. தோன்றி, 1253. தோன்றின், 236, 884, 885, 958. தோன்றிய, 1328. தோன்றுக, 236. தோன்றா, 479. தோன்றாமை, 236. தோற்றம் 'appearance,' 124, 272, 1003, 1059.

ந.

நகு (§ 56, II.), 'laugh, be kindly, deride.' நகல் 'laughing, cheerfulness,' 860, 999. நகுதல், 784. நகும் 'will deride,' 271, 774, 1040, 1094, 1095, 1098. நக, 187, 685, 786, 829, 873, 927, 1173. நகுப, 1140. நகுக, 621. நகாஅ, 824. நகை 'laughter,' 182, 304, 694, 817, 871, 953, 995, 1274.

நசை (§ 57), 'desire.' [Comp. அவா.] நசைஇ 'desiring,' 1263. (See அளபெடை.) நசைஇயார் 'the object of my desires,' 1199. நசை 'desire,' 1043, 1156.

நச்சு (§ 62), 'desire.' [நசை, நயம்.] நச்சப்படாதவன், 1004.

நஞ்சு 'poison,' 580, 926. நச்சு 'poisonous,' 1008.

நட (§ 66) 'walk.' நடை 'gait, method,' 59, 712, 1014.

நடு 'middle,' 1008. [நள்.] நடுவு 'justice, impartiality,' 113, 116, 117, 171, 172. நடுவுநிலைமை 'equity,' Ch. XII.

நடுக்கு 'trembling.' நடுக்கற்ற 'firm.' நடுங்கு (§ 62), 'tremble.' நடுங்கஞர் 'fearful war,' 1086. நடுங்கல் 'trembling,' 680.

நண், நள், நட் 'nearness.' [Opp. சேண்.] நணியது 'it is near,' 353. நணித்து 'it is near,' 856. நண்ணு (§ 62), 'draw near.' நண்ணேன் 'I draw not nigh,' 1311. நண்ணார் 'foes,' 1088. நள் (§ 56, III.), 'be friendly.' நள்ளா, 912. நட்டல், 784, 791. நட்பது, 786. நட்பின், 781. நட்டு, 812, 830. நட்ட, 791. நட்டார், 192, 679, 804, 805, 808, 826, 908, 1293. நண்பு 'friendship.' 74, 998. நட்பு 'friendship' [தொடர்பு, பழைமை], 106, 107, 187, 338, 381, 782–89, 790–98, 800–7, 821, 829, 830, 874, 1122, 1165, Ch. LXXIX. நட்பாராய்தல், Ch. LXXX. தீநட்பு, Ch. LXXXII. கூடாநட்பு, Ch. LXXXIII.

நத்தம் 'advantage, gain,' 235. [S. ஆக்கம், ஆயம்.]

நயம், நயன், 'benefit, gain, pleasure, reason,' 97, 103, 192, 193, 194, 197, 216, 219, 314, 783, 860, 994, 998, 912. [Comp. நல், நசை.]

நய (§ 66), 'desire.' [Comp. நசை.] நயத்தக்க, 580. நயவற்க, 439. நயந்தவர், 1181, 1232. நயவாமை, 150. நயவாதவன், 147. நயப்பித்தார் (§ 160), 1189, 1190.

நரி 'a jackall,' 500.

நல் 'good.' [Opp. தீ, புல், சிற்.]

I. In comp. நன், நற், 2, 314, 860, 138, 171, 60, 335, 460, 719, 746, 908, 1000, 1026, 1030, 1111, 1133, 1134, 1189, 1322, 1247. நல்லாறு, 41, 222, 242, 324. நற்பால், 659. நல்விருந்து 'a worthy guest,' 84, 86.

II. நன்மை 'goodness, worth,' 103, 194, 292, 511, 712, 1013. நன்கு 'what is good'; adv. 'well,' 458, 513, 534, 712, 719, 728, 1046. நன்றி 'a benefit,' 67, 97, 102, 104, 108, 110, 117, 138, 422, 439, 652, 685, 994. செய்(ந்)நன்றியறிதல் 'gratitude,' Ch. XI. நன்றியிற்செல்வம் 'wealth without benefit,' Ch. CI. நலம், நலன் 'goodness, beauty,' 407, 457–59, 499, 511, 641, 651, 914–16, 958, 960, 982, 984, 1007, 1019, 1305. வாழ்க்கைத்துணைநலம், Ch. VI. நலம்புனைந்துரைத்தல், Ch. CXII. உறுப்புநலனழிதல், Ch. CXXIV. நலக்குரியர் 'men to whom goodness is a special property,' 149.

III. As வினைக்குறிப்பு (§ 184). நல்லாள், 924, 1040. நல்ல(ா)ர், 403, 408, 450, 729, 903, 905, 1305, 1011. நல்ல(-வை), 96, 213, 300, 375, 379, 416, 679, 823, 826, 905, 981, 1115. நல்லது, 323. நன்று 'what is good, 'tis good,' 38, 49, 92, 108, 109, 111, 113, 125, 128, 150, 152, 157, 197, 222, 236, 253, 297, 308, 323, 328, 379, 404, 456, 469, 655, 673, 715, 815, 908, 932, 967, 1072, 1038, 1190, 1225.

IV. Deriv. நல்கு (§ 62), 'grant a favour, be kind.' நல்குவ(ா)ர், 1150, 1156. நல்கார், 1199, 1248. நலகாதவர், 1213, 1244, 1249. நலகா, 1217. நலகாமை, 1181, 1190, 1232.

V. நல்கூரு (§ 57) 'be poor' [? 'seek for good']. நலகுரவு 'poverty,' Ch. CV., 1043, 1045, 1047, 657. நல்கூர்ந்தார் 'the poor,' 219, 1046, Nâl. 301.

நவில் (§ 70), 'learn.' நவிறொறும் (வி. தொ.), 'whenever you learn,' 783.

நறு 'fragrant,' 1231. [Comp. நாறு.] நறா 'palm-tree sap, toddy,' 1090.

நனவு 'a state of wakefulness,' 1213–20. [Opp. கனவு 'dream.']

நனி 'much,' 403.

நனை (§ 57) 'become wet.' வி. தொ., 678.

நா 'tongue,' 127, 129, 335, 641, 1066.

நாகம் [S.], 'snake, dragon,' 763.

நாகரிகம் [S.], 'urbanity,' 580.

நாடு. 1. (§ 62), 'search out,' Nâl. 15, 101. [Used often with தேடு in common.] நாட, 739. நாடி, 96, 242, 504, 511, 516, 553, 561, 948, 1214. நாடிய, 518. நாடுக, 520. நாடா, 739, 74. நாடாது, 791. நாடாமை, 833. 2. 'A country,' 397, 553, 731–740, 966, 1323. நாட்ட 'they belong to the land,' 545.

நாண், நாணு. 1. 'Modesty, shame'; *verecundia*, αἰδώς, 502, 902, 903, 907, 924, 951, 952, 983, 1011–17, 1020, 1089, 1132–34, 1151, 1157, 1162, 1163, 1183, 1247, 1297. நாணின்மை 'shamelessness,' 1019. நாணுடைமை, Ch. CII., 960, 1012, 1014. நாணுத்துறவுரைத்தல், Ch. CXIV. (§ 62), 'be ashamed of.' நாண, 314, 1018, 1149. நாணுதல், 1011. நாணுவார், 433, 794, 1015. நாணுபவர், 172. நாணின, 1231. நாணார், 506, 1018, 1205. நாணாமை, 833. 2. 'A cord.' ஞாண், 1020.

நாள் 'day' [நாளை], 38, 156, 326, 334, 520, 553, 776, 808, 1146, 1169, 1206, 1278, 1261, 1266, 1269, 1233. நாளேம் 'I am seven days,' 1278.

நாமம் [S.]. 1. 'Name,' 360. 2. 'Fear,' 149. [Beschi says 'âm *nil* significat.']

நார் 'affection.' நாரின்மை 'want of affection,' 833, 958.

நாவாய் 'a ship,' 496 [S. *nau*; *navis*, ναῦς.]

நாறு (§ 62), 'emit fragrance.' நாறு, 650. நாற்றம் 'fragrance,' 27, 1113, 1274.

நான்கு 'four,' 35, 146, 382, 390, 501, 513, 605, 743, 766, 953.

நிகழ் (§ 57), 'go on.' நிகழ்பவை 'things that happen,' 582.

நிச்ச = நித்திய 'perpetual.' [S. *nitya*.]

நிணம் 'fat,' 1260.

நிர (§ 66), 'arrange.' நிரந்தவர் 'those arranged,' 821. நிரந்து 'setting in order,' 648.

நிரப்பு 'poverty,' 532, 1048, 1049, 1060, Nâl. 287.

நிரம்பு, நிரப்பு (§ 62), 'be full, fill.' நிரப்பிய 'abundance,' 229. நிரம்பிய 'full, ample,' 401.

நில் (§ 70), 'stand, abide.' நிற்க (§ 140), 'stand!' 391; inf. 708. நிற்கும், 145, 232, 288, 544, 765, 946, 1141. நிற்பேம், 1260. நிற்பவை, 636. நிற்பது, 233. நின்று, 11, 13, 184, 286, 468, 771, 1053, 1055. நின்றன்னார் 'those who seemed to stand as . . .,' 898. நின்ற 41, 698, 1019, 1157. நின்றவர், 771. நின்றார், 6, 29, 142, 806. நின்றான், 176, 552. நின்றது, 543. நில்லாது, 592; pl. 331. நில்லன்மின், 771. Forms compounds with எதிர், முன், கண்.

நிலம், நிலன் 'earth, ground, soil, country,' 3, 28, 68, 151, 239, 307, 383, 386, 413, 452, 496, 499, 526, 544, 990, 959, 898, 1039, 1040, 1094. நிலவரை, 234. நிலக்கு, 570, 572, 1003.

நிலை 'position, standing-place, permanence,' 124, 325, 449, 716, 745, 789, 964, 966, 1189, 1036. நிலையின 'things permanent,' 331. உயிர்நிலை 'body,' 80, 255, 290. நிலைமை = நிலை, 273. நடுவுநிலைமை, Ch. XII. நிலையாமை 'instability,' 349, Ch. XXXIV., Nâl. ch. I.–III. அந்நிலையே, 370, 489, 967. நிலைமக்கள் 'soldiers, rank and file,' 770. கனவுநிலையுரைத்தல், Ch. CXXII.

நிழல் 'shadow,' 208, 742, 881, 1309. நீழல், 1034.

நிறு (§ 64), 'place, put a stop to'

(caus. of நில்). நிறுத்து, 1132, 1174.

நிறை (§ 57), 'become full' (caus., § 64). [Comp. சாலு, நிரம்பு.] நிறைய 'so as to be full,' 1282. நிறைந்த 'which is full *or* fills,' 1117, 1272. நிறைந்தற்றே 'as though it were full,' 215, 523.

நிறை. 1. வி. தொ., 28, 782, 1315. 2. 'Fulness, excellence, modest reserve (=சால்பு), 57, 864, 917, 1138, 1251, 1254. நிறையழிதல், Ch. CXXVI., 'reserve overcome.' நிறையுடைமை, 154.

நினை (§ 64 or 57), 'think, reflect, devise.' [Syn. கருது, உள்ளு.] நினைக்க, 169; imp. 250. நினைப்ப, 1202. நினையும், 674. நினைத்து, 1241, 1320. நினைத்த, 1296. நினைப்பான், 519. நினைப்பவர், 1203. நினைந்து, 1209. நினைந்தவர்புலம்பல் 'lamentation at thought of the past,' Ch. CXXI. நினையார், 1203. நினைப்பினும், 1208.

நீள் (§ 70, as கேள்). [Comp. நெடு.] நீளும் 'it will be extended,' 1022; 'grow,' 1147. நீள 'so as to be prolonged,' 1302. நீடு (§ 62), 'extend, prolong, delay.' நீடுக, 1330. நீடுவது, 1307. நீட்டு (§ 62), 'stretch out,' 796. [நீட்டல்.] நீள (adj.), 'prolonged,' 234, 1022. நீட்டம் 'length,' 595. நீடு 'prolonged duration,' 3, 6, 566, 1312.

நீ 'thou,' 1123, 1221, 1242, 1249, 1291. நீர் 'you,' 1319, 1320. நின் 'thy,' 1151, 1222, 1271, 1288, 1311. நின்னொடு, 1294. நின்னினும், 1111. நுமர் 'your,' 1318.

நீ (§ 64), 'remove' (act.).

நீ-ங்கு, நீ-க்கு (§ 62), 'remove' (a. and n.).

I. நீத்து, 1262. நீத்தார் 'he, they, who left,' 21, 325, 1220. நீத்தார்பெருமை 'the greatness of those who have renounced all.' அற, Ch. III. நீத்த, 1149. நீப்பின், 370, 969, 1154. நீப்பர், 969. நீப்பினும், 327.

II. நீங்கும், 195, 1124, 519, 1265. நீங்கியான், 341. நீங்கி, 246, 352, 353, 502, 592, 1234. நீங்கிய, 98. நீங்கின், 495, 1104, 1155. நீங்க, 358. நீங்கா, 383. நீங்காமை, 154, 562. நீங்கலர் [அல்], 1216. நீங்கான், 864.

III. நீக்கும், 194, 327. நீக்க, 920. நீக்கின், 853. நீக்கியார், 330. நீக்கி, 384, 436, 685, 787, 1132, 1160, Nâl. I.

நீந்து (§ 62), 'swim.' நீந்தல், 8. நீந்தல 'they swim not,' 1170. நீந்தி, 1167. நீந்தும், 1164. நீந்துவர், 10. நீந்தார், 10.

நீர். I. 'Water,' 13, 20, 149, 215, 298, 452, 523, 660, 701, 718, 742, 881, 929, 1038, 1066, 1093, 1121, 1147, 1161, 1170, 1174, 1309, 1323. க(ண்)ணீர் 'tears,' 71, 780, 828 [comp. 1315]. நீராடி, 278. தெண்ணீர், 1065.

II. 'Quality, essence,' 34, 881. நெடுநீர் 'procrastination,' 605. நீரர் 'those who possess a quality,' 1319, 527, 782. நீரது 'it has (this) nature,' 221, 745. நீர்மை 'quality,' 17, 219, 1272, 195. நீர்த்து 'it is thus,' 431, 596, 777, 1143. நந்நீரை 'thou hast a good nature,' 1111. மென்னீரள் 'she is tenderer,' 1111. பின்னீர 'things having a nature that deteriorates,' 782. நிறைநீர 'things that improve,' 782. கெடுநீரார் 'men doomed to, fitted for, destruction,' 605.

நுசுப்பு 'the waist,' 1115.

நுண், நுட் 'fine, subtle,' 407, 424, 726. நுண்ணிய 'subtle,' 373. நுண்ணியர் 'a penetrating one,' 1126. நுண்ணியம் 'we are sagacious,' 710. நுணங்கு (§ 62), 'be subtle.' நுணங்கிய 'refined,' 419. நுணக்கம் 'refinement.' புலவிநுணக்கம், Ch. CXXXII., 'the artifices of jealousy.' நுட்பம் 'subtlety.'

நுதல் 'brow,' 1238, 1327. நன்

னுதலாள், 908. திருநுதல், 1123. திருநுதனல்லவர், 1011. ஒண்ணுதல், 1088, 1240.

நுது (§ 64), 'extinguish.' நுதுப் பேம், 1148.

நுமர். See நீ.

நுழை (§ 57), வி. தொ., 'enter, penetrate,' 407. நுழைந்து, 130, ['B. reads உழைந்து.']

நுனி 'tip,' 476.

நூல் 'a scientific treatise,' *lit.* 'thread' [Nannûl 24], 401, 410, 440, 543, 560, 636, 683, 726, 727, 743, 783, 1273. [Comp. பனுவல்.] நுண்ணியநூல், 373. உரைசான்றநூல், 581. நூலோர் 'scientific writers,' 322, 533, 683, 941.

நூறு 'hundred,' 932.

நெகிழ் (§ 57), 'become loose, flaccid; slip off.' நெகிழ, 1236.

நெஞ்சம் 'mind, heart, conscience,' 116, 253, 272, 706, 910, 917, 1252, 1259, 1299, 1300, 1310. [Syn. மனம்.]

நெஞ்சு, 276, 281, 288, 293, 842, 917, 1053, 1081, 1200, 1284, 1242, 1246, 1248, 1249, 1264, 1291, 1292, 1295–98. நெஞ்சே, 1112, 1237, 1241, 1243, 1244, 1245, 1247, 1291, 1293, 1294. நெஞ்சத்து 'in *or* of mind,' 115, 161, 288, 928, 1072, 1204, 1205, 1250. நெஞ்சினார், 243, 1260. நெஞ்சத்தான், 169, 185, 1128, 1218. நெஞ்சொடுகிளத்தல் 'colloquy with one's own heart,' Ch. cxxv. நெஞ்சொடுபுலத்தல் 'quarrel with one's own heart,' Ch. cxxx.

நெடு 'long, extensive,' 605. [Comp. நீள்.] நெடும், 17, 495, 496, 566. நெடுநீர் 'tardiness,' 605. நெடிய, 1169. நெடிது, 562, 943.

நெய் 'ghî,' 1148.

நெருஞ்சி 'a thorny plant: *tribulus terrestris.*'

நெருநல் 'yesterday,' 336, 1048. நெருநற்று, 1278.

நெறி 'way,' 6, 324, 356, 477. [வழி.]

நேர் 'similarity.' (§ 57), 'yield; agree; vow.' நேர்வது, 733. நேரார், 821. நேர்ந்தேன், 1181.

நோ (§ 58), 'suffer pain, grieve, complain of.' [Comp. நோவல்.] நோ 'suffering pain' (=நோய்), 157; for நோவ 'things which are meet to bring pain,' 805. நோவல் 'I shall suffer,' 1236. நோதல், 341, 1308. நோவார் 'they should complain of,' 237, 1219. நோவற்க 'don't bewail your sorrows,' 877. நோவது 'the complaining of,' 237, 1242. நொந்து, 1236. நொந்தது, 877. நொந்தார், 1308.

நோய் 'pain, disease,' 261, 286, 315, 320, 359, 360, 429, 848, 851, 853, 941, 946, 947, 948, 1091, 1102, 1147, 1159, 1160, 1161, 1162, 1171–76, 1183, 1200, 1226, 1227, 1241, 1243, 1255, 1266, 1280, 1301, 1303.

நோக்கு (§ 62), 'regard, look at.'

I. Act. நோக்க, 90, 1047, 1098. நோக்கி, 93, 189, 528, 542, 673, 701, 708, 1093, 1173, 1279. நோக்கின், 528. நோக்கினும், 1320. நோக்கிய, 1172. நோக்கினீர், 1320. நோக்கினாள், 1082, 1093. நோக்குதல், 1082, 1099. நோக்கும், 1094, 1114.

II. Neg. நோக்கா, 1094, 184. நோக்காத, 148. நோக்காது, 1009. நோக்கான், 528, 865. நோக்காமை, 1095.

III. Deriv. நோக்கு 'a look,' 976, 1082, 1089, 1091, 1099. நோக்கம். 'look, glance,' 1085, 1092.

நோல் (§ 70, as கல்), 'suffer, perform penance.' [Comp. நோ.] நோன்றல், 261. நோற்றல், 269. நோற்றான், 70. நோற்பார், 48, 160, 270. நோற்கிற்பவர் (Intro. p. xxii. 9), 159, 267. நோனு, 1132, 1163. நோலாதவர், 270. நோன்மை

'penance, suffering,' 48, 984. நோன்பு, 344.

பசை 'tenderness.' [பசு.] பசையினள் 'the tender maiden,' 1098.

பசு 'green, tender.' [Comp. பைம், பச, பச்சை, பசை.] பசும்புல் 'the green grass,' 16. பசுமண் 'unburnt clay,' 660.

பசி 'hunger,' 13, 225, 227, 656, 734. அழிபசி 'ravening hunger,' 226. (§ 64) 'suffer hunger,' பசிப்பர், 837. பசித்து, 944.

படர் 'sorrow.' படர்மெலிந்திரங்கல், Ch. CXVII. தனிப்படர்மிகுதி, Ch. CXX. (§ 57) படர்தரும் 'will spread.' [Comp. தா.]

படாம் 'a veil,' 1087.

படி 'the earth,' 606.

படிவத்தர் 'ascetics,' 586 [corr. of S. பதிவிருத்தன்.]

படிறு 'deceit,' 91. படிற்றொழுக்கம் 'pretended good conduct,' 271, 275.

படு. It is often added to trans. verbs and forms a passive; comp. § 92, 262.

I. படு (§ 56, II.; root, for பட்ட or படும்), 'will be, turn out to be, result, accrue,' 172, 279, 676, Nâl. 7, 239, 246. படல் (v. n.), 'closing,' 1175, 1136 [comp. 1049]. படுதல் (v. n.), with பாழ், 83; with என, 967; with இரக்க, 224, Nâl. 18, 29, 277. பட (inf. mood, § 97, 41), 524, 922, Nâl. 295, 364; ='to become spring' (with a noun), 231, 237; forming an adv. (§ 168), 640, Nâl. 116, 156. பட்டு (part., § 77), 'having suffered,' 127, 597, 996; 'fallen under,' 1074, 1297, 111, 266, Nâl. 47, 66, 317. படின் (§ 95, 97), 216, 217, 272, 558, 886, 977, Nâl. 154. படினும் (§ 100), 654, 896. பட்டது (past tense, § 70*), 1176; (as part. noun, § 87), 49, Nâl. 117, 160, 196, 212. பட்டன்று (=பட்டது; அன்று for அது), 999. பட்டேம் (ஏம்=ஓம்), 699. பட்டார், 105, 348, 819, 920, 936, Nâl. 229, 285, 287, 325. பட்ட (§ 74), 'endured, enjoyed,' 408; 'felt,' 878, 1140, Nâl. 6, 38, 91, 108, 110, 129, 180, 197, 237, 291. படும் (fut. tense, § 72.) The 3rd neut. used for all genders and both numbers; ='will be *or* suffer,' 50, 114, 169, 185, 186, 214, 191, 298, 349, 388, 405, 525, 575, 625, 665, 822, 824, 826, 836, 850, 947, 958, 1037, 1045, 1046, 1047, 1096, 1138, 1254, 1327, 1078, Nâl. 6, 9, 150, 176, 236, 242, 274, 288, 306, 326, 340, 345, 347, 350, 373, 100; ='should be,' 131, 154, 202, 265, 335, 412, 501, 589, 698, Nâl. 37, 42, 89, 133; =rel. part. (§ 74), 453, 1145. படுவர்='they will be,' 927, 1078, 356. படுப (ப=வார்), 810, 626. படுவ (§ 88) ='things that will be,' 172. படுவார் (§ 87)='those (that) will be,' 1193, 1194, 1289, Nâl. 139, 180, 208, 272. பட்டார் (§ 87)='those that have endured,' 895, Nâl. 21, 136. படுவது='that which will be,' 291, 324, 379, 438, 591, 801, 844. பட்டவர் (§ 87), 269. படுபாக்கு (§ 97)='that (it) will ensue,' 136, 164. பட்டாங்கு 'as it suffers,' 1189. (See ஆங்கு.) படாஅர் (§ 110), 921, 1194. படாதி (§ 121, poet. for படாதே), 'set not!' 1210. படாது, 702, Nâl. 134, 183. படாத (§ 121), 776, 418. படா(அ) (§ 121), 1140, 1108, 1087, 1115 (§ 110), Nâl. 142, 169, 250, 255. படாதவர் (§ 121), 623, 1004. படாதார், 88. படாமை (§ 154, used for படாமல்), 38.

II. படுப்பது (§ 64, 87), 'that which will cause to be,' 460, 465. படுத்து (§ 77), 512. படுக்கும் (§ 72), 372. படுப்பர்

(§ 72), 623. படுத்தான், 590. படுத்தும் (§ 100), 747.

III. பாடு, (1) 'anything that befalls, or is suffered'; then (2) 'dignity, honour,' 409, 597, 768, 906, 995, 1237, 1322, Nâl. 105, 187, 252, 281, 340. In compounds:—இடர்ப்பாடு 'affliction,' 624. உடம்பாடு 'agreement,' 890. ஊறுபாடு 'hindrance,' 945. ஏதப்பாடு 'disgrace,' 464. ஐயப்பாடு 'doubt,' 587. கடப்பாடு 'duty, obligation,' 211, Nâl. 261. கண்பாடு 'sleep,' 1049, Nâl. 366 [comp. Nâl. 169]. திறப்பாடு 'ability,' 640. தொடர்ப்பாடு 'connection,' 345. மாறுபாடு 'disagreement,' 945. வன்பாடு (வன்பாட்டது 'what pertains to impudence'), 1063.

IV. படு is compounded with புறம், பாழ் ('become waste,' 83), கை, பால் ('behave,' 111), கோள்(ட்), பயன் (1078), கடை, தலை ('attain to,' 1289 [see தலை], 348), அடி, வடு, தீ, கீழ் (='fall under,' 558), வேறு, முனை, உள்.

படை. 1. 'Instrument,' 555, 828, 985, 1228, 1258, 1324. [படு.] 2. 'Army' (=தானை), 253, 381, 498, 761–69. படைமாட்சி, Ch. LXXVII. படைச்செருக்கு, Ch. LXXVIII.

பட்டடை 'anvil,' 821. [படு + அடி.]

பட்டி 'meanness,' 1074. (See அகம்.)

பணி (§ 57), 'bow down, be humble.' பணி (வி. தொ.), 1121, 1258. பணிதல், 125, 963, 985. பணியும், 978. பணிவு, 95, 960. பணிந்து, 680.

பணை 'strength,' 1234.

பண் 'melody; sound of musical instrument,' 573. பண்பு 'quality, good quality, excellence, courtesy,' 45, 97, 389, 469, 579, 681, 683, 688, 783, 810, 811, 912, 937, 955, 993–995, 1181. பண்புடைமை 'right conduct, courtesy,' Ch. c., 991–1000. பண்பினோர், 579. பண்புடையார், 996. பண்புடைமக்கள், 62. மக்கட்பண்பில்லாதவர் 'those destitute of human feelings,' 997. பண்பாற்றார் 'those who act not worthily,' 998. பண்பிலன் 'a worthless person,' 865, 1000. பண்பின்மை, 851. பண்பிலதனை, 871. பண்பல்ல, 700. பண்பில்செல், 194. பண்புடையாளன், 874.

பண்டம் 'material, goods,' 475.

பண்டு 'formerly,' 1083, 1133.

பதம் 'foot, manner,' 548 [S. *pada*; see தண்]. எண்பதம் 'easiness of access,' 548, 991.

பதடி 'chaff' (B. *scoria!*). [Comp. பதர்.]

பதி [S.] 'place,' 1116, 1229. உறைபதி 'abode,' 1015.

பத்து 'ten,' 450, 817. (§ 172.)

பயன் 'profit, fruit.' [Comp. பலன், பழம். S. *phala*.] பயன்மரம், 216, 2, 45, 87, 97, 103, 104, 128, 177, 198, 200, 239, 354, 524, 560, 606, 646, 676, 901, 912, 994, 1100, 1109. பயம், 728, 740. பயத்த, 705. என்னபயத்ததோ 'of what use is it?' 987. பயன்சாரா 'useless,' 194. படுபயன், 172. பயன்படு, 1078. பயனிலசொல்லாமை, Ch. xx., 191–200.

பய (§ 66), 'yield, produce.' பயத்தல், 202. பயக்கும், 97, 123, 292, 351, 461, 659, 669, 854. பயந்தற்று, 1192. பயப்பினும், 690. பயப்பது, 685, 690. பயவா, 406, 439, 652.

பயில் (§ 70, as வெல்), 'practise, enjoy.' பயிற்றும், 783.

பர (§ 66), 'be extended.' பரந்து 'wandering,' 1062.

பரத்தன் 'a profligate.' பரத்த! 'thou profligate!' 1311.

பரி (§ 57) 'compassionate, endure, defend, dread.' [? S. *bri*.] பரியும் 'ward off,' 862; 'dread,' 502. பரிதல் 'suffering,' 1243.

பரிந்து 'having compassion,' 1248, 1243; 'having suffered, toiled,' 132, 1172; '*laborare*,' B. பரியினும் 'though you toil,' 376. பரியது (=பெரியது) 'great.'

பருகு (§ 62), 'drink.' பருகுவன் 'I shall taste of joy,' 1266. பருகவார் 'those who will devour you with affection,' 811.

பருவம் [S.] 'season,' 1028. பருவத்தும் 'even in the season,' 218. பருவத்து 'in the season,' 490. பருவத்தோடு 'cling to the favourable season,' 482.

பருவரு 'suffer.' (See பரி, வரு.) பருவரல் 'suffering,' 1197, 1240. பருவந்து 'suffering, 83. பருவரார் 'he suffers not,' 1126. பசப்புறுபருவரல் 'suffering from the wanness of hue,' Ch. CXIX.

பல் 'many' (§ 184), 242, 322, 735, 1045. [Opp. சில்.] பன், 1258. பல, 140, 337, 342, 373, 649, 823, 868, 934, 1034. பலவும், 275, 492, 522, 884, 885. பல்லவை, 728. பலர், 270, 278, 468, 473, 514, 528, 771, 1112, 1119, 1141, 1149, 1160. பல்லார், 191, 192, 194, 450, 873.

பழ 'old.' [பழவினை, Nâl. 123, Ch. XI.]

I. பழம் 'fruit,' 1120. [S. *phal*; comp. பயன்.] பழு (§ 64), 'fruit.' பழுத்தற்றால் 'as though it fruited?' 216, 1008.

II. 'Old,' 955. [Comp. கிழ, கெழு.] பழைமை 'old intimacy,' Ch. LXXXI., 801, 521. பழையார் 'old friends,' 810. பழையம் 'we are old friends.' பழகு (§ 62), 'become accustomed.' பழகுதல் 'habit,' 785. பழகிய 'wonted,' 803, 937.

பழுது 'fault; evil,' 639. [பழ.]

பழி 'guilt'; '*vituperium, censura*' (B.), 40, 44, 62, 137, 145, 146, 172, 186, 433, 506, 618, 657, 794, 865, 1015, 1051, 1285. [பழ.] (§ 64), 'blame,' பழிக்கும், 656. பழிப்பார் 'those who will malign,' 820. பழித்தது 'what it has condemned,' 280. பழிப்பது, 49. [Comp. பழவினை.]

பளிங்கு 'crystal,' 706.

பள்ளி 'bed,' 840.

பறி (§ 64), 'pluck out.' பறியா (=பறித்து; § 97), 774.

பற (§ 66), 'fly away.' பறந்தற்றே 'it is as the flight,' 338.

பறை 'a drum,' 1076, 1115, 1180.

பற்று. 1. (§ 62), 'Seize, hold, cling to.' பற்றி, 347, 956. பற்றற்கு, 747. பற்றார் 'enemies,' 865. பற்றுக, 350. பற்று 'deeds of variance,' 852. பற்றியார், 748. 2. 'A grasp, what one clings to, attachment,' 88, 275, 347, 350, 506, 521, 606, 748. பற்றுள்ளம் 'an avaricious soul,' 438. [Comp. S. *bhaj*.]

பனி 'dew; coolness,' 1223, 1232, 1121 (*or* பணி).

பனுவல் 'a book,' 21. [நூல்.]

பனை 'a palmyra tree,' 104, 433, 1282, Nâl. 96, 105. (See தினை and துணை.)

பா (§ 64), 'distribute.' [பகு.] பாத்து=பகுத்து, 44, 227, 1107.

பாகம் [S.], 'portion, half,' 1092.

பாக்கியம் [S.], 1141. பாக்கியத்தால் 'happily.'

பாடு. 1. See படு. 2. (§ 62), 'Sing.' பாடல் 'singing.'

பாத்தி 'a garden-bed,' 718. [பகு.] பாத்திப்படுப்பது 'plant out,' 465. (See படு.)

பாய் (§ 57), 'leap, spring.' பாய்பவர் 'those who will leap into,' 1287.

பாயிரம் 'introduction,' Ch. I.

பாராட்டு. See பார்.

பார்ப்பான் 'a Brâhman,' 134. [? corr. of S.]

பார். I. (§ 62), 'See, watch for, behold.' [காண், நோக்கு.] பார்த்து, 86, 487, 676. பார்க்கும், 130, 1186. பார்ப்பார், 285. பார்வல் 'sight,' 1152. புரராட்டு (see ஆடு), 196, 521, 994.

II. 'A sandbank, rock, *bar*,' 1068, Nâl. 122. [Comp. பாடி.]

பாரி (§ 64), 'spread, make much of.' பாரிப்பார், 916. பாரித்து, 193. பாரிக்கும், 851. [Comp. பற.]

பால். 1. 'Milk,' 1000, 1121. 2. 'Portion, division' (=பகல்). (1) அறத்துப்பால், Ch. v.–xxxviii.; (2) பொருட்பால், Ch. xxxix.–cix.; (3) காமத்துப்பால், Ch. cx. *ad fin.* பாலது, பாற்று, பால 'thing *or* things that pertain to.' தீவினைப்பால் 'evil things,' 209, 206, 437, 871, 82, 825, 515, 376, 378, 659, 40, 342, 672. 3. 'Side,' 118, 422. 4. 'Kind, sort,' 533, 950, 279. 5. 'Land.' வன்பால் 'barren soil,' 78. 6. As வினைக்குறிப்புமுற்று. (Intro. p. xxiii.) பாற்று 'it is meet to be,' 11, 829, Nâl. 1. பாற்பட்டு 'as befits each *order* of men,' 111. பாற்பட்டது 'has fallen into, is in the *state* of,' 999.

பாம்பு 'a snake,' 890, 1146.

பாழ் 'desolation.' [பழைய.] பாழ்படுதல் 'becoming void,' 83. பாழ்செய்யும் 'which lays waste,' 735.

பாவம் [S.], 'sin,' 146. [Syn. தீவினை, தீப்பால, தீமை, இன்னாதது, குற்றம், மாசு, பழி.] பாவி 'a sinner' (personification), 168, 1042.

பாவை 'puppet; image on the retina,' 407, 1020, 1058. பாவாய்! 'O image!' 1123.

பிடி (§ 64), 'sieze.' பிடித்து 'a handful,' 1037. கடைப்பிடித்து (see கடை), 'persevering,' 944.

பிணம் 'a corpse,' 913.

பிணி. 1. 'Disease,' 949, 1014, 1102. தீப்பிணி, 227. பிணியின்மை, 738. ஒவாப்பிணி, 734. 2. (§ 64), 'Bind.' பிணிக்கும் 'will bind,' 570; 'which will enchain,' 643.

பிணை 'hind: *cerva*,' 1085, 1089.

பிரி (§ 57, 64), 'separate; go apart.' பிரிதல், 394. With தலை:—தலைப்பிரிதல் (see தலை), 'departing from,' 955; தலைப்பிரியா, 97; தலைப்பிரிந்த, 258; தலைப்பிரியாதார், 810. பிரிந்தவர், 633, 1248, 1264. பிரிந்து, 530. பிரிவு, 839, 1152, 1153, 1156, 1158, 1160, 1295. பிரிவாற்றாமை, Ch. cxvi. பிரியலன் 'I sever myself not,' 1315. பிரித்தல், 633. பிரிப்பர் 'they will put asunder,' 187.

பிழை (§ 64), 'miss, sin against.' [Comp. பிசு.] பிழைப்பின் 'if you err in,' 1019. பிழைத்து 'erring, offending,' 417, 896. பிழைத்த 'which has missed,' 772. பிழைத்தது 'what has been done wrong,' 779. பிழையாது 'it misses not,' 307. பிழையாமை 'avoiding offence.' பெரியாரைப்பிழையாமை, Ch. xc. பிழை 'a fault,' 535.

பிற. I. [Comp. S. *para.*] 'Other (things),' 8, 34, 61, 95, 213, 297, 300, 302, 304, 321, 495, 661, 710, 909, 917, 982, 1011, 1102, 1181, 1184. பிறவும், 120. பிறன், 49, 141–50, 163, 178, 186, 204, 282, 316, 508, 1047. பிறனில்விழையாமை, Ch. xv. பிறர், 72, 160, 206, 311, 319, 424, 436, 646, 834, 1009, 1015, 1018, 1076, 1079, 1319. பிறிது, 251, 257, 315, 327, 645, 841, 842.

II. [Comp. S. *pra.*] (§ 66), 'Be born.' பிறத்தல், 303, 681, 992. பிறக்கும், 1044. பிறந்தார், 409, 951–59, 1044. பிறந்து, 502, 794. பிறந்தும், 409. பிறந்த, 603, 1026. பிறவாமை, 362. பிறவி 'birth,' 10. பிறப்பு

'birth,' 62, 107, 133, 134, 339, 345, 349, 351, 357, 358, 361, 1002, 1315.

பிறங்கு (§ 62), 'appear, shine forth.' [பிற.] பெருமைபிறங்கிற்று 'it has shone forth,' 23. பழிபிழங்காப்பண்பு 'faultless excellence,' 62.

பிறை 'the crescent moon,' 782. [Comp. மதி.] நால், 125.

பின் (§ 225), 'after.' **1.** Adv. 'afterwards,' 535, 780. **2.** As prep. gov. case with இன் or அன், 160, 225, 323. **3.** As conj. with rel. part., 293, 391, 467, 491, 509, 662, 693, 791. பின்றை=பின், 518. **4.** வி. கு., பின்னது 'it comes after,' 1031. **5.** Forms compounds:—(1) With verbs: பின்செல் 'follow after,' 207, 966, 967, 1033, 1248, 1255, 1256, 1293; பின்னோக்கு 'regard the future,' 184; பின்னிரு 'survive,' 1160; பிற்பய 'yield after,' 659. (2) With nouns: பிற்பகல் 'afternoon,' 319; பின்னீர 'things that deteriorate,' 782.

பீடு 'pride, greatness,' 59, 968, 1014, 1021, 1088. [Comp. பாடு.]

பீலி 'peacock's feather,' 475.

பீழை 'affliction,' 658, 839, 843. [Comp. பிழி.] பீழி (§ 64), 'afflict.' பீழிக்கும், 843. பீழிப்பது, 1217.

புகழ் (=இசை) 'praise,' 5, 39, 59, 156, 296, 457, 532, 652, 966, Ch. XXIV., 232–37. புகழ்மை=புகழ், 533. (§ 57), புகழ்ந்தவை 'things praised,' 538.

புகு (§ 56, II.), 'enter.' புகல் 'entering,' 144, 243, 840. புகும் 'will enter,' 346. புகின் 'if it enter,' 937. புக்கு 'having entered,' 835, 996. புகுத்தி (§ 160), 'having caused to enter,' 608, 616. புகுத்து (§ 62). புக்கில் 'a dwelling,' 340. [இல்.]

புடை 'place' (§ 251). With பெயர்: 'I changed my place,' 1187.

புண் 'a wound,' 129, 257, 393, 575, 776. [வடு.]

புணர் (§ 57), 'join, embrace.' புணர்தல், 1109, 1326. புணரின் 'if you can,' 308. புணர்ந்து, 1260. புணர்வது, 1307. புணர்பவர் 'those who embrace,' 917. புணர்வு 'reunion,' 1152, 1155. புணர்ச்சி 'union, intimacy,' 785. புணர்ச்சிமகிழ்தல், Ch. CXI. புணர்ச்சிவிதும்பல், Ch. CXXIX.

புணை 'raft,' 306, 1134, 1164.

புதல் (=புதர்) 'thicket,' 274.

புதல்வர் (=மக்கள்) 'children.' [? corr. of புத்திரர்.] புதல்வரைப் பெறுதல் 'the obtaining of children,' Ch. VII.

புதை 'a sheaf (of arrows),' 597.

புத்தேள் 'a deity,' 213, 234, 290; pl. புத்தேளிர், 58. புத்தேளுடு 'the celestial world,' 966, 1323.

புயல் 'a cloud,' 14.

புரந்தரன் 'a king,' 780. [S.=Indra.]

புரளு (§ 56, III.), 'roll away.' புரளவிடல் 'let it go!' 755.

புருவம் [S.], 'an eye-brow,' 1086.

புரை. **1.** 'Worth,' 919. **2.** 'Fault,' 292. [Comp. பெறு, பிழை.]

புல (§ 66), 'sulk, feign dislike,' புலத்தல் 'affecting anger,' 1323. நெஞ்சொடுபுலத்தல், Ch. CXXX., 'finding fault with the mind.' புல, 1316, 1305. புலந்து 'being sulky,' 1039, 1246, 1287. புலந்தார் 'those that sulk with one,' 1303. புலத்தை 'be reserved, as if angry,' 1301. புலப்பல் 'I will show myself angry,' 1259. புலப்பேன் 'shall I stand aloof?' 1267. புலவி, Ch. CXXXI., 1302, 1306, 1309, 1324. புலவிநுணக்கம், Ch. CXXXII.

புலம், (1) 'place,' 43. (2) 'field,' 85. (3) 'knowledge,' 407, 716; புலவர் 'the learned,' 234, 394. (4) 'senses,' 174, 343; '*objecta: ponit objecta pro potentiis ad illa tendentibus.*' ஐம்புலன் 'enjoyment coming through the five senses,' 1101.

புலம்பு (§ 62), 'lament.' நினைந்தவர் புலம்பல், Ch. CXXI.

புல். 1. 'Grass,' 16. 2. 'Mean, trifling, wan,' 71, 189, 331, 719, 815, 846, 914, 915, 916, 1222. புல்லறிவாண்மை 'folly,' Ch. LXXXV. புலை=புன்மை: புலைவினையர் 'vicious persons,' 329. புன்கண் 'sorrow,' 1152. (See கண்.) புன்மை 'meanness,' 174, 185, 329. புல்லென்னும் 'it will be low,' 790. (See என்.) புற்கை 'a decoction of vegetables,' 1065.

புலி 'a tiger,' 273, 599.

புல்லு (§ 62), 'embrace.' புல்லல் 'embracing,' 827. புல்லுதல், 1290. புல்லி 'having embraced,' 1187, 1324. புல்லுவேன் 'shall I embrace,' 1267. புல்லினேன் 'I embraced,' 1259. புல்லா, 1303. புல்லாது, 1301. புல்லார், 755. புல்லாள், 1316.

புரி (§ 57), 'desire, aim at.' புரிந்தார், 5, 287. புரிந்து '*concupiscere*' (B.), 59, 541, 607, 143. புரிந்த, 511, 977, 994.

புலால் 'flesh,' 257, 259. புலான் மறுத்தல், Ch. XXVI.

புழுதி 'dust, earth,' 1037. [S. *pritvî.*]

புள் 'a bird,' 274, 338.

புறம், புறன். I. 'Outside' [opp. அகம்], 277, 298, 487, 933.

II. வி. கு. (Intro. p. xxiii.) புறத்த 'are things externe,' 39. புறத்ததா 'as a thing outside,' 82.

III. Compounds: 1. Verbs. புறப்படுத்தான் [படு (56, III.)], 'make known,' 590. புறங்காத்து 'defend,' 549. புறங்கொடுக்கும் 'forsake,' 924. புறங்கூறு 'defame,' 181, 183. புறங்கூறுமை, Ch. XIX. புறஞ்சொல்லும், 185. புறநோக்கி 'watching for his absence,' 189. புறனழீஇ 'defaming,' 182.

2. Nouns. புறத்துறுப்பு 'external members,' 79. புறத்தாறு 'foreign course,' 46.

புற்கை. See புல்.

புற்கென்ற, 1261. (See என்.) புற்கு 'dimness.' [என்ற=என்றன.] Sub. கண்கள் 'my eyes have grown dim.'

புனல் 'a stream of water,' 495, 737, 1134, 1167, 1287.

புனை. 1. 'Fetters,' 836. 2. (§ 57), 'adorn, laud.' புனையினும் 'though you adorn it, laud it,' 790. புனை (வி. தொ.) 'adorned,' 407. நலம்புனைந்துரைத்தல், Ch. CXII.

பூ 'a flower,' 1112, 1115, 1305, 1313. [Comp. அரும்பு, போது, மலர்.] (§ 64), 'bloom.' பூப்பர், 248.

பூசல் 'clamour,' 61, 1237.

பூசனை 'worship,' 18. [S. *pûja.*]

பூண் (§ 56, II.), 'put on as an ornament.' அறம்பூண்டார் 'those who have arrayed themselves in virtue,' 23. பூண்டு 'having put on,' 30. பூணும் 'will put on,' 836.

பூதம் [S.], 'the elements,' 271.

பூரியார், பூரியர்கள் 'the vile,' 241, 919.

பூழ் 'a quail,' Nâl. 122.

பெள், பெட், பெண் (§ 70). [See வேள்.] 1. 'Desire.' பெட்டக்கதாகி [பெள் for பெட்க], 'being to be desired,' 732. பெட்டார் 'he who desired,' 1178. பெட்ப, fut. inf., 'so as to give pleasure,' 1276; v. noun, 'things one desires,' 1257, 1283. பெட்டு 'having desired,' 141. பெட்டாங்கு 'as — has desired,' 908, 1293. 2. பெண் 'a woman,' 54, 56, 902, 907, 910, 1137. In comp., 'womanly,' 907, 909, 1083, 1084, 1311; 'womanhood,' 402, 1272, 1280. பெண்வழிச்சேறல் 'being under woman's guidance,' Ch. XCI.; pl. பெண்டிர், 58, 913, 920. பெண்மை

'womanhood,' 147, 150, 1280, 1258.

பெயர் (§ 57, 64), n. and a., 'change.' [Spelt also பேர். I have retained the spelling of all the editions.] பேரும் 'will change,' 486. பேரா 'unchanging, remediless,' 370, 892. பெயர்ந்தேன் 'I changed,' 1187. ஊழி பெயரினுந்தாம் பெயரார் 'though eternal fate be moved, they move not,' 989. பெயர்த்து 'again,' 205, 344. பேர்த்து, 357.

பெய் (§ 58), 'drop (as rain), pour in, place, assemble.' பெய்யெனப்பெய்யுமழை 'it will rain when she bids it,' 55. பெய, 580. பெய்து, 660. பெய் (வி. தொ.), 475. பெயின், 475. பெயல், 545, 559, 1174. பெய்தாள் 'she put on as a girdle,' 1115. [Comp. தலைப்பெய் 'assemble.' See தலை.]

பெரு (பெரிய, பேர்), 'great.' [Comp. அரு, அரிய, ஆர், § 131.] பெரு, பெரும், 10, 54, 58, 198, 217, 332, 380, 526, 565, 571, 732, 805, 816, 837, 847, 866, 924, 968, 1000, 1001, 1006, 1137, 1239, 1255. பெருமிதம் 'pride, greatness,' 431, 979. [S. பரிமிதம்.] பெரிது, 69, 102, 103, 124, 328, 839, 947, 1092, 1166, 1272, 1276. பெரியது, 902. பெரியார், பெரியர், 26, 160, 443, 444, 680, 694, 892, 896, 976. பெரியாரைப்பிழையாமை, Ch. xc. பெரியாரைத்துணைக்கோடல், Ch. xlv. பெருமை 'greatness,' 21–28. 336, 416, 451, 505, 611, 907, 1021. Ch. xcviii., 974–980. நீத்தார்பெருமை, Ch. iii. பேர், 744, 1083. பேரறிவாளன், 215; பேரிரையான் 'glutton'; comp. பேராண்மை, 148, 773, 962. பெருகு (§ 62), 'grow great.' பெருகும், 96, 604. பெருக்கு (§ 62), 'multiply.' பெருகல் 'increase,' 811. பெருக்கம் 'prosperity,' 115, 170, 431, 963. பெருக்கல் 'increasing, feeding,' 251. பெருக்கி 'increasing *revenue*,' 512.

பெறு (§ 56, II.) 'obtain, bear, or beget children; come to pass.' புதலவரைப்பெறுதல், Ch. vii.

I. பெறல், 213, 1180. பெறுதல், 1190. பெறின் 'if (you) obtain, if it come to pass, if,' 54, 58, 62, 92, 111, 119, 123, 162, 257, 334, 403, 540, 648, 666, 680, 708, 709, 838, 869, 988, 1270, 1295, 1330. பெறினும், 311, 812, 954. பெறுவர், 58. பெறுவான், 842. பெறும், 61, 768, 1322. பெறுவது 'what can be gained,' 46, 813. பெறுகுவம் 'we shall gain,' 1328. பெறுதியோ 'wilt thou gain?' 1237.

II. பெற்ற, 524, 1000, 1109, 1270. பெற்றார், 1191. பெற்றான் 'a husband, one who has obtained,' 58, 226, 268, 943. பெற்றாள், 1067, 1104. பெற்றேம், 626. பெற்றவர், 1191. பெற்றால், 333. பெற்றன்ன, 1143. பெற்றத்தால் (=பெற்றதால்), 524.

III. பெறாது, 1143, 1198. பெறாமை, 1295. பெறாஅ, 238.

IV. பேறு 'gain,' 60, 61, 162. பெற்றம் 'a cow,' 273. பெற்றி (யார்), 442 [பெற்றி='nature'].

பேடி 'hermaphrodite,' 614, 727. [பெண்.]

பேணு (§ 62), 'cherish.' [பெண், பெள்.] பேண, 866. பேணி, 56, 120, 442, 443, 633, 917, 976. பேணியார் 'my lover,' 1257. பேணாமை, 833, 866. பேணா, 924. பேணாது, 163, 892, 902, 1178, 1283. பேணான், 526. பேணலர் 'they cherish not,' 1016. [அல்.]

பேதை. 1. 'A simple person,' 603, 816, 833–88. பேதைப்படுக்கும் 'will stultify,' 372. 2. 'A woman,' 1084, 1106, 1136, 1238, 1239, 1248, 1272, 1274. பேதையார், 142, 782, 797, 834, 839. பேதைமை 'folly,' 141,

358, 417, 428, 507, 805, 831, 832, 910, 1242, Ch. LXXXIV.

பேய் 'a demon,' 565.

பேர். See பெயர் and பெரு.

பேறு. See பெறு.

பைதல் 'pining grief,' 1172, 1175, 1197, 1223, 1239, 1243, 1266; with உழ. [Comp. with நோய்.]

பைம். See பசு. பைஞ்சுழ் 'green grain,' 550. மைந் தொடி 'yellow (golden) armlet,' 1234, 1238.

பைய 'softly,' 1098.

பொச்சா (§ 66), 'forget.' பொச்சாந்தும் 'though they forget,' 199, 719. பொச்சாந் தார் 'those oblivious of,' 246. பொச்சாப்பார், 533. பொச் சாப்பு (=சோர்வு), 285, 532, 534. பொச்சாவா, 537. பொச்சாவாமை 'not being oblivious of duties,' Ch. LIV.

பொது 'common, alike,' 528, 915, 1099, 1311.

பொதி (§ 57), 'store up.' பொ திந்து, 155.

பொத்து 'hole.' [Comp. பொந் து.] பொத்துப்படும் 'will fail,' 468.

பொய். 1. 'A lie, what is false,' 6, 836, 938, 1246. [Opp. மெய்.] In comp. = 'false.' 2. (§ 64) 'deceive, lie.' பொய்த் தல், 1287. பொய்த்த, 293. பொயற்க, 293. பொயப்பின், 13. பொய்யா, 299, 753. பொய்யாது, 294. பொய்த்து, 182, 183. பொய்ம்மை, 292, 913. பொய்யாமை, 296, 297.

பொரு (§ 60) 'fight, attack.' பொருதகர் 'the fighting ram' (வினைத்), 486. பொருது, 888. பொருத, 888. போர் 'war,' 758, 767.

பொரு-த்து (§ 62), 'join.' பொருத்தல், 633. [Opp. பிரித் தல். √பொர்.]

பொருள். 1. 'Reality,' 5, 351, 434. Book II.: பொருட்பால். [√பொர்.] 2. 'Meaning,' 424, 509, 1046, 583, 199. 3. 'Property,' 63, 122, 128, 141, 176, 212, 226, 241–49, 252, 254, 282, 285, 307, 501, 477, 644, 660, 732, 592, 741, 909, 911, 913, 914, 925, 933, 938, 1230, 751, 753, 755, 756, 757, 759, 1001, 1002. 4. 'A thing, matter,' 355, 423, 462, 675, 695, 746, 901, 588, 751; with பயன, செல்வம், ஆட்சி, உடைமை, ஆக்கம். மெய்ப் பொருள், 249, 355, 356, 423, 857. செம்பொருள், 358, 91. எண்பொருள, 424. எண்பொ ருள், 760. நுண்பொருள், 424. அருட்பொருள், 914. கைப் பொருள், 178, 371. சிறுபொ ருள், 870. அரும்பொருள். ஒண்பொருள், 760, 1009. வான் பொருள், 897. நன்பொருள், 171. பொருளார், 914. பே ருள்செயல்வகை, Ch. LXXVI. பிறன்பொருளாள் 'neighbour's wife'; '*mulier propria*' (B.), 141, 1001, 1002. பொருட்டு 'for the sake of,' 81, 212, 725, 784. பொருட்டால், 256, 1017.

பொழுது (1) 'time' (=காலம்), 481; (2) 'day'; (3) 'evening.' பொழுதே 'when,' 1215. பொ ழுதின் 'than in the time,' 69. ஒருபொழுதும் 'even one day,' 337. போழ்து, 412, 539, 1229. போழ்தின் 'in the time,' 569, 930, 1105. பொழுதுகண்டிரங் கல் 'mourning at eventide,' Ch. CXXIII.

பொள்ளென 'suddenly,' 487. [என், § 82.]

பொல்லாத 'evil things,' 176. [? from v. பொல்லு (§ 62)='be fitting.']

பொறி. 1. 'A sense, organ of sense,' 6, 9. 2. 'Fate.' பொ றியின்மை 'want of luck.'

பொறு (§ 64), 'bear, endure.' பொறுத்தல், 151, 152. பொ றுக்கும், 389. பொறுத்து, 579, 1032. பொறேன், 1247.

பொறுத்தான், 37, 155, 156. பொறுத்த, 239.
பொறை (1) 'patience,' 153, 154. பொறையுடைமை, Ch. XVI. (2) 'burthen,' 189, 570, 572, 733, 990, 1003, 1027.

பொன் 'gold, any metal,' 155, 267, 888, 931.

பொன்று (§ 62), 'die.' [Comp. போ.] பொன்றும், 36, 156. பொன்றி, 171. பொன்ற, 36. பொன்றது, 233. பொன்றமை, 886.

போ (§ 58, 258), 'go.' Causal: போக்கு (§ 62). போகூழ் (வி. தொ.), 371. போகாறு 'expenditure,' 478. போய், 46, 933. போம், 659, 848, 1070. போதாய் 'go thou!' 1123. போக, 831. போகா, 376. போகார், 1126. போக்கி, 774. போக்கு 'the dismissal,' 332. அறைபோகாது 'not capable of being undermined,' 764.

போர். 1. See பொரு. 2. (§ 64), 'cover.' போர்த்த, 80. போர்த்து, 273.

போது 'a flower,' 1227. [Comp. பூ, அரும்பு, மலர்.]

போழ் (§ 57), 'pass between.' [போ.] போழ, 1108, 1239.

போழ்து. See பொழுது.

போலு (§ 70), 'resemble' [comp. § 227]. போல், 59, 118, 120, 126, 155, 190, 235, 267, 276, 253, 315, 334, 395, 574, 706, 781, 826, 882, 887, 940, 946, 957, 1078, 1090, 1096, 1097, 1118, 1180, 1186, 1222, 1253, 1269, 1273, 1274, 1285, 1287. போல, 77, 151, 283, 288, 435, 454, 479, 614, 674, 788, 822, 888, 974, 1027, 1047, 1095, 1099, 1117, 1159, 1161, 1196, 1224. போலும், 339, 552, 783, 997, 1048, 1054, 1105, 1228, 1232, 1233. போலினும், 811. போல்வர், 997, 1071. போன்று, 135, 822, 1097, 1170, 1203. போலக 'be like!' 691.

போற்று (§ 62), 'make much of, extol, defend, ward off.' போற்றல், 693, 891. போற்றி, 154, 493, 477, 537, 538, 942. போற்றின், 693. போற்றினும், 468. போற்றுவார், 891. போற்றுபவர், 741. போற்ற, 315. போற்றது, 234. போற்றதார், 252. போற்றர், 493.

ம

மக 'child.' [Pronounced by the Tudas *maχ*.] மகன் (used with 'father,' தந்தை), 'son,' 67, 69, 70, 196; 'man,' 110. மகள் 'daughter'; pl. மகளிர் = 'women,' 57, 822, 912, 918, 974. வரைவின்மகளிர், Ch. XCII. மக்கள் [syn. புதல்வர்], 'children,' 196, 388, 60–68; 'sons of men,' 410, 600, 993, 997, 1071. நிலைமக்கள் 'private soldiers,' 770. தலைமக்கள் 'officers,' 770. மாக்கள், irreg. pl. 'human beings,' 329, 420. [Syn. பிள்ளை and குமாரன்.]

மகிழ் (§ 57), 'rejoice, exult'; 'gladness,' 1090, 1201. மகிழ்ச்சி, 531, 539. மகிழ்தல், 1281. மகிழ்ந்து, 1057. புணர்ச்சிமகிழ்தல், Ch. CXI.

மங்கலம் [S.], 'blessing,' 60.

மடங்கு 'become bent, folded, indolent.' மடங்கின், 1036. [மடி.]

மடம் [S.], 'simplicity, folly,' 1297, 1089. மடமை 'folly.' மடவார் 'fools,' 89, 153. மடந்தை 'a maiden,' 1116, 1122, 1273. மடவரல் 'a woman,' 1085.

மடல் 'a palmyra leaf-stem; a horse made of such stems, on which a suffering lover mounted to proclaim his grief,' 1131–37.

மடி [மடங்கு]. 1. 'The fold of a garment,' 1023. 2. 'Laziness,' 371, 601–10, 1028. மடியின்

மை 'alertness,' Ch. LXI. மடிமை 'laziness,' 608.

மடி (§ 57, 64), perish, destroy,' 604. மடியா=மடித்து (§ 97, Note), 602. மடியும், 603. மடிமடிக் கொண்டு, 603. The former மடி is வி. தொ. 'possessing the laziness *which should be destroyed.*'

மடு (§ 64), 'hinder.' மடுத்த, 624.

மண (§ 66), 'wed.' மணந்தார் 'wedded folks,' 1221, 1226. மணந்தநாள் 'the wedding-day,' 1233, Nâl. 23, 25.

மணல் 'sand.' [மண்.] மணல் கேணி 'a well in the sand,' 396.

மணி. 1. 'A gem' [S.], 1273. 2. 'Apple of the eye,' 1123. 3. 'Beauty,' 742.

மண் 'earth,' 660, 407, 576, 742, 996; 'an earthern vessel,' 883. [Opp. விண். See மணல்.]

மதலை 'a pillar,' 449.

மதி [S.], 'the full moon,' 1116–1119, 782, 957, 1210. [Comp. பிறை, திங்கள்.]

மதி [S.] (§ 64), 'esteem, honour.' மதிப்பின் 'if . . . esteem,' 898. (n.) 'intellect,' 636, 915, 1229.

மந்திரி [S.], 'counsellor'; = அமைச்சு, 639.

மயங்கு (§ 62), 'be confused' [S.]. [Comp. மை, மயல், மாயம், மருள்.] மயங்கி, 348. மயக்கம் 'confusion,' 360.

மயல் 'confusion,' 344. [Comp. மை.]

மயில் [S. *mayūra*], 'pea-fowl,' 1081. [மயிலாப்பூர், மயிலை. Intro. p. ii.]

மயிர் 'hair,' 964, 969.

மரபு 'nature.' மரபினர், 188.

மரம் 'a tree,' 78, 216, 217, 600, 576, 879, 997, 1008; prefixed= 'wooden,' 1020, 1058.

மருங்கு 'side' [பக்கம்], 210, 526.

மருள் (§ 56, III.), 'be bewildered.' மருண்டு, 1139, 1229; 'bewilderment,' 351, 352, 1002, 1222, 1230. மருட்டு (§ 62), 'pretend, imitate.' மருட்டியற்று, 1020.

மருந்து 'medicine,' 82, 217, 942, 950, 968, 1091, 1102, 1241, 1275, Ch. xcv. ['Corr. of S. *amṛita.*']

மருவு (§ 62) 'cherish.' மருவுக, 800. மரீஇ, 227. (See அளபெடை.)

மலர் 'a flower full-blown,' 3, 1142, 1289, 1112, 650, 1231, 1119; 'the lotus-flower,' 595. [Comp. பூ, அரும்பு, போது.] மலரு (§ 57), 'blow as a flower, expand.' மலர்தல், 425. மலரும், 1227.

மலை. 1. 'Mountain,' 124, 737, 742. 2. (§ 57), 'abound.' மலைந்த, 657.

மல்கு (§ 62), 'abound.' [Comp. மலை, மல்லல்.] மல்க 'with copious tears,' 780.

மல்லல் 'abundance,' 245.

மழலை 'babbling,' 66.

மழி (§ 64), 'shave.' மழித்தல், 280.

மழை 'rain,' 12, 15, 55; in comp. = 'weeping, tearful,' 1239; 'cloud,' Nâl. 361.

மற (§ 66), 'forget.' [பொச்சா.] மறத்தல், 32, 152, 303. மறவற்க 'forget not,' 106. மறந்து, 1284. மறந்தும், 204. மறந்தேன், 1297. மறந்தார், 263. மறந்திர், 1316. மறப்பர், 560. மறப்பின், 1125, 1207, 1262. மறப்பினும், 134. மறப்பது, 108. மறக்கல்லா, 1297. மறிப்பு, 1207, 1125. மறவி, 'forgetfulness,' 605.

மறம் 'sin,' 76.

மறன் 'bravery,' 384 ('*generositas,*' B.), 766. மறவர் 'heroes,' 778.

மறு. 1. 'Spot,' 957, 1117. [களங்கம், மாசு.] 2. 'Other.'

In மறுமை 'the other world,' 98, 459, 904, 1042, Nâl. 1. **3.** (§ 62) 'Refuse, deny, reject.' மறுத்தல் : புலான்மறுத்தல், Ch. XXVI. மறுத்தான், 260. மறுத்து, 945; (='again'), 312.

மற்று. [Comp. மறு.] **1.** A particle which often seems to have no meaning, a mere அசைநிலை; but often marks an antithesis = 'but,' 15, 16 (with ஆங்கே), 30, 802, 490, 506, 1316, 266, 695, 773, 356, 359, 362, 364, 1178, 60, 36, 65, 323, 966, 591, 1308, 596, 905, 923, 968, 1122, 1166. **2.** 'Other' (with எல்லாம்), 'all else,' 39, 221, 226, 655, 95, 588, 1033, 1206, 380, 459. மற்றின்பம், 173. மற்றுதல், 248. மற்றும 'afterwards,' 540, 344; 'other,' 345, 205; 'nevertheless,' 373, Nâl. 19. **3.** 'Otherwise,' 349, 1294, 1151, 1155. மற்றையார் 'others,' 365, 348, 214, 263. மற்றைய(வை) 'other things,' 400, 289, 661.

மறுகு. **1.** 'Street,' 1139. **2.** (§ 62), 'wander abroad.' மறுகும், 1139.

மறை. [Comp. மற.] **1.** 'A secret, concealment,' 590, 697, 847, 1076, 1180, 1138, 1254. மறைமொழி, 28. **2.** (§ 57, 64), 'be hidden; conceal.' மறைந்தவை 'hidden things,' 587. மறைந்து, 278, 274 ('hypocritically'). மறைக்குமு, 980. மறைத்தல், 846. மறைத்திர், 1318. மறைப்பேன், 1161, 1253. மறைப்பான், 1029. மறைப்பின், 1086.

மனம் 'mind,' 253, 295, 454, 822, 823, 825, 7, 661, 317, 453-59, 920, 34. [S. *manas*. Comp. உள்ளம்.] மனத்தது 'what is in the mind,' 278. மனத்தான் 'he whose mind is —,' 271.

மனை 'a house' [comp. இல்], 51, 52, 60, 820, 1268; 'a house-wife' (so இல் for இல்லாள்), 148, 901. மனையான் 'wife,' 904. [The com. மனைவி is not found in K.]

மன். **1.** An emphatic particle, 378, 540, 996, 1086, 1125, 1161, 1184, 1189, 1212, 1216, 1253, 1254, 1265, 1266, 1284. மன்னே, 819, 990, 1016, 1170, 1178, 1206, 1329. With கொல், 1165, 1207. **2.** (§ 62), 'Endure, last.' மன்னும், 1146, 1164, 1327. In comp. (வி. தொ.) மன்னுயிர், 68, 190, 244, 268, 318, 457, 1168; '*homines in mundo existentes*' (B.). மன்னியர் 'very tender,' 138. மன்னுதல, 556. மன்னு, 556. மன்னிய, 692. மன்னன், மன்னவன் 'a king,' 386, 388, 455, 458, 542-46, 553, 556, 558, 559, 581, 583, 610, 692.

மன்ற 'certainly,' 143 (B has மன்றம்=*certò*), 229, 649, 867, 880, 1136. [Comp. மன்.]

மன்று 'the street,' 820. [Opp. to மனை. Comp. மறுகு.] மன்றுபடும் 'will become public,' 1138, 1154.

மா [S. *mahā*]. **1.** 'Great,' 68, 245, 526, 544, 617, 999, 1058. [Comp. மாண்.] **2.** 'Horse,' 814. [Comp. மான்.] கவரிமா, 969.

மாசு 'stain,' 278, 601. [Comp. ஆசு.] மாசற்ற 'stainless,' 956, 649. மாசற்றார் 'the spotless ones,' 106, 311, 312, 646. மாசிலன் 'one without spot,' 34. மாசறுகாட்சியவர் 'those who have seen the vision pure,' 192, 352.

மாடு. **1.** 'Prosperity.' (See மா, மாண்.) **2.** 'Place.' Its inflex. base மாட்டு (§ 251) is used as a prep. sign of 7th case (III. Gr. 63)='near, unto, in regard to'; 5, 94, 175, 188, 211, 303, 536, 541, 991, 1054, 1110, 1199. யார்மாட்டும் 'unto any one whatsoever.'

மாண் (மாட்). [Comp. மா.]
I. மாண், adj. 'glorious, re-

splendent, excellent, worthy,' 3, 407, 606, 901, 919, 1114.
II. v. 'excell' (56, III., like உண்). 1. Inf. (§ 168, used as an adverb), மாண 'exceeding, much,' 102, 124, 883; '*valde.*' 2. Past (§ 87; = மாண்டவர்), மாண்டார் 'men of excellent virtue,' 278, 665. மாண்டது 'that which has excelled,' 631, 632, 749. மாண்ட (§ 74), '(which has become) excellent,' 604, 607, 766, 897, 915. 3. மாண்டல் (=மாணுதல்), v. noun (§ 148), 'the excelling,' 177. 4. Neg. (§ 121): மாணார், *lit.* 'those who are without excellence'='foes,' 823. மாணா 'not possessing excellence, undignified, degraded,' 53, 317 (v.n.), 351, 432, 884, 1002, 1297. மாணாத 'things not excellent,' 867 [comp. 317].
III. Nouns. (§ 190). 1. மாட்சி 'excellence, glory,' 52, 60, 646, 750. [Commonly மாட்சிமை; syn. சிறப்பு, பெருமை.] இறைமாட்சி, Ch. XXXIX. படைமாட்சி, Ch. LXXVII. பகைமாட்சி, Ch. LXXXVII. 2. மாண்பு 'excellence (moral) in virtue,' 51, 53, 432. [Comp. பண்பு.]

மாதர் 'a woman,' 1081, 1117, 1118, 1120, 1087. [மாது, S.]

மாத்திரையார் [S.], 406. *Lit.* 'those who are a measure.' As in coll. மாத்திரம்='only,' so here: 'they have the measure and nothing more; they are *only* persons who exist.'

மாந்தர் 'men, human beings,' 28, 278, 396, 452, 453, 499, 514, 595, 964, 1012. [Comp. S. *manushya.* Other forms, மனிதர், மானிடர், மாக்கள்.]

மாயம் [S.], 'deceit,' 918, 1258. [Comp. மையல்.]

மாய் (§ 57), 'perish.' [மாயம்.] மாயும் 'will perish,' 878, 1230. மாய்வர் 'they will perish,' 898. மாய்வது 'it is that which will perish,' 996. மாய்ந்து 'perishing,' 601. மாயா (=மன்) 'enduring,' 1230.

மாரி 'rain-cloud,' 211, 1010. [Comp. மறை.]

மார்பு 'breast,' 1288, 1311.

மாலு (§ 62), 'be bewildered.' [மையல.] மாலும், 1081.

மாலை. [Comp. S. *mālā.*] 1. 'இயல்பு.' மாலையவர், 1035, 1230. 2. 'Evening,' 1135, 1221–30, 1268.

மாழ் (§ 62), 'become dim.' மாழ்கும், 653.

மாறு (§ 62), 'vary, be changed.' [மறு='other.' Comp. S. *mār,* causalfrom *mṛi.*] மாற்று (§ 62), 'change.' மாறா (§ 121), 'unchanging,' 701. மாற்றும்படை = 'repel,' 985. மாற்ற 'to amend,' 609. மாற்றல் 'changing, relieving,' 7; 'exchange, giving in exchange; *permutare,*' 101. மாற்றுவார் 'those who will relieve,' 225. மாற்றலர் 'enemies,' 749. மாற்றான் 'foe,' 471, 868, 985. மாறு (n.), 'hostility,' 861; 'disagreement,' 944. மாறுபாடு [படு], 945. கைம்மாறு 'equivalent,' 211, 1183. மாற்றம் 'word,' reply,' 689, 725.

மானம் [S.], 'honour,' Ch. XCVII., 970, 384, 766, 432, 1028; 'dishonour,' 968 (=அவமானம்).

மிசை. 1. 'Upon, over,' 3. [Comp. மீ, மீமிசை, மேல்.] 2. v. (§ 57), 'Eat.' மிசைவான், 85.

மிச்சில்=எச்சில் 'what is left,' 85. [Comp. மிசை.]

மிகு (§ 56, II.), 'exceed.' [Comp. S. *mahâ.*] மிகும் 'will prevail,' 373, 928, 1161. மிக 'much,' 829, 1007, 1074. மிகல் 'prevalence of,' 855–59. மிக்க 'what exceeds,' 504, 724. மிக்கவை 'acts of overweening pride,' 158. மிக்கற்று 'as though (it) were in excess,' 1302. மிக்கார் 'those who excel,' 724. முகுதி 'pride, insolence,' 158, 784. தனிப்படர்மிகுதி, Ch. CXX. மிகை 'excess, preponderance,' 345, 504. மிகினும் 'if it be in excess,' 941.

மீ 'above.' மீக்கூறும் 'will extoll,' 386. [கூறு.] [Comp. மிகல், மேல், மிகுதி.]

மீன். 1. (S. *mînam*) 'a fish,' 931. 2. (from மின் 'glisten') 'a star,' 1116.

முகடி (மு, முது), 'the elder sister of fortune, misfortune,' 617. மா, 936.

முகம், முகன் [S.], 'face, forefront,' 84, 90, 92, 224, 706–8, 786, 1116, 1118, 1119. முகத்த, 500. முகத்தான், 93, 565. முகத்து 'in presence of,' 393, 574, 749, 923, 1117. முகத்தின், 824.

முகை 'bud,' 1274.

முடி (§ 57, 64), 'come to an end; accomplish.' முடிக்கும, 517. முடிந்தாலும், 658. முடியார், 908. முடிவு 'end,' 640, 671, 676, 1024.

முட்டு (§ 62), 'hinder.' முட்டா, 547.

முதலை 'a crocodile,' 495.

முதல். [√MU.] 1. 'Beginning.' முதல, முதற்று, 1. முதலா = '*et caetera*,' 941. 2. 'Stem,' 1304. 3. 'Cause,' 948. 4. 'Capital,' 449, 463. முது 'old.' முதுகுறை (§ 57), 'what is experienced, wise.' முதுகுறைந்தது, 707. [Comp. மூ. See குறை.] முதுவர் 'the elders,' 715.

முத்தம் [S.] 'pearl,' 1113.

முந்து (§ 62) 'precede.' [முன். Comp. பிந்து, ஏந்து.] முந்தியிருப்ப 'so as to take precedence,' 67. முந்து seems an adverb in 380, 603, 707, 715, 1023.

முயங்கு (§ 62), 'embrace.' முயங்கிய, 1238. முயக்கம் 'embrace,' 913. முயக்கு, 918, 1107, 1186, 1239, 1108. முயங்க, 1330.

முயலு (§ 70, as வெல்), 'use effort.' முயல, 265. முயல்வார், 47. முயற்சி 'effort,' 611, 616, 619. முயற்றின்மை 'absence of effort,' 616.

முயல் = முசல் 'a hare,' 772.

முரண் 'strength,' 492, 567.

முரி (§ 57), 'break' [comp. முறி]; (§ 64) Nâl. 123. முரிந்து, 473, 899 (with இடை).

முலை 'female breast,' 402, 1087.

முள் 'thorn.' முண்மரம், 879.

முறி 'tender shoot.' [தளிர்.]

முறுவல் 'tooth,' 1113.

முறை. 1. 'Manner, course, order,' 677, 508, 541. கடைமுறை 'at last,' 792. 2. 'Relation,' 885, 698. 3. 'Justice,' 388, 547, 548, 553, 558, 559. முறைப்பட, 640.

முற்று (§ 62), (1) 'end'; (2) 'besiege.' முற்றும் 'it will end,' 491. முற்றாது 'not blockading,' 747. முற்றி, 679, 747. முற்று 'a siege,' 748. முற்றிய, 748.

முனி (§ 57), 'be angry.' முனிய, 191.

முனை 'edge of battle,' 749. [முன்.]

முன் (§ 225). 1. Prep. 'before,' 59, 192, 250, 395, 403, 714, 718, 720, 722, 724. 2. Adv. 335; (with நில்), 184, 636, 771, 1053, 535, 442. 3. In comp.: முற்பகல் 'forenoon,' 319; முற்கை 'forearm,' 1157. முன்னர், 435, 716 முன்னம், 1277. [Comp. முந்து, முனை.]

மூ. 1. 'Three' (§ 172). மூவர், 41, 589. மூன்று, 383, 682, 941, 952, 1085. மூன்றின், 360, 684, 688. 2. 'Old' [முது]; 'grow old' (§ 64), மூத்தவறிவு, 441. மூத்தற்று, 1007.

மூக்கு 'nose,' 277.

மூடு (§ 64), 'cover.' மூடப்பட்டார், 936.

மெய். 1. 'Body,' 65, 619, 774, 925. 2. 'Reality,' 249, 354, 355, 356, 423. மெயுணர்தல், Ch. XXXVI. மெய்யா, 300.

மெல் 'soft.' மென், 919, 1103, 1111, 1265, 1279, 1325. மெல்ல 'softly,' 562, 1094. மெலியார், 250, 561. மெல்லிது, 1289. மென்மை, 877. மெலி (§ 57), 'wasting away.' படர்மெலிந்தி ரங்கல், Ch. cxvii.

மேய் (§ 57), 'graze.' மேய்ந்தற்று, 273.

மேல். [Comp. மிகல்.] **1.** 'A great man,' 627. மேலல்லார், 973. **2.** Prep. 'above, over, against,' 232, 250, 861, 973, 1016, 1079, 1087, 1182, 1262. **3.** With verbs: செல், கொள், வரு, 262, 326, 335, 409, 551, 713, 733, 765, 784, 836, 845, 938, 981, 1055. **4.** (வி. கு.) மேல, 320. மேற்றே, 1027. மேலர், 1218. **5.** Comp. மேலுலகம் 'heaven,' 222. மேன் மேல் 'more and more,' 368. மேன்மை 'superiority,' 137.

மேவு (§ 62), 'desire, join.' [விரும்பு; பொருந்து.] மேவார், 1059. மேவும், 857. மே-க (=விரும்ப), 861. மேவற்க (=மேவிட்டுக்கொள்ள), 877. மேவன, 1073.

மேனி 'body' ('உடல்'), 1113, 1182, 1185, 1189, 1278. [மேல்.]

மை. **1.** இம்மை, 459, 1042; மறுமை, 98, 1315, 126. ஒருமை 'in this life,' '*in hac viâ, propriè est unus ortus*' (B.), 126 (see ஒரு); எழுமை 'the life to come'; '*alterâ vitâ, propriè est septem ortûs*' (B.). **2.** In சிறுமை, &c. 98, 645, 153. **3.** மை யாத்தி 'bewilderment,' 1112. [மைந்து.] மை-ந்து 'confusion,' 539 [comp. மயக்கம்]. மை-யல் 'confusion,' 838.

மொக்குள் 'bud,' 1274. [Comp. முகை.]

மொய்ம்பு 'courage.' மொய்ம்பினவர், 492.

மொழி. **1.** (n.) 'A word,' 28, 1121, 1258, 567, 1258 [always with epithet, நிறை, மறை, பணி, *or* பனி, கடு]. **2.** (§ 57), 'Speak.' மொழிவது, 643. மொழியின், 295.

மோ (§ 60, as இரு), 'smell.' [முகரு.] மோப்ப, 90.

ய

யா. I. (§ 64), 'tie, join.' [Comp. ஆர்.] யாக்க 'join thou,' 793. [For the இ comp. III. Gr. 24, *Nannûl*, 164.] யாப்பு 'a tie, tying,' 777, 1093. யாக்கை 'body, compacted,' 79, 239, 942. யாக்கைநிலையாமை, Nâl. 21–30.

II. For எ (§ 47), 'which.' [Comp. அ, இ, உ, எ.] (1) யா (sub. and obj.), 'what *or* which things?' 54, 127, 380. யா before a noun and உம் after: 'any whatsoever,' 641. (2) யாது 'what?' 178, 254, 291, 321, 324, 341, 397, 462, 703, 789, 801, 831, 833, 842, 986, 1041, 1049, 1212 [with உம், ஒன்றும், ஆனும்]. (3) யார் 'who?' (m.f.), 94, 149, 162, 175, 256, 509, 536, 541; Without ய்: ஆர், 991, 1249, 1294, 1314, 1317, Nâl. 2. யாரே (double int.), 477, 779, 855, 1299. யார்க்கும், 317, 618, 647, 664, 693, 864, 960, 1181. யார்யார்க்கும், 20. யார்யார் வாய், 423. யாங்கு 'where?' 1070. யாங்கணும் 'everywhere,' 864. யாண்டு, யாண்டும், 4, 585, 895, 1104.

யாமம் [S.] 'midnight,' 1136, 1167, 1252. யாமத்து 'at midnight.'

யாழ் 'lute,' 66, 279. [ஆழ்.]

யானை 'elephant' [ஆனை], 599, 678, 758, 772, Nâl. 3, 21. [களிறு, வேழம்.]

யான் = நான் (§ 10), 'I.' Sing.—(1) யான், 116, 346, 1071, 1094, 1098, 1161, 1167, 1125, 1184, 1206, 1212, 1225, 1247, 1253, 1254. (2) என்னை, 1316, 1244,

1256, 1296. (3) . . . . (4) எனக்கு, 1151. (5) என்னினும், 1290. (6) என், 771, 1081, 1185, 1136, 1139, 1292, 1295, 1296, 1297, 1284, 1264, 1252, 1254, 1175, 1316, 1310, 1324, 1230, 1262, 1242, 1246, 1248, 1249, 1209, 1213, 1237, 1170, 1163, 1168, 1181, 1182, 1189. எனது, 346. (7) என்கண், 1174.

PLUR.—(1) யாம், 61, 300, 790, 844, 1111, 1123, 1140, 1150, 1171, 1204, 1245, 1278, 1265, 1312, 1329. நாம், 1195. (2) எம்மை, 1205, 1217, 1318. (3) . . . . (4) நமக்கு, 1195, 1231. எமக்கு, 790, 1142, 1176, 1291. (5) நம்மினும், 1277. (6) நம், 1220, 1258. எம், 1278, 1180, 1126, 1185, 1204, 1205, 1222. (7) எம்மிடை, 1122.

வ

வகு (§ 64). [Comp. பகு.] வகுத்தல், 385. வகுத்தான், 377. வகுத்த, 377. வகை 'manner,' 33, 377, 465, 514, 953. தெரிந்துசெயல்வகை, Ch. XLVII. வினைசெயல்வகை, Ch. LXVIII. குடிசெயல்வகை, Ch. CIII. பொருள்செயல்வகை, Ch. LXXVI. வகையறி, 713, 721, 878. வகைதெரி, 27. வகைமாண்ட 'possessed of all manner of excellence,' 897. வகையர், 817. வகைமை = வகை, 709.

வசை 'disgrace, reproach, blame,' 238-40. [Opp. to இசை.]

வஞ்சம் [S.] 'deceit.' வஞ்சர், 824. வஞ்சமனத்தான், 271. வஞ்சி (§ 64), 'deceive.' வஞ்சித்து, 276. வஞ்சிப்பது, 366.

வடு. 1. 'Scar, ulcer,' 129. 2. 'Fault,' 502, 549, 689, 1079.

வணங்கு (§ 62), 'reverence, bow, bend. [வளை.] வணங்கிய, 419. வணங்கா, 9. வணக்கம் 'reverence, bending,' 827.

வண்ணம் [S.] 'method,' 561, 664; 'colour,' 714.

வண். See வள்.

வயிறு 'belly,' 412.

வயின் (§ 251), 'place'; used as sign of 7th case: 'in oneself,' 846; 'where it springs up,' வி. தொ., 177. [Comp. வழி.] அவர்வயின் விதும்பல் 'mutual longing,' Ch. CXXVII.

வரன் [S.], 'a boon; bliss,' 24. [Comp. வரம்.]

வரிசை 'order of merit' [தகுதி], 528. [Comp. வரி.]

வருந்து (§ 62), 'suffer, take pains.' [Comp. பருவரல்.] வருந்தினர் 'those who suffer,' 1131. வருந்தா, 468. வருத்தம் 'trouble, pains,' 468, 619.

வரை. 1. 'Limit,' 480. இறுவரை 'the time to destroy,' 488. உளவரை 'the measure of one's means,' 480. பிறன்வரையாள் 'she who is within the limits, *possession* of an other,' 150; '*quae est intra limites*' (B.). நிலவரை 'to the ends of the earth,' 234. 2. (§ 57) 'Take, accept as one's limit.' அறன்வரையான் 'who takes not virtue as his limit, measure of conduct,' 150. வரைத்து 'it has as its limit, measure,' 105. வரையும் 'as far as,' 748. வரைவு 'limit of decorum, *modestia*,' 919. வரைவின்மகளிர், Ch. XCII., 'women who are immodest.'

வல். வன் 'strong, hard cruel; prompt,' 273, 496, 721, 737. [Comp. பல, பெல, S.] வன்சொல் 'harsh words,' 99. வன்பால் 'rocky, sterile soil,' 78. வன்கண் 'a hard eye; pitilessness *or* cool determination,' 228, 276, 632, 689, 726, 762, 764 775, 1027, 1156, 1198, 1222.

வலி 'strength,' 273, 380, 471, 473, 1131. வலியறிதல், Ch. XLVIII. அறன்வலியுறுத்தல் Ch. IV. வன்மை 'strength,

153, 444, 682, 1063, 1151. சொல்வன்மை, Ch. LXV. வன்பாடு 'strength.' (See படு.) வன்பட்டது 'what possesses strength,' 1063. வலியார் 'those who are strong,' 250, 861. [Opp. மெலியார்.] வல்லறிதல் 'prompt discernment,' 582. [Comp. வல்லே.]

Conj. app. (Intro. p. xxiii.), வல்லே 'thou art able,' 1118. வல்ல(ா)ன், 387, 446, 647 (pl.), 683, 578, 648, 717, 795, 808, 855, 999. வல்லது, 385, 585, 633, 634, 713, 845, 1321, Nâl. 101. வற்று, 587, 1079. வல்லே (adv.), 'swiftly,' 480. [Comp. வல் in 1151, 582.]

வலை 'net,' 348. [? வளை.]

வழ-ங்கு (§ 62), 'be current, be in use, pass round, give.' [Comp. பழ, வழி, ஒழுங்கு.] வழங்கி, 11. வழங்கும், 245, 477. வழங்காது, 19. வழங்குவது, 99, 955. வழக்கு 'method; cause,' 73, 75, 795, 991, 992.

வழி. **1.** 'A way,' 38, 766, 1170. பெண்வழிச்சேறல், Ch. XCI. **2.** 'After, the sequel,' 865, 508, 461. **3.** 'Posterity,' 44. **4.** With verb. root or adj. part. ='when,' 770, 846, 1224, 1299, 1300, 1308. வழியுரை 'deliver a message,' 688. வழியது 'what is in the way of,' 80. வழிவந்த 'old, veteran, hereditary,' 764, 807, 809.

வழுக்கு (§ 62), 'slip.' வழுக்கியும் 'though they slip,' 139, 165. வழுக்காமை 'not failing' (= வழுக்காமல்), 536. வழுக்கு 'a slip, failure,' 776. [Comp. பழு, பழி.]

வழுத்து (§ 62), 'salute, bless.' [Comp. வாழ்.] வழுத்தினள், 1317.

வளரு (§ 57) 'grow.' வளர்வது 'what is growing,' 718. வளர 'so as to increase,' 1223.

வளா for வளைவு 'a circuit, bank,' 523. [வளை.] குளவளா 'the compass of a tank.'

வளி 'wind' [காற்று], 245, 1108, 1239; வாதம் in med., 941.

வளை 'a bangle, bracelet,' 1157, 1277. [வளை 'encircle.']

வள், வண் 'strong, prosperous,' 239. வள்ளியம் 'we are prosperous,' 598. [Comp. பெரிய.] வளம் 'produce, income, plenty, prosperity,' 14, 480, 512, 736, 739. வளத்தன 'yielding plenty,' 739. வளத்தக்காள் 'she who expends according to her husband's means,' 51.

வள்ளி 'a creeper, a species of convolvulus,' 1304.

வறு 'dry.' [வல்.] வறுமை 'poverty,' 408, 769, 934. வறங்கூர் 'grow dry.' [வறு+அம்; see கூர்.] வறியார் 'poor people,' 221. [Comp. பெரியார்.] வறிஞர், Nâl. 1.

வற (§ 66), 'grow dry.' வறக்குமேல், 18. வற்றல் 'dryness,' 78.

வா (§ 70), 'come, result.'

I. (வரு, வந்த்.) வருக 'may he come!' 1266. (வி. தொ.) வரு, 83, 86, 737, 1269. வருப 'things which come,' 961. வரல், 1205, 1263. வருதல், 11, 642. வருவது, 39, 429, 1048, 1202. வரும், 63, 220, 264, 303, 319, 362–68, 455, 529, 621, 1042, 1223, 1224. வருங்கால் 'when it comes,' 733, 830, 859. வருமுன்னர் 'before it comes,' 435. வருபவன், 774. வரின், 969, 970, 1052, 1179, 1267, 1282. வரினும், 433, 625, 669, 765.

II. வந்து, 1058. வந்தான், 530. வந்த, 609, 754, 767, 968; with வெரு, இளி, அறி, வழி seems=nearly to உள்ள or term. '-tive,' &c., 563, 569, 654, 764, 807, 809, 1044, 1066.

III. வாரா, 335, 356, 755, 1179.

IV. வரவு 'a coming,' 1043, 1151, 1165, 1264.

வாடு 'wither.' வாடு (வி. தொ.), 1237. வாடிய, 1234, 1235. வாடினும், 1322.

வாட்டு 'draughts: game,' 401.

வாணிகம் [S.], 'merchandise,' 120.

வாதம் [S.], 'word,' 685.

வாய் (§ 64, 57), 'succeed, be fitting; exist.'

I. வாயின் 'if it be obtained,' 536. வாய்ந்த 'suitable,' 737. வாய்ப்ப 'things which are fitting,' 948. வாய்ப்பன், 865.

II. 'Place,' 33, 624, 673, 789, 948, 1001, 1117; 'mouth,' 91, 139, 159, 415, 420, 423, 424, 689, 721, 959, 1100. வாயினர், 419.

III. வாயில் (=வாசல்) 'gate, way,' 6. வாய்மை 'truth,' Ch. XXX., 291, 292, 295, 298, 300, 364, 688, 952, 953, 983.

வாரு (§ 62), 'pour.' வாரும், 1232.

வாரி [S.], 'income,' 512; 'water,' 14.

வால், வான் 'pure, white,' 2, 714, 1121. [Comp. வெள்.]

வாழ் (§ 57), prosper, live prosperously.' Comp. வழு.]

I. வாழ் (வி. தொ.), 38, 326. வாழ்தல், 183, 231, 967, 1062, 1124, 1158. வாழி 'hail! *salve!*' 1111, 1118, 1210, 1221, 1222, 1242. வாழிய, 1200. வாழ்கு, 1312. வாழுர், 58, 392, 542, 557. வாழுநம், 1193. வாழ்வான், 41, 42, 147, 214, 1025. வாழ்வார், 3, 6, 240, 276, 528, 1033, 1160, 1192, 1198. வாழ்பவன், 47, 50. வழ்வது, 81, 337. வாழ்வாங்கு, 50. வாழ்தும் 'we have lived; *viximus!*' 956, 971. வாழாதான், 479. வாழா, 969. வாழாதவர், 240, 237. வாழாத, 970. வாழினும், 420, 906.

II. வாழ்க்கை 'prosperity, happiness, happy life,' 44–49, 51, 52, 78, 83, 330, 435, 479, 523, 856, 890, 897, 968. இல்வாழ்க்கை, Ch. V., 46, 47. வாழ்க்கைத் துணைநலம், Ch. VI.

III. வாழ்த்து 'praise,' Ch. I. கடவுள்வாழ்த்து.

வாள் 'sword,' 334, 726, 727, 882; 'brightness,' 1261 [ஒளி]. வாளாண்மை 'swordsmanship,' 614.

வான், வானம், forms of the same word; the change is கடைக்குறை, III. Gr. 41. [Comp. S. *varuṇa*.]

I. வானம். 1. மழை 'rain,' 19. 2. மேகம் 'cloud,' 559. 3. ஆகாசம் 'sky,' 18, 1192. 4. வீட்டுலகம் 'the heavenly world,' 353. வானத்தவர் (§ 184), 'the inhabitants of heaven,' 86.

II. வான். 1. மழை 'rain,' 11, 20. 2. ஆகாசம், 542. வான்சிறப்பு 'the excellence of rain,' Ch. II. வானோர் (§ 184), 'the heavenly ones,' 18, 346. வானகம் [opp. வையகம்], 'the heavenly place, *coelum*,' 101. வானுறையுந்தெய்வம் [opp. வையம்], 'the divinity that dwells in heaven,' 50. வான்பொருள் 'great wealth, *heaped up to heaven*,' 897. வானுயர் தோற்றம் 'a form that is high as heaven,' 272. [Syn. விண், விசும்பு, புயல், எழிலி.]

III. See வால்.

விக்குள் 'hiccough,' 335.

விசும்பு. [Comp. S. *vrish.*] 1. 'Cloud,' 16. [மேகம்.] 2. 'Firmament,' 25, 957. [ஆகாயம்.]

விடு (§ 68, 254), 'leave; emit; put.' It is often redundant.

I. விடு (imp.), 1247; (வி.தொ), 689. விடுக, 928. விட, 1118. விடல், 113, 158, 203, 314, 343, 350, 697, 517, 818, 830, 831, 876, 979, 912, 961, 1245, 450, 755, 797, 1302, 1203. விடுதல், 1038. விடும், 28, 121, 128, 138, 167, 168, 267, 451, 476, 498, 535, 592, 608, 616, 980, 1039, 1068, 1253. விடுவார், 799, 1310. விடின்=

'if,' 17, 238, 280, 1159. விடினும், 876.

II. விடா, 347, 422, 1324. விடாது, 1210. விடார், 809. விடாதவர், 347.

III. விட்ட, 695. விட்டேம், 1036.

IV. வீடு (=விடுதல்), 'relinquishment,' 791.

விண், a variation of வான், 'cloud,' 13.

விதிரு (§ 64), 'sprinkle.' விதிரார், 1077.

விதும்பு, விதுப்பு (§ 62), 'desire.' [விரும்பு] அவர்வயின் விதும்பல், Ch. CXXVII. புணர்ச்சிவிதும்படல், Ch. CXXIX. கண் விதுப்பழிதல், Ch. CXVIII. விதுப்பு 'desire,' 1290.

வித்தகர் [S.], 'learned men,' 235.

வித்து [S.], 'seed,' 24, 85, 138, 361. [விதை.]

விய (§ 66), 'admire, praise.' விய-வற்க, 439. விய-ந்து, 978. விய-ந்தான், 474. விய-ன் 'wide,' 13, 19, 716, 1016.

வியர்ப்ப (§ 64), 'perspire,' 1328. (See வேர்.)

விரல் 'finger,' 1261, Nâl. 123.

விரி (§ 57, 64), 'expand.' வி. தொ, 13. விரி-த்து, 650.

விருந்து. 1. 'A feast,' 1211, 1268. [Com. says it means 'a novelty'; hence = '*hostis*.'] 2. 'A guest,' 43, 81–90. விருந்தோம்பல் 'hospitality,' Ch. IX.; opp. 'விருந்தோராஅல்,' 153.

விருப்பு 'desire,' 522. [விரும்பு.]

விரை 'hasten.' விரைந்து, 474, 1080, 1218. விரைந்தது, 679.

விலங்கு 'beast,' 410.

விலை 'price,' 256. [வில், விற்.]

வில் 'bow,' 827, 872. [Comp. வளை.]

விழி (§ 64), 'see, awake.' விழிப்பது, 339. விழித்த, 775. விழிக்கும், 1218.

விழு. 1. (§ 57), 'fall.' விழுமம், 107 [B. has விழுமம்]. விழுப்புண் 'a deadly wound,' 776 (B. '*speciale ac notabile vulnus*'). 2. 'Affliction' [துன்பம்]. விழுமம், 107 (?), 284, 313, 663 (diff. epi. in each). 3. 'Excellence,' 162, 363. சிறப்பு '*celsitudo*' (B.). விழு-ப்பம், 21, 131. விழு-மியார், 201.

விழுங்கு (§ 62) 'swallow,' 931. [விழுகியற்று.]

விழை (§ 57), 'desire eagerly.' விழை (வி. தோ.), 804. விழைய, 810. விழை-யும், 630, 911, 809. விழை-ப, 692. விழைவது, 1036. விழை-வான், 615, 901, 902. விழை-யான், 615, 628, 911, 810. விழை-யாதான், 629. விழை-யாமை, 692. பிறனில்விழையாமை, Ch. XV.

விள-ங்கு (§ 62), 'shine.' [Comp. ஒள்.] விள-ங்கும், 717, 957. விள-க்கு, 299, 1186. விள-க்கம், 601, 753, 853.

விளி. 1. (§ 57), 'die, disperse.' விளி-ந்தார் 'the dead,' 143. விளி-யும், 1209. விளி-யாது, 145. விளி-ந்தற்று 'it is as the dispersing,' 332. 2. (§ 64), 'call.' விளித்தற்று 'it is like summoning,' 894.

விளை (§ 57), 'grow.' [Comp. வள-ம்.] விளை-வது, 732. விளை-வு 'growth,' 284, 738. விளையுள் 'produce,' 545, 731. [Comp. பொரு-ள.] விளை-வயின் (வி. தொ.) 'where they grow,' 177.

விறல் 'victory,' 180. ['வெற்றி.']

விற், வில் (§ 70, as கல்), 'sell.' விற்று, 220. விற்றற்கு, 1080. [See விலை.]

வினவு (§ 62), 'enquire.' [வினா.] அதர்வினாய் (=வினவி) 'asking the way,' 594.

வினை. [? S. *vi+nî*.] I. 'Action in general,' 279, 367, 439, 483, 519, 631, 612, 697, 758, 901, 1022, 456, 584, 684, 819, 836. ஆள்வினை 'activity,' 618, 632, 1022. ஆள்வினை யுடைமை, Ch.

LXII. வினையாண்மை, 904. தெரிந்துவினையாடல், Ch. LII., 512–20. வினைத்தூய்மை, Ch. LXVI. வினைத்திட்பம், Ch. LXVII. வினைசெயல்வகை, Ch. LXVIII., 651–80. செய்வினை 'action,' 455, 953, 677.

II. 'Deed, with idea of retribution,' 63, 244, 327, Nâl. 3, 101–10. [Comp. பழவினை, Nâl. Ch. XI.] அறவினை 'virtuous action,' பிறவினை 'other (vicious) action,' 321, 909. வினைப்பகை 'nemesis,' 207. நல்வினை, 335. தீவினை, 201, 209, 210. தீவினையச்சம், Ch. XXI. Hence இருவினையும், 5.

III. 'Warlike operations,' 471, 491, 749, 750, 1268. வென்றிவினை 'the action that gains the victory,' 683.

IV. 'Hostility,' 781. வினையர் 'doers,' 329.

வீ (§ 57), 'fail.' [விழு.] வீ-வர் 'they will fail,' 289. வீ-யாது 'unfailing,' 207, 208. வீ-யா, 284.

வீங்கு (§ 62), 'swell.' வீங்கிய, 1233.

வீழ் (§ 64), 'let down, fasten' (causal of விழு='fall'); (§ 57), 'fall, love' [poet. for விழு and விழை). வீழ 'to be loved,' 1191, 1193, 1194. வீழின் 'if it fall,' 16. வீழ்-வர் 'will love,' 1103, 1191, 1192, 1194, 1198, 1202, 1325. வீழும் 'will fall,' 1030; 'who love,' 1108, 1123. வீழ்-த்த 'fastened,' 1251. வீழ்-ந்த 'fallen,' 955. வீழுநர் 'lovers; loved one,' 1193. வீழ்-பவள் 'she whom I love,' 1111. வீழ்-நாள் 'a lost day,' 38.

வீறு 'greatness, majesty,' 665, 749, 904 (with எய்). வீற்றிருக்கை 'supreme greatness,' 789.

வெ 'hot, swift, severe.' வெம், வெய், வே.

I. வெ-ஞ்-கோல் (=கொடுங்கோல்) 'tyranny.' வெங்கோலன் 'a tyrant,' 563. வெ-ந்-துப்பு 'hot anger.' வெந்துப்பின் வேந்து 'an angry king,' 895. வெ-ய்து 'anything hot; quickly,' 569, 1128. வெ-யில் 'sunshine.'

II. வெ-குளு (§ 62) 'be angry.' வெகுளும், 870. வெகுளி 'wrath,' 29, 35, 309, 864. [=சினம், கதம்.] வெகுளாமை 'absence of wrath,' Ch. XXXI., 303, 308, 360, 526, 531, 1060.

III. வெ-ரு 'fear.' [Comp. *fear*; Lat. *ver-eor*.] வெருவு (§ 62) 'fear.' வெரூஉம்= வெருவும் (அளபெடை) 'will fear,' 599. வெருவரு (see வா) 'fear.' வெருவந்த 'things that cause fear, tyrannical acts,' 563. வெருவந்த செய்யாமை, Ch. LVII. வெருவந்து 'dreading,' 569.

IV. வெ-ஃகு (§ 62), 'desire, covet.' [Comp. விழை, வீழ், விரும்பு.] வெ-ஃகுதல், 174. வெ-ஃகின், 171, 180. வெ-ஃகி, 172–77. வெ-ஃகா, 179. வெ-ஃகாமை, Ch. XVIII.

V. வெ-று (1) 'detestable.' வெறிய 'hateful things,' 175. (2) (§ 64), 'detest. வெறுப்பு 'detestation,' 696. (3) 'Admiration.' வெறுத்தக்க 'admirable,' 993. (4) வெறு-க்கை 'glory,' 600 ('*sedes*,' B.), 761, 971.

VI. வே (§ 58), 'burn.' வெ-ந்து, 899. வே-பாக்கு (§ 97, Note), 'it will burn,' 1128.

வெண்மை. See வெள்.

வெல் (§ 70), 'conquer.'

I. வெல் (வி. தொ.), 761. வெல்-லல், 647. வெல்-லும், 481, 495, 645, 769. வெல்-வது, 748.

II. வென்-று, 931, 1268. வென்-ற, 174. வென்-றார், 1327. வென்-றது, 931.

III. வென்-றி 'victory,' 546, 683.

IV. வேல் 'a javelin,' 500, 546, 552, 772, 774, 775, 1113. வேலார் 'javelin-bearers,' 683.

வேலை (§ 184), 'thou art a dart,' 1221.

வெள் 'white.' வெள்ளம் 'a stream of water,' 595, 622, 1170. வெளிறு 'ignorance,' 503. வெண்மை 'ignorance.' 844. வெளி 'open.' வெளிப்படு 'become manifest,' 1145. வெளியார் 'ignorant persons,' 714.

வெறி 'fragrance,' 1113.

வேட்டுவன் 'a hunter,' 274. [? வேள்.]

வேண்-டு [வேள்; comp. பேண்] (§ 62), 'want, ask, require.' வேண்டுதல் 'desire,' 4. வேண்டல், 82, 871. வேண்ட, 364. வேண்டற்க 'seek not,' 177, 931. வேண்டுவான், 281. வேண்டுக, 960. வேண்டுப, 696. வேண்டுபவர் 'those who want,' 173, 320, 562, 580, 602, 962. வேண்டும் 'will require,' 21; 'is needed,' 178, 85, 257, 316, 362, 343, 481, 470, 538, 652, 653, 611, 667, 794, 867, 960, 963, 1150, 1282, 1060; '(when, as) you seek,' 362, 367. வேண்டி, 263, 265, 777, 804, 1256. வேண்டிய, 265, 343, 651. வேண்டியவர், 1177. வேண்டின், 154, 342, 893, 960, 1150, 1062. வேண்டார், 670. வேண்டாது, 670, 1037. வேண்டா 'it is not necessary,' 37, 211, 280, 357, 497, 777, 785, 901, 942, 1003. வேண்டாதான், 163, 206, 584, 922. வேண்டாமை 'absence of desire,' 4, 180, 362. [வேண்டும் is used impersonally as in common Tamil. For the neg., in 942, வேண்டாவாம் is found, and simply வேண்டா, not வேண்டாம்.]

வேந்தன் 'king' (see √வெ), 382, 389, 390, 481, 528, 530, 549, 557, 564, 567–69, 582, 665, 689, 691, 756, 761, 899, 1268. வேந்து, 550, 551, 561, 681, 735, 740, 895.

வேய் 'bambu,' 1113. [மூங்கில்.]

வேர் (§ 64), 'perspire, be angry' [வியர்ப்ப]. (See √வெ.) வேரப்பர், வேரார், 487.

வேல். See √வெ.

வேலி 'a hedge,' 1016.

வேள் [வேண்டு], 'favour, desire.' வேளாண்மை 'beneficence,' 81, 212, 613, 614. வேள்-வி 'beneficence,' 87, 88; 'offering': five are enumerated, (1) study of the Vêdas, to Bramhâ; (2) fire-offerings, to gods; (3) food-offerings, to all living creatures; (4) water-offerings, to the Manes; (5) alms, to the needy. [Comp. S. *yâga.*] (§ 70), 'sacrifice; desire eagerly.' வேட்டல் 'offering,' 259. வேட்ப 'so as to desire,' 643, 646, 696. வேட்பன 'desirable things,' 697. வேட்ட 'when — desired,' 1105.

வேறு 'other.' [Comp. மறு 'vary.'] Also, as a noun, = 'kind,' 374, 143, 514, 600, 704, 819, 822, 926, 1012, 1209. வேற்றுமை, 972.

வை. **1.** 'The earth.' வையம், 189, 50, 353. வையத்து 'on earth,' 22, 850. வையகம், 75, 101, 547; *terra.* வையக்கு, 701. வையத்தார், 238. **2.** (§ 64, 261), 'Place, put, consider,' Nâl. 1. வைக்க, 50, 214, 388, 850. வைக்கும், 776. வைத்து, 228, 840, 1269. வைத்தான், 1001. வைப்பர், 155. வையார், 155. வையாது, 117, 841. வைப்பு 'land,' 24, 149; 'place,' 226. **3.** 'Straw,' 435.

வைகல் 'a day.' வைகலும் 'daily,' 83, Nâl. 7, 39.

சிந்தைக் கினிய செவிக்கினிய வாய்க்கினிய
வந்த விருவினைக்கு மாமருந்து
முந்திய
நன்னெறி நாமறிய நாப்புலமை வள்ளுவனார்
பன்னிய வின்குறள் வெண்பா.

Sweet to the thought, sweet to the ear, sweet to the mouth,
Great cure for twofold deeds' disease, is *Vaḷḷuvar's*
Sweet *Kurraḷ-Veṇpâ* verse, with tongue right eloquent
Set forth, that we the way of good may know.

INDEX.